Teaching Mainstreamed, Diverse, and At-Risk Students in the General Education Classroom

SHARON VAUGHN

University of Miami

CANDACE S. BOS

University of Arizona

JEANNE SHAY SCHUMM

University of Miami

Allyn and Bacon

Boston ∎ London ∎ Toronto ∎ Sydney ∎ Tokyo ∎ Singapore

Series Editor: Ray Short
Developmental Editor: Mary Ellen Lepionka
Series Editorial Assistant: Christine Svitila
Marketing Manager: Kris Farnsworth
Composition and Prepress Buyer: Linda Cox
Manufacturing Buyer: Megan Cochran
Cover Administrator: Linda Knowles
Cover Designer: Studio Nine
Photo Director: Susan Duane
Production Administrator: Rob Lawson
Production Coordinator: Deborah Schneck
Editorial Production Service: Schneck-DePippo Graphics
Copyeditor: Gail Burlakoff
Text Designer: Melinda Grosser

Copyright © 1997 by Allyn & Bacon
A Simon & Schuster Company
Needham Heights, MA 02194

Library of Congress Cataloging-in-Publication Data
Vaughn, Sharon, 1952–
      Teaching mainstreamed, diverse, and at-risk students in the general education
classroom / Sharon R. Vaughn, Candace S. Bos, Jeanne Schumm.
            p.   cm.
      Includes bibliographical references and index.
      ISBN 0-205-19954-2
      1. Mainstreaming in education—United States. 2. Special education—
United States. 3. Handicapped children—Education—United States. 4. Socially
handicapped children—Education—United States. 5. Disabled children—
Education—United States. I. Bos, Candace S., 1950– . II. Schumm, Jeanne
Shay, 1947– . III. Title.
LC3981.V28 1996
371.9'046—dc20   96-28482
                                                                                 CIP

Photo Credits

Will Hart: pp. 2, 25, 53, 55, 66, 73, 104, 109, 187, 214, 221, 244, 260, 276, 327
332, 337, 342, 348, 360, 369, 374, 394, 398, 406, 410, 419, 433, 441, 458, 471;
Will Faler: pp. 11, 28, 81, 98, 151, 162, 181 (top) 190 200, 202, 206, 228 (right),
267, 272, 282, 317, 365, 375, 438 (top), 446, 461, 469, 478; Brian Smith: pp. 34,
40, 134, 235, 290, 293, 306, 314, 315, 385, 426, 462; Robert Harbison: pp. 83,
85, 128, 166, 175, 311; Stephen Marks: pp. 140, 226; Robert Finken/The Picture
Cube: p. 114; David Young-Wolff/PhotoEdit: pp. 195, 355; Bob Daemmrich/Stock
Boston: p. 254; Richard Hutchings/PhotoEdit: p. 267 (bottom).

Printed in the United States of America

10   9   8   7   6   5   4   3   2   01   00   99   98   97

BRIEF CONTENTS

CONTENTS

CHAPTER THREE
Managing Student Behavior and Promoting Social Acceptance   66

CHAPTER FOUR
Collaborating and Coordinating with Other Professionals and Family Members   98

CHAPTER FIVE
Teaching Students with Learning Disabilities or Attention Deficit Disorders   128

CHAPTER SIX
Teaching Students with Communication Disorders   160

CHAPTER SEVEN
Teaching Students with Emotional and Behavioral Disorders 190

CHAPTER EIGHT
Teaching Students with Mental Retardation and Severe Disabilities 214

CHAPTER NINE
Teaching Students with Visual, Hearing, Physical, or Health Impairments   244

CHAPTER TEN
Teaching Culturally and Linguistically Diverse Students   272

CHAPTER ELEVEN
Teaching Students at Risk   306

CHAPTER FOURTEEN
Facilitating Writing   394

CHAPTER FIFTEEN
Helping All Students Succeed in Mathematics   426

CHAPTER SIXTEEN
Teaching in the Content Areas   458

A P P E N D I X
Making a Difference through Action Learning:
Teaching Study Skills, Learning Strategies and Self-Advocacy 488

TIPS FOR TEACHERS

PREFACE

Today's elementary and secondary teachers are assuming considerably more responsibility for meeting the educational needs of students from diverse backgrounds and with diverse learning needs. Teachers identify students with special needs as their greatest challenges and often their greatest rewards. Unfortunately, most general education teachers feel at a loss as to how to educate these students. They are eager to provide appropriate instruction and yet often feel inadequately prepared to do so. Furthermore, teachers tell us that what they most want to learn are specific instructional practices that "make a difference" for diverse learners and that they want these practices to enhance the learning of all the students in their classrooms.

The central theme of this book is that general education teachers can "make a difference" in the lives of all students, particularly students with special needs, by using the tools and strategies presented by the authors. Our confidence in the effectiveness of these suggested practices comes from our ongoing and continued work in teachers' classrooms where these practices have been successfully implemented. The many teachers whose stories appear throughout this book interpret and extend the recommended practices.

Organizational Format

By presenting information that can be easily retrieved and applied, we hope this book will serve as an indispensable resource for teachers seeking effective strategies for meeting the needs of exceptional learners.

The book is organized into three major sections. The first section, Chapters 1–4, is entitled "Mainstreaming and Inclusion Strategies for Classroom Teachers." This section first addresses issues regarding mainstreaming, inclusion, and laws, and then provides guidelines and suggestions for how teachers can orchestrate their classrooms for stu-

dents with special needs. It includes strategies for planning, grouping, classroom management, and working collaboratively with parents and professionals.

The second section of the book, Chapters 5–12, is entitled "Teaching Students with Disabilities and Diverse Needs." Chapters 5 through 9, on teaching students with disabilities, cover learning disabilities, attention deficit disorders, communication disorders, mental retardation and severe disabilities, visual impairments, hearing impairments, physical disabilities, and health impairments. Chapters 10 through 12 focus on teaching

In every section of the book, the authors provide **Tips for Teachers** with specific advice, guidelines for teaching practice, and step-by-step procedures. These tips can empower readers to meet all students' needs.

students who are culturally and linguistically diverse, students at-risk, and gifted or talented students. We have presented instructional practices and specific accommodations in each of these chapters to ensure that teachers not only will better understand students with special needs but also will know what to do to meet their needs.

The third section of the book, Chapters 13–16, is entitled "Curriculum Adaptations for Special Learners." This section provides specific instructional practices for curricular areas, including reading, writing, mathematics, and content area learning. Students in our university classes as well as practicing teachers *urged* us to do more than describe curriculum adaptations; they encouraged us to provide the step-by-step procedures for how to implement curriculum adaptations in the classroom. After reading this book, students and teachers will have more than increased knowledge about students with special needs; they will have

the tools and more confidence to adequately meet their students' academic and social needs.

The organizational structure of each chapter is the same so that readers can readily locate critical information. Each chapter opens with **Focus Questions** that provide an invitation to learn and an orientation to the key ideas presented in the chapter. Next is an **interview** or vignette that presents a teacher's, student's or parent's story that directly relates to the central ideas of the chapter. Each of these stories also identifies issues and personal responses that set the tone for the material that follows.

Each chapter's figures, tables, photos, and informational sidebars are designed to stimulate interest and aid in comprehension. Each chapter closes with a **Summary** that highlights the key points that are contained in the chapter. **Key Terms and Concepts** are presented as a list following the summary and are highlighted in text for ease of location. A **Think and Apply** section at the end of each chapter provides questions, activities, and interesting problems that challenge the reader to integrate and apply the material presented. **Read More about It** follows and provides a list of books and materials related to the chapter topic with brief descriptions of their content.

In addition to the organizational features that open and close each chapter, the following features are used within chapters.

Special features such as *Making a Difference: The 60 Second Lesson* and *Making a Difference: Action Teaching* provide specific lesson plans and activities that can be used immediately in the classroom. A special appendix, *Making a Difference: Action Learning*, contains lessons and activities for teaching secondary learners study skills, learning strategies, and student self-advocacy.

- **Making a Difference: The 60-Second Lesson**—These brief mini-lessons appear in every chapter of Section 1 and Section 2 and provide specific, concrete examples of how a teacher can make a difference for students with disabilities or diverse needs in only a minute of time.
- **Making a Difference: Action Teaching**— These sample lessons are provided at the ends of the curriculum chapters in Section 3. Each lesson includes objectives, procedures, and application suggestions for classroom implementation.
- **Tips for Teachers**—Teaching tips are featured in every chapter and include lists of concrete suggestions for how to teach a particular skill or how to address a particular student need.
- **Tech Talk**—This illustrated feature, provided in every chapter, describes a technological

application that can be used in the classroom to enhance success for all learners, particularly students with special needs.

- **Research Brief**—Every chapter highlights brief summaries of essential research studies that relate to key points in the chapter.

To provide adequate coverage at the secondary level, we have provided examples in each chapter that illustrate how to apply accommodations and instructional practices at the secondary level. We also designed the content area curriculum chapter to include issues relating specifically to instruction at the secondary level. Finally, a special appendix, **Making a Difference through Action Learning**, contains more than 20 specific examples of how to instruct secondary students with emphasis on study skills, learning strategies, and student self-advocacy.

Supplements

The combined **Instructors' Manual and Text Bank** with transparency and handout masters is a comprehensive resource that comes with this textbook. Some masters are drawn from the text, but many new ones are provided to give instructors more options for augmenting chapter content. For each chapter the Instructor's Manual also provides an instructor's overview, teaching outline, focus questions, activities, teaching strategies, and discussion questions.

The Text Bank contains multiple choice items with answer feedback and essay or case-based applications with answer guidelines. For your convenience, the Text Bank is also available in electronic format for both IBM and Macintosh.

In addition, adopters of this textbook receive a free **Inclusion Video**, which traces the progress of three students with disabilities—Josh, Eric, and Tonya—as they are mainstreamed into general education classes. This 23-minute video spans the elementary school, middle school, and high school levels and illustrates environmental, instructional, technological, and curricular adaptations. The video also highlights professional cooperation and collaboration as parents, classroom teachers, special education teachers, and school administrators work together to help Josh, Eric, and Tonya succeed in inclusive classrooms.

Acknowledgments

We have many people to thank for their generous contributions of time, knowledge, experience, and sound advice. We are deeply grateful to the many teachers who have shared their classrooms, students, and experiences with us. In particular, we would like to extend our heartfelt thanks to the teachers and principals of Flamingo Elementary School. We would also like to thank the many students in the initial teacher preparation programs at the University of Arizona and the University of Miami who have helped us better understand the important attitudes, knowledge, and skills for new teachers preparing to teach diverse learners.

Just a few of the many people whose names should be in lights for their generous contribution to this book follow.

A special thanks to Sandra Bowen, Penny Rosenblum, and Andrea Morrison. Their expertise in educating students with hearing impairments, visual impairments, and mental retardation/severe disabilities, respectively, was a valuable resource. Sandra played an important role in writing the section on hearing impairments in Chapter 9. Penny took on a similar role in writing the section on

Research Briefs in every chapter briefly summarize essential research findings that relate to key chapter topics.

visual impairments in the same chapter. Andrea not only worked on the physical disabilities and health impairments section of Chapter 9, but also played a significant role in writing Chapter 8 on Mental Retardation and Severe Disabilities.

Mary Hinson for sharing her valuable knowledge as a job developer and university instructor for the mainstreaming course for secondary teachers.

Sharon Kutok for sharing her valuable knowledge as a speech/language pathologist.

Elba Reyes for reviewing and providing insights for Chapter 10 on teaching students with cultural and linguistic diversity.

Jeanne Bergeron and Michelle Sobol for their help with Chapter 12 on gifted and talented students.

Maria Arguelles, Kristine Kalamani, Patrick Kinner, Tina Stanton Chapman, and Tiffany Newell for their assistance in manuscript preparation.

Jane Sinagub who assisted with all aspects of manuscript preparation including expert editorial

work and good judgment. Her contribution to the book is extensive.

We also benefited form the suggestions and revision of outstanding reviewers. Like all authors, we were not always anxious to rewrite but soon realized the benefits form their helpful suggestions and resources. Thank you for your generous assistance:

Philip C. Chinn, California State University, Los Angeles
Gary A. Davis, University of Wisconsin, Madison
Bill Davis, University of Maine, Orono
Mary Kay Dykes, University of Florida
Patricia Edwards, University of Akron
John Garrett, University of Louisville
Jane F. Hogan, SUNY-Genesco
Marie C. Keel, Georgia State University
Henry Earl Knowlton, University of Kansas
Linda Duncan Malone, Ball State University
Thomas Mihail, Purdue University, Calumet
Sharon Raimondi, Buffalo State College
Colleen M. O'Rourke, Georgia State University
Katherine (K.C.) Sacca, Buffalo State College
Sandra K. Squires, University of Nebraska, Omaha
Beth Lorene Tulbert, Ball State University

The personnel at Allyn and Bacon provided ongoing support for this book. Mary Ellen Lepionka, Development Editor, worked closely with us on the overall design for the book as well as assuring that the central ideas and features were carried consistently throughout each chapter. Her fine editorial skills improved our organization and writing. We would also like to thank the many personnel at Allyn and Bacon for their assistance: Rob Lawson, Production Administrator, Debbie Schneck, Coordinator, Editorial Production Services, Gail Burlakoff, Copyeditor, and Melinda Grosser, Text Designer.

We also would like to give a very special thank you to our husbands for their steadfast support and personal sacrifices: Jim Dammann, Bob Bos, and Jerry Schumm.

An illustrated **Tech Talk** feature in each chapter presents specific information on sourcing and using assistive technology, educational software, and other products and services for students with special needs.

Teaching Mainstreamed, Diverse, and At-Risk Students in the General Education Classroom

CHAPTER ONE

Special Education and Inclusive Schooling

FOCUS QUESTIONS

1. What basic laws and procedures govern special education and mainstreaming?

2. As a classroom teacher, what are your responsibilities toward your students with special needs?

3. What systems and resources are in place in your school to help you teach students with special needs in your classroom?

4. How are professional collaboration and family involvement critical to the success of inclusive education?

5. What concerns do teachers, parents, and schools have about inclusion, and how can these issues be addressed?

6. What are some opportunities and challenges you can expect to find in your mainstreamed classroom?

Tiffany Royal

Tiffany Royal is a fifth grade teacher at Flamingo Elementary School in Miami, Florida. During the past two years she has worked in an inclusive classroom in which seven of her 34 students have been identified as students with disabilities. For up to two hours a day, a special education teacher, Joyce Duryea, works in Tiffany's classroom as a co-teacher. Each week, Tiffany and Joyce also meet for an hour or more to discuss students' progress and plan instruction for the following week.

Tiffany has been successful in maintaining her students with special needs in her inclusive classroom on a full-time basis. To honor her achievement, in 1994 the Dade County Council for Exceptional Children named her "Mainstreaming Teacher of the Year."

Here is Tiffany's advice for teachers working in mainstreamed classrooms:

Don't worry that you have to know everything about students with disabilities to be successful with them as a teacher. At first, I was concerned that I didn't know what to do and that I hadn't been specially trained. Then I realized that they are like the other students in my class, and many of the instructional practices I use work for all students. I just have to think about the special needs of students and make accommodations. It sounds hard but it really isn't. My advice is get to know each of your students really well, and you will learn what types of adaptations work for them. I spend a few minutes at the end of the day making a list of students I need to be sure to spend a few minutes with the next day on a one-on-one. I think about what I want to accomplish with them. That really helps a lot. Also, the special education teacher is a big help. Joyce Duryea has given me many ideas, and I learn from watching her with the students.

I think about communicating frequently with parents. Our class publishes a newsletter every other week that gets sent home to every parent. Also, the parents of students with disabilities really appreciate the weekly notes that Joyce and I take turns sending home.

Like many new teachers, I was worried about the special education laws, IEPs, and conferences. I kept saying to myself, "What if I mess something up?" Again, the special education teacher was a big help. I realized I wasn't responsible for everything, that there are many shared responsibilities. The most important thing to remember is that the IEP is not a legal contract but a plan to define goals for each of the students with disabilities. Actually, I do something like an IEP for my entire class.

I must admit, ever since I was little I wanted to be a teacher. When I imagined myself as a teacher I never thought about students with disabilities in my class. Now I cannot imagine teaching without them. It sounds corny, but they add so much. I'll never forget Jose. The teachers here tell stories about him, you know, how he acted when he first came to school and all. You should see him now. I'm not saying he does all the work other students do, but he is making great progress. When he raises his hand and gets the answer right, he just beams and looks around the room to see that everyone noticed. I don't think I could teach any other way.

Introduction

Tiffany's account reflects the philosophy of this book. Our philosophy rests on the belief that teachers make a difference, that we must teach purposefully to empower all of our students to learn, and that even small steps matter. The aim of this book is to offer you the basic knowledge, tools, and strategies that will empower you as a classroom teacher to skillfully, confidently, and successfully promote learning for all your students.

The basic knowledge you need includes an understanding of the laws and procedures that govern special education and mainstreaming, and so this is where we begin.

IDEA and the Vocational Rehabilitation Act

Legislation for individuals with disabilities has provided them with education, employment, housing, and other rights that they previously were denied because of their disabilities. You can imagine how important the following two landmark pieces of legislation have been. The Individuals with Disabilities Education Act (IDEA), P.L. (Public Law) 94–142, and Vocational Rehabilitation Act, P.L. 93–112, have significantly improved the opportunities for individuals with disabilities.

P.L. 94–142, originally referred to as the Education for All Handicapped Children Act, was enacted in 1975, and later reauthorized and expanded as the **Individuals with Disabilities Education Act (IDEA)**. This legislation was designed to ensure that all children with disabilities receive an appropriate education through special education and related services. Figure 1.1 provides a summary of the history of laws governing special education.

According to Turnbull (1990), IDEA includes the following primary characteristics:

- **Zero reject/Free appropriate public education.** No child with disabilities can be excluded from education. Mandatory legislation provides that all children with disabilities are provided a free appropriate public education.

Before IDEA, school officials who felt they were not equipped to address the special needs of particular students would not accept them into their schools.

- **Child find.** States are required to identify and track the number of students with disabilities and to plan for their educational needs.
- **Age.** The ages during which children with disabilities must be educated are defined by the law, and these ages exceed those provided for nondisabled students. IDEA provides for special programs and services for all students with disabilities between the ages of three and twenty-one. Infants and toddlers with developmental delays (birth to two years of age) are also eligible to receive early intervention services.
- **Nondiscriminatory evaluation.** An evaluation that does not discriminate on the basis of language, culture, and students' background, must be provided for each individual identified for special education. This is particularly challenging in states such as California, Florida, and Texas where students identified for special education services represent more than 100 languages.
- **Individualized education program (IEP).** A plan—developed to meet the special learning needs of each student with disabilities—must be written, implemented, and reviewed.
- **Least restrictive environment.** IDEA defines the educational settings in which students are placed. The least restrictive environment is the setting most like that of nondisabled students, which also meets each child's educational needs. Inherent within the least restrictive environment is the notion of continuum of services. Continuum of services means that a full range of service options for students with disabilities will be provided by the school system. These service options include self-contained classrooms, resource rooms, and homebound and general education programs.
- **Due process.** Due process not only ensures that everyone with a stake in the student's educational success has a voice, but also addresses written notification to parents for referral and testing for special education, parental consent, and guidelines for appeals

History of the Federal Laws for the Education of Learners Who Are Exceptional

1973 Vocational Rehabilitation Act (VRA) (Public Law 93–112, Section 504)
- Defines "handicapped person"
- Defines "appropriate education"
- Prohibits discrimination against students with disabilities in federally funded programs

1974 Educational Amendments Act (Public Law 93–380)
- Grants federal funds to states for programming for exceptional learners
- Provides the first federal funding of state programs for students who are gifted and talented
- Grants students and families the right of due process in special education placement

1975 Education for All Handicapped Children Act (EAHCA) (Public Law 94–142, Part B)
- Known as the Mainstreaming Law
- Requires states to provide a free and appropriate public education for children with disabilities (ages 5 to 18)
- Requires individualized education programs (IEP)
- First defined "least restrictive environment"

1986 Education of the Handicapped Act Amendments (Public Law 99–457)
- Requires states to extend free and appropriate education to children with disabilities (ages 3 to 5)

- Establishes early intervention programs for infants and toddlers with disabilities (ages birth to 2 years)

1990 Americans with Disabilities Act (ADA) (Public Law 101–336)
- Prohibits discrimination against people with disabilities in the private sector
- Protects equal opportunity to employment and public services, accommodations, transportation, and telecommunications
- Defines "disability" to include people with AIDS

1990 Individuals with Disabilities Education Act (IDEA) (Public Law 101–476)
- Renames and replaces P.L. 94–142 (EAHCA)
- Establishes "people first" language for referring to people with disabilities
- Extends special education services to include social work and rehabilitation services
- Extends provisions for due process and confidentiality for students and parents
- Adds two new categories of disability: autism and traumatic brain injury
- Requires states to provide bilingual education programs for students with disabilities
- Requires states to educate students with disabilities for transition to employment, and to provide transition services

and record keeping. IDEA guarantees the right to an impartial hearing if appropriate procedures outlined by IDEA are not followed and parents or schools believe that programs do not meet the educational needs of the student.

- **Confidentiality of records.** IDEA requires that all records and documents regarding students with disabilities remain both confidential and accessible to parents.

- **Advocacy.** Advocates are assigned for individuals with disabilities who lack known parents or guardians.

- **Noncompliance.** IDEA requires that states mandate consequences for failure to comply with the law.

■ **Parent participation.** Parents' participation and shared decision making must be included in all aspects of identification and evaluation of students with disabilities.

The Individuals with Disabilities Education Act of 1990 differs from the original legislation P.L. 94–142 in that it:

■ Puts the person first and the use of the term "disability" second; for example, "students with learning disabilities" rather than, "LD students."
■ Requires that transition services be included in the individualized education programs of all students by at least age 16.
■ Provides for states, as well as school districts, to be sued if they violate IDEA.
■ Includes two additional categories: traumatic brain injury and autism.
■ Adds assistive technology as a support service.

The Vocational Rehabilitation Act (P.L. 93–112) prevents any private organization that uses federal funds, or any local or state organization, from discriminating against persons with disabilities solely on the basis of the person's disability. This law made a significant difference in the provision of equal opportunities and services for individuals with disabilities, because agencies that accept state or federal moneys must comply with the law. This law prohibits discrimination not only in public education, but also in the employment of persons with disabilities, and in social and health services. Because of this law, many individuals with disabilities now have greater access to colleges and universities (Cartwright et al., 1995). Take, for example, the case of Kathy Carter. "Access to facilities has opened up the world for me and Kathy," said Amy Carter, Kathy's mother.

> Since Kathy's mobility is limited to scooting around or the use of a wheelchair, there were many places we could not go. The movie theater closest to our house has a show upstairs where they often show children's movies. I either have to go with another adult who can help me get Kathy up the stairs or we can't go at all. I must say, I've noticed a big difference recently. The new shopping mall near our house is completely wheelchair accessible.

The Concept of Least Restrictive Environment

According to IDEA (P.L. 94–142), a continuum of educational services must be available for students with disabilities. This continuum of services ranges from the full-time general education classroom to a special day school or residential facility. Figure 1.2 shows the continuum of services in terms of the major placement alternatives.

Consideration for educational placement is dynamic and ongoing. Students' placements are continually reevaluated for opportunities to move to less restrictive environments. Fundamental to the law is the notion that students cannot be educated in more segregated settings simply because it is easier to do so (Osborne & DiMattia, 1994). The principle behind the least restrictive environment is that students are best served in the settings (most like those of their nondisabled peers) in which they can learn, ideally moving to less and less restrictive settings. A checklist for determining the least restrictive environment is provided in Figure 1.3. Most students will receive services in the general education classroom, with support services provided as necessary. There are times, however, when students' needs are best met in other settings. Thus, the decision must be made on a student-by-student basis, with any level on the continuum potentially serving as the least restrictive environment for a target student. For example, many parents of children who are deaf prefer that they be educated in settings with other children who are deaf so that they have opportunities to learn the culture and language of deafness.

In addition to defining the continuum of services, special education laws also identify the types of services to which students with disabilities are entitled. These related services include: speech therapy, audiology, psychological services, physical therapy, occupational therapy, recreation, early identification and assessment, counseling, medical services for diagnostic or evaluation purposes, school health services, transportation, and social work services. Related services can be an extremely important part of a student's program. The requirements for related services follow:

> The term "related services" means transportation and such developmental, corrective, and other supportive services (including speech

FIGURE 1.2

Continuum of Educational Services for Students with Disabilities from Least to Most Restrictive

Least restrictive

Level I General education classroom with consultation from specialists:
Student functions academically and socially in general education classroom full time. Specialists provide consultation.

Level II General education classroom; cooperative teaching or co-teaching:
Special education teacher and classroom teacher co-plan and co-teach for part of school day. For entire school day, student is included in general classroom, where support services are provided.

Level III Part-time placement in special education classroom:
Student is placed in the general education classroom for part of the school day and in the special education classroom, usually the resource room, for a certain number of hours daily.

Level IV Full-time special education classroom in a general education school:
Student is educated in a special education classroom housed in a general education school. This arrangement—of being educated in the special education room so students have contact with general education peers only during nonacademic periods—may include part-time involvement with general education students for activities such as physical education and lunch.

Level V Special school:
Student is provided special education services in a special education school.

Level VI Residential school, treatment center, or homebound instruction:
Student is provided special education services at home, or resides in a school or treatment center in which education is provided.

Most restrictive

---

pathology and audiology, psychological services, physical and occupational therapy, recreation, including therapeutic recreation, social work services, counseling services, including rehabilitation counseling, and medical services, except that such medical services shall be for diagnostic and evaluation purposes) only as may be required to assist a child with a disability to benefit from special education, and includes the early identification and assessment of disabling conditions in children (United States Department of Education, 1992).

Part-Time Placement in Special Education Some students whose educational and social needs cannot be met solely within the general education classroom receive special education and related services (that is, counseling, speech, language, occupational or physical therapy, instruction, and so on) outside the classroom. Related services may be provided individually or in small or large groups.

A common educational placement, designed to meet the educational needs of students with disabilities outside the general education classroom, is the special education resource room. The resource-room model provides specialized, individualized, and intensive instruction to meet students' needs. Reading, writing, and math are the three academic areas most frequently addressed by the special education teacher in the resource room. Students can work in the resource room for as little as a few hours per week in an elementary school, or one period per day in a secondary setting. Depending upon their needs, students may work nearly full time in a resource setting.

Some resource rooms are designed to meet the needs of students identified as having a particular kind of disability—learning disabilities, for example. Other resource rooms are designed to meet the needs of students with varying exceptionalities. The term varying exceptionalities refers to the placement of students who represent a range of disability categories (e.g., students with emotional disorders, learning disabilities, physical impairments, and students who are gifted).

Full-Time Placement in Special Education The educational and social needs of some students cannot be met through part-time placement in the general education classroom. These students may be placed in a special education classroom located in a general education school. Students placed in full-time special education classrooms often attend electives classes (such as physical education, music, art, and vocational education) with their nondisabled peers. If there are no full-time special education classrooms in the home school, students may be transported to schools outside their neighborhood. Many educators and parents, believing that the relocation of students to another school interferes with the students' social and personal adjustment, discourage such placements. Students placed full-time in special education classes should be closely monitored so that they can be placed as quickly as possible in the general education classroom.

Special School or Residential Settings When the problems of students with disabilities are so severe and complex that adequate education cannot be provided in general education classrooms, students may be placed in special schools. These schools may be part of the school system, or the system may contract private schools that specialize in programs for students with special needs. One advantage of special schools is that total enrollment is usually small, with technical services and individual attention more easily provided. One disadvantage to the school system is cost—special schools are expensive, and transportation also can be expensive. Disadvantages for students are that travel to and from the school can be time consuming, and that they have limited opportunities to interact during the school day with children who do not have disabilities.

Homebound Instruction Students with health or physical problems that prevent them from attending school regularly, or students who have been expelled from school, may receive homebound instruction. The primary role of a homebound teacher is to provide direct instruction and to coordinate instructional programs between the school and the home. Although students with disabilities sometimes receive long-term homebound instruction, it usually is a short-term remedy until the student is able to return to school. Mariel Simpson explains,

> Over the past eight years my son Jalena, who has spina bifida, has been operated on six times. After each of these operations he needed to stay at home for eight to twelve weeks to recover. I felt very fortunate to have the homebound teacher come to my home to work with Jalena so that he would not get too far behind in his school work.

RESEARCH BRIEF

STUDIES OF MAINSTREAMING EFFECTIVENESS

Ongoing studies of the effectiveness of mainstreaming and inclusion practices are important to the future of the education of students with special needs. A summary of early research by Lloyd Dunn (1968) contributed to the widespread acceptance of the concept and practice of mainstreaming. Dunn reviewed the effectiveness of self-contained separate classrooms for students with mental retardation and found that those classrooms were no more effective in promoting students' academic and social development than were general education classrooms. Subsequent research has supported this finding, indicating further that students with mental retardation, regardless of the severity of the condition, benefit from placement in general education environments where planned, structured opportunities for interaction with students without disabilities are made available (e.g., Halvorsen & Sailor, 1990; McDonnell et al., 1991).

People's perceptions play a major role in the effectiveness of mainstreaming and inclusion programs (National Center on Educational Restructuring and Inclusion, 1994). For example, Stainback and Stainback (1990) reported that

classroom teachers who have opportunities to interact with students with severe or multiple disabilities are not fearful or intimidated by the presence of those students in their schools. A common perception of teachers and schools is that full-inclusion is not for everyone. Schools and teachers report the greatest difficulty in successfully integrating students with emotional and behavioral disorders and students with learning disabilities who need a more distraction-free learning environment than general education classrooms can provide.

The Individualized Education Program (IEP)

IDEA (P.L. 94–142) requires that an individualized education program (IEP) be developed for each student with special educational needs. The purpose of an IEP is to provide an appropriate education. IEPs are developed and implemented by the multidisciplinary team (MDT). The multidisciplinary team serves two purposes. First, the team determines whether the student has a disability and is eligible for special education services. If this is the case, then the team develops the IEP, which provides the foundation for establishing the educational program for the student. The multidisciplinary team includes a representative of the local education agency, the classroom teacher, the special education teacher, parents or guardians and, when appropriate, the student. Depending on the student's needs, the team also includes professionals from the related services (such as social workers, speech and language pathologists, psychologists, occupational therapists) and may include other professionals, such as doctors.

Each IEP must include the following information:

- Student's present level of educational performance
- Annual educational goals for the student, including short-term instructional objectives
- A description of the specific educational services provided for the student
- The initial starting date and anticipated duration of these services
- Criteria and procedures for regularly evaluating student progress and determining

whether instructional objectives have been achieved

- Related services, such as transportation, counseling, speech and language therapy, occupational therapy, and so on
- At least by the time a student reaches the age of 16, a transition plan and transition services
- Percentage of time in general education
- Special instructional media and materials
- Service providers with primary responsibility
- Justification for the type of educational placement
- Committee members present
- Parents' signatures

The IEP is a method for planning and assessment that reflects the judgments and inputs of the school system, specialists, teachers, parents, and students themselves. The IEP is a safeguard not only for students, but also for families and school systems. An example of an IEP is presented in Figure 1.4.

Participants in IEP Meetings IEPs are intended to serve as planning guides for the student with special needs, not as mere paperwork. IEPs provide guidelines for educators for the daily education of the individual. Unfortunately, classroom teachers at the middle and secondary levels often do not participate in the IEP process and do not know which students in their classrooms have been identified as having special needs (Schumm & Vaughn, 1992). Carl Turner, a middle school teacher, put it this way,

> I know that Mike has an IEP and I read it at the beginning of the year, but I haven't really used it in my planning. There may be other students who have learning disabilities in my class, but I won't know until the special education teacher tells me.

Persons who are *required by law* to attend the IEP meeting include:

- A school representative other than the teacher, such as a person designated by the school system.

- Parents or guardians—to ensure that they are informed and involved in the student's placement and progress.
- The student, when appropriate—involving students in the planning of their educational goals is often appropriate, particularly at upper elementary grades and secondary grades.
- The student's teacher (general and/or special education)—the teacher is involved in identifying realistic and appropriate educational goals for the student.
- Others whom the parents or school believe can help develop the IEP. (As mentioned earlier, this may include representatives from a range of related services and professions (e.g., medicine, physical therapy, and psychology).

The school should ensure that parents attend IEP meetings, by making every reasonable attempt to contact parents and accommodate their schedules. This includes scheduling meetings at times that are convenient for parents, giving ample advance notice of the meeting, securing mutual agreement for the time and place of the meeting, meeting through phone calls or home visits if parents cannot attend, and providing a copy of the IEP to parents upon request. If parent involvement cannot be obtained, the school should document

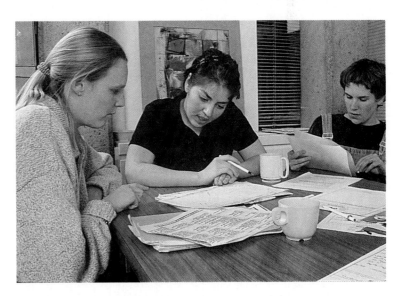

How do classroom teachers participate in the IEP process? What are three ways that teachers participate in the referral and planning process for students with special needs?

FIGURE 1.4

Sample IEP

NAME **Alan Brenner**   D.O.B. **5-19-83**   I.D. NO. **1234567**   ADDRESS **4141 SW 40th Terrace**

HOME SCHOOL **Southend Elem.**   ASSIGNED SCHOOL **Southend Elem.**   GRADE **4**   TELEPHONE **593-8986**

PARENT NOTIFICATION: 1) **10-27-94 phone call**   2) **11-3-94 letter sent**   3) **11-7-94 phone call**

(Dates and Methods)

COMMUNICATION IN BASIC LANGUAGE OF PARENT: **English**

PRESENT PERFORMANCE LEVELS

INSTRUMENT	DATE	LEVELS	INSTRUMENT	DATE	LEVELS
Key Math	5/94	2.8			
Spelling	5/94	2.0			
Dolch Word List	5/94	80% 1st			
PIAT	5/94				
Read Recog.	5/94	1.9			
Read Comp.	5/94	2.2			
Woodcock Johnson	11/94				
Word I.D.	11/94	K.5			
Word Attack	11/94	1.7			
Passage Comp.	11/94	1.7			
Key Math	11/94	3.0			

BEHAVIORAL OBSERVATIONS **Has trouble staying on task, very talkative, often disrupts class.**

STUDENT WILL PARTICIPATE IN THE STANFORD ACHIEVEMENT TEST
NO ☐   YES ☑

☐ INITIAL
☐ REEVALUATION
☑ ANNUAL REVIEW
☐ OTHER _____

RECOMMENDATION:
☐ STANDARD HIGH SCHOOL DIPLOMA
☐ SPECIAL HIGH SCHOOL DIPLOMA
☐ CERTIFICATE OF COMPLETION
☐ SPECIAL CERTIFICATE OF COMPLETION

Not Applicable

MODIFICATIONS:
☑ FLEXIBLE SCHEDULING   ☐ REVISED FORMAT
☑ FLEXIBLE SETTING   ☐ AUDITORY AIDS
☐ RECORDING OF ANSWERS

REGULAR/VOCATIONAL EDUCATION PROGRAMS
40% of day, content, Art, Music, P.E.
☐ PT   ☑ FT   INITIATION DATE: **11/10/94**   ANTICIPATED DURATION: **11/9/94**

E.S.E. PROGRAM(S) **Specific Learning Disabilities**
☐ PT   ☐ FT   INITIATION DATE **11/10/94**   ANTICIPATED DURATION **11/5/94**

PERSONS RESPONSIBLE **Exceptional Student Education Teacher**

RELATED SERVICES **Counseling**

PERSONS RESPONSIBLE **School Counselor or Exceptional Student Education Teacher**

OTHER PERTINENT DATA (Medication, etc.) **Ritalin 2 X a day — Morning and at lunch.**

FIGURE 1.4

STUDENT'S WEEKLY CALENDAR

R = REGULAR EDUCATION   E = EXCEPTIONAL EDUCATION

TIME	MONDAY	R/E	TUESDAY	R/E	WEDNESDAY	R/E	THURSDAY	R/E	FRIDAY	R/E
8:30	Jrnl. Writing	R	Jrnl. Writing	R	Jrnl. Writing	R	Jrnl. Writing	R	Jrnl. Writing	R
9:00		E		E		E		E		E
9:30	Math	E	Math	E	Math	E	Spanish	E	Math	E
10:00		E		E		E		E		E
10:30		E	Sustained silent reading	E		E		E		E
11:00	P.E.	R	P.E.	R	P.E.	R	P.E.	R	P.E.	R
11:30	Lunch	R	Lunch	R	Lunch	R	Lunch	R	Lunch	R
12:00		E		E	Art	R		R		E
12:30	Lang. Arts	E	Lang. Arts	E		R	Lang. Arts	E	Lang. Arts	E
1:00		E		E	Music	R		E		E
1:30		E		E		R		E		E
2:00		R		R				R		R
2:30	Content	R	Content	R			Content	R	Content	R
3:00		R		R				R		R

ADDITIONAL NOTES: ___60___ % EXCEPTIONAL EDUCATION   PLUS   ___40___ % REGULAR EDUCATION TIME = 100% PROGRAM TIME

A current calendar must be maintained to account for all program aspects (100% total) of the child's school time, including regular education.

SIGNATURE (ESE TEACHER) *Kimberly Davidson*   PROGRAM *Specific Learning Disabilities*   DATE *11/10/94*

LEA REPRESENTATIVE *Linda McKeon*   POSITION *Principal*

FIGURE 1.4

Include academic, behavioral, emotional, social, vocational, speech, physical/occupational therapy, adaptive p.e., as needed.

ANNUAL GOALS	SHORT-TERM INSTUCTIONAL OBJECTIVES	EVALUATIVE CRITERIA AND TIMELINES	OBJECTIVE MET	DATE
A. Alan will demonstrate improvement in Language Arts Skill by 4–6 months.	A. Alan will:			
	A1. Read sight words at 2nd grade level.	Teacher observation and/or teacher made test with at least 85% accuracy to be evaluated every grading period.	+	3/95
	A2. Improve phonics ability by identifying spelling patterns such as digraphs, ccvc words, and cvcv (silent) words.		+	12/94
	A3. Use structural analysis to obtain mng. of words when reading such as prefixes/suffixes.			
	A4. Participate in various prewriting techniques such as reading, brainstorming, charting, and webbing.		+	3/95
	A5. Produce first drafts independently.		+	12/94
	A6. Participate in the revision process through conferencing w/peers and/or teacher.		+	6/95
	A7. Use context of a sentence to determine unfamiliar word meaning.			
	A8. Identify story elements such as setting, characters, problem/goal events, resolution.			
	A9. Read orally with expression at a 2nd grade level.		+	3/95
	A10. Identify the main idea from selected material that is read.		+	6/95
	A11. Locate and use dictionaries and encyclopedias.			
	A12. Spell words correctly at a 2nd grade level.			

FIGURE 1.4

Sample IEP (continued)

B. Alan will	B. Alan will:			Teacher-made test and/or teacher observation with at least 85% to be evaluated every grading period.
demonstrate improvement in Math Skills by 4–6 months.	B1. Identify place value of whole numbers from 11, 10, 100, and 1000.	+	12/94	
	B2. Identify rote memory times tables up to 9 X 9.	+	3/95	
	B3. Identify the proper unit of measurement through the 3rd grade.			
	B4. Solve word problems requiring addition and subtraction.	+	6/95	
	B5. Identify and compare attributes of geometric figures.			
	B6. Use manipulatives to show relationships of fractions.			
	B7. Demonstrate and use a calculator effectively for simple operations.			

LEA REPRESENTATIVE _Linda McKeon_   ELIGIBILITY CERTIFIED   YES ☑   NO ☐

CONFERENCE DATE _11-8-94_

SIGNATURES OF PERSONS PARTICIPATING IN MEETING:

Julie Brenner   **PARENT**

Jason Brenner   **PARENT**

Kimberly Davidson   ESE   **TEACHER**

Arlene Eaton   Reg. Class   **TEACHER**

John Smith   Counselor   **PSYCHOLOGIST**

Linda McKean   **ADMINISTRATOR**

all attempts to involve parents, including correspondence and a log of phone calls and visits. Some school districts have a placement specialist who takes responsibility for managing the placement and program development for students with IEPs. In other schools the special education teacher takes this responsibility.

The role of the general education teacher in the IEP process varies because each school district handles IEP meetings a little differently. As the classroom teacher, however, you will be an important resource.

Each person is at the meeting because he or she has knowledge and experience that can assist

TECH TALK

Individualized Education Program Software

Multidisciplinary teams (MDT) can develop individualized education programs (IEP) with the aid of computer software. Generally, these programs provide a standardized outline to which the MDT can add particular information specific to each student (e.g., name, academic difficulties, strengths). In addition, an extensive database of possible long-term goals and short-term objectives is provided, and the MDT can select which are appropriate for any given student. Some of the more sophisticated programs are capable of producing administrative reports and updates for teachers and parents (Lewis, 1993).

One program that is compatible with both IBM and Apple II systems is TALLEY™ Goals and Objectives Writer. This software affords the MDT the opportunity to select goals and objectives for the IEP from preexisting databases, such as the BRIGANCE® CIBS, or to develop their own bank of goals and objectives. Data, including diagnostic information and the selected goals and objectives, are coded and input into the computer. Goals and Objectives Writer II is available for Windows and Macintosh. These products are available from Curriculum Associates®, Inc. tel. 1-800-225-0248.

Portions of a sample IEP report developed through Goals and Objectives Writer II, using goals and objectives from CIBS, follow:

INDIVIDUAL EDUCATIONAL PROGRAM

Goals and Objectives

Student's Name	Newell, Tiffany	ID #	123456789
Birth Date	12/9/88	Grade	Third
Parent Name	Newell, Tara and Jason	Teacher Name	Pinne, Tom
Address	100 Main St., Apt. 2	School	Lake Elementary
Referral date	5/29/96	Placement date	4/12/96
Primary Placement	Third grade, General education	I.E.P. Date	6/23/96

Additional Data/Notes

SIGNATURES OF MEETING ATTENDEES   TITLES   DATE

_____   _____   _____

_____   _____   _____

_____   _____   _____

_____   _____   _____

_____   _____   _____

_____   _____   _____

Goals and Objectives

Goal File #10

  TO INCREASE WRITING SKILLS

Objective File # 136

  J-8   BY (11/23/96), WHEN GIVEN AN ADDRESS AND AN ENVELOPE, STUDENT WILL CORRECTLY AND LEGIBLY ADDRESS THE ENVELOPE USING HIS OR HER OWN ADDRESS AS THE RETURN ADDRESS.

Criteria for Evaluation:

Schedule for Evaluation:

MASTERED ( )   CONTINUE ( )   CONTINUE WITH MODIFICATION ( )
DISCONTINUE ( )

BRIGANCE® *Diagnostic Inventory of Basic Skills,* ©1976, 1977, Curriculum Associates, Inc. Reprinted by permission.

in designing the best educational program for the student. Not everyone knows the same things, and so each person's contribution is unique and necessary. For example, the school psychologist often provides expertise on diagnostic test results and interpretation. You, however, are the expert on the curriculum for your content areas and grade levels. Your responsibility is to ensure that the goals designed to be implemented in your classroom reflect appropriate content and skills for your classroom. At the same time, everyone's knowledge of the student is useful to establish high, realistic behavioral and academic goals.

The IEP Process   Most school districts have developed their own format and procedures for writing IEPs. All members of the team contribute to the IEP, which should include everyone's ideas about the educational goals and objectives. The person who most frequently incorporates what the team agrees upon and who writes the IEP is the special education teacher.

Responsibilities of Classroom Teachers

General education teachers often express concerns about the extent to which they need to know and understand the law as it pertains to individuals with disabilities. Daniele Ferguson put it this way,

> As a classroom teacher, I'm concerned about all of the children in my classroom. I want to do as good a job as I can, but I also realize that I cannot know everything about every difficulty, learning and behavioral, that the children in my classroom will manifest. I know that I need to know who to contact when I have questions. But I suppose what is of the most interest to me is exactly what I'm responsible for and what I need to know so that I can successfully implement education programs for the students with special needs. Probably my biggest questions center around the law and what I need to do.

When asked what questions she had, Daniele provided the following list:

Who's responsible for the IEP?
The multidisciplinary team is responsible for developing the IEP; the person principally responsible for the IEP, however, is the special education teacher. The general education teacher and the parent might be responsible for particular objectives described in the IEP.

Can I be held responsible if a student in my class does not accomplish all of the objectives in the IEP?
The IEP is not a contract, but rather an agreement in which the teacher undertakes the optimum educational procedures to help ensure that the student meets the IEP objectives. Teachers cannot be held responsible for students' lack of progress on IEP goals unless it can be proven that teachers have not made efforts to fulfill their responsibilities.

What if I was unable to attend the meeting at which the child's IEP was developed?
Obtain a copy of the student's IEP from the special education teacher or meet with the special education teacher to identify the IEP objectives for which you are responsible.

What should I do if I feel a student is not making adequate progress on his or her IEP?
Communicate your observations to other members of the multidisciplinary team. Regular meetings with the special education teacher and other professionals who are providing services to the student will ensure that the student's progress is monitored. Also, meetings that involve parents or guardians will help you explain a student's progress and find ways to enhance his or her performance.

Although knowledge of the law is important, you should also be aware of the resources available to you when you have questions and need further information. Many people in your school and district can help you. Experienced teachers tell us that their best

> The IEP is a plan, not a contract, and teachers cannot be held responsible for students' lack of progress toward IEP goals if they do everything feasible to ensure that the plan is implemented.

resources are the special education teachers in their building, other teachers, the school psychologist, and the principal (Schumm & Vaughn, 1992). IDEA is a law aimed at enhancing the quality and equity of education for all students. The law requires reasonable expectations of teachers. Your role is to help students fulfill the objectives in the IEP and to provide an appropriate education for all students (See Tips for Teachers 1.1).

Octavio Gonzalez, a ninth grade English teacher, has three students with disabilities in two of his five sections of English. These students receive support services during the school day from the special education teacher, and Octavio meets occasionally with the special education teacher to plan and get suggestions for accommodating their needs in his English class. Octavio comments,

> At first I was nervous about having students with disabilities in my class. One of the students has a learning disability, one student has serious motor problems and is in a wheelchair, and the third student has vision problems. Now I have to say that the adaptations I make to meet their special learning needs actually help all of the students in my class. I think that I am a better teacher because I think about accommodations now.

An eighth grade teacher, Lin Chang, put it this way,

> At first I was worried that it would be all my responsibility. But after meeting with the special education teacher, I realized that we would work together and I would have additional resources if I needed them. Furthermore, I think more about keeping in touch with the parents so that they are always informed of progress. Doing all of this communication on the telephone is not always possible, so I send a lot of notes home.

Unfortunately, monitoring the progress of students mainstreamed into general education sometimes becomes the sole responsibility of the special

TIPS FOR TEACHERS

1.1 How Can You Meet Your Special Education Responsibilities?

- Ask special education teacher what reports are relevant to successful instruction of students with disabilities in your class, then read these reports.
- Ask special education teacher for suggestions for enhancing the learning of students with disabilities in your classroom.
- Ask special education teacher to co-teach your class or demonstrate lessons that show how his or her suggestions can be implemented.
- Attend relevant meetings (about your students with disabilities) that involve parents and other school personnel.
- Reexamine IEPs quarterly, and check that you monitor the progress of students with disabilities in your classroom.

- For each student with disabilities in your classroom, keep a folder of relevant work samples to document progress.
- Maintain parent contact through occasional phone calls and written notes.
- Meet regularly with special education teacher. If he or she does not already work in your classroom, extend an invitation to come in and help you instruct students with special needs.
- If you are concerned about a student's progress, don't hesitate to inform the special education teacher.

education teacher. This is not an effective procedure. An appropriate education for the students with disabilities is most likely to occur when the special and general education teachers work together. Our studies with middle and high school teachers reveal that obtaining access to students' IEPs and psychological reports (to be used to guide teacher planning for students with disabilities) is difficult (Vaughn & Schumm, 1994). Teachers believe that their best sources of information are parents, former teachers, or the students themselves (Schumm & Vaughn, 1992). Thus, middle and high school teachers need to consider adaptations that provide for the special learning needs of students with disabilities and also enhance instruction for all their students. Remember, a few minutes of one-on-one purposeful teaching is an effective way to assess progress and provide directed instruction. We have found several accommodations general education teachers can make that not only assist students with disabilities in the general education classroom but also enhance instruction for all students. These approaches, described in detail later in this book, are summarized in Tips for Teachers 1.2.

Participating in the Referral and Planning Process

Approximately 10 percent of the school-age population receives special education services (United States Department of Education, 1994). These are students whose educational and social/emotional needs are not expected to be met through traditional instructional procedures alone.

The term "disabilities" refers to conditions that include mental retardation, hearing impairments, vision impairments, speech and language disorders, learning disabilities, serious emotional disturbance, orthopedic impairments, other health impairments, autism, deafness and blindness, and multiple disabilities. The classification of students into categories of disability is controversial. Many people feel that labels are necessary because they provide a common understanding of the needs of the student and help identify appropriate special education services. Others feel that the labels conjure negative stereotypes, harm students' self-concepts, and cause confusion because each category subsumes many different defining characteristics.

Regardless, labels and categories can be used in ways that are helpful as well as harmful. You need to consider how to think of the person first, rather than the type of disability. Figure 1.5 shows the system of federal categories and the percentage (by category) of students who are provided special education.

Students are identified as having special needs through a system of referral. Students who have obvious disabilities (such as significant hearing, visual, or physical impairments or significant mental retardation) are usually referred and identified prior to age five. For these children, the disabilities are obvious to parents and pediatricians, and intervention begins early in the child's life. Students with mild to moderate disabilities are often identified, after they begin school, by classroom teachers or parents.

> This book takes a cross-categorical approach—that is, accommodations for exceptional learners are discussed in terms of their shared needs rather than in terms of their identification as members of a disability category.

The Prereferral Assistance Team Referrals for assessment and appropriate intervention services are often initiated by classroom teachers. Many schools have established school-based prereferral assistance teams (PATs) to screen students for assessment. The prereferral assistance team is a group of teachers from the same school who meet regularly to discuss the specific progress of students brought to their attention by other teachers in the school. This school-based, problem-solving team is designed to help teachers make classroom accommodations that maximize opportunities for students to succeed in the general education classroom and might make referral for special education unnecessary. The model provides a forum where classroom teachers can meet and participate in a collaborative, problem-solving process.

Prereferral assistance teams work toward the following goals:

■ Provide suggestions to the classroom teacher
■ Accommodate students' academic and behavioral needs

TIPS FOR TEACHERS

1.2 Adaptations for Students with Disabilities in the General Education Classroom

- Respect all students as individuals with differences (e.g., be aware of their capabilities and problems, and make exceptions accordingly), and encourage all students to respect mainstreamed students.
- Establish appropriate routines (e.g., establish a setting so that students know what is expected; be consistent).
- Adapt effective classroom management strategies for students with special needs (e.g., time out, point systems).
- Provide reinforcement and encouragement (e.g., encourage effort, provide support when students get discouraged).
- Establish personal relationships with students (e.g., get to know students as individuals, determine student interests and strengths).
- Help students find appropriate ways to deal with feelings (e.g., by expressing their feelings through drawings or writings; provide brief periods of time away from class).
- Communicate frequently with mainstreamed students (e.g., plan frequent short, one-on-one conferences, and discuss potential modifications with students).
- Communicate with the special education teacher (e.g., exchange notes and talk informally with the special education teacher).
- Communicate with parents of mainstreamed students (e.g., exchange notes and talk informally with parents, encourage parents to provide support for students' education).
- Establish expectations for all students (e.g., expect the best from every student).
- Make adaptations for students when developing long-range (yearly/unit) plans (e.g., establish realistic long-term objectives).
- Make adaptations for students when developing daily plans (e.g., be alert to problems that could pose special difficulties for students).
- Plan assignments and activities that allow mainstreamed students to be successful (e.g., try to structure assignments to reduce frustration).
- Allot time for teaching learning strategies as well as content (e.g., test-taking skills, note-taking skills, and so on).
- Adjust physical arrangement of room (e.g., modify seating arrangements).
- Adapt regular classroom materials (e.g., different textbooks, supplemental workbooks).
- Use alternative materials (e.g., different textbooks, supplemental workbooks).
- Use computers to enhance learning (e.g., as a tool for writing, as a tool for practicing skills).
- Monitor the mainstreamed students' understanding of directions and assigned tasks (e.g., ask students to repeat or demonstrate what you have asked them to do, check with students to be sure they are performing assignments correctly).
- Monitor the mainstreamed students' understanding of concepts presented in class (e.g., attend to, comment on, and reinforce understanding of vocabulary, abstract ideas, key words, time sequences, and content organization).
- Provide individual instruction (e.g., plan for one-on-one sessions after school, allocate time for individual instruction during class).
- Pair students with a classmate (e.g., to provide assistance with assignments, provide models for behavior and academics, and for social support).
- Involve students in small-group activities (e.g., allow students from different levels to work in small groups).
- Involve students in whole-class activities (e.g., include mainstreamed students in class participation).
- Provide extra time (e.g., schedule extra time for skill reinforcement and extra practice).
- Adapt pacing of instruction (e.g., break down materials into smaller segments, use step-by-step approaches).
- Keep records to monitor students' progress (e.g., keep a folder of students' papers, keep a progress chart).
- Provide students with ongoing feedback about performance (e.g., meet periodically with students to discuss academic and behavioral performance).
- Adapt evaluations (e.g., use oral testing, give more time for tests, modify administration procedures).
- Adapt scoring/grading criteria (e.g., alter criteria for grades).

Reprinted with permission from: Schumm, J. S., & Vaughn, S. (1991). Making adaptations for mainstreamed students: General classroom teachers' perspectives. *Remedial and Special Education, 12*(4), 18–27. ©1991 by PRO-ED, Inc. Used by permission.

- Reduce the need for referral to special education
- Assist the teacher with the referral process, if necessary

Although prereferral strategies take different forms in different school districts, there are three general models (Strickland and Turnbull, 1990):

- The resource consultation model
- The special education teacher as part-time consultant model
- The teacher assistance team (TAT) model

Consultation Models The special education teacher as a consultant is a traditional prereferral intervention model. Classroom teachers who have students with learning and behavioral difficulties and other disabilities in their classrooms frequently look to the special education teacher for advice and support (Schumm & Vaughn, 1992). Teachers

might ask the special education teacher to observe students in the classroom and in other settings to provide initial suggestions for assistance.

In a second consultation model, the special education teacher works part-time in general education classrooms to assist teachers with students who have been identified as requiring special education but whose needs generally can be met in the general education classroom. The special education teacher also assists teachers in implementing practices to enhance academic and social outcomes for students at risk for referral to special education.

The Teacher Assistance Team The teacher assistance team (TAT) (Chalfant & Pysh, 1989, 1993; Chalfant et al., 1979) provides initial strategies and support for classroom teachers prior to referring a student for assessment for special education services. According to Chalfant and colleagues, schools may benefit in several ways by using teacher assistance teams:

FIGURE 1.5

System of Federal Categories and the Percentage of Students Served

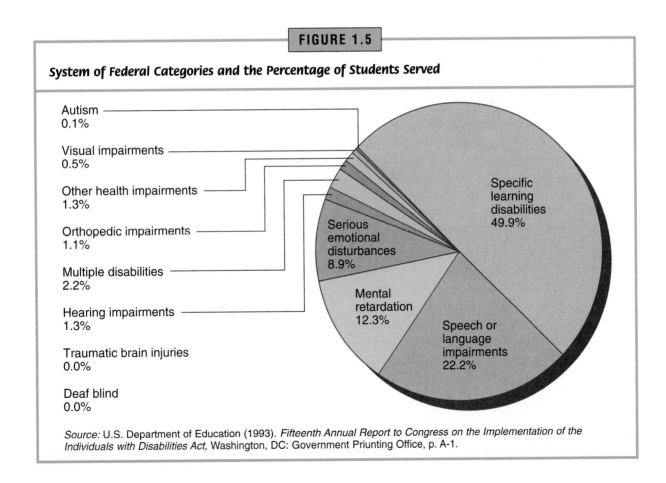

Autism
0.1%

Visual impairments
0.5%

Other health impairments
1.3%

Orthopedic impairments
1.1%

Multiple disabilities
2.2%

Hearing impairments
1.3%

Traumatic brain injuries
0.0%

Deaf blind
0.0%

Specific learning disabilities
49.9%

Serious emotional disturbances
8.9%

Mental retardation
12.3%

Speech or language impairments
22.2%

Source: U.S. Department of Education (1993). *Fifteenth Annual Report to Congress on the Implementation of the Individuals with Disabilities Act,* Washington, DC: Government Priunting Office, p. A-1.

- Classroom teachers have considerable knowledge and talent and can assist each other in meeting the needs of targeted students.
- Classroom teachers can and do help many students with disabilities. Every effort should be made to meet students' needs in the classroom before referral for special education.
- Teachers who work together can solve more problems more effectively than when they work alone.
- Teachers can increase their skills and knowledge through solving the academic and social problems of students.

Figure 1.6 provides an example of a form that might be used to assist with prereferral. During a TAT meeting, team members (using the guidelines in Tips for Teachers 1.3) participate in a problem-solving process that lasts approximately 30 minutes.

Adapting Instruction

In addition to participating in planning, prereferral, and referral procedures, the chief responsibility of classroom teachers is to adapt curriculum and instruction to accommodate students' special needs. "What does it mean to adapt instruction for students with disabilities?" asked Anna

---

FIGURE 1.6

Prereferral for Special Education Services

Directions: Please complete all sections of this form. The form should be sent to the Teacher Assistance Team. Complete and specific information will assist the team in providing as much assistance as possible. Use behavioral descriptions whenever possible.

Teacher

Grade/Class

Date

Student

Age

1. Describe what you would like the student to be able to do that he or she does not presently do.

2. Describe what the student does (assets) and what he or she does not do (deficits).

3. Describe what you have done to help the student cope with his or her problem.

4. Provide background information and/or previous assessment data relevant to the problem.

TIPS FOR TEACHERS

1.3 Problem-Solving Guidelines for TAT Meetings

- Present and review summary information about students from your prereferral form or notes.
- Identify primary concern and describe interventions you and other teachers have tried.
- Brainstorm and evaluate ideas for potentially solving the problem.
- Select a goal to address the problem and identify objectives and procedures for solving it.

- Discuss suggestions with classroom teacher and further refine your classroom intervention plan.
- Develop a means of measuring success of intervention plan.
- Establish a date and time for a 15-minute follow-up meeting to evaluate effectiveness of plan.

Schmidt, a tenth-grade social studies teacher. "I have certain objectives I need to meet for all of my students. Does this mean I alter these objectives?" Anna's questions are important and are the subject of Parts II and III of this book. Classroom teachers can greatly help their students with special needs by making adaptations that positively affect learning for all students in the classroom.

Many of the adaptations you make for students with disabilities will enhance learning for all students in your classroom. For example, Marie Trajeho, an eighth grade teacher, develops an outline of her lectures. She projects this outline on a screen, pointing out her location in the outline as she presents key information. This procedure not only helps students with disabilities who have difficulty organizing information, taking notes, and identifying key ideas, but also enhances learning for all the students in her classroom.

Looking for students' strengths, and ways to say "good job" also promotes learning for all students. Jane Gordon, a fourth grade teacher, was a pro at this. She realized that motivation is the key to success, particularly for the students with disabilities in her classroom, and she put considerable effort into knowing the strengths and interests of each student and recognizing the strengths and interests whenever possible.

RESEARCH BRIEF

MODELS FOR ADAPTING INSTRUCTION

A study of 53 teachers who planned and developed a program to integrate students with moderate or severe disabilities into general education schools and classrooms yielded guidelines for key stakeholders at the school (Janney et al., 1995).

District Administrators—(1) Provide a clear and open message that you want to support what is best for all students and that you want to encourage integration of students with moderate or severe disabilities. (2) Teachers do not want a mandate that they must include every student full-time in general education no matter what. (3) Provide a "green light" to go ahead with integration of students with moderate to severe disabilities when appropriate.

Principals—(1) Key to success is a positive tone from the principal regarding integration and acceptance of students with moderate or severe disabilities. (2) Start with teachers who volunteer to participate, rather than forcing all teachers to participate. (3) Involve everyone in the planning and preparation for the inclusion of students with moderate and severe disabilities. (4) Provide information, new resources, and training so that teach-

MAKING A DIFFERENCE

The 60-Second Lesson

Teaching on Purpose

The philosophy of this book is that classroom teachers can help their students who have special needs by teaching "on purpose," that is, by being mindful and proactive in using opportunities to make a difference in these students' classroom experiences. Contrary to common belief, purposively teaching students with special needs need not take a great deal of time. You can make a difference in only a minute. For example,

think about having one or two 60-second lessons with each of your special-needs students every day. How is Darnell progressing on a given IEP objective? What directed feedback can you provide to Marlene to help her achieve her goals? To reflect the value of 60-second lessons in classroom practice, a feature, called "Making a Difference," provides an example in every chapter of this book.

ers feel knowledgeable and prepared to meet the needs of exceptional learners. (5) Provide the resources so that the program can be implemented effectively, and handle the logistics from central administration, parents, and other key stakeholders. (6) Start small (a few teachers and students) and then build the program as it succeeds.

General Education Teachers—(1) Have an "open mind" about the process. Many teachers reveal that their anxieties and concern were not warranted. (2) Work collaboratively with other teachers, most importantly the special education teacher. (3) Help the student with disabilities acquire full membership in the school and class community.

Transition: Expanding the Impact of IDEA

With the amendments of IDEA, the impact of IDEA has expanded to include: (1) services for infants, toddlers, and young children from birth to age five, and (2) transition planning and services for adolescents as they move from high school to post-secondary education, adult life, and the world of work.

Early Intervention and Transition from Early Childhood to School

The 1986 IDEA amendments mandated services for young children with developmental delays (beginning at age three) and also made infants and toddlers with or at risk for developmental delays (birth to two years of age) eligible to receive early intervention services. Early intervention services are comprehensive services that incorporate goals in education, health care, and social services (Hanson & Lynch, 1989). The important role played by the IEP in program planning for school-age students with disabilities is played, for children from birth to three years of age, by the individualized family

The National Association for the Education of Young Children (NAEYC) has more than 80,000 members who provide services to young children (birth to age 8). NAEYC has developed guidelines entitled, *Developmentally Appropriate Practice in Early Childhood Programs Serving Children from Birth Through Age 8* (Bredekamp, 1986).

service plan (IFSP). As the name suggests, however, the IFSP broadens the focus to include not only the child but the family and their needs in supporting a young child with disabilities.

If you are a kindergarten teacher, you probably will have the opportunity to teach young children who, having received early intervention services, are making the transition from preschool to your classroom. It is important for you to remember that for families and children with disabilities, these transitions are among the most significant times in their lives, filled with uncertainty and concern. Following are some comments from parents:

> "I was scared to have him go to public school. I worry about him a lot . . . If I had it my way, I'd never send him to school" (Johnson et al., 1986, p. 15).
>
> "I saw making the transition to a preschool program in the school district as an extremely traumatic experience, second only to learning of Amy's diagnosis" (Hanline & Knowlton, 1988, p. 116).

As a teacher, you can help parents of children with special needs by recognizing that their fears and concerns are expected and realistic and by providing information about your classroom and the school to help alleviate their concerns (Fowler et al., 1991; Wolery, 1989). You can also help to facilitate this transition by doing the following:

- Attending the IEP or IFSP meeting prior to transition so that you are aware of the child's strengths, the goals planned, and techniques and strategies that have been successful. You can meet the child's parents and current teachers, ask questions, and determine how this child's goals fit with goals for your other students.
- Meeting with the child's parents prior to the transition to learn about their goals for their child, the child's strengths and needs, and strategies they have found help their child succeed in preschool.
- Setting up a regular means of communication with the child's parents and former teachers, particularly for the first several months. Invariably, questions will arise that can be answered easily by the parents and those who have been working with the child. Do not hesitate to use these resources.

Transition from School to Work and Other Post-School Activities The 1990 amendments to IDEA mandated transition planning and transition services for students from 16 years of age (or 14 years and even younger, if appropriate) to age 21. In IDEA, transition services are defined as "a coordinated set of activities for a student, designed within an outcome-oriented process, which promotes movement from school to post-school activities including post-secondary education, vocational training, integrated employment (including supported employment), continuing and adult education, adult services, independent living, or communication participation" (P.L. 101–476, 602[a][19]). The law also notes that these activities should be based on the student's needs, preferences, and interests. The activities include instruction, community experiences, the development of employment and other adult-living objectives, and when appropriate, vocational evaluation, rehabilitation counseling, and the acquisition of daily living skills.

This emphasis on transition planning and services came in response to the growing concern about the number of students with disabilities who were unemployed or underemployed as adults, and the limited emphasis on vocational education and adult living in many secondary programs for students with disabilities. For example, a 1994 Harris poll found that three of ten adults with disabilities were working full- or part-time, and that 79 percent of those not working and of working age indicated that they would like to have jobs (Harris, 1994). A study in Vermont linked successful employment and higher wages following school to vocational education and support services during high school (Hasazi et al., 1989). As the Vermont study implies, an important part of changing this pattern is the provision of transition services, including supported employment during high school, so that students can develop the social and job skills needed to obtain and continue employment.

A key component of these transition services is the transition plan incorporated into the IEP. This transition plan should state what transition services are necessary and, when appropriate, should include a statement of the interagency responsibilities and linkages (P.L. 101–476, 1990). Many districts interpret this by including in the IEP specific goals and objectives for transition, then adding a list of classes and activities that would provide opportunities for students to meet these goals and objectives. Sample objectives follow:

- By the end of the semester, Jason will develop the skills to successfully complete job applications. (Taught in career exploration class and by completing job applications with job developer.)
- By the end of the school year, Nancy will develop positive work habits (e.g., arriving on time, interacting with co-workers). (Taught in career exploration class and during work experiences supported by the job developer.)
- Within the next three years, Maria will develop computer skills in word processing, databases, and spreadsheets to the degree that she can effectively use them on a job. (Taught in computer classes and during work experiences supported by the job developer.)

With the increased emphasis on transition, vocational education, and work experience

Why was IDEA expanded to include eligibility for transition planning for individuals with disabilities from birth to age 21? In what transition activities might this student be involved when he is in high school?

opportunities during high school for students with disabilities, many districts have special education personnel who work in this area. Mary Hinson, a job developer at Catalina High School, is one such person. She comments on her job and the difference it makes for her students,

> I believe that the work I do as a job developer makes the difference for many students with disabilities and lets them leave high school already employed and adjusted to the world of work. I also believe that the opportunities provided through Catalina's transition program are the best dropout deterrent for students with disabilities, particularly with learning and emotional disabilities. What I do is work with the students, their teachers, and parents to plan a program that allows them to develop job and independent living skills, take relevant coursework both at the high school and at the community college, and have relevant work experiences. I also network with agencies and post-secondary institutions. For example, I will assist college-bound students in exploring possible community colleges and universities, in learning about support programs for students with disabilities at those institutions, and in completing the application process.
>
> A big part of my job is developing partnerships with businesses that will provide initial training and "the first job" for students with disabilities. One of these partnerships that I am particularly proud of is with AutoZone. Through this partnership, we have a classroom that is set up like an AutoZone store. Students with disabilities and their nondisabled peers take this class and learn the various facets of running an auto parts store. The class is co-taught by the marketing teacher and myself. I've learned more about sales and fixing a car in the last four years than you can imagine. And the students participating in this class find themselves prepared not only in general job skills but specific skills related to sales and auto repair.

Important to making a successful transition from school to adult life is developing self-determination and self-advocacy skills, including the skills of considering options, making appropriate choices, and communicating choices to others (Schloss et al., 1993; Van Reusen et al., 1994).

Clearly, Mary has a different role than that of a typical special education teacher. If you teach in high school, you will want to take the time to find out about transition services and the job developers or persons in charge of transition planning and services. Knowing about a student's transition goals will help you tailor your accommodations so that they are relevant for the student's long-term career goals. For example, if a student with a learning disability is planning to enter the field of drafting, then emphasizing measuring skills in Basic Math class and computer-assisted design in computer classes may be particularly beneficial for this student.

Role of Collaboration in Meeting Students' Special Needs

Collaboration between general and special education teachers is a growing trend in schools across the nation (Dettmer et al., 1993; Sugai & Tindal, 1993). Greater collaboration among education professionals has grown out of increased awareness that students with disabilities are more likely to succeed in general education classrooms if they receive targeted support services in the classroom. The goal of collaboration models is to ensure that mainstreamed students remain in the classroom while continuing to receive the accommodations they need to succeed. The goal of collaboration is to achieve ongoing dialogue between all persons who can provide support for the education and social needs of the students.

At the center of the collaboration model is the classroom teacher. Research suggests that three conditions must be met for collaboration models to work (West & Idol, 1990):

- Teachers need access to opportunities for training and professional development.
- School administrators need to support the model.
- Teachers' and students' schedules must be flexible.

With increased interest in including students with disabilities in general education classrooms full-time, there has been increased movement toward a collaboration model. Despite this increased interest, there is limited research data documenting the effectiveness of this approach to meeting the needs of students with disabilities (Fuchs & Fuchs, 1988). Many administrators support consultation and collaboration models because they view them as opportunities to cut the costs of educating students with disabilities. This is a misunderstanding, because the consultation and collaboration model, when appropriately done, does not reduce costs. Figure 1.7 outlines some perceived benefits and challenges of collaboration models that you should be aware of.

Cooperative Teaching

Cooperative teaching, or co-teaching, occurs when general and special education teachers work together to coordinate curriculum and instruction and to teach heterogeneous groups of students in the general education classroom setting (Bauwens et al., 1989). The benefits of cooperative teaching are that the teachers have the opportunity to co-plan and co-teach and thus to coordinate and assess the ongoing educational programs of all students. Furthermore, the responsibilities and rewards of meeting the needs of students with disabilities are shared. Finally, all students in the classroom are likely to benefit from the teachers' expertise and coordination.

The teachers broadly plan their overall goals and desired outcomes for the class, identify students for special accommodations, and design adaptations and supports to meet the individual needs of students and enhance the learning of all students. The teachers also decide which instructional period they will co-teach and when and how they co-plan.

How might co-teaching actually work in the classroom? While one of the teachers delivers some instruction to the group as a whole, for example, the other teacher works with small groups or individual students. The special education teacher is not limited to working only with students who have disabilities, but can include in the group other students who benefit from the accommodations provided.

Patty Cohen is a special education teacher who works in a cooperative teaching arrangement with Karen Feller, a fifth grade teacher. Karen has

---

FIGURE 1.7

Benefits and Challenges of Consultation and Collaboration Models

Benefits:
- Students with special needs are served in the classroom.
- Learning for all students is enhanced through spillover effects.
- Social stigma of exceptionality is reduced.
- Teachers gain new knowledge and skills.
- Teachers develop more integrated curriculum and instructional variety.
- Teachers share both burdens and rewards of working with students with disabilities.
- Importance of labels and categories of disability decreases.
- Models work at all grade levels.

Challenges:
- Teachers need greater communication and problem-solving skills.
- Special educators' case loads need to remain realistic.
- Expectations of results need to remain realistic.
- Results need to be evaluated for effectiveness.
- Students need continued access to the continuum of services.
- Adequate funding, administrative support, and flexible scheduling need to be maintained.

---

six students with disabilities in her classroom, and Patty spends two hours each day in her room. Additionally, Karen has a teaching assistant for four hours a day. During a 90-minute language arts period, three teachers are in the classroom. Patty and Karen take turns as lead teacher and small-group teacher. Patty has time to work with students individually or in pairs to teach specific skills. Patty and Karen make cooperative teaching look simple. As you observe them in the classroom you are aware of how easily the class grouping arrangements flow from one configuration to the next and how comfortably the teachers move from lead teacher to small-group instructor. "It's very easy for us," they say almost in unison. "Both of us have very high expectations for the students and we strive never to waste a minute of instructional time. This requires planning on our part, but it's worth it."

Zigmond and Baker (1995) have investigated the many ways special and general education teachers work together to meet the needs of students with disabilities. As described in the preceding paragraph, sometimes co-teachers share responsibilities for small-group and large-group instruction. This is not always the case, however. In some settings, the special education teacher works only with the students with disabilities.

Family Collaboration

Parents are the most influential persons in a child's life. This is particularly true for exceptional students whose parents serve multiple roles, including those of advocate and information source. Fundamental to the implementation of IDEA is parent involvement and collaboration (Turnbull et al., 1992). Parent permission is obtained prior to assessment for identification and then through every step in the process. Parents participate in the development of the IEP and are provided yearly reports of the progress of their child. During the middle and high school years, students are encouraged to participate with their parents (Van Reusen & Bos, 1994).

The intention of the law is that parent involvement will benefit the student in many ways (Shea & Bauer, 1991), including those that follow:

- Parents will be able to provide knowledge about the student that should influence what and how he or she is taught.
- Parent knowledge of the student's educational program will ensure school-to-home continuity so that many skills can be reinforced in both settings.
- Parent knowledge and involvement will increase expectations for the student, and result in academic and social gains.
- Parent involvement ensures a safeguard so that the needs of the student are discussed and met by the school system.

In many cases and many school systems, parents' roles are collaborative. They provide essential information to the multidisciplinary team that assists in the development of an appropriate IEP and a high-quality educational program. This, however, is not always the case. Parents often feel overwhelmed by the amount of information they are provided, the technical terms used, and can be intimidated by the number and qualifications of professionals present at meetings. This results in parents who are present but are not active, collaborative members (Vaughn et al., 1988). Often, too much emphasis is placed on compliance rather than on genuine communication (Harry et al., 1995).

What can you do so that parents serve as active, collaborative resources? Some key ideas are provided by Dettmer, et al. (1993):

- Remember that a teacher's place is on the parents' side as a team member working for a common goal, the student's success.
- Become aware of your own feelings of defensiveness. Taking a deep breath and putting feelings aside will help teachers to continue building positive relationships. If that is not possible, teachers should postpone interactions until the defensiveness can be handled.

In what type of professional collaboration are these teachers engaged? What other forms of collaboration are important for achieving goals in meeting students' special needs?

- Remember that the focus must be on the needs and interests of parents and their children, not on their values. It is important to attack the problem, not the person.
- Accept people as they are and stop wishing they were different. This applies to parents as well as to their children.
- Remember that most parents are doing the best they can. Parents do not wake up in the morning and decide, "I think today I will be a poor parent."
- Respect parents' right to have their own values and opinions. Different values are not better or poorer values.

Mainstreaming and Inclusion

How does mainstreaming relate to the continuum of services? Mainstreaming, the placement (from part-time to full-time) of students with disabilities in the general education classroom, is not required by law but is one way to achieve placement in the least restrictive environment. The essential element of mainstreaming is shared responsibility on the part of all educators in the school toward the student with disabilities. Mainstreaming includes accommodations designed to facilitate the participation of students with disabilities in all aspects of public education including transportation, instruction, extracurricular activities, and access to facilities.

In practice, the terms mainstreaming and inclusion are used interchangeably. They can have very different meanings, however. Mainstreaming refers to the participation of students with disabilities in general education classrooms to the extent it is appropriate to meet their needs. Inclusion refers to the situation in which students with disabilities are educated with their nondisabled peers, with special education supports and services being provided as necessary. Advocates of full–inclusion feel that all students with disabilities should be educated in the general education classroom all the time (Stainback & Stainback, 1992). Pull-out services (e.g., special education resource room models) are not options for full-inclusion advocates because students with disabilities are not educated

entirely in the same setting (i.e., the general education classroom) as nondisabled students.

At issue is the extent to which a continuum of services is maintained. Earlier in this chapter, the range of educational options for students with disabilities (e.g., the self-contained special education classroom, homebound instruction, and resource room) was presented. This is the continuum of services, which advocates of inclusion want to maintain. Advocates of full inclusion are concerned, however, that maintaining a continuum of services will prevent real integration of students with disabilities. The concern is that if the option for separation or pull-out from the regular classroom is available, then educators will too easily choose it. Debate continues over the extent to which full–inclusion should be required for all students with disabilities. We believe that the central issue is the extent to which the academic and social progress of students with disabilities is monitored and adjustments provided if progress is not adequate (Vaughn & Schumm, 1995).

The Regular Education Initiative (REI) is a concept that promotes the placement of students with disabilities in the general education classroom for all or most of the school day. One primary thrust of the REI is that students with disabilities benefit from placement in general education classrooms. The idea is that general and special education teachers, working cooperatively to meet the individual learning needs of all students in the general education classroom, can better educate the increasing number of students who demonstrate learning problems but do not qualify for special education. The REI has not been without criticism, however,

> Mainstreaming is not required by law. The law requires that youngsters with disabilities be educated in the least restrictive appropriate educational placement, which for most students includes at least partial inclusion in the general education classroom.

and many educators (e.g., Fuchs & Fuchs, 1994) express concern about the wholesale return of students with disabilities to general education classrooms on a full-time basis.

Recently, the movement within the REI has been expanded to include not only individuals with disabilities, but also other support services, such as Chapter 1 reading and migrant education. Individuals who support the REI believe, fundamentally, that the separation of services between special and general education creates an unnecessary burden, restricting the use of funds and limiting the educational opportunities available to all children. Many advocates believe that too many students are identified for special programs and that these students' needs can best be served in general education classrooms.

There are some areas in which people do agree. One is that students with disabilities need to be educated in the most normalized environment available and that extensive experience with nondisabled persons is essential to the social and academic growth of students with disabilities. The extent to which these experiences can be provided while not abolishing required special education support services should serve as the guiding principle.

Parents must receive written notification before an evaluation for special education services for their child can be conducted. The notification must be in a language parents can understand.

The arguments presented in Figure 1.8 are really not for or against inclusion. All advocates feel that students with disabilities should be educated in general education settings to the extent possible. Of concern is the extent to which specialized support services aimed at meeting the learning and behavior needs of students with disabilities should be available.

Cortina Fernandez describes the strategy she uses to successfully incorporate students with disabilities into her general education classroom,

First, I work very closely with the special education teacher. Before a student is placed into my classroom I find out as much as I can about what the student likes, what they can do, what their academic strengths are, what they enjoy doing outside of school, and what they can teach me and other students in the classroom.

Second, I find out what they need to know, where they are in terms of their academic progress, and what skills they need to learn, both academically and socially. I get this information from the student's IEP, from the

FIGURE 1.8

Arguments for Full Inclusion and Maintenance of the Continuum of Services

Arguments for Full Inclusion:
- Students with disabilities should be educated in general education classes all the time.
- Students with disabilities should not be pulled out of the general education classroom to receive specialized education.
- Benefits of placing students with disabilities in specialized classes, for either their academic or social growth, have not been demonstrated.
- Comprehensive, professional development that prepares teachers to meet the educational and social needs of all students is required.
- All students with disabilities have the right to education in the most normalized setting, the general education classroom.

Arguments for Maintaining Continuum of Services:
- Students with disabilities should be educated in general education classes to the extent it meets their educational and behavioral needs.
- Some students with disabilities need to have their educational needs met outside the general education classroom for part or all of the school day. A continuum of services to meet the needs of students with disabilities is required.
- Benefits and pitfalls of full-inclusion models for all students with disabilities have not been empirically documented.
- General education teachers are inadequately prepared to meet the specialized needs of all students with disabilities.
- Inclusion is a philosophy, not a place. Students have the right to receive the appropriate educational services to fill their learning needs in the most suitable site.

previous teacher, usually the special education teacher, and, if possible, by interviewing the student and the parent before the student is placed into my classroom.

Third, I work with all of the students in my classroom to assure that every child is a member of our community. Our learning community provides support and assistance for every other member and provides social support as well. This ongoing philosophy maintains a classroom environment in which all children are accepted, an essential ingredient to the success for mainstreaming of students with disabilities. I also make the success of every student in the class the responsibility of every other student. While I'm the teacher in the classroom and take that responsibility seriously, our learning community is one in which each child teaches each other. Thus, it's important to find out what everyone knows and what everyone needs to know so we can all work together. I also closely monitor the progress of every student in my classroom, particularly students with disabilities. I frequently check in with them, make sure they know what they're doing, and assure that they are making expected progress.

Fourth, communication is essential to the successful mainstreaming of students with disabilities. This communication occurs between myself and all the specialists, myself and the parent, as well as myself and other students in my class. However, I do not feel the communication is solely a one-way street. I hold the special education teacher and other specialists responsible for communicating with me, as well as encourage the parents to talk to me as frequently as they feel necessary. In addition, communication is part of the responsibility of students. They need to inform me about what they are doing well and where they need help. I encourage this communication by being open and receptive when they want to talk to me. Successful mainstreaming is more than just what I do as a classroom teacher. It's how I think and how I convey this to all the students and teachers in my school.

SUMMARY

- The Individuals with Disabilities Education Act (which incorporates and extends P.L. 94–142) and the Vocational Rehabilitation Act (P.L. 93–112) are the two primary laws that have increased the opportunities and services available to individuals with disabilities.
- According to IDEA (P.L. 94–142) a continuum of educational services needs to be available for students with disabilities.
- The principle behind the concept of least restrictive environment is that students are best served in settings, most similar to those of their nondisabled peers, in which they can learn (ideally, moving to less and less restrictive settings).
- A common educational placement, designed to meet the educational needs of students with disabilities outside the general education classroom, is the special education resource room. Other placements include: (1) full-time special education, (2) special school or residential settings, (3) homebound instruction, and (4) mainstreaming.
- The individualized education program (IEP) is developed and implemented by the multidisciplinary team, with the goal being the appropriate education of all students.
- In the last ten years, IDEA has been expanded to include services for young children (birth to five years) and to incorporate transition planning and services for students in secondary schools.
- The goal of collaboration models and practices is to ensure that mainstreamed students continue to receive the accommodations they need to succeed.

Key Terms and Concepts

advocacy

child find

confidentiality of records

continuum of services

cooperative teaching, co-teaching

cross-categorical approach

due process

early intervention services

educational placement

exceptionalities

free appropriate public education

full–inclusion, inclusion

individualized education program (IEP)

individualized family service plan (IFSP)

Individuals with Disabilities Education Act (IDEA)

least restrictive environment

mainstreaming

multidisciplinary team (MDT)

noncompliance

nondiscriminatory evaluation

prereferral assistance teams (PAT)

Public Law 94–142

Regular Education Initiative (REI)

related services

special education resource room

teacher assistance team (TAT)

Vocational Rehabilitation Act

zero reject

Think and Apply

1. Now that you have read Chapter 1, review Tiffany's account of her experience at the beginning of this chapter. If you could talk with Tiffany directly, what other questions would you ask her? List any questions or concerns you currently have about teaching in mainstreamed classrooms. Then, after you read each chapter, consult your list again and check off any questions that you can answer satisfactorily. File your personal inquiries in your teaching portfolio and record your answers as you progress through the book.

2. The primary components of the Individuals with Disabilities Education Act are described in this chapter. Select three of the components (e.g., zero reject/free appropriate public education, child find, nondiscriminatory evaluation) and write a brief description of what could happen to a student with disabilities if this component were not part of the legislation.

3. Obtain a copy of the IEP form used in a local school district. Work with a partner to complete as much of it as you can. Which aspects of the development of the IEP were challenging for you? Which aspects taught you the most?

4. Interview one or more teachers who have students with disabilities in their classrooms. Ask these teachers to identify any key practices they implement that they believe make a difference. Ask also what they wish they knew more about?

5. Interview a preschool teacher who works with students with disabilities, or a secondary teacher or job developer who coordinates transition services for students with disabilities. What do they view as their major roles and responsibilities? What do they think is more important for you as a general educator to know and do, so that these students are successful?

Read More about It

1. Blatt, B., & Kaplan, F. (1966). *Christmas in purgatory: A photographic essay on mental retardation.* Boston: Allyn & Bacon.

   Though taken more than 30 years ago, the photographs in this book tell a moving story about progress for individuals with disabilities and the importance of the laws described in this chapter. This book provides pictures of individuals living in institutional settings prior to the deinstitution movement.

2. Council for Exceptional Children. (1994). *Creating schools for all our students: What 12 schools have to say.* Reston, VA: Council for Exceptional Children.

   Provides a practical guide for developing inclusive schools for students with disabilities. Representing the work of 12 school districts from around the United States, common themes about what practices need to be in place to implement inclusive schools for all students are described.

3. Fuchs, D., & Fuchs, L. S. (1994). The inclusive schools movement and the radicalization of special education reform. *Exceptional Children, 60*(4), 294–309.

   Provides an overview of issues regarding the Regular Education Initiative, inclusion, and the merger of general and special education. The article describes the controversy surrounding the push for full–inclusion for all students with disabilities, and explains various positions on this issue.

4. Montessori, M. (1912). *The Montessori method.* New York: Stokes.

   Maria Montessori was a physician in Italy who successfully developed approaches for teaching students who were "unable to learn." Her approaches have been implemented with a wide range of students, including young children, gifted students, and students with cognitive impairments.

5. Strickland, B. B., & Turnbull, A. P. (1990). *Developing and implementing individualized education programs* (3rd ed.). Columbus, OH: Charles E. Merrill.

   Provides a complete overview of the development, writing, use, and implementation of individualized educational programs and plans. Forms and samples of individualized education plans are provided.

6. Vaughn, S., & Rothlein, L. (1994). *Books to prepare children for inclusion: Read it again!* Glenview, IL: GoodYear Books.

   Designed for teachers and parents, to assist them in identifying children's books that address the topic of or include key characters with disabilities. Activities are provided to help children better understand individuals with disabilities.

CHAPTER
TWO

Planning and Grouping Strategies for Special Learners

FOCUS QUESTIONS

1. What are the elements of the Flow of the Planning Process Model, including types of planning and factors that influence planning?

2. In thinking about long-term planning, what parameters must be considered and what resources need to be identified?

3. What are the key components of the Course Planning Routine?

4. What are the key components of the Planning Pyramid, and how can it be used for unit and lesson planning?

5. What kinds of instructional adaptations can be used in general education settings to promote learning for students with disabilities?

6. What are the differences between traditional grouping practices and current trends in instructional grouping?

7. What are the advantages and disadvantages of same- and mixed-ability groups?

8. When are whole group, small group, student pairs, and individual instruction most appropriate?

9. What is cooperative learning, and how can it be used to facilitate positive academic and social outcomes for all students?

10. How can you plan for flexible grouping in your classroom?

Interview

Lisa Geller

Lisa Geller is a third grade teacher at South Pointe Elementary School in Miami, Florida. Of the thirty-five students in Lisa's class, five have learning disabilities. Lisa's faculty has chosen an inclusion model of service delivery for students with disabilities. Ellen Fascano is the special education teacher who works with Lisa. Her role is to provide instruction for students with learning disabilities in the general education classroom during the reading and language arts block, and then to pull individual students, as necessary, to work on specific objectives identified on the IEP. Because Lisa and Ellen work daily in the same classroom, collaborative planning is a must.

Each week, Ellen and I sit down to talk about what the students with disabilities are doing. This is really important because we have parent conferences with the parents of all of our students four times a year, and Ellen and I both meet with the parents of the special education students. Although Ellen actually is responsible for the grades of the students with disabilities, we confer about their progress and decide on their grades jointly.

At the beginning of the year Ellen and I review the IEP for all of the children and develop plans for individual students. But really our planning is ongoing. We also conduct an informal reading test at the beginning, middle, and end of the year for the students so that we can keep track of their progress in reading and make revisions and additions to our plans. We also do a great deal of informal observation and keep checklists about student progress, and we input our observations into the computer every week. The philosophy of our school is to record one observation per subject area per week. As you can imagine, this takes a great deal of work, and we need to meet every week to accomplish it all. But it is really important as we think how to meet individual student needs.

When I do my unit and lesson planning, I talk with Ellen about what areas might be difficult for the students with disabilities. She lets me know the most sensitive areas and gives me suggestions for how I can make adaptations to help students learn the material.

Part of our planning is related to how we group students for reading instruction. The philosophy at our school is for each student to feel that he or she is important and one person is not better than the other, so we use a variety of grouping patterns—and most of the grouping is mixed, in terms of student achievement levels. If you came into our reading class, this is what you'd see. First we do whole class activities, such as reading a literature book together, and then some follow-up activities. Once again, Ellen is really helpful here because she lets me know where the students with disabilities might have some trouble and suggests some adaptations that I might make. I'm getting better at being sensitive to what they can and can't do while I'm teaching and making on-the-spot changes to help them learn.

During the follow-up activities, my kids always have a "study buddy." Usually we try to choose the buddy that they work with so that a high achiever is working with a student who is having difficulty reading. It's great because the high achievers feel that they are being teachers, and they are learning something too. The low achievers are only working with one student, so they don't feel embarrassed or feel that they can't do it. It works well.

During part of the reading time we divide up into smaller groups for skill lessons. Ellen pulls all the students with disabilities into one group. The other students are placed in mixed achievement-level groups of six to ten students. I teach one group, and three other teachers come to our class to teach the other groups. This is unusual, but it really works. The other three teachers rotate from class to class to provide individual attention to students. I really like this small-group time because we can zero in on what each student in the class needs to work on.

You can see that the students with disabilities don't really feel that they are in a lower group. In our class we just say Ms. So-and-so's group is this table, and so on. The special education group is just another group. They look forward to that time because Ellen is a wonderful teacher, she's very caring, she loves the kids.

So we have whole-class instruction, student pairing for activities, and small-group instruction for skills. We also have cooperative learning groups for special projects, and also Ellen or I pull students who might need to work on a specific skill in phonics or comprehension. As you can see, we use many different grouping formats, which involves a great deal of planning and coordination. I've been very happy with the way we grouped our students this year. Next year I probably would take even more time, pull the students who are really having difficulty, and really try to focus more on the ones who can achieve more and try to challenge them. That's just my own personal goal.

Introduction

Planning for the success of all students in your class involves careful consideration of the needs of individuals as well as of those of the class as a whole. As our interview with Lisa indicates, she recognizes that in order for this to happen she needs to "plan time for planning" every week. Part of this planning time is hers alone and part is for collaborative planning with other professionals in the school. Although Lisa is meticulous with her beginning-of-the-year planning, she recognizes that it is important to keep setting new goals for meeting the individual needs of her students.

Part of Lisa's instructional planning is the way she organizes students for instruction through grouping. She knows that sometimes whole-class instruction is appropriate and necessary, but also realizes that at times she must incorporate small groups and student pairing into her plans in order to meet individual student needs.

In this chapter you'll learn strategies for planning for individual student needs within the framework of planning for the class as a whole. You'll also learn about how to incorporate a variety of grouping strategies to promote student suc-cess in your instructional planning. The focus of this chapter is not on your role in planning the IEP for students with special needs. Rather, the chapter focuses on how to make plans for your own classroom—plans that will attend to the learning needs of all students.

Model of the Planning Process

If you ask experienced teachers how they plan, you are likely to get a collection of very different answers. Like any kind of planning (planning a budget, planning a personal schedule, planning a trip) individuals have different styles—and it is important for you to learn from other professionals and then develop your own.

In developing your own planning routines, it is helpful to think about how and when planning occurs and the factors that influence planning. The **Flow of the Planning Process Model** (Figure 2.1) can help structure your thinking (Schumm et al., 1995). This model indicates the sequence and relation among three types of planning and the factors that influence planning.

FIGURE 2.1

The Flow of the Planning Process Model

Used by permission of *EEC* and the University of Calgary Press.

Types of Planning

For most teachers, planning is not just what is written in plan books, which often include only a general outline of what is going to happen in class. The "real" plan is in the head of the teacher and is developed and revised on an ongoing basis. Whether planning is for an entire school year, for a unit, or for an individual lesson, planning occurs at three stages—preplanning, interactive planning, and postplanning—as the Flow of the Planning Process Model indicates.

Preplanning Preplanning involves decisions about what to teach and how to teach it. This advance preparation, which occurs at many levels, includes activities such as developing unit or lesson plans, gathering materials, identifying resources, and deciding on instructional methods. Preplanning also involves gathering information about students' prior knowledge of the topic being taught, and their level of skill development, so that instructional plans are appropriate for meeting individual needs.

In a survey of 775 classroom teachers, 98 percent reported that their knowledge and skills for planning for general education students was excellent or good, but only 39 percent said that their knowledge and skills for planning for special education students was excellent or good (Schumm & Vaughn, 1992).

Interactive Planning Your goals for the year, plans for a unit, or outline for a lesson may be carefully drawn on paper and imagined in your head, but as you begin to implement your plans, you may need to make changes to promote learning for all students. For example, you may observe that one or more students are having difficulty learning a skill or concept. That's when interactive planning comes in. **Interactive planning** involves monitoring students' learning, and adapting your plans in response to their needs.

You might say to yourself, "Isn't interactive planning just teaching?" The two certainly overlap, but interactive planning differs somewhat, in that it focuses on the way students are learning and making appropriate adjustments.

Lampert and Clark (1990, p. 21) have noted, "teaching is a complex act requiring the moment-by-moment adjustments of plans to fit continually changing and uncertain conditions." Thus, interactive planning involves the on-the-spot decisions you make as a teacher to respond to student needs and to ensure that learning takes place.

Postplanning Postplanning is follow-up planning, and frequently occurs at the end of a lesson. After a lesson you may reflect on the way students performed, then use that information to guide your planning for subsequent instruction. For example, you might realize that you covered less material than you anticipated, and might need to adjust your plans for the next day.

Or perhaps many students did not grasp what you were teaching, and you may need to develop plans for reteaching the lesson—in a different way.

When evaluating a lesson, you may also reflect on how you would teach it in the future, or simply think, "When I teach that lesson next year, I'll be certain to make some changes." In other words, you evaluate what occurred and decide what to keep and what to leave out in the future.

Overall, postplanning involves thinking about and evaluating a lesson, and determining how student needs can best be met in future lessons, units, or in school years to come.

Factors That Influence Planning

The Flow of the Planning Process Model includes four interrelated factors that influence planning: teacher, environment, student, and topic. These factors can have a strong impact on what you plan, how you plan, and even how much you plan.

Teacher-related factors are those that pertain to you as a planner not only for your class as a whole, but also for students with special needs. **Environment-related factors** pertain to the context in which you teach and include state, local, and class-level factors. **Student-related factors** pertain to who your students are, how they learn, and how they respond to instruction—both academically and socially. **Topic-related factors** concern specifically what you are teaching.

Table 2.1 presents examples of each of the four factors that influence planning.

TABLE 2.1

Four Factors That Influence Planning

Teacher-Related Factors
- attitudes and beliefs about planning in general, and motivation to do so
- attitudes and beliefs specific to planning for students with special needs, and motivation to do so
- knowledge and skills in planning and making accommodations for students with special needs
- knowledge of and experience and interest in the subject matter you are teaching
- amount of planning time
- confidence in planning and making adaptations

Environment-Related Factors
- state and school-district guidelines and policies regarding planning and curriculum
- school-level guidelines and policies regarding planning and curriculum
- grade-level, department, or subject-area guidelines and policies regarding planning and curriculum
- state-adopted textbooks and available materials
- access to specialists (i.e., reading resource specialists, special education teachers, school counselors)
- scheduling of special classes: physical education, special education, ESL classes, music, and art

- scheduling of special holidays, assemblies, and special activities
- physical arrangement and condition of school and classroom

Student-Related Factors
- class size
- engagement and interest in the topic and tasks
- motivation
- learning strategy preferences
- level of background knowledge
- behavior patterns
- acceptance of adaptations
- language and cultural differences
- difficulty with basic skills

Topic-Related Factors
- new or review material
- prior knowledge of topic
- interest level of topic
- number and complexity of new concepts or skills introduced
- clarity of topic presentation in curricular materials
- importance of topic in relation to overall curriculum

RESEARCH BRIEF

FACILITATORS AND BARRIERS TO PLANNING INSTRUCTION FOR STUDENTS WITH SPECIAL NEEDS

Prior to 1990, the topic of general education teachers' planning for students with disabilities was restricted to research on the classroom teachers' role in the IEP process. Because larger numbers of students with disabilities were being placed in general education settings for all or part of the school day, research was needed in the ways teachers plan and make adaptations for exceptional students.

To explore this topic, Schumm and Vaughn (1992) conducted a survey with 775 general education teachers (elementary, middle school, and high school) to determine what they do to plan and make adaptations for students with disabilities. The survey included a section in which to identify factors that can impact planning for mainstreamed students: both facilitators and barriers to planning.

Responses to survey items among teachers in various grade groupings were similar. In general, classroom teachers viewed fellow professionals (special education teachers, school-based curriculum specialists such as reading resource teachers, fellow teachers, department chairs, and guidance counselors) as those who help in the planning process. Budgetary factors (particularly the need for larger classes) were identified as the greatest barriers. Need to cover curriculum objectives, access to equipment and materials, and lack of planning time were also identified as factors that inhibit planning.

Meeting the instructional needs of all your students takes careful advance planning (preplanning), adjustments during lessons to be certain that learning is taking place (interactive planning), and reflection and evaluation to improve instruction in the future (postplanning). The need for conscientious planning of all three types is particularly important when you teach diverse learners, including students with disabilities. The task might seem awesome, but it can be done. First, it can be accomplished by considering the reality of your situation: the teacher, student, environmental, and topic-related factors. It can also be accomplished by using planning procedures specifically designed to focus on individual needs within the framework of planning for the class as a whole. In the next sections, you'll read about procedures for long-term, unit, and lesson planning.

Long-Term Planning

It is interesting to observe three or four teachers in the same school who teach the same grade (at the elementary level) or the same grade and subject (at the secondary level). Even in schools in which teachers use the same state-adopted textbooks and follow the same state or district curriculum objectives, you are likely to see differences, particularly in the ways teachers accommodate individual student needs. Many of these differences stem from the type of **long-term planning** (planning for the whole school year) teachers do to meet individual student needs. This section presents suggestions for ways to include individual student needs in your long-term preplanning, interactive planning, and postplanning for your class as a whole.

Few travelers would start out on a cross-country trip without a map. Long-term planning is your map for the school year. Long-term preplanning is essential to helping you get the big picture in respect to curriculum and classroom management. It can help you set a plan for moving from unit to unit and developing a sense of continuity. Most important, it can help you set a framework for meeting the individual needs of your students throughout the year.

Procedure for the Course Planning Routine

If you are an elementary teacher, you'll probably teach a number of subjects: language arts, reading, mathematics, science, social studies, and so on. If you are a secondary teacher, you'll need to prepare for one or more courses. In either case, it's important to develop a master plan for what you'll teach and how to teach it. Of course, you'll need to work within your "planning parameters," but even so you'll have many decisions to make for your own class.

The six-stage **Course Planning Routine**, developed by researchers at the University of Kansas (Lenz et al., 1993), is a guide for long-range planning for classrooms with diverse learners. This guide includes procedures for setting goals for the

What process did this teacher undertake in planning this geography lesson? What factors influenced this process?

course, getting the course off on the right foot, monitoring and managing the course during the year, and closing the course. As an elementary teacher you can use this routine in your planning for each subject. As a secondary teacher you can use this routine for planning each course. In either case, the Course Planning Routine can help you get the big picture:

Stage 1—ReflActive Planning Process—consists of seven steps designed to help teachers think through an overview of the course. The steps are easy to remember because they're organized by the acronym **SMARTER** (Lenz et al, 1993, p. 14–15):

- Select the critical content outcomes and turn them into a set of 10 questions that everyone in the class will be able to answer at the end of the course.
- Map the organization of the critical content of the entire course and create a visual device that will help students see their progress in mastering course content.
- Analyze why the critical course content might be difficult to learn, based on:

quantity	complexity
interest	student background
relevance	organization
abstractness	external conditions (e.g., calendar)

- Reach decisions about the types of routines, devices, or learning strategies that should be used throughout the course to address learning difficulties.
- Teach using these routines regularly throughout the year to inform students about the devices and strategies being used and to involve students in constructing the devices and strategies in explicit ways.
- Evaluate mastery of the critical course content and related processes for high achievers, average achievers, low achievers, and others.
- Reevaluate course decisions and revise plans for the next unit or for next year.

Stage 2—Community of Learners—guides teachers through a series of questions related to creating a community of learners in the classroom,

one in which every student feels accepted as a full participant:

- How can I nurture the community of learners enrolled in this course so that connections among them are strengthened and students help each other learn?
- How can I include everyone enrolled in the course in the learning process, such that each person becomes an involved learner?
- How can I determine the strengths and resources of course participants to ensure they can be contributed to the community?
- How can I circumvent and compensate for the limitations of course participants?

Stage 3—Target Students—helps teachers focus on individual needs by identifying four types of student: high-, average-, and low-achieving students, as well as those with disabilities. (In some classes, identifying a student who speaks English as a second language may also be helpful.) The teacher keeps these target students in mind during all aspects of planning. In planning for diversity in the classroom it's difficult, if not impossible, to plan for the needs of every single student for every single lesson. This is particularly true in high schools where teachers may instruct over 100 students in a day! Identifying target students is a practical, realistic technique that helps make teaching more sensitive to diversity.

Stage 4—Course Launching—involves developing a plan for getting the course under way. Launching involves a plan for:

- developing rapport with students
- communicating course goals and expectations to students
- describing classroom routines and procedures
- generating enthusiasm and interest in the course

Stage 5—Course Maintenance—revisits the course map developed during Stage 1 periodically to make certain that everything is on track and to make any necessary revisions. At the beginning of the school year, it will be helpful to mark specific dates on your calendar for conducting a review of the course map.

Stage 6—Course Closure—serves as a course evaluation. The 10 questions outlined in the course map are once again revisited to determine how well all students have fared in learning the content. During this stage the teacher and students also discuss issues related to the learning community and how well goals were achieved.

The Course Planning Routine can serve as your road map for a grading period, a semester, or an entire school year. Its strengths include a system for considering individual student needs through target students, planning for academic goals through 10 questions, and planning for social goals through questions about the community of learners. As with any planning, the Course Planning Routine takes time. But the payoff is having a clear idea of where you're going and how you're going to get there! Tips for Teachers 2.1 provides time-management suggestions.

TIPS FOR TEACHERS

2.1 Time Management for Teachers

As you begin to plan for a new school year, you may start wondering, "How am I going to get all of this done?" Time management for teachers is complex—so much to do and so little time. With careful planning and prioritizing, however, you can accomplish a great deal. Here are some tips:

1. Keep your radar out for time-management tips from other teachers. They know the job and can give you hints for getting things done.
2. Write "to do" lists, and keep them short. Use the 80–20 rule suggested by Alan Lakein (1973). Twenty percent of the items on your list should yield 80 percent of the value. In a list of ten items, identify two and have a plan for getting them done.
3. As you look at your "to do" list, identify 5-minute tasks, 15-minute tasks, and 1-hour tasks (and try to figure out when they can be done). You'd be surprised at what you can accomplish during in-between times, with a little planning.
4. Set realistic goals. For example, you may not be able to contact every parent every week, but you can make a commitment to contacting five parents a week. Before you know it, you'll have contacted all the parents of students in your class.
5. Schedule time for contacting fellow professionals, for planning and coordinating. Say to yourself, "I'll contact two fellow professionals per week. This week I'll talk to the teacher of the gifted and talented students in my class and to the teacher of the special education students."

6. Learn how to delegate. Can someone help you with all or part of a project? Perhaps a parent, paraprofessional, volunteer, or student can assist you with tasks.
7. Think about how technology can help. Keep your eye out for computer programs to help with your grading, planning, and so on.
8. Avoid the temptation to overplan. As a teacher, you will be interrupted by parents, administrators, and, naturally, by students. It is important to keep these interruptions in mind and to realize that they are part of the job.
9. Plan for long-term, monthly, weekly, and daily goals, but be prepared to change your plans. Be flexible with your plan when legitimate situations arise.
10. Schedule a time every day for conferences. Meet with certain students on Monday, others on Tuesday, still others on Wednesday, and so on.
11. Plan for 60-second lessons while students are engaged in seatwork.
12. Take note of students who arrive early or leave late, and meet with them during those times.
13. Once or twice a week, make an appointment for lunch with a student.
14. Schedule conference times, and have students sign up for a conference with you.
15. This is the tough part: schedule time for planning. The payoff for a short time spent planning is tremendous.

An Example of the Course Planning Routine

Jeanette Robinson teaches a self-contained fifth grade class in a suburban elementary school. Of the 24 students in Jeanette's class, three are students with learning disabilities who are mainstreamed into the class for science and social studies.

Jeanette used the Course Planning Routine to plan her overall goals for teaching a semester-long course on earth science. Her questions were based on overall objectives presented in her textbook and in her district science curriculum guide. Figures 2.2 and 2.3 illustrate Jeanette's Course Organizer and Course Map for science instruction during the school year.

Unit Planning

After you establish "the big picture" for what you want to accomplish during the school year, the next step is to plan for units of study. An **instructional unit** is actually a series of lessons related to the same topic. For example, your school district's mathematics curriculum guide may require you to teach a series of lessons on measurement, which includes lessons on liquid measurement, distance, and so on. The length of the unit will depend on the topic. Some may last only a few days, others may last a month or more. In this section, you'll read about a unit-planning framework for planning for diverse student needs, the **Planning Pyramid** (Schumm et al., 1994).

Procedure for the Unit Planning Pyramid

The Unit Planning Pyramid is a framework or a way of thinking about planning instruction to enhance learning for all students. The Pyramid is designed as a flexible tool that teachers can adjust to their personal style of planning and teaching. It involves careful identification of what needs to be taught, and careful attention to individual student's needs to determine how the information will be taught.

FIGURE 2.2

Course Organizer

Name of Course: _____*Earth Science*_____

is about

Our planet, its place in space, how it changes naturally and due to pollution, and what we need to do to preserve it.

Course Questions:

1. What is the atmosphere?
2. How do storms form?
3. How do scientists predict weather changes?
4. What is the Earth's crust?
5. What is the Earth's surface made of?
6. What are sources of energy and how are these energy resources used?
7. What are the sources of air, water, and land pollution?
8. How does pollution affect natural resources?
9. What is the solar system and what objects can be found in space?
10. How has space been studied and what instruments are used to study it?

Adapted from Vaughn, S., Schumm, J. S., Lenz, K., Schumaker, J., Deshler, D., Morocco, C., Gordon, S., Riley, M., Fuchs, L., & Fuchs, D. (1995). *Planning for academic diversity in America's classrooms: Windows on reality, research, change, and practice.* Lawrence, KS: Universoty of Kansas Center for Research on Learning.

FIGURE 2.3

Course Map

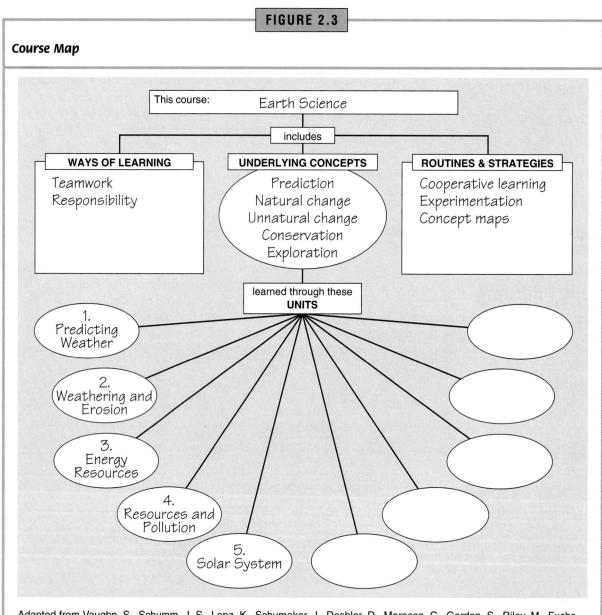

This course: **Earth Science**

includes

WAYS OF LEARNING

Teamwork
Responsibility

UNDERLYING CONCEPTS

Prediction
Natural change
Unnatural change
Conservation
Exploration

ROUTINES & STRATEGIES

Cooperative learning
Experimentation
Concept maps

learned through these
UNITS

1. Predicting Weather

2. Weathering and Erosion

3. Energy Resources

4. Resources and Pollution

5. Solar System

Adapted from Vaughn, S., Schumm, J. S., Lenz, K., Schumaker, J., Deshler, D., Morocco, C., Gordon, S., Riley, M., Fuchs, L., & Fuchs, D. (1995). *Planning for academic diversity in America's classrooms: Windows on reality, research, change, and practice.* Lawrence, KS: Universoty of Kansas Center for Research on Learning.

Degrees of Learning The primary component of the Planning Pyramid (see Figure 2.4), the **Degrees of Learning,** make up the body of the Pyramid and will help you examine the content to be taught and prioritize concepts in an instructional unit. The Degrees of Learning are based on the premise that although all students are capable of learning, not all students will learn all the content covered. The three Degrees of Learning are the base of the Pyramid, the middle level of the Pyramid, and the top of the Pyramid.

The base of the Pyramid, considered the foundation of the lesson, consists of information that is essential for all students to learn. This section of

FIGURE 2.4

Planning Pyramid

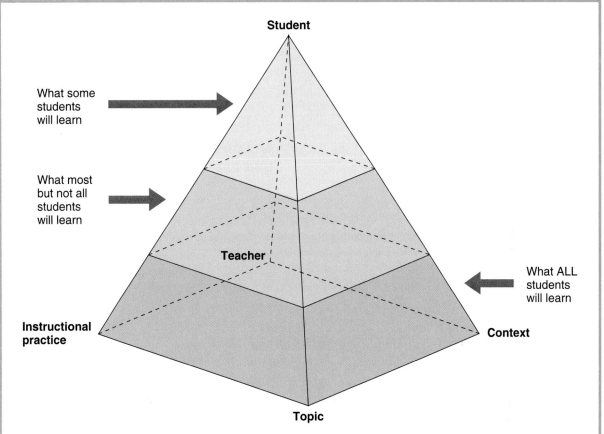

Schumm, Jeanne Shay, Vaughn, Sharon, & Leavell, Alexandra G. (1994, May). Planning Pyramid: A framework for planning for diverse students' needs during content area instruction. *The Reading Teacher, 47* (8), 608–615. Nancy Padak and Timothy Rasinski, Eds.) Copyright by the International Reading Association.

the Pyramid is directed by the question, "What do I want *all* students to learn?"

The middle part of the Pyramid represents information that is next in importance. This is information that *most* (but not all) students are expected to learn or grasp. This level of the Pyramid includes supplementary facts and information about ideas and concepts presented at the base of the Pyramid. The guiding question is "What do I want *most* students to learn?"

The top of the Pyramid represents information that the teacher believes will enhance basic concepts and facts about the topic or subject. This type of information will be acquired only by a few

students who have an added interest in and desire to learn more about the subject. It is information that the classroom teacher may not emphasize or elaborate upon during a class, but that students might read in a text or retain from a brief mention in class. The guiding question at this level is, "What information will a *few* students learn?"

Cautions and Comments A few cautions and comments about the Planning Pyramid:

■ All students must have the opportunity to be presented with or exposed to the same information, although presentation of the information may vary somewhat according to a student's needs.

- All students must have equal access to information that represents all levels of the Pyramid.
- Students should not be assigned to a particular level of the Pyramid based on their ability—students who learn at the middle and top levels do so based on their interests, prior knowledge, or personal experience.
- Activities at the base of the Pyramid should not be less stimulating (e.g., dittos, worksheets) than those at the other levels, nor should the upper levels be viewed as the place for creative, fun activities.

Deciding What Concepts to Teach   After teachers have used the Planning Pyramid for a while, it is easier to determine what concepts belong at each degree of learning. Initially, teachers find it helpful to use a self-questioning process to determine what concepts to teach. Table 2.2 provides a list of questions you might ask to guide your thinking.

After you decide on the concepts to be taught, you can record them on the Unit Planning Form (see Figure 2.5). This form also provides areas in which to record the unit title, materials and resources needed, instructional strategies and adaptations to be used, and evaluation or products that will serve as unit outcome measures.

An Example of the Unit Planning Pyramid

Jeanette used the Planning Pyramid to structure a unit on weathering and erosion. She predicted that this would be a difficult unit for her students because they had little prior knowledge of this

---

TABLE 2.2

Questions to Guide Thinking about Concepts to Be Taught

Questions Pertaining to the Topic

    Is the material new or review?

    What prior knowledge do students have of this topic?

    How interesting is the topic to individual students?

    How many new concepts are introduced?

    How clearly are the concepts presented in the textbook?

    How important is this topic in the overall curriculum?

Questions Pertaining to the Teacher

    What prior knowledge do I have of this topic?

    How interesting is the topic to me?

    How much time do I have to plan for the lesson?

    What resources do I have available to me for this unit?

Questions Pertaining to the Students

    Will a language difference make comprehension of a particular concept difficult for a student?

    Is there some way to relate this concept to the cultural and linguistic backgrounds of my students?

    Will students with reading difficulties be able to function independently in learning the concepts from textbooks?

    Will there be students with high interest or prior knowledge of these concepts?

    Will my students have the vocabulary they need to understand the concepts to be taught?

    What experiences have my students had that will relate to this concept?

Schumm, Jeanne Shay, Vaughn, Sharon, & Leavell, Alexandra G. (1994, May). Planning Pyramid: A framework for planning for diverse students' needs during content area instruction. *The Reading Teacher, 47* (8), 608–615. (Nancy Padak & Timothy Rasinski, Eds.) Copyright by the International Reading Association.

FIGURE 2.5

Unit Planning Form

UNIT PLANNING FORM

	Date: _____ Class Period: _____
	Unit Title: _____
What some students will learn.	Materials/Resources:
	_____
	_____
	_____
	_____
	_____
What most students will learn.	Instructional Strategies/Adaptations:
	_____
	_____
	_____
	_____
	_____
What ALL students should learn.	Evaluation/Products:
	_____
	_____
	_____
	_____
	_____
	_____

Schumm, J. S., Vaughn, S., & Harris, J. (1995). Collaborative planning for content area instruction. Published by TEC.

topic. She knew that it would be important for her to identify the key concepts she wanted students to learn—and to predict adaptations necessary for special learners in her class. She liked the way the textbook presented the material, and wanted to follow it closely. Because two of the students with learning disabilities were nonreaders, however, she knew she would need to enlist a volunteer to make audiotapes of the chapters and to arrange cooperative learning groups for in-class reading of the text. Jeanette also planned to have in-class study time (with study buddies) before tests. To plan the weathering and erosion unit, Jeanette used the Unit Planning Form shown in Figure 2.6.

Lesson Planning

Your overall plan for the school year is in place. Your plan for a unit of study is detailed. Now it's time to focus on a particular instruction session—the lesson. The earlier recommendation that you develop your own planning style is particularly important for lesson planning. As you consider

FIGURE 2.6

Jeanette's Sample Unit Plan

UNIT PLANNING FORM

Date: __Sept. 1–30__   Class Period: __1:30 – 2:30__

Unit Title: __Weathering and Erosion__

What some students will learn.	• How Earth looked during Ice Age • Disasters caused by sudden changes • Geographic examples of slow and fast changes
What most students will learn.	• Compare and contrast weathering and erosion • How humans cause physical and chemical weathering • Basic types of rocks
What ALL students should learn.	• Basic components of Earth's surface • Forces that change crust are weathering and erosion

Materials/Resources:
Guest speaker on volcanoes
Video: erosion and weathering
Rock samples
Library books – disasters, volcanoes, etc.
Colored transparencies for lectures

Instructional Strategies/Adaptations: Experiments!
Concept maps
Cooperative learning groups to learn material
  in textbook
Audiotape of chapter
Study buddies to prepare for quizzes and tests

Evaluation/Products:
Weekly quiz
Unit test
Learning logs (daily record of "What I learned")
Vocabulary flash

your lesson-planning style, you'll want to think about how to plan to promote learning for all students. The Lesson Planning Pyramid can help.

Procedure for the Lesson Planning Pyramid

The Lesson Planning Pyramid can be used for an individual lesson or to add depth and detail to the Unit Planning Pyramid described earlier. The Lesson Planning Pyramid does not necessitate a great deal of paperwork, and contains most of the elements teachers think are necessary to plot out a lesson.

With the Lesson Planning Pyramid, as with the Unit version, you focus on identifying concepts to be taught by asking, "What do I want all, most, and some of the students to learn as a result of the lesson?" As you can see from Figure 2.7, the Lesson Planning Form also provides areas in which to record materials, evaluations, in-class assignments, and homework assignments. In addition, there is an agenda area on which to list activities that will occur during the lesson.

In lesson planning it is important to think not only about the teacher, student, and topic, but also about the environment and the instructional strategies you will use. The questions in Table 2.3

Planning Software for Teachers

More and more teachers are using word processors to plan their lessons. With word processors, teachers can easily copy a lesson plan framework (including spaces for lesson objectives, materials, assignments, homework, assessment, and procedures), move information, and make frequent changes.

For teachers who want to use more sophisticated systems, computer software specifically designed for instructional planning is available. For example, *Bradford Lesson Planner* and *Bradford Class Manager* (William K. Bradford Publishing Company, 1-800-421-2009) are Windows programs for developing and printing lesson plans and student data. The *Bradford Lesson Planner* includes formatted lesson plans with spaces for lesson objectives, textbook information, supplemental materials, and lesson notes. Another example, published by Teaching, Inc. (206-774-0755), is entitled *Plan to Teach*. This software for Apple and Macintosh helps you develop daily and weekly plans, as well as plans for individual students. It also provides guidelines for setting up beginning-of-the-year classroom routines and seating charts.

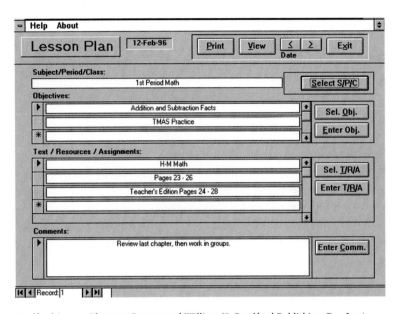

Bradford Lesson Planner (Courtesy of William K. Bradford Publishing Co., Inc.)

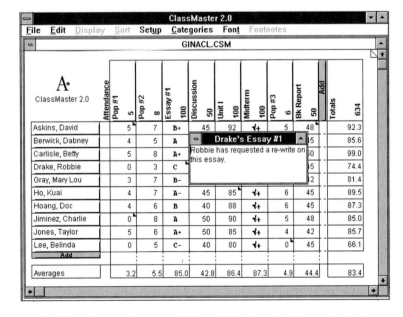

Bradford ClassMaster (Courtesy of William K. Bradford Publishing Co., Inc.)

FIGURE 2.7

Lesson Planning Form

Date: _____ Class Period: _____ Unit: _____

Lesson Objective(s): _____

_____

_____

Materials	Evaluation

In Class Assignments	Homework Assignments

LESSON PLANNING FORM

Pyramid	Agenda
What some students will learn.	_____ _____ _____ _____
What most students will learn.	_____ _____ _____ _____ _____
What ALL students should learn.	_____ _____ _____ _____ _____

Schumm, J. S., Vaughn, S., & Harris, J. (1995). Collaborative planning for content area instruction. Published by TEC.

can guide your thinking about the environment and instructional strategies.

An Example of the Lesson Planning Pyramid

Jeanette used her Lesson Planning Form as a guide for her lesson plan for the science lesson on the earth's surface. This lesson included many new terms that she knew would be unfamiliar to her students. The vocabulary was important for students to learn because it would be used throughout the unit. Her lesson plan included specific strategies for teaching the vocabulary, and visuals to help the vocabulary come alive. Also, by having students write in learning logs, she could monitor what they were learning. She knew that while they were working on the learning logs, she'd need to check in with students with writing difficulties to monitor their learning orally. Figure 2.8 shows Jeanette's plan.

Monitoring Student Learning During the Lesson

As you read earlier in this chapter, interactive planning is planning that occurs during a lesson. When you recognize that students are not "getting it," you adjust or alter your plans to respond to student needs. Monitoring what students understand is critical for interactive planning. Monitoring helps you keep in touch with what students are learning and remain sensitive to the troubleshooting you must do when students experience difficulty. The most typical kinds of monitoring are to ask questions during class and to circulate around the room, checking in with students during individual or group seatwork. Some quick strategies for monitoring follow.

Informal member checks are frequent, quick checks to see whether students understand. For example, after Susan Moore taught her third graders a lesson about the four food groups, she asked for a "thumbs up" hand signal if they understood, "thumbs down" if they did not.

At frequent intervals during a lesson you can ask students to summarize key points. This helps keep students on their toes while helping you keep tabs on what they are learning.

McTighe and Lyman (1988) described the **Think-Pair-Share** method, which can be used during peer monitoring activities. This strategy yields high student involvement and verbal interaction. Students are first encouraged to think individually about a topic for two minutes. Then students pair up to discuss the topic. The teacher then signals the pairs of students to share their responses with the entire class. The Think-Pair-Share method involves all students in active idea processing throughout the school day.

Class notes are the most tangible record of what students have learned during a lesson. Often students with learning disabilities have a difficult time taking notes during class, and thus have difficulty preparing for tests. One way to provide

---

TABLE 2.3

Questions to Guide Thinking about Environment and Instructional Strategies

Questions Pertaining to Environment:

Are there any holidays or special events that are likely to distract students or alter instructional time?

How will the class size affect my teaching of this concept?

How well do my students work in small groups or pairs?

Questions Pertaining to Instructional Strategies:

What methods will I use to motivate students and to set a purpose for learning?

What grouping pattern is most appropriate?

What instructional strategies can I implement?

What learning strategies do my students know (or need to learn) that will help them master these concepts?

What in-class and homework assignments are appropriate for this lesson?

Do some assignments need to be adapted for students with disabilities?

How will I monitor student learning on an ongoing, informal basis?

Schumm, Jeanne Shay, Vaughn, Sharon, & Leavell, Alexandra G. (1994, May). Planning Pyramid: A framework for planning for diverse students' needs during content area instruction. *The Reading Teacher, 47* (8), 608–615. (Nancy Padak & Timothy Rasinski, Eds.) Copyright by the International Reading Association.

support is to have **collaborative open-note quizzes** (Schumm & Lopate, 1989). After completing a lecture, divide the students into small cooperative learning groups. Allow students some time to discuss the lecture and summarize key points. Students should also revise their notes, adding information from their fellow students. Then, give students questions about the lecture to answer as a group. Through sharing, students with learning problems are provided the opportunity to "fill in the gaps" of what they missed during a lesson and also to see examples of the way other students take notes.

FIGURE 2.8

Jeannette's Sample Lesson Plan

Date: _Sept. 1_____   Class Period: _1:30 – 2:30_____ Unit: _Weathering and Erosion_____
Lesson Objective(s): _The students will describe components of the earth_____

Materials	**Evaluation**
Colored transparencies Rock samples	Learning logs Oral summaries

In Class Assignments	**Homework Assignments**
Write in learning log	Draw diagram of Earth's layers Make vocabulary flash cards

LESSON PLANNING FORM

Pyramid		Agenda
What some students will learn.	• Examples of 3 types of rocks	Introduce key vocab. using transparencies
		Work in coop. groups to read chapter
		Discuss chapter
What most students will learn.	• Crust made of 3 types of rock • How rocks are formed	Show rock samples
		Have students write in learning logs
What ALL students should learn.	• Earth has 3 layers • Outer layer is where we live • Crust is constantly changing	Have several students read log entries aloud Assign homework — Recommend extra reading for students who want to learn more about rocks

An Overview of Instructional Grouping

As you make your long-range, unit, and lesson plans, you'll want to plan for a variety of grouping patterns. At the beginning of the chapter you read that Lisa uses a variety of grouping patterns: sometimes whole class, sometimes small groups, and sometimes pairs of students. Sometimes Lisa combines students with similar achievement levels; sometimes she mixes high and low students. Part of Lisa's planning is to think about which grouping pattern seems most appropriate for each learning objective.

MAKING A DIFFERENCE

The 60-Second Lesson

Using Lesson Reaction Sheets

Student monitoring provides an excellent opportunity for 60-second lessons. Lesson Reaction Sheets are one quick way to monitor students' understanding. After a lesson is completed, have your students write a brief reaction to it. Provide your students with the following questions:

• What did you learn from this lesson?

• What was confusing about the lesson?
• What else would you like to know about the topic?

It should take students only a few minutes to write answers to these questions. You may need to find another time to ask these questions of students who have difficulty writing, so that they can answer orally.

There is no easy answer to the question of how best to group students for instruction. Consequently, the issue of grouping has triggered vigorous debate among educators, parents, and students. Our experience is that almost everyone has an opinion based on personal experience as a teacher, parent, or student. Your personal experience has already helped you shape ideas about how grouping should occur in the school and in the individual classroom. In this section you'll learn more about grouping from an historical standpoint, as well as current trends and issues associated with grouping students. The section

also includes a description of various grouping configurations you might use in the classroom, as well as suggestions for implementing flexible grouping patterns to promote successful learning for all students.

Traditional Instructional Grouping

In the mid-1800s, preoccupation with improving the productivity of public education in the United States gave rise to "graded" schools. A teacher assigned to a specific grade could teach the entire class. The graded system spread widely across the United States, thus establishing the most durable form of grouping in our educational system, age-level grouping, or grades.

John Philbreck of the Quincy, Massachusetts, school system initiated the graded system in 1847. It is likely that Philbreck was influenced by Horace Mann's and Colonel Francis W. Parker's reports of the ordered curriculum they had observed in Prussia (Button & Provenzo, 1983).

Teachers quickly realized, however, that a single grade included a wide range of academic levels. As Berliner and Casanova note (1993, p. 6), teachers often resort to grouping by ability because of an "inescapable fact of life: students differ dramatically from one another."

How could using unit and lesson planning pyramids help this teacher to adapt instructional activities for students with special needs? How should this teacher plan ways of grouping students for instruction?

Homogeneous or same-ability grouping is the practice of putting students at approximately the same achievement level together for instruction. School-level ability grouping is called tracking. At the school level, students might be assigned to a particular class. In an elementary school, for example, one teacher might be assigned all the high-achieving students, another teacher all the average-achieving students, and a third teacher all the low-achieving students. At the middle- or high-school level, high-achieving students might be assigned to accelerated courses, average-achieving students to regular courses, and low-achieving students to remedial courses. Students are assigned to tracks based on their grades, achievement test scores, and (in some cases) behavior. The idea of homogeneous grouping is that the content and pacing of instruction can be better controlled to meet individual needs.

> The first ability-grouped classes originated in 1862 in the St. Louis, Missouri, Public Schools, under the direction of superintendent William T. Harris (Otto, Wolf, & Eldrige, 1932).

Although research on the effectiveness of homogeneous grouping was inconsistent, early reviewers of such literature generally recognized the positive impact of homogeneous grouping, particularly for children with learning difficulties (Miller & Otto, 1930; Whipple, 1936). In 1957, the launching of the Soviet satellite, Sputnik, caused many people in the United States to think our country trailed in the space race, and prompted a definite increase in the practice of grouping students in classes, tracks, or streams according to their level of achievement. The reasoning was that the brightest students should be grouped together to get the training in science and mathematics they would need to compete internationally. Thus, tracking became an integral part of education in the United States.

> The Joplin Plan, started in Joplin, Missouri (Floyd, 1954), involves regrouping students across grade levels. For example, all first, second, and third grade students reading on the first grade level would be moved to the same group during reading time.

During the 1950s, the practice of within-class same-ability grouping for reading and mathematics began to take hold in elementary classes (Harris & Sipay, 1980). Within-class same-ability grouping occurs when students in a single classroom are placed with other students of similar abilities for an entire school year. The goal of same-ability small groups is to reduce the range of abilities between group members so that the teacher can instruct students who are functioning on approximately the same level. For example, the reading and math groups in an elementary school classroom might be based on similar student achievement (high, medium, or low) in each area. The teacher would pull one group at a time for instruction while the other groups focused on completing workbook assignments or silent readings. Within-class same-ability grouping for reading and mathematics was a dominant practice in elementary schools until recent years.

The early 1960s witnessed the ultimate attempts at homogeneity: the resource room for students with disabilities (Cruickshank et al., 1961) and special programs for the gifted. More recently, with the new influx of non-English-speaking immigrants to the United States, separate classes for students with limited English proficiency (LEP) have been established in many areas of the United States.

Current Trends in Instructional Grouping

Ability grouping, tracking, and placing students in resource rooms have been the norm in the United States for years. Schooling in the United States is now in a phase in which educators are exploring new alternatives to traditional ways of organizing students for instruction (Barr, 1995). The trends described here summarize current thinking about grouping.

Trend #1: A critical examination of homogeneous grouping

Although many alternatives to homogeneous grouping had been proposed, the trend toward homogeneous grouping—including the expansion of pull-out programs—continued (Barr & Dreeben, 1991) into the early 1990s. Recently a number of criticisms of homogeneous grouping have been raised, including the following (Oakes, 1992):

- There is little evidence that homogeneous grouping results in substantial academic advantages (Slavin, 1987).
- Homogeneous grouping "widens the gap" between high and low achievers (Slavin, 1987).
- Homogeneous grouping restricts friendship choices (Hallinan & Sorensen, 1985).
- Although homogeneous grouping may enhance the motivation and self-esteem of high-achieving students, it lowers the motivation and self-esteem of low-achieving students (Oakes et al., 1991).
- Homogeneous grouping frequently results in social stratification, in which students representing minority groups are overrepresented in low-ability tracks (Oakes, 1990).
- The quality of instruction in low-ability classes is frequently inferior. Emphasis in typical low-ability classes is more on lower-level skills and discipline, and less on higher-level thinking (Goodlad, 1984; Hiebert, 1983).

The trend in general education is toward **heterogeneous** or **mixed-ability grouping**, in which students with a range of achievement levels are put together for instruction. Heterogeneous grouping (rather than lock-step same-ability grouping) is being advocated to avoid the inevitable stratification resulting from traditional ability groups and tracking policies (Marshall & Weinstein, 1984; Webb & Cullian, 1983).

RESEARCH BRIEF

STUDENTS' PERCEPTIONS OF GROUPING

What do students think about grouping practices for reading instruction? Elbaum, Schumm, and Vaughn (1995) surveyed 549 elementary students (grades 3, 4, and 5), including 23 students with learning disabilities, to find out what students think. Results revealed that students at all levels of reading ability liked mixed-ability groups and mixed-ability pairs most, followed by whole-class instruction. Same-ability groups and working alone were the least popular formats. Students in mixed-ability groups were perceived as getting more help from classmates, working more cooperatively, and making more progress in reading than those in same-ability groups. Same-ability groups were perceived to be desirable for nonreaders only.

Trend #2: Movement of inclusion of students with disabilities in general education settings

Students with disabilities are spending more and more of their school day in general education settings. This movement toward inclusion broadens the range of student diversity in the classroom. Inclusion, coupled with the movement toward heterogeneity discussed earlier, means that classroom teachers must learn new strategies and organizational procedures for meeting the needs of individual students.

What are the six key elements of effective cooperative learning? What are some special considerations for students with disabilities when working in cooperative learning groups?

Trend #3: A critical examination of "what's best" for all students

- Those who oppose—or at least question—mixed-ability grouping do so out of concern for what will happen to students at the extremes of the ability spectrum. Two typical questions follow:
- Will mixed-ability grouping slow down the academic progress of gifted and high-achieving students?
- Can mixed-ability grouping enable teachers to provide the intensive, direct instruction needed by low-achieving students?

The answer to the first question is that there is no conclusive evidence about the effect of mixed-versus same-ability grouping for the academic success of gifted and high-achieving students. Indeed, an examination of the literature on grouping can be interpreted in very different ways. Allan (1991) concluded from such an examination that students who are gifted and high-achieving benefit from some form of same-ability grouping, and that opportunities should be maintained for accelerated instruction of such students with their high-achieving peers. Allan concluded, "The strongest positive academic effects of grouping for gifted students result from either acceleration or classes that are specially designed for the gifted and use specially trained teachers and differentiated curriculum and methods" (p. 65). Slavin (1991) examined the same literature and determined that the evidence to support same-ability grouping for high achievers was sparse, and that the modest academic benefits cannot compensate for maintaining an unequitable system. Slavin's conclusion is that students who are high achieving "will do well wherever they are" (p. 70).

Similarly, there is no clear-cut answer to the second question. There is little definitive evidence that ability grouping (including pull-out programs) positively impacts the academic achievement of low-achieving students. "Nor—given the widespread practice of undifferentiated whole-class instruction in general education classrooms—is there much encouragement that low-achieving students in that setting will receive the intensive, direct instruction they need (Baker & Zigmond 1990; McIntosh et al., 1993). It is abun-

dantly clear that the type of instruction needed to improve the basic skills of students who are low achieving needs to be improved, regardless of the setting.

Trend #4: Exploration of alternatives to same-ability grouping

For many years, educators continued with tracking and other forms of same-ability grouping simply because other alternatives were not available. Recently, however, researchers and teachers have begun to explore alternatives to traditional practices. These alternatives are not necessarily "new," but they are "improved" in respect to meeting the needs of a wide range of students. For example, whole-class instruction—teaching the whole class at the same time—is hardly "new." What is "improved" is that ways to meet diverse individual needs during whole-class instruction have been developed and tested in classrooms.

Trend #5: Emphasis on flexible grouping

Research has not identified one "best" grouping pattern, in terms of academic and social benefits to students. Many teachers are beginning to realize that using a variety of grouping patterns is most appropriate for classrooms with a wide range of student diversity. These teachers are beginning to recognize that different grouping patterns are appropriate for different purposes.

The use of a variety of grouping patterns is called **flexible grouping**. As Table 2.4 demonstrates, when grouping students you can think about different group sizes, composition, materials, purposes, and leadership.

Unsworth (1984, p. 300) listed five principles of flexible groups:

- There are no permanent groups.
- Groups are periodically created, modified, or disbanded, to meet new needs as they arise.
- At times there is only one group consisting of all pupils.
- Groups vary in size from two or three to nine or ten students, depending on the group's purpose.
- Group membership is not fixed; it varies according to needs and purposes.

TABLE 2.4

Grouping Decisions

Size
  Individuals
  Pairs
  Small groups
  Half-class
  Whole class

Composition (placement in group determined by)
  ability
  interests
  skill levels
  prior knowledge (content)
  prior knowledge (strategies)
  random
  friendship
  sex
  English proficiency
  cultural background
  behavior
  teacher selection
  student selection
  standardized test scores
  administrator preference
  parent preference
  previous success with group

Materials
  teacher-chosen
  student-chosen
  same materials for all groups
  different levels of different topics
  different levels of similar topics
  different materials and different activities—
    same level

Purposes
  skill development
  skill practice
  projects
  written assignments
  reading assignments
  problem solving
  discussions

Leadership
  teacher-led
  student-led

Adapted from: Flood, J., Lapp, D., Flood, S., & Nagal, G. (1992). Am I allowed to group? Using flexible patterns for effective instruction. *The Reading Teacher* 45(8), 608–616. Copyright by the International Reading Association, James Baumann, Editor.

Trend #6: *Emphasis on helping students learn the process of working in various grouping patterns*

Teachers can group students for the purpose of working together to complete an assignment or project, to solve a problem, or to practice basic skills. It is unwise, however, to assume that students will automatically know how to work with each other. The current trend is not only to group students so that they can accomplish tasks together, but also to show students *how* to work together. Working collaboratively, students can learn such lessons as how to give and receive help, how to listen and respond to the ideas of others, and how to complete a task as a team. The teacher needs to structure group work, however, so that these valuable lessons are not lost.

In the upcoming sections you'll read about different grouping patterns and how to implement them in your classroom. Particular emphasis is placed on how to meet the needs of students with disabilities in each grouping pattern. You will also learn to teach students how to work effectively in groups. Finally, you'll learn how to incorporate different grouping patterns as part of a flexible grouping plan.

Planning for Flexible Grouping

For flexible grouping to be successful, careful planning is essential. Without thoughtful preplanning, flexible grouping sometimes doesn't occur. The temptation becomes not to group at all, but to fall into the pattern of whole-class teaching followed by individual practice, a less than ideal pattern for meeting individual needs (Radencich & McKay, 1995). As you think about a lesson, keep grouping in mind by asking yourself the following questions:

- What is the best group size for teaching this lesson?
- What is the best group size for seatwork and follow-up activities?
- What is the best composition of learners for each group, with respect to student academic ability and work habits?
- What materials are needed for each group?
- Will the groups be teacher-led, student-led, or cooperative?

- What room arrangement is necessary for the grouping plan?
- When students move from one group to another, how can I ensure quick and smooth transitions?

Grouping Patterns

There are many ways to group students of varying abilities for instruction. This section describes different grouping patterns and includes guidelines for classroom implementation of these grouping arrangements. The discussions focus on ways to create student groups of different sizes (whole class, small group, pairs, and single student).

Whole Class

Whole class grouping is the pattern most students in the United States have experienced most often. Indeed, whole class is the most frequently used grouping pattern. Whole classes can comprise students of same or mixed ability. Quite often the decision of whether to track students or group them by ability is a districtwide or schoolwide decision. You may or may not be part of that decision-making process. Even in a "same ability" class, however, you'll quickly note that students in your class have a range of differences to which you, the teacher, need to attend.

Keeping the whole class together is appropriate for a variety of reasons:

- building classroom community
- establishing classroom routines
- introducing new units of study
- introducing new skills and concepts
- conducting whole-class discussions
- developing common experiences
- listening to guest speakers
- viewing educational videos

Many teachers like whole-class grouping because it makes planning fairly simple, with one instructional plan (including one set of instructional activities) for the whole group. Whole-class grouping also makes classroom management easier, in that teachers do not have to divide their time among different groups. Being in a mixed-ability whole class can improve the self-esteem of low-achieving students by helping them feel less isolated from their higher achieving peers.

There are some drawbacks to whole-class grouping, however. The primary problem is that it is more difficult to attend to individual needs during whole-class grouping. Students with learning difficulties are likely to try to fade into the woodwork and not participate fully in class activities (Brozo, 1990). The pace of instruction might be too fast for some students and too slow for others. Moreover, the content might be too difficult for some students and too easy for others.

The Planning Pyramid discussed earlier in this chapter is particularly important to use when planning whole-group instruction. With whole-class grouping, it is important not only that you monitor what students are learning, but also that you think about necessary adaptations to ensure success for all students. For example, if whole-class instruction involves a reading assignment followed by a discussion, you'll need to plan adaptations, such as listening to an audiotape of the reading assignment, for students who are non-readers.

Small Groups

Small groups consist of three or more students. In this section you'll read about same-ability small groups, mixed-ability small groups, and cooperative learning groups.

Same-Ability Small Groups Students in same-ability groups are at approximately the same level (as determined by achievement tests, informal tests, or teacher judgment). Although the current trend is away from permanent same-ability groups, some teachers still prefer to have same-ability groups as part of their overall grouping plan. In Yvette Myers' fourth grade class, for example, six students are reading below the second grade level. Yvette finds it necessary to provide this group of students with direct instruction in word recognition, three times a week, but she also includes many other types of grouping patterns during the school day so that the students don't feel isolated from the class as a whole.

The pros and cons of same-ability groups were discussed earlier in this chapter. If you elect to use same-ability groups as part of your total

TIPS FOR TEACHERS

2.2 Effective Grouping Strategies for Small, Same-Ability Groups

1. Instead of having an arbitrary number of groups (for example, three groups), make sure that you have enough groups to handle individual differences.
2. Plan for appropriate pacing of instruction.
3. For students who have difficulty learning, plan to reteach concepts and skills, using different methods and explanations.
4. Keep student assignment to groups fluid, so that students can be moved to more appropriate groups, as necessary.
5. Disband groups that have served their purpose.
6. Be flexible about the time spent with each group. A rigid schedule will not permit you to work with groups that need extra or reduced time.
7. Avoid using student membership in a same-ability group to determine involvement in other activities. For example, if students are in the "yellow" group for extra help in reading, don't put the "yellow" students together for science or social studies projects.
8. A good rule of thumb is to keep groups of students who need extra help small, and to provide students with the intensity of instruction they need.

Adapted from: Good, T. L., & Brophy, J. E. (1994). *Looking in classrooms* (6th ed.). New York: HarperCollins Pubs., Inc.

---

grouping plan, Tips for Teachers 2.2 includes some suggestions for their most effective use.

Mixed-Ability Small Groups Students in mixed-ability groups represent a wide range of levels. Group placement may be determined by many different criteria, from student interest to needed skill lessons. Mixed-ability groups are created for special purposes and are fluid, in that they tend to change throughout the school year and even throughout the school day. In fact, students can belong to more than one group at one time. Once the goals of the project are achieved, the groups are reorganized.

Mixed-ability groups can be organized for a variety of purposes, including the following:

- conducting minilessons on an as-needed basis
- completing a project
- preparing a presentation for the class
- completing a follow-up assignment
- practicing new skills
- discussing a reading assignment

The composition of students can be grouped in a number of ways, some of which follow:

- Interest. Students with similar interests can be placed together in small groups. Teachers can determine student interests through surveys and group discussions, and place students together for an assignment such as creating a volcano during science time. Interest groups tend to yield impressive products because students in the group are highly motivated.
- Skills to be learned. Several students who are experiencing difficulty with a particular skill, such as antonyms, may be placed in a small group. This may give them the extra time and support they need. If necessary, the teacher can intervene with this group for the purpose of reinforcing the needed skill. Once the skill is mastered by individual group members, they no longer need to be in this particular group.
- English proficiency. For students who need help understanding English, you can provide very necessary support by including in the group a bilingual classmate with greater proficiency.
- Level of basic skills. Depending on the purpose of the group and the task to be

completed, it may be helpful to group students who are better readers, writers, or mathematicians with students who may need assistance.

- Prior knowledge. Students can be grouped according to how much they already know about a topic. If you are teaching a lesson on dinosaurs, for example, you may want to develop mixed-ability groups of students who know a great deal about dinosaurs and students who are new to the topic.

Finally, two types of groups do not depend on students' knowledge or needs:

- Student-selected. The teacher may give students time to create their own small groups at specific times during the week. One instance of this type of grouping occurs when the teacher asks students to discuss with their classmates the books they read independently over the weekend.
- Random assignment. Random assignment to groups for special projects can be done to expose students to different classmates throughout the year.

The advantages of small, mixed-ability groups are both social and academic. Socially, students learn how to work collaboratively, communicate effectively in groups, and give and receive help. Academically, students become more engaged in their learning and spend more time on-task.

The disadvantages mainly concern classroom management. Teachers can be in only one place at a time. When the class is divided into groups, the possibility for misbehavior increases. Therefore, guidelines for student responsibilities during small-group activities need to be communicated clearly and reinforced consistently. The research conducted in cooperative learning groups has yielded classroom procedures for maximizing productivity in small, mixed-ability groups. Those procedures are discussed in the next section.

Cooperative Learning Groups

The purpose of this section is to provide an overview of cooperative learning. In **cooperative learning groups**, students work together toward a common goal, usually to help one another learn academic material (Slavin, 1991). Students not only help explain material to each other and provide mutual support, but also give group members multiple perspectives (Morrow & Smith, 1990). In cooperative learning groups, students perceive that the main goal of the group is that all students learn and that each member of the group is critical for group success. As the Research Brief indicates, research in cooperative learning has yielded positive outcomes.

RESEARCH BRIEF

BENEFITS OF COOPERATIVE LEARNING

The benefits of cooperative learning are well documented in the research literature. Slavin (1991) synthesized the research in this area with the following highlights:

1. Cooperative learning is most successful when there are group goals coupled with individual accountability.
2. Achievement effects of cooperative learning have been positive for high-, average-, and low-achieving students across grade levels— elementary through high school.
3. Social effects of cooperative learning have been demonstrated in terms of improving self-esteem, intergroup relations, acceptance of students with disabilities, and attitudes toward school.

Goor and Schwenn (1993, p. 8) identified six key elements of cooperative learning:

- Teams are formed to maximize heterogeneity.
- Positive interdependence is structured through shared goals and rewards.
- Management systems are established to maximize group learning.
- The room is arranged to facilitate small-group activity.
- Students are taught skills necessary to cooperate and teach one another.
- The structure of each cooperative learning activity is chosen to match the goals of the lesson.

Cooperative groups consist of three to six students, with typically about four per group (Wilcox et al., 1987) and should include high, average, and low achievers (Slavin, 1987). Some teachers create permanent cooperative learning groups that are seated together for an entire school year. Other teachers keep the groups together for a grading period; still others for a single project.

To ensure full student participation, each member of a cooperative learning group is assigned a role. It is the teacher's responsibility to explain the roles thoroughly, including why each role is important. For example, one student can serve as timekeeper, another as quiet control, another as secretary or scribe, and still another as an encourager or "cheerleader."

While the cooperative learning groups are in session it is the teacher's job to listen and observe how students work as a group. When necessary the teacher models collaborative behaviors, such as how to give and receive help, and how to ask what others think. It is also important to praise groups that are following guidelines and to redirect groups that are not. The teacher also needs to clarify directions or clear up any misconceptions students may have about the topic. As you can see, cooperative learning time is an active time for the teacher as well as for the students.

Many teachers are concerned about how to grade students for cooperative learning work. What happens if one student does all the work for the group? Should everyone get the same grade? What happens if one group member does nothing? In determining a grade for the group product, it's probably best to have both an individual score and a group score. When making the cooperative learning assignment, announce a group goal and an individual goal. For example, you might be teaching a lesson on the layers of the Earth. The group project might be to complete a drawing of the Earth and its layers, and to ensure that each group member can name the layers. The group goal is to complete the drawing and teach the names of the layers to group members. The individual goal (followed by a quiz) is to demonstrate knowledge of the layers.

It is important for students to evaluate the group process, as well as to earn a "grade" for a project. Evaluating the process makes students aware of the importance of working together and of the steps necessary for enhancing group dynamics.

Goor and Schwenn (1993) offer some special considerations for students with disabilities working in cooperative learning groups. Students with learning and behavior disorders may have difficulty monitoring their own learning, following directions, and in social skills. Some students may have difficulty participating fully in groups when their basic skills in reading, writing, and mathematics are not on a par with those of their peers. Goor and Schwenn make the following recommendations:

> Of all recent education innovations, cooperative learning has undergone the most extensive research, including research on both academic and social outcomes for students of different grade levels, achievement levels, and cultural backgrounds (Slavin, 1961).

1. Make certain that students with disabilities are clear about the procedures for working in cooperative groups.
2. Be sure that students are assigned to a group that provides the necessary support.
3. Make certain that the role you assign a student with disabilities is appropriate for that student. For example, the job of recorder may be inappropriate for a student who cannot write, unless that student is allowed to tape record the session and then make an oral summary.
4. For students who have difficulty staying on task, develop signals for keeping excess movement and noise to a minimum.
5. Monitor student learning consistently to make certain that students are picking up on key concepts and not becoming more focused on group process than on learning the designated material.

Learning Partners in Pairs

Pairing occurs when students work together in groups of two, sometimes called **dyads**. Depending on the task, pairs can be either same- or mixed-ability. When two students of the same ability level are placed together for an assignment, they can offer each other support, corrective feedback, and praise. For example, two students who are about the same level in mathematics might work together to solve word problems.

Pairing also can be effective when students of differing ability levels work together. When one students in such pairs acts as teacher to the other student, **peer tutoring** occurs (Cohen, Conway & Gow, 1988). When peer tutoring involves a student with learning disabilities, that student can serve as either the tutor or the tutee of a general education student (Eiserman, 1988). Academic and social benefits for both tutor and tutee have been documented in research (King, 1982). An example of mixed-ability pairs might be a more able reader serving as partner to a less able reader to complete the reading of a science chapter.

Another way to place two students together for reading instruction is known as **cross-age pairing**. In this scenario, an older and younger student are "buddies" in a mutually beneficial reading activity (Morrice & Simmons, 1991). Benefits of this method include motivation to read (for the younger student), and application and reinforcement of previously learned language arts concepts (for the older student). Cross-age pairing has been shown "to boost the self-esteem of each of the buddies" (Morrice & Simmons, 1991, p. 573). Some suggested activities to use during cross-age pairing are creating Big books, making cards and writing letters for the holidays, and participating in science projects (Morrice & Simmons, 1991). In a study on the effectiveness of cross-age pairing, it was concluded that both students in the pairs improved in their ability to work cooperatively with another student (Morrice & Simmons, 1991).

Pairs can also be based on friendships, interests, or can be random. The important things to think about when planning for student pairing are the task to be completed and the kind of support your students need to complete that task.

Student pairing can be used for the following activities:

- revising written assignments
- practicing new skills
- developing fluency in reading or computation
- preparing for tests
- completing reading assignments
- solving problems
- conducting library research
- conducting science experiments
- reflecting about stories or books read

TIPS FOR TEACHERS

2.3 *Making the Most of Working with Pairs*

Set procedures for peer tutoring, such as:
1. Give everyone a chance to be a tutor—every student has something to share with a peer.
2. Give the tutor very specific suggestions about what to teach and how to teach it.
3. Keep tutoring sessions short for students with short attention spans.

Set procedures for collaborative pairs, such as:
1. Give specific guidelines about the responsibilities of each partner.

2. Hold each partner accountable for fulfilling responsibilities.
3. Give students the opportunity to work with a variety of partners.

Set rules, such as:
1. Talk only to your partner.
2. Talk only about your assignment (project).
3. Use a low voice.
4. Cooperate with your partner.
5. Try to do your best.

Used by permission of Douglas and Lynn Fuchs, Vanderbilt University.

TIPS FOR TEACHERS

Many teachers like to use student pairs because pairing provides students with additional support and helps them learn how to work as a team. Pairing involves minimal planning and is easily implemented in the classroom. Many students like pairing because it makes learning more fun and helps them feel less isolated. Students like to give and receive help. As one third grade student put it, "Two heads are better than one."

One potential pitfall of student pairing is that students can get off-task and spend more time socializing than working. Another problem is that a student who is asked to "tutor" another student may simply not know what to do, and both students get frustrated. In some classrooms, higher achieving students are asked too often to help their lower achieving peers, and resentment occurs. Finally, some students may simply prefer to work alone. These problems can be minimized. Tips for Teachers 2.3 suggests ways to make the most of student pairs.

When students work together, they can learn to encourage each other. Tips for Teachers 2.4 provides a list of encouraging words and phrases you can post in your class to serve as a reminder. You can also model the use of encouraging words during whole-group, small-group, and one-on-one instruction.

One-on-One Instruction

Research indicates that general education teachers rarely make extensive individualized plans for students (Schumm & Vaughn, 1991). However, teachers do have one-to-one instructional encounters with students throughout the day. For example, while you are monitoring students as they complete seatwork, you may observe that one student doesn't understand. So you do some quick reteaching. During writing instruction you may have one-to-one conferences with students about their writing.

In yet another scenario, a student assigned to a special education resource room might be in your class for only 15 minutes of a language arts period. In such cases, you may want to consult with the special education teacher to plan activities for the best use of that 15 minutes each day. The advantage of one-to-one instruction is that you can zero in on a student's individual needs. The obvious disadvantage is finding the time to do it.

SUMMARY

- The Flow of the Planning Process Model indicates the sequence and relation between three types of planning (preplanning, interactive planning, and postplanning) and factors that influence planning (teacher, environment, topic, and student).

- In long-range planning, planning parameters such as state, district, and school guidelines for curriculum and instruction must be considered.

- The Course Planning Routine, a guide for long-range planning, includes procedures for setting goals for the course, getting the course off on the right foot, monitoring and managing the course during the year, and closing the course.

- The Planning Pyramid, a framework for unit and lesson planning, helps you examine the content to be taught and prioritize concepts to ensure learning for all students.

- Current trends in instructional grouping include a critical examination of homogeneous grouping, a movement toward inclusion of students with disabilities in general education settings, critical examination of "what's best" for all students, exploration of alternatives to ability grouping, and an emphasis on flexible grouping as well as on helping students learn how to work in various grouping patterns.

- A variety of group sizes—whole class, small group, pairs, and individual student—can be used for instruction. The decision about which size is most appropriate depends on student needs and the learning activity being planned.

- Students can be grouped in a number of ways, including interests, skills to be learned, English proficiency, and prior knowledge.

- In cooperative learning groups, students work together toward a common goal, usually to help each other learn academic material. Students in cooperative learning groups perceive that the group's main goal is that all students learn and that each member of the group is critical for group success.

Key Terms and Concepts

collaborative open-note quizzes

cooperative learning groups

Course Planning Routine

cross-age pairing

Degrees of Learning

environment-related factors

flexible grouping

Flow of the Planning Process Model

heterogeneous grouping

homogeneous grouping

informal member checks

instructional unit

interactive planning

long-term planning

mixed-ability grouping

peer tutoring

Planning Pyramid

postplanning

preplanning

same-ability grouping

SMARTER

student-related factors

teacher-related factors

think-pair-share

topic-related factors

tracking

whole-class grouping

within-class same-ability grouping

Think and Apply

1. Now that you have read Chapter 2, reread the interview with Lisa. How does Lisa plan with Ellen, the special education teacher? How does she use flexible grouping?
2. Use the Course Planning Routine to develop initial plans for a course you might teach. Compare your plans with those of a classmate who is teaching the same (or a similar) course.
3. Use the Planning Pyramid to develop a unit plan and for an individual lesson within that unit. Compare your plans with those of a classmate.
4. Imagine that you have been assigned to a task force to make a proposal about whether or not to keep tracking at your school. In preparation for the first meeting you have been asked to draft a position statement explaining your stance on the issue. Develop a brief statement explaining your thoughts.
5. Describe an appropriate instructional activity that would be appropriate for each of the following group sizes: whole class, small group, pairing, individual.

Read More about It

1. Cohen, E. (1994). *Designing groupwork: Strategies for the heterogeneous classroom* (2nd ed.). New York: Teachers College Press.

   Comprehensive handbook to help make your students' small groupwork productive. Includes chapters on planning groupwork, preparing students for cooperation, setting expectations, and applications for groupwork in classrooms in which some students speak English as a second language.

2. Johnson, D. W., & Johnson, R. T. (1991). *Learning together and alone: Cooperative, competitive, and individualistic learning* (3rd ed.). Boston: Allyn & Bacon.

   Comprehensive overview of cooperative learning, with specific instructions for ways to implement different cooperative learning methods, such as Cooperative Integrated Reading and Composition (CIRC), Student Teams-Achievement Divisions (STAD), and Teams-Games-Tournaments (TGT).

3. Moran, C., Stobbe, J., Baron, W., Miller, J., & Moir, E. (1992). *Keys to the classroom: A teacher's guide to the first month of school.* Newbury Park, CA: Corwin.

   How do you get the school year off on the right foot? This teacher-friendly guide for elementary teachers provides specific suggestions for preparing the classroom, structuring routines, planning the first day, and activities for the first month. It also includes sample letters to parents, in both English and Spanish.

4. Radencich, M. C., & McKay, L. J. (Eds.). (1995). *Flexible grouping for literacy in the elementary grades.* Boston: Allyn & Bacon.

   Provides guidelines for planning and implementing flexible grouping for reading and writing instruction in elementary classrooms. Provides detailed descriptions of ways to implement a variety of grouping options.

5. Slavin, R. E. (1990). *Cooperative learning: Theory, research, and practice.* Englewood Cliffs, NJ: Prentice-Hall.

   A detailed manual for structuring cooperative and individualized learning. Includes a chapter on teachers' concerns about cooperative and individualized learning that is particularly helpful in considering students who are low and high achieving as well as students who are socially isolated and disruptive.

6. Vaughn, S., Schumm, J. S., Lenz, K., Schumaker, J., Deshler, D., Morocco, C., Gordon, S., Riley, M., Fuchs, L., & Fuchs, D. (1995). *Planning for academic diversity in America's classrooms: Windows on reality, research, change, and practice.* Lawrence, KS: University of Kansas Center for Research on Learning.

   This monograph reports findings from a series of investigations conducted by four research groups. Each group investigated general education teachers' planning for students with disabilities. The monograph includes practical suggestions for planning and implementing instruction for students with disabilities.

THREE

Managing Student Behavior and Promoting Social Acceptance

FOCUS QUESTIONS

1. What are some basic principles of classroom management?

2. What does it mean to establish a few clear rules with known consequences?

3. What procedures can you implement to decrease inappropriate behavior?

4. What mistaken behavioral goals do students have? How can teachers recognize these goals?

5. How can you establish a classroom climate that promotes appropriate behaviors and acceptance of all students?

6. What are some examples of social skills intervention programs that can be used by classroom teachers?

7. What are the principles teachers can apply to enhance the self-concept and social skills of their students?

8. What steps can you implement to teach self-management skills to your students?

9. How should teachers manage the behavior of students from diverse ethnic and socioeconomic backgrounds?

Interview

Nina Zaragoza

Nina Zaragoza, a third grade teacher at Morningside Elementary School, asked to be placed in an inner city school. She has spent her entire 20-year career teaching in different inner city schools. A visit to Nina's classroom is a most rewarding experience. Students work in pairs, small groups, alone, and sometimes with the class as a whole. The atmosphere of the classroom is much like that of a workshop. There is the healthy "buzz" of activity, without the noise of students who are lost or off task. The students are not the only ones who are busy. Nina moves from student to student, group to group, asking questions, listening, and teaching. She stops the entire group to teach a mini-lesson when she realizes they are all having difficulty with a particular concept. The students in Nina's classroom know the rules and routines and seem to be able to work without prodding from the teacher. During several interviews with Nina, she revealed what she considered the critical components to successful classroom management.

> First, you have to teach that all students are valuable, contributing members to the classroom community and that it is everyone's job to be sure everyone is learning. This is not the usual "teacher is responsible for everyone" mentality. In my class everyone is responsible for themselves and for everyone else. Second, students have to know that you care and respect them. For some students this is a difficult task because they have been told by many of the adults they have previously encountered that they are not worthwhile. Third, you need to establish a few rules and a lot of routines. What

I mean by this is that the class needs to have some rules that we all agree on as important. We occasionally revisit these rules during our class meetings. But I don't like to have too many rules because then we don't follow any of them. Respect for others, following directions, and safety for self and others are the three basic rules I apply. The routines are the minute-by-minute, day-by-day procedures for how the classroom runs. As much as possible I turn routines over to the students so that I have as much of my time devoted to teaching as possible. For example, I never collect or pass out materials, take attendance, or other activities that the students can learn to do. Fourth, I have established consequences for inappropriate behavior. I do not get emotional or upset, just enforce the consequence. It saves me energy and is more effective for students. Fifth, and maybe the most important, I look and recognize what is going well. I praise and provide positive feedback to my students individually, in small groups, and to the class as a whole. I don't think teachers can ever be too positive. I also spend time teaching social skills to my class as a whole. In the beginning of the year I teach interpersonal problem solving skills that students apply during our class meetings. Teaching interpersonal social skills at the beginning of the year is time consuming, but I find it pays off because over the year I spend less and less time on it and students get more and more skillful. I have to add one more thing. I think a lot of behavior problems are a result of students being involved in "busy work" that is not productive. They get bored with what they are doing so they start to bother their neighbors, and the next thing you know there is a behavior problem.

Introduction

What are some of the principles Nina uses that allow her to spend so much of her time teaching and so little of her time managing student behavior? How did she establish in her classroom a community in which students work together and all students feel accepted and valued? The purpose of this chapter is to familiarize you with the principles of responding to students and promoting social acceptance so that you will be prepared to create a classroom similar to Nina's. This chapter addresses several issues, which include:

- an overview of the basic principles of managing student behavior
- ways to establish a harmonious classroom climate
- procedures for enhancing the acceptance of students with disabilities by peers and professionals
- procedures for teaching social skills, enhancing self-esteem, and self-management
- considerations of students' behavior, based on ethnicity and socioeconomic factors

Basic Principles of Managing Student Behavior

Glen Nichols, a seventh grade science teacher, felt frustrated. One of his science classes included several students with special needs, and he was interested in modifying his usual routine to ensure that they had an adequate opportunity to learn. He had spent considerable time preparing a science experiment for the laboratory, one he thought students would learn from and enjoy. He arranged the materials ahead of time, identified the key concepts he wanted to teach, and was optimistic that the lesson would go well. What happened? Glen described it this way:

> First of all, the students came to the lab and were more interested in who their lab partner would be than the topic. They seemed to have a more difficult time settling down than usual and talking seemed to occur during the entire session. There were a few students who seemed to follow the procedures and get something out of it, but for the most part I think it was a waste of my time.

Often teachers need to change their own behavior in order to change the behavior of students in their classrooms (Hunter, 1982; Rosenshine & Stevens, 1986). Glen is a good example. He understood well the content he was teaching, but was less able to manage student behaviors so that he could teach effectively. Glen is not alone. Teachers not only identify classroom management as a cause of stress, but many also cite it as their reason for leaving the profession (Elam & Gallup, 1989; Fettler & Tokar, 1982). The following sections describe some guiding principles that might help you establish more effective classroom management.

Look for the Positive

Told he needed to look for positive behaviors, Glen threw up his arms and said, "There weren't any. The poor behavior far outweighed the good." But when Glen examined the videotape of his lesson and was asked to make a written list of student behaviors that he found acceptable, he noticed quite a few. "Actually, there were more students behaving appropriately than I thought."

Glen, like many teachers, got into the habit of noticing and calling attention to *misbehavior* instead of noticing appropriate behavior and providing reinforcement. He was asked to list behaviors he most wanted to see in his students. He was then asked to look for and say something positive to students who were performing those behaviors.

In addition to focusing on negative rather than positive behavior, teachers often think they speak positively to students more often than they actually do. When someone "counts" the positive comments in the classroom, teachers are surprised at how few they actually made. McIntosh, Vaughn, Schumm, Haager, and Lee (1993) found that even general education teachers identified as effective and accepting of students with special needs made very few positive statements during a lesson. You need to provide much more positive feedback than you think is necessary.

Positive feedback to students must be specific, and presented immediately after you witness the target behaviors you want them to continue (and other students to model). At the elementary level, teachers can comment on which students are displaying the desired behavior, "Mark, Jacob, and Cynthia are looking at me with their books open. I can tell they are ready. Who else knows what to do to show me they are ready?" At the secondary level, teachers can state the desired behavior and then ask students to summarize the request. For example, Glen could have said, "Today we are going to work in pairs in the lab. You can talk with your lab partner while you are conducting the experiment, but I do not want you to talk while I am preparing you for it—which will take about 15 minutes. You need to look at me and remain quiet during this time. Daniel, in your own words, what is the request?"

How effective is positive reinforcement with students in middle and high school? Because positive reinforcement is more effective with younger students than with older students, it is more useful at the elementary level than in middle school, and least effective with high school students (Forness, 1973; Stallings, 1975). This does *not* mean that you should not have a positive attitude and look for appropriate behavior with older students. All students like to be told when they are doing something right. They all like a classroom in which the atmosphere is positive and upbeat, and a teacher they can count on to look for good things, not only bad behaviors.

Several authors distinguish between positive feedback and encouragement (Dreikurs & Cassel, 1972; Dreikurs et al., 1982). The primary difference is that **positive feedback** often provides some judgment from the teacher about the appropriateness of the behavior, whereas *encouragement* recognizes the behavior but does not provide judgment from the teacher. An example of positive feedback is a teacher saying, "Shana is waiting in line quietly. Good job, Shana." An example of encouragement is to say, "I'm sure that you know how to stand in line when we get ready for lunch." Both encouragement and positive feedback are effective procedures for "noticing what is positive" about the behavior of your students.

> Students do not always interpret teachers' positive recognition in the positive ways that teachers intend. For some students, receiving praise in front of their peers is embarrassing and therefore not rewarding (Grossman, 1995).

Use Reinforcers to Encourage Positive Behavior

How do positive and negative reinforcement differ? **Positive reinforcement** is the presentation, following the target behavior, of a **stimulus** (a verbal response, a physical response, such as touching, or a tangible response, such as a reward) to maintain or increase the target behavior. **Negative reinforcement** is the removal of a stimulus to increase engagement in desirable behaviors. If a teacher rings a bell until the students are quiet, then the removal of the bell sound is a negative reinforcer for quieting student behavior. Because "negative" is often misinterpreted to mean "harmful," the implication is that positive reinforcement is good and negative reinforcement is bad. Although negative reinforcement can be effective, positive reinforcement is the best way to increase desirable student behaviors (see Tips for Teachers 3.1).

Table 3.1 provides a list of reinforcers teachers can use to increase appropriate behavior. In most classrooms, teachers do not have to use tangible and/or consumable reinforcers to maintain student behavior. Some teachers, however, particularly those who have students with emotional and behavioral problems in their classrooms, may need to establish a token system in which the tokens are exchanged for tangible and or consumable rewards.

Juanita Cowell is a middle school teacher who has five students with special needs in her classroom. One of her students has emotional and behavioral disorders and had difficulty staying on task, not disrupting others, and raising his hand when he had something to say. Unfortunately, several students seemed to be learning his "bad" behavior instead of him learning the good behavior of other students. Juanita had tried many of the reinforcers mentioned in Table 3.1 (such as adult, peer, and activity reinforcers, as well as privileges), and although the class had more good days than bad, she was still concerned about the behavior of several students. She decided to establish a **token system** (or token economy), whereby she would place a token in a glass "bank" at the following times:

■ At the end of every period (usually about 50 minutes) if students followed rules during the period

TABLE 3.1

Reinforcers Teachers Can Use to Increase Appropriate Behavior

Students Provide Self-Reinforcers:
- Students give themselves points for behaving well.
- Students say positive things to themselves ("I'm working hard and doing well.")
- Students monitor their own behavior (see Making a Difference: The 60-Second Lesson).

Adult Approval:
- Teacher provides verbal recognition that student is behaving appropriately ("John, you are following directions on this assignment.")
- Teacher provides physical recognition of appropriate student behavior. Teacher moves around classroom, touching the shoulder of students who are behaving appropriately.
- Teacher informs parents or other professionals of students' appropriate behavior. This can be accomplished orally or with "good news notes."

Peer Recognition:
- Teacher informs other students of a student's appropriate behavior. ("The award for student of the day goes to the outstanding improvement in behavior demonstrated by [student's name].")
- Students can place in a special box the names of students who have demonstrated appropriate behavior. These names can be read at the end of the week.
- A designated period of time is allocated at the end of the class period (high school) or day (elementary school) to ask students to recognize their fellow classmates who have demonstrated outstanding behavior.

Privileges:
- Students are awarded free time after displaying appropriate behavior.
- Students are allowed to serve in key classroom roles after demonstrating outstanding behavior.
- Students are awarded passes that they can trade for a night without homework.

Activities:
- Students can perform an activity they like (e.g., drawing) after they complete the desired activity (e.g., the activity during that class period).
- Students can perform their tasks on the computer.
- Students can perform their tasks with a partner they select.

Tokens:
- Tokens are items (e.g., chips, play money, points) that can be exchanged for something of value.
- Use tokens to reward groups or teams who are behaving appropriately.
- Allow groups or individuals to accumulate tokens they can "spend" on privileges, such as no homework or free time.

Tangibles:
- Tangibles are rewards, objects that students want, but usually not objects they can consume (e.g., toys, pencils, erasers, paper, crayons).
- Tokens can be exchanged for tangible reinforcers.
- Tangible reinforcers can be used to reward the class for meeting a class goal.
- Tangible reinforcers may be needed to maintain the behavior of a student with severe behavior problems.

Consumables:
- Consumables are rewards that students can eat (e.g., raisins, pieces of cereal, candy).
- Tokens can be exchanged for consumable reinforcers.
- Consumable reinforcers can be used to reward the class for meeting a class goal.
- Consumable reinforcers may be needed to maintain the behavior of a student with severe behavior problems.

- At the beginning of each new period if the students made a quiet transition to the new task
- For exceptional student behavior, such as ignoring another student's interfering behavior or helping a student who was distracted get back to work
- For successfully completing activities

She removed a token from the jar when rules were broken. Students added up the tokens at the end of each day. When the number of tokens totaled 200 (approximately 10 days of good behavior) the class could exchange the tokens for a pizza party at lunch. Juanita soon found that she could shake the jar as a signal to the class to quiet down or as a warning that they were about to lose a token.

TIPS FOR TEACHERS

3.1 *Suggestions for Positive Reinforcement*

Suggestions for Natural Positive Reinforcement:
- access to lunchroom snack machines (student supplies money)
- attend school dances
- attend school assemblies
- be first in line (to anything)
- be team captain
- care for class pets
- choose activity or game for class
- class field trips
- decorate the classroom
- eat lunch in cafeteria rather than in classroom
- extra portion at lunch
- extra P.E., recess, or break time
- free time to use specific equipment or supplies
- give student a place to display work
- have use of a school locker
- help custodian
- omit certain assignments
- pass out papers
- run errands
- run film projector or video player for class
- serve as class or office messenger or aide
- sharpen class pencils
- sit at teacher's desk for a specified period
- sit by a friend
- time with a favorite adult or peer
- tutor in class, or with younger students
- use of playground or P.E. equipment
- use of class "walkman" or tape recorder
- use of magic markers and/or art supplies
- visit the principal (prearranged)
- visit the school library (individual or group)
- water class plants
- work as a lunchroom server
- write on chalkboard (regular or colored chalk)

Suggestions for Material/Tangible Reinforcement:
- address book
- art supplies
- audiocassette tapes
- badges
- ball
- balloons
- bean bags
- book
- bookmark
- bubble-blowing set
- calendar
- chalk
- clay or play dough
- colored paper
- coloring books
- comics
- cosmetics
- crayons
- eraser
- games
- good student certificates
- grab-bag: toys, candy, decals
- hackey sack
- jacks
- jewelry
- jump rope
- key chains
- magic markers
- marbles
- miniature cars
- model kits
- new pencils
- paint brushes/paints
- play money
- positive note home
- positive phone call home
- posters
- puzzles
- real money
- rings
- school supplies
- seasonal cards
- self-stick skin tattoos
- stickers
- stuffed animals
- surprise treats or rewards (random)
- toiletries
- toys
- wax lips and teeth
- yo-yo

Establish a Few Clear Rules with Known Consequences

Effective management of student behavior requires clearly specified guidelines, and consequences when students do not follow those guidelines. *Guidelines* in the classroom consist of procedures and rules (Brophy, 1988). *Procedures* are classroom routines that occur at specified times and allow the classroom to run effectively. These procedures need to be taught to students and used consistently so that the classroom will run smoothly. Each teacher needs to establish procedures for record keeping (taking attendance, for example), passing out papers and materials, storing materials and books, collecting papers and materials, entering and leaving the room (alone and with the class), and making the transition between tasks.

Rules provide the structure for acceptable and unacceptable classroom behaviors. Instead of trying to develop a rule to govern every possible misbehavior, teachers should develop a few general rules that guide students in determining whether behavior is or is not acceptable. These rules should be based on the teacher's criteria for what constitutes a behavior problem (Emmer et al., 1989). Some teachers involve students in determining class rules and consequences. **Consequences** are the repercussions associated with appropriate (e.g.,

gaining a token in a token economy) and inappropriate behavior (e.g., losing a token). When students are involved in the development of the consequences, the teacher needs to play an active role. Students often want to establish consequences far harsher than those established by the teacher.

Examples of general rules follow:

- Raise your hand if you have something to contribute.
- Do not interfere with the learning of your fellow students.
- Do not interfere with the teacher's instruction.
- Complete tasks and homework on time.
- Do not bring to school materials (e.g., toys, action figures) that interfere with your learning.

Some teachers show each new class the rules from the previous year and allow the current students to make changes.

Think about Nina's introductory comments. As you may recall, she indicated that she had few rules but many routines. She also stated that procedures and rules are not enough. The teacher and students need to know what the consequences are of not following a procedure or rule. Nina said that during her first year as a teacher, establishing consequences was difficult. She had a hard time anticipating the kinds of problems she would have, and had limited experience in providing consequences for student behavior. She implemented a strategy in which consequences for breaking class rules were as closely related to the problem as possible. For example, students who interfered with the learning of others suffered the consequences of being removed from the group for a designated period of time.

Nina also established a system for classroom procedures. Every Friday, two students were selected to distribute and collect papers and materials during the following week. She identified these students with a "lottery"

What reinforcer is being used in this classroom? What other kinds of reinforcers might be used to encourage positive behavior? If this were your classroom, how might you respond to misbehavior?

system, with eligibility based on meeting weekly behavior goals. Also, so that students would understand what was expected of them, all students practiced procedures for transitions between centers, going to and from their classroom, and other routines. Rules were handled through the new "token system" she established. On Friday, she counted the number of tokens for the week and students solved math problems about the number of tokens needed to win the prize.

Help Students to Change Inappropriate Behavior

What should a teacher do when focusing on positive behaviors does not change the negative behaviors? Three alternative techniques are ignoring on purpose, time out, and punishment. Effective procedures for implementing these techniques follow.

Ignoring on Purpose The goal of **ignoring on purpose** is to eliminate (extinguish) a student's undesirable behavior, which is being reinforced through the teacher's attention. The technical term for this elimination is **extinction**. For example, a teacher may want to extinguish a student's behavior of shouting out. Having determined that telling the student to raise his hand provides the attention the student wants and therefore reinforces the student's shouting-out behavior, the teacher decides to ignore the student (and reduce the behavior). Ignoring can be a very effective strategy to reduce undesirable behaviors, but is harder to implement than most people think. Often the teacher does not say anything, but looks at the student—and that may be enough to reinforce the student's undesirable behavior.

Ignoring can be an effective means of decreasing undesirable behaviors. It is often slow, however, and can be impractical for many behaviors that occur in the classroom because the reinforcers for an undesirable behavior may not be completely under the teacher's control. Let's return to the example of the student who continually shouted out in class. This student's behavior was reinforced not only by the attention of the teacher, but also by that of his classmates. Thus, for planned ignoring to work in this situation, both teacher and classmates needed to ignore the undesirable behavior.

Another characteristic of extinction as applied through ignoring is the rate at which the target behavior continues to occur. During extinction, the target behavior will increase in rate or intensity before decreasing. Although ignoring can be an effective means of decreasing undesirable behaviors, it requires patience and the ability to control reinforcement.

Time Out Time out occurs when the student is removed from the opportunity to receive reinforcement. In the classroom, the student receives reinforcement from classmates, the teacher, and hopefully the environment. When a student is removed from this setting, he or she is no longer able to receive these reinforcers. The underlying principle behind the successful use of time out is that the environment the student leaves must be reinforcing, and the time-out environment must not. In busy classrooms and schools where there is little space, time out is often difficult to accomplish.

For example, a tenth grade teacher asked students who were interfering with his lesson to sit in a chair in the corner of his classroom. Laurence, a student with learning problems, was frequently asked to remove himself from the class lesson and sit in that chair. Because Laurence did not like Geography and could sleep when he was in the chair, however, his behavior never really improved during class. The teacher moved the chair so that it was just outside the door. Laurence's desire to be with his classmates served as a motivator, and his behavior in class quickly improved.

> The record keeping procedure for monitoring time out should include the student's full name, the date and times the student was placed in and removed from time out, the behavior that led to the use of time out, the context in which the behavior occurred (e.g., where, with whom), and the student's behavior during and after time out.

The efficacy of time out is strongly influenced by environmental factors (Burke, 1992). If the environment the student is leaving is unrewarding, then time out is not an effective means of changing the student's behavior. Guidelines for implementing time out in the classroom are provided in Tips for Teachers 3.2.

TIPS FOR TEACHERS

3.2 Guidelines for Implementing Time Out

1. Time out should be used as a last resort.
2. Time out procedures should be discussed with school administrators and parents before implementation.
3. Students should be provided in advance with information about behaviors that will result in time out.
4. The amount of time the student is in time out should be brief (between 15 to 20 minutes).
5. The amount of time the student is in time out should be specified ahead of time.
6. The student should be told to go to time out. If the student does not comply, the teacher should unemotionally place the student in time out.
7. Time out should be implemented *immediately* following the inappropriate behavior.
8. Contingencies should be established in advance for the student who fails to comply with time out rules.
9. Do not leave the time out area unmonitored.
10. When time out is over, the student should join his or her classmates.
11. The teacher should look for ways to provide reinforcement for appropriate behavior after time out.

Punishment Punishment is the opposite of reinforcement, in that it follows a behavior and decreases the strength of the behavior or the likelihood the behavior will continue to occur. Although punishment often reduces the undesired behavior, it does not ensure that the desired behavior will occur. Thus, instead of teaching students to do what the teacher wants them to do, punishment simply teaches them to avoid doing what the teacher does not want them to do. For example, a student who is punished for talking in class may stop talking, but may not attend to his or her studies for the remainder of the day.

Following are some of the many significant arguments against the use of punishment:

- Punishment is often ineffective in the long run.
- Punishment often causes undesirable emotional side effects such as fear, aggression, and resentment.
- Punishment provides little information about what to do, teaching the individual only what *not* to do.
- The person who administers punishment is often associated with it and subsequently viewed as harsh or negative.

- Punishment frequently does not generalize across settings, thus it needs to be readministered.
- Fear of punishment often leads to escape behavior.

Unfortunately, despite the many arguments against the use of punishment, it is frequently used by parents and teachers. Why is punishment so frequently used? There are several reasons:

- because teachers may be unfamiliar with the consequences of punishment
- because teachers are unable to effectively implement a more positive approach
- because it is often reinforcing to the person who administers it. Often, punishment rapidly changes the undesirable behavior; the person who implements the punishment is highly rewarded.

Punishment should be used as a last resort and when behaviors are harmful to a student or others. For example, Marleen Sugai decided to implement punishment with Latrene Jackson, whose fighting on the playground was harmful to others. Despite positive attempts to change her behavior, Latrene continued to attack others when they did

TABLE 3.2

Summary of Behavioral Techniques that Can Be Used to Increase and Decrease Students' Behaviors

Procedures for Increasing Desirable Behaviors:

- *Positive reinforcement.*
  The application of a pleasurable consequence following the display of a desirable behavior. Positive reinforcement increases the target behavior that it follows. Positive reinforcement can be social (e.g., a smile, pat on the back) or tangible (e.g., a sticker or food).

- *Negative reinforcement.*
  The removal, following a behavior, of an unpleasant consequence that increases the likelihood of that behavior being maintained or increased.

- *Contract.*
  An oral or written agreement between student and teacher that identifies the expected behavior and the consequences for exhibiting or not exhibiting that behavior. For example, the teacher and student write up the specific behavior to be demonstrated, how often it should occur, and the positive consequences of fulfilling the contract.

- *Premack principle.*
  The Premack principle provides the opportunity for behaviors (acceptable to both teachers and students) to serve as reinforcers for behaviors that teachers want, as well as other behaviors acceptable to teachers but less acceptable to students.

Methods for Decreasing Undesirable Behaviors:

- *Extinction.*
  The removal of positive reinforcement. For example, when a student shouts in class and other students laugh at this behavior, that laughter can be a positive reinforcer for the shouting behavior. In such cases, the teacher may want to have a class meeting when the target student is not present and elicit the cooperation of classmates, asking them to help reduce or extinguish the shouting behavior by not laughing when the student shouts.

- *Punishment.*
  The application of an unpleasant or aversive consequence immediately following an undesirable behavior. In many cases, teachers think only of physical punishment. Other forms of punishment include any behavior that is extremely unpleasant or undesirable to the student and that reduces the occurrence of the student's target behavior. Sometimes staying after school or staying in the classroom during lunch is used as punishment. It is important for teachers to remember that a consequence is punishing only if it reduces the occurrence of the target behavior.

- *Time out.*
  The removal of a student from a positively reinforcing situation. Many teachers use time out ineffectively, removing students from classroom situations that are not positively reinforcing. Also, time out should be for a very specific period of time, not more than 15 to 20 minutes, and students should be told ahead of time when they will be allowed to return to the reinforcing situation.

---

not do what she wanted. Marleen implemented the following procedures, which are necessary to effective punishment:

- Tell the student ahead of time what the punishment will be for implementing the behavior.
- Deliver punishment immediately following the undesirable behavior (e.g., fighting).
- Consistently apply punishment when the behavior occurs.
- Unless a sharp decrease in the frequency and intensity of the behavior occurs, the punishment is ineffective and should be altered.

- Identify and reinforce the appropriate behaviors of the target student.

Table 3.2 provides a summary of behavioral techniques for increasing students' desirable behavior and decreasing undesirable behavior.

Recognize Students' Mistaken Goals

Rudolf Dreikurs, a follower of Alfred Adler and director of the Adler Institute, is well known for his contribution to understanding the classroom behavior of students (Dreikurs & Cassel, 1972; Dreikurs et al., 1982). He believed that all behav-

TABLE 3.3

Students' Mistaken Goals

Student's Goal	Student's Behavior	Teacher's Feeling
Attention	Repeats aversive behavior.	Annoyed
Power	Refuses to stop behavior.	Threatened, loss of control
Revenge	Becomes hostile, tries to hurt others.	Hurt
Exhibition of inadequacy	Refuses to participate or cooperate.	Helpless, gives up

ior was purposeful and that student behavior and misbehavior could be better dealt with by teachers if they better understood the purpose behind the behavior.

The following principles form the foundation of Dreikurs' approach to discipline:

■ Students (like the rest of us) are social beings and their behaviors are attempts to be liked and accepted.

■ Students can control their own behavior.

■ When students display inappropriate behavior, they do so because they have the **mistaken goal** that it will get them the recognition and acceptance they want.

Many students learn that they can garner the acceptance and recognition they need by behaving appropriately and completing school tasks. Other students do not feel capable or worthy of obtaining recognition in these ways; they attempt to obtain the acceptance and recognition they need by displaying inappropriate behavior and not completing their school tasks. Over time, they begin to feel that the only way to get recognition is through inappropriate behavior.

Dreikurs identified four mistaken goals that categorize the behavior of most students:

■ attention
■ power or control
■ revenge or getting even
■ display of inadequacy

According to Dreikurs, the best way to determine the "mistaken goal" of the student is to identify what the student is doing and how you feel about or react to the behavior. Table 3.3 provides a description of a student's mistaken goal, the student's behavior, and the teacher's reaction.

Dreikurs indicates that the teacher's job is to identify the student's mistaken goal and to discuss it with him or her. Teachers also need to identify their own reaction to the student's behavior, and how that might contribute to the student's mistaken goal. See Charles (1989) for further information on the application of Dreikurs' approach to classroom management.

RESEARCH BRIEF

BEHAVIOR MANAGEMENT CONSIDERATIONS IN CULTURALLY DIVERSE CLASSROOMS

Educators tend to have low expectations of poor, African American, Native American, and Hispanic students (e.g., Cortes, 1978; Dusek & Joseph, 1983; Ford, 1992; MacLeod, 1987; Ogbu, 1990).

Beginning in preschool and continuing through their college careers, educators and education students tend to expect the European American middle-class students in their classes to do better academically than non-European American and poor students. In addition, they expect European American middle-class students to be more intelligent, even when students' achievement test scores, grades, and school histories would predict otherwise. (Grossman, 1995, pp. 69–70).

It is likely that teachers also hold low expectations for individuals with disabilities, and these low expectations influence the extent to which they interact with students.

How might these low expectations influence the ways in which teachers manage the behavior of students? This question is particularly relevant, since disproportionate numbers of students from minority groups are identified as needing special education, although many of them remain in the general education classroom for all or part of the school day (Robertson et al., 1994). Although there is little information about ways that teachers' attitudes might influence their treatment of the behavior problems of students in their classrooms, there is little doubt that lowered expectations for students do *not* yield positive benefits. Teachers are likely to expect the behavior of students from traditionally underrepresented groups to be worse, and (in an attempt to stop problems before they get out of control) provide overcorrection for problems they would be willing to overlook with other students. The primary solution to the problem is awareness of prejudices and the subtle and not so subtle ways these prejudices might influence the way you manage the behavior of students in your classroom. Keep the following questions in your desk, and frequently read and reflect on them:

■ What behaviors bother me as a teacher? Who is exhibiting these behaviors? Am I sure that *all* students who behave in these ways are treated in the same way?
■ Who are the students I have the most difficulty managing? What socioeconomic, cultural, and linguistic background do they represent? How does this affect my attitude?
■ To what extent have I "reached out" and demonstrated genuine caring and concern to *all* students in my class?
■ If students were asked to identify which students in the class I like best and least, what would they say? What does this say about me?
■ How are students from traditionally underrepresented groups performing in my class? What behaviors do I demonstrate to promote their success?

Teachers often misinterpret the behavior of minority students and thus respond inappropriately to their behavior (Irvine, 1991; Morgan, 1980). The miscommunication between minority students and their teachers may cause misunderstandings that lead to discipline problems and ultimately discouragement on the part of the minority student. Following are cautions and considerations that should help you cope more effectively with the behavior of minority students. For a complete review of these issues, see Grossman (1995).

■ Behaviors that are acceptable and encouraged in home and community may be incompatible with behaviors at school. Students may not only receive conflicting messages about their behavior, but also be forced to choose between loyalty to home and community or to school. Teachers should avoid placing all students in this position, by learning as much as they can about the expectations of students' home and community, and communicating acceptance of these practices. So informed, teachers can help students distinguish which behaviors are acceptable in which settings. For example, aggressive, emotionally charged behavior may be expected of African American males at home and in their community but unacceptable in classrooms. Another example is the behavior of Hispanic students, many of whom are viewed by teachers as dependent, passive, and reticent about participating and responding to the teacher. Yet these behaviors are expected and nurtured in the Hispanic family and community.
■ Behaviors that are indicative of problems in one group of students may not be so in another. For example, teachers may overlook signs of internalizing behaviors in African American students, who may express such behaviors differently. Also, teachers who know that Hispanic students may not ask for help may need to check frequently with these students to determine how they are proceeding. Finally, behaviors of some African American students may be viewed as aggressive and acting out, when their intention is merely to "fit in" and be recognized.
■ Some behaviors students exhibit may be wrongly attributed and interpreted by teachers who do not understand the students' culture or background. For example, some stu-

dents who are limited speakers of English may fail to respond, make limited eye contact with the teacher, or appear defiant because they lack confidence. Some students from other cultures (e.g., Asian groups) are accustomed to clearly defined rules and regulations and may have difficulty interpreting more implicit rules.

If, after implementing the suggestions in this section, you are not satisfied with your students' progress in increasing desirable classroom behavior and decreasing undesirable behaviors, ask yourself the questions shown in Figure 3.1.

Establishing the Classroom Climate

You cannot control certain aspects of your classroom's climate. The condition of the building, the size of your classroom, the type of furniture, and the nature of the ventilation in your classroom are examples of important elements in your environment that affect you and your students but over which you are likely to have little or no control. You can attempt, however, to optimize the environmental conditions you have and to utilize classroom space in a way that is most likely to

---

FIGURE 3.1

Implementation Checklist

If your intervention is not working, consider the following:

✔ Have you adequately identified and defined the target behavior?

✔ Have you selected the right kind of reinforcer?
(What you decided on may not be reinforcing to the student.)

✔ Are you providing reinforcement soon enough?

✔ Are you providing too much reinforcement?

✔ Are you giving too little reinforcement?

✔ Are you reinforcing too often?

✔ Are you being consistent in your implementation of the intervention program?

✔ Have you made the intervention program more complicated than it needs to be?

✔ Are others involved following through (e.g., principal, parent, "buddy")?

✔ Is social reinforcement by peers outweighing your contracted reinforcement?

✔ Did you fail to give reinforcers promised or earned?

Reprinted with permission from: Larrivee, B. (1992). *Strategies for effective classroom management: Creating a collaborative climate* (p. 259). Boston: Allyn and Bacon.

enhance students' learning. In addition to the physical environment, the students' seating arrangement is likely to influence management of the classroom (Levin & Nolan, 1991). Consider the following questions as you think about seating arrangements:

- Based on the seating arrangement in my class, is any student not an obvious member of the group?
- What grouping arrangement is used for students' seating? Are students arranged in small-group pods, individual seats, pairs, and so on?
- How often during the day does the seating arrangement change? For what reasons? Are any students not involved? Why?

Perhaps an even more important factor than the physical arrangement of the room are the procedures you, the teacher, implement to create a classroom climate that is respectful and accepting of all students.

Create a Learning Community

Reread the beginning of this chapter, with its focus on the third grade teacher, Nina. What did she say that leads you to believe that establishing a classroom community was important to her? In a subsequent interview, Nina described how she establishes a classroom community:

> There are three things I emphasize. First, all students in the room are full members and participants in the community. It is all of our responsibility to assure that they are active, involved, and engaged. Second, everyone in the classroom has a role. These roles rotate but tend to focus on students' interests and expertise. Third, the class belongs to all of us (teachers and students) not just to me. I serve as the leader who is responsible for learning and [for] creating a classroom environment that promotes acceptance, but I engage all of the students in the process.

What are some things you can do to establish a classroom that fosters acceptance of all students? A list of guiding principles follows:

- *Students are children or adolescents first.* Teachers who remember this look beyond the visible and less obvious ways in which stu-

dents differ, and respect their common needs and goals—to be accepted, recognized, and valued members of the community. The classroom community is one of the most important places this needs to occur. An attitude which places children or adolescents first recognizes that students are more alike than different.

- *Focus on abilities.* To foster an accepting classroom climate, you must establish an environment in which teachers and students seek and use knowledge about the abilities and expertise of *all* class members. In Laureen Rankin's third grade class, a picture of each student was framed in a decorated star and hung in the classroom. Attached to each star were lists of self- and teacher-identified strengths or abilities. In addition, all students were encouraged to recognize their fellow students' abilities (which, when identified, were added to the appropriate star).
- *Celebrate diversity.* Diversity can be viewed by teachers as something to be tolerated, mildly accepted, or celebrated. *Celebrating diversity* means conveying to students the value of students who represent different learning styles, behavior profiles, physical abilities, languages, and cultural backgrounds. Sharon Andreaci, a sixth grade teacher, was delighted that many of the students in her classroom spoke Spanish and represented the cultural backgrounds of several Hispanic groups (e.g., Cuban, Nicaraguan, Colombian, Mexican). She often asked students about their backgrounds and encouraged them to share their knowledge and practices with others in the classroom. For example, she routinely asked such questions as, "Juan, how would you say that in Spanish? Ana, do you agree with Juan? Is there another way to say it in Spanish?"
- *Demonstrate high regard for all students.* Students know when teachers prefer particular students, even when teachers go out of their way to disguise this information. Demonstrating high regard for all students means treating each of them as the most important student in the class. Carlos Rivera, a ninth grade science teacher, provides this advice:

Listen carefully and attentively to each student's responses, not just those of the brighter students. Look for ways to connect each student's response to what you are talking about now or in a previous lesson. Make eye contact with each student, do not always look at the brighter students. Be sure to call on each student at least every day. Get to know a few personal things about each student and check on them periodically.

- *Provide opportunities for students to work in mixed-ability groups.* Students prefer, and benefit from, opportunities to work with their peers in groups that represent a range of abilities. Be sure that each group member plays a genuine role, in which he or she contributes to the group process.

Use Class Meetings

Joan McGinnis and Laura Prinstein are fifth grade teachers who use **class meetings** to involve students in the management of their classes, but who do not approach class meetings in the same way. Joan has a regularly scheduled Friday afternoon meeting. Laura calls class meetings when she needs them. She has one meeting some weeks, two meetings other weeks, and at times several weeks pass without a meeting. Laura uses class meetings to solve crises and to deal with immediate problems. Joan uses class meetings to prevent problems, identify potential or occurring problems, teach problem solving, and foster class responsibility for the cohesion and functioning of the classroom. Joan's application of class meetings is more likely to be effective in the long run (Nelson et al., 1993).

The format of the class meeting is much the same at both the elementary and secondary level. Nelson, et al. (1993) emphasize the importance of starting the class meeting by forming a circle so that everyone can see everyone else. The change in the seating structure of the classroom reminds students that this is a special time.

The first ten minutes are used for compliments and appreciations, which can be handled in several ways. Joan uses a recognition box, a decorated shoe box into which students and teachers place written recognitions of classmates or teachers who have done helpful or special things, such as helping a classmate, doing well on a paper, or ignoring someone who is bothering them. Recognitions also include personal information, such as winning a swim meet. When the class meeting starts, Joan brings the recognition box and passes it around the circle. Each student selects one slip, until all the slips have been removed from the box. Students take turns reading the recognitions. Joan often allows several minutes during which students can contribute recognitions they did not submit to the recognition box.

> "I expect as much from the students with disabilities in my class as I do from each of my other students. I understand that their goals and expectations often have to be altered, but I set high expectations for them, and it surprises me and them how often they live up to those expectations."
> —a fifth grade teacher

What instructional and management goals can be met through a class meeting format? How might class meetings increase students' stake in the day to day cohesion and operation of their classroom?

The second part of the class meeting—follow-up on prior solutions—takes approximately fifteen minutes. During this time, problems brought up at previous meetings are discussed and evaluated. Students and teachers share their perceptions in answer to the following questions:

- How frequently does the problem occur? More or less than before?
- How well are people implementing the selected solution? Is this still a problem? Is the solution effective?

The third part of the meeting—new problems—takes approximately fifteen minutes and gives students and teachers an opportunity to identify problems and work with the group to identify potential solutions to the problems. Joan cautions that it is important not to let this part of the meeting turn into a "gripe session" and to be sure not to allow students to complain about a selected student. Joan teaches all her students how to solve problems and encourages them to use those skills.

Conveying acceptance of all students in the classroom is one of the teacher's most important roles.

The fourth part of the meeting—future plans—takes approximately ten minutes. Joan describes this section of the meeting:

> I try to keep this part of the meeting very upbeat with an emphasis on future projects, school events, or field trips. I use this time to engage the students not just in the social plans of the class and school but also in my academic plans for the future weeks. If I have a special project planned, I use this time to introduce the new project to the students.

Joan has used class meetings for different grade levels, including middle and high school. She comments:

> I feel that it is an essential aspect of a successful classroom. The students in my room are not only better behaved, they work more as a team. They take more responsibility for their own behavior as well as that of other students in the class. I think the benefits go way beyond classroom management and include academic gains as well. I guess you can tell I'm pretty enthusiastic about their function.

Increase Social Acceptance of Students with Disabilities and Exceptional Learners

Judith Warner, a veteran fifth grade teacher, is well respected by her students, their parents, and her fellow teachers for the effective way she manages students' behavior. "I probably take advantage of Judith," said her school principal, "because I can always give her the students who are the biggest behavior problem and I know she will be successful with them." Judith indicates that the secret to her success is to establish a personal relationship with each student in her class. She says:

> I spend the first month of class getting to know each of my students, what they are like, what they do outside of school, who is special to them at home and in their community, what their strengths are, and what makes them tick. I use this information to facilitate their adjustment to the classroom community and to establishing a relationship with me that will influence our year together. Yes, you can say that each student learns very early in the year that I genuinely respect and care about each of them.

What are some of the things Judith does to ensure acceptance of all students in her classroom?

- All students are treated with respect. Her classroom is not segmented into those who know and those who do not. She genuinely communicates the importance of learning what each member of the classroom community can contribute and of ensuring that all students are respected.
- Concern for each other. The students in Judith's classroom learn quickly that they are responsible for themselves and for each other. The following are examples of the types of questions Judith asks her students during the day:
- "Jonathon doesn't know how to complete his writing project. Who is going to help him?"
- "There are several students who are not involved in the activity centers. Who should be involving them in their group?"
- "One of the groups is too noisy. What should they be doing?"
- "Is everyone ready to go to lunch? What do you need to do to ensure that everyone is ready?"

TECH TALK

Using Computer Games to Promote Student Acceptance

Computer games can be used to promote the social acceptance and peer interaction of students with special needs (Lewis, 1993). *Interaction Games, Interaction Games II,* and *Games 2 Play*™ for Apple II from Don Johnston Developmental Equipment, Inc. (800-999-4660) provide opportunities for students to engage in both competitive and cooperative games. The cooperative games require that each student manipulate an independent switch, but it is only through the combined efforts of both students that the game can be won. Such interactions can foster the idea that students with special needs have strengths and abilities that are beneficial to others in the class, and can provide a context for students to relate with their classmates with special needs. Teachers can manipulate the competitive games so that students of different ability levels can compete from more equal starting positions. Similar products exist for Windows and Macintosh platforms, including curriculum-related applications, such as cooperative storytelling and math problem solving games.

- Point out students' abilities. Judith insists that when a negative statement is made about a student, something positive about that student must be said.
- "Yes, Myla (a student who uses a wheel chair) does slow us down going to lunch, but Myla is the class artist. She helps us and we help her."

Conveying acceptance of all students in the classroom is an important role the classroom teacher can play. Serving as an advocate for all of your students with other professionals is another critical role. Students with special needs may be more likely than other students in your class to receive criticism from other professionals.

The classroom teacher needs to serve as advocate for the student, both in the classroom and with other professionals.

Enhancing Students' Self-Concepts

Ask parents what they most want for their children and a frequent response is that they want their children to be happy. They want their children to like themselves and be proud of what they do and who they are. What role do teachers play in ensuring that students are able to develop positive relationships with others? Most students come to school feeling good about themselves. The self-concept of most kindergartners is very high, but it gradually decreases, stabilizing somewhat in about the second grade (Vaughn et al., 1992). Teachers as well as parents play an important role in ensuring that students view themselves positively and are able to use skills that enable them to make and maintain appropriate relationships with others. This section of the chapter identifies procedures teachers can implement to enhance self-concept and social skills.

> Individuals with positive self-concepts feel worthwhile, competent, and deserving of others' respect and caring.

How do you feel about yourself? Do you think you are a valuable person, worthy of love and appreciation from others? Do you think you have friends and are liked by others? Do you think you do well in school and are likely to succeed? How do you feel about the way you look? What about your ability to play sports? Your answers to these questions provide insight into your self-concept. Individuals with positive self-concepts generally feel as though they are worthwhile and deserve the respect, recognition, and appreciation of others. They have positive feelings about themselves in multiple settings including at school, with friends, and with family. They generally like the way they look and who they are.

What about students who are disabled, "at-risk," or exceptional? What are their self-concepts like? Because these students are not a homogeneous group, no general statements can be made about their self-concept. But because individuals who are at-risk or disabled often receive more negative feedback than other students do, their self-concepts probably are lower, on the average, than those of other students (Haager & Vaughn, 1995).

What are some of the ways teachers can enhance the self-concepts of students with learning and behavior problems?

- Discover students' talents, abilities, or interests and recognize them personally. Every student in the classroom can be an expert on something. Be sure to find out what expertise every student in your classroom possesses.
- Provide opportunities for students who do not succeed academically to succeed in other ways. One parent described it this way:

  > The best thing that happened to my son is swimming. He joined a swim team when he was six and all his friends know he has won many swimming awards. No matter how discouraged he is about school, he has one area in which he is successful.

- Recognize students' difficulties with learning, and explain their problems to them in a way they can understand. Sometimes teachers and parents try to protect students and do not explain to them why they are having problems in school. An honest explanation (that they have attention problems, learning problems, physical problems, and so on) often helps students understand why some things are more difficult for them than for other students. The explanation should help the student understand that we are all different from each other in many ways, and this is one way the student is different from others.
- Hold all students to high standards and then provide the encouragement and support to meet those standards (Canfield & Wells, 1994). Teachers often have lower expectations for students who demonstrate learning and behavior problems than for other students. These lowered expectations, however unintentional, nevertheless limit the opportunities available to these students as compared to those for whom we have high standards.
- Remember the important role you play in influencing (both negatively and positively)

As a teacher, what is your role in promoting the social acceptance of students with disabilities? How will you model social acceptance for your students, and what other strategies will you use?

students' self-concepts. Teachers exert an enormous influence on the self-perceptions of students, even those students whom you feel pay too little attention to you. Students know (much better than you might imagine) what you think and how you feel about them (Babad et al., 1991).

Teaching Social Skills

Have you ever met someone who seems to know the right thing to say and do, no matter what the situation may be? We often watch these people with envy as they move from person to person,

always seemingly at ease. We refer to these people as demonstrating good social skills, or demonstrating social competence. **Social competence** is defined as ". . . those responses, which within a given situation, prove effective, or in other words, maximize the probability of producing, maintaining, or enhancing positive effects for the interactor" (Foster & Ritchey, 1979, p. 26), and, it should be added, while causing no harm to others. Social skills allow one to adapt and respond to the expectations of society. Social competence is a process that begins at birth and continues throughout life. Many students with learning and behavior problems exhibit difficulties with social skills (see Figure 3.2).

Interpersonal Problem Solving

Interpersonal problem solving is an important skill for many students to learn, particularly students with special needs. The goal of **interpersonal problem solving** is to teach students to identify their problems, goals, and a wide range of alternative strategies for effectively solving their problems. Some students learn to problem solve with little assistance from adults, but many students, particularly those with special needs, must be taught the skills for interpersonal problem solving. Interpersonal problem solving has been used successfully with different groups, including adult psychiatric patients (Platt & Spivack, 1972), preschoolers (Ridley & Vaughn, 1982), kindergartners (Shure & Spivack, 1978), children with mental retardation (Vaughn et al., 1983), children with learning disabilities (Vaughn et al., 1988; Vaughn et al., 1991), and aggressive children (Vaughn et al., 1984).

Four components appear in most interpersonal problem-solving programs (Spivack et al., 1976): problem identification, generation of alternative solutions, identification and evaluation of consequences, and solution implementation. For example, an interpersonal problem-solving program was implemented with students identified as having serious emotional and behavioral disorders (Amish et al., 1988). The intervention was taught once a week for approximately 40 minutes, for a total of 15 weeks. Students who participated in the program improved their interpersonal

FIGURE 3.2

Examples of Social Skill Deficits

- deficits in social perception and social cognition, which inhibit students' abilities to interact with others
- lack of consequential thinking
- difficulty expressing feelings
- difficulty in feeling empathy for others
- difficulty delaying gratification (impulsive)
- inappropriate grooming and hygiene
- failure to understand and fulfill the role of listener
- inability to take the perspective of another
- less time spent looking and smiling at a conversational partner
- unwilling to act in a social situation to influence the outcome
- less likely to request clarification when given ambiguous or incomplete information
- lack of self-confidence and tendency to portray learned helplessness behaviors
- aggressive or antisocial behaviors
- tendency to talk more or less than non-LD peers
- more likely to approach teacher and ask inappropriate questions
- less proficient in interpersonal problem solving
- less proficient in planning for the future

FIGURE 3.3

Problem Log

 What is the problem?

Describe it (who is involved, where did it happen, and what happened?).

 What do you want to happen?

 What did you do or say to solve the problem?

 Did your choice solve the problem?

 How well did it work?

1	2	3	4	5
Poorly	Not so well	Okay	Good	Great

Homework:

Reprinted with permission from: Goldstein, A. P. (1988). *The Prepare Curriculum: Teaching prosocial competencies* (p. 47). Champaign, IL: Research Press. Copyright 1988 by A.P. Goldstein.

problem-solving skills and were able to generate more alternatives to interviewing and role-playing measures. The following steps were taught:

1. Say what the problem is and how you feel.
2. Decide on a goal.
3. Stop and think before you decide what to do.
4. Think of many possible solutions to the problem.
5. Think about what will happen next (after each possible solution).
6. When you find a good solution, try it.

A sample worksheet for recording interpersonal problems and identifying procedures for addressing them is provided in Figure 3.3.

Vaughn and colleagues (McIntosh et al., in press; Vaughn & Lancelotta, 1990; Vaughn et al., 1988; Vaughn et al., 1991) have developed the FAST and SLAM strategies as part of an overall interpersonal problem-solving program. The purpose of **FAST** is to teach students to consider problems, identify alternatives, and evaluate consequences to their interpersonal problems. A description of the FAST strategy (see Figure 3.4) follows:

FIGURE 3.4

FAST: An Interpersonal Problem-Solving Strategy

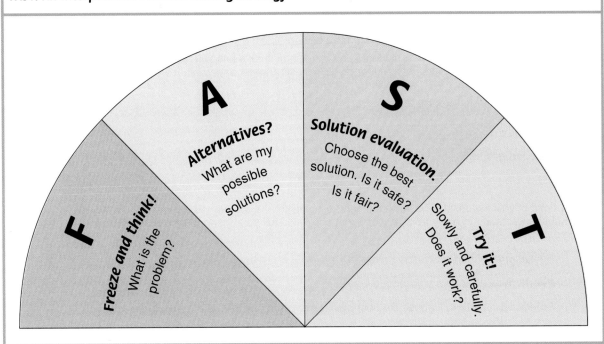

Step 1. Freeze and Think. Students are taught to identify the problem. They are encouraged to view the problem from their own perspective as well as that of the other student.

Step 2. Alternatives. Students are taught to generate many possible alternative solutions to each problem. Students learn to categorize the solutions to ensure that they represent many different types.

Step 3. Solution Evaluation. Students select several of the most feasible alternatives generated in step 2 and evaluate the likely consequences if the alternatives were implemented. Students also select an alternative that is safe and fair. The goal is to teach students to identify solutions that are effective in the long run.

Step 4. Try It. Students rehearse and implement the solution, and evaluate its effectiveness.

If that solution is not effective, students go back to step 2.

Figure 3.5 presents an activity sheet for implementing FAST in your classroom.

The purpose of **SLAM** (see Figure 3.6) was to develop a strategy, compatible with FAST, that would teach students to accept and respond appropriately to negative feedback from others. This is how SLAM works:

Step 1. Stop. Students are taught to stop what they are doing and take a breath when someone gives them negative feedback. Through role play and rehearsal, teacher and students identify the typical response to negative feedback—saying something negative or stopping work. This step teaches students to stop, take a breath, and simply listen.

FIGURE 3.5

Activity Sheet for Use with the FAST Strategy

This activity sheet can be used to give students written practice in using the FAST strategy.

You are in the cafeteria. Another student keeps bugging you. He hits you, pokes you, tries to steal your food, and will not stop bullying you. You start to get angry. What would you do? Use FAST to help you solve the problem.

1. Freeze and think. What is the problem?

2. Alternatives. What are your possible solutions?

3. Solution evaluation. Choose the best one. Remember: safe and fair; works in the long run.

4. Try it. Do you think this will work?

A friend of yours is upset. She is teased a lot, especially by a boy named Kenny. She told you that she wants to run away from school. What could you tell your friend to help her solve the problem? Use FAST to help you.

1. Freeze and think. What is the problem?

2. Alternatives. What are your possible solutions?

3. Solution evaluation. Choose the best one. Remember: safe and fair; works in the long run.

4. Try it. Do you think this will work?

Reprinted with permission from: Bos, C. S., & Vaughn, S. (1994). *Strategies for teaching students with learning and behavior problems* (3rd ed., p. 373). Boston: Allyn & Bacon.

Step 2. **Look.** Teaches students that the best thing to do when someone is giving them negative feedback is to stop what they are doing and look at the other person. Sometimes students look down or away when they are given negative feedback.

Step 3. **Ask.** Teaches students to ask questions to clarify what the other person means. Often students feel as though they do not deserve the negative feedback that teachers or parents give them. Instead of saying, "I didn't do that," students are taught to ask questions for clarification before they respond.

Step 4. **Make.** Teaches students to make an appropriate response to the other person. Students role-play these responses, which include agreeing with the other person,

agreeing to stop the behavior, or explaining their point of view. Figure 3.7 provides the lyrics to a rap song developed to help teach the SLAM strategy.

Mutual Interest Discovery

The purpose of **Mutual Interest Discovery** (Fox, 1989) is to increase peer acceptance of students with special needs in the general education classroom. Students who do not know each other very well are paired so that they have a structured opportunity to discover things they

> Mutual Interest Discovery is a method of providing structured opportunities for students to increase peer acceptance.

FIGURE 3.6

The SLAM Mnemonic to Aid in Accepting Negative Feedback SLAM Strategy

S	**L**	**A**	**M**
STOP	**LOOK**	**ASK**	**MAKE**
Stop whatever you are doing.	Look the person in the eyes.	Ask the person a question to clarify what he or she means.	Make an appropriate response to the person.

Reprinted with permission from Council for Exceptional Children, McIntosh, R., Vaughn, S., & Bennerson, D. (1995), FAST social skills with a SLAM and a rap. *Teaching Exceptional Children, 28,* 37–41.

FIGURE 3.7

Lyrics to the SLAM Strategy Song

Accepting negative feedback, feedback, feedback.
Accepting negative feedback, feedback, feedback.
Stop what you're doing. Look them in the eye.
Fix your face. We'll tell you why.

Accepting negative feedback, feedback, feedback.
Accepting negative feedback, feedback, feedback.
Listen with your ears to what they say.
This is no time for you to play.

Accepting negative feedback, feedback, feedback.
Accepting negative feedback, feedback, feedback.
Ask a question if you don't understand.
Don't stand there in wonderland.

Accepting negative feedback, feedback, feedback.
Accepting negative feedback, feedback, feedback.
Make a response to their concerns.
Accepting negative feedback is the way to learn.

Reprinted with permission from Council for Exceptional Children, McIntosh, R., Vaughn, S., & Bennerson, D. (1995), FAST social skills with a SLAM and a rap. *Teaching Exceptional Children, 28,* 37–41.

have in common. The rationale is that the better we understand someone, the better our chances of accepting them. Structured opportunities for students to interact and get to know each other better are provided. The following procedures describe the implementation of Mutual Interest Discovery:

1. Students who are well accepted in the class are paired with those who are less well accepted. This is an opportunity for the teacher to pair popular students with students with special needs.

2. Student pairs work in semistructured activities once a week for periods of approximately 40 minutes.

3. Students design and conduct interviews with each other about such topics as entertainment, hobbies, and sports. Following the interview, each person writes three items discovered during the interview to be of common interest to both partners.

4. Students keep a written record (e.g., diary, log, book) about their partner and themselves. This information is shared with the class, so that all students have an opportunity to know and accept each other better.

Example of a Social Skills Program for Adolescents

The purpose of **ASSET** is to develop the social skills of adolescents with special needs who demonstrate difficulties in social functioning (Hazel et al., 1982). The program also has been used successfully in regular classrooms.

ASSET provides a comprehensive social skills training program that emphasizes the following eight fundamental skills:

- giving positive feedback
- giving negative feedback
- accepting negative feedback

- resisting peer pressure
- negotiation skills
- personal problem solving
- following directions
- conducting conversations

Each fundamental skill is further divided into component skills that are sequenced for instruction. For example, the fundamental skill, following directions, includes the following twelve component skills:

1. Face the person.
2. Keep eye contact.
3. Keep a neutral facial expression.
4. Use a normal voice tone.
5. Keep a straight posture.

6. Listen closely to the instruction so that you will know what to do, and remember to give feedback with head nods and by saying "mm-hmm" and "yeah."
7. Acknowledge the instruction.
8. Ask for more information if you don't understand the instruction. "But I don't understand ..."
9. Say that you will follow the instruction. "I'll do it...."
10. Follow the instruction.
11. Throughout, give polite, pleasant responses.
12. Do not argue with the person about the instruction: go ahead and follow it; you can talk to the person later about the problem.

FIGURE 3.8

Teaching Social Skills to Secondary Students

Each social skill is taught by implementing the following nine-step procedure:

Step 1: Review. Previously learned skills are reviewed and homework is evaluated and integrated.

Step 2: Explain. The skill that is the focus of the lesson is explained and discussed.

Step 3: Rationale. A rationale for why the skill is important and why the students need to learn it is provided.

Step 4: Example. Examples of situations in which the skill can be used are provided. These examples relate directly to the experiences and interests of the students.

Step 5: Examined. A skills sheet that lists the component skills (refer to text for list of skills for following directions) is provided to each student.

Step 6: Model. Through videotapes that can be purchased with the curriculum, or as implemented by the teacher, the skills are demonstrated and modeled.

Step 7: Verbal Rehearsal. The procedure of verbally stating the components of each skill so that they can be learned by the student is implemented. The students practice saying the skill components and play games and engage in activities that teach them the skills.

Step 8: Behavioral Rehearsal. Students practice performing each subskill and overall skill, and demonstrate proficiency.

Step 9: Homework. Designed to enhance generalization, homework provides students with directed activities that allow them to practice the subskills and skills outside the classroom.

TIPS FOR TEACHERS

3.3 Instructional Materials to Enhance Students' Social Skills

Anderson, J. (1981). *Thinking, changing, rearranging: Improving self-esteem in young people*. Eugene, OR: Timberline Press.

Intended for students age 10 and older, the activities in this book examine students' cognitions as related to social interaction.

Bash, M. A. S., & Camp, B. W. (1985). *Think aloud: Increasing social and cognitive skills: A problem-solving program for children*. Champaign, IL: Research Press.

Developed for elementary students, this program is organized into three sections for grades one through six. Students are taught how to think through and successfully deal with social conflicts.

Canfield, J., & Wells, H. C. (1994). *100 ways to enhance self-concept in the classroom* (2nd ed.). Boston, MA: Allyn & Bacon.

Provides 100 strategies to help teachers build a positive classroom community and promote the growth of their students. Particularly useful are the references for instructional books, videotapes, and organizations.

Cautela, J. R., & Groden, J. (1978). *Relaxation: A comprehensive manual for adults, children, and children with special needs*. Champaign, IL: Research Press.

Provides different techniques for teaching relaxation training.

Elardo, P., & Cooper, M. (1977). *Aware: Activities for social development*. Menlo Park, CA: Addison Wesley.

Provides specific exercises (e.g., games, role-play activities) to develop social competence in elementary students.

Gerald, M., & Eyman, W. (1981). *Thinking straight and talking sense*. New York: Institute for Rational Living.

This workbook, designed for students in the sixth grade and above, helps students examine the cognitions behind their behavior.

Goldstein, A. P., & Glick, B. (1987). *Aggression replacement training: A comprehensive intervention for aggressive youth*. Champaign, IL: Research Press.

This multifaceted program includes activities to help students improve their behavior, affect, and cognitions.

Goldstein, A. P., Sprafkin, R. P., Gershaw, N. J., & Klein, P. (1980). *Skillstreaming the adolescent: A structured learning approach to teaching prosocial skills*. Champaign, IL: Research Press.

Provides explicit methods for enhancing the social skills of adolescents. The inclusion of a transcript from a skills training session is particularly illustrative and helps to crystallize the procedures necessary for effective instruction.

Jackson, N. F. (1983). *Getting along with others: Teaching social effectiveness to children*. Champaign, IL: Research Press.

This program, designed for elementary students, provides guides, exercises, and lessons targeted to develop skills in cooperating, accepting feedback, responding to criticism, dealing with peer pressure, and reacting to harassment.

Mannix, D. (1993). *Social skills activities for special children*. West Nyack, NY: Center for Applied Research in Education.

This workbook provides 142 lessons and accompanying activity sheets that teachers can reproduce and use with their sudents. The activities focus on skills, both in the classroom and at home.

McGinnis, E., Goldstein, A. P., Sprafkin, R. P., & Gershaw, N. J. (1984). *Skillstreaming the elementary school child: A guide for teaching prosocial skills*. Champaign, IL: Research Press.

Based on the skillstreaming model, this book provides instruction and activities for teaching social skills to elementary-age students.

Vaughn, S., Levine, L., & Ridley, C. (1986). *PALS: Problem-solving and affective learning strategies*. Chicago: Science Research Associates.

This skills training program targets students between four and eight years of age. A teacher's guide outlines recommended activities, which are designed for small-group and whole-class instruction.

Walker, H. M., McConnell, S., Holmes, S., Todis, B., Walker, J., & Golden, N. (1983). *The Walker social skills curriculum: The Accepts program*. Austin, TX: PRO-ED.

A tool for teachers to help students with disabilities make the transition into less restrictive settings. Association with classmates and coping strategies are some of the topics focused on.

Figure 3.8 provides a description of the steps in the ASSET program, The Leader's Guide (Hazel, et al., 1982) from the ASSET program provides instructions for running the groups and teaching the skills. Eight teaching sessions are provided on videotapes that demonstrate the skills. Program materials include skill sheets, home notes, and criterion checklists.

Teachers might want to implement the specific approaches to social skills instruction identified in this section of the chapter, and to use some or all of the social skills materials described in Tips for Teachers 3.3.

Principles for Conducting Social Skills Training

There are several principles of social skills training that generalize across social skills programs (Vaughn & La Greca, 1993):

1. *Use principles of effective instruction.* These principles include:

   - Obtain a student's commitment to learn the targeted social skill.
   - Assess social skills and target skills appropriate for the students with whom you are working.
   - Explain the targeted social skills to students and demonstrate and model appropriate uses of the skills.
   - Identify the steps in implementing the social skill and provide adequate time to rehearse the skill.
   - Allow students to role-play the implementation of the social skill in controlled and natural settings.
   - Teach students to monitor and evaluate their use of and progress in implementing the targeted social skill.

2. *Involve peers in the training program for low social status students.* Students who do and do not demonstrate social skills problems need to be included in the training. Why? Because when social skills programs target only students with social skills diffi-

culties, the changes those students make in their behavior are not noticed by students of higher social status. (Bierman & Furman, 1984; Vaughn et al., 1988). Thus, despite positive changes in their social behavior, targeted students are often still rated by their peers as undesirable social partners.

For example, Vaughn et al. (1988) found that popular students who were involved in social skills training with students low in popularity were more likely to increase their acceptance of the low social status students than were popular students who were not involved in the training.

3. *Teach for transfer of learning and generalization.* As with other skills (e.g., learning strategies), social skills training programs often effectively increase students' social skills within the context of social skills training, but do not effectively generalize the skills to other settings (Berler et al., 1982; Vaughn & Ridley, 1983). Program plans for teaching generalization have been developed (Vaughn et al., 1986) and include such strategies as varying the setting, the trainer, the materials, the task, and the cues. The extent to which these components of generalization are built into the training will increase the likelihood that the learned social skills will generalize to other settings. Michelson and Mannarino (1986) provide a summary of strategies for promoting generalization of social skills. These strategies include:

   - Teach social behaviors that will be supported naturally in the setting.
   - Teach alternative response patterns, not just "pat" phrases.
   - Teach students to adapt the procedures of the social skill taught so that it becomes their own.
   - Rehearse skills in a variety of settings.
   - Use natural and logical consequences to maintain the target skills.
   - Use peers as change agents.

Teaching Self-Management Skills

The purpose of teaching students **self-management** skills is that such skills enable them to be more aware of their own behaviors and to govern the reinforcers for their behaviors. Furthermore, teaching students self-management skills enables them to depend less on the teacher. You may recall, from the basic principles of managing student behavior introduced earlier in this chapter, that much of the responsibility for targeting behavior, identifying reinforcers, and implementing a behavior-change plan rested with the teachers. Self-management skills require that students learn some principles of behavior management and then implement the selected reinforcers. Self-management requires a more active role from the student and a more collaborative role from the teacher.

Margarite Rabinsky is a fourth grade teacher whose student, Eduardo Cora, is not completing assignments. Although Margarite worked closely with Eduardo to ensure that the assignments were not too difficult and that Eduardo understood how to complete them, he was still unsuccessful at turning in completed assignments on time. Deciding to involve Eduardo in a self-management plan, she implemented the following steps for developing a self-management plan with a student:

Step 1. *Teacher and student identify and agree on the behavior to be changed.* Margarite and Eduardo agreed on the behavior to change and put it in writing (see Figure 3.9).

Step 2. *Identify when and where the behavior most frequently occurs.* Margarite stated, "First, let's think about what classes it occurs in most and then let's think about whether there are certain days when it occurs." Eduardo volunteered that he started the week off pretty well and then felt he got worse on Thursday and Friday. Margarite indicated that she did not think he had difficulty with math, "where" he most frequently turned in his work, but seemed to have trouble with social studies and science. Eduardo agreed and they summarized this on the form shown in Figure 3.9.

Step 3. *Establish realistic goals for changing the behavior.* Margarite and Eduardo discussed his behavior and then established the goals listed in Figure 3.9.

Step 4. *Identify a time line showing how long the behavior-change plan will be in effect.* Because neither Margarite nor Eduardo had done this before, they decided to meet for five minutes every Friday to review the progress for the week, and to have a longer meeting in three weeks to determine how effective the program had been.

Step 5. *Identify reinforcers and consequences.* Margarite and Eduardo reexamined their goals and discussed what reinforcers should be provided if Eduardo met the goals. They also discussed consequences if the goals were not met. These reinforcers and consequences were written into the plan in Figure 3.9.

Step 6. *Self-evaluate the success of the program each day.* Margarite explained to Eduardo that he would be responsible, at the end of each day, for writing a brief evaluation of how effective the plan was for that day.

FIGURE 3.9

Self-Management Plan

Name: *Eduardo Cora*

Target Behavior: Submit completed assignments to teacher on time, or meet with teacher before assignment is due to agree on alternative date and time.

When Behavior Occurs: Mostly on Thursdays and Fridays.

Where Behavior Occurs: Social Studies and Science.

Goals:

1. Eduardo will write down assignments and due dates in a separate assignment book for each subject.

2. Eduardo will look at each assignment and be sure that he knows how to complete it. Eduardo will ask questions, as necessary.

3. Eduardo will tell the teacher ahead of time if an assignment is going to be late.

Time Line: Meet each Friday to review the progress on the plan, and then revise plan in three weeks.

Reinforcer: Edwardo will receive 15 minutes of extra time to work on the computer each day his assignments are completed.

Evaluation: Edwardo will write a brief description of the program's success.

MAKING A DIFFERENCE
The 60-Second Lesson

Encouraging Self-Monitoring

Purpose: To have students monitor their own behavior during an activity.

Procedure:

1. Clearly write the directions for the activity on the chalkboard, overhead projector, or writing pad so that all students can see them.
2. Explain the following to your students: While you are working on this project I want you to monitor how well you are following the directions I have pro-vided. Every ten minutes I will say stop, and I want you to give yourself a rating from 1–5. Five means I am following the directions and working all the time, four means I am mostly following the directions and working, three means sometimes I do and some-times I don't, two means I am more frequently not following directions and working, and one means I have done very little since the last time we stopped.
3. At the end of the activity period, ask students to report their scores.

SUMMARY

- Teachers need to continually monitor how their perspectives, attitudes, beliefs, expectations, and experiences influence the ways in which they interpret the behaviors of their students.
- Often teachers first need to change their own behavior in order to change the behavior of their students.
- Teachers tend to focus on negative student behaviors, and to estimate that they praise students *more* than they actually do.
- Positive reinforcement is the most significant means of increasing desirable student behaviors.
- Reinforcers can be intangible (e.g., verbal praise) or tangible (e.g., food, tokens), and supplied from a variety of sources (e.g., adults, peers, self).
- The effective management of student behavior requires the implementation of guidelines, procedures, and rules in the classroom as well as the specification of consequences for nonadherence.
- Additional techniques for decreasing undesirable student behaviors include ingoring on purpose, time out, and punishment.
- The learning environment itself can help students maintain appropriate behavior in the classroom.
- Social competence is a multifaceted construct. Many instructional programs (e.g., FAST, ASSET) aimed at improving students' social skills are available to teachers.
- Principles for effectively conducting social-skills training include: principles of effective instruction, involving peers in the training, and teaching for transfer of learning and generalization.
- Procedures for teaching students self-management skills that will enable them to govern and reinforce their own behavior are described.
- Considerations for teachers regarding behavior management for students from diverse ethnic and socioeconomic backgrounds are provided.

Key Terms and Concepts

ASSET

class meetings

consequences

extinction

FAST

ignoring on purpose

interpersonal problem solving

mistaken goal

Mutual Interest Discovery

negative reinforcement

positive feedback

positive reinforcement

Premack principle

punishment

self-management

SLAM

social competence

stimulus

time out

token system

Think and Apply

1. Nina Zaragoza identified several key principles of effective classroom management. On a sheet of paper, list the principles of effective classroom managment she followed. Now add several others to the list, based on information provided in this chapter and your own experience. Rank these principles according to their importance to you. As you continue reading, return to your list of classroom-management principles and see whether there are any you would rewrite or reorder.

2. This chapter provides several suggestions for developing forms, and describes forms that have already been developed. For example, in the section of the chapter on time out, a set of procedures for effectively monitoring time out is provided. The procedures (e.g., student's name, date, and time student was placed in time out) could be used to develop a record form for time out. Develop and copy the forms you think will be helpful to you as a teacher. Keep them in your portfolio. As you read each chapter, develop additional forms.

3. Many teachers identify classroom management as the issue they are most concerned about prior to teaching, and practicing teachers identify it as the issue with which they have the most difficulty. Interview five practicing teachers and ask the following questions:

   a. What classroom management strategies do you find most useful?

   b. What aspects of classroom management do you wish you knew more about?

   c. What advice about classroom management would you offer?

   Summarize the results of the interviews, and write guidelines for classroom management. How do your guidelines compare with those provided in the chapter?

4. This chapter provided several practices teachers can implement to enhance the self-concept of students. Think about your own experiences as a student, the teachers who enhanced your self-concept, and those who affected your self-concept negatively. What did these two types of teachers say and do? How do your experiences compare with this chapter's recommendations for enhancing students' self-concepts?

5. Return to the Research Brief entitled, "Behavior Management Considerations in Culturally Diverse Classrooms." Think about the questions posed (e.g., What behaviors bother you as a teacher? Who is performing these behaviors? Are you sure that *all* students who perform these behaviors are treated in the same way?) What additional questions might be important to add to this list? Based on your experiences as a student and as a teacher, why are these questions important?

Read More about It

1. Branden, N. (1987). *How to raise your self-esteem.* New York: Bantam.

   Provides a sequenced approach to better understanding your self-esteem, and methods you can apply to improve your self-esteem and that of others. The author provides a practical step-by-step sequence to improving self-esteem.

2. Canfield, J., & Wells, H. C. (1994). *100 ways to enhance self-concept in the classroom.* Boston, MA: Allyn and Bacon.

   Packed with ideas about what teachers can do in the classroom to positively affect the self-concept of their students. The activities are divided into seven sections: getting started, my strengths, who am I?, accepting my body, where am I going?, the language of self, and relationships with others.

3. Dreikurs, R., & Stoltz, V. (1964). *Children: The challenge*. New York: Dutton.

   Though over 30 years old, this book continues to provide teachers and parents with guidance for better understanding and coping with children's behavior problems. The major principles of understanding why children do what they do and how the reactions of teachers and parents affect behavior are very informative.

4. Grossman, H. (1995). *Special education in a diverse society*. Boston, MA: Allyn and Bacon.

   Provides excellent materials regarding ways in which socioeconomic status, gender, and cultural and linguistic background are likely to affect the behavior of students. Describes what teachers can do to be sensitive to these issues as they develop behavior-management strategies.

5. Larrivee, B. (1992). *Strategies for effective classroom management*. Boston, MA: Allyn and Bacon.

   This two-part training package consists of a Leader's Guide and a Teacher's Handbook that provides practical strategies and procedures for effectively managing behavior in the classroom. The format is an alternative to traditional textbooks, with multiple examples and forms to help teachers implement the suggested practices.

6. Nelson, J., Lott, L., & Glenn, H. S. (1993). *Positive discipline in the classroom*. Rocklin, CA: Prima.

   An easy-to-read book written more like a trade book than a textbook. The major principles in the book are related to positive discipline strategies and illustrated with examples and suggestions for application.

Collaborating and Coordinating with Other Professionals and Family

FOCUS QUESTIONS

1. What is collaboration? Describe two collaboration models that can be used in schools. What components of these models make them effective?

2. What is cooperative teaching, or co-teaching? What parts of co-teaching are necessary to make it effective? How might it be used to provide an educational program for students with disabilities?

3. What are the issues and dilemmas to consider when implementing collaboration models?

4. To communicate effectively with parents and professionals, what skills does a teacher need? Can you identify some good and bad examples of communication with parents and professionals?

5. Why is family adjustment an important factor for students with disabilities? How might teachers assist in the family adjustment of their students?

6. Working effectively with parents requires several skills. What are they? What techniques presented in this chapter might you use to more effectively communicate with parents?

Interview

One Parent's Experience

I knew my daughter, Sheena, wasn't right even when she was very little. She always had trouble getting along with other kids, fighting, and not wanting to play with others. Also, she was never interested in books or anything like that the way her older brother was. Everybody always said that when she went to school she would be different but it didn't happen. She was just the same at school as at home. She was always in trouble, and couldn't seem to sit still and do what she was supposed to.

I was relieved to learn that Sheena's problems aren't just because she's stubborn. From my meetings with her teachers I've learned that she has attention deficit disorder and behavior problems and learning problems too. Meeting with Sheena's teachers has really helped Sheena, her teachers and me. I remember very distinctly when we had our first meeting at the school. It was me and my sister.

All of these people from the school were going to be there and I was a little scared to go alone, but everyone at the school was very nice, and they told me to go ahead and bring my sister for support. Sheena's (special education) teacher, Mrs. Cohen, greeted me ahead of time and talked to me as if we already knew each other and were friends. She sat next to me at the meeting and when the other people there would go off talking about something I didn't understand, she would explain it to me. I liked the way she would stop them and say, "OK, now say it again so we can all understand it." Anyway, I liked her right away and I was happy that Sheena was going to get the help she needed.

At our last meeting, Mrs. Cohen and Mrs. Chamber (a general education teacher) told me about a program that they thought would be better for Sheena. This program put her in the classroom all day and then Mrs. Cohen was going to work with Mrs. Chamber to help Sheena learn and help with her behavior. I cannot say I was really for it when they first told me about it. My first reaction was, "Hey, why mess with something that is going good." Now, after Sheena has been in the program this year we all think it worked out. Sheena liked staying in the classroom all day with her friends. She had some trouble at first because I think she missed getting up and leaving the classroom, but after they got the routine down it worked out really well. Also, I really liked the way the teachers kept me informed. They sent me weekly messages and would call frequently. Also, I know that if I needed to speak with one of them I could send a note with Sheena and then one of them would call me. With all of us working together so closely, Sheena just had to give up and behave because she couldn't get away with anything anymore.

Introduction

Sara Cohen, a special education teacher, says, "Some teachers are fine in the classroom, but are unable to work effectively with their fellow teachers. Some even have difficulty communicating with parents." Being successful as a teacher is an important but insufficient part of the job. Increasingly, teachers are required to work with other professionals and parents, and need skills to collaborate and communicate effectively. The increasing diversity in our classrooms, including second-language learners, students with disabilities, and students who are gifted requires collaboration with other professionals and parents.

Consultation and Collaboration

What is collaboration? According to Friend and Cook (1992), "Interpersonal **collaboration** is a style for direct interaction between at least two coequal parties voluntarily engaged in shared decision making as they work toward a common goal" (p. 5). Collaboration describes the interaction that is occurring—people are working together as equal partners in shared problem solving.

Whether you are an elementary or secondary teacher, you can expect to work collaboratively with the special education teacher, the counselor, parents, and other teachers. You might also work with the school psychologist or nurse, the Chapter 1 teacher, the ESL teacher, the teacher of gifted students, and an inclusion specialist. You might have students in your class who need specialized services from the speech and language teacher or the occupational or physical therapist. Most of your ongoing collaboration, however, will be with the special education teacher, the school counselor, and the students' parents. Table 4.1 describes the qualities of collaborative professionals.

What are some ways to collaborate with other professionals? The next section of this chapter describes various models for effective collaboration with professionals and parents.

A Consultation Model

Collaboration in the Schools (West et al., 1988) is a consultation model outlining procedures for the

---

TABLE 4.1

Qualities of Collaborative Professionals

- Realize that goals are often complex and that the success of achieving these goals requires joint effort. Everyone's effort is needed to solve problems and make schools more effective in meeting the needs of all students.
- Recognize the creativity that occurs when people work together to solve common problems. Collaborative professionals realize that working together makes the problem more manageable and often yields more effective and creative solutions.
- Enjoy the social aspect of problem solving with others. Collaborative professionals respect the other members of the group even when they do not always agree with them. They are able to express their point of view without hostility or "put downs" toward others in the group.
- Recognize and value the benefits from working collaboratively. Collaborative professionals realize that many ideas and experiences could not be developed independently; thus, they value the work of the group.
- Interested in reflecting on and changing their own practices. Collaborative professionals are willing to consider alternative instructional practices and to think about suggestions and comments that arise during collaboration.

Adapted from: Pugach, M. C., & Johnson, L. J. (1995). *Collaborative practitioners, collaborative schools.* Denver, CO: Love.

---

special education teacher to work as a consultant to general education teachers and help them successfully mainstream students with disabilities. The underlying principle of the **consultation model** is that it is,

> An interactive process that enables people with diverse expertise to generate creative solutions to mutually defined problems. The major outcome of collaborative consultation is to provide comprehensive and effective programs for students with special needs within the most appropriate context, thereby enabling them to achieve maximum constructive interaction with their nonhandicapped peers. (Idol et al., 1986, p. 1)

West and Idol (1990) cite three reasons for using consultation models for students with disabilities in the schools:

1. *Prevention.* Many of the expenses of assessing and placing students with disabilities in special education can be eliminated through the use of effective consultation models.
2. *Effective schools.* Collaborative planning and problem solving promotes the collegial relationships associated with effective schools.
3. *Coordinated instruction.* Consultation models can provide opportunities to coordinate instruction between special and general education and to exchange knowledge regarding effective practices for enhancing instruction.

Factors to be considered in implementing consultation and collaboration models include systematic and ongoing staff development, administrative support, and flexible scheduling (West & Idol, 1990).

Collaboration in the Schools is based on a six-stage consultation process that a collaborative team completes. Typically the team includes those professionals who have primary responsibility for the student's educational program, often the general education and special education teachers.

Stage 1. *Goal/Entry.* The team discusses roles, objectives, responsibilities, and expectations. Topics include the role of each member of the team, what is expected (e.g., number of meetings, implementation tactics), the type of paperwork to be maintained and who will do it, and the responsibilities of each team member.

Stage 2. *Problem Identification.* The student(s) is identified and the specific nature and extent of the problem is defined. Each member of the team receives a written copy of the problem description, which helps the group stay focused on the problem at hand.

Stage 3. *Intervention of Recommendations.* The team brainstorms potential interventions and predicts outcomes. In this stage, the team can discuss possible alternatives and their consequences before recommendations are prioritized and selected. Team members decide how, and by whom, recommendations will be implemented. They develop objectives to specify the intervention details, the procedures, and the means for determining whether the problem has been solved.

Stage 4. *Implementation of Recommendations.* The intervention plan is implemented. Individuals responsible for the implementation keep notes on the effects so that they can report back to the team.

Stage 5. *Evaluation.* The team completes an evaluation of the intervention, which includes any data collected, evidence from the student's work, and reports from persons who implemented the intervention. The evaluation includes a report on the impacts on the student, the consultants, and the context in which the intervention is occurring.

Stage 6. *Redesign.* Evaluation informs the revision process. The intervention is continued, redesigned, or discontinued based on the evaluation, and the process begins again with Stage 2, Problem Identification.

Figure 4.1 presents a consultation problem-solving worksheet to use in conjunction with this consultation process. The team completes a worksheet for each member, and each member takes notes on the progress of his or her role in the intervention.

Consultation is increasingly used in schools and districts throughout the United States. The **Mainstream Assistance Team** (MAT; Fuchs et al., 1990), for example, was designed as a prescriptive approach to problem solving, in which a specialist (e.g., the special education teacher) serves as consultant, and the classroom teacher as the consultee. The MAT follows four common problem-solving steps:

- problem identification
- problem analysis
- plan implementation
- problem evaluation

The team works with a list of preidentified potential interventions to facilitate the process and save time. Research indicates that both special and general education teachers are satisfied with the concept, process, and outcomes of the MAT program.

FIGURE 4.1

Consultation Problem-Solving Worksheet

Collaborative Team Member Name and Position:

_____

Team Member's Responsibilities Include:

a) _____

b) _____

c) _____

d) _____

_____

Target Student's Name: _____

Problem Behavior Student is Exhibiting: _____

_____

_____

Potential Interventions and Consequences Include:

a) _____

b) _____

c) _____

d) _____

Implemented Intervention: _____

Procedures Include: _____

_____

Team Members Involved and Their Responsibilities: _____

_____

_____

Summary Evaluation of the Intervention: _____

_____

Future Interventions/Objectives: _____

A Peer Collaboration Model

The **Peer Collaboration Model** (Johnson & Pugach, 1991; Pugach & Johnson, 1995) was developed to help classroom teachers solve problems by providing time and structure to do so. The model was designed for teachers to work with one or two other teachers. By engaging in a structured conversation about a specific problem, teachers can increase their awareness of the problem and develop potential solutions.

How might you participate in peer collaboration? Collaboration may occur at varying levels of teacher and school involvement. For example, Michelle Canner is a high school English teacher who has several students with learning disabilities mainstreamed into her classes. These same students are also mainstreamed into Jonathan Wood's social studies classes and Maria Rodriguez's science classes. The special education teacher and these three teachers established a collaborative team to more effectively meet the needs of the target students. At a middle school, the special education teacher and the speech and language teacher work cooperatively with the general education teachers to develop strategies for facilitating vocabulary and concept learning of target students.

According to Johnson and Pugach (1991), 86 percent of the teachers who participated in peer collaboration indicated that the problems that they worked on were eliminated and referral rates for special programs were reduced.

Procedures for peer collaboration include the following five steps:

1. *Initiation or facilitation.* Each participant takes a role as either an **initiator,** the teacher with the problem to be addressed, or **facilitator,** the teacher who guides his or her peer through the process and helps to generate solutions.
2. *Clarifying questions.* The initiator states the problem and the facilitator asks questions that clarify the problem.
3. *Summarization.* The team takes time to examine and summarize the problem. The format for summarizing the problem includes: (a) establishing the pattern of behavior, (b) acknowledging the teacher's feelings about the problem, and (c) identifying aspects of classroom and school environment that the teacher can modify (Pugach & Johnson, 1995).

4. *Interventions and predictions.* The team tries to develop at least three interventions for the problem and to predict the likely outcomes of each one.
5. *Evaluation.* The team develops an evaluation plan that includes strategies for keeping track of the intervention, recording the student's progress, and meeting on an ongoing basis.

Resources Needed for Collaboration

Time is the most precious and necessary resource for effective collaboration. Unless time is built into teachers' and other professionals' schedules and work loads, collaboration simply does not occur regularly. Also, if the special education teacher is going to work collaboratively with the social studies teacher, both need to have a planning period at the same time. What are some ways planning time can be arranged?

■ Administrators designate a common time for collaborating professionals (e.g., all fourth grade teachers who are members of the same team).
■ School boards pay professionals for one extra time period each week that is used for collaboration or for meeting parents.

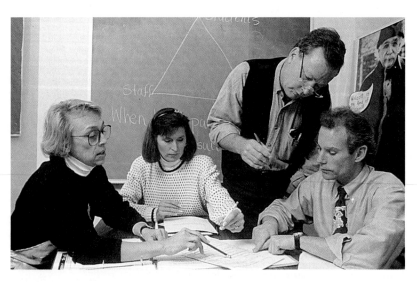

What are the hallmarks of the peer collaboration model? What steps should these teachers follow in planning and problem solving to achieve a successful peer collaboration?

- School districts provide early dismissal for students one day a week so that team members have a common planning time.
- Teachers schedule brief but focused planning periods with each other, as necessary.

Participants must be familiar with the procedures for collaborating. Having a regular time to meet to collaborate is the first step. Knowing what to do with that time is the next step. Which collaboration model does the school use, and what are the designated procedures? What paperwork is required, and how should it be completed and submitted? All teachers involved in collaboration should participate in an orientation that addresses basic questions about their roles and responsibilities.

Space for meeting is another necessary resource. In some schools, overcrowding is such a problem that classroom space is never available for meetings with colleagues. Designated meeting rooms or other conference space may be needed for collaboration to occur.

RESEARCH BRIEF

TEACHERS' PERCEPTIONS OF COLLABORATION

According to a study conducted by Voltz, Elliott, and Cobb (1994), general education and special education teachers have similar perceptions of collaboration in an idealized setting. For example, both groups were positive about the idea of: (a) exchanging student progress information, (b) working together to develop coping strategies to meet students' needs, and (c) participating in joint problem solving. The extent to which these behaviors actually occurred was rated considerably lower, however. Time was identified by both groups as a significant barrier to collaboration. The findings of this study support the premise that specific time must be established during which the general education and special education teacher work together; otherwise, collaboration is unlikely to occur.

Cooperative Teaching

Aside from using consultation and collaboration models, general and special education teachers can work together to enhance instruction for students with disabilities through co-planning and co-teaching. As you may recall, Chapter 1 introduced the concept of cooperative teaching. The key aspects of cooperative teaching include long-range co-planning, lesson co-planning, lesson co-teaching, and grading.

Co-Planning

In *long range co-planning*, the general education and special education teachers broadly plan their overall goals and desired outcomes for the class and for specific students with disabilities in the class. This co-planning of broad goals occurs quarterly (or more frequently, if necessary). This planning fits in with the IEP of each student with disabilities.

In *lesson co-planning*, the general education and special education teachers plan specific lessons and desired outcomes for the week. The teachers decide who will take the lead in the lesson, who will ensure that target students' needs are met, and who will provide individual or small-group instruction. A form for weekly co-planning is provided in Figure 4.2 and a model co-teaching lesson form is provided in Figure 4.3.

Joyce Duryea, a special education teacher, has a set day and time for co-planning with each teacher. Meetings take place during the school day while students are in other classes, such as Spanish, art, or music. "We discuss the planning for the following week and how we can best work together," explains Joyce. Once a month she and the other teachers go over the goals and objectives from the students' IEPs and discuss "whether we are meeting them or whether we need to switch over to another goal if the students have accomplished the one previously established, and we discuss each student's progress in depth."

Co-Teaching

For *lesson co-teaching*, the special education and general education teachers are both in the classroom during the same lesson and both participate

FIGURE 4.2

Weekly Co-Planning Form

Day(s)   Mon. _____   Tues. _____   Weds. _____   Thurs. _____   Fri. _____

Objective(s) _____

Material(s) _____

Activities: _____

_____

GE 1. _____   2. _____   ESE 1. _____   2. _____

3. _____   4. _____   3. _____   4. _____

Assessment: Student Performance _____   Discussion _____

Quiz _____   Exam _____   Paper _____   Other _____

Notes: _____

_____

in the instruction. Because lessons are co-planned, the specific roles and responsibilities of each teacher are decided ahead of time. Sometimes the general education teacher works with the class as a whole and the special education teacher adapts assignments for special needs students, accommodating their learning needs or working with small groups of students. At other times the class is divided into groups, with each teacher working with a different group. Sometimes the special education teacher takes the lead in providing instruction to the class while the general education teacher moves from student to student, conducting individual lessons or conferences. The roles of both teachers vary according to the goals of the lessons and the needs of the students.

Joyce, a special education teacher in an inclusive setting, explains her role this way:

> I work in three general education classrooms, and in each classroom I do something differ-

ent. Teachers differ in the extent to which they are willing to share control of their classrooms. Ruby, a second grade teacher, prefers that I take the lead role when I'm in her class, and she likes to provide me support. Tiffany, the fifth grade teacher, likes to share control through either co-teaching or alternating the role of lead teacher. Juan, on the other hand, prefers to maintain the lead role in his class.

Cooperative teaching requires that both teachers work with all students. When general education and special education teachers co-teach in the same classroom, the goals of the instruction and the needs of all students are the responsibility of both teachers.

Co-Assessment

Grading is an important consideration when students with disabilities are in general education classrooms. Often the special education co-teacher

FIGURE 4.3

Co-Teaching Lesson Form

Curriculum area: _____

IEP objectives of student(s) with disabilities: _____

_____

Adaptations for student(s) with disabilities: _____

_____

Academic objective(s): _____

_____

Collaborative skill objective(s): _____

_____

Group size: _____

Who will be assigned to each group? _____

_____

Materials: _____

Time required: _____

Plan the lesson (creating goal/resource/reward interdependence):

Academic task: _____

_____

Criteria for success: _____

_____

Positive interdependence: _____

_____

Individual accountability: _____

_____

Expected cooperative behaviors: _____

_____

Monitoring will be done by: _____ Special Education Teacher

_____ Classroom Teacher _____ Students

Monitoring will focus on: _____ Whole Class _____ Group _____ Student

Collaborative behaviors to be monitored: _____

_____

Closure (How will students summarize what they have learned? How will feedback on group performance be given? How will students plan their future use of specified social skills?):

_____

_____

Results: _____

Suggested changes for future lessons: _____

_____

Reprinted with permission from: Putnam, J. W. (1993). *Cooperative learning and strategies for inclusion: Celebrating diversity in the classroom* (pp. 50–51). Baltimore: Paul H. Brookes. P.O. Box 10624, Baltimore, MD 21285-0624.

makes adaptations to homework, assignments, and tests. How do these modifications affect the way students are graded? To what extent should students' motivation affect their grades? Persistence? Ability? How can these qualities be measured? These issues need to be openly discussed by teachers who have students with disabilities in their classrooms.

The questions about assessment are often easier for elementary teachers to answer than for middle and high school teachers. At the elementary level, teachers often consider a student's ability and then assign a grade based on the extent to which the student's progress matches his or her ability. At the middle and high school levels, however, student performance is often assessed on the basis of established standards. Grading procedures for students with disabilities are often an IEP item, and grading guidelines are written and agreed upon during the development of the IEP. This means that students with special needs who are mainstreamed into general education classrooms often do poorly in these classes. Even when students do their best, their grades are often in the failure range. Students with disabilities need grades that reflect more than the extent to which their performance compares with that of other students in the class. They need encouragement and reinforcement for their work and effort, and reasonable accommodations in assessment and grading.

RESEARCH BRIEF

STUDENTS' PERCEPTIONS OF ASSESSMENT ADAPTATIONS

What do students think when teachers make adaptations to meet the needs of students with learning problems? Vaughn and colleagues (Vaughn, Schumm, Niarhos, & Daugherty, 1993; Vaughn, Schumm, Niarhos, Gordon, 1993) have studied this question with elementary, middle, and high school students. For the most part, students' decisions about grading and testing are driven by what they perceive as fair. On the whole, students believe that all students should have the same tests; however, they feel that modifications in testing procedures are acceptable. Students at the elementary level accept that there are times when different tests are needed to match the different abilities of students. Students feel that their classmates have varied abilities and that tests should reflect this difference. One elementary student said, "I want the teacher that changes the test for some students because some students need easier tests. If the test is too hard the students do not do well because they get nervous." Another elementary student said, "If they can't read, the teacher should read the test out loud so they could understand."

Middle and high school students prefer the teacher who makes adaptations to meet the individual learning needs of students. Students who prefer instructional adaptations are more likely to be higher achievers than those who do not prefer these adaptations. The exception are issues related to testing and homework, areas in which middle and high school students think all classmates should be treated the same.

Collaboration Issues and Dilemmas

At some time most general education teachers will work with special education personnel in consultation, collaboration, or cooperative teaching roles. Following is a description of issues and dilemmas that frequently occur. Perhaps by considering these issues now you will be able to work more effectively in future collaborative situations.

Student Ownership When students with special needs are placed in general education classrooms for all or part of the day, both general education and special education teachers are responsible for their education. It is not uncommon, however, for teachers to claim "ownership" of or responsibility for some students and not others. Effective programs for all students require teacher attitudes that say, "All students are members of the learning community in my classroom and I welcome them all."

Individual versus Class Focus Research confirms that for the most part general education teachers at all grade levels plan instruction for the class as a whole rather than for individual learning needs

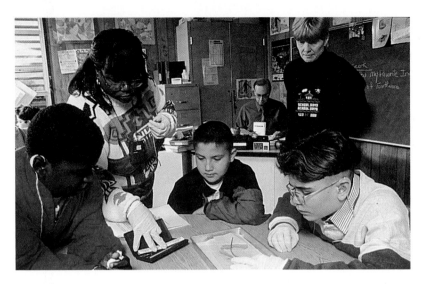

What is involved in co-planning, co-teaching, and co-assessment? What are some issues that might arise in collaborations between classroom teachers and special education teachers?

(McIntosh et al., 1993; Schumm et al., 1995). This approach to planning reflects the need to cover the content for a subject area. Special education teachers, on the other hand, focus on meeting students' individual needs. Neither perspective is inherently better than the other (Glatthorn, 1990), but the difference can lead to conflict. Teachers need to understand and respect each other's perspectives. Sallie Gotch, an elementary special education teacher, puts it this way:

> I am a special education teacher, and so the direction of my interest is always with the individual student and how the educational setting can be altered to meet his or her needs. During the last few years I have been working in a cooperative teaching situation with general education teachers and I realize that I've needed to adjust my perspective if I am to work effectively with them. When they think about planning they think about the class as a whole. I have to work cooperatively to think about meeting the needs of individual students without slowing the progress of the class as a whole.

Content versus Accommodation When classroom teachers discuss planning and instruction, one of the most consistent themes is content coverage (Schumm et al., 1995; Vaughn & Schumm, 1994). Classroom teachers feel they must cover more content to meet local and state guidelines and to ensure that students are prepared for the next grade level. Teachers acknowledge that this need often conflicts with some students' knowledge acquisition, but feel obliged to continue teaching new material (Schumm et al., 1995). Judy Schloss, a seventh grade science teacher, puts it this way, "I know that when I complete a science unit some of the students understand the main concepts and others do not, but I do not have time to reteach. We just move on to new material." As a result of such moving on, many students, particularly students with learning problems, are introduced to a lot of material but learn little about any of it. As Ed Glover, a ninth grade social studies teacher says, "If I waited until the students got it, we would never be able to cover all the material."

The issue of content coverage directly influences the instruction of students with special learning needs in general education classrooms. You can imagine the difficulty you might have if you felt pressured to cover extensive amounts of content and at the same time felt pulled to meet the needs of individual students who failed to learn the material. Professional development programs for general education teachers address this issue. Teachers learn to make adaptations and accommodations that will help all students learn, even if the content coverage and pace are reduced.

Real World versus Student's World Some general education teachers feel that treating all students fairly means treating them "the same." Making adaptations in homework or tests is perceived as providing undue advantage for some students. Furthermore, some general education teachers define their mission as preparing all students for the real world, where, they believe, accommodations and adaptations will not be made. Judy McDowell, a secondary special education teacher, explains the issue from her perspective:

When general education teachers talk to me about preparing students for the real world, I'm prepared. First, I present them with the idea that students are never going to be successful in the real world if they do not have an opportunity to learn and experience success in their present world. Their present world is that teacher's classroom. Second, I present them with the fact that employers are required by law to make reasonable accommodations for individuals with disabilities. I never ask classroom teachers to make adaptations or accommodations that I could not justify as necessary to enhance students' learning success.

This section covered several of the issues involved in collaboration and cooperative teaching, such as student ownership, focus on individuals versus the class, content versus accommodation, and the real world versus the student's world. The next section addresses ways to communicate effectively with professionals and parents.

Critical Communication Skills

Some teachers communicate effectively with parents and other professionals with seemingly little effort. They seem to have acquired the skills to listen effectively and express their point of view. Jacob Levitz, an eighth grade English teacher, conveys an accepting attitude and is able to make parents feel at ease and willing to disclose information. He is also able to express his views in ways that make parents *want* to listen.

> In a working alliance, all professionals are invested in a common goal, centered on the student. All members of a working alliance feel that they are working together as a team to enhance the student's educational and social development.

The following sections and Tips for Teachers 4.1 describe basic principles for communicating with parents, teachers, and other professionals.

Acceptance

People know when you accept them and are interested in their point of view. Acceptance by the teacher is critical to parental and professional participation in the student's program. Lucia Corzo, a third grade teacher, has been working with parents and professionals for twelve years. Despite expected frustrations and disappointments, she communicates her care and concern to the parents and professionals with whom she interacts, and always manages to find the few minutes necessary to meet with them. She says:

> Parents have a great deal to teach me about their child. They have spent a lot of time with their child and have seen patterns of behavior that can help me as a teacher. Also, if I can get the parent on my team we can work together to solve problems.

Listening

As a teacher, your willingness to genuinely listen to parents and professionals is important to your ability to learn and to work effectively with others. **Effective listening** is more than waiting politely for someone to finish before you speak. You must hear the message the other person is sending, and must often ask questions to clarify that you truly understand what others are saying. Effective listening involves the following elements:

- *Listening for the real content in the message.* The **real content** in the message is the main idea or the key information the person wants to convey.
- *Listening for the feelings in the message.* As you listen, consider what the message conveys about the person's feelings about the issue.
- *Restating content and reflecting feelings.* After the person has talked for a while, consider all that he or she has said. Then either ask a question to clarify what you know or restate the main idea to verify that what you heard is correct.
- *Allowing the speaker to confirm or correct your perception.* Give the speaker a chance to correct any misunderstanding you may have or to say more.

An example of a special education teacher listening effectively to a parent is provided in Figure 4.4.

FIGURE 4.4

Effective Listening: An Example

Anna Martinez is the mother of Michael, a student with spina bifida and learning problems who has been placed full-time in a fifth grade classroom. Michael's special education teacher, Joyce, works with him in the general education classroom for part of the school day. Anna made an appointment to meet with Joyce about her son's progress. Their conversation models effective listening.

Anna (parent): I'm worried about Michael in this new program. I liked it better last year when I knew he was being pulled out of class and getting the help he needed. He seems to have a lot more work and he complains about homework.

Joyce (teacher): Let me see if I understand the problem. First, you are concerned about his progress in this new program and second, Michael seems to have too much work. Is this right? Is there anything else you are concerned about?

Anna: Well, I can't help him with the work because I don't read English that well. He needs help when he comes home and it can't be from me.

Joyce: The homework he is getting is too hard for him and there isn't someone to help him at home.

Anna: That's right. He's going to flunk if he doesn't do his work and yet I can't help him with it, and we are both very worried about it.

Joyce: What if I met with Michael at the end of every day to assure that he knows how to do his homework by himself. I could also meet with him in the morning before school to make sure he completes it and to help with what he doesn't know. How does that sound?

Anna: I would like to try that. That sounds good.

Joyce: Now let's get back to his placement this year. You indicated some concern about his being in the fifth grade class all day.

Anna: No, it was really the homework in the class. If we solve that it will be okay.

Joyce: Well, let's give this plan a try.

Questioning

Questions, an important part of the communication process, can have multiple purposes. They can be used not only to teach, to establish relationships, to inquire, and to investigate, but also to bully or intimidate. As teachers work with parents and professionals, they need to consider the questions they ask, to ensure that they set a tone of acceptance.

Knowing which types of questions to ask helps you obtain the information you need. Questions can be open or closed. An **open question** allows a full range of responses (often beginning with "How," "What," or "Tell me about," for example), and discourages short "yes" or "no" answers. Following are several examples of open-ended questions:

- How do you explain the change in your son's behavior?
- What suggestions do you have about how I might help Mark get a better grade in social studies?
- Tell me your opinion about ways I might adjust my math instruction for Jose.
- How does what I've said about Tanika relate to her behavior at home?

- What do you suggest?
- How would you describe Gilbert's behavior?

Antoinette Kavale, a seventh grade science teacher, was concerned about Naomi, who was not paying attention in class, seemed sleepy and disinterested, and was not completing assignments. She called Naomi's mother, explained the behavior, and let Naomi's mother give her point of view.

> *Antoinette (teacher):* Naomi has not been paying attention in class and has generally seemed tired and disinterested. What do you think might be happening?
>
> *Tracey (parent):* Well, I don't know. Maybe she just isn't that interested in science. I don't know why.

> *Antoinette:* Well, the reason I'm concerned is that her behavior in class has gotten worse in the last few weeks and I wonder if you might be able to help me understand.
>
> *Tracey:* Maybe it's because there have been so many people in the house the last few weeks. My family is visiting and they were supposed to only stay one week and now they are starting on their third week. We really don't have room for all of them, so Naomi's had to give up her room. Maybe I need to make sure she is sleeping well enough.

The teacher's questions gave the parent a chance to consider the relationship between her

TIPS FOR TEACHERS

4.1 Facilitating Effective Communication with Parents and Professionals

1. Indicate respect for parents' knowledge and understanding of their child.
2. Demonstrate respect for the diverse languages and cultures parents and their children represent.
3. Introduce parents to other members of the education team in a way that sets the tone for acceptance.
4. Give parents an opportunity to speak and be heard.
5. Represent the parents to other professionals and ensure that a language of acceptance is used by all professionals and parents.
6. Even when you are busy, take the time to let parents and professionals know that you value them, and that you are simply unable to meet with them at *this* time.
7. Avoid giving advice unless it is requested. This does not mean that you can never give suggestions; however, suggestions should be given with the expectation that the person may or may not choose to implement them.
8. Avoid providing false reassurances to colleagues or parents. Reassurances may make them and you feel better in the short run, but are harmful in the long run. When things do not work out as you predicted, everyone can become disappointed and potentially lose trust.
9. Ask specific questions. Unfocused questions make a consistent, purposeful conversation difficult to conduct.
10. Avoid changing topics too often; you must monitor the topic and direct others to return to it.
11. Avoid interrupting others or being interrupted (interruptions disturb conversation and make effective collaboration difficult.
12. Avoid using clichés. A cliché as a response to a problem situation makes the other person feel as though you are trivializing the problem.
13. Respond to colleagues and parents in ways that attend to both the content of their message and their feelings.
14. Avoid jumping too quickly to a solution. Listening carefully and fully to the message will help you get at the root of the problem.

child's behavior and what was occurring at home. This parent was able to identify a change in the household that might be related to her child's poor performance. The parent and teacher were able to identify a possible solution and felt better about their working relationship.

Staying Focused

Staying focused in your communication and keeping others focused is an important skill that contributes to successful collaboration. One thing you can do when someone has difficulty keeping to the topic is redirect them, saying, for example, "Go back to talking about Mildred. You were providing some suggestions for note-taking skills that might be helpful to her." Another thing you can do is remind them of the purpose of the meeting (for instance, "Jackie, let's stick to talking about content-area reading instruction.") Sometimes parents have so many problems of their own that they want to spend their time with you discussing their issues (including such personal problems as financial or marital difficulties) rather than the student's. When this occurs, a good strategy is to have ready a referral list for specialized assistance. It is your responsibility to remind parents that you cannot assist them with *these* problems and to suggest others who can.

Working with Parents

School systems have expended considerable effort to involve parents in their child's educational program. The rationale is that parent involvement is related to their child's adjustment in the educational setting, as well as to academic achievement (Hughes, 1995). Also, both federal laws and state regulations require parental involvement for students with disabilities (refer to Chapter 1, for review). This section discusses family adjustment and the roles parents can play in supporting their children's education.

Family Adjustment

Much of what has been written about **family adjustment** to having a child with disabilities addresses family reaction to children with severe disabilities, mental retardation, or physical disabilities (Turnbull & Turnbull, 1990). Considerably less attention has been paid to how families adjust to having family members with learning disabilities, communication problems, attention problems, and emotional or behavioral problems. This occurs because the more obvious or severe disabilities, such as mental retardation or physical disabilities, are apparent before children start school, whereas other problems, such as learning and behavior disorders, are often not expressed until children are older (age three and older). Although many parents are aware long before diagnosis that their child is different, they continue to hope that their observations are incorrect or that their child will outgrow the problem.

From a systems perspective, the family is an important force in the student's learning and development. For this reason, many mental health and social work professionals recommend an integrated approach to working with students with disabilities. In an integrated approach, all family members and other important caretakers are involved in some way.

Simpson (1982) suggests that the needs of parents of children with disabilities fall into five broad categories:

1. *Information exchange.* Parents need conferences, program and classroom information, progress reports, interpretations of their child's academic and social needs, and informal feedback about their child. Teachers can rarely provide too much information to parents (particularly parents of children with special needs, who are already aware of their child's differences).
2. *Consumer and advocacy information.* Parents of students with disabilities sign seemingly endless numbers of forms and permissions. Be sure to summarize for parents not only the purpose of the forms, but also what they are agreeing to by providing their signature.
3. *Home/community program implementation.* Parents want to assist their children at home and also to involve them in appropriate community activities. How can you help? Provide helpful information. If possible, ask other professionals or community resource people

to offer a program to all parents on these topics. Work with other teachers to develop an informational handout or brochure, and provide it in the languages parents read.

4. *Counseling, therapy, and consultation.* When parents request information about support groups, counseling, therapy, and other consultation services, what should you do? First, identify the information sources available from your school or school district, and keep them handy in a folder. Second, ask the school counselor or principal what procedures they want you to follow.

5. *Parent-coordinated service programs.* Parents need to be able to provide services to and receive services from other parents through advisory councils, parent-to-parent participation, advocacy, and other options. In a study reported by Simpson (1988), the services most widely requested by parents were program information and informal feedback.

Parents and Homework

Often parents are so interested in helping their child that they get deeply involved in assisting with school work at home.

Homework gives parents a daily idea of your curriculum and instruction. Many parents want to

help but often do not know what to do. It is your responsibility to provide parents with guidance so that they can help their child as effectively as possible. Here are some suggestions for providing that guidance.

Establishing Homework Policy   Start the school year with a written policy statement that begins with a rationale assigning homework. According to Epstein and Becker (1982), teachers assign homework for a number of reasons:

- practice (to help students strengthen skills learned in class)
- participation (to increase involvement with learning activities)
- personal development (to build a sense of responsibility, and time-management skills)
- parent-child relations (to increase involvement in home-learning activities)
- policy (to conform to school and district mandates)
- public relations (to communicate to parents what students are learning in school)
- punishment (to correct misbehavior in school)

As you might expect, using homework for punishment is not particularly effective—and counterproductive, besides. It is important to communicate why you think homework is important, and what positive outcomes it might have for students.

Your policy statement should also include a set of expectations: what you expect of the student, what you expect of the parent, and what both the parent and student can expect of you. Whenever possible, involve parents in developing the policy statement.

Tips for Teachers 4.2 is an outline of issues to address in your policy statement.

One suggestion is to send home biweekly progress reports. By taking 30 minutes every other week to complete a progress form, you can eliminate problems that arise when parents are uninformed about the student's progress.

How does the family's response to having a child with disabilities affect the child's learning and development? How can teachers help in family adjustment? How can teachers promote effective parental involvement?

TIPS FOR TEACHERS

4.2 Communicating Homework Policy

What you expect of the student:
- Record homework assignments on an assignment sheet or in an assignment notebook.
- Complete homework assignments in a neat and timely manner.

What you expect of the parent:
- Assist the student in setting up a homework center.
- Assist the student in determining a regular homework schedule.
- Monitor and assist as necessary in the completion of homework.
- Write note if confused about the assignment.

What the parent and student can expect of you:
- Create homework assignments that are meaningful and provide for independent practice of skills taught in class or enrichment of content covered in class.
- Write homework assignments on board daily.
- Provide parents with a general homework schedule (e.g., Monday night, math and spelling; Tuesday night, math and composition).
- Provide a system for reporting missing or late homework to parents and students.
- Grade homework in a timely fashion and provide feedback to students.

Encouraging Student Independence Parents are often unsure about how much or how little they should help with special projects such as term papers, book reports, and science fair projects. Parents' resources for providing assistance vary widely. Your policy statement should clarify expectations, such as arranging transportation to the public library, and access to a typewriter or word processor for term papers. When a major project is assigned, let parents know the purpose of the assignment, its components, due dates, and precisely when and how their assistance may be needed. A special project checklist and contract (see Figures 4.5 and 4.6) will help clarify the responsibilities of the teacher, parents, and students for the completion of long-term assignments.

Parents as Teachers

Free or inexpensive brochures about parents as teachers are available from various professional organizations. These brochures can be sent home as report card or progress report inserts, and bibliographies and other helpful resources can be sent home during the school year.

RESEARCH BRIEF

PARENTAL INVOLVEMENT IN LITERACY INSTRUCTION

Hughes (1995) conducted a study of Hispanic parents of children with learning disabilities to determine their involvement in literacy instruction. The study addressed the types of reading and writing activities practiced in the home, and parents' perceptions of the desirability and feasibility of different reading and writing activities.

The Hispanic parents involved in this study reported that they regularly provided their children with different reading and writing activities at home. The most frequent activities involved parents reading to children and children reading to parents. Parents emphasized reading activities more than writing activities. The writing activities in which parents and children did engage included writing related to homework assignments, writing letters to relatives, or writing lists.

In telephone interviews to determine what reading and writing activities they thought were

FIGURE 4.5

Special Project Checklist

Step		Date Done
☐	1. Decide on a project theme.	_____
☐	2. Have theme approved by a teacher.	_____

Theme: _____

☐ 3. Make a list of what needs to be done and the order in which the tasks should be completed. (List, then number each task.)

☐ 4. Decide who is going to do what. (Initial each task.)

☐ 5. Set deadlines for completion of each task. (Write in the dates.)

Task	Date Due	Date Done	Person Responsible
_____	_____	_____	_____
_____	_____	_____	_____
_____	_____	_____	_____
_____	_____	_____	_____

☐ 6. Make a list of materials needed to do the project.

☐ 7. Make a projected budget. (Write the estimated cost of each item.)

Item	Cost
_____	_____
_____	_____
_____	_____

☐ 8. Send away for resource materials needed.

Resource Material	Date Requested	Date Received
_____	_____	_____

☐ 9. Contact community resources.

Community Resource	Date Contacted
_____	_____

☐ 10. Visit the library.

Purpose of Visit	Date of Visit
_____	_____

☐ 11. Complete the project ON TIME.

Date Handed In: _____   **Year:** _____

FIGURE 4.6

Special Project Agreement Form

Today's Date: _____   Due Date: _____

Project Theme: _____

I, _____ , agree to do the following tasks by myself. I agree to do them on time.
  (Student's Name)

Task   **Date Due**

_____

_____

_____

I, _____ , and I, _____ ,
  (Parent's Name)   (Student's Name)
agree to do the following tasks together. We agree to do them on time.

Task   **Date Due**

_____

_____

_____

desirable and feasible to do at home, parents indicated that many suggested activities were desirable and that prior to the interview they had not thought of doing so many activities. They also indicated, however, that many activities were not feasible to do at home because their children had difficulties with reading and writing and they (the parents) did not know how to help their children with these difficulties.

Parents identified the following activities as helpful:

- more communication with the teacher about reading and writing activities they could do at home
- further information about how to do the reading and writing activities with their children since their children had trouble learning to read and write

- providing information to the parents both orally and in writing in the parents' first language (Spanish)

The goal of helping students with homework and providing an academic support system at home is to enable them to develop independent study skills. For this to happen, parents and teachers need to work cooperatively.

What happens when students with special needs fall behind their same-age peers, and parents want to help? Particularly for students with disabilities, it is rarely a good idea for an untrained parent to become the child's tutor. This does not mean that the parent should not help with homework, coach the child for a spelling test, or assist with a school project. Providing assistance and serving as a tutor are two different roles, however.

FIGURE 4.7

Tips for Tutors

1. Have specific, realistic goals developed *with* the classroom teacher or the special education teacher.

2. Begin and end each tutoring session with an activity that is fun and with which the child is successful.

3. Keep the tutoring session brief—not more than fifteen minutes for students up to grade six, and not more than thirty minutes for older students.

4. Work on small segments of material at a time.

5. Use creative, novel ways of reviewing and teaching new material.

6. Prevent the student from making mistakes. If the student does not know the answer, give it.

7. Keep a tutoring log in which you record a couple of sentences about what you did and how the student performed.

8. Provide encouragement and support. No one learns more by being "corrected" more.

9. Practice the activities in fun ways that prevent boredom.

10. Work should be challenging but not so difficult that there is not considerable opportunity for success.

11. Tutor at the same time and in the same place, so that the student develops an expectation set for what will happen. Do not extend the designated time.

12. If you are frustrated or your interactions with your child are strained or stressful during the tutoring, stop. Your relationship with your child is much more important than what you can teach him or her during the tutoring session.

Our use of the term **tutoring** refers to a systematic plan for supplementing the student's educational program. Ask parents who are providing their own home tutoring to comply with the suggestions provided in Figure 4.7.

Planned and Unplanned Parent Conferences

The opportunity for a planned conference with parents occurs often. This conference could be part of the multidisciplinary team meeting, part of an annual parent–student meeting, or a specific meeting scheduled because of an academic or behavioral problem. Figure 4.8 is a sample letter teachers can send to parents to confirm a planned meeting.

With a planned conference the teacher is able to prepare materials and provide background knowledge. To prepare for a planned conference, teachers should do the following:

1. Review the student's materials, grades, and work progress.
2. Meet with and learn the perspectives of other professionals who also work with the student.
3. Review the student's folder, portfolio, and previous assessment information.
4. Obtain samples of the student's most recent work.
5. Make an outline of topics to discuss.

What happens when conferences are unplanned? At the end of the day, as students line up to go home, you notice a parent waiting by the door to speak with you. There is little question that unplanned conferences with parents will occur (Turnbull & Turnbull, 1990). Often parents who come to school to talk with the teacher do so

It's a Date

Dear Parent of _____ ,

Thank you for your response to my request for a meeting about your child. Your appointment has been set for _____ (time) on _____ (day), _____ (date).

I have set aside _____ minutes for our visit. If you will be bringing any guests, please let me know in advance. If this time is no longer convenient, please let me know.

Looking forward to seeing you,

_____

Teacher's Name

because they are concerned about something they have seen or heard. Their source of information might be their own child, who may not have told the story accurately. The guidelines in Tips for Teachers 4.3 will help you work effectively with parents in such situations.

Forms of School-to-Home Communication

Communicating with parents must be an ongoing part of your routine as a teacher. Communication with all parents is important, but it is particularly important with parents of students with special needs. What are some ways to communicate? Letters, notes, calendars, newsletters, and phone calls are but a few described in this section.

There are many letters you can send home to all parents. In the beginning of the year it is a nice idea to send home with students a note that intro-

TIPS FOR TEACHERS

4.3 Working toward Effective Parent Conferences

1. *Listen until they are finished.* As difficult as it may be to hear them out, particularly when the statements they are making are inaccurate, the best way to begin the meeting is to allow them to say everything that is on their minds. Chances are they have thought for a long time about what to say, and have even rehearsed it. Listening does not mean you agree. Let them finish.

2. *Take notes.* Write down key phrases the parent says, summarize key points, and jot down notes of things you want to remember to tell them. While you are doing this, be sure to maintain eye contact and composure. Your getting upset increases the likelihood of the parent growing more upset.

3. *Summarize their major concerns.* As stated previously, good communication includes effective summarization of the speaker's words and their meaning. Your summary shows parents not only that you have been listening, but also that you care about what they say.

4. *State your position calmly.* After you have listened thoroughly and let parents know that you understand their key points, state your position calmly and succinctly. If parents have inaccurate information, now is the time to provide accurate information. Be sure that they understand your point of view. Speak calmly while stating your position and addressing their concerns.

5. *Come to closure.* Getting to closure differs according to the situation. Sometimes, for example, you hear a parent's concern and quickly find a solution. "Oh, Mrs. Garcia, Lucy can stay in during lunch while she is sick. That is no problem. Just be sure she remembers to bring her own lunch." At other times, an issue needs to be negotiated. "Well, Mrs. Garcia, I do not think that Lucy has too much homework. The main reason it takes her so long is that she does not work on her math homework during the time allotted at school. Let's first set up a plan to increase her working on math at school."

FIGURE 4.9

Sample Beginning of School Year Letter

Dear Parents:

   The purpose of this letter is to welcome you and your child to my classroom. I have taught at West Elementary School for four years and at two other schools in this school district before moving to West Elementary. I am confident that this school year will be an interesting and productive one for your child and me.

   You are welcome to visit the classroom; however, I would appreciate receiving notice ahead of time to be sure your visit will not be interrupted. Feel free to call me at 544-1257 and leave a message. I will return your call as quickly as possible. I look forward to meeting you in person in the near future.

Sincerely,

Julia Anderson, 4th grade teacher

FIGURE 4.10

Parent Bulletin

Name: _____   Date: _____

Subject: _____

_____

_____

_____

You can help at home by: _____

_____

_____

_____

duces you and provides a means for parents to contact you (see Figure 4.9).

You may also want to send home a letter or bulletin (see Figure 4.10) prior to any long break (one week or more) to alert parents to activities they can do with their children to reinforce learning while they are out of school or to introduce a new unit of study, such as measurement or space. Remember, parents want to receive notification of things that are going well, progress reports, your expectations of their child, materials the child needs, problems (early on), and general ideas of how to help their child learn.

Another letter that many parents appreciate is a progress report for the year. Joyce (special education teacher) and the classroom teachers with whom she works send the letter shown in Figure 4.11 to parents of children with disabilities who are included full-time in general education classes.

Students appreciate having their parents receive good news, and notes are a quick and easy way to communicate with parents. A major advantage is that after you have developed and photocopied a supply of notes, it takes virtually a second to jot a note to a parent. Good News Notes (see Making a Difference on the following page) have

---

FIGURE 4.11

Year-End Progress Report

Dear Parents and Guardians:

We thank you all for your cooperation and support this school year. As the school year ends, we always ask parents how they feel the special education program met the needs of their children. We hope you have been satisfied with the results.

Following are your child's scores from the beginning of the year and from the end of the year. Please feel free to call one of us at 666–0000 and leave a message. We will return your call as soon as we can.

	Beginning Scores	*End of Year Scores*
Reading Comprehension	_____	_____
Word Recognition	_____	_____
Math Computation	_____	_____
Math Application	_____	_____

Thank you,

Joyce Duryea, Special Education Teacher
Maggie Lowe, Classroom Teacher

Suggestions or Comments:

_____

_____

_____

MAKING A DIFFERENCE

The 60-Second Lesson

Reinforcing Parent Involvement through
Positive Feedback about Their Child

When you keep a supply of photocopied notes on hand, sending feedback to parents takes only a minute.

GOOD NEWS!

Name _____

Date _____

_____

_____

_____

_____

Sincerely,

_____

been used to communicate effectively regarding academic and behavioral progress of students (Kelly, 1990). There are many different types of notes; you can create some of your own. It is also possible to use notes written by the student and structured by the teacher to send home to parents. An example of a student note is provided in Figure 4.12.

Teachers also use weekly and monthly calendars to communicate key information and to record homework assignments. You can fill in events on a calendar and then copy and distribute it to students to take home. A fourth grade teacher who regularly sends home a weekly calendar reports that it takes her about 10 minutes to do. Or you and the special education teachers you work with might decide that providing parents with a weekly list of accomplishments (see Figure

FIGURE 4.12

My Behavior Can't Be Beat

How I worked at school: _____

_____

How I got along with friends: _____

_____

What I tried for the first time: _____

_____

How I helped others: _____

_____

My most amazing deed: _____

_____

_____

Student's Name

4.13) will help a student.

Another option, newsletters, can be written by the teacher or by students. The purpose of a newsletter is to keep parents informed of what is happening in the classroom. Newsletters should not target the poor performance or behavior of a particular student. If your newsletter recognizes student accomplishments, be careful not to name certain students repeatedly but never mentioning others.

Phone calls are an important and often effective means of communicating with parents. Make a list each week of several parents you want to contact with positive reports. Allow three to five minutes for each call, and make one call at the end of each day. Be sure to keep a phone log of parents contacted by phone during the year.

FIGURE 4.13

Mechanical Genius' Accomplishment Sheet

Name _____

Week of _____

Teacher's Signature _____

Subject	Monday	Tuesday	Wednesday	Thursday	Friday
_____	_____	_____	_____	_____	_____
_____	_____	_____	_____	_____	_____
_____	_____	_____	_____	_____	_____
_____	_____	_____	_____	_____	_____
_____	_____	_____	_____	_____	_____
_____	_____	_____	_____	_____	_____
_____	_____	_____	_____	_____	_____

Collaboration and Computers

Through the use of computer software, teachers can collaborate with school personnel in other cities, states, and even different countries. Synchronous collaboration occurs when the individuals involved interact at the same time (Collis & Heeren, 1993). *Aspects* is an example of a computer program that enables the user to engage in synchronous collaboration. This computer program allows its users to open and work on the same file(s). Changes made to the file by one user will appear on the screens of all of the current participants. In this manner, users can work together, simultaneously changing text files and drawing files of a shared document. *Aspects* is available from Group Logic (telephone 1-800-476-8781).

Asynchronous collaboration occurs when the participants communicate with each other not only from different places, but also at different times (Collis & Heeren, 1993). For example, *Common Knowledge* allows its users to modify a shared document at any time. Each user then has access to the most recent version of the document, as well as its original version. Commands within the program allow the user to view which specific changes have been made to the document, when these changes were made, and by whom. *Common Knowledge* is available from On Technology (telephone 1-800-548-8871).

The importance and value of collaboration is underscored throughout this chapter. Technological advancements such as *Aspects* and *Common Knowledge* provide teachers with greater opportunities and increased flexibility in collaboration.

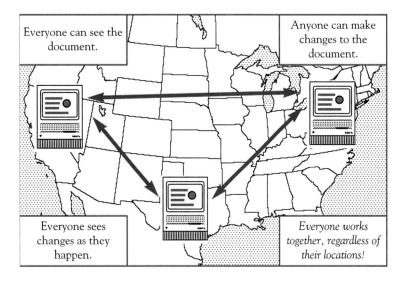

Everyone can see the document.

Anyone can make changes to the document.

Everyone sees changes as they happen.

Everyone works together, regardless of their locations!

Courtesy of Group Logic Inc.

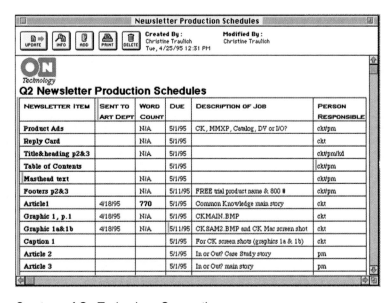

Courtesy of On Technology Corporation.

SUMMARY

- Teachers' ability to collaborate with significant people in a student's life (e.g., special education teacher, psychologist, parent) is a vital skill, growing in importance to general education teachers whose classrooms include increasingly diverse students.
- Collaboration may take many different forms. For example, one common form allows for the special education teacher to serve as a consultant, assisting general education teachers who are instructing students with special needs. Such consultation programs usually involve a collaborative team of parents, general and special education teachers, and other people who contribute to a student's educational program.
- This chapter describes the six steps upon which one consultation program is based: (1) goal/entry, (2) problem identification, (3) intervention of recommendations, (4) implementation of recommendations, (5) evaluation, and (6) redesign.
- Peer collaboration involves the regular participation of two or three teachers in structured conversations so that each teacher assists and receives assistance from the other teachers regarding planning, problem solving, and instructing.
- For any collaboration model to be effective, several criteria must be in place, including: (1) time to co-plan, (2) knowledge of the procedures involved in the particular model, and (3) a location where participants can meet.
- Effective collaboration also requires particular skills, such as: (1) effective listening, (2) appropriate questioning, and (3) focus. Procedures for communicating with other school personnel and parents are delineated in this chapter.

Key Terms and Concepts

collaboration	effective listening	open question
consultation model	facilitator	Peer Collaboration Model
cooperative teaching	family adjustment	real content
co-planning	initiator	tutoring
co-teaching	Mainstream Assistance Team	

Think and Apply

1. How did the teachers in the opening interview help Sheena's parent feel at ease and become more willing to cooperate? Trace Sheena's parent's adjustment to having a child with disabilities. What events contributed to this adjustment?

2. With a partner from your class and using the Consultation Problem-Solving Worksheet (see Figure 4.1) as a guide, work through the six stages of the consultation process outlined in this chapter. Be sure to target a student, define the nature of the problem, and generate as many practices for effective implementation as you can. As you work through the problem-solving worksheet, make a list of your questions (then keep the list in your portfolio). As you read through the book, answer your questions.

3. This chapter's "Collaboration Issues and Dilemmas" section lists four issues you might need to consider if you are involved in a consultation or cooperative teaching model with another professional. Write your current feelings about each issue (student ownership, individual versus class focus, content versus accommodation, and real world versus student's world). What knowledge and experiences might support your perspectives? What knowledge and experiences might cause you to change your views?

4. Consider the five qualities of effective collaborators (see Table 4.1). To what extent do you feel you have displayed these qualities in past collaborative efforts? Select one quality to improve and monitor over a designated time period (e.g., one month), then evaluate your progress.

5. Have you ever had a conversation during which you did not feel connected? Think about what the other person(s) did and what you did. Using the principles of effective listening identified in this chapter, make a checklist of things you should consider during a conversation.

6. Make a list of the ways you want to ensure that you are working effectively with parents. What are some of the materials and resources you need to do your job effectively? Contact parent and professional organizations for information about parent involvement.

Read More about It

1. Anderson, W., Chitwood, S., & Hayden, D. (1990). *Negotiating the special education maze: A guide for parents and teachers* (2nd ed.). Kensington, MD: Woodbine House.

    A valuable resource for parents and professionals about terminology, legal issues, and procedures for better understanding special education.

2. Friend, M., & Cook, L. (1992). *Interactions: Collaboration skills for school professionals*. White Plains, NY: Longman.

    A practical orientation to developing and using knowledge and skills with which to work effectively with other professionals. Procedures for team building, team meetings, conferences with parents, co-teaching, and problem-solving formats are provided.

3. Jordan, A. (1994). *Skills in collaborative classroom consultation*. New York: Routledge.

    An application of collaboration skills as a tool for creating change in educational practice. Topics include: collaborative consultation in context; alternative school delivery models; consulting skills; contracting; assessment and feedback; developing action plans; difficult consulting situations; working with parents, administrators, and service professionals; drawing on the resources of the school; and classroom consultation.

4. Kelly, M. (1990). *School–home notes: Promoting children's classroom success*. New York: Guilford Press.

    A resource for teachers interested in examples of "Good News Notes." Includes many examples of uses of these notes, as well as procedures for using them to increase academic achievement and appropriate behavior in the classroom.

5. Pugach, M. C., & Johnson, L. J. (1995). *Collaborative practitioners, collaborative schools*. Denver, Co: Love.

    An orientation to teaching by working collaboratively with others. Teaches adults to form a "community of learners" and to grow professionally. Includes descriptions of teamwork approaches, communication skills, group work, problem solving, and team teaching.

6. Radencich, M., & Schumm, J. S. (1988). *How to help your child with homework*. Minneapolis: Free Spirit.

    This practical guide for parents who want to provide homework support while helping their children learn independent study habits includes general guidelines for homework sessions, as well as specific suggestions for reading, language arts, mathematics, and other content areas.

Teaching Students with Learning Disabilities or Attention Deficit Disorders

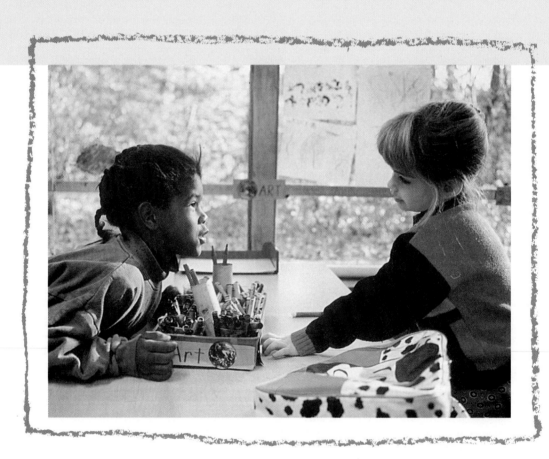

FOCUS QUESTIONS

1. According to IDEA, what are the major components of the definition and criteria for determining a specific learning disability?

2. What are the characteristics of students who have learning disabilities?

3. What percentage of students in school have learning disabilities?

4. What techniques could you incorporate into your teaching to benefit students with learning disabilities?

5. What is an attention deficit disorder? How does it affect a student in school?

6. What are the characteristics of inattention, hyperactivity, and impulsivity?

7. What is the percentage of students who have ADD?

8. What are some possible reasons that more boys than girls are identified with learning disabilities and attention deficit disorder?

9. What are some strategies you can use to help students with ADD be successful in school?

Tammy Gregory

Tammy Gregory is one of four second grade teachers at Canyon Verde Elementary School in Tucson, Arizona. This is Tammy's third year teaching. In her class of 31 students, Tammy has one student with learning disabilities, Adrian, and one student with attention deficit disorder, Lenny.

When you talk with Tammy and watch her teach, it is clear that she believes all students can be successful learners, and that her job is to modify the content and the curriculum for the different learners in her classroom. This is certainly the case with Adrian, whose learning disabilities relate most to the speed at which he processes information. It takes him longer to understand what is being said during classroom discussions and presentations. He reads slowly whether he is reading aloud or to himself. His responses to questions are often slow and labored, and the ideas are not clearly stated. He also writes slowly. He is almost always the last or next-to-last student to finish a written assignment, and often does not complete work in the time allowed.

Tammy regularly makes accommodations for Adrian so that he is a successful learner in her classroom. Because his writing is slow, she sometimes reduces the length of the assignment so that he can complete it in the time allowed. Tammy says, "The key is that Adrian understands and has mastered the skill. If he can demonstrate mastery answering five problems instead of ten problems in math, then he has learned and reached his goal."

Tammy has also set up an informal buddy system in her room. Students regularly help each other with assignments. Tammy has Adrian sitting next to one student who is an able helper and high achiever and another student who is an average achiever and who likes to problem solve and work with Adrian on assignments. This arrangement gives Adrian the opportunity to work with two very different students who like to work with other students and provide support for him. Although speed of processing can make Adrian appear slow and not very adept at many skills, his teacher has taken the time to learn about his interests and his strengths and to share those with the other students. It is not unusual to hear Tammy say to the class, "Check with Adrian on that, he's a real expert."

Tammy has also made accommodations for Lenny, a student with attention deficit disorders including hyperactivity and impulsivity. At the beginning of the year, Tammy thought that Lenny would be "the child that led her into early retirement." He moved constantly (even when sitting), and was out of his seat, sharpening his pencil, talking to and bothering the other students. During class discussion he would answer before Tammy had a chance even to ask the students to raise their hands. He rarely completed assignments. Tammy felt that Lenny could do much of the work, but that his attention problems got in the way of his being a successful learner. To help Lenny, Tammy thought about and modified the structure of her classroom and schedule. Tammy comments,

> Lenny attends best when he knows what is "on tap" for the day. Each day I review the schedule for the day and put a copy of it on the board, on the corner of Lenny's desk, and on my desk. As each activity is completed, Lenny checks it off and rates himself for that activity on three criteria: paying attention, effort, and work completed. At first I also rated Lenny, but now I am comfortable with his self-monitoring. At lunch and during the end of the day wrap-up, I take several minutes to review with Lenny his self-monitoring. Based on his performance, Lenny receives good work day certificates to take home for his parents to sign, and on Friday afternoon he can receive a "Job Well Done" pass to watch a video or participate in other activities with the other good workers in the school. For me, taking this extra time with Lenny is well worth the progress Lenny has made and the sanity that has been restored to my classroom.

Tammy also makes other modifications for Lenny, such as reducing the number of math problems assigned by having him complete only the odd or even numbered problems. She also helps Lenny, Adrian, and other students in her class break multiple-step or complex tasks and projects into smaller tasks. Tammy comments, "Even reading a book and writing a book report can be divided into five or six steps the students can complete one-by-one. This substantially increases the likelihood of students getting these projects done in a timely manner."

Adrian and Lenny have made good progress this year in school, both in terms of their learning and their positive self-concepts as learners. Tammy is concerned, however, about their transition into third grade, where more emphasis will be placed on written work and complex assignments and less time will be spent on teaching basic skills and individualizing for different students' needs. She is wondering what to communicate to Adrian and Lenny's teachers next year, so that they can continue as successful learners.

Introduction

Think about Tammy's philosophy and practice of teaching students with learning disabilities and attention problems. To what extent do the practices she implements with Adrian and Lenny reflect the type of teacher you are or want to be? The first section of this chapter provides an overview of students with learning disabilities (LD), and the second section focuses on students with attention deficit disorder (ADD). As you read, think about ways the strategies suggested for these students can also be used for other students in elementary and secondary classrooms.

Learning Disabilities

The disabilities of students who have visual impairments, are deaf or hard of hearing, or have overall cognitive delays usually are obvious. In contrast, you probably will not recognize students with learning disabilities in your classroom until you have the opportunity to interact with them and see how they learn. Only in the last twenty-five years have learning disabilities, sometimes referred to as the "invisible disability," been recognized in our schools. This section provides definitions and characteristics of learning disabilities, as well as suggestions for meeting the needs of students with learning disabilities in your classroom.

Definitions and Types of Learning Disabilities

The issue of how to define learning disabilities has received considerable attention in the field since 1963, when Samuel Kirk suggested the term "specific learning disabilities" at the organizational meeting of the Learning Disabilities Association (LDA) (formerly called the Association for Children with Learning Disabilities, ACLD). At that time, children with learning disabilities were referred to by such terms as perceptually handicapped, brain-injured, and neurologically impaired and were served in classrooms for students with mental retardation or, in most cases, were not receiving any specialized services in the public schools.

The term **specific learning disabilities** represents a heterogeneous group of students who, despite adequate cognitive functioning and the ability to learn some skills and strategies quickly and easily, have great difficulty learning other skills and strategies. For example, students with specific reading disabilities may participate quite well in class discussions but have difficulty reading the text and taking tests. Other students may have great difficulty with math, but have little difficulty with tasks that incorporate reading and writing.

> The Learning Disabilities Association is a parent and professional organization that provides many resources related to learning disabilities. Contact information: Learning Disabilities Association, 4156 Library Road, Pittsburgh, PA 15234, telephone: (412) 341-1515.

The operational guidelines for the definition of specific learning disabilities are specified in the rules and regulations for IDEA, and indicate that a multidisciplinary team may determine that a child has a specific learning disability if:

- the student does not achieve commensurate with his or her age and ability level in one or more of several specific areas when provided with appropriate learning experiences
- the student has a severe discrepancy between achievement and intellectual ability in one or more of these seven areas:

  a. oral expression
  b. listening comprehension
  c. written expression
  d. basic reading skills
  e. reading comprehension
  f. mathematics calculation
  g. mathematics reasoning

- the student needs special education services

A student is not regarded as having a specific learning disability if the discrepancy between ability and achievement is primarily the result of any of the following:

- visual, hearing, or motor disability
- mental retardation
- emotional disturbance
- environmental, cultural, or economic disadvantage

FIGURE 5.1

IDEA Definition of Learning Disabilities, and Major Components of the Definition

DEFINITION

The term "children with specific learning disabilities" means those children who have a disorder in one or more of the basic psychological processes involved in understanding or in using language, spoken or written, which disorder may manifest itself in imperfect ability to listen, think, speak, read, write, spell, or to do mathematical calculations. Such disorders include such conditions as perceptual handicaps, brain injury, minimal brain dysfunction, dyslexia, and developmental aphasia. Such terms do not include children who have learning problems which are primarily the result of visual, hearing, or motor handicap, of mental retardation, of emotional disturbance, or of environmental, cultural, or economic disadvantage.

MAJOR COMPONENTS

✔ difficulty with academic and learning tasks

✔ discrepancy between expected and actual achievement

✔ disorder in basic psychological processing

✔ exclusion of other causes

Although many definitions of learning disabilities have been developed (see Figure 5.1), secondary science teacher Joseph Blankenship's ideas about learning disabilities are similar to those of many other general education teachers. He comments that initially these students often do not seem different from other students. They participate in classroom discussions and appear to understand the content covered. But as assignments are submitted and tests given, he quickly realizes that students with learning disabilities have difficulties with reading, writing, studying, and organizing their time.

Learning disabilities represent a group of disorders that cause students to have learning and academic difficulties. Currently, although no generally accepted classification systems exist for students with learning disabilities (Keogh, 1993; Speece, 1994), types of learning disabilities have been discussed in the literature and used in medical and psychological reports for many years. Some of the most frequently used terms follow:

- **Dyslexia**—severe difficulty in learning to read, particularly as it relates to decoding
- **Dysgraphia**—severe difficulty learning to write, including handwriting
- **Dyscalculia**—severe disability in learning mathematical concepts and computation (Baroody & Ginsburg, 1991)

As a teacher, when you find these diagnostic terms in medical and psychological reports, you need to ask the following question:

What behaviors or learning characteristics should I expect when a student has been identified as having learning disabilities?

For example, when Lynn Ann Chang reviewed the special education files of students who would be in her fourth grade classroom the following year, she noticed that an evaluation in second grade identified Jessica as having dyslexia. Lynn Ann met with Jessica's current third grade teacher, special education teacher, and mother to learn more about what this meant for Jessica and to plan for having Jessica in her classroom. Lynn Ann learned that Jessica had experienced significant difficulties in learning to read, particularly learning to understand the relationship between sounds in the oral language and the symbols they represented. In second grade, Jessica was reading at a preprimer level and could not consistently identify the beginning or ending sounds of words. Jessica liked books, however, and when they were read to her, could retell and answer questions about stories written for children her age. Since that evaluation, Jessica has been receiving small-group reading instruction from the special education teacher and tutoring in an after-school program. Lynn Ann decided to assign a buddy to assist Jessica in reading her science and social studies texts, and she also incorporated high-interest, low-vocabulary books into her reading instruction. Jessica's teachers have encouraged her to use different strategies to help her decode and remember words. Her sight vocabulary has grown significantly, and she is now reading at a second grade level.

RESEARCH BRIEF

DEVELOPMENTAL, NEUROLOGICAL, AND GENETIC NATURE OF READING DISABILITIES

Currently, the National Institute for Child Health and Human Development is sponsoring a number of research centers and projects that are investigating the nature of reading disabilities, particularly as it relates to learning to read (Lyon, 1994). This work has been summarized by Lyon (1994), with the following findings:

- Although schools identify approximately four times as many boys as girls as having reading disabilities, studies show that as many girls are affected as boys.
- Reading disabilities persist. Of the students who have reading disabilities in the third grade, about 75 percent still have significant problems in ninth grade.

- The ability to read and comprehend depends upon rapid and automatic recognition of words. Slow and inaccurate decoding are the best predictors of difficulties in reading comprehension.
- The ability to decode words depends on the ability to segment words into syllables and sounds. Difficulty with this task is central to dyslexia.
- There is strong evidence that reading disabilities are inherited, and affect the processing of information by the brain.

In addition, two major types of dyslexia have been identified (Eden et al., 1995; Lyon et al., 1991). The most prevalent type is language-based and results in students having difficulty processing sounds, which in turn affects the use of phonics rules to decode words and spell (Olson et al., 1990; Stanovich, 1988). The second, less frequent type relates to the visual aspects of reading and results in students having difficulty remembering words and developing sight vocabulary (Stanovich et al., 1991; Van Strien et al., 1995; Vellutino et al., 1994).

Characteristics of Students with Learning Disabilities

Because learning disabilities are heterogeneous, it is very difficult to list a set of characteristics that describe them all. You will find that students with learning disabilities seem more different from each other than alike, in relation to how they learn, but certain overriding characteristics will help you in identifying these students:

- *unexpected* difficulty or low performance in one or more academic areas (unexpected in that your general impressions of the student would not lead you to predict that he or she would have difficulty)
- has ineffective or inefficient information-processing or learning strategies in the area(s) of difficulty

Furthermore, the reasons for this low performance vary according to the strengths and weaknesses of the learner, and the learning strategies he or she employs. For example, Tamara and Randy, two students in Carla Huerra's third grade classroom, were identified as having specific learning disabilities and were reading and spelling at an early first grade (primer) level. Both students have difficulty developing an automatic sight vocabulary to use when reading and writing, but the strategies each of them uses are very different, as are the individualized educational programs Carla and the special education teacher use with each student.

Carla *observes* the students to better understand their learning styles, including their strategies and motivation for learning, and their interests. She listens to each of them as they read aloud and retell what they have read. She notes the miscues each of them makes when reading, and watches for the strategies they use when they come to a word they do not recognize automatically or to something they do not seem to understand. She also observes both students during writers' workshop, as they compose first (and subsequent) drafts of their work.

Carla's observations reveal that Tamara has strong oral language skills. She capitalizes on these skills when she reads, and uses the meaning and the syntax (word order or grammar) of the language as her primary strategies for figuring out unknown words. When she does not know a word, she skips it or substitutes a word that more or less makes sense. She shows little evidence of using phonics to figure out unknown words. Carla notes that even though Tamara sees a word many times, either in context or written by itself, it is not easy for her to recognize it automatically, so that it becomes part of her sight vocabulary. When Carla observes Tamara's writing, she notes that Tamara has wonderful ideas but spends much of her time asking other students how to spell words,

Approximately 85 percent of the elementary-age students with learning disabilities have difficulties reading, particularly in decoding words.

What are some learner characteristics that might help you identify a student with possible learning disabilities? How might you work with an inclusion specialist or special education teacher to plan and design an education program to support such a student?

or changing what she was originally going to write so that she can use words she knows how to spell. She does this despite the classroom rule that, "Spelling doesn't matter on drafts; spell it the way you think."

Like Tamara, Randy has difficulty memorizing words so that they become part of his sight vocabulary and can be retrieved automatically when he reads or writes. Randy's strategies for reading are very different from Tamara's, however. Randy's reading is very slow because he tries to sound out the words (uses his phonic analysis skills). He is able to get a number of the individual sounds, but has trouble blending them together to make a word. Although the words that result may not make sense, he does not seem to monitor this by going back and rereading. Randy's writing also reflects his use of his somewhat successful phonic analysis, in that even high-frequency, irregular words are spelled phonetically (e.g., *cum* for *come*, *wuz* for *was*).

In talking with David Ross, Tamara and Randy's special education teacher, Carla learned that her observations were the same as his. Both students have visual-memory and auditory-processing difficulties that make it hard for them to learn to automatically recognize words. Each student, however, uses very different strategies and strengths to compensate (i.e., Tamara relies on her strong oral language skills and Randy relies on "somewhat successful" phonic analysis).

Together, Carla and David have *planned and designed* educational programs to support these students. For studying content areas such as science and social studies, Carla relies on partner reading and the use of trade books written at different reading levels. She also allows students to demonstrate their knowledge through oral reports, posters, and pictures, rather than only through traditional written reports and tests. During writers' workshop, Carla has helped each student develop a spelling dictionary. For reading, Carla and David work together to help Tamara and Randy expand the strategies they use to decode unknown words. For Tamara, this includes learning to identify the first sound(s) in the words and to use this information, along with meaning, to help her identify the unknown word. They are also helping Tamara to see similar patterns in words (e.g., word families: -ake, make, take, lake). For Randy, their help includes getting him to ask himself the question, "Does this make

sense?" and to take more risks, instead of laboriously sounding out each word.

Table 5.1 presents some characteristics that, although they might not apply to all students with learning disabilities, have helped signal to general education teachers which students might have specific learning disabilities. Several of these characteristics refer to difficulties in attention. Students with learning disabilities often have difficulties with attention and, in some cases, hyperactivity. About 35 percent of students with learning disabilities also have attention deficit disorders (Barkley, 1990) which are discussed later in this chapter.

As students with learning disabilities continue to fail in school, they are likely to develop emotional and behavioral disabilities, depression, and low self-esteem as learners (Huntington & Bender, 1993; Montgomery, 1994). A longitudinal study of the self-concept of students with and without LD indicated, however, that the self-concepts of the other achieving groups decreased from kindergarten through fifth grade, and that students with LD did not have lower self-concepts than other students (Vaughn et al., 1992).

What are the lifelong outcomes for students with learning disabilities? There is no single

---

TABLE 5.1

Signals for Possible Learning Disabilities

Signals for learning disabilities are characteristics of students with learning disabilities. Because these students are a heterogeneous group, only certain signals will apply to any one student.

- has trouble understanding and following directions
- has a short attention span; is easily distracted
- is overactive and impulsive
- has difficulty with handwriting and fine motor activities
- has difficulty with visual or auditory sequential memory
- has difficulty memorizing words or basic math facts
- has difficulty allocating time and organizing work
- is unmotivated toward tasks that are difficult

- has difficulty segmenting words into sounds, and blending sounds
- confuses similar letters and words, such as *b* and *d*, and *was* and *saw*
- listens and speaks well, but decodes poorly when reading
- has difficulty with tasks that require rapid naming of pictures, words, and numbers
- is not efficient or effective in using learning strategies

answer for all students, but we do have evidence that some individuals with learning disabilities are quite successful in adult life and that they learn to adjust and make accommodations for the disabilities. (For example, Albert Einstein, Nelson Rockefeller, and Thomas Edison all had significant learning disabilities.) What are the social and education factors that predict success for individuals with learning disabilities? Research indicates that successful adults with learning disabilities make realistic adaptations for their learning disabilities, take control of their lives, are goal oriented, and persist at these goals. Successful adults with learning disabilities have indicated that one or more significant people have supported their adjustments during school, post-secondary training, and young adult life (e.g., Speckman et al., 1993). Increased access to vocational training programs and support programs in colleges has also served to increase success (Gerber et al., 1992; Vogel et al., 1993).

RESEARCH BRIEF

LEARNING DISABILITIES AND JUVENILE DELINQUENCY

The incidence of learning disabilities is generally much higher in delinquents (18 to 55 percent) than in the general population. Similarly, teens who have learning disabilities report more contact with the law than their non-learning-disabled peers (e.g., Bryan et al., 1989; Keilitz & Dunivant, 1986; Spreen, 1988).

Two theories have been suggested as to why this is the case. The *school failure theory* suggests that school failure, including poor academic achievement, leads to persistent delinquency. The *susceptibility theory* suggests that learning disabilities may be linked to certain underdeveloped personality skills, such as general impulsiveness and poor judgment, which lead to increased susceptibility to delinquent behavior through unwise social choices. Waldie and Spreen (1993) conducted follow-up interviews with sixty-five individuals with

learning disabilities who were diagnosed between ages eight and twelve and reported police contact during an interview at age eighteen. During an interview at age twenty-five, 62 percent had persisting problems with the law. Data analysis, which demonstrated that poor judgment and impulsivity were the two factors involved, supports the susceptibility theory.

Prevalence of Learning Disabilities

Today, more students are identified as having specific learning disabilities than any other type of disability. According to the *Sixteenth Annual Report to Congress on the Implementation of the Individuals with Disabilities Education Act* (United States Department of Education, 1995), 10 percent of school-age children were identified as disabled, and over 5 percent were identified as having learning disabilities. During the last two decades, the number of students identified as having learning disabilities has increased substantially. For example, during the 1979–80 school year, 1,281,379 students with learning disabilities were identified and served in the public school system. This number increased to 2,064,892 by 1989–90, and to 2,444,020 in 1993–94..

Why does the percentage of students with learning disabilities continue to increase? Several factors are related to the answer, including the following (Hallahan, 1992; Lerner, 1993):

- *Growing public awareness of learning disabilities.* As more parents and general education teachers learn about the characteristics of students with learning disabilities, they become more attuned to watching for signs and seeking assistance within the school system.
- *Greater social acceptance.* Learning disabilities are among the disabilities viewed as more socially accepted and with fewer negative connotations than others.
- *Limited alternatives for other students at-risk.* Due to limited alternative programs, the tendency is to identify students who may be failing for reasons other than specific learning disabilities, so that they may receive services.
- *Social and cultural influences on central nervous system integrity.* Demographics would suggest that more children are being born of

parents whose income falls below the poverty level, who may be addicted to drugs and alcohol, and who are teenagers (all factors that increase chances of these children being at risk for learning disabilities).

- *Increasing needs for literacy at work and in daily life.* As we move into an information age that requires better educated individuals, schools are demanding more of students, and higher literacy levels are necessary for jobs and the tasks of daily life.

Also of interest is the number of boys versus girls identified as having learning disabilities—with boys identified from twice to as many as eight times more often than girls (Shaywitz & Shaywitz, 1988). Data from the U.S. Department of Education (1994) indicates a ratio of approximately four boys to every girl. Recent research on the genetic bases of dyslexia would suggest that the ratio of boys to girls should be more equal (Shaywitz et al., 1990). Males may be more vulnerable to referral and identification, however, because boys generally exhibit more disruptive behaviors that are difficult to manage in school.

Identification and Assessment of Students with Learning Disabilities

Most students with learning disabilities are identified because of difficulties with academic achievement. Teachers—usually the first professionals to notice the students' learning strengths and weaknesses and academic skills—play an important role in identifying students with learning disabilities.

Louise Parra, a first grade teacher, comments on the importance she places on being alert for students who may have learning disabilities. She comments,

> As a first grade teacher, it is very important that I understand learning disabilities and keep alert for children who are not learning at the same rate or with the same ease that I would expect of them. If I notice these children in the first grade and begin collaborating with the special education teacher, other specialists, and the children's families, then I can assist in preventing these children from developing the poor self-esteem that frequently develops if they continue to fail and are not supported.

Of all the members of a prereferral or multidisciplinary team, classroom teacher(s) and parent(s) have the most experience with a student. Referral from the classroom teacher is one of the most important predictors as to whether a student will be identified as learning disabled. A recent study of 236 referrals made in an intermediate school district in the midwest, for example, indicated that 128 students (approximately 45 percent) were identified by the multidisciplinary teams as eligible for special education as learning disabled (Fugate et al., 1993).

Although some students with learning disabilities receive direct instruction in a resource room, more and more of these students receive all their education in the general education classroom, with support from the special education teacher or a paraprofessional.

Jackie Darnell, a classroom teacher, shared observations and information (see Figure 5.2) about a student, Cassandra, at a multidisciplinary conference during which it was decided that, because of math disabilities, Cassandra was eligible for special education services.

The information Jackie provided clearly identified her concerns in the area of math computation. She also provided information about strategies she had already tried with Cassandra. Because Jackie felt that the computer programs were the most helpful, she and the special education teacher decided to work together to identify additional computer programs for Cassandra. The special education teacher would work with Cassandra on how to use a calculator and build skills in computation of multiplication problems. Both teachers would use manipulatives to build Cassandra's understanding of division and fractions. Tips for Teachers 5.1 suggests what classroom teachers should consider before referring a student who seems to have learning disabilities.

Instructional Techniques and Accommodations for Students with Learning Disabilities

Because the group of students with learning disabilities is so diverse, no one approach or tech-

Name: Cassandra

Age: 10–10

Grade: 5th

Literacy:
- 4th to 5th grade level
- Enjoys reading as a leisure-time activity, and uses the library on a regular basis.
- Enjoys writing fantasy and drama, and uses both character and plot development; patterns many of her stories after the popular girl-oriented series.
- Participates in literature discussion groups and can answer a variety of questions about the literature, including underlying theme and application questions.
- Can write a report with introduction and two supporting paragraphs.
- Spells at fourth-grade level, using phonic and structural analysis for unknown words.
- Can use a word processor to write and revise written work.

Math:
- Second-grade achievement level.
- Adds and subtracts with regrouping, but makes computation errors in the process and basic facts.
- Understands basic concept of multiplication but does not know basic facts or how to use for computations.
- Has difficulty understanding simple, one- and two-step word problems.
- Has not yet memorized 50% of the basic addition and subtraction facts.
- Knows multiplication facts 0, 1, 5, and 10.
- Understands concept of multiplication as repeated addition. Does not compute multiplication problems.
- Does not demonstrate concept of division and does not know division facts.
- Demonstrates concept of simple fractions 1/2, 1/3, 1/4.
- Solves word problems. Errors are generally in computation and basic facts rather than problem representation.
- Describes math as least favorite subject.
- Struggles to learn basic math facts, despite incentive program, coordination with parents, and use of computer programs at school.

Social/Emotional:
- Well liked by peers, both boys and girls.
- Quiet, does not ask for help when needed.
- Works well in cooperative groups but usually does not take leadership roles.
- Good sense of humor.

TIPS FOR TEACHERS

5.1 What to Consider in Referring Students Suspected of Learning Disabilities

- **In which academic areas of learning** (e.g., listening comprehension, oral expression, basic reading skills, reading comprehension, basic writing skills, written expression, math computation, math reasoning and problem solving) is the student successful, and in which areas is the student having difficulties?
- **What are the academic achievement levels in these areas** and what are representative examples of the student's work?
- **How does the student compare with other students** in the classroom in areas of success and difficulty?
- **What factors (other than specific learning disabilities)** might be contributing to the learning problems experienced by the student (e.g., frequent moves, absences, recent traumatic life events, vision or hearing impairments, emotional disorders)?
- **Are the student's first language and language of instruction the same,** or is the student learning academics while also acquiring a second language or dialect?
- **What learning or compensatory strategies** does the student currently use to aid in learning?
- **How does the student perceive him- or herself** as a learner, and what is the student's attitude toward school and learning?
- **What strategies and accommodations have been tried,** and how did they work?

---

nique is relevant for all students with learning disabilities. In fact, many special education teachers describe themselves as having to be necessarily eclectic in their philosophy and approaches to teaching to match the different learning styles these students exhibit. Effective classroom teachers report that they must use their "best teaching practices" to teach students with learning disabilities.

Len Hays, a seventh-grade English teacher elaborates on "best teaching practices,"

> When I work with students who have been identified as learning disabled or who are at risk, it requires my best teaching. By this I mean that I must be very organized in the manner in which I present a literature unit or an English lesson. First, I give an overview of the lesson and explain the activities and what is expected of the students. I also make sure that when I lecture, I use an overhead projector to write important information. If I want the students to understand a process, such as how to revise an essay to add "color," then using the overhead projector lets me demonstrate the process and my thinking as I edit. I find that using the overhead allows me to model not only the questions I ask myself as a writer, but to show the changes I make. It is also important that I organize the learning activities and working groups so that students have the opportunity to practice the skills that are the focus of the lesson. Whether we are working on editing skills or doing a critical analysis of a book, I always work to relate the learning to the students' daily lives. Finally, I try to be creative and humorous. That is just part of being a middle school teacher and dealing with adolescence.

This section presents some general teaching strategies that are effective for students with learning disabilities. You will find many more ideas in the chapters about teaching reading, writing, content area subjects, mathematics, and the Appendix on Learning Strategies. The general strategies in this chapter include the following:

- Provide a framework for learning.
- Model the processes and strategies.
- Present information in multiple ways.
- Allow students to demonstrate learning in multiple ways.
- Teach students to use memory strategies.
- Teach self-regulation and self-monitoring.

- Provide opportunities for extended practice and application.
- Use learning tools and aids (e.g., computers, calculators, spell checkers).
- Adjust work load and time requirements.

These strategies have been shown to be effective when teaching students with learning disabilities.

Provide a Framework for Learning Students are more successful when they have a good idea of where they are going. Research on the use of advance organizers would suggest that this is even more important for students with learning disabilities, learning problems, or limited background knowledge for the task being taught (Mayer, 1979). The concept of advance organizers was introduced in the 1960s by David Ausubel. He defined an **advance organizer** as information presented "in advance of and at a higher level of generality, inclu-

What are nine general teaching strategies that are helpful for all students but are especially effective for students with learning disabilities?

TIPS FOR TEACHERS

5.2 Steps in Using an Advance Organizer

1. Inform students of advance organizers:
   - Announce advance organizer.
   - State benefits of advance organizer.
   - Suggest that students take notes on the advance organizer.
2. Identify topics of tasks:
   - Identify major topics or activities.
   - Identify subtopics or component activities.
3. Provide an organizational framework:
   - Present an outline, list, or narrative of the lesson's content.
4. Clarify action to be taken:
   - Explain your actions.
   - State actions expected of students.
5. Provide background information:
   - Relate topic to the course or to a previous lesson.
   - Relate topic to new information.
6. State the concepts to be learned:
   - State specific concepts and ideas from the lesson.
   - State general concepts and ideas broader than the lesson's content.
7. Clarify the concepts to be learned:
   - Clarify by examples or analogies.
   - Clarify by nonexamples.
   - Caution students about possible misunderstandings.
8. Motivate students to learn:
   - Point out relevance to students.
   - Be specific, personalized, and believable.
9. Introduce vocabulary:
   - Identify and define new terms.
   - Repeat and define difficult terms.
10. State the general outcome desired:
    - State objectives of instruction and learning
    - Relate outcomes to test performance.

Adapted with permission from: Lenz, B. K. (1983). Promoting active learning through effective instruction. *Pointer*, 27(2), 12.

siveness, and abstraction than the learning task itself" (Ausubel & Robinson, 1969, p. 606).

Keith Lenz and his colleagues (Lenz 1983; Lenz et al., 1987) developed ten steps for using an advance organizer. Lenz found that when content area teachers in middle and high schools used this framework for learning, adolescents with learning disabilities could experience significant improvements in both the quality and quantity of learning.

Three factors seem important to the success of advance organizers. First, students with learning disabilities are taught how to listen for and use the advance organizer. Students might complete a worksheet (see Figure 5.3) as they listen to the teacher introduce each part of the advance organizer. Second, after using the advance organizer worksheet, the teacher and students discuss the effectiveness of its use and how and when it might be used in various content classes. Third, before an advance organizer is presented, the teacher cues the students that it is going to be used.

One critical aspect of the advance organizer is that it provides basic information or activates the students' background knowledge (refer to Step 5 in Tips for Teachers 5.2). Students with learning disabilities often have information about the topics, skills, or strategies being taught but do not automatically think about this information (e.g., Borkowski et al., 1989; Bos & Filip, 1984; Wong, 1991; Wong & Wong, 1986). The chapters on reading and content-area instruction discuss specific techniques for activating students' background knowledge.

Model Processes and Strategies One key to success for students with learning disabilities is to make the learning visible. Think back to your experiences as a student. How did you learn to find the main idea when you were reading? Many teachers traditionally used the technique of repeatedly asking students questions such as, "What is the main idea of this story?" until a student provided the right answer (e.g., Durkin, 1978–79). Students were expected to infer how to find the main idea. In the last twenty years, however, intervention research on teaching reading comprehension and other cognitive processes has emphasized that teachers and students should model and discuss the **cognitive strategies** (i.e., thinking processes) they use for tasks such as finding the

FIGURE 5.3

Headings and Questions to Include on a Student Worksheet for Advance Organizer

Advance Organizer Worksheet

Name:
Date:
What is the topic?

What is the framework or picture for the information?

What do I need to do or what are the assignments?

What do I need to learn?

What is the important vocabulary?

What are the due dates for the assignments and test?

main idea of the story (e.g., Echevarnia, 1995; Moll, 1990; Palincsar, 1986; Tharp & Gallimore, 1988). Teachers use discussions (referred to as **instructional conversations**) to make visible the thinking processes needed for understanding.

In the following dialogue, the teacher is helping students to better understand story elements, using an instructional conversation to make learning more visible (Englert et al., 1994). In this example, the teacher is working with two students who have partner-read a narrative story about a bear and are now telling the rest of the students about the story.

T: Tell us about the story.
Ann: [Begins ... by retelling random incidents from the story]
T: You already said we were going to talk about the characters, setting, and problem. Who are the characters in that story?

Dee: There is Brother Bear, Papa Bear, and ... [Shows pictures from the book]

T: Who would you say is the main character?

Ann: They were all main characters because they were all together throughout the story.

T: When we try to figure out the main character, what is the question we ask ourselves?

Ann: What the author wants us to know.

T: Remember when we try to figure out the main character, we ask ourselves, "Who is ..."

Ann: [Ann fills in] ... "The story mostly about."

T: Could you answer that question by saying it's mostly about everybody there? (p. 21)

Rather than providing the answer, the teacher is modeling what question to ask to determine who the main character is.

Whether teaching reading, math, or written expression, research on students with learning disabilities consistently has demonstrated that making the learning visible improves learning significantly (e.g., Bos & Anders, 1990; Englert et al., 1991; Wong, 1991).

Present Information in Multiple Ways

Students with learning disabilities have difficulty processing information when it is presented in only one way. To assist these students, it is important to present the information in multiple ways. Bruce Ford incorporates a number of activities, materials, and ways of presenting information as he plans a unit on cells for his ninth grade science class.

> Modeling strategies and processes and using instructional conversations as the major means of teaching may be uncomfortable at first for teachers accustomed to more traditional lecture or question/answer formats.

When I think about planning for biology class, I think about what are the key knowledge and skills that I want the students to understand and use. I know that if I just present the information, using a lecture, and have the students read the textbook, a good number of the students will not be able to access the informa-

tion. So I find myself being creative and constantly on the lookout for additional resources that I can integrate into the unit. Right now, when we do the unit on cells, I have a great video from "Nova" that I use. I have also developed a study guide that I have students complete as we go through the unit. It incorporates pictures of cells and allows them to label the parts of the cell and their functions. The study guide also provides the outline for my lecture notes. The study guide is critical because many of the students in my class cannot take adequate notes. One activity that I always use is an experiment where students have to view cells during the reproduction cycle with a microscope. This activity allows the students to work in teams and develop a group report of their findings. I ask the students to be sure to include drawings. I have found that some of my students with learning disabilities excel at this activity. The experiment allows them to work in teams and move around the room. Having them incorporate drawings is something that these students often excel in, even though they struggle with writing.

Allow Students to Demonstrate Learning in Multiple Ways

The majority of students with learning disabilities have writing problems that persist over time (Graham & Harris, 1989; Mather & Roberts, 1995). A high school teacher of students with learning disabilities explains the situation this way, "The adolescents in my program do not want to write. They do not even want to answer questions in writing. Writing a theme for a class is torture" (Bos & Vaughn, 1994, p. 214). Yet writing and tests are the major vehicles used to demonstrate learning. Modifying the manner in which students demonstrate learning enables students with learning disabilities to be more successful in the classroom.

Tips for Teachers 5.3 gives ideas for presenting information in multiple ways.

Teach Students to Use Memory Strategies

Research has consistently demonstrated that students with learning disabilities are less effective at employing memory strategies than their peers (Swanson, 1993; Swanson & Cooney, 1991, Torgesen & Goldman, 1977). For the classroom teacher, this means that students with learning dis-

TIPS FOR TEACHERS

5.3 *Ideas for Presenting Information and Demonstrating Learning in Multiple Ways*

Ideas for Presenting Information

- Demonstrate the process or strategy.
- Lecture, writing key points on an overhead projector as you talk.
- Lecture, stopping at natural breaks so that students, working in pairs, can discuss what they see as the major ideas.
- Use a graphic organizer or map to show the relationship among the ideas you are presenting.
- Use a video or movie that presents the key points.
- Have students listen to books on tape.
- Have students conduct experiments to test hypotheses or discover relationships.
- Use pantomimes and skits to explain concepts.
- Have students role-play.
- Use computer simulations.
- Use manipulatives to demonstrate and then have the students use manipulatives.
- Use analogies, metaphors, and examples to further explain concepts.
- Have students use visualization and imagery to see ideas and their relationships.

Ideas for Demonstrating Learning for Math

- For students who have difficulties aligning numbers, use graph paper.
- Have students draw a visual representation of the story problem and then complete the math computation. Give partial credit for correct visual representation, even if math computation is incorrect.
- Allow students who do not know their math facts to use math fact matrixes or calculators.
- Allow for time extensions.

Ideas for Demonstrating Learning for Content Areas:

- Give tests orally and have students respond orally (students can tape-record their responses). (The special education teacher or paraprofessional can often assist in this activity.)
- Allow time extension on tests and projects.
- For projects, help students divide the project into steps and develop a timeline for completing each step.
- Have students use a picture or sequence of pictures to demonstrate understanding of a concept or process.
- Have students develop a skit or pantomime and present it to the class.
- Use word processing and spell checkers.

---

abilities will not automatically use **memory strategies** such as rehearsing information they are learning, categorizing the information to make it easier to learn, using visual imagery to "see" the information mentally, and using acronyms to remember lists. By teaching students with learning disabilities how to organize and associate information, how to use mnemonic devices and key words, and how to use rehearsal strategies, you can help them remember information, whether they are beginning readers developing an automatic sight vocabulary or high school students studying for a science test. Take, for example, the use of acronyms to remember lists of information.

The sentence, "Kings play cards on fine green sofas," can help students remember the biological classification system:

> Kingdom
> Phylum
> Class Order
> Family Genus
> Species

It is important not only to teach students memory strategies, but also to *cue students to use their memory strategies when they work on a task.* (For more information about teaching memory strategies, see the appendix, "Making a Difference through Action Learning: Teaching Study Skills, Learning Strategies and Self-Advocacy." This chapter's 60-Second Lesson describes a fun way to have students develop acronyms.

Teach Self-Regulation and Self-Monitoring By having students keep track of how well they are understanding or performing, they can gain incentives for learning and change their learning patterns to more effective ones. Research suggests that students with learning disabilities are not as adept as their peers at monitoring their own performance (e.g., Bos & Filip, 1984; Harris et al., 1994, Wong, 1991). One way to help students with learning disabilities is to teach them to ask themselves questions about their learning and performance. General questions that students can ask themselves include the following:

- What is my purpose for learning or doing this?
- What is my plan for doing this task?
- Does what I am learning, reading, or doing make sense?
- What do I already know about this topic?
- How am I doing with my work?
- What are the main points I am learning?
- How can I use this elsewhere?

The use of **self-recording** and graphing has been shown to be effective for students with learning and attentional problems (e.g., Martin & Manno, 1995; Rooney et al., 1984; Trammel et al., 1994). Teaching students to self-monitor assignment completion, using an assignment sheet

such as the one in Figure 5.4, has been shown to be effective in increasing assignment completion (Trammel et al., 1994).

Following are several important aspects to consider:

- Students should record when assignments are due, then mark not only for assignment completion but also for turning in the assignment.
- General education teachers can initial the assignment sheet, thereby providing an easy means of communicating to the special education teacher and parents. The special education teacher can review and discuss the assignment sheet and the assignments with the student.
- Students should set goals to increase their assignment completion, rewarding themselves when they reach their goals.

Provide Opportunities for Extended Practice and Application Students with learning disabilities need extended practice and additional opportunities to apply their learning, to ensure continued mastery (Bos & Vaughn, 1994; Kameenui & Simmons, 1990). To create these opportunities when other students in the class may not benefit from them, teachers must be adept at instructional management.

Margaret Duran, a fifth grade teacher, comments on the way she organizes her classroom to promote opportunities for extended practice and maintenance of skills and strategies,

MAKING A DIFFERENCE

The 60-Second Lesson

Teaching Students to Develop Acronyms

One activity that students of all ages seem to enjoy and profit from is learning to develop and memorize acronyms for lists of information that must be learned. When you teach a list to students, have them form

cooperative groups, with each group working on developing an acronym to help them remember the list. Then each group can report on its acronym.

FIGURE 5.4

Assignment Sheet for Monitoring Assignment Completion

X = Completed and Turned In
I = Incomplete/Not Turned In
O = No Assignment

Name _____

1	2	3	4	5	6
Mon.					
	X I O	X I O	X I O	X I O	X I O
Tues.					
	X I O	X I O	X I O	X I O	X I O
Wed.					
	X I O	X I O	X I O	X I O	X I O
Thurs.					
	X I O	X I O	X I O	X I O	X I O
Fri.					
	X I O	X I O	X I O	X I O	X I O

Reprinted with permission from: Trammel, D. L., Schloss, P. J. & Alper, S. (1994). Using self-recording, evaluating, and graphing to increase completion of homework assignments. *Journal of Learning Disabilities, 27,* 75–81.

One of the most difficult aspects of teaching is juggling the grouping of students and scheduling of activities to assure that students who need more time to learn have that opportunity available. I find that using readers' and writers' workshops have allowed me the flexibility I need. Within these workshops I embed lessons that focus on different skills and strategies. I select the skills/strategies based on students' needs, and we usually work on those skills/strategies for one to three weeks. I usually teach nine 10-to-15-minute lessons a week so that I focus on three skills/strategies at the same time. The students who are most academically at risk usually work on two of the three skills/strategies. This allows the students who need the most guidance to receive regular small-group instruction and to work consistently on a specific skill or strategy. In their writing folders, there is a list of these skills/strategies and space to record when we worked on them and for the student and me to judge mastery level. When I do individual conferences with the students, we review the skill/strategy list, update the records, monitor progress, and set goals. I find that for students with learning disabilities or who are academically at risk, I have more individual conferences to monitor progress, and we do more maintenance checks to see that the students are continuing to use the skills/strategy effectively in their writing.

As for materials, the fourth and fifth grade teachers have been working on these lessons for several years and regularly add lessons and materials for each lesson, particularly materials for extended practice.

Use Learning Tools and Aids

With the new technology and its increasing availability, more students with reading, writing, and math disabilities are able to overcome their academic problems through the use of technologically based learning tools (Lewis, 1993). The best known tool is the computer, with its peripherals and programs. Students with handwriting and spelling disabilities have been helped by word processors and their built-in spell checkers. Through speech synthesizers and such software as *Talking Text Writer,* students with reading and writing difficulties have had the opportunity to hear what they write and then to read along with the computer. More and more children's literature is available on CD-ROM, an increasingly available medium that allows readers to hear as well as read the text, to have words and pictures in the text explained, and to have words provided in another language. Drill and practice programs for math facts, such as *Math Blasters Plus,* have provided many students with the opportunity to review and practice their math facts in an interac-

> Whether learning skills or strategies, students with learning disabilities have difficulty transferring or applying these skills and strategies to other learning situations (Borkowski, & Turner, 1990; Wong, 1994).

tive game format. See Tech Talk on page 147 for more information about **computer-assisted instruction** (CAI).

Although computers and multimedia learning environments can play an important role in assisting students with learning disabilities to reach academic success, limited access to hardware and software, classroom constraints, lack of professional development in technology, and unavailability of special education technology specialists will continue to serve as barriers to making full access a reality (Okolo et al., 1993). Other learning tools recommended for students with learning disabilities include calculators, spell checkers, and tape recorders.

Adjust Work Load and Time

Adjustments of work load and time allocations can be useful accommodations for students with learning disabilities. Adjustments to the work load can include both the amount of work given and the manner in which it is given. Reducing the amount of work may be a very reasonable accommodation when the goal of an assignment or test is for the student to demonstrate mastery (and it can be demonstrated with less work). For example, if the purpose of a math assignment is to demonstrate mastery in using addition and subtraction with regrouping to solve verbal math problems, then completing the odd-numbered problems rather than all the problems may provide adequate evidence of mastery. This type of accommodation is reasonable for students who are slow in math computation because their knowledge of math facts is not at an automatic level. Another accommodation—providing time extensions for tests or completion of large projects—has been helpful to students with learning disabilities.

Another way to adjust work is to divide it into smaller sections or tasks. Having students work on groups of five problems at a time rather than the complete set of twenty can make a task more manageable for the student and give the teacher additional opportunities to provide feedback and encouragement as each five-problem set is completed. Helping students break a complex task, such as reading a book and writing a report, into smaller tasks and develop a timeline for completing each task can also improve successful task completion. As a teacher you will find that many

Computer-Assisted Instruction

Computer-assisted instruction (CAI) involves learning through the use of computers and multimedia systems. In contrast, computer-managed assessment and instruction uses computers and multimedia systems to obtain and manage information about the learner and learning resources so as to prescribe and better individualize instruction for the students.

What does the research have to say about the effectiveness of computer-assisted instruction? Word processing, paired with writing instruction, consistently produces a positive though relatively small impact on students' writing and their attitude toward writing (Bangert-Drowns, 1993; Cochran-Smith, 1991). Critical to the success of word processing for students with learning disabilities, however, is that it be coupled with systematic instruction in writing (MacArthur, 1993).

The research in reading is also encouraging, although at this point most of the research conducted has been on drill and practice word-recognition programs rather than on multimedia computer systems and CD-ROM books (Higgins & Boone, 1993). Computer-assisted instruction in math has also shown promise (for reviews see Mastroprieri et al., 1991; Woodward & Carnine, 1993).

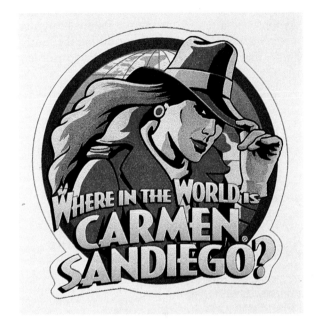

In *Where in the World is Carmen Sandiego?* ® by Broderbund, students explore and learn about dozens of the world's great cities and diverse cultures. School Editions include teacher guides and classroom activities to help teachers provide follow-up activities for the game in which students practice their writing and research skills. Courtesy of Broderbund.

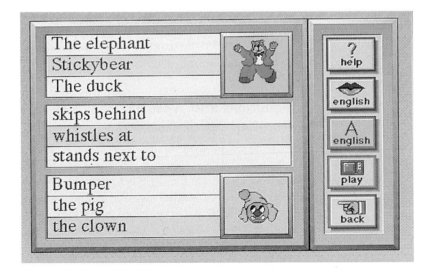

Screen from *Reading Rabbit.* Courtesy of Optimum Resource, Inc.

of the accommodations and teaching ideas suggested in this section will also assist students with attention deficit disorders.

Attention Deficit Disorders

Many students with learning disabilities also demonstrate attention problems. Danny Moreira, a tenth-grade student, found out during the ninth grade that he has an attention deficit disorder (ADD):

> It has been an enormous relief to me, because all of my life I have been called names like "spaced out," "lazy," "hyper," and "daydreamer," yet I always knew that I was doing the best I could and that it was difficult for me to behave any other way. Ever since I was very young I was very intense and had extra energy to work on areas of interest, but I also became easily bored and distracted. I've been reading and talking to my counselor about ADD, and what they say is that people with ADD have a hard time making friends. That has sure been true for me. I get bored with what people are saying. I interrupt. I am also somewhat impulsive so that if I am thinking something I just blurt it out and sometimes I say the wrong thing. I've gotten much better and the friends I have now understand me. I must say, though, that finding out I had an attention deficit really took the weight off of me. I feel like I've had a boulder removed from my shoulders.
>
> School was a disaster for me. Largely because I was so bored and the work all seemed so repetitive and tedious. I've only had one teacher who I felt understood me, Mrs. Golding, my third grade teacher. I'll never forget her. For math, she would tell me I only had to do the problems until I got five in a row right, then I could stop. At recess she would help me get involved in games with other children and insist that I be included.

IDEA does not recognize Attention Deficit Disorder as a separate category of disability. In 1991, the United States Department of Education clarified that students with ADD may be eligible for special education services under IDEA as "Other Health Impaired" or they may be served if they have another disability (e.g., learning disability, serious emotional disturbance).

Students with attention deficit disorder have been identified for well over a century (e.g., Still, 1902), but only recently have we begun to address the educational implications of their disorder in schools. Parent groups such as Children and Adults with Attention Deficit Disorders (CH.A.D.D.) have applied pressure at the local, state, and national levels so that appropriate educational services would be developed for their children (Children and Adults with Attention Deficit Disorders, 1988, 1992). Additionally, teachers and other school personnel, recognizing that students with ADD come to school with behaviors that interfere with their successful learning, are increasingly requesting information that provides instructional guidelines that will help them meet the needs of students with ADD. Linda Wellens, a veteran kindergarten teacher, explains her experiences with ADD this way.

> I know that every year at least one of the students in my class will have serious attention problems. I don't mean the usual behaviors that a five-year-old and six-year-old display. I mean serious problems focusing on what we are doing, controlling themselves, and following directions even after everyone else in the room has caught on to the routines. I can usually tell after the first two weeks of school, but I try everything I can think of to structure the classroom for the child before I mention it to the parents or school counselor. I find that parents are relieved to discover that another adult has confirmed what they know about their child. Most of these parents are totally stressed out having to deal with the problems day and night and are looking for help.

Definitions and Types of Attention Deficit Disorders

Some teachers wonder whether there is such a thing as ADD, or whether parents and children use it as an excuse for their behavior (Reid et al., 1993). Research studies provide compelling evidence that ADD is a true disorder (Barkley, 1990; McBurnett et al., 1993). According to the *Diagnostic and Statistical Manual of Mental Disorders* (DSM-IV) (American Psychiatric Association,

1994), **attention deficit disorder** has two distinct factors: (1) inattention and (2) hyperactivity–impulsivity (McBurnett et al., 1993). Students who display either or both of these characteristics can be identified as having ADD.

Inattention refers to consistent (over six months) and highly inappropriate levels of the following behaviors:

- failing to pay close attention to details, and making careless mistakes that are inconsistent with the child's developmental level
- failing to sustain attention to tasks and/or play activities
- failing to listen, even when spoken to directly
- failing to complete tasks
- having difficulty with organization
- resisting to work on tasks that require sustained attention
- losing materials and objects
- becoming easily distracted
- being forgetful

Students need to display six or more of the above symptoms for a sustained period of time.

Hyperactivity refers to consistent (over six months) and highly inappropriate levels of the following behaviors:

- fidgeting or squirming
- having a difficult time remaining seated during class, even when other students are able to do so
- running or climbing excessively when it is not appropriate
- having difficulty playing quietly
- acting as though he or she is "driven by a motor"
- talking too much

Impulsivity refers to consistent (over six months) and highly inappropriate levels of the following behaviors:

- blurting out answers
- difficulty waiting for their turn
- interrupting others or butting into activities

Students must display six or more of the preceding characteristics to be identified with hyperactivity–impulsivity.

Characteristics of Students with Attention Deficit Disorders

There is general agreement that ADD manifests itself early in a youngster's life. In fact, the precursors to ADD have been identified in infancy (Ross & Ross, 1982). Some early indicators of ADD include poor sleeping and eating habits, difficult temperament, and high levels of activity. By the time youngsters are three years old, approximately 50 percent of those who will later be identified as having ADD demonstrate such behaviors as high levels of activity, behavior problems, and short attention span (Barkley, 1990). Therefore, it is not uncommon that many of the behaviors associated with ADD will be demonstrated by children as early as kindergarten and first grade. The core characteristics of ADD include the following:

- poor sustained attention and vigilance
- impulsive or poor delay of gratification
- hyperactivity or poorly regulated activity
- diminished rule-governed behavior
- increased variability of task performance

The common developmental features that distinguish ADD from mild attention or hyperactive problems follow:

- onset in early childhood
- chronic over time
- generally pervasive across situations
- deviant from age-based standards
- increased co-morbidity with other learning and psychiatric disorders

Typically, teachers notice that these students are restless, inattentive, and have a difficult time with routines. These observations are often confirmed by parents. Tips for Teachers 5.4 describes what teachers and parents can do to explain ADD to others.

Individuals with ADD do get better as they get older, but more than half of them continue to complain of impulsivity, inattention, low self-esteem, and restlessness as adults (Hechtman et al., 1980). See Table 5.2 for a description of the characteristics of ADD in adolescents.

Perhaps one of the most distinctive characteristics of ADD is the likelihood that it will co-occur with another disability, such as learning disabilities or conduct disorders. Many students with

TIPS FOR TEACHERS

5.4 Ten Tips for Parents and Teachers for Explaining ADD to Children and Others

- *Tell the truth.* This is the central, guiding principle. First, educate yourself about ADD, then put what you have learned into your own words, words the child can understand. Don't just hand the child a book or send the child off to some professional for an explanation. Explain it to yourself, after you have learned about it, then explain it to the child. Be straightforward and honest and clear.

- *Use an accurate vocabulary.* Don't make up words that have no meaning, or use inaccurate words. The child will carry the explanation you give him or her wherever he or she goes.

- The *metaphor of nearsightedness is useful* in explaining ADD to children. It is accurate and emotionally neutral.

- *Answer questions.* Ask for questions. Remember, children often have questions you cannot answer. Don't be afraid to say you don't know. Then go find the answer. Books by professionals who deal with ADD are good sources of information; see for example, Paul Wender's *Hyperactive Children, Adolescents, and Adults,* and Russell Barkley's *Attention Deficit Hyperactivity Disorder.*

- *Be sure to tell the child what ADD is not.* ADD is not stupidity, retardation, defectiveness, badness, and so on.

- *Give examples of positive role models.* Use role models either from history, such as Thomas Edison, or from personal experience, such as a family member (mom or dad).

- *If possible, let others know the child has ADD.* Let others in the classroom know (after discussing this with the child and parents), and let others in the extended family know. Again, the message should be that there is nothing to hide, nothing to be ashamed of.

- *Caution the child not to use ADD as an excuse.* Most kids, once they catch on to what ADD is, go through a phase of trying to use it as an excuse. ADD is an explanation, not an excuse. They still have to take responsibility for what they do.

- *Educate others.* Educate the other parents and children in the classroom, as well as members of the extended family. The single strongest weapon we have to ensure that children get proper treatment is knowledge. Spread the knowledge as far as you can; there is still a great deal of ignorance and misinformation out there about ADD.

TABLE 5.2

Characteristics of Attention Deficit Disorder in Adolescents

Adolescents with attention deficit disorder will manifest many of the following characteristics (Shaywitz & Shaywitz, 1988):

- less active than younger children with ADD
- restlessness
- behavior problems or antisocial conduct
- low self-concept
- inattentiveness
- impulsiveness
- depression
- academic difficulties in school
- problems with relationships
- difficulty maintaining jobs
- difficulty following through on tasks
- problems with drugs/alcohol
- difficulty following directions
- procrastination
- impatience, easily frustrated or bored

What are some signs of hyperactivity and impulsivity in students identified as having attention deficit disorder? What can you do to help students with ADD in your classroom?

Again, however, as in the case of IDEA, the number of students with ADD is not recorded.

Prevalence estimates of students with ADD consistently report higher rates for males than for females. Some reports indicate that the ratio of males to females is 3 to 1, with other studies reporting ratios as high as 6 to 1 (e.g., Rapport, 1994). It is difficult to determine why the rate is so much higher for boys, but there is some reason to believe that ADD may manifest itself differently in girls than in boys and that the identification instruments are based on the behavioral manifestation of ADD in boys. There is evidence that girls with ADD are more likely to be withdrawn (and thus less likely to be identified) than boys with ADD, who are likely to be hyperactive.

ADD (25 to 68 percent of them) are also identified as learning disabled (McKinney et al., 1993; Shaywitz & Shaywitz, 1988). Approximately 30 percent of students with ADD also display conduct disorders (Fowler, 1992). Thus, students with ADD frequently have other behavior or academic difficulties.

Prevalence of Attention Deficit Disorders

A conservative estimate of the number of students with ADD is 3 percent (Schiller & Hauser, 1992). Current best estimates of the prevalence rate of ADD are from 3 percent to 5 percent (Barkley, 1990). As with learning disabilities, the exact number of individuals with ADD is difficult to determine because many children with ADD have not been identified (Rapport, 1994). Furthermore, recording the number of students with ADD is difficult because there is no separate category for ADD under the Individuals with Disabilities Education Act. Students with ADD may be identified as having a health impairment or a secondary condition, when ADD and another disability (e.g., learning or emotional disabilities) overlap. Other students, who do not qualify under IDEA as students with ADD, do qualify under Section 504 of the Vocational Rehabilitation Act (discussed in Chapter 1).

Instructional Guidelines and Accommodations for Students with ADD

Because students with ADD are likely to spend all or most of their school time in general classroom settings (Fowler, 1992), much of their educational program is likely to be the responsibility of the classroom teacher. What are the characteristics of teachers who are effective with students with ADD? According to Lerner and colleagues (Lerner et al., 1995), "in many respects, they are simply good teachers" (p. 96). Lerner and colleagues indicate that the following characteristics help teachers to work successfully with students who have ADD:

- *Positive attitudes toward mainstreaming and inclusion of students with ADD.* These attitudes are reflected in the way teachers accept students and promote students' acceptance by the classroom community.
- *Ability to collaborate as a member of an interdisciplinary team.* Teachers who have students with ADD in their classrooms have an opportunity to work with other

professionals and family members who will be monitoring the students' academic and behavioral progress, response to medication, and self-esteem.

■ *Knowledge of behavior-management procedures.* Most students with ADD in your classroom will demonstrate difficulty following directions, remembering routines, attending to task, and organizing themselves and their work. Behavior-management skills are essential to adequately meet the needs of students with ADD.

■ *Personal characteristics.* To teach students with ADD, you need understanding, compassion, patience, concern, respect, responsiveness, and a sense of humor.

In addition to the preceding characteristics, educational and medication-related interventions can also be helpful in your work with students with ADD.

Educational Interventions As indicated in Chapter 2, teachers should begin any educational intervention with planning. Maria Nahmias has served as a consultant to parents and teachers on how to effectively meet the needs of students with ADD in the classroom. Based on her extensive experience she recommends that teachers consider the following key points when planning **educational interventions** for students with ADD (Nahmias, 1995):

■ *Use novelty in instruction and directions.* Highlight important instructions and key points with colored pens, highlight markers, or flair-tip pens. Bold key information or underline it. Use "oral cuing" to identify key words or ideas in the directions.

■ *Maintain a schedule.* As indicated earlier, students with ADD have a difficult time learning rules and routines; thus, it is critical that these be changed as infrequently as possible. Change is difficult for students to adjust to and often promotes behavior problems. Post rules and schedules in the room and on index cards on the students' desks.

■ *Provide organizational assistance.* Provide guidelines for how the students should maintain their desks, materials, and schedules.

Provide opportunities at the beginning of each week for students to organize and then reward them for doing so. Ask students to keep a notebook for each of their classes and to write their assignments and due dates in the notebook.

■ *Provide rewards consistently and often.* All students like to receive positive feedback about their performance and behavior; however, the frequency, intensity, and consistency of rewards needs to be increased for students with ADD. Whenever possible, involve the student in selecting the rewards.

■ *Be brief and clear.* Think about instructions before stating them, and provide them as briefly and in as well organized a way as possible. Present the critical information in chunks so that it is more easily understood and remembered. Keep instructional lessons brief to maintain students' attention.

■ *Arrange the environment to facilitate attention.* Consider where the student is sitting. Are there other students who might promote good behavior and organizational skills? Are you able to quickly and easily maintain eye contact as well as physical contact with the student? Be sure to consider how to minimize distractions.

Planning lessons for students with ADD within the context of planning for the class as a whole is a challenge. The primary focus of planning should be on what accommodations are needed to make the lesson effective for all students, including a student with ADD. Figure 5.5 names the types of problems frequently manifested by students with ADD, and provides potential solutions. Figure 5.6 provides a sample lesson plan with supports identified for a student with ADD.

A problem frequently noted by parents and teachers of students with ADD is homework. These students have a difficult time recording assignments, knowing when they are due, and establishing an organizational sequence that enables them to complete the task on time. For this reason, homework record sheets are often developed and implemented by teachers and then monitored by parents. Figure 5.7 provides an example of a daily assignment log.

| | FIGURE 5.5 | |

Educational Interventions

PROBLEM	SOLUTION
Listening	Provide visual displays (flowcharts, pictorials, wheels); prereading questions/terms at end of chapter; assigned reading; keyword note-taking system to expand memory jogs during daily review; advance note-taking organizers from subtitles in textbook.
Distractibility	Minimize visual distractors in the environment; don't have interesting activities going on in one corner of the room while expecting the student to do his or her seatwork.
Attention Span	Have student work in short units of time with controlled activity breaks (i.e., reading break or magazine break); activities need to be interspersed throughout instruction.
Short-Term Memory	Offer review systems in a flashcard style so frequent practice can be done independently; material may need to be reviewed frequently.
Task Completion	Present work in short units (i.e., five problems on paper cut into quarters rather than on one sheet); timeframes should be short, with clear deadlines and checkpoints to measure progress; have a model available so product can be examined if directions can't be retained.
Distractibility	Have as few distractions as possible; provide a "quiet corner" for anyone who wishes a distraction-free place to work.
Impulsivity	Show the student how to do the work; have a checklist for what he needs to do, and have a reward system tied to the completion of all the steps.
Inattention to Detail	Emphasize detail through color coding or isolation.
Test Taking	Have the student review systems on critical detail and main ideas in a flashcard system to support attention and practice specific retrieval.

Reprinted with permission from: Rooney, K. J. (1995). Teaching students with attention disorders. *Intervention in School and Clinic, 30*(4), 221–225. Copyright 1995 by PRO-ED, Inc. Reprinted by permission.

FIGURE 5.6

Lesson Plan for Students with Attention Deficit Disorder

Objective:
Students will understand the difference between an adverb phrase and an adjective phrase.

Methods for Presentation:
Demonstrations, examples, overheads, worksheets, student samples for analysis.

Materials Needed:
Overhead projector, worksheets, examples.

Workplan and Timeframes for Presentation

2:00 PM – 2:05 PM   Review definition of adverb/adjective; have students write definition of each term from memory and then correct them to the book's definition.

2:05 PM – 2:15 PM   Explain and discuss the difference between an adjective phrase and an adverb phrase; demonstrate examples on the overhead.

2:15 PM – 2:25 PM   Have students write an operational rule and share their versions.

2:25 PM – 2:35 PM   Have students produce an example of an adverb phrase and an adjective phrase.

2:35 PM – 2:40 PM   Explain and demonstrate assignment.

Supports for Attention:
Frequent shifts in activities.
Activities interspersed with instruction.
Demonstration as well as oral presentation.

Review System:
Record of instruction will be written in a bound notebook. Study card (homework) will be produced for the grammar review system.

Demonstration of Knowledge (Independent Use):
Homework. Study card from the grammar book section (pp. 54–56). The card will include the topic, the rule or instruction, and an example of each. Examples corrected in class, and errors highlighted and corrected on the card.

FIGURE 5.7

Daily Assignment Log

Name _____

Date _____

Materials	Subject	Class Assignment	Done	Homework	Done
□Y □N			□Y □N		□Y □N
□Y □N			□Y □N		□Y □N
□Y □N			□Y □N		□Y □N
□Y □N			□Y □N		□Y □N
□Y □N			□Y □N		□Y □N
Totals Y__ N__			Totals Y__ N__		Totals Y__ N__

Reprinted with permission from: Kemp, K., Fister, S., & McLaughlin, P. J. (1995). Academic strategies for children with ADD. *Intervention in School and Clinic, 30*(4), 203–210. Copyright 1995 by PRO-ED, Inc. Reprinted by permission.

The following guidelines will help reduce the trauma often associated with homework for students with ADD.

■ *Unfinished classwork remains in class.* This helps students to differentiate between classwork and homework. If unfinished classwork becomes homework (as an "add on" to the already assigned homework), students can easily become overwhelmed.

■ *Identify the minimum amount to demonstrate learning.* Understanding and mastering the task is more important than completing an extensive amount of work. Consider shortening the task for these students. It is better that they do a small amount well than a lot of work poorly.

■ *Provide timelines for tasks associated with long-term assignments.* Rather than telling students the date a long-term assignment is due, help them problem solve a timeline for completing the key components of the assignment. Pair them with a buddy or work cooperatively with parents to ensure that each component in the timeline is completed.

Although no one educational treatment package has been demonstrated to yield successful outcomes for students with ADD (Fiore et al., 1993), the best treatment procedures to date are those that involve a range of instructional supports and accommodations.

Effects of Stimulant Medications Students with ADD are frequently identified by a team that includes a physician. The physician often recommends that these students be provided **stimulant medications** to assist in the treatment of their disorder. This decision can be a tumultuous one for parents who, unsure about the outcomes associated with medical treatment, fear negative side effects. Parents need to be informed as to how to recognize possible side effects so that, should they occur, they can inform the physician. Linda Wellens, a kindergarten teacher comments,

> This year I had a student, Alex, who was identified as hyperactive–impulsive. His mother called me frequently to check on how he was doing in school. He had been kicked out of three preschools before he even started kindergarten, and she was worried about how he

would perform. Alex just couldn't sit still. He would try to stay in his seat and then would jump up and start playing with toys or building with blocks. He just seemed to need a frequent release. He was a handful, but I managed to set up a behavior modification program that was highly effective. One of the things that helped the most is that his parents, his physician, and the psychologist agreed that he would benefit from medication. Then we worked as a team to monitor his reaction and progress.

Several medications can help alleviate many of the symptoms of ADD. The medication works like a pair of eyeglasses, helping the individual to focus. It can also reduce the sense of inner turmoil and anxiety that is so common with ADD. Stimulant medication works by adjusting a chemical imbalance that affects the neurotransmitters in the parts of the brain that regulate attention, impulse control and mood (Hallowell & Ratey, 1994). Swanson and colleagues (Swanson et al., 1993) have completed a comprehensive review of the effect of stimulant medication on children with ADD. Table 5.3 provides a summary of the treatment outcomes you should expect when youngsters with ADD are provided stimulant medication.

The one thing all professionals agree on about treatment of ADD with medication is that it should always be considered as one component of an overall treatment plan (Accardo et al., 1991; Barkley, 1990; Goldstein & Goldstein, 1990; Swanson et

---

TABLE 5.3

Treatment of Children with Attention Deficit Disorder with Stimulant Medication

What You Should Expect:	
▪ improved ability to modulate motor behavior and overactivity	▪ possible side effects such as facial tics, loss of appetite, difficulty sleeping, and psychological effects on cognition and attribution
▪ increased concentration or effort on tasks	▪ no significant improvement of academic skills
▪ improved self-regulation and reduced impulsivity	▪ no significant improvement of athletic or game skills
▪ increased compliance and effort	▪ no significant improvement of positive social skills
▪ decreased physical and verbal aggression	▪ no long-term improvement in academic achievement
▪ decreased negative behaviors during social interactions	▪ no long-term reduction in antisocial behavior or arrest rate
▪ increased amount and accuracy of academic work	

Adapted from Swanson et al. (1993). Effect of stimulant medication on children with attention deficit disorder: A "review of reviews." *Exceptional Children, 60,* 154–162.

al., 1993). As Lerner and colleagues state (Lerner et al., 1995), "Medication should not be considered a 'silver bullet' or the single solution to the problems the student is facing. Rather, medical treatment should be recognized as one part of a total inter-disciplinary management and intervention program" (p. 175). Schools, parents, the physician, and the counselor or psychologist all need to work as a team to develop a coordinated effort to meet the needs of students with ADD.

SUMMARY

- The term "learning disabilities" is used to describe a heterogeneous group of students who, despite adequate cognitive functioning, have difficulty learning, particularly academics.
- Dyslexia, dysgraphia, and dyscalculia are three types of learning disabilities that refer to extreme difficulty learning to read, write, and do mathematics, respectively.
- Students with learning disabilities represent a range of characteristics that include low performance in one or more academic areas, unexpected low performance considering their overall ability, and ineffective or inefficient information processing.
- The number of individuals identified as learning disabled is approximately 5 percent of the school-age population, which accounts for over half of all students identified as having disabilities.
- Because the characteristics of students with learning disabilities are heterogeneous, the types of learning accommodations vary. Accommodations that generally assist students with learning disabilities include: providing a framework for learning, modeling the processes and strategies, presenting information and allowing students to demonstrate learning in multiple ways, teaching students to use memory strategies, teaching self-regulation, providing opportunities for extended practice and application, using learning tools and aids, and adjusting work loads and time requirements.
- Attention deficit disorder (ADD) refers to difficulty in attention and has two factors: inattention and hyperactivity–impulsivity. Students can display one or both of these factors.
- A conservative estimate of the number of students with ADD is 3 percent.
- The core characteristics of ADD are poor sustained attention and vigilance, impulsivity with poor delay of gratification, hyperactivity and poorly regulated activity, diminished rule-governed behavior, and increased variability of task performance.
- Classroom interventions to assist students with ADD include: using novelty in instruction and directions, maintaining a schedule, providing organizational assistance, providing rewards consistently and often, communicating briefly and clearly, and arranging the environment to facilitate attention.

Key Terms and Concepts

advance organizer

attention deficit disorder (ADD)

cognitive strategies

computer-assisted instruction (CAI)

dyscalculia

dysgraphia

dyslexia

educational interventions

hyperactivity

impulsivity

inattention

instructional conversations

memory strategies

self-recording

specific learning disabilities

stimulant medications

Think and Apply

1. Now that you have read Chapter 5, review Tammy's experiences in working with Adrian and Lenny. If you could talk to Tammy and the parents of Adrian and Lenny, what other questions would you ask them? What would you suggest Tammy tell Adrian and Lenny's third grade teachers to help them succeed next year? List any questions or ideas you have now about teaching students with learning disabilities and attention deficit disorder. Discuss your questions and ideas with your fellow students, your instructors, and teachers in the field. Also check the list of questions or concerns you developed from reading Chapter 1, and see whether you can check any of them off your list. Record your answers and file your personal inquiry in your teaching portfolio.

2. Think about several students you know, have taught, or are currently teaching who are not achieving as you would expect. Using the definition of learning disabilities and the exclusionary factors, predict whether their learning difficulties are due to specific learning disabilities or other reasons.

3. Select a lesson in which you are going to teach a new skill or strategy. Think about how you can modify the lesson to provide more opportunities for you and the students to model or demonstrate the skill or strategy, and more opportunities for the students to practice the skill or strategy.

4. Modify a lesson or unit you are going to teach, increasing the number of ways in which students can learn the information or skills, and the number of ways in which they can demonstrate learning. Think about the needs of students with learning disabilities or attention deficit disorders.

5. Write or call the following organizations, request copies of their publications and resources, and keep them in a designated file for use in your classroom with parents or other teachers.

   ■ Attention Deficit Disorder
       Advocacy Group
       8091 South Ireland Way
       Aurora, CO 80016
       (800) 487–2282

   ■ Children and Adults with
       Attention Deficit Disorder
       499 N.W. 70th Avenue, Suite 308
       Plantation, FL 33317
       (305) 587–4599

   ■ A.D.D. Warehouse
       300 Northwest 70th Avenue, Suite 102
       Plantation, FL 33317
       (305) 792–8944
       (800) 233–9273

   ■ Learning Disabilities Association of
       America
       4156 Library Road
       Pittsburgh, PA 15234
       (412) 341–1515

Read More about It

1. Bos, C. S., & Vaughn, S. (1994). *Strategies for teaching students with learning and behavior problems* (3rd ed.). Boston: Allyn & Bacon.

   Provides specific strategies that teachers, school personnel, and parents can use to facilitate the academic and personal growth of students with special needs. Also describes the major theories and approaches to learning.

2. Hallowell, E. M., & Ratey, J. J. (1994). *Driven to distraction: Recognizing and coping with attention deficit disorder from childhood through adulthood.* New York: Touchstone.

   Useful to different audiences, including those who know little about ADD and those who are well informed. Topics addressed include: definition, the child with ADD, the adult with ADD, ADD in couples, ADD and the family, subtypes of ADD, diagnosis, treatment, and biology.

3. Hampshire, S. (1982). *Susan's story: An autobiographical account of my struggle with dyslexia.* New York: St. Martin's Press.

   Provides an interesting account of a young woman's experiences in school and life. Her dyslexia was difficult for her to deal with, and in many cases even more difficult for others.

4. Lerner, J. (1993). *Learning disabilities: Theories diagnosis, and teaching strategies* (6th ed.). Boston: Houghton Mifflin.

   Provides an explanation of learning disabilities, characteristics, assessment, and procedures for effective instruction. Separate chapters address specific content areas such as reading, mathematics, and written language.

5. Lerner, J. W., Lowenthal, B., & Lerner, S. R. (1995). *Attention deficit disorders: Assessment and teaching.* Pacific Grove, CA: Brooks/Cole.

   Provides an overview of ADD from an educational perspective. Topics covered include: definition, ADD and the law, assessment, educational interventions, working with families, medical treatment, and the biological bases of ADD.

6. Moss, P. B. (1990). *P. Buckley Moss: The people's artist.* Waynesboro, VA: Shenandoah Heritage.

   Ms. Moss has become a successful artist and advocate for individuals with learning disabilities. This book conveys her feelings concerning the need to look for the creative strengths many students with learning disabilities hide because of fears related to their difficulties learning in school.

7. Smith, S. (1986). *No easy answers.* Cambridge, MA: Winthrop.

   Sally Smith is a successful woman with learning disabilities who owns a private school for students with learning disabilities. She explains the difficulties of growing up with learning disabilities, and describes some of the strategies used in her school to effectively meet students' educational and social needs.

Teaching Students with Communication Disorders

FOCUS QUESTIONS

1. Communication is a powerful tool. What are communication disorders and in what areas of communication might students have difficulty?

2. Many speech and language skills develop before students enter school. What speech and language skills develop during the school-age years? Think of language skills in terms of content, form, and use.

3. What percentage of students have communication disorders, and how does this percentage change from preschool to elementary school to secondary school?

4. What key signs might make you suspect that a student has a communication problem? With whom would you work to determine whether a student needs further assistance in the area of communication?

5. What techniques could you incorporate into your teaching that would help a student with a language disorder? Are these techniques helpful only for students with language and communication problems?

Interview

Lorrie Perrodin

Lorrie Perrodin is one of five third grade teachers at Drexel Elementary School. This is her first year of teaching. In her class of thirty-one students, one (Samatha) has a communication disorder. She also has two students with learning disabilities, one of whom receives support from both the speech and language pathologist (SLP) and the special education teacher.

Lorrie believes that all children can learn and that her job is to create a learning community that supports this belief. Although she utilizes the district-wide curricula, she is quick to modify, supplement, and augment the curricula to fit her students' needs. For example, she uses the language arts textbook only as a resource for activities to build communication and written language skills. These activities she embeds in thematic units on such typical third grade topics as fantasy and weather.

Samatha, the student with communication disorders, works with the speech and language pathologist, Nancy Meyers, for 30 minutes twice a week. Nancy and Lorrie check in with each other informally about once a week regarding Samatha's progress and what is working. This communication often occurs during lunch or when both teachers are in the teachers' work room.

As Lorrie describes Samatha, it is clear that she understands Samatha's needs and makes accommodations to help her communicate successfully in the classroom. Lorrie notes,

> The way I would describe Samatha is as a late bloomer when it comes to language. Early in the year, Nancy and I sat down with Samatha's file, and we discussed her history and needs. Samatha did not start talking until she was almost three years old, despite the fact that she is an only child. Although she babbled and seemed to be talking to herself when she played as a toddler, she did not use words in her play or to communicate with others. Her mom reported that she did appear to understand what others were saying to her for she responded appropri-

ately. At age 4, Samatha began attending Head Start and was identified as a child with speech and language disabilities. She started working with a speech and language pathologist at that time. She has continued to receive services since then. Both Nancy and I agree that talking is difficult for Samatha. Her sentences are short, and she continues to have difficulty producing complex sentence structures, does not use adjectives and adverbs to elaborate, and has significant difficulty with verb tenses and irregular verbs. Samatha also has a limited vocabulary when she speaks, and I am oftentimes unsure if she is getting the concepts that I am teaching.

I feel that I work to make my class successful for Samatha in several ways. First, I usually don't call on Samatha in large class discussions unless she raises her hand. We have a deal that she can't use this rule to escape listening and learning and that I expect her to contribute to large group discussions at least several times a day. But this way she gets to pick the opportunities. Second, I have a habit of frequently "checking for understanding." During lessons, I regularly ask students if they are understanding. To keep the class active, I have them use thumbs up, stand up, clap hands, etc. to indicate if they understand. I think Samatha and the other students feel comfortable telling me they don't understand, for I encourage and praise them for the questions they ask. Third, I have Samatha take leadership roles that require her to talk when we work in small groups, and I encourage her to help other students when doing independent seat work. Finally, through reading and writing, I can focus on the areas that are difficult for her in oral language. For example, we have been working on using adjectives to make our writing more interesting. Samatha has really improved in this area of writing, and now I am asking the students to take their new descriptive written language and use it more when they talk.

I guess overall, I feel that Samatha is a successful learner in my class, but I would like to know more about communication disorders so I can provide more encouragement and assistance.

Introduction

Lorrie and many other teachers (both elementary and secondary) share these feelings. They learn a lot about teaching reading and writing, but much less about the development of oral communication, the characteristics of students with communication disorders, strategies for identifying these students, and techniques for promoting oral communication and language development in general education classrooms. This chapter focuses on those areas and should provide you with a number of techniques and strategies for working with students who have communication disorders or other disabilities that result in delayed communication development.

Communication Disorders

Communication is a natural part of life, and society places high value on oral communication. Both in school and society, communication is a powerful resource. We use communication to do the following:

- develop and maintain contact and relationships with others
- gain and give information
- control and persuade
- create and imagine
- communicate feelings
- monitor our own behavior when we talk to ourselves

Even though written communication plays a key role in school, speaking and listening are the most frequently used means of learning. Consequently, students with communication disorders may experience difficulties in many aspects of school, including both learning and social situations.

The term **communication disorders** refers to difficulties with the transfer of knowledge, ideas, opinions, and feelings (Oyer et al., 1987). Communication disorders range in severity from mild to profound. They may be developmental or acquired through injuries or diseases that affect the brain. A communication disorder may be the primary disability, or it may be secondary to other disabilities (ASHA, 1993). For example, students with learning disabilities often have secondary language disabilities and receive services from a speech and language pathologist.

When students enter school, they are expected to communicate by listening and speaking. Some students may have difficulty transmitting the message or information. For example, when Sarah entered kindergarten her speech was so difficult to understand that both the teacher and students had to listen to her for several days before they began to figure out what she was trying to communicate. Sarah has difficulty with speech, or the vocal production of language. Jeffrey, on the other hand, has difficulty understanding the message of others and communicating his message to others. His speech (vocal production) is adequate, but the message is unclear. Jeffrey's difficulties lie in the area of language. Language, the major vehicle humans use for communicating, is a "code whereby ideas about the world are represented through a conventional system of arbitrary signals for communication" (Bloom & Lahey, 1978, p. 4). The American Speech–Language–Hearing Association (1993) has divided communication disorders into the three broad categories: speech disorders, language disorders, and hearing disorders. This chapter deals with speech and language disorders, whereas Chapter 9 discusses students with hearing disorders.

> Of students with communication disorders, 53 percent have speech disorders. By far the most typical speech disorders are articulation disorders (47 percent), with voice disorders (4 percent) and fluency disorders (2 percent) far less frequent (Leske, 1981).

Speech Disorders

Individuals have **speech disorders** when their communication is unintelligible, unpleasant, or interferes with communication (Van Riper & Emerick, 1984). The vocal production of language has three components: articulation, fluency, and voice. **Articulation** has to do with the production of speech sounds, **fluency** refers to the flow and rhythm of language, and **voice** focuses on the quality of speech, including resonance, pitch, and intensity.

Articulation Disorders By far, the most common speech disorders, **articulation disorders** occur when students are unable to produce the various sounds and sound combinations of language (Hulit & Howard, 1993). It is not unusual for speech and language pathologists to work with elementary-age children who have a delay in the development of articulation, because the ability to produce the speech sounds continues to develop through age eight. Learning to produce the speech sounds, no matter what the language, usually proceeds in a fairly consistent sequence, but there may be as much as a three-year variance between the time early learners start producing a particular sound and the time late learners start producing the sound. Figure 6.1 demonstrates the developmental progression of speech sounds and clarifies why many children enter school still in the process

of learning to produce such sounds as *r, l, s, ch, sh, z, j, v,* and voiced and voiceless th and zh.

It is also interesting to note that the production of speech sounds generally develops earlier in girls than in boys. Table 6.1 compares the development of girls and boys, noting the age at which 90 percent of the girls and boys can articulate the sounds. If you teach kindergarten through second grade, you will have the opportunity to hear these sounds developing in some of your students. Even if these sounds are not fully developed, children's speech by the time they enter kindergarten should be at least 90 percent intelligible.

The types of articulation disorders are sound substitutions, omission, additions, and distortions. Substitutions and omissions are the most common errors. In *substitutions,* one sound is substituted for another. Common substitutions include /w/ for

---

FIGURE 6.1

Developmental Sequence for the Production of Speech Sounds

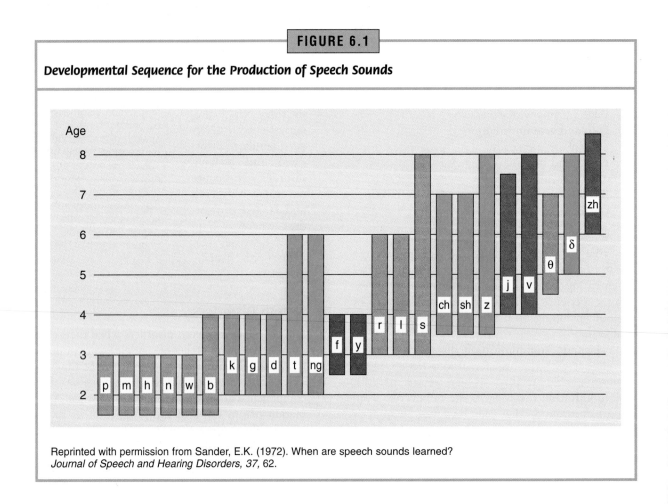

Reprinted with permission from Sander, E.K. (1972). When are speech sounds learned?
Journal of Speech and Hearing Disorders, 37, 62.

TABLE 6.1

Comparison of the Development for Speech Sound Production in Boys and Girls

BOYS

Age	3	4	5	6	7
	p	ng	y	zh	f
	b			wh	l
	m			j	r
	h				ch
	w				sh
	d				s
	n				z
	k				th (voiceless)
	t				v
	g				th (voiced)

GIRLS

Age	3	4	5	6	7
	p	l	j	sh	s
	b	t	y	ch	z
	m			r	th (voiceless)
	w			zh	v
	d		f	f	th (voiced)
	n			wh	
	k				
	g				
	h				
	ng				

*The age at which 90 percent of boys and girls can articulate sounds. *Note:* Vowel sounds are produced correctly by 90 percent of all children by age 3. Consonant blends—tr, bl, pr, and so on—develop between ages 7 and 9.

Reprinted with permission from Work, R.S. (1994). Articulation disorders. In S. Adler & D.A. King, (Eds.), *Oral communication problems in children and adolescents* (p. 3). Boston: Allyn & Bacon.

/r/ (*wabbit* for *rabbit*), /t/ for /c/ (*tat* for *cat*), /b/ for /v/ (*balentine* for *valentine*), and /f/ for /th/ (*free* for *three*). *Omissions* occur when a sound is not included in a word. Because blends are later developing, many omission errors have the second sound in the blend omitted (e.g., *boo* for *blue*, *pity* for *pretty*). Final sounds also are commonly omitted, particularly the later-developing sounds such as /s/, /sh/, /z/, and voiced and voiceless /th/. As a

classroom teacher, it will be important for you to listen for children whose articulation is developmentally delayed or whose articulation errors are so frequent that they significantly affect intelligibility. You will want to talk with the speech and language pathologist about these children.

Articulation is affected not only by development but also by regional dialects and culturally specific uses. For example, Bostonians often use /er/ for /a/ (as in idea/ider and data/dater), and Southerners draw out vowels. **Black Vernacular English** (BVE) is used by some African Americans and reflects the complex racial and economic history of the African American in the United States. The features of BVE are characteristic of the dialect as a whole but vary in individual speakers.

Articulation of English sounds is also affected when English is a second language (ESL). Sounds made in one language may not be made in another language or may not be made in the same manner. As a classroom teacher, it is important for you to remember that differences in articulation due to regional dialects or English as a second language should not be considered disorders. (For more information about BVE and ESL, see Chapter 10, "Teaching Culturally and Linguistically Diverse Students.")

> Variations in speech or language that are used by a group of individuals from a geographic region or from a social or cultural group are not communication disorders. Rather, these variations (e.g., Black Vernacular English and Appalachian English) are dialects.

Fluency Disorders Whereas articulation disorders involve difficulty with the production of the sounds, **fluency disorders** refer to difficulty with the rate and flow of speech. **Stuttering**, the most common fluency disorder, is an interruption of the forward flow of speech (Palmer & Yantis, 1990). All of us are nonfluent to some degree when we communicate. We hesitate in the middle of sentences, break the flow of language with meaningless sounds and fillers

> Boys are four times more likely to stutter than girls.

(e.g., ah, um, you know, like), repeat parts of words, and speak very quickly. We are more nonfluent in stressful, novel, or exciting situations. When we have difficulty thinking of a word, we may stutter.

This normal dysfluency becomes stuttering when the disruptions in speech are accompanied by awareness, anxiety, or compensatory behavior (Cantwell & Baker, 1987). Most young children, at different times during the preschool years, are nonfluent in a manner that resembles stuttering. Four of five children move through these times spontaneously usually by age five (Sheehan & Martyn, 1970), and fewer than 1 percent of school-age children have stuttering problems. Although Sharon Kutok, a speech and language pathologist in Tucson, serves few students at the high school level, several of these students have problems with stuttering.

> Students who have had corrective surgery for a cleft palate may have difficulties with resonance, and often receive speech therapy to learn to control the flow of air.

Voice Disorders Voice disorders relate to the quality of the voice itself. Usually, four dimensions are considered:

- Quality
- Resonance (nasality)
- Pitch (high or low)
- Intensity (loud or soft)

The most typical type of voice disorder found in school-age children is the presence of vocal nodules caused by yelling and other forms of vocal abuse that affect voice quality. Vocal nodules, which develop because the vocal mechanism is used incorrectly or overused, are somewhat like calluses on the vocal folds. If the nodules become too large, students can lose their voices and require surgery. Generally, it takes consistent and prolonged abuse for nodules to develop, but it is important to caution students about "yelling till they are

hoarse" or talking a great deal using "pretend or contrived voices," such as the guttural, hoarse voices that monsters or aliens might make.

Few school-age children have the other types of voice disorders—resonance (e.g., difficulty producing the nasal sounds of /m/, /n/, and /ng/), pitch and intensity. Should you notice students with these difficulties, talk with your speech and language pathologist.

School-Age Language Disorders

Language disorders are the other major area of communication disorders discussed in this chapter. Language functions as an integral part of the communication process because it allows us to represent ideas, using a conventional code. A person's ability to understand what is being communicated is referred to as **comprehension** or **receptive language**, whereas a person's ability to convey the intended message is referred to as **production** or **expressive language**.

Students with language disorders may have developmental delays in comprehension or receptive language. These students frequently ask for information to be repeated or clarified. In school these students may have difficulties with the following processes:

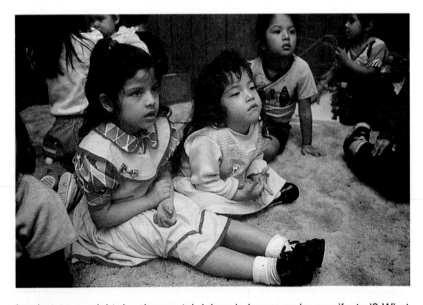

In what ways might developmental delays in language be manifested? What aspects of communication are important in identifying students with possible language-learning disabilities?

- following directions
- understanding the meaning of concepts (particularly technical or abstract concepts)
- seeing relationships among concepts (e.g., temporal, causal, conditional relationships)
- understanding humor and figurative language
- understanding multiple meanings
- understanding less common and irregular verb tenses
- understanding compound and complex sentences
- detecting breakdowns in comprehension

Students with production or expressive language difficulties generally communicate less frequently than their peers. These students may have difficulty doing the following:

- using correct grammar
- using compound and complex sentences
- thinking of the right word to convey the concept (word retrieval or word finding)
- discussing abstract concepts
- changing the communication style to fit different social contexts
- providing enough information to the listener (e.g., starting a conversation with "He took it to the fair," when *He* and *it* have not been previously identified)
- maintaining the topic during a conversation
- repairing communication when the listener doesn't understand

To help us think about language and language disorders, language has been divided into **content** (semantics), **form** (phonology, morphology, and syntax), and **use** (pragmatics) (Bloom & Lahey, 1978). It is the interaction of content, form, and use that creates language.

Language Content

Semantics (content) refers to the ideas or concepts we are communicating, and the relationships among those concepts. When you teach content (as in social studies or science), you are teaching concepts and the labels for those concepts (vocabulary). For example, students often ask for the label for an idea (e.g., "What is that?" or "What are you doing?"), and they ask about what a word

means (e.g., "What is a penguin?" or "What does freedom mean?"). By providing that information, we teach content.

Teaching content focuses on teaching vocabulary, word categories and relationships, multiple meanings, and figurative language. Gloria Huerra, a high school social studies teacher, comments,

> Grouping words by categories and using relationship words (like *if . . . then* and *because*) are often difficult for students with language impairments or second-language learners. It is also the multiple meanings of words and the figurative language that holds up their learning. I consistently highlight these in our discussions of social studies. One way that I highlight them is by writing them on the overhead projector and discussing them prior to reading. Then I cue the students to look for them when they read. We discuss them after reading by finding them in the text and reviewing their use.

Vocabulary As students develop language, their **vocabulary** and their ability to understand and talk about abstract concepts increase quickly. For example, children's speaking vocabulary when they enter school is estimated to be about 2,500 words (Owens, 1995). In comparison, when technical words are discounted, average adult speakers use about 10,000 words in everyday conversation, and an estimated 60,000 to 80,000 words are known and used by the average high school graduate (Carroll, 1964). In comparison, students understand or comprehend even more words. Owens (1995) suggest that at age six, students' comprehension vocabulary is between 20,000 and 24,000 words, increasing (by age 12) to more than 50,000 words. Even in math, vocabulary increases, with second grade vocabulary focusing on such terms as *addition, estimation, subtraction,* and *regrouping* (in comparison to eighth grade terms such as *absolute value, circumference, equation,* and *finite set*). School provides an important opportunity for children to expand their vocabularies.

Word Categories and Word Relationships During school-age years, students' ability to understand and organize abstract concepts increases significantly (Owens, 1995). Students learn to group concepts by abstract features (such as animate and

TABLE 6.2

Semantic Feature Analysis for a Chapter on Fossils

Relationship Chart

Key:
  + = positive relationship
  − = opposite or negative relationship
  o = no relationship
  ? = uncertain

Important Words	Type of Life		Location			Extinct?	
	Plant	*Animal*	*Sea*	*Lakes*	*Land*	*Extinct*	*Not Extinct*
trilobites							
crinoids							
giant cats							
coral							
bryozoans							
guide fossils							
dinosaurs							
fresh water fish							
brachiopods							
small horses							
ferns							
enormous winged bugs							
trees							

inanimate), spatial features, temporal relationships, or by function. For example, in learning about fossils, students learn to simultaneously classify different types of fossils (e.g., trilobites, crinoids, brachiopods) according to plant/animal, extinct/not extinct, and location (e.g., sea, fresh water, or land). By using **semantic feature analysis**, in which the categories or critical features are placed along one axis of a matrix and the specific vocabulary along the other axis, teachers can guide student discussion about the relationships among concepts and then visually represent those relationships (see Table 6.2). Relationships can be noted as positive, negative, or no relationship, or can be rated as to the degree of relationship along a scale. Instructional research shows a substantial increase in the comprehension and learning of students with learning disabilities and language disorders when these kinds of feature analysis are incorporated into the teaching routine (Bos & Anders, 1990; 1992).

Clearly, the ability to understand the relationships among concepts is important to successful learning. Types of relationships include the following categories:

- Comparative (taller than)
- Spatial (above, under)
- Temporal-Sequential (before, first)
- Causal (because, therefore)
- Conditional (if . . . then)
- Conjunctive (and)
- Disjunctive (either . . . or)
- Contrastive (but, although)
- Enabling (so that, in order that)

Teaching relationship vocabulary is important for students' understanding of content subjects such as science, social studies, and math.

Multiple Meanings Students also learn to deal with **multiple meanings** of words during school-age years (Menyuk, 1971). For example, *bank* has several meanings and can function as both a noun and verb:

> Lou sat on the *bank* fishing.
> You can *bank* on him to be there.
> Put your money in the *bank* for now.

Students with communication disorders and other disabilities generally have more limited vocabularies, and their word meanings are generally more concrete and less specific than those of other students (Bishop & Adams, 1992; Gerber, 1993). These students also have greater difficulty understanding multiple meanings and when to apply which meaning.

As Mary Armanti got to know Krista, a student with communication disorders in her third grade class, she discovered that Krista's vocabulary was very limited. During sharing or small-group discussion, Krista used simple words and did not expand on her ideas (compared to the other students). Concerned about Krista's limited vocabulary, Mary worked with the speech and language pathologist to develop some classroom strategies to increase Krista's vocabulary. These

strategies included Mary elaborating on what Krista said, that is, to model for Krista how to use a more complex, rich vocabulary. For example, when Krista volunteered, "The egg hatched," as she watched a bird nest outside the classroom window, Mary elaborated on her statement, "Yes, the bird's egg just hatched. The new bird is so tiny and fuzzy."

Figurative Language Another area of language content, **figurative language**, represents abstract concepts and usually requires an inferential rather than literal interpretation. Figurative language allows students to use language in truly creative ways (Owens, 1995). The primary types of figurative language include:

- *idioms* (It's raining cats and dogs.)
- *metaphors* (She watched him with an eagle eye.)
- *similes* (He ran like a frightened rabbit.)
- *proverbs* (The early bird catches the worm.)

Table 6.3 presents some common American English idioms.

Students with language disorders and other disabilities, and students from other cultures or for whom English is a second language, tend to have difficulty with figurative language. Yet figurative language, particularly idioms, prevail in the classroom. Classroom research shows that teachers use idioms in approximately 11 percent of what they say, and that approximately 6.7 percent of the sentences in third- to eighth-grade reading programs contain idioms (Lazar et al., 1989).

Language Form

Difficulties with the form of language are usually quite noticeable to classroom teachers. Students not only have difficulty pronouncing certain sounds and using prefixes, suffixes, and endings on words, but they also use sentences that have poor word order and grammar. As mentioned earlier, form refers to the structure of the language and includes phonology, morphology, and syntax.

Phonology Phonology focuses on the sounds of language and the rules that determine how those sounds fit together. **Phonemes** are the smallest lin-

TABLE 6.3

Common American English Idioms

Animals
> a bull in a china shop
> as stubborn as a mule
> going to the dogs
> playing possum
> a fly in the ointment
> clinging like a leech
> grinning like a Cheshire cat

Body Parts
> on the tip of my tongue
> raised eyebrows
> turn the other cheek
> put your best foot forward
> turn heads

Clothing
> dressed to kill
> hot under the collar
> wear the pants in the family
> fit like a glove
> strait laced

Colors
> grey area
> once in a blue moon
> tickled pink
> has a yellow streak
> red-letter day
> true blue

Games and Sports
> ace up my sleeve
> cards are stacked against me
> got lost in the shuffle
> keep your head above water
> paddle your own canoe
> ballpark figure
> get to first base
> keep the ball rolling
> on the rebound

Foods
> eat crow
> humble pie
> that takes the cake
> a finger in every pie
> in a jam

Plants
> heard it through the grapevine
> resting on his laurels
> shrinking violet
> no bed of roses
> shaking like a leaf
> withered on the vine

Tools and Work
> bury the hatchet
> has an axe to grind
> hit the nail on the head
> jockey for position
> throw a monkey wrench into it
> doctor the books
> has a screw loose
> hit the roof
> nursing his wounds
> sober as a judge

Vehicles
> fix your wagon
> like ships passing in the night
> on the wagon
> don't rock the boat
> missed the boat
> take a back seat

Weather
> calm before the storm
> haven't the foggiest
> steal her thunder
> come rain or shine
> right as rain
> throw caution to the wind

Reprinted with permission from Owens, Jr., R.E. (1995). *Language disorders: A functional approach to assessment and intervention* (2nd ed., p. 347). Boston: Allyn & Bacon. Compiled from Boatner, Gates, & Makkai (1975); Clark (1990); Gibbs (1987); Gulland & Hinds-Howell (1986); Kirkpatrick & Schwarz (1982); Palmatier & Ray (1989).

guistic units of sound that can signal a meaning difference. In English there are approximately 45 phonemes or speech sounds, classified as either consonants or vowels. (The section on articulation disorders also includes information relevant to the development of phonemes.)

The ability to listen to and produce sounds is important not only for oral language but also for reading and writing (written language). As students learn to decode unknown words while reading, one strategy they use is to "sound out the word." Students who have difficulty generating rhyming words, segmenting words into their individual sounds, or producing individual sounds and then blending them together to make words often have difficulty using the "sound out" strategy. These skills develop in the early elementary years as students experiment with sounds and sound patterns while they learn to read and write. These skills, referred to as **phonological** (or phonemic) **awareness**, pertain to students' ability to understand that words contain sounds and that sounds can be used as linguistic building blocks to construct words (Mann, 1984). This difficulty with phonological awareness has been identified as the most common type of reading disability (Goswami & Bryant, 1990; Mann, 1984; Pennington, 1991; Wagner & Torgesen, 1987). Consequently, the ability to listen and produce sounds plays an important role in the development not only of oral language but also of written language.

> Different languages have different sounds. When sounds are not made in a student's first language, the student does not listen for or discriminate those sounds. One aspect of learning a second language is "retraining the ear" to listen for the sounds unique to that second language.

Morphology Whereas phonology focuses on sounds, **morphology** focuses on the rule system that governs the structure of words and word forms. And as phonemes are the smallest sound units, **morphemes** are the smallest units of language that convey meaning. There are two different kinds of morphemes: *root words*, or words that can stand alone (e.g., cat, run, pretty, small, inside), and *affixes* (prefixes, suffixes, and inflectional endings) that, added to words, change the meaning of the words (e.g., cats, *re*run, small*est*, *trans*form*ation*).

Learning the different affixes and their meanings can help elementary and secondary students to decode words and determine the meaning of words. For example, students who do not recognize or know the meaning of the word *predetermination* can break it into the root word *determine* (to decide), the prefix *pre* (before), and the suffix *tion* (denoting action in a noun). Then the students can decode the word and decide that the meaning of *predetermination* is "a decision made in advance."

Developmentally, inflectional endings are the easiest to learn, followed by suffixes, and then prefixes (Owens, 1995; Rubin, 1988). Although inflectional endings can be taught through conversation, suffixes and prefixes usually require more formal instruction in both oral and written form (Moats & Smith, 1992). The most frequently used prefixes in American English are *un-*, *in-*, *dis-*, and *non-*. You can use the common prefixes, suffixes, and inflectional endings presented in Table 6.4 as a guide for teaching morphology.

Syntax Syntax (sometimes referred to as *grammar*) focuses on the rules that govern the order of words in sentences. During the school-age years, students continue to grow in their ability to use more complex sentence structures (Scott, 1988). Even though most students understand and generate basic sentences by age five (McNeill, 1970), first graders produce sentences that are neither completely grammatical (*He'll might go to jail*) nor reflect the syntactical complexities of the English language. Table 6.5 presents the sequence of development for selected syntactical structures (Wiig & Semel, 1984).

Some of the most difficult structures are complex sentences that express causation (*because*), conditionals (*if ... then*), and enabling relationships (*so that*). Passive sentences (*The boy was chased by the girl*) also are developed later, often not until age seven. Students with language impairments, and second-language learners, are often delayed in the development of syntax. In the case of second-language learners, students may understand complex syntax, particularly if similar syntax is found in their first language, but may be

TABLE 6.4

Common Prefixes, Suffixes, and Inflectional Endings

Derivational		Inflectional
Prefixes	Suffixes	
a- (in, on, into, in a manner)	-able (ability, tendency, likelihood)	-ed (past)
bi- (twice, two)	-al (pertaining to, like, action, process)	-ing (at present)
de- (negative, descent, reversal)	-ance (action, state)	-s (plural)
ex- (out of, from, thoroughly)	-ation (denoting action in a noun)	-s (third person marker)
inter- (reciprocal between, together)	-en (used to form verbs from adjectives)	-'s (possession)
mis- (ill, negative, wrong)	-ence (action, state)	
out- (extra, beyond, not)	-er (used as an agentive ending)	
over- (over)	-est (superlative)	
post- (behind, after)	-ful (full, tending)	
pre- (to, before)	-ible (ability, tendency, likelihood)	
pro- (in favor of)	-ish (belonging to)	
re- (again, backward motion)	-ism (doctrine, state, practice)	
semi- (half)	-ist (one who does something)	
super- (superior)	-ity (used for abstract nouns)	
trans- (across, beyond)	-ive (tendency or connection)	
tri- (three)	-ize (action, policy)	
un- (not, reversal)	-less (without)	
under- (under)	-ly (used to form adverbs)	
	-ment (action, product, means, state)	
	-ness (quality, state)	
	-or (used as an agentive ending)	
	-ous (full of, having, like)	
	-y (inclined to)	

Reprinted with permission from Owens, Jr., R.E. (1995). *Language disorders: A functional approach to assessment and intervention* (2nd ed., p. A–62). Boston: Allyn & Bacon.

uncomfortable producing it, particularly in the classroom.

Regardless of the reason for the delay, one helpful strategy is to listen to the students' language and determine where they are in the developmental sequence. For example, Rebecca Blair, a third grade teacher, noticed that several of her students with language-learning disabilities were not using the past participle during class discussions, on the playground, or during small-group discussions (*has/ have + verb*). She talked with Jean Gleason, the speech and language pathologist, who agreed that this would be a good skill to work on, since all three students were able to use simple past tense. To teach the skill directly, Rebecca worked with the three students as they wrote a language-experience story in which she controlled the use of verb tense by requiring them to use the past participle. The story follows:

> Once upon a time there was a very hungry boy named Jason. Jason decided that he would eat everything he could find in the refrigerator. All day long he has gone to the refrigerator and eaten whatever food he could find. By the end of the day,
>
> Jason has eaten 3 pickles.
> Jason has eaten 5 olives.
> Jason has eaten 8 slices of cheese.
> Jason has eaten 25 grapes.
> . . . .
> Now Jason has a stomach ache.

In discussing the story, Rebecca compared the simple past tense with the past participle and had

TABLE 6.5

Developmental Sequence for Comprehension of Sentence Types

Syntactic Structure	Sentence	By 75%		By 90%
		Age of Comprehension		
Simple imperative	Go!	4-6*	to	6-0 years
Negative imperative	Don't cross!	5-6	to	7-0+ years
Active declarative				
Regular noun and present progressive	The girl is jumping.	3-0	to	3-0 years
Irregular noun and present progressive	The sheep is eating.	6-6	to	7-0 years
Past tense	The man painted the house.	5-6	to	7-0+ years
Past participle	The lion has eaten.	6-0	to	7-0+ years
Future	He will hit the ball.	7-0	to	7-0+ years
Reversible	The car bumps the train.	6-6	to	7-0+ years
Perfective	The man has been cutting trees.	7-0+	to	7-0+ years
Interrogative				
Who ...	Who is by the table?	3-0	to	3-0 years
What ...	What do we eat?	3-6	to	5-0 years
When ...	When do you sleep?	3-6	to	5-6 years
Negation				
Explicit	The girl isn't running.	5-6	to	7-0+ years
Inherent	These two are different.	6-6	to	7-0 + years
Reversible passive	The boy is chased by the dog.	5-6	to	6-0 years
Conjunction				
If ...	If you're the teacher, point to the dog; if not, point to the bear.	7-0+	to	7-0+ years
... then	Look at the third picture; then point to the baby of his animal.	7-0+	to	7-0+ years
neither ... nor	Find the one that is neither the ball nor the table.	7-0+	to	7-0+ years

*4-6 = 4 years, 6 months.

Reprinted with permission of Wiig, E.H., & Semel, E., (1984). *Language assessment and intervention for the learning disabled* (2nd ed.). Columbus, OH: Merrill.

the students think of other instances in which they could use the past participle. Rebecca had the students write other stories with similar formats, and Jean, at the same time, worked on the same skill with the students. Rebecca also gave each student a quick "thumbs up" whenever she heard them use the past participle. Within three months, the past participle became part of their language.

As sentence complexity increases, so does the average length of the sentences. Table 6.6 shows the growth in the number of words per communication unit. From early elementary school to high school, students grow from an average of seven words per communication unit to almost twelve words. During the early elementary grades, students also continue to increase in their ability to

TABLE 6.6

Average Number of Words per Communication Unit

Grade	Average Number of Words per Communication Unit (mean)		
	High Group	Random Group	Low Group
1	7.91	6.88	5.91
2	8.10	7.56	6.65
3	8.38	7.62	7.08
4	9.28	9.00	7.55
5	9.59	8.82	7.90
6	10.32	9.82	8.57
7	11.14	9.75	9.01
8	11.59	10.71	9.52
9	11.73	10.96	9.26
10	12.34	10.68	9.41
11	13.00	11.17	10.18
12	12.84	11.70	10.65

Reprinted by permission of Loban, W. (1976). *Language development: Kindergarten through grade twelve* (p. 27), Res. Report #18. Urbana, IL: National Council of Teachers of English.

use irregular noun plurals (e.g., *mice, sheep, men*) and irregular verbs (see Table 6.7). In students with communication disorders and other disabilities, development of these irregular forms is often delayed by several years (Koziol, 1973).

TABLE 6.7

Development of Irregular Verbs

Age in Years	Irregular Verbs
3-0 to 3-5	Hit, hurt
3-6 to 3-11	Went
4-0 to 4-5	Saw
4-6 to 4-11	Ate, gave
5-0 to 5-5	Broke, fell, found, took
5-6 to 5-11	Came, made, sat, threw
6-0 to 6-5	Bit, cut, drove, fed, flew, ran, wore, wrote
6-6 to 6-11	Blew, read, rode, shot
7-0 to 7-5	Drank
7-6 to 7-11	Drew, dug, hid, rang, slept, swam
8-0 to 8-5	Caught, hung, left, slid
8-6 to 8-11	Built, sent, shook

Adapted from Shipley, K., Maddox, M., & Driver, J. (1991). Children's development of irregular past tense verb forms. *Language, Speech, and Hearing Services in Schools, 22,* 115–122.

Language Use

The area of most important linguistic growth during the school-age years is language use, or pragmatics (Owens, 1995; Reed, 1994). **Pragmatics** refers to the purposes or functions of communication, or how we use language to communicate (Roberts & Crais, 1989). During the school years, students become quite adept in using communication for a variety of functions. During later school years students use language proficiently including figurative language, sarcasm, jokes, and multiple meanings (Schultz, 1974). Students also learn to vary their communication style, or **register,** according to the listener's characteristics and knowledge of the topic. By the age of thirteen, students can switch from peer register to adult register (depending on the person with whom they are talking) and from formal register to an informal register, depending on the setting and circumstances (McKinley & Larson, 1991; Owens, 1988).

Young children use language for such functions as gaining and holding attention, obtaining and giving information, directing and following others, expressing feelings, and role playing (White, 1975). By adolescence, students demonstrate communication competence (Mobbs et al., 1993; Owens, 1995; Wiig & Semel, 1984) in that they are able to do the following:

- express positive and negative feelings and reactions to others
- present, understand, and respond to information in spoken messages about persons, objects, events, or processes that are not immediately visible
- take the conversational partner's perspective
- comprehend the speaker's mood
- comprehend nonverbal communication
- understand and present complex messages
- adapt messages to the needs of others
- use clarification and repair in conversation
- based on prior experience, approach verbal interaction with expectations of what to say and how to say it

- relate a narrative cohesively and sequentially
- communicate a point of view logically
- select different forms of messages according to the age, status, and reactions of listeners
- use sarcasm, humor, and multiple meanings
- make deliberate use of figurative language

Language is used for many different communication activities. One activity that occurs frequently in school and in other settings is conversation.

To determine whether students are having difficulty with the use of language, you can assess their conversational skills. Take a few minutes to think about several students you know or with whom you are currently working. Think about how they use language to communicate in social contexts. Do they vary their communication style depending on the listener? Do they present enough information for the listener to understand the message? If the listener is not understanding, do they take action to clarify what they said? For students who do have difficulty with these areas, working on language use may be an appropriate goal.

Metalinguistics

Students who use **metalinguistics** can think about, analyze, and reflect on language as an object in much the same way one can describe tables or

What competencies in the pragmatics of language do these students probably possess? How does the way children typically use language change as they mature into adolescence?

friends (Wallach & Miller, 1988). Metalinguistics also involves understanding that language is a code for representing sounds, words, and ideas. The Research Brief presents the results of developmental research on metalinguistics.

RESEARCH BRIEF

DEVELOPMENT OF METALINGUISTIC ABILITIES

Young children learn to use language without really understanding how it operates and functions. They use the linguistic rules that govern language, but if you asked them to tell you about or explain the rules, they would have great difficulty. As children mature, however, they become more sophisticated language learners. They develop *metalinguistics* skills, or the ability to talk about and reflect on language as if it were an object. Reed (1994) notes that metalinguistics involves talking about language, seeing it as an entity separate from its function. It is the ability to judge the correctness of language and to correct it. Wallach and Miller (1988) have arranged information on the development of metalinguistic skills to correspond in rough approximation to Piaget's stages of cognitive development (see Table 6.8).

It is evident from this table that during stage two (ages 2 to 6), children develop the metalinguistic skills critical for decoding words (when reading) and for learning to spell (when writing) (Blachman, 1989; Hill & Haynes, 1992; Kamhi 1987; van Kleeck, 1990). These skills include ascertaining word boundaries in spoken and printed sentences, rhyming, making sound substitutions, segmenting words into syllables and sounds, and blending syllables and sounds into words. Research consistently demonstrates the reciprocal relationship between early reading and writing and the development of these metalinguistic skills (e.g., Blachman, 1989; Bradley & Bryant, 1985; Kamhi & Catts, 1989).

As a teacher, you will want to talk about language, how it works, and the rules that govern language. Playing word games such as the ones suggested in the 60-Second Lesson is one way to build this type of language learning into those free moments during the day.

TABLE 6.8

Stages of Children's Metalinguistic Development

Stage One (Ages 1 1/2 to 2):
- Distinguishes print from nonprint
- Knows how to interact with books: right side up, page turning from left to right
- Recognizes some printed symbols, e.g., TV character's name, brand names, signs

Stage Two (Ages 2 to 5 1/2 or 6):
- Ascertains word boundaries in spoken sentences
- Ascertains word boundaries in printed sequences
- Engages in word substitution play
- Plays with the sounds of language
- Begins to talk about language parts and about talking (speech acts)
- Corrects own speech/language to help the listener understand the message (spontaneously or in response to listener request)
- Self-monitors own speech and makes changes to more closely approximate the adult model; phonological first; lexical and semantic speech style last
- Believes that a word is an integral part of the object to which it refers (word realism)
- Able to separate words into syllables
- Inability to consider that one word could have two different meanings

Stage Three (Ages 6 to 10):
- Begins to take listener perspective and use language form to match
- Understands verbal humor involving linguistic ambiguity, e.g., riddles
- Able to resolve ambiguity: lexical first, as in homophones; deep structures next, as in ambiguous phrases ("Will you join me in a bowl of soup?"); phonological or morphemic next (Q: "What do you have if you put three ducks in a box?" A: "A box of quackers.")
- Able to understand that words can have two meanings, one literal and the other nonconventional or idiomatic, e.g., adjectives used to describe personality characteristics such as *hard, sweet, bitter*
- Able to resequence language elements, as in pig Latin
- Able to segment syllables into phonemes
- Finds it difficult to appreciate figurative forms other than idioms

Stage Four (Ages 10+):
- Able to extend language meaning into hypothetical realms, e.g., to understand figurative language such as metaphors, similes, parodies, analogies, etc.
- Able to manipulate various speech styles to fit a variety of contexts and listeners

Reprinted with permission from Wallach, G.P., & Miller, L. (1988). *Language intervention and academic success* (p. 33). San Diego: College Hill.

The 60-Second Lesson

Promoting Language through Word Games

Often teachers find themselves before or just after a transition with several minutes that need to be filled. Playing word games is a great way to fill the time and to promote language and metalinguistic skills. Listed here are several word games you and your students can play. You may want to make lists based on the words you generate from these games and post them for student reference.

For Younger Students

Rhyming Words: Select a word. Use a word from a word family (e.g., *-at, -ight, -an, -end*) to provide lots of opportunities for rhyming. Or have a student select a word. Then have the other students give rhyming words. You may want to write the words so that students can see the similarities between words. If you want students to select the words, put each word on a slip of paper and place them in a container such as a hat or jar, then have students draw words from the container.

Sound Substitutions: Select a word (e.g., hat). (Again—use of word-family words helps.) Say the word and write it on the board. Then ask students what word will be made if the first sound (e.g., /h/) is changed to another sound (e.g., /b/).

Syllables: Have a student select a word and say it. Then repeat the word slowly and have the students clap once for each syllable in the word.

Opposites: Select pairs of simple word opposites (e.g., hot/cold, easy/hard, big/little, happy/sad). Say one word from each pair and have students say the opposite.

For Older Students

Antonyms: Select pairs of word opposites (e.g., cool/warm, hard/soft, cruel/gentle, empty/full, tame/wild). Write one word from the pair on a card and put it in a container. Have student draw a card, say the word, and have other students say or write the opposite word.

Synonyms: Select a word with several synonyms (e.g., eat, pretty, pants, laugh). Say one word and have students name as many synonyms as they can.

Homonyms: Select a word with at least one homonym (e.g., fare, sale, male). Say and spell one word and have students give the homonyms.

Multiple meanings: Select a word that has several meanings, write it on the board, and have students give examples of sentences that use the different meanings of the word (e.g., I have a **run** in my stocking. Let's go for a **run**. In the long **run**, it isn't very important. I have to **run** and pick up a sandwich.)

Suffixes: Select a suffix (e.g., -tion). Discuss its meaning, and then have students provide examples of words that use this suffix (e.g., determination, nomination, participation). Have students also tell what the root word is. (You can play the same game with prefixes.)

Prevalence of Communication Disorders

Approximately 7 to 10 percent of school-age children receive services for communicative disorders, but only 2 to 3 percent of these children have a primary disability of communication disorders (United States Bureau of the Census, 1993). Why is this the case? Many school-age children who receive services from a speech or language pathologist have another disability that is considered the primary disability (e.g., learning disabilities, mental retardation, hearing impairment, severe or multiple disabilities). For example, nearly 50 percent of children with mild retardation have some type of communication disorder (National Institute of Neurological Disorders and Stroke, 1988). Of school-age children with communication disorders, most have difficulties in the areas of language and articulation. In comparison, only 4 percent of students with communication disorders have voice disorders, and only 2 percent have fluency disorders (stuttering) (Leske, 1981). Over 85 percent of the students with communication disorders are mainstreamed into general education classes (United States Department of Education, 1994).

Over 85 percent of students with communication disorders spend most of the school day in general education classes.

Within this population, communication disorders occur three to four times more often in boys than girls (National Advisory Neurological Disorders and Stroke Council, 1990). Recall that speech sounds develop later in boys than girls (refer to Table 6.1). This trend is evident in most aspects of communication, including the development of language, and may be responsible for the higher identification of boys than girls.

A greater percentage of preschool-age children than school-age children are identified with communication disorders as their primary disability (approximately 10 to 15 percent of the population, or 70 percent of preschoolers with disabilities) (ASHA's Committee on Prevention of Speech, Language, and Hearing Problems, 1984; National Institute of Neurological Disorders and Stroke, 1988). Children identified as having communication disorders at the preschool age are often classified as having learning disabilities as they move into elementary school and experience academic difficulties (Mallory & Kerns, 1988).

Evaluation of students for possible language delays or disorders often includes collecting a language sample. Sampling involves tape recording students as they interact, then analyzing the students' utterances for characteristics such as mean length of utterance, types of utterances, vocabulary, topic maintenance, and turn taking.

Identification and Assessment of Students with Communication Disorders

Most students with communication disorders are identified in preschool or during the early elementary grades. If a speech disorder is suspected, it will be important for the student to have a hearing screening and to determine if there is a history of chronic ear infections. One role that general education teachers play is that of observer and listener for students who may have significant difficulty communicating.

Particularly in the elementary grades, the classroom teacher spends more time with the students than any other individual in school.

When Sharon Kutok, a speech and language pathologist, spoke about what teachers should watch, she commented, "Classroom teachers are good at identifying students with language disabilities. When identifying students with receptive language problems, typical teacher comments are, 'When these students are listening to a presentation they look away and don't focus. When I ask a question, they don't seem to know what is going on. I don't know if the students don't understand me or if they can't answer my question.'"

Sharon also talked about teachers' comments about expressive language difficulties, noting that, "Classroom teachers indicate that these students give answers that have no relationship to the question. They use short sentences or just words, and sometimes the words are out of order. Those are the kinds of symptoms that teachers notice when identifying students with language difficulties."

As a classroom teacher, you have the opportunity to observe students using language in the classroom (during both academic and social activities), as well as on the playground, and during other activities such as art, music, and physical education. What should you look for in the area of language? Tips for Teachers 6.1 presents questions you can ask about your students to determine the possibility of difficulties with language. The questions are grouped according to the three areas of language: form, content, and use. If a language delay is evident, then you should consider making a referral to the speech and language pathologist.

If students are second-language learners, or if their first dialects are other than Standard English, consult with a speech and language pathologist and a bilingual education or ESL teacher when observing students for language differences associated with second language/dialect acquisition or possible language difficulties. (See Chapter 10 for additional information.)

TIPS FOR TEACHERS

6.1 Identifying a Student with Possible Language Disorders

Language Form
- Does the student mispronounce sounds or words and omit endings?
- Does the student comprehend and produce types of sentences similar to those of other students in the classroom?
- Is the student's language as elaborate and descriptive as that of other students in the classroom?
- Are the student's comprehension and production of grammatical rules similar to those of other students in the classroom?

Language Content
- Does the student comprehend and produce vocabulary as rich and varied as that of other students in the classroom?
- Does the student comprehend others' ideas and express his or her ideas as effectively as other students in the classroom?
- When talking, does the student have significant difficulty finding the word he or she wants to use (i.e., word-finding difficulties)?

- Does the student comprehend and use figurative language similar to that of other students in the classroom?

Language Use
- Does student use language for different purposes, including: to gain attention, ask for and tell about information, express and respond to feelings, use imagination to understand and tell stories and jokes, express opinions and persuade, and for greetings, introductions, and farewells?
- Does student take turns appropriately in conversations?
- Does student initiate conversations?
- Does student maintain topic during a conversation?
- Does student have more than one style of interacting, depending upon the listener, situation, and topic?
- Does student recognize when the listener is not understanding, and act to clarify communication for the listener?

Instructional Guidelines and Accommodations for Students with Communication Disorders

Most students with communication disorders are educated in general education classrooms. Although these students may work (individually or in small groups) with a speech and language pathologist several times a week for 30 minutes or so, they spend the rest of their school days with the classroom teacher and students. Consequently, students with communication disorders have many more opportunities to develop effective communication in the classroom than in the lim-

ited time spent with the speech and language pathologist. You, the classroom teacher, play a major role in facilitating the development of effective communication for these students.

Speech and language pathologists are one of your best resources for ideas facilitating speech and language development. As more schools adopt inclusion policies, speech and language pathologists are more frequently teaming with classroom teachers. Two major benefits of these teams are that you and the SLP have more opportunities to learn from each other, and students others than those identified as having communication disorders profit from the communication activities (Haynes et al., 1990).

Facilitating Speech Development

Generally, specific remediation of articulation errors, voice disorders, and stuttering is provided by the speech and language pathologist. The major goal of the general education teacher is to provide opportunities for the student to communicate in the classroom using the most natural, nonthreatening situations possible (LaBlance et al., 1994). If students are to generalize what they are learning in therapy, you will also need to work with the SPL to get specific information on the skills students are targeting and to discuss strategies you can use to help them generalize those skills. One such strategy is to develop a personal cueing system for students who have difficulty responding in a large groups. Robert Encino, a seventh grade science teacher, explains how he developed such a system with Kim.

> Kim was a student in my fifth period who stutters. I was aware that she often knew an answer and wanted to share her knowledge, but I was unsure of when she felt confident enough to do so. I met with Kim one day during planning period, and we agreed on a system where she would open her hand, palm-side up on her desk if she wanted to respond. What I found was that this reduced her anxiety, and during the semester her hand was open more and more frequently. Eventually, we discontinued the system because she felt that she didn't need it any longer.

It is also important for students with speech disorders that the classroom be a safe environment in which to practice oral communication. Tips for Teachers 6.2 provides some strategies for helping promote a classroom community that accepts and encourages meaningful student communication.

Some students with physical disabilities and other severe disabilities cannot communicate effectively through speech, gestures, or writing. **Augmentative communication** systems attempt to compensate for, temporarily or permanently, the impairment and disability patterns of individuals with severe expressive and language comprehension disorders (ASHA, 1993). Augmentative communication is a means for students with limited or no speech to join the classroom community. Tech Talk describes different types of augmentative communication.

TIPS FOR TEACHERS

6.2 Creating an Accepting Classroom Community for Students with Speech Disorders

- Create an atmosphere of ease and comfortable pacing. Avoid an atmosphere that creates time pressures and tensions.
- Listen in a calm and thoughtful manner to what students have to say. Allow time for students to finish their thoughts. Don't disregard ideas just because students have difficulty expressing them.
- Do not criticize or point out speech errors. You may, however, demonstrate correct speech by correctly repeating what the students said.
- Classroom rules should not allow for ridicule of students or their speech errors.
- Take care not to place students with speech problems in situations in which their communication difficulties might interfere or are highlighted.

- Allow time for students to respond. Students often need time to get their ideas organized and to plan their communication. Speech may be labored and slow.
- Develop cueing systems in which students can let you know when they are comfortable responding.
- Reading aloud in a slow, easy manner can be a good opportunity for students to practice fluency strategies or new sounds they are learning. Students become more fluent with multiple readings, so the use of repeated reading may be beneficial.
- Avoid competition among students, particularly when it highlights oral communication.

Augmentative Communication

Augmentative communication is used to supplement the communication skills of persons for whom speech is not possible or is unintelligible (Lewis, 1993). There is a long history of the use of alternative means of communicating. Suddath and Susnik (1991) suggest such traditional methods as "multiple choice questions, eye blinks, gestures, sign language, communication boards, communication books, alphabet boards, and even primitive Morse Code Systems" (p. i).

What has changed the type of augmentative communication in the recent past is the availability of the computer and voice synthesizers. One approach focuses on the method the individual uses to make choices—by scanning or by direct selection. Other approaches focus on unaided or low technology devices, such as communication boards, alphabet boards, and communication books. In contrast to low technology devices, high-technology devices require external devices, such as voice output or a speech synthesizer with a large vocabulary, multiple input modes, and a built-in printer. For example, the Liberator by the Prentke Romich Company (800-262-1990) allows for input through direct selection and one of several scanning modes. Output is through a printer, the eight-line LCD display, or a speech synthesizer. Another system, the DeltaTalker, has both prerecorded speech and a speech synthesizer. This communication device also has a menu-type computer touch screen. Pegasus LITE by Words+ (800-869-8521) is a talking screen for Windows and features all the latest developments in high-tech augmentative communication systems.

Lewis (1993) suggests considering the following questions when making decisions about high technology communication devices:

- What type of speech output does the device offer? Is the speech intelligible? Is it appropriate for the student in terms of age and gender?
- Are other types of output provided?
- What input modes are available to the student? Direct selection? Scanning? What physical abilities does the student need to operate the device?
- How are message choices presented to the user? Does the student see letters, words, graphics, or a combination of these?

A child using a low-tech communication board

A high school student using a Liberator communication board with computer and voice synthesizer from Prentke Romich Company. Courtesy of Prentke Romich Company.

- How much vocabulary can be stored in the device? Are there strategies for increasing the quantity of vocabulary? For increasing the user's speech in selecting vocabulary?
- How easy is the device for the student to use in communication situations? Can the student (or a teacher or parent) change or add messages easily?
- Is the device portable and durable enough to withstand daily use?
- Is the communication device compatible with other technologies that the student uses, such as computers and environmental control units?
- What is the cost of the device? (p. 393).

Facilitating Language Development

Opportunities for teaching oral language abound during general education classroom activities—whether they occur in the classroom itself or on the playground, during field trips, or in the lunch room. It is also in these settings that language becomes more natural and purposeful than is the case in the therapy setting.

As a classroom teacher, you are constantly teaching oral language. When you teach students new concepts and vocabulary in content area subjects, you are teaching oral language. When students learn how to give oral reports or retell a story, how to introduce themselves, or how to use irregular verbs, they are developing language skills. What are some general guidelines you can use to facilitate language development in your classroom? Bos and Vaughn (1994) suggest the following guidelines to help shape your instruction:

- Teach language in purposeful contexts.
- Teach comprehension (receptive language) and production (expressive language).
- Use effective teaching strategies when presenting a new concept.
- Help students see the connections or relationships among concepts.
- Use conversation as the major milieu for teaching rather than questions or drill and practice.
- Give students enough time to respond.
- Adjust the pace, chunk information, and check for understanding.
- Use self-talk to explain what you are doing or thinking.
- Use parallel talk to describe what others are doing.
- Use modeling to help students get practice and feedback on a specific language skill.
- Use expansion and elaboration to demonstrate how an idea can be expressed in a more complex or mature manner, and more information provided.
- Use language as an intrinsic motivator.

Specific ideas for using these guidelines are presented in the following section.

Teaching Language in Purposive Contexts

Whether you are teaching students causal relationships such as the effect of heat on water, or how to request information by telephone, it is important to teach language in the context of meaningful activities. It is difficult to imagine teaching someone how to use a screwdriver or a needle and thread without having the tools at hand, demonstrating how to use them, and then letting students practice. The same is true for language. Hence, when you cannot create a "real" situation, use such techniques as simulations and role-play to create authentic learning experiences. Tips for Teachers 6.3 explains how to use barrier games to teach language.

Teaching Comprehension and Production Give students opportunities to develop both their understanding (comprehension) and their ability to express (production) the new structures (form), vocabulary (content), and ways of using language (use) that they are learning. When teaching the vocabulary associated with a new unit, for example, provide students with opportunities not only to listen to explanations but also to discuss their knowledge of the vocabulary and to use the new terms in their discussion and writing. The pause procedure provides these opportunities (Di Vesta & Smith, 1979; Ruhl et al., 1990). Using this procedure, the teacher pauses at logical breaks in the lecture or discussion, and the students discuss what they are learning (with a partner or in a small group) and review their notes.

Presenting New Concepts Critical to new content or concepts is the use of effective teaching strategies. As you may recall from the earlier discussion of vocabulary development, students' knowledge of concepts grows exponentially during the school-age years. By using effective teaching strategies (see Tips for Teachers 6.4), you help students with language impairments and second-language learners to gain the concepts and content necessary for success in content-area classes.

Demonstrating Connections among Concepts One important way we learn about concepts is by understanding the relationships or connections between concepts. If you listen to a conversation in which a new idea is being explained, you'll undoubtedly hear statements such as, "It's like ...," or "You can compare it to ..." or "It's like ... except that ..." or "It's almost the opposite of ...." These phrases all help students understand and see

TIPS FOR TEACHERS

6.3 Using Barrier Games to Promote Language

It is not always possible to create authentic learning environments when you teach language, but we know that the best, quickest way to learn language is when it is purposeful and taught in context. One way to promote purposeful language and to help students build their comprehension and production of descriptive language, particularly locative prepositions, is to use barrier games. These games (frequently used by speech and language pathologists to teach prepositions) can be a great activity for the entire class or used as a filler activity after students complete their work.

The Game: Students work in pairs, with a barrier placed between them so that they cannot see each other's work. The materials usually consist of blocks for building or paper and colors for making a picture. The lead student builds a simple structure or colors a simple design or picture. Then the lead student describes to the second student how to make what he or she has built or drawn. The second student is encouraged to ask questions when the directions are unclear. After the second student has finished his or her project, the barrier is removed, the two projects are compared, and differ-

ences discussed. Then the roles are reversed. Students can keep track of the number of projects they make accurately.

If you use competition, do not have the students in one pair compete against each other. Instead, have one team compete against another team. Also, this should not be a timed task, because the goal is to promote the use of descriptive language.

---

the connections among concepts. Because students with language problems have difficulty making those connections, it is important that you highlight them as you and the students discuss new concepts. For example, when Peggy, a first grade teacher, was introducing the concept of *squirm* because it was important for understanding the book her students were to discuss and read, she asked the students, "What does squirm mean?" "Show me with your body how you can squirm." "What other things can squirm?" "Now that we know what squirm is, what other words mean something similar to squirm?" "Is squirm similar to wiggle?" "What would be the opposite of squirm? If you weren't squirming, you would be ____."

At more advanced levels, when students make comparisons among books written by the same author, when they compare the relationships between addition and multiplication versus subtraction and division, and when they compare the similarities between the Korean and Vietnam Wars, the emphasis is on making connections. These kinds of discussions help students see the relationships among concepts and better understand semantic relationships (such as contrastives, comparatives, causals, conditionals). The use of feature analysis (refer to Table 6.2) and other graphic organizers (see Chapter 16) can help students see the relationships.

Using Conversation As students with language impairments work, think, and play in your classroom, you need to create opportunities for them to engage in conversations with you and with other students. One way to do this is to use dis-

TIPS FOR TEACHERS

6.4 Presenting New Language Concepts or Content

When teaching new language concepts or patterns, keep the following strategies in mind:

- Gear the activities to the students' interests and cognitive level.
- Get the students' attention before engaging in communication activities.
- Bombard the student with the concept or skill frequently throughout the day in a functional manner.
- When speaking, place stress on the target concept or language pattern.
- Pause between phrases or sentences so that the student has time to process the new concept or language pattern.
- Decrease the rate of presentation when first introducing the concept or language pattern.
- When introducing a new concept or language pattern, use familiar, concrete vocabulary and simple sentence patterns (Bloom, Miller, and Hood, 1975; Reed, 1994).
- If possible, present the new concept or language pattern by using more than one input mode (e.g., auditory, visual, kinesthetic). Gestures and facial expressions that are paired with a specific language pattern often assist students in understanding the form. For example, giving a look of puzzlement or wonder when asking a question can serve as a cue to the students.
- Pair written symbols with oral language. For instance, demonstrating morphological endings such as s (plurals) and ed (past tense) can be done in writing. The students can then be cued to listen for what they see.

Reprinted with permission from Bos, C.S., & Vaughn, S. (1994). *Strategies for teaching students with learning and behavior problems* (3rd ed., p. 81). Boston: Allyn & Bacon.

---

cussion groups rather than a question–answer format for reviews of books and current events. Nancy Meyers, the speech and language pathologist who works with Lorrie Perrodin, chose to work in Lorrie's classroom while the literature groups meet. Once a week she joins Samatha's literature group. As she listens and joins in the conversation about the book being discussed, Nancy has the opportunity to model language patterns on which Samatha is working.

At least several times a week, engage students in conversations. (This may take some forethought and effort on your part, for observational research has shown that classroom teachers, in general, are not as responsive to students with language impairments as they are to average and high-achieving students [Pecyna-Rhyner et al., 1990]). Let the students direct the topics of these conversations, which need not be long and, in secondary settings, can be accomplished as students enter the room. Tips for Teachers 6.5 provides more ideas for promoting language through conversations—use these ideas and share them with parents.

Using Wait Time When speech and language pathologist, Sharon Kutok, talks about the most important principles in teaching students with language impairments, the first one she mentions is **wait time**. For some students, waiting is important. Wait time gives students the opportunity to understand what has been said and to construct a response. These students may have particular difficulty with form (e.g., syntax), and need the extra time to think about the form they should use in constructing their response.

Students who have difficulty with content may have difficulty also with **word retrieval** or word finding (German, 1992). A word retrieval problem is like having the word on the tip of your tongue but not being able to think of it. Two examples demonstrate how difficulty with word retrieval can affect the flow of communication. The first conversation (about making an Easter basket) is a dialogue between two third graders—one with typical language and the other with word-retrieval problems (Bos & Vaughn, 1994).

Susan: Are you going to make, uh, make, us . . . one of these things (pointing to the Easter basket on the bookshelf)?

Cori: Oh, you mean an Easter basket?

Susan: Yeh, an Easter basket.

Cori: Sure, I'd like to, but I'm not sure how to do it. Can you help me?

Susan Yeah, first you need some, uh, some, uh . . . the things you cut with, you know. . .

Cori: Scissors.

Susan: Yeah, and some paper and . . . uh, the thing you use to stick things together with.

Cori: Tape?

Susan: No, uh, uh, . . . sticky stuff.

Cori: Oh, well let's get the stuff we need.

Susan: Let's go, to, uh, uh, the shelf, uh, where you get, you know, the stuff to cut with.

Cori: Yeh, the paper, and let's also get the glue.

In the second example, an adolescent explains how to fix a tire:

"Well . . . to fix a tire . . . or your wheel . . . you gotta take the tire off . . . you gotta lift up . . . you jack up the car and use this thing . . . it's square metal wrench . . . to loosen the bolts . . . you know the nuts . . . then you take the wheel off the axes. First you ask the guy at the garage if he will fix the tire. You lock up the car so it won't . . . you put the car in gear so it stays put" (Chappell, 1985, p. 226).

It is clear from these two examples that wait time is important for students with word-retrieval problems. In addition to increasing wait time, strategies that teachers can use during classroom

TIPS FOR TEACHERS

6.5 Promoting Language through Conversations

- Talk about things in which the child is interested.
- Follow the child's lead. Reply to the child's initiations and comments. Share his/her excitement.
- Don't ask too many questions. If you must, use questions such as *how did/do . . .*, *why did/do . . .*, and *what happened . . .* that result in longer explanatory answers.
- Encourage the child to ask questions. Respond openly and honestly. If you don't want to answer a question, say so and explain why. (*I don't think I want to answer that question; it's very personal.*)
- Use a pleasant tone of voice. You need not be a comedian, but you can be light and humorous. Children love it when adults are a little silly.

- Don't be judgmental or make fun of a child's language. If you are overly critical of the child's language or try to catch and correct all errors, he/she will stop talking to you.
- Allow enough time for the child to respond.
- Treat the child with courtesy by not interrupting when he/she is talking.
- Include the child in family and classroom discussions. Encourage participation and listen to his/her ideas.
- Be accepting of the child and of the child's language. Hugs and acceptance can go a long way.
- Provide opportunities for the child to use language and to have that language work for him/her to accomplish his/her goals.

Reprinted with permission from Owens, Jr., R.E. (1995). *Language disorders: A functional approach to assessment and intervention* (2nd ed., p. 416). Boston: Allyn & Bacon.

discussions include:

- using multiple-choice formats so that students need only recognize one word in a group, rather than generate the word
- providing a cue, such as the initial sound or syllable, the category name or function, a synonym or description, or a gesture demonstrating the word
- restating a question so that it requires a yes or no response rather than an open-ended answer (German, 1992)

By teaching students with word-finding problems to categorize words, make visual images of words, learn synonyms, and make word associations (e.g., bread/butter; plane/fly), you can help them recall words, thereby increasing the accuracy and fluency of their expressive language (Gerber, 1993; German, 1992).

Adjusting the Pace Students with language delays and other disabilities, and second-language learners, often have difficulty comprehending what is being said during class, particularly in content-area classes. Teachers need to adjust the pace so that these students have time to process language input. The flow of instruction does not have to suffer, but when you discuss new or difficult concepts or ideas, slow the pace and highlight key ideas by writing them on the board or overhead projector and repeating them.

Reducing the amount of information in each segment is helpful also. For example, Bob Stern, a high school science teacher, used to introduce the terms for a new science chapter by writing them on the board and discussing them as a group when he introduced the chapter. After Bob noticed that his students with language problems listened to the first five words and recorded three of them in their science notebooks, he decided to chunk the words into groups of three to five, introducing them when they were needed.

Checking for understanding is also important for facilitating language development in classroom

> Students with word-retrieval problems may use circumlocutions (talking around the word) when they are having difficulty retrieving a word, as in "It's the thing, you know, the thing you write on" (Owens, 1995).

settings. Teachers generally identify a group of several students by whom to gauge the pace of instruction and the decision as to when to move on. Make sure that your group includes the students with language problems.

Using Self-Talk and Parallel Talk Students, particularly young students with language delays, need to hear language that is connected to activities. In **self-talk**, teachers describe what they are doing or thinking; in **parallel talk**, teachers describe what students are doing or thinking. As you and the students work or play, describe what everyone is doing. Maria Ferraro, a first grade teacher who works in an inner-city school, regularly uses parallel and self-talk when she joins students at the different centers in her classroom.

> When I join a center, I try to sit down and join in the activities rather than asking students questions. My goal is to become part of the group. As I join in the activity, I describe what I am doing and what other students in the group are doing. For example, I might say, 'José is making a clay animal. It's blue and right now he is putting a ferocious snarl on the animal's face. I wonder what kind of animal it is? I think I'll ask José.' In this way, the students get to hear how words can describe what someone is doing, and it focuses the attention on José and the ongoing activities.

Using Modeling Modeling plays an important role in the process of learning language. Whether students are learning a new sentence structure, new vocabulary, or a new function or use for language, modeling is a powerful tool. For example, Sharon Kutok and Armando Rivera, the speech and language pathologist and the eighth grade English teacher at Vail Middle School, decided to improve their students' conversational skills during literature groups. Both Armando and Sharon were concerned about the number of students who did not clarify what they were saying when other students clearly did not understand (but did not request clarification).

To teach clarification skills, Armando and Sharon began discussing clarifying conversations. During their discussion they role-played, first as students who could not effectively clarify what they were saying, then as students who clarified effectively. They exaggerated the examples, and the students seemed to really enjoy their modeling. Next, Armando and Sharon joined the literature groups and continued to model as they participated in discussions. At the end of the period, they asked students to summarize what they had learned, and whether they thought they could become more effective at clarifying what they said and asking others to clarify if they did not understand. During the next two weeks, Armando had the students in each literature group rate the group's effectiveness in clarification. When Sharon returned in two weeks, both teachers observed a difference in the students' discussions, particularly in their ability to clarify ideas and ask for clarification. The students also thought that their skills had improved. In discussing the change, both teachers and students agreed that the modeling Armando and Sharon had done on the first day was an important key to their learning. Peer modeling, discussed in Chapter 2, can also be a powerful tool.

Promoting Language through Expansion and Elaboration Language **expansion** is a technique used to facilitate the development of complex language form and content. By repeating what students say, but in a slightly more complex manner, the teacher demonstrates how their thoughts can be more fully expressed. For example, Susie Lee, a first grade teacher, is working to get Rob to use adverbs to describe his actions. As he finished several math problems, Rob reported, "I got the first one easy. The second one was hard." Susie replied, "Oh, you got the first one *easily*. The second one was hard." Note that you do not want to imply that you are correcting the student, but simply showing him or her a more complex way of expressing the thought. Note also that you should expand only one of two elements at a time. Otherwise, the expansion will be too complex for the student to profit from it.

You can use language **elaboration** to build upon the content of the student's language and provide additional information on the topic. For example, Chris, a fourth grade student with language disabilities, was explaining that snakes have rough skin. Teacher Peggy Anderson elaborated on Chris's idea by commenting, "Yes, and snakes have smooth skin on their bellies and so do lizards. Are there other animals in the desert that have smooth skin on their bellies?"

Using Language as an Intrinsic Motivator

Language, a powerful enabling tool, carries a great deal of intrinsic motivation for students. Rather than using praise (e.g., "I like the way you said that" or "Good talking"), you can capitalize on the naturally reinforcing nature of language. During a cooking activity, for example, teacher Jon Warner asked students, "How can we figure out how much two-thirds of a cup plus three-fourths of a cup of flour is?" After Lydia explained, Jon said, "Now we know how to figure that out. Shall we give it a try?" Later, Jon asked how to sift flour. After Randa explained, Jon said, "I've got it, how about the rest of you? Do you think you can sift the flour just the way Randa explained to us?" Instead of commenting on how "good" their language was and disrupting the flow of communication, Jon complimented Lydia and Randa by letting them know how useful the information was.

When students' purposes and intents are fulfilled because of their language, their language is naturally reinforcing, and students learn that language is a powerful tool for controlling the environment (Bos & Vaughn, 1994; Owens, 1995; Reed, 1994).

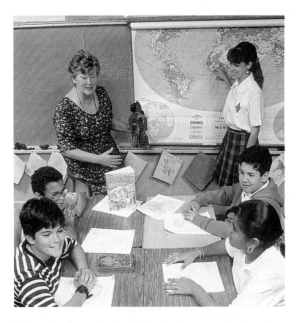

These students are working in a cooperative learning group. Which instructional accommodations described in this chapter might the teacher use for her students who have communication difficulties?

SUMMARY

- Communication is a powerful tool in school and society. For example, we communicate to develop and maintain relationships, to gain and give information, to express feelings, and to control others and the environment.
- Communication disorders include speech and language disorders. Speech disorders involve difficulties with articulation, fluency, and voice. Language disorders involve difficulties with content (semantics), form (phonology, morphology, and syntax), and use (pragmatics).
- Language can be divided into comprehension (receptive language) and production (expressive language).
- Although most basic language skills develop before children enter school, language continues to evolve through the school-age years, a process that includes a large growth in vocabulary, more complex sentence structures, use of prefixes, suffixes, multiple meanings, figurative language, complex semantic relationships (e.g., causal, conditions, enabling), and more sophisticated uses of language (e.g.,

adjustments to the register of communication, use of sarcasm and humor).
- Approximately 7 to 10 percent of school-age children are identified as having communication disorders, but only 2 to 3 percent have communication disorders as their primary disability. Approximately 10 to 15 percent of the preschool population is identified as having communication disorders.
- An important role classroom teachers play is to identify students who may have speech and language impairments.
- For students with speech disorders, the classroom teacher's role is to create a nonthreatening environment in which students can communicate.
- Classroom teachers play an important role in facilitating the development of language. The classroom is an ideal setting to use such language techniques as self and parallel talk, expansion and elaboration, modeling, and conversations. It is also important to adjust the pace and wait time.

Key Terms and Concepts

articulation disorders
augmentative communication
Black Vernacular English
communication disorders
comprehension
content
elaboration
expansion
figurative language
fluency disorders

form
language disorders
language use
metalinguistics
morphemes
parallel talk
phonemes
phonological awareness
pragmatics

production
register
semantics
speech disorders
stuttering
syntax
voice disorders
wait time
word retrieval

Think and Apply

1. Now that you have read Chapter 6, review Lorrie's experiences in working with Samatha. If you could talk to Lorrie, what other questions would you ask her? List any questions or concerns you have now about teaching students with communication disorders. Discuss your questions with your fellow students, your instructor, and a speech and language pathologist. Also, check the list of questions or concerns you developed from reading Chapter 1 to see whether you can check any of them off your list. Record you answers and file your personal inquiry in your teaching portfolio.

2. What are the major components of oral language? Listen to a conversation between two students and think about how the components function and interact.

3. Listen to students as they move from one school setting to another (e.g., classroom, playground, lunchroom). Determine how their use of language and its formality varies.

4. Interview a speech and language pathologist. Get information about the number and type of students served, typical ages, type of speech or language problems, ideas for classroom teachers.

Read More about It

1. Haynes, W. O., Moran, M. J., Pindzola, R. H. (1990). *Communication disorders in the classroom.* Dubuque, IA: Kendall/Hunt.

   Provides information about the normal development of communication, and different communication disorders. For each type of disorder, strategies for assessing and facilitating development in the classroom are provided.

2. Langdon, H. with Cheng, L. L. (1992). *Hispanic children and adults with communication disorders: Assessment and intervention.* Gaithersburg, MD: Aspen.

   Provides important information about speech and language assessment and intervention with Hispanic children whose first language is Spanish. Also provides information about the acquisition and development of English as a second language in Spanish speakers.

3. Owens, Jr., R. E. (1995). *Language Disorders: A functional approach to assessment and intervention* (2nd ed.). Boston: Allyn & Bacon.

   Provides a comprehensive look at language disorders and presents a model for assessment and teaching that stresses the use of functional environments, conversations as the instructional milieu, and meaningful contexts. Also provides information about second-language and second-dialect learners.

4. Reed, V. A. (1994). *An introduction to children with language disorders* (2nd ed.). New York: Macmillan.

   Reviews normal language development and includes a chapter about the language of students with different types of disabilities (e.g., mental retardation, autism, learning disabilities, deaf/hard of hearing). Also includes information on language assessment and intervention.

5. Shames, G. H., Wiig, E. H., & Secord, W. A. (Eds.) (1994). *Human communication disorders* (4th ed.). New York: Merrill/Macmillan.

   Provides a comprehensive introduction to the field of communication disorders, discusses language differences and disorders, and the communication disorders of special populations.

6. Wiig, E. H., & Semel, E. (1984). *Language assessment and intervention for the learning disabled.* Columbus, OH: Merrill.

   Provides many ideas for facilitating the development of semantics, morphology, syntax, and pragmatics, as well as an overview of several language curriculums.

Teaching Students with Emotional and Behavioral Disorders

FOCUS QUESTIONS

1. What information can teachers use to decide whether a student has emotional or behavioral problems?

2. Many students may exhibit emotional and behavioral problems occasionally, but what percentage of the students in your class would you expect to have emotional and behavioral disorders? What types of problems would you expect them to have?

3. Classification of students with emotional and behavioral problems can be viewed from what two broad categories, and which subtypes?

4. How should classroom teachers decide whether a student's behavior is problematic enough to warrant referral to special education or other specialized services?

5. What characteristics of the teacher–student relationship enhance positive outcomes for students with emotional and behavioral problems?

6. What types of instructional practices are likely to facilitate the learning and social development of students with emotional and behavioral problems?

Interview

Juline Truesdell

Juline Truesdell has been a primary teacher for five years, during which time she has worked with many students who were identified as emotionally and behaviorally disordered. We interviewed her about one of her students who was identified as "seriously emotionally disturbed" as a preschooler.

My greatest challenge as a teacher was a student named Lenox, who was identified as seriously emotionally disturbed and placed in my classroom for part of the school day. Lenox was in my class during his first grade year. The first day of school he ran into my classroom swinging his lunch box, bumping into other students on his approach to me. When no more than four inches from me he looked up and shouted, "Are you my teacher?"

The first two months of school were difficult for both of us. Lenox was very rebellious and aggressive and he had a very hard time controlling himself. He wanted the other children to like him but he threw tantrums when they did not give him his way, and so many of the children were afraid of him. I worked very hard with him so that he could sit with one of the groups of children during the day, but I found I often had to separate him from other students. He often sat at a desk by himself, away from the other children. I know he didn't like that because he continued to say to me, "Why can't I sit with my group?" I always told him why he was separated but he seemed to forget seconds later. He just didn't seem to be able to control himself and when he sat with the other students he would call them bad names and hit them and interfere with their work. The other students would complain and say that they didn't want him to be in their group.

Once in a while he would have a good day and he would get a smiley face on his report to take home and I could tell that made a difference. But then the next day he would come in and have a terrible day. It was very difficult to predict his behavior. Then I decided to try something new. Lenox really liked me, and so I set up a program with him where he would get a point for each of the five periods in the day. If he got all five points, I would spend five minutes with him at the end of the day. Sometimes we would talk, color together, play games or read a book, but it would be time just for the two of us. If he got five points for four days in a row, I would bring lunch for him and the two of us would eat together alone in the room. The program made a big difference in how Lenox behaved. He started to work better with other students and he reduced considerably the amount of hitting and fighting. He was able to work with his group most of the day. I can truly say I hated to see him leave at the end of the year. I loved this child. I always have. He gave me so many problems and such a hard time, but there was something about him I'll never forget.

Introduction

The relationships established between classroom teachers and their students with emotional and behavioral disorders, like that of Juline and her student Lenox, are often among the more meaningful relationships experienced by both. Sharon Andreaci, a sixth grade teacher, describes a student with emotional problems who was mainstreamed into her classroom part-time and spent the rest of the day in the special education resource room.

> Diana was her name, and you could just tell by looking into her eyes that something was wrong. She had been raped by a member of her family, and she never seemed to recover. She would see spirits and think evil things were coming to get her. She would say very strange things to me and to other students in the class. I felt that the support she got that year from me and the [other] students ... really helped her feel better accepted. I have followed her in school, and checked to see how she is doing. Now she is in a regular ninth grade class and is participating in counseling.

General education teachers indicate that the students they feel are the most difficult to mainstream into their classrooms are students who demonstrate serious emotional and behavioral disorders (Schumm & Vaughn, 1992). Even special education teachers find students with serious emotional and behavioral problems to be a challenge. As Mark Stitz, a sixth grade teacher, indicates, "Teaching the content that I am interested in is the fun part. Meeting the needs of students with behavior problems is the work." Teaching students with emotional and behavioral disorders is indeed a challenge, but for teachers who understand and implement the types of instructional adaptations necessary to meet these students' educational needs, the results can be very satisfying. And as experienced teachers have reported, the positive impact their efforts have on their students' lives can greatly reward teachers, and stay with them forever.

Although some students with emotional or behavioral disorders receive at least part of their educational program in self-contained special education classrooms or in specialized settings (e.g., alternative schools for students with specific problems, hospital settings), approximately 50 percent of students identified as having emotional or behavioral disorders spend part or all of their school day in general education classrooms (Knitzer et al., 1990). Therefore, general education teachers must be knowledgeable in the techniques and skills necessary to work with these students.

Definitions of Emotional and Behavioral Disorders

What does it mean to be emotionally disturbed? What types of behaviors would you expect to see? As with many other disabilities, there is no clear line between those who have disabilities and those who do not. Often the question is decided by how severe the problem is, and how persistent. As a teacher, you will come in contact with students who display a range of emotional and behavioral problems.

The National Mental Health Association's National Mental Health and Special Education Coalition Workgroup on Definition (Forness & Knitzer, 1992) uses the descriptor **emotional or behavioral disorders** for students whose behavior falls considerably outside the norm. The federal government uses the term *serious emotional disturbance* in its criteria for placement of students in special education. The federal definition of serious emotional disturbance is provided in Figure 7.1.

It is not the responsibility of general education teachers to determine whether a student qualifies as seriously emotionally disturbed, but teachers do have the responsibility of referring students for possible special education placement (by requesting evaluation of students who present significant emotional or behavioral problems in their classrooms). The federal definition of serious emotional disturbance can help you determine whether the behaviors of a student warrant referral.

> Although the terms *behaviorally disordered* and *serious emotional disturbance* are often used to mean the same thing, a movement exists to emphasize the term "behaviorally disordered," which professionals believe is the less stigmatizing label. Nevertheless, the Individuals with Disabilities Education Act still uses the term "serious emotional disturbance."

FIGURE 7.1

The Federal Definition of Serious Emotional Disturbance

The federal government defines seriously emotionally disturbed as follows:

(i) The term means a condition exhibiting one or more of the following characteristics over a long period of time and to a marked degree, which adversely affects educational performance including:

   (A) An inability to learn which cannot be explained by intellectual, sensory, or health factors;

   (B) An inability to build or maintain satisfactory interpersonal relationships with peers and teachers;

   (C) Inappropriate types of behavior or feelings under normal circumstances;

   (D) A general pervasive mood of unhappiness or depression; or

   (E) A tendency to develop physical symptoms or fears associated with personal or school problems.

(ii) The term includes children who are schizophrenic. The term does not include children who are socially maladjusted, unless it is determined that they are seriously emotionally disturbed.

The Individuals with Disabilities Education Act: 25C.F.R.

Prevalence of Students with Emotional or Behavioral Disorders

Higher prevalence rates are reported for mild emotional or behavioral disorders, and lower prevalence rates for more severe disorders. Prevalence varies, depending on the criteria used. Estimates for emotional and behavioral disorders range from 0.5 percent to 20 percent or more of the school-age population (Kauffman, 1993). Recent reports indicate a general prevalence rate of 3 percent to 6 percent of the student population (Achenbach & Edelbrock, 1981; Brandenburg et al., 1990). Approximately 0.8 percent of students receive special education services because of emotional disturbance (U.S. Department of Education, 1990). Thus, students with emotional or behavioral disorders are regarded as underserved.

The National Mental Health Association (1986) summarized the following issues as reasons for the *underidentification* of students with emotional and behavioral disorders:

- Social stigma is associated with the label "seriously emotionally disturbed."
- Eligibility for categorization as emotionally disordered is not clearly explained.
- There is a lack of uniformity in the identification process.
- A lack of funding may limit school districts' willingness to identify these students.
- There is often a lack of appropriate services when students are identified.

Although few professionals disagree that students with emotional and behavioral disorders are underidentified, there is less certainty as to why so many of the students identified are males. Males consistently outnumber females in all prevalence reports for serious emotional disturbance (Quay

In the first few years following the implementation of IDEA, McLaughlin and Owings (1992) found that rural school districts identified fewer students with learning disabilities and emotional disturbance than did more populated areas. The authors suggest that this lower identification rate is the result of social, cultural, and economic factors.

& Werry, 1986; Rosenberg et al., 1992). Particularly in specialized programs for students with emotional and behavioral disorders, males outnumber females by as much as 8 to 1.

Types and Characteristics of Emotional or Behavioral Disorders

Think about classrooms you have observed or taught in. Which students got your attention first—those who were quiet and withdrawn, or those who were acting out and disturbing others? Not surprisingly, students who demonstrate such **externalizing behaviors** as aggression, hitting, and shouting are much more likely to come to the teacher's attention and therefore to be identified as behavior-disordered than are students who exhibit more **internalizing behaviors**, such as shyness, withdrawal, or depression.

Emotional and behavioral disorders can be classified broadly as externalizing or internalizing. Students who exhibit externalizing behaviors (e.g., conduct disorders, acting out, aggression, tantrums, and bizarre behaviors) tend to interfere with others. Conversely, students who exhibit internalizing behaviors (e.g., fear, immaturity, tenseness, withdrawal, worry) tend to be more harmful to themselves than to others.

Considering the behaviors of students as either externalizing or internalizing can be useful for classroom teachers. First, it helps you become aware that students with internalizing problems also need help, even though they do not call attention to themselves in the same way as those with externalizing problems do. Second, being able to identify the type of behavior problem gives you a basic idea of what to do.

Quay and colleagues (Quay & Peterson, 1987; Quay & Werry, 1986) have identified the major subtypes of externalizing

and internalizing emotional and behavioral disorders that teachers are likely to encounter. These subtypes include: conduct disorder, motor excess and attention problems, socialized-aggression, pervasive developmental disorder, immaturity, and anxiety–withdrawal. During your career as a teacher, you will have students who display a range of these behaviors, some mild and some severe. Understanding these categories will help you not only to more accurately describe your students' behavior to professionals, but also to respond appropriately to your students. One classification system frequently used by counselors, psychologists, and physicians is described next.

The *Diagnostic and Statistical Manual of Mental Disorders* (DSM) classification system is based on the reference book of the same name, published by the American Psychiatric Association. Currently in its fourth edition, the book is commonly referred to as the *DSM-IV*. Its purpose is to provide a uniform nomenclature from which clinicians and researchers may discuss, research, diagnose, and treat mental disorders.

The book describes specific criteria necessary for the diagnosis of each disorder, as well as symptoms, indicators of severity, and any variations of the disorder.

What internalizing behaviors might signal the possible presence of emotional or behavioral disorders? How are externalizing behaviors different?

Symptoms affected by culture, age, sex, or other variables are discussed, along with the prevalence and progression of the disorder. Each disorder is given a code (usually four or five numbers).

Counselors, psychologists, psychiatrists, and medical doctors who have had extensive training in diagnostic procedures generally use the DSM-IV. Although teachers need not be fluent in its content, familiarity with its use can facilitate communication with school counselors, psychologists, and doctors who may use DSM-IV disorder classification titles, symptoms, and codes.

A copy of the DSM-IV should be available from the school counselor or psychologist, or a local library or bookstore.

It is important to remember that the DSM-IV is an independent classification system. The disorders delineated and their characteristics may be different from those in other classification systems, although some overlap can be expected.

Conduct Disorders

Behaviors associated with **conduct disorder** include hitting, fighting, throwing, temper tantrums, teasing, acting defiant or disobedient, being irritable or overactive, difficult to get along with, uncooperative, inconsiderate, resistive, jealous, quarrelsome, distractable, irresponsible, and inattentive. Some students with conduct disorders provoke peers into hitting them or others. Students with conduct disorders who are defiant often resist direction from adults. When teachers call home to describe a student's lack of compliance, they often find frustrated parents who feel their child is not as responsive to them as they would like.

Not surprisingly, teachers have no difficulty recognizing students who display conduct disorders. Their aggressive, interfering behaviors are probably the greatest source of frustration for classroom teachers. Identifying students with extreme conduct disorders may be easy, but developing successful strategies for managing them can be difficult.

Students with mild-to-moderate conduct disorders can be handled in the general education classroom by effective behavior-management strategies and cooperation with the school counselor, psychologist, and parents. Students with more extreme conduct disorders are challenging to

all adults and may be removed from the classroom for all or part of the school day for special education. More than 50 percent of students with conduct disorders continue to demonstrate difficulties as adults and often have adjustment problems throughout their lifetimes (Kazdin, 1993). Although their intelligence is often well within the normal range (Sattler, 1988), students with conduct disorders often display low academic achievement (Gold & Mann, 1972; Vaughn et al., 1992). Research on conduct disorders is ongoing.

RESEARCH BRIEF

DEVELOPMENTAL PATHWAYS TO CONDUCT DISORDERS

Loeber and colleagues (1993) conducted a long-term study of the **developmental pathways** associated with conduct disorder. Some students follow one pathway, others follow more than one. Those who follow multiple pathways are most at risk. The pathways (covert, overt, and disobedience) and related behaviors follow:

Covert behavior: stealing, lying, burglary, use of drugs and alcohol

Overt behavior: aggression, coercion, bullying, manipulation of others, escalated interactions with teachers, parents, and peers

Disobedience: noncompliance, oppositional–defiant behavior, resistance to adult influence

Motor Excess

Although most parents of two-year-olds perceive **motor excess** as a perfect descriptor of their child, the term refers to the restless, overactive behavior (also referred to as *hyperactivity*) displayed by some students. These students cannot sit still for long periods of time, even when they are doing something they enjoy. Described as acting as though they were driven by a motor, they tend to be tense, unable to relax, and overtalkative. Note that motor excess does *not* refer to students who have difficulty remaining quiet all day or who seem restless in their seats. As a teacher you will find that many students dislike sitting still and remaining quiet. Wise teachers build into the day brief, structured transition times during which students can move around and visit with their classmates.

Socialized-Aggression

Few people have not engaged in some type of antisocial behavior at some point in their lives (Bullis & Walker, 1994). The term **socialized-aggression** is used to refer to students who routinely engage in antisocial behavior. Adults describe them as hanging around with the wrong kinds of kids, displaying behaviors that are not typical of others in their age-group, harassing others, and stealing and damaging property. School behaviors that get these students into trouble include truancy and cutting classes. Socialized-aggression is also associated with **group behavior**; that is, behaviors are displayed in the presence of other group members. Parents and teachers often worry that they have little influence over the behavior of students loyal to delinquent friends. Students with socialized-aggression often belong to gangs. Students' attraction to gang life is apparent in many inner cities as well as in suburban and rural areas (Jankowski, 1991; Morales, 1992). Law enforcement agencies categorize **gangs** into the following four groups:

- *delinquent* youth gangs that are loosely structured and recognize each other by the way they dress and look
- *turf-based* gangs—also loosely structured, but committed to defending a reputation or neighborhood
- *crime-oriented,* or drug gangs—engage in robbery, burglary, or sale of controlled substances for monetary gain
- *violent* hate gangs whose members commit assaults or hate crimes against specific types of people

Students may be attracted to gangs through a desire for companionship, acceptance, and success. Many such students feel that they have not been accepted by traditional society (Goldstein & Huff, 1993).

A high rate of overlap exists among conduct disorders, attention problems, and socialized-aggression. For example, many students who have attention problems might also display behaviors associated with conduct disorders, such as aggression and acting out.

RESEARCH BRIEF

FIVE TYPES OF AGGRESSION

Lancelotta and Vaughn (1989) examined five subtypes of aggression. In *provoked physical aggression,* one student hits or taunts another, who retaliates. In *unprovoked physical aggression,* a student acts aggressively with no apparent prompting. In *verbal aggression,* one student screams, yells, or uses other verbal expression to attack another. In *outburst aggression,* a student "blows up." In the last type of aggression, *indirect aggression,* a student does something sneaky or tricky to get back at another student. Neither boys nor girls like students who use indirect aggression. Both sexes are the most tolerant about provoked aggression, but girls are less tolerant of all types of aggression than are boys. All subtypes of aggression were related to low social acceptance by classmates except provoked physical aggression. Teachers' ratings were closer to boys' ratings of peer acceptance than to similar ratings by girls.

Pervasive Developmental Disorder

Pervasive developmental disorder can be classified as either externalizing or internalizing, depending upon the type(s) of behavior manifested. Students who exhibit behaviors characterized as **pervasive developmental disorder** express farfetched, unusual, or unbelievable ideas. These students may say strange things to the teacher (e.g., "The blue dog is in the hallway and it is going to get me when I leave.") and may also exhibit repetitive speech, and unusual behaviors such as excessive rocking, nail biting, or head knocking. Students with this disorder may relate to others (including family members) as if they were inanimate objects rather than people. Students may also ignore or resist signs of affection and love and fail to interact with or adapt to others. You are unlikely to have students identified with pervasive developmental disorders in your classroom.

Immaturity

Behaviors associated with **immaturity** include lack of perseverance, failure to finish tasks, short attention span, poor concentration, and frequent day dreaming or preoccupation. Students might stare into space excessively; appear absentminded, inattentive, or drowsy; and seem clumsy or poorly coordinated.

Immature students often come to the attention of teachers because they show little interest in schoolwork and need prodding to participate. Teachers might feel frustrated at the amount of effort necessary to keep these students interested and involved.

These students often seem overly dependent on parents or caretakers and have difficulty being responsible members of a group (whether the classroom or the family). Students with severe immaturity often have difficulty interacting with other people, using social skills, and playing with children their own age. They may frequently retreat into fantasy and develop fears that are out of proportion to the circumstances.

> The categories of emotional and behavioral disorders described in this chapter are cultural constructs and may be regarded differently in different cultural settings. Teachers need to consider the cultural and ethnic background of students and how their behavior would be interpreted in light of that background. Students from diverse cultural backgrounds need to be assessed carefully, with consideration of their community and environment (Rogoff & Morelli, 1989).

Depression

Many students with emotional and behavioral disorders are also prone to depression (Klein & Last, 1989; Kovacs et al., 1988). Mental health workers and educators have realized only recently that depression is a widespread, serious problem among children and adolescents (Forness, 1988). Whereas depression is more prevalent in adult women than men, school-age boys are as likely as girls to exhibit depression (e.g., Lefkowitz & Tesiny, 1985; Lobovits & Handal, 1985).

Teachers often have difficulty identifying students who are depressed (Sarcco & Graves, 1985). The following behaviors may indicate depression:

- acting sad, lonely, and apathetic
- exhibiting low self-esteem
- displaying avoidance behaviors (particularly, avoiding social experiences)
- having chronic complaints about eating, sleeping, and elimination
- refusing or fearing going to school or other public places
- talking of suicide

Anxiety–Withdrawal

The term **anxiety–withdrawal** includes two highly related major behaviors. *Anxiety* refers to extreme worry, fearfulness, and concern (even when little reason for those feelings exists). Simple reassurance is rarely effective. *Withdrawal* describes the typical behavior of students who are anxious or depressed; they frequently withdraw from others and appear seclusive, preferring solitary activities. Withdrawn students are often timid or bashful around others, even people they know, thinking of themselves (and described by others) as loners with few friends, if any. Often preferring to work alone, in class these students may avoid group work, volunteering, or answering questions. Teachers and parents often attribute such behavior to low self-confidence and poor self-concepts.

As you can see from the preceding descriptions, students with behavior disorders display a wide range of characteristics. Perhaps the most consistent characteristic of these students is their inability to maintain satisfying relationships with others (e.g., Kauffman, 1993; Walker et al., 1995).

Causes of Emotional and Behavioral Disorders

Although the rate of sexual abuse among individuals with disabilities is unknown, 62 percent of the 13- to 18-year-old females with emotional disorders in one study were sexually abused before the age of 16 (Brooks, 1985).

Despite a general understanding that the emotional and behavioral disorders of students do not reflect directly on parents, teachers still wonder where the behaviors come from. On the basis of the research we currently have, our best understanding is that emotional and behavioral disorders result from both environmental and genetic factors, and that in some cases one set of factors plays a greater role than the other. For example, a student exposed to family violence may be more likely to display violent behaviors (Jacobs, 1994; Sanson et al., 1993), but some students who are mentally ill may have heritable explanations for their symptoms (e.g., Lombroso et al., 1994; McGuffin et al., 1994).

Whether emotional or behavioral disorders have social or organic causes, they are treated with three groups of medications: stimulants, antidepressants, and antipsychotics.

Stimulants target the central nervous system and are believed to help the brain release certain chemicals that make it possible to focus on particular stimuli rather than be overwhelmed by all present at a given moment. Thus, stimulants increase attention and reduce impulsive and intrusive behavior. Examples of stimulants include Cylert, Ritalin, Dexedrine, and Benzedrine. Some of the possible side effects caused by stimulants include a loss of appetite, insomnia, growth retardation, muscle tics, depression, and nervousness.

Antidepressants are often used in the treatment of depression, anxiety disorders, bed wetting, compulsive and obsessive behavior, stomachaches, anxiety attacks, and muscle tics. Antidepressants have a sedative effect; they reduce mood swings and levels of stress, making tasks seem less overwhelming. Examples of antidepressants include Elavil, Tofranil, and Prozac. Some of the possible side effects of antidepressants include nausea, dry mouth, loss of appetite, insomnia, and seizures.

Antipsychotics are tranquilizers used in the treatment of severe cases of behavioral disorders. These drugs reduce delusions and hallucinations, severe anxiety, depression, and hyperactivity. Examples of antipsychotics include Haldol, Thorazine, Mellaril, Navane, and Stelazine. Possible side effects of antipsychotics include listlessness, passiveness, impaired cognitive performance, dry mouth, increase in appetite, weight gain, enuresis, and motor difficulties.

Although not included in the preceding classifications, lithium is another commonly used medication in the treatment of emotional and behavioral disorders. Lithium is used in the treatment of severe mood disorders, such as manic-depression. Some of the possible side effects include nausea, excessive need to urinate, thirst, tremors, dizziness, diarrhea, vomiting, abdominal pain, shaking, exhaustion, and distorted or slurred speech.

Identification and Assessment of Students with Emotional and Behavioral Disorders

How are students with emotional and behavioral disorders identified? Some students with severe disorders are recognized by parents and other adults before they start attending school. These students may receive early treatment through a combination of educational interventions, medications, play therapy, and family counseling. Other students have emotional and behavioral disorders that remain latent until students are older or that become apparent in structured settings such as the school. Older students may not have received specialized services outside the school setting.

How should classroom teachers decide whether a student's behavior is problematic enough to warrant referral to special education or other specialized services? The following criteria provide indications of disturbance and the likelihood for referral (e.g., Clarizio & McCoy, 1983; Morgan & Reinhart, 1991):

■ *Behavior–Age discrepancy:* The social and behavioral problems exhibited must be unusual or deviant for the student's age. For example, clinging to adults is common in very young children but is deemed inappropriate for school-age children.

- *Frequency of occurrence of the behavior:* Under stress, all people exhibit characteristics of emotional or behavioral disorders, such as whining, withdrawal, mood swings, or depression. These behaviors and feeling states are not considered problems if they occur only occasionally.

- *Number of symptoms:* Display of one or more behavior problems at some time does not indicate that a person has an emotional or behavioral disorder, but students who frequently display several related symptoms should be considered for referral. The greater the number of symptoms, the greater the likelihood of a serious emotional disturbance.

- *Inner suffering:* Signs of inner suffering include low self-esteem, less interaction with others, appearance of sadness or loneliness, and general malaise. Inner suffering interferes with learning, social relationships, and achievement.

- *Persistence of the behavior:* Persistence refers to the continuation of the emotional or behavioral problems over time, despite substantive efforts on the part of adults and the student to change the behaviors. A behavior problem is persistent when several types of interventions have not resulted in long-term change.

- *Self-Satisfaction:* Students who appear to be generally happy with themselves reflect a measure of self-satisfaction. They show positive affect, and the willingness to give and receive affection and pleasure. A lack of self-satisfaction contributes to problems that interfere with personal growth and development as well as academic and social success but that may not signal the presence of an emotional or behavioral disorder.

- *Severity and duration of the behavior:* All dimensions of a student's behavior can be

Self-stimulation—repetitive sensory stimulation, such as twirling, patting, flapping, staring at lights, and swishing saliva—is common behavior in students with severe emotional disturbance.

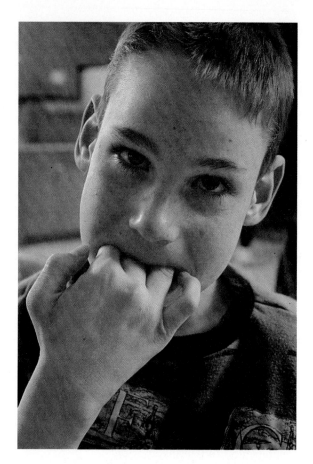

What criteria would you use to determine whether this student's behavior warrants referral for evaluation for the presence of an emotional or behavioral disorder?

classified in terms of two important criteria: severity and duration. *Severity* refers to how extreme the problem is and the extent to which it varies from expected behavior. *Duration* (or persistence) refers to the length of time the problem has occurred. A problem that persists over a long period of time is said to be *chronic*. Most students who are identified as having emotional or behavioral disorders must deal with their problems throughout their lifetimes.

When identifying a student with possible emotional or behavioral disorders, ask the following questions:

- How often does the behavior occur? How long has the problem persisted?

TIPS FOR TEACHERS

7.1 Making Referrals for Students with Emotional or Behavioral Disorders

- Keep a journal that includes the dates, times, and contexts of student behaviors that you regard as deviant or bizarre.
- Be specific, using behavioral terms to describe what occurs. As much as possible, avoid including value judgments. For example, a journal entry might read, "Mark got up from his seat, pushed John out of his chair, and then ran around the room flapping his arms."
- Record any relevant information from parents, such as their descriptions of the student's behavior

at home or telephone calls concerning the student. Keep parents informed of the problem, both in writing and by telephone.
- Also record relevant information from other teachers or school personnel who know the student.
- Keep samples of the student's work in different subjects, and a record of skills the student can and cannot perform. If student's academic performance is inconsistent, note this as well.

- Under what conditions does the behavior occur? To what extent does this behavior occur in different settings, such as the classroom, playground, or home?
- What are the *antecedents* of the behavior; that is, what events occur before the behavior is exhibited, triggering the behavior? What are the *consequences,* that is, what occurs as an outcome of the behavior?
- Does the problem not arise in certain situations?
- To what extent does the student develop and maintain positive relationships with other people? Does the student seem happy or display satisfaction at any time?
- How severe is the problem? To what extent is the behavior deviant from that of other students of the same age?
- To what extent is this a problem in the relationship between you and the student, or a problem in the student?

Tips for Teachers 7.1 offers suggestions for gathering information in preparation to referring a student with possible emotional or behavioral disorders.

Teaching Guidelines and Accommodations for Students with Emotional or Behavioral Disorders

Many teachers realize that understanding and recognizing the behaviors of students with emotional and behavioral disorders is the first step in providing appropriate interventions. The most important role of the teacher is to establish an academic community and climate that promotes the learning and acceptance of all students, including students with emotional and behavioral problems. How can you do this? This section provides an overview of teaching accommodations to facilitate the academic and social growth of students with emotional and behavioral disorders.

Teachers usually realize that providing appropriate intervention is not sufficient, but that the student's day-to-day environment is essential to promoting mental health. Students who return to abusive families or inappropriate environments that maintain their emotional or behavioral problems are unlikely to achieve much success without changes in these environments. In working with students with serious emotional or behavioral problems, some teachers feel hopeless and give up. Remember, however, that the small things you do often make a big difference in the life of a student, even if the student does not say so or demonstrate significant changes.

No single approach to intervention works for all students with severe emotional and behavioral problems. A systematic, well-organized plan, and documentation of changes in behavior will help you determine whether an intervention is working, however.

What physical characteristics of the classroom environment support the learning of students with emotional or behavioral disorders? What characteristics of the classroom climate contribute to a positive emotional environment in which academic and social learning can take place?

Maintaining an Organized Physical Environment

Look around your classroom or that of another teacher, and evaluate whether the physical environment supports or detracts from the student's ability to behave appropriately (Fimian et al., 1983). The physical arrangement may have a significant effect on the classroom climate as well as on student behavior, particularly that of students with emotional and behavioral problems. Consider the following:

- Is the classroom uncluttered, clean, attractive, and uncrowded?
- Are necessary materials accessible, organized, and stored appropriately?
- Is there sufficient natural light in the classroom?
- Is the classroom well ventilated?
- Is the noise level appropriate? What objects might be removed or changed to make the room less noisy?
- Is there evidence that housekeeping chores have been taken care of? Is the room clean and orderly?
- Does each student have his or her own physical space, desk, and materials?

Students with emotional and behavioral disorders work best in organized, structured environments in which materials, equipment, and personal items are well maintained, neatly arranged, and presented in a predictable way. You can establish a classroom committee composed of elected students or students you appoint on a rotating basis that allows all students to participate over the school year. This committee might meet weekly to assess the classroom environment and address issues raised by students (perhaps in a student suggestion box).

Establishing Positive Relationships

Think about the teachers that you remember most from your elementary and secondary school days. What made these teachers special to you? Chances are that you felt they really cared about you, what you learned, and how you felt. The importance of your establishing good relationships with all students is important, but especially so for students with emotional and behavioral disorders. These students probably have had few positive relationships with adults and may act as if they dare you to care about them.

Trust is the foundation for success with students with emotional and behavioral disorders (Henley et al., 1993). Students learn to trust you when you act in predictable ways and do what you say you are going to do. They also learn to trust you when they believe you will do what is best for them, rather than what is best for you.

Remember that disliking the student's behavior is not the same as disliking the student, who needs your respect and caring. "Respect the student—dislike the behavior" is an important motto when you work with students with emotional and behavioral disorders. Think about the language you use when you reprimand students or enforce consequences for inappropriate behavior. Be sure you convince them that their behavior is unacceptable, not they. Jason Landis, a high school English teacher, says it this way:

> When I correct students I always talk about the behavior and I always let the student know that anyone who behaves like this will be treated the same way. For example, the other day in class I needed to remind a student that no one swears in the class and those who swear will get a detention and therefore, here is your detention. Later on in the period, I encouraged the same student to respond to a

question and provided positive feedback for the part of the answer he got correct.

Caring for students with emotional and behavioral disorders should not come with strings attached or expectations that students will reciprocate (Webber et al., 1991). Many of these students have little experience with giving or receiving kindness and warmth. Some are hurting and cannot cope with giving to others. All children need our concern, and students who do not reciprocate need it the most.

Be empathic. Empathy requires genuine concern and interest in understanding the student, no matter how deviant or difficult his or her behavior. Students know when teachers are empathic and concerned about them.

Tips for Teachers 7.2 offers further suggestions for creating an appropriate emotional environment.

TIPS FOR TEACHERS

7.2 Creating an Appropriate Emotional Environment

- *Respond to students' feelings and intentions* rather than to overt behavior. When students with emotional and behavioral disorders act out or become aggressive, the teacher's first reaction might be to respond with anger or hostility—but the student is really saying, "I'm hurting. Pay attention to me."
- *Listen.* Before responding, no matter how certain you are that the student is in the wrong, give the student an opportunity to explain and give his or her version of what occurred. You may not always agree with the interpretation, but by taking the time to listen you demonstrate caring and concern to the student. Listening is a sign of acceptance, an important first step in helping students.
- *Develop a positive relationship* with the student about one topic. All students are interested in and can succeed at something that you can recognize. Discover what this area is and what the student knows about it, then make him or her the class expert.

- *Establish rules and consequences* to help provide the structure that students with emotional and behavioral disorders need.
- *Consider changes you can make.* Evaluate the classroom routines, instructional procedures, and discipline practices you use that may be contributing to the student's behavioral problems.
- *Catch the student being good.* You have many opportunities to recognize the student's inappropriate behavior. A greater challenge is to catch the student being good and recognize that appropriate behavior several times a day.
- *Use humor* to build relationships and to decrease tension. Look for the fun in the way students relate to each other and to you.
- *Create an emotionally safe classroom* environment in which students accept each other's strengths and weaknesses and treat each other with respect and consideration.

Changing Behavior

The student behaviors teachers most want to change are those they regard as undesirable, such as those that interfere with instruction, other students, or the student's learning. Desirable behaviors—those that enhance instruction, relations with others, and the student's success—are the behaviors teachers most want to see increased. In addition to the behavior-management procedures discussed in detail in Chapter 3, the following guiding principles will help you use consequences for desirable and undesirable behaviors (Morgan & Reinhart, 1991):

■ Carefully select the rules you apply, and then follow through consistently. If you try to clamp down on every rule you may find yourself continually at war with the student.

■ Consider consequences carefully, because you must follow through on stated consequences. Do not use threats. When you make remarks such as, "You're going to do this math paper if you have to sit here all day," students soon learn that consequences are not real and that your words cannot be trusted.

■ Establish consequences that are not punishing to you. If you are stressed or inconvenienced by the consequence, you might resent the student (a circumstance that would surely interfere with the quality of the relationship you need to establish). For example, staying in at lunch, giving up your planning period, or driving the student home may punish you as much as the student.

■ Listen and talk to the student but avoid the trap of arguing. Listen to what the student has to say, and say what you have to say. If you are tempted to argue, recognize that you need a break and set another time to finish the discussion.

■ Use logic, principles, and effective guidelines to make decisions. Avoid flaunting your authority as a teacher to make students do something, without giving them a clear sense that it is the right or best thing to do.

■ Focus on the problems that interfere most; that is, ignore minor misbehaviors and focus on the important things.

■ Inform students that the work they complete is necessary and meaningful for their educa-tion. Avoid asking them to complete work "for you."

■ As you know, each student is an individual with his or her own attributes and problems. Avoid comparing a student with emotional or behavioral problems to other students. Comparisons do not help students understand and accept themselves, or be understood and accepted by others.

■ Students' problems belong to them. They may interfere with your work, but they are not your problems. Resist the temptation to solve students' problems for them. Students need to learn how to resolve conflicts for themselves.

■ Recognize your feelings and do not let them control your behavior. When you are upset by a student's behavior in class, it is important not to respond by further upsetting the student. Never "strike back" by humiliating, embarrassing, or berating a student.

■ Let the student know how many chances he or she has before a consequence will be applied (and do not add chances later). When you tell a student, "This is the last chance," and he or she continues to behave inappropriately, you need to follow through on whatever consequence was designated.

■ Give yourself positive feedback for what you do to enhance student learning and social functioning. Do not be too hard on yourself, especially when you make mistakes. Although there are limitations to what any effective teacher can do, there are always opportunities to be successful in teaching students with emotional and behavioral disorders.

The following procedures should remind you how to target key behaviors you want students to change:

■ Whenever possible, involve students and parents in identifying the target behavior. In this way, you work at changing the behavior both at school and at home.

■ As when making referrals, describe the behavior in as much detail as possible, including when and with whom it typically occurs.

■ Get the student's input on the behavior, as well as his or her suggestions for what might help reduce it.

FIGURE 7.2

Sample Student–Teacher Contract

Date: _____

Ms. Gonzalez will draw a star next to Paul's name on the bulletin board, and give Paul one point when he does any of the following in her classroom:

1) When the teacher asks a question, he raises his hand and waits for the teacher to call on him before talking.

2) He stays seated in his chair while working on class assignments.

3) When other kids in the class are bothering him, he tells the teacher about their behavior instead of yelling at and/or hitting the other kids.

After Paul has earned 12 points from his teacher, Ms. Gonzalez, he may select one of the following rewards:

1) He may have extra time to work on the computer.

2) He may serve as the teacher's helper for a day.

3) He may be in charge of caring for the class pet for the day.

4) He may serve as a peer tutor for a day (for a subject decided upon by the teacher).

After Paul has received 12 points he begins earning the points again. Another reward will be given when 12 points have been earned.

I, Paul B. O'Brien agree to the conditions stated above, and understand that I will not be allowed any of the rewards until I have earned 12 points by doing the activities stated above.

_____
(student's signature)

I, Ms. Gonzalez, agree to the conditions stated above. I will give Paul one of the aforementioned reinforcers only after he has received 12 points.

_____
(teacher's signature)

■ Describe the target behavior in writing, using the terms expressed by the student, the parent, and yourself so that everyone involved understands the problem.

■ Establish a procedure for eliminating the behavior and providing positive consequences when the behavior does not occur. Involve parents in distributing positive consequences as well.

Many techniques exist for helping students change their behavior. Figure 7.2 provides an example of a behavior contract between a student and a teacher. The 60-Second Lesson on the following page shows how even simple devices can work.

Resolving Conflicts and Promoting Self-Control

Dealing with conflict between students and between a student and a teacher is an ongoing issue for teachers at all grade levels. Conflicts are

MAKING A DIFFERENCE

The 60-Second Lesson

Using a Timer to Change Behavior

Purpose: To increase appropriate behavior, such as "on-task" behavior, and to reduce inappropriate behavior, such as being "out-of-seat"

Materials: Kitchen timer

Procedure:

1. Show students the kitchen timer and indicate that you will be using it to cue students to look for on-task behavior in the class. Discuss with students what behaviors will be included (e.g., working, performing an assignment, asking a question, reading a text).

2. Indicate that the timer will ring at different intervals and that all groups or individuals who are on task when the timer rings will be awarded a point.

3. Set the timer initially for a range of times (from five to ten minutes), then for longer periods of time.

Adapted from: Wolf, M. M., Hanley, E. L., King, L. A., Lachowicz, J., & Giles, D. K. (1970). The timer-game: A variable interval contingency for the management of out-of-seat behavior. *Exceptional Children, 37,* 113–117.

---

inevitable in a classroom community; they occur with students who have emotional and behavioral disorders as well as among other students.

Morgan and Reinhart (1991) suggest the use of conflict reports as a strategy for **conflict resolution.** Conflict reports not only enable students to debrief after a conflict, but also give them an opportunity to practice writing skills. A conflict report might include the following items:

- Describe the conflict you were involved in (fighting, taking an object that belongs to another, pushing).
- Briefly list who was involved in this conflict.
- Briefly list who else winessed (but was not involved in) the conflict.

- Describe where the conflict took place (in the back of the classroom, in line going to lunch, at recess).

What steps should this teacher take to help the students resolve their conflict? What specific skills can students be taught to use in preventing future interpersonal conflicts?

- Briefly describe how the conflict started. What did you do? What did they do? Describe what you said. Describe what they said.
- What else would you like to say or do to the other people involved in the conflict?
- What did you do to try to stop the conflict?
- What did they do to try to stop the conflict?
- Whom do you think might be able to help stop or resolve the conflict?
- Write a brief set of procedures for resolving the conflict. Be specific. Be sure to tell who will do what, and when.

One of the advantages of a conflict report is that both participants have an opportunity to write all they know about it and to give their side of the story. Furthermore, the process of reporting provides time to debrief and let anger or resentment subside. Some teachers train students in conflict resolution as part of the regular curriculum. Students serve on an informal hearing board to resolve conflicts without teacher intervention. This training lets students practice the important skill of conflict negotiation.

By teaching students to set personal goals you also help them to develop self-control. Setting and monitoring positive personal goals contributes to students' positive self-concept and higher self-esteem. The 60-Second Lesson below describes a simple activity for helping students establish personal goals.

Using the Life-Space Intervention

The Life-Space Intervention (LSI) (Wood & Long, 1994), originally discussed by Redl (1959), can be used to help students with emotional and behavioral problems cope with a crisis situation. According to Redl, the LSI has two primary goals:

- to provide emotional "first aid" so that the student can regain composure and return to as normal an activity level as possible
- to take advantage of the conflict situation to assist students in confronting and resolving their own personal conflicts

Although many professionals feel that the Life-Space Intervention is best applied by trained professionals familiar with counseling procedures, teachers can apply the key principles of the Life-Space Intervention. When the emotional problem or conflict is serious and warrants the help of a

MAKING A DIFFERENCE

The 60-Second Lesson

Helping Students Establish Personal Goals

Purpose: To establish personal goals

Materials: Index card or small piece of paper; pencil or pen

Procedure:
1. Ask students to think about people they most admire. For younger students, discuss the meaning of *admire.*
2. Ask students to identify the qualities of people they admire and examples of their behavior that demonstrate these qualities.
3. Now ask each student to write on the index card one quality for which they would like to be admired.
4. Ask students to keep the card in a prominent place (taped on their assignment folder or inside their desk, for example).
5. Throughout the year, ask students to look at the card and assess the extent to which they express the quality or trait for which they most want to be admired.

trained counselor, however, the teacher needs the good judgment to make an immediate referral.

Long, Morse, and Newman (1980) provided the following suggestions for the application of the LSI by teachers:

- Shake off or drain off the frustration and upset through the use of humor, physically shaking the problem away, or diffusing tension by allowing the student to talk about the problem. Drain off enough frustration so that the student can talk about the issue.

- Be as courteous as you would be if you were dealing with a friend or another adult. Give the student time to adequately explain his or her side of the story, and listen attentively. If you ask questions, be sure to give the student time to think and respond to them.

- Conduct the LSI in as private a place as possible. No one wants to exhibit problems, throw tantrums, or be extremely upset in front of others. Find a private, quiet place to conduct the session.

- Eliminate barriers between you and the student. Position yourself at eye level, for example. With a young child, pull up small chairs and sit down so that you are at the same level.

- Ask the student to provide his or her interpretation of the event. Listen carefully and be sure that you clarify any misunderstandings, but do not give in to his or her misperceptions of the situation. Confront the student, if necessary, to point out that there is another way to view the situation.

- Discuss what needs to be done to resolve the situation. If an apology is needed, role-play and rehearse how that can be done. If the conflict needs to be further discussed and resolved with another person, plan procedures for doing so.

- Discuss what to do the next time a similar situation develops. How can you prevent a conflict? Discuss procedures for eliminating problems in the future.

- Do not assume that you understand how the student feels. Many times teachers assume that the student is angry, hurt, or disappointed. Ask how the student is feeling (to check whether you are correct).

- Avoid invalidating students' feelings by claiming that they could not possibly feel the

TIPS FOR TEACHERS

7.3 Providing Opportunities for Student Success

- When you correct papers, point out correct responses rather than mistakes.
- Before students submit papers, ask them to look carefully to see whether they can find an error. Call on students to describe mistakes they find, and praise them for finding and correcting the mistakes. Point out that everyone makes mistakes and that with practice we can reduce the number and types of mistakes we make.

- When a student with emotional or behavioral disorders asks for help, start by asking him or her to find something correct on his or her paper.
- Find opportunities for a student to "shine" in front of classmates. Even small recognitions are valuable.
- Notice improvement. If the student usually gets three right on the weekly spelling test and this week gets five right, let the student know that you notice the change. Recognition of progress toward a goal motivates students more than recognition that comes only after the goal has been attained.

way they say they do. Students with emotional and behavioral disorders often say outrageous things that they mean at the time. Listen carefully without judging or denying their feelings. Allow time for students to ask you questions and to prepare a follow-up.

■ Teach problem solving skills (such as those presented in Chapter 4).

Adapting Instruction

Students with emotional and behavioral problems often have academic difficulties (Vaughn et al., 1992) and are underachievers in school (Kauffman, 1989). An important factor that positively affects students with emotional and behavioral disorders is the extent to which they are busy in purposeful, authentic activities. Activities need to be viewed by students as personally relevant and related to learning skills they need. Effective teachers explain to students *why* they are studying a topic, *why* they do an assignment, and *how* their learning will contribute to their success as students and in the future. Teachers can also adapt instruction in the ways described in the following sections.

Provide Instruction that Allows All Students to Succeed
Academic failure or frustration can exacerbate a student's emotional or behavioral disorder. Without creating a parallel program or watering down the curriculum, teachers can adapt and modify assignments and expectations so that students can succeed. One simple strategy is to look for opportunities to reinforce and reward students for what they know or have done correctly. Another is to enhance motivation and performance by changing activities when students are failing. Students with emotional and behavioral disorders may have difficulty accomplishing particular types of tasks. In many cases, you can change the task so that students can demonstrate knowledge without performing tasks that upset them. Tips for Teachers 7.3 offers additional suggestions for giving students opportunities for success.

Provide Opportunities for Students to Learn Academically and Socially
Use different groupings—individual, small group, paired, and large group—to give students opportunities to acquire academic and social skills. Students with emotional and behavioral disorders may have difficulty learning in whole-class instruction but do well in small-group or paired learning situations. Also provide opportunities for students to be tutored and to serve as tutors themselves. Learning to work with others is an important skill for students with emotional and behavioral disorders. Recall from Chapter 2 the specific suggestions for grouping practices that enhance learning for all students.

Social learning also contributes to the success of students with emotional and behavioral disorders. **Social learning** involves observing and modeling or imitating the behavior of others (e.g., Bandura, 1971, 1973). To what extent can you expect students to imitate the appropriate behaviors of classmates, and what can you do to accelerate this process? Research suggests that students with emotional and behavioral disorders are unlikely to imitate "better" behaviors in the classroom unless teachers provide directed experiences to promote this behavior (Hallenbeck & Kauffman, 1995). Tips for Teachers 7.4 offers a strategy for guiding students to learn appropriate behaviors from classmates.

Use a Variety of Commercial and Individually Created Materials
Assignments built to maximize success and capture students' interest reduce inappropriate behaviors. By providing high interest materials, you can keep students involved in the task. High interest is a characteristic of educational technologies, for example. Having students compose essays, complete tests, and practice skills on the microcomputer may provide better motivation than more traditional activities.

Also provide alternative ways for students to complete tasks and demonstrate learning. For example, students might give oral recitations, describe what they know to other students who have already mastered the material, or perform learning outcomes. Allow students to express their individual learning-style preferences. For instance, some students work better standing up, others while sitting on the floor, still others while sitting in bean bag chairs. As long as students are working, learning, and not interfering with the progress of others, appropriate alternatives for completing tasks make sense.

Interactive Multimedia

Today teachers and students can design and create multimedia programs of their own to address instructional goals. Interactive multimedia combines on a CD-ROM or videodisc different kinds of information (such as graphics, photos, sound, video, and text) that can be accessed in any order through hypermedia. Hypermedia refers to links in a program that give the "hyperlearner" random access to the contents by clicking on words or images.

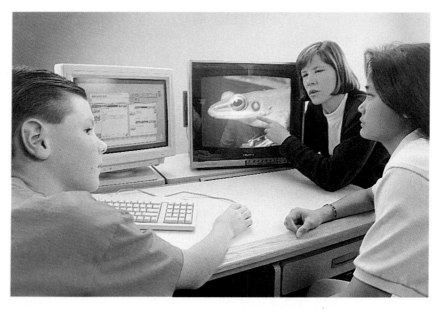

Courtesy of Video Discovery.

Authoring tools such as HyperCard, The Digital Chisel, and PowerPoint permit teachers to create their own interactive multimedia lessons. As an alternative to starting from scratch, teachers can also select, reorder, and customize components from databases called "tool kits." For example, the *Bio-Sci II* videodisc tool kit from VideoDiscovery (800-548-3472) is a large database of images, film clips, and textual data on the natural sciences. Teachers can use key words to locate specific topics and resources. They then select, resequence, and add their own material to incorporate their selections into a lesson. Software manufacturers offer many services for "adaptive software" users. For example, Pierian Spring Software (800-472-8578), which publishes the *Digital Chisel*, offers a monthly subscription to educational "clip media" that teachers can integrate into multimedia lessons.

Students and teachers can both benefit from being involved in a cutting-edge creative process.

Teachers can develop unique and effective teaching materials, and involving students in creating interactive multimedia can boost motivation and support active learning, cooperative learning, interdisciplinary learning, and individualized instruction.

For more information, see:

Abrams, Arnie H. (1996). *Multimedia Magic* (Boston: Allyn and Bacon).

Collin, Simon. (1994). *The Way Multimedia Works.* (Redmond, WA: Microsoft Press)

Gertler, Nat. (1994). *Multimedia Illustrated.* (Indianapolis, IN: Que Corporation)

Murie, Michael. (1994). *Multimedia Starter Kit for MacIntosh* (Indianapolis, IN: Hayden Books).

TIPS FOR TEACHERS

7.4 *Guiding Students to Learn Appropriate Behaviors From Classmates*

1. Identify student "models" and their behaviors that you want other students to emulate. For example, "Joaquin has his math book open to page 38 and is looking at me to indicate that he is ready. Show me that you are ready by doing the same thing."

2. Monitor whether the student with emotional or behavioral disorders follows the model. Look for approximations and provide positive reinforcement. For example, "Sheilah (student with emotional or behavioral problems) is getting her math book out. What are the next two things you need to do, Sheilah, to indicate that you are ready?"

3. Provide frequent feedback when the student performs the desired behaviors. Look for as many chances as possible to recognize desirable behaviors.

4. Students who view themselves as "like" a model are more likely than not to imitate desirable behaviors. You can facilitate this process by identifying ways in which students' behaviors are similar. For example, "Sheilah (student with emotional or behavioral disorder) and Joaquin are not talking while they are getting ready for the homework assignment. Good for them!"

SUMMARY

- Students with emotional and behavioral disorders exhibit behaviors that are significantly different from the norm, and that persist over a long period of time.
- Emotional and behavioral disorders are grouped into two broad categories: externalizing and internalizing.
- Externalizing behaviors are characterized by acting out, aggression, and interfering, attention, and conduct problems.
- Internalizing behaviors are viewed as more self-directed, such as being anxious, worried, and depressed.
- There are six major classifications of emotional and behavioral disorders: conduct disorder, attention problems, socialized-aggression, pervasive developmental disorder, immaturity, and anxiety–withdrawal. Some of these classifications fit the externalizing category, some the internalizing category, and some fit both, depending on the specific manifestation of the problem behavior.
- The criteria considered when interpreting emotional or behavioral problems include: behavior–age discrepancy, frequency of occurrence of behavior(s), number of symptoms, inner suffering, persistence of behavior, self-satisfaction, and severity and duration of behavior(s).
- Points to consider when teaching students with emotional and behavioral disorders include: altering the environment, targeting

and changing behavior, promoting academic and social factors that enhance learning, providing successful experiences, providing ample opportunities for students to learn, monitoring and changing activities, and using alternative behavior-management strategies.

Key Terms and Concepts

anxiety–withdrawal

conduct disorder

conflict resolution

developmental pathways

Diagnostic and Statistical Manual of Mental Disorders (DSM)

emotional or behavioral disorders

externalizing behaviors

gangs

group behavior

immaturity

internalizing behaviors

motor excess

pervasive developmental disorder

social learning

socialized-aggression

Think and Apply

1. Now that you have read Chapter 7, consider the behaviors of Lenox, the student in Juline's first grade class described at the beginning of the chapter. Make a list of the types of behaviors you would expect Lenox to exhibit. Consider the suggestions provided in the chapter and list instructional and behavior-management practices you could implement to enhance this student's success. File your responses in your teaching portfolio and add ideas as you read this book.

2. Identify a practicing teacher you can interview, and ask him or her the following questions:

   a. To what extent have students in your class exhibited symptoms of emotional and behavioral disorders? What kinds of problems do you see?

   b. Do you think that more students have emotional and behavioral problems today than in the past? Why or why not?

   c. To what do you attribute students' emotional and behavioral problems?

   d. What advice would you give to teachers about working effectively with students with emotional and behavioral disorders?

   Compare the teacher's answers with your own ideas and those of your classmates.

3. Most school districts have special classrooms or programs for students with severe emotional and behavioral disorders. Make arrangements to visit one of these classrooms or programs. How do these educational settings differ from the general education classroom? What types of resources are available to meet the special learning needs of these students?

Read More about It

1. Knitzer, J., Steinberg, Z., & Fleisch, B. (1990). *At the school house door: An examination of programs and policies for children with behavioral and emotional problems.* New York: Bank Street College of Education.

    A comprehensive examination of the types of programs available for school-age children with emotional and behavioral disorders, this book also describes the educational, political, and social policies that influence intervention programs for these students.

2. MacCracken, M. (1973). *Circle of children.* Philadelphia: J. B. Lippincott.

    This personal account of one teacher's experiences instructing students with emotional disorders poignantly describes the frustrations and successes teachers are likely to encounter when working with this student population.

3. Quay, H. C., & Werry, J. S. (1986). *Psychopathological disorders of childhood.* New York: Wiley.

    A comprehensive overview of the classification, research, and intervention effects of treating students with emotional and behavioral disorders. This book identifies the types of problems frequently found in students and expands on the subtypes presented in this chapter.

4. Walker, H. M., Colvin, G., & Ramsey, E. (1995). *Antisocial behavior in school: Strategies and best practices.* Pacific Grove, CA: Brookes/Cole.

    Provides background on identification, classification, and intervention strategies for addressing antisocial behavior of students in school settings.

EIGHT

Teaching Students with Mental Retardation and Severe Disabilities

FOCUS QUESTIONS

1. What are the major concepts presented in the new AAMR definition of mental retardation? How does the new definition change and broaden previous concepts about mental retardation? Do you consider it to be an improvement? Why?

2. What are some characteristics of students with autism? With dual sensory impairments?

3. Describe some alternative or augmentative methods of communication for persons with severe disabilities and mental retardation.

4. Describe two planning systems you could use to help plan for a student with mental retardation and severe disabilities. How are the two systems different in their purposes?

5. Why are functional assessment and functional practice important for increasing the learning of students with mental retardation and severe disabilities?

6. As a classroom teacher, describe how you could have peers assist students with disabilities in your classroom.

Susie Speelman, Mary Robinson, and Steve Canty

Susie Speelman is an **inclusion support teacher** at Sunrise Elementary School, Tucson, Arizona. Susie's job involves supporting students with mental retardation, severe disabilities, physical disabilities (e.g., cerebral palsy), and visual impairments in general education classrooms. To do this Susie works closely with the general education teachers at Sunrise to learn what the different classes will be doing and to make the necessary accommodations or adaptations so that students with disabilities can be successful and learn at their level.

Susie has been in this position for three years and, therefore, knows well the children whom she supports. Susie does not work alone—besides herself there are six *educational assistants* (EAs) or paraprofessionals who support the ten children with whom she works in ten different kindergarten-through-fifth-grade classrooms. When talking about making accommodations, Susie comments:

> The key to making inclusion work is to have good working relationships with the classroom teachers and to assist them in feeling that they are capable of teaching students with significant disabilities. In working in the different classrooms, one generalization that I can make is that it is the attitude and knowledge of the classroom teacher that is oftentimes the key to a student's success. If the teacher has a "can do" attitude and considers the student a viable member of the class, then the stage is set for the student's success. My job becomes one of providing the supports for the student's learning. This may be an EA who works in the classroom part- or full-time, using assistive technology such as a communication board, or my directly working with the student. While it may appear more challenging to support these children at the upper elementary level where the work includes more pencil and paper tasks, I have found that many of my students have become fascinated with the various hands-on projects and activities that are emphasized at the upper elementary level in content subjects such as math, science, social studies, and art.

Melody's work in Mary Robinson's fifth grade class is a good example of how a student with mild to moderate mental retardation is integrated into the classroom community. One of Melody's strengths is math. With the help of the EA and peer tutors, she is developing many functional math skills, such as reading prices and knowing how much money is necessary to make a purchase. Melody is also memorizing basic addition and subtrac-

tion facts. While the other students are working on timed tests or on the computer, Melody also works on a timed test or on computer programs for math facts. In this way she participates like the other students, but the content of her work is different.

Many of Melody's goals focus on communication and social development and are worked on throughout the school day. Mary, Susie, and the EA know that Melody is working on asking for help instead of waiting for someone to notice her, and also on looking up and speaking clearly. The team finds opportunities throughout the day to work on these goals. Mary comments on how she integrates Melody's goals into the class routines:

> Now that I know Melody, it is easy to integrate her goals with the other students' goals. For example, students are expected to be independent in this classroom, and we use lots of semistructured activities such as writer's workshop and literature study groups. Each requires that the students take responsibility for getting materials, working on projects, and evaluating their own learning. Melody is responsible for getting and putting away her writing folder, her literature log, and her reading folder just like the other students. As a reminder, I have a picture of each taped on her desk. When she has difficulty remembering to get or put away her materials, I can point to the picture of what she needs to get or put away. This serves as a cue, without calling undue attention to her.

José, another student Susie supports, is in Steve Canty's third grade class. José has severe disabilities, is nonverbal, and uses a wheelchair. One of the most difficult challenges with José is to get him actively involved in the classroom activities. Steve comments:

> José tends to let others make decisions for him and he sits back and watches instead of participating. Therefore, making choices is one of José's major goals. Susie and I have worked hard at providing José lots of opportunities and helped his peers also give José choices throughout the day.

> For example, when the students were designing their own money, one of José's classmates gave him three choices of designs for their joint project.

Susie, Mary, and Steve all agree that an important key to the successful integration of Melody and José is co-planning and ongoing communication not just among themselves, but with the EAs, with parents, and with other specialists who work with these students, including the speech and language pathologist and the occupational therapist.

Introduction

Like Mary and Steve, you will probably have students like Melody and José in your class. This chapter provides information about students like them. It also presents a process for curriculum modification and describes strategies you can use to support students with mental retardation and severe disabilities in your classroom.

Definitions and Types of Mental Retardation and Severe Disabilities

The populations of individuals considered to have mental retardation or severe disabilities are quite heterogeneous, as is evident in our interview with teachers at Sunrise Elementary. This section discusses the definitions and types of mental retardation and severe disabilities.

Mental Retardation

Students with mental retardation have limited intellectual functioning, which affects their learning. These students have slower rates of learning and are particularly challenged by complex and abstract tasks. Students with mental retardation are just like other students in your class in that they are members of families, have friends and neighbors, have personalities shaped by both their innate characteristics and life experiences, and have aspirations to become adults, get jobs, and fall in love (Smith & Luckasson, 1995). Yet, to be successful in general education classrooms, they also need additional support and accommodations. In planning for this support, it is helpful to have some knowledge about mental retardation and how it affects learning.

The underlying concept associated with mental retardation is that students have limited abilities to learn. Historically, definitions of mental retardation focused on limitations in intellectual functioning (as measured by intelligence tests). More recent definitions are broader, focusing on four major concepts:

- **Intellectual functioning:** Individuals who have mental retardation have substantial limitations in **intellectual functioning** and have been characterized as having "significantly subaverage intellectual functioning." On measures of intellectual functioning, "significantly subaverage" has been defined as an IQ of 70 to 75 or less, and includes about 3 percent of the population.

- **Adaptive behavior:** Students who have mental retardation also have significant limitations in adaptive skills or behavior. **Adaptive behavior** refers to "the effectiveness or degree with which individuals meet the standards of personal independence and social responsibility expected for age and cultural group" (Grossman, 1983, p.1).

- **Developmental period:** Students who have mental retardation demonstrate limitations in intellectual functioning and adaptive behavior during the **developmental period**, before the age of 18. Persons who acquire limited intellectual functioning after that age are not referred to as having mental retardation but instead as having traumatic brain injury, or whatever the cause of the disability (Smith & Luckasson, 1995).

- **Systems of support:** This term refers to the coordinated set of services and accommodations matched to a student's needs, and can include teachers and specialists, specialized programs and methodologies, and assistive technology. When appropriate supports are provided over a sustained period, the life functioning of students with mental retardation will generally improve (AAMR, 1992).

Using these four themes, in 1992 the American Association on Mental Retardation (AAMR) defined **mental retardation** as follows:

> Mental retardation refers to substantial limitations in present functioning. It is characterized by significantly subaverage intellectual functioning, existing concurrently with related limitations in two or more of the following applicable adaptive skill areas: communication, self-care, home living, social skills, community use, self-direction, health and safety, functional academics, leisure and work. Mental retardation manifests before age 18 (p. 1).

The following four assumptions are essential to the application of this definition:

- Valid assessment considers cultural and linguistic diversity, as well as differences in communication and behavioral factors.
- The existence of limitations in adaptive skills occurs within the context of community environments typical of the individual's age peers and is indexed to the person's individual needs for supports.
- Specific adaptive limitations often coexist with strengths in other adaptive skills or other personal capabilities.
- With appropriate supports over a sustained period, the life functioning of the person with mental retardation will generally improve (AAMR, 1992, p. 5).

In comparison to previous definitions, the current definition stresses the interaction among: (1) the environment in which the person functions, (2) the person's capabilities, and (3) the need for varying levels of support (Beirne-Smith et al., 1994).

In addition, the new definition reflects a change in the classification system. The traditional system emphasized the individual's degree of retardation (i.e., mild retardation [IQ scores of 50–55 to 70–75], moderate retardation [35–40 to 50–55], severe retardation [20–25 to 35–40], profound retardation [below 20–25]). The new classification system emphasizes the level of supports needed to facilitate the individual's integration into the community (Meyen & Skrtic, 1995). Figure 8.1 presents this new classification system, along with examples of support at each level. The classification system incorporates a multidimensional approach that includes emotional, psychological, and related health factors.

The cause of the mental retardation, although known only about 50 percent of the time (Beirne-Smith et al., 1994), is one way people think about different types of mental retardation. Chromosomal disorders are probably the best known cause of mental retardation. **Down syndrome**, one of the most common chromosomal disorders, is often what people think of when mental retardation is mentioned. Yet Down syndrome occurs in only about one in seven hundred live births and accounts for less than 10 percent of all individuals with mental retardation (Kozma & Stock, 1993). **Fetal Alcohol Syndrome** (FAS) refers to a spectrum of birth defects caused by the mother's drinking during pregnancy, and is fast becoming the leading cause of mental retardation (March of Dimes, 1992). Children with FAS may experience some degree of mental retardation, poor coordination, learning disabilities, and psychosocial behavior problems.

Severe Disabilities

Severe disabilities are often described as a condition in which typical life activities are significantly affected. The Association for Persons with Severe Handicaps (TASH), defines persons with severe disabilities as:

> individuals of all ages who require extensive ongoing support in more than one major life activity in order to participate in integrated community settings and to enjoy a quality of life that is available to citizens with fewer or no disabilities. Support may be required for life activities such as mobility, communication, self-care, and learning as necessary for independent living, employment and self-sufficiency (Meyer et al., 1991, p. 19).

Among those considered to have severe disabilities are students whose mental retardation is severe or profound, who are autistic, who have dual sensory impairments (i.e., deaf–blind), or who have multiple disabilities (e.g., significant mental retardation and physical disabilities, or mental retardation and a sensory disability).

Autism Autism is a physical disorder of the brain that causes a developmental disability. Although persons diagnosed as autistic are considered to have a severe disability, the range in ability levels within this group is varied (Powers, 1989). Some individuals with autism may function independently or almost independently. Kim Peek, the character played by Dustin Hoffman in the movie *Rainman,* is an example of an individual who has autism but generally functions independently (and even has some specific cognitive abilities in the genius range).

The physical features of people with autism may not suggest a disability. Rather, the disability generally is manifested in their language and personal, social behavior. According to the

FIGURE 8.1

1992 Classification System for Mental Retardation

LEVEL OF SUPPORT	DESCRIPTION OF SUPPORT	EXAMPLE
Intermittent	Support on an "as needed basis." Characterized by episodic nature, person not always needing the support(s), or short term supports needed during life-span transitions (e.g., job loss or an acute medical crisis). Intermittent supports may be high or low intensity when provided.	Counseling support needed as student adjusts to school at the beginning of each year and as the student begins job training programs in high school.
Limited	An intensity of supports characterized by consistency over time, time-limited but not of an intermittent nature, may require fewer staff members and less cost than more intense levels of supports (e.g., time-limited employment training or transitional supports during the school to adult period).	Support provided to a high school student with mild mental retardation as they take specially designed courses in learning strategies/study skills, functional English, and applied math. Support provided by a job developer as student works in the afternoons.
Extensive	Supports characterized by regular involvement in at least some environments (such as work or home) and not time limited(e.g., long term support and long term home living support).	Support provided to an elementary age student with a moderate or severe disability who works in the general education classroom. An educational assistant provides the major support during reading, language arts, math, and science, with peers and the classroom teacher providing the major support at other times of the day.
Pervasive	Supports characterized by their constancy, high intensity; provided across environments; potentially life-sustaining nature. Pervasive supports typically involve more staff members and intrusiveness than do extensive or time-limited supports (Luckasson et al., 1992, p. 26).	Ongoing support provided to a student who is medically fragile and in need of constant support by a staff member.

Adapted from Luckasson, R., Coulter, D.L., Polloway, E.A., Reiss, S., Schalock, R.L. Snell, M.E., Spitalnik, D.M., & Stark, J.A. (1992). *Mental retardation: Definition, classification, and systems of supports.* Washington, DC: American Association on Mental Retardation, p. 26.

Individuals with Disabilities Education Act (1992) autism means:

> A developmental disability significantly affecting verbal and nonverbal communication and social interaction, generally evident before age 3, that adversely affects a child's performance.

When autism was first identified in the 1940s, it was thought to be a psychosocial problem caused by parents' aloof or hostile behavior. Later, autism was classified under physical impairments. Not until the IDEA amendments of 1990 was autism treated as a separate disability category.

Other characteristics often associated with autism are engagement in repetitive activities and stereotyped movements, resistance to environmental change or change in daily routines, and unusual responses to sensory experiences. The term does not apply if a child's educational performance is adversely affected primarily because the child has a serious emotional disturbance (34 C.F.R., Part 300, Sec. 300.7[b][1]).

After having Jason, a student with autism, in his fourth grade class for several months, Robert Hernandez expressed these thoughts, "I was worried about how it would work with the other children; if it would take away from them. I was concerned that Jason would be a distraction to the students. But now that Jason has been part of our class for several months, I feel that the more he is in the classroom, the less the children even notice the noise or occasional outbursts. The students had to learn that Jason will do things that are not okay for them to do." Tips for Teachers 8.1 presents Robert's advice for working with students like Jason in the classroom.

Multiple Disabilities Individuals with multiple disabilities have mental retardation that is severe or profound, as well as one or more significant motor or sensory impairments or special health needs. For example, a person with severe mental retardation might also have cerebral palsy or epilepsy (Westling & Fox, 1995). Types of multiple disabilities include: mental retardation with physical disabilities (e.g., cerebral palsy, spina bifida, seizure disorders), or mental retardation with severe behavior disorders, or mental retardation with a visual or hearing impairment. It is reasonable to expect that two of every five students with severe and multiple disabilities will have a sensory impairment (Sobsey & Wolf-Schein, 1991).

Like all students, students with multiple disabilities have learning needs that require a *holistic*

TIPS FOR TEACHERS

8.1 A Teacher's Advice for Working with Students with Autism

- *Don't let the behavior overwhelm you.* Develop a behavior-management plan and implement small steps. Decide what you will put up with and what behaviors must stop, and target those.
- *Systematically expect more and more of the student.* At first the student might only be required to sit with the class with whatever it takes (a favorite object), then the student may be required to hold the reading book.
- *Develop a picture and word schedule for daily activities.* Use this to prepare the student for transitions to new activities. Introduce changes in routine slowly, and let the student know in advance that these changes are going to occur.
- *Talk to the student's parents and other teachers,* and find out what works and what does not work with this student.
- *Use peers to help redirect the student's behavior* and to interest him or her in the task.
- *Take "ownership" of the student* so that he or she feels like a real member of the class.

TIPS FOR TEACHERS

8.2 Environmental Accommodations for Students with Dual Sensory Impairments

- Develop a tactile schedule for your student. Each activity of the day has an object that represents it. For example: math—calculator, lunch—spoon, reading—a small book.
- Along with the schedule, objects can be used to make choices, get information from the environment or convey a message (e.g., handing the teacher a small pillow might mean the student wants his or her position changed, choosing a small ball would communicate what the student wants to do during recess).
- Tactually or visually identify your student's belongings with a consistent, meaningful symbol. This will help facilitate independence (e.g., a pencil taped on the desk, a safety pin on the tag of his or her coat).
- Have clear pathways marked with objects that serve as cues. Consistent furniture, or tactile or visual run-

ners on the wall help promote orientation and the student's independent mobility. Important places should be distinguished by special cues.

- To encourage your student to use his or her remaining hearing or vision, add light, color, sound, vibration, interesting textures, and colors to objects.
- Firmly touch the student's shoulder to signal that an interaction is going to occur.
- Introduce yourself by using a consistent symbol for your name. This could be a ring, watch, or other piece of jewelry you always wear that the student could easily touch. Or it could be a distinguishing feature, such as your hair or glasses. Name signs or the finger spelling of the first letter of your name could also be signed in the palm of the student's hand as a consistent symbol for your name.

Adapted from Rikhye, C.H. Gotheif, C.R., & Appell, M.W. (1989). A classroom environment checklist for students with dual sensory impairments. *Teaching Exceptional Children, 22*(1), 44–46; California Deaf–Blind Services (1992). *How to interact with individuals with dual sensory impairments* (Fact Sheet). California: Author.

approach to education (an approach in which the student is viewed as a whole person). In determining educational goals and teaching strategies, professionals consider factors such as the student's emotions, cognitive processes, and other factors that interact with the environment to produce behavior (Siegel-Causey et al., 1995).

Dual Sensory Impairments Students with **dual sensory impairments** (also referred to as **deaf–blind**) present unique challenges in that the two main channels (auditory and visual) of receptive communication and learning are impaired. Although difficult to

What factors must be taken into account when planning instruction for students with severe or multiple disabilities?

determine, the cognitive abilities of students with dual sensory impairments can vary from severe retardation to giftedness. Downing and Eichinger (1990) noted that individuals who are deaf–blind may have diverse combinations of vision and hearing impairments with normal or gifted intelligence, or they may have additional mental, physical, and behavioral disabilities. Because these individuals do not receive clear and consistent information from either sensory modality, a tendency exists to turn inward. These individuals may appear passive, not responding to or initiating interactions with others. Tips for Teachers 8.2 provides a list of teaching strategies and guidelines for interacting with individuals with dual sensory impairments.

> Fifty to sixty percent of persons with cerebral palsy also experience a mental disability.

Prevention of Mental Retardation

The President's Committee on Mental Retardation reported that more than 50 percent of all cases of mental retardation could have been prevented. Maternal use of alcohol and drugs during pregnancy, as well as maternal infections (such as HIV) are among the fastest-growing causes of mental retardation that can be prevented. McLaren and Bryson (1987) estimated that as many as 15 percent of the cases of mild retardation are a result of child abuse or neglect, and that one in thirty newborns will experience a serious head trauma before the age of eighteen. Poverty can cause mental retardation through increased chances of lead poisoning, inadequate diet, inadequate health care (including immunizations), unsafe neighborhoods, and environmental pollutants (Smith & Luckasson, 1995). In fact, Menolascino and Stark (1988) stated that poverty is a determinant in 75 to 80 percent of people with mental retardation at higher IQ levels. Following are some simple prevention strategies:

Prenatal
- avoid using alcohol, drugs, and smoking
- avoid sexually transmitted diseases
- obtain appropriate medical care

- maintain good health and nutrition
- immediately treat infections
- obtain genetic testing and prenatal tests, if indicated

Postnatal
- provide proper nutrition and medical care
- obtain proper immunizations
- use infant and child car seats and seat belts in automobiles
- prevent lead or other chemical intake
- eliminate child abuse and neglect
- eliminate poverty and associated conditions

Prevalence of Mental Retardation and Severe Disabilities

Prevalence of persons with mental retardation is difficult to determine because different definitions and methodologies are used to determine retardation. Generally, however, prevalence is estimated to be about 1 to 2 percent of the population. According to the federal government, slightly less than 1 percent of the school-age population is identified as having mental retardation and requiring special education services (U.S. Department of Education, 1994), with approximately 90 percent of those students having mild retardation. Prevalence of multiple disabilities is difficult to determine, as different states use different classification systems (e. g., some states include students with multiple disabilities under the category of physical disabilities). The United States Department of Education (1994) reports that about .13 percent of the general population has multiple disabilities or dual sensory impairments.

It is interesting to note that the prevalence of children born with severe disabilities is on the rise. Some screening and early intervention has led to a reduction in causes (e.g., most hospitals now screen to determine whether babies have phenylketonuria [PKU], so that it can be treated before mental retardation occurs), but the number of children being born exposed to drugs and alcohol is increasing. In addition, because medical advances have also resulted in more high-risk and low birth weight babies living and living longer, more children with disabilities are reaching school age.

Characteristics of Students with Mental Retardation and Severe Disabilities

When you consider the characteristics of students with mental retardation and severe disabilities, not every student will have all the characteristics discussed. As a group, however, students with mental retardation and severe disabilities display these characteristics more often than the general population (Mihail, 1995). The characteristics are grouped into four areas: intellectual functioning, social skills, motor skills, and communication.

Intellectual Functioning

Students with mental retardation and severe disabilities, although they have many diverse learning characteristics, generally learn slowly and often fail to notice relevant features of what is being taught, do not demonstrate learned skills spontaneously, and have difficulty generalizing learned skills to new situations (Noonan Siegel-Causey, 1990). These students also have difficulty learning complex skills and abstract concepts, and learn less overall than other students learn. Many students with mental retardation and severe disabilities experience memory deficits, either remembering incorrectly or not remembering automatically. These students frequently need additional cues to help them focus their attention.

Students with mild retardation learn academic tasks such as reading, writing, and math—sometimes achieving up to a sixth-grade level in some areas by the end of high school. These students, however, usually have more success with basic academic skills (such as decoding and math computation) than with more abstract and applied skills, such as reading comprehension and math problem-solving (Thomas & Patton, 1990). Students also have significant difficulty making connections among ideas and generalizing newly learned knowledge and skills to new situations (Drew et al., 1996). The following strategies promote skill and strategy acquisition and generalization:

- Engage students actively in learning.
- Teach the strategy or skill in small steps or segments.
- Teach students to use self-talk to "talk themselves through" activities.
- Have students perform the skill or strategy repeatedly.
- Provide many examples to promote generalization.
- Use the skill or strategy in several different learning situations to promote generalization.

Given that students with mental retardation have slow learning rates and significant difficulty learning higher-level thinking skills and abstract concepts, what they learn should be necessary to their daily functioning and serve them in their adult lives. The *Brigance Diagnostic Inventory of Essential Skills* (Brigance, 1981) provides one means of assessing higher-level functional skills (see Table 8.1).

Because students with mental retardation have many opportunities to experience failure, they can develop poor motivation for learning, and set low goals (Balla & Zigler, 1979). They also learn not to trust their own solutions, and look to others for cues (Zigler & Burack, 1989). Many students with mental retardation display **biased responding**—saying "yes" because they want to please the teacher or hide their confusion (Sigelman et al., 1981).

For Lilly, an eighth grader with Down syndrome and mild mental retardation, it is important that her teachers accommodate her slower rate, more concrete style of learning, and low level of confidence in her ability to learn. Lilly, who attends Madison Middle School, is mainstreamed for physical education, art (her favorite class), and home economics.

Grace Fong, her home economics teacher, makes several accommodations for Lilly. Although Lilly can decode the words in many recipes, directions, and other readings in the class, Grace found that Lilly often does not understand what she is reading. To help Lilly and several other students in her class, Grace uses paired reading and has the students check often for understanding. The students read with partners, stopping at the end of each paragraph or section to discuss that paragraph (or section), consistently using the

TABLE 8.1

Functional Skills Assessed by the Brigance Diagnostic Inventory of Essential Skills

AREA	SUBTESTS	AREA	SUBTESTS
Functional Word Recognition	Basic sight vocabulary Direction words Abbreviations Warning/safety signs Reads number words	Health and Safety	Medical vocabulary Medical labels Health evaluation form Health practices and attitude rating scale Self-concept rating scale Warning labels
Schedules and Graphs	Reads class schedule Reads television schedule Identifies and interprets graphs	Money and Finance	Price signs Computes totals for amounts of money Making change Comprehends and computes purchase savings
Forms	School information form Computer base form		Computes expenses using charts and tables Balancing a checking account
Measurement	Equivalent values of coins and the dollar bill Total values of collections of coins and bills Conversion of coins Time Equivalent units of time Conversion of units of time Equivalent calendar units Conversion of calendar units Calendar Dates Ruler Equivalent units of measurement Conversion of units of measurement Meters and gauges Concepts of Fahrenheit temperature		Manages a checking account Computes interest on loans Reads and comprehends a credit agreement Application for a credit card Reads and comprehends monthly credit statement
		Travel and Transportation	Traffic signs Traffic symbols Car parts vocabulary Identifies car parts Application for driver's instruction permit Auto safety rating scale Gas mileage and cost Mileage table Bus schedule and map of route Road map
Vocational	Attitude rating scale Personality rating scale Responsibility and self-discipline rating scale Job interests and aptitudes Health and physical problems/handicaps Application for a social security number Choosing a career Employment signs Employment vocabulary Employment abbreviations "Help wanted" advertisements Simple application for employment Complex application for employment Job interview questions Job interview preparation rating scale Job interview rating scale W-4 form Future time on clock Past time on clock Time duration on clock Payroll deductions Federal income tax return—Form 1040A Unemployment compensation form	Food and Clothing	Food vocabulary Food preparation vocabulary Basic recipe directions Food labels Conversion of recipes to different servings Foods for a daily balanced diet Computes cost of purchasing different quantities Food quantity at best price Personal sizes of clothing Clothing labels
		Oral Communication and Telephone Skills	Speaking skills Speaking skills rating scale Listening skills Listening skills rating scale Telephone Telephone book Telephone Yellow Pages

Reprinted with permission from Brigance, A.H. (1981). *Brigance Diagnostic Inventory of Essential Skills*. North Billerica, MA: Curriculum Associates.

cue, "What was this mainly about?" Lilly can check for understanding as she reads, instead of reading the entire assignment and then realizing that she has not understood. When reading recipes and directions for sewing, the pairs stop after each ingredient or direction and discuss what to do. Grace finds that this approach helps increase not only Lilly's success in comprehending what she reads, but also her confidence in her reading skills. Grace also finds that, in the long run, with paired reading all her students do better (and enjoy the interactions that naturally occur).

Social Skills

Students with mental retardation and severe disabilities have friends and participate in social activities, but often have difficulties developing friendships. Such difficulties may be due to behaviors that deter interactions or to the lack of opportunity (Westling & Fox, 1995). With the move toward inclusive learning communities, students have more opportunities to make friends.

The "Circles of Friends" (Forest & Lusthaus, 1989) is one example of an activity that can promote social support for students with disabilities as they are integrated into general education classrooms. In this activity, each student in the classroom completes a picture of his or her circles of friends, following the steps in Tips for Teachers 8.3.

Some students, particularly those with autism, may seem uninterested in the people around them, seldom making eye contact, or initiating, or responding to interactions. Students with severe disabilities often engage in isolated inappropriate behaviors such as stereotypic or self-injurious behaviors. **Stereotypic behaviors** include rocking, flapping fingers, twirling or spinning objects, and grinding teeth. **Self-injurious behavior**, which occurs in only 5 to 15 percent of individuals with severe retardation, may consist of head banging, scratching, or biting oneself, and is difficult to understand. One of several theories about why students exhibit these behaviors is that they are a means of communicating or regulating their own level of awareness (Helmstetter & Durand, 1991). Because students are unable to express their desires or dislikes verbally, they express them through their behavior.

Motor Skills

Some students with mental retardation, and most students with severe disabilities, have physical disabilities (Beirne-Smith et al., 1994) and also experience delays in sensory and motor development. The physical disabilities commonly found among individuals with severe disabilities include cerebral palsy, spina bifida, seizure disorders, hydrocephalus, and cardiovascular disorders. (Chapter 9 discusses physical disabilities in more detail.) Many students with severe disabilities cannot move independently, and need assistance through wheelchairs, walkers, and braces. Other students may have limited voluntary movement of any type, and may experience difficulty grasping items, holding their heads up, and rolling over.

Communication Skills

Students with mental retardation and severe disabilities often have difficulties communicating. Delayed speech and other speech problems are more common in students with severe disabilities than in other students. Additionally, language development may be inhibited or significantly delayed in students who have more limited cognitive abilities on which to build language skills, fewer experiences, and less exposure to activities than their nondisabled peers.

For many students with mild mental retardation, speech problems also are mild and can be corrected with help from a speech and language pathologist. Mental retardation affects not only how students communicate, however, but also the content and quality of their communication. These students use shorter, less complex sentences with fewer relative clauses and words with more concrete meanings. They also exhibit poorer recall of sentences (Bernstein & Tiegerman, 1993).

Students with severe disabilities may not acquire speech, or their speech may be difficult to understand for those who do not interact with them often. It is important to realize that a lack of speech does not preclude communication. Communication can occur through gestures, facial expressions, eye blinks, behavior, and through alternative and augmentative communication (such as the high- and low-technology communication devices introduced in Chapter 6). Low-technology

8.3 Providing School Support through Circles of Friends

Circles of Friends (Forest & Lusthaus, 1989) is an activity that can be used when students with disabilities are going to be integrated into general education classrooms. In this activity, each student in the classroom completes a picture of his or her circles of friends, using the following steps:

1. Students draw four circles.
2. In the first circle, students list the people closest to them, the people that they love.
3. In the second circle, students list the people they really like (but not enough to put in the first circle).
4. In the third circle, students list groups of people they like or people they do things with (e.g., scouts, soccer team).
5. In the fourth circle, students list people paid to be in their lives (e.g., doctor, dentist).

After students have completed their own circles of friends, the teacher describes the circles for a "fantasy person" who is similar to the student who will be joining the class. For example, a student might have only Mom listed in the first circle, with the second and third circles empty. In the fourth circle are a number of doctors and therapists. Through discussion, the teacher and students talk about how the student must feel and how this fantasy person is similar to the student with disabilities who is going to join the class. Finally, the teacher and students plan on how they can become part of the circles of friends for the student with disabilities through such activities as classroom ambassadors, telephone buddies, lunch buddies, and reading buddies.

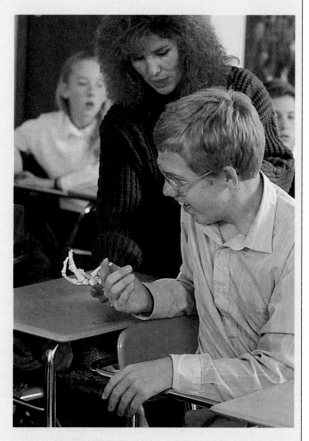

How might the Circles of Friends activity contribute to providing social support for students with disabilities in your classroom?

Adapted from Forest, M., & Lusthaus, E. (1989). Promoting educational equality for all students: Circles and maps. In S. Stainback, W. Stainback, and M. Forest (Eds.), *Educating all students in the mainstream of regular education.* (pp. 45–57). Baltimore: Brookes.

devices can involve pictures or drawings at which the student points to convey a message. High-technology devices can provide voice output (speech synthesizers) and can be programmed with many messages.

A **communication board** is one example of augmentative communication. The essential elements are the board itself and the symbols or pictures. The board can be made of sturdy paper or a board, or it can be a regular or simplified computer keyboard, or a computer screen. The symbols or symbol systems selected depend on the learner and the environment in which he or she lives. Symbols should be selected according to what students need and want to communicate. In constructing communication boards, Lewis (1993) suggests that the following questions need to be addressed:

- What choices will the student be able to make?
- How will the choices be represented on the board?
- How will the student make his or her selections?
- How many choices will be available and how will they be arranged on the board?
- How will the communication board be constructed?

Figure 8.2 presents examples of common symbol systems, which include: *Core Picture Vocabulary* (Johnston, 1985), *Talking Pictures* (Leff & Leff, 1978), *Pic Syms* (Carlson, 1984), *Oakland Schools Picture Dictionary* (Kirstein & Bernstein, 1981), *Picture Communication Symbols* (Johnson, 1985), and *Blissymbols* (Bliss, 1965).

This chapter's Tech Talk describes a computer program (The Communication Board-Maker) teachers can use to create communication boards.

Communication is an important area for students with mental retardation and severe disabilities because it gives them some control over their environment and a way to fulfill their wants and needs. It is also an important key to being socially accepted.

The students in Robert Hernandez's fourth grade class imitated the noises that Jason, a student

---

FIGURE 8.2

Picture Symbol Systems for Communication Boards

Core Picture Vocabulary	Talking Pictures	Pic Syms	Oakland	Picture Communication Symbols	Blissymbols
Man					
Wash					
Want	No Symbol				
Hello	No Symbol		No Symbol		
Happy	No Symbol				
House					
Car					

Reprinted by permission from Glennen, S. (1992). Augmentative and alternative communication. In G. Church and S. Glennen (Eds.), *The handbook of assistive technology,* (p. 100). San Diego, CA: Singular Publishing Group.

Communication Board-Maker

The Communication Board-Maker™ (Mayer-Johnson Co. [619-550-0084]) is a software program that allows teachers to create and print communication boards, using the Picture Communication Symbols (Johnson, 1985). This software is available for both Macintosh and IBM compatible systems. The boards are easy to design by using either a menu at the top of the screen or an index of the words for the pictures, or by clicking on the find button at the bottom of the screen and typing in the desired word.

More than 3,000 picture communication symbols are available. The arrangement of the pictures can be modified. Each picture has the written word. The written word for each picture can be deleted or it can be displayed in English, Spanish, or another language. This program provides a simple and efficient way for teachers to construct and modify communication boards.

Adapted from Lewis, R.B. (1993). *Special education technology: Classroom applications* (pp. 388–389). Pacific Grove, CA: Brooks/Cole.

Courtesy of Mayer-Johnson Co.

with autism, made. Robert and the special education teacher discussed with the class how Jason is learning to communicate. "Right now he does not use words, but he makes noises and uses his communication board. The noises he makes are [the way] he communicates, so . . . you need to respect this communication and not make fun of it. Your job is to listen closely and watch the communication board to learn what Jason is saying." Ideas to help students with mental retardation and severe disabilities develop communication skills are discussed in Tips for Teachers 8.4.

Approximately 40 percent of children with autism do not speak, and many others use **echolalia,** a repeating of what was said without necessarily understanding the meaning (Powers, 1989). For students with mild retardation, speech difficulties most often occur in articulation and include omissions, substitutions, or distortions of sounds (Beirne-Smith et al., 1994). Speech and language problems are the most frequently diagnosed secondary disability for students with mild retardation (Beirne-Smith et al., 1994).

TIPS FOR TEACHERS

8.4 Helping Students Develop Communication Skills

Following are areas to consider when assisting students with mental retardation and severe disabilities to develop their communication skills:

Reason to Communicate
By anticipating the needs of students with mental retardation and severe disabilities, we often deprive them of reasons to communicate. We need to create situations that motivate students to communicate. An example might be to "accidentally" forget to give them their lunch tickets when the rest of the class receives their tickets, or having every student tell you about the drawing they just did before they can go out to recess. Working on communication skills during everyday activities significantly increases the students' desire to communicate.

Mode of Communication
We need to make sure that students have a way, as well as a reason, to communicate. If your students do not use speech, they should have an augmentative communication device. If your students do not have a mode of communication, talk with the school's speech and language pathologist or inclusion specialist about developing or purchasing one.

Way to Make Choices
Self-stick notes provide a quick and easy way to provide students with disabilities on-the-spot choices (choosing a word to fill in the blank, choosing a color) to facilitate their participation in class. Just write the choices on the notes and stick them on the students' desks so that they can make the choices.

To help students choose a partner, take pictures of all the students in the class (or use individual class photos) and paste them in a little book or on a board, so that the student with a disability can chose the person with whom he or she wants to work on a class assignment.

Identification and Assessment of Students with Mental Retardation and Severe Disabilities

Before the passage of IDEA in 1975, many students with severe disabilities and mental retardation were not allowed to attend public schools. This federal legislation required that educational services be provided all students, including students with severe and profound retardation and severe disabilities, with the resulting need for better methods of identification and assessment for educational purposes. With the passage of IDEA amendments in 1986 (P.L. 99–457), these children became eligible to receive special education services as infants, toddlers, and in preschool (see Chapter 1).

Initial identification for students with all but mild mental retardation is usually a medical diagnosis at birth or shortly thereafter. For students with mild mental retardation, initial identification often occurs during preschool when the child's rate of development in cognitive, language, and motor skills is not typical. For these students the emphasis is on developmental and educational assessment, which usually includes measures of general intelligence and measures of adaptive behavior.

Although intelligence tests are still used to determine whether students have mental retardation and severe disabilities, a number of concerns have been raised. First, it can be difficult to know whether the tests accurately reflect the abilities of the students, particularly given their difficulty with communication and their delayed responses.

Second, there is continuing concern regarding cultural influences and biases in tests of intellectual functioning. In 1984 the California courts ruled that standardized IQ tests (e.g., Weschler, Stanford-Binet, and Leiter) could not be used to determine eligibility for special education for African American students (*Larry P. v. Riles*, 1984). Currently, emphasis continues to move toward a more functional definition, with intellectual functioning seen as only one aspect to consider in determining mental retardation and severe disabilities.

Another area used to determine evidence of mental retardation is the student's adaptive behavior. One frequently used adaptive behavior scale is the *AAMR Adaptive Behavior Scale—School* (2nd ed.) (Lambert et al., 1993), which includes domains for both adaptive and social behaviors (see Table 8.2).

Educational assessments are also used to determine instructional goals and objectives for individual students. According to Westling and Fox (1995), the process of determining instructional needs includes:

- collecting information from existing records
- interviewing parents to determine educational goals
- using adaptive behavior scales, activities, and skill lists to help decide students' needs
- conducting ecological inventories of the students' learning environments

Functional assessments determine the skills needed to complete a particular activity or task. **Ecological inventories** assess the different skills a student needs in his or her specific environments. Related service providers also assess the student's speech and physical needs (including vision and hearing, if necessary). The needs and strengths determined by these assessments are then incorporated into the student's IEP goals and objectives.

TABLE 8.2

Domains and Subdomains of the AAMR Adaptive Behavior Scale—School

Part One

I. Independent Functioning
   A. Eating
   B. Toilet Use
   C. Cleanliness
   D. Appearance
   E. Care of Clothing
   F. Dressing and Undressing
   G. Travel
   H. Other Independent Functioning

II. Physical Development
   A. Sensory Development
   B. Motor Development

III. Economic Activity
   A. Money Handling and Budgeting
   B. Shopping Skills

IV. Language Development
   A. Expression
   B. Verbal Comprehension
   C. Social Language Development

V. Numbers and Time

VI. Prevocational/Vocational Activity

VII. Self-Direction
   A. Initiative
   B. Perseverance
   C. Leisure Time

VIII. Responsibility

IX. Socialization

Part Two

X. Social Behavior

XI. Conformity

XII. Trustworthiness

XIII. Stereotypical and Hyperactive Behavior

XIV. Self-Abusive Behavior

XV. Social Engagement

XVI. Disturbing Interpersonal

Lambert, N., Nihira, K., & Leland, H. (1993). *AAMR Adaptive Behavior Scale—School: Examiner's manual* (2nd ed.). Austin, TX: Pro-Ed.

Instructional Guidelines and Accommodations for Teaching Students with Mental Retardation and Severe Disabilities

Teachers who have students with mental retardation and severe disabilities in their classrooms are asked to participate in the development of the students' educational plans, work with the students, and communicate and work with the paraprofessionals and specialists who provide support. Douglas Akers, a fifth grade teacher, has been working for several months with Amy, a student with Down syndrome and moderate retardation who is being included in general education classes for the first time. Reflecting about Amy's entering his class, Doug comments,

> I wanted to establish a good rapport with Amy. I wanted her to take directions from me, ... not just to rely on her aide or the special education teacher. I wanted Amy to develop a relationship with me and feel comfortable coming to me or the other students for assistance. I knew this would take time because she has always been in a self-contained special education class. But now she does come to me with her work and with questions.

The instructional guidelines and accommodations discussed here will help you to include students with mental retardation and severe disabilities in your class and to develop a social support network that will facilitate these students' success.

Role of the General Education Teacher

With the move toward inclusive schools, the roles of special education and general education teachers are less clearly defined. The role of the general education teacher is to be involved in and problem-solve adaptations and curriculum modifications for all students. Chris Johnson is a good example of a teacher whose role changed as he worked with a student with disabilities.

Upon hearing that he would have Darrell, a student with mild mental retardation, in his eighth grade applied math class, Chris shared these concerns, "One of my main concerns was what am I going to do for Darrell? How am I possibly going to teach him anything? I don't have a special education degree. I feel as if I need one in order to teach him. How is Darrell going to fit in as a member of the class?"

To alleviate these feelings, Chris met with Darrell's special education teacher, Martha Anderson. They reviewed the applied math curriculum in relation to Darrell's IEP goals and objectives. What they quickly realized was that many of Darrell's goals (including skills in measurement, making change, and using fractions and percentages) could be met within the general curriculum.

Each week Chris discussed the activities and assignments with Martha and she gave him ideas for modifications. Once a week, Martha worked in the room with Chris so that she could keep up with the curriculum and Darrell's progress. At the end of the first month, Chris commented, "Darrell is a member of our class, just like any of the [other] students. He works on math assignments, although I usually modify them by giving him less to complete, by allowing him to use manipulatives and a calculator, and in some cases giving him different assignments from the other students. What I have come to appreciate is that Martha is there to assist me."

One of the teacher's most important roles is to take "ownership" of students with disabilities by demonstrating that these students are members of the class. When this happens, students with disabilities develop a sense of belonging and being accepted. The need for this sense of belonging is part of the reason that spending only part of the day in class may not work for some students with mental retardation and severe disabilities. Schnorr (1990) found that part-time integration negatively affected the acceptance of a student with a severe disability as a class member. For Chris and his class, Darrell was just another member of the applied math class.

> Despite the movement toward inclusion, less than 10 percent of students with mental retardation and severe disabilities are educated primarily in general education classrooms. Thirty-five states use separate classrooms for educating more than half the students with mental retardation (the ARC, 1992).

Planning Systems

Planning—critical for all students—is particularly important for students with mental retardation and severe disabilities, whose learning goals may differ substantially from those of other students in the class. One planning system is the Planning Pyramid, introduced in Chapter 2 (Schumm et al., 1994). In the example in Chapter 2, Jeannette Robinson planned a unit on Weathering and Erosion (refer to Figure 2.6).

As she planned, Jeannette wrote in the base of the pyramid what she wanted *all* students to learn. This goal was appropriate for all the students in her class that year, but when Jeannette taught this unit the next year, Steven, a student with autism and limited language and cognitive skills, and Sandra, a student with mild mental retardation, were in her class. During weekly planning time, Jeannette talked about the unit with the inclusion specialist and assistant who supported Steven and Sandra. They decided that Steven's content goals would be to identify three types of weather (i.e., sunny, rainy, and snowy) and the type of clothing worn in each type, and Jeannette noted these specific goals on the unit planning sheet (see Figure 8.3).

Although Steven would participate in a number of the activities planned for the unit and continue to work on his general language and social goals (e.g., working with others and sharing, communicating wants and feelings), the assistant would work with him on these content goals. In discussion, Jeannette and the team decided that for Sandra a more limited depth of learning and modified quizzes would be appropriate accommodations. You should find the Planning Pyramid helpful for planning lessons and units and making instructional decisions about how to accommodate the various learners in your classroom.

When working with a student with severe disabilities you may also participate in planning for the student's long-range goals, which are incorporated into the IEP. **The McGill Action Planning System** (MAPS) (Lusthaus & Forest, 1987) is one example of such a planning system. The purpose of this planning activity is to foster relationships to improve the quality of life for persons with severe disabilities and to facilitate participation in inclusive settings such as a general education classroom.

In the MAPS process, the student, his or her family and friends, and special and general educators establish a team. Because peers are important to the process, students from the classroom generally participate in the team (Vandercook, York, &

Adults with mental retardation and severe disabilities, most of whom lived in institutions before the 1970s, now live in group homes and supported apartments. In a supported apartment arrangement, the person chooses his or her roommates, and the apartments are located in different areas on the community.

FIGURE 8.3

Planning Pyramid with Modifications for a Student with Significant Disabilities

What some students will learn.	• How earth looked during Ice Age • Disasters caused by sudden changes • Geographic examples of slow and fast changes
What most students will learn.	• Compare and contrast weathering and erosion • How humans cause physical and chemical weathering • Basic types of rocks
What ALL * students should learn.	• Basic components of earth's surface • Forces that change crust are weathering and erosion

* Steven— identify 3 types of weather and the appropriate clothing.

FIGURE 8.4

MAPS Questions and Ideas Generated for Tyrone

1. What is the individual's history?

   Tyrone developed meningitis shortly after birth, which resulted in brain damage. He learned to walk and talk much later than normal.

2. What is your dream for the individual?

   Tyrone will find a job in the community, where he can interact with many people, and a place to live with friends.

3. What is your nightmare?

   Tyrone will be alone after we (parents) pass away.

4. Who is the individual?

   Tyrone is a young man who loves music and talking to people. He is an only child. He is a sophomore in high school. He loves sports. He gets lonely and bored when alone for long periods of time.

5. What are the individual's strengths, gifts, and abilities?

   He loves to laugh and smiles a lot. He works hard. He has a great sense of humor. He's energetic. He is sensitive to others' moods.

6. What are the individual's needs?

   He needs friends his own age with whom to do things. He needs to be more assertive and ask for help, when necessary. He needs to be more independent in food preparation and in getting around the community.

7. What would the individual's ideal day at school look like and what must be done to make it happen?

   A Circle of Friends should be done with Tyrone so that he has friends to meet when he gets off the bus and to hang out with during lunch and breaks. Tyrone should participate in some community-based instruction. Tyrone should take a Foods class.

Forest, 1989). This team answers seven questions, using them to brainstorm methods to plan the student's future in an inclusive environment. Answers to the seven questions help determine the goals and objectives. Figure 8.4 provides an example of the MAPS questions and ideas for Tyrone, a high school student with severe mental retardation.

Functional Assessment, Discrepancy Analysis, and Task Analysis

Functional assessment, discrepancy analysis, and task analysis help determine the skills the student needs to reach established goals. In a functional assessment each goal or activity is broken into steps or subskills, and the student's present performance level is determined for each subskill or step in the activity. For example, the first column of Figure 8.5 shows the steps involved in the activity of getting to school, with the student's performance noted in the second column.

A **discrepancy analysis** reviews each specific step or skill and determines how the student does the step or skill, compared to nondisabled peers (the third column in Figure 8.5). If the student is unable to perform a step or skill (i.e., a discrepancy exists), then the teacher determines whether the student should be taught that particular step or skill or whether an adaptation should be made to help the student perform the skill. The fourth column in Figure 8.5 shows the adaptations and

---

FIGURE 8.5

Functional Assessment/Discrepancy Analysis

Student: Marta is an eighth grade student with moderate mental retardation and cerebral palsy

Activity: Arriving at school

Steps of the Activity	Student Performance	Discrepancy Analysis	Teach or Adapt
1. Arrives at school by bus	+		
2. Goes to locker	−	Cannot propel herself	Peers will wait by bus
3. Opens locker	−	Doesn't remember combination	Use key lock
4. Gets notebooks, etc. out	−	Can't reach items	Put items in backpack on hook
5. Hangs out/does hair until class	−	Doesn't initiate conversations	Develop a Circles of Friends
6. Goes to class when bell rings	−	Can't self propel that far	Ask classmates to help
7. Listens to announcements in homeroom	+		
8. Raises hand to indicate will eat lunch	+		
9. Goes to first hour when bell rings	−	Doesn't know which class is at this time	Teach to review a picture schedule and ask for help

Code: + = can do step   − = cannot do step

teaching that will occur as a result of the functional assessment and discrepancy analysis.

Next, a **task analysis** (a further breakdown of each individual step or skill, with the necessary adaptations) is used to guide teaching the step or skill to the student. For example, Making a Difference: The 60-Second Lesson describes how to develop a picture task analysis.

The same goals can be assessed across the different environments in which the activities occur. Mary Hinson, Marta's high school job developer, assessed "arriving and getting started" as part of placing Marta in her first job in an office—putting on labels and doing simple packaging. For a number of steps, the adaptations made at school could easily be made at work.

Partial Participation

When you look at a skill to determine whether a student can do it, it is important to remember the concept of **partial participation**, which assumes that an individual has the right to participate in all activities to the extent possible (Falvey, 1995). An opportunity to participate should not be denied because a person cannot independently perform the needed skills; instead individualized adaptations should be developed to allow participation

How might functional assessments have aided in placing this student in a work setting? How would you identify the skills the student needs to succeed? What opportunities does this learning situation provide for the functional practice of these skills?

and learning, even of only part if the skill. Ferguson and Baumgart (1991) stress the importance of active partial participation by having students make choices, manipulate objects, or communi-

MAKING A DIFFERENCE

The 60-Second Lesson

Developing a Picture Task Analysis

Picture task analyses, by providing visual cues of the steps of a task, enable students with mental disabilities to gain meaningful skills and independence. A picture is taken of each step in a task. Then the pictures are glued (in sequential order) in a manila folder, with a number under each picture. Laminating the whole folder helps preserve the photographs. An erasable pen enables students to cross off pictures as the steps are completed. How might you develop a picture schedule for Marta (see Figure 8.5)?

For more information, see "Using a Picture Task Analysis to Teach Students with Multiple Disabilities," by W. Roberson, J. Gravel, G. Valcante, and R. Maurer in *Teaching Exceptional Children, 1992, 24*(4), 12–16.

cate. Active participation not only helps maintain students' physical health, but also enhances their image as peers see them partaking in a meaningful activity. Say, for example, that a class is working on writing sentences, using correct punctuation. A classmate randomly selects three small pictures and places them on Heather's desk. Heather, a student with a severe disability, has to reach out and point to one of the pictures. Her goals are to reach and point, look at her peer, and make decisions in a timely fashion. The peer then holds up the picture for the class to see. The class writes a sentence about it, and Heather must answer a question about it.

Curriculum Adaptations

An important component of adapting materials or instruction is joint planning by the special education and classroom teachers. When Jeannette Robinson heard she was going to have two students with mental retardation and severe disabilities in her classroom (i.e., Steven and Sandra, discussed earlier in this chapter), she was concerned that she would be responsible for writing lesson plans and making all the adaptations. She felt overwhelmed until she realized it was a team process and that the special education teacher and assistant would help her plan. She commented, "I'm so relieved. I feel much more positive now. I didn't know how I was going to do it." Realizing that it is a team process, and that everyone has knowledge to contribute, is important.

The following hierarchy of curriculum-modification questions can be used to help guide teams in making decisions about a student's participation:

1. Can the student participate in the unmodified activity?
2. Can the student participate in the activity with adapted materials, support, or modified expectations?

   - Can the student participate with peer support or with extra adult support?
   - Do materials need to be modified or substituted?
   - Do expectations of the activity (e.g., learning goals, amount of work, method of evaluation) have to be modified?

3. Can the student participate in this activity by working on embedded communication, motor, or social skills?

If the answer to these questions is "no," the team might consider a parallel activity related to the student's educational priorities (as Jeannette and her team did for Steven, when planning the unit on Erosion and Weathering).

Peer Support

Another important component of teaching accommodations is the development of peer support. Peers may be the most underrated and underused human resource available in general education classrooms. Nondisabled peers are often creative problem solvers and staunch supporters of students with mental retardation and severe disabilities (York & Vandercook, 1991).

It is important, however, that students not always take the role of "helping" a student with disabilities, which can get in the way of their developing a friendship. Initially, peer support requires adult facilitation as needs and strategies are identified, but adult participation should be reduced as friendships develop. Teachers using Circle of Friends for a student with disabilities often find that classmates want to add the student to their circles and try to finish their work early so they can work with the student. Some teachers find that so many students volunteer, they must use a sign-up sheet, limiting the number of times per month peers can work with a student.

Strategies to Support Students in General Education Classes

A number of general strategies can be used to support students with mental retardation and severe disabilities in general education classrooms.

Increasing a Student's Sense of Belonging One key to success is to create a community to which the student with disabilities has a sense of belonging. Frisbee and Libby (1992) suggest the following strategies to increase this sense of belonging:

- Give the student the same "things" as the other students (e. g., desk, typical seating, locker, name on classroom charts).

- Demonstrate respect for the student by using age-appropriate language, and being a good role model.
- Involve the student in the typical classroom routine.
- Work with your educational team and students to find ways for the student to participate actively in classroom activities.
- Consult with specialists for ideas, and express your concerns.
- Encourage students to find ways to increase learning opportunities for classmates who are challenged.
- Promote equality and interactions with other classmates (e.g., remember to use the word "friend" instead of "peer tutor," and say "go together" rather than "take _____ with you."

Accepting Varied Learning Goals The most frequently asked question about inclusion is, "How are students going to benefit from my class—what will they get out of it?" Students with mental retardation and severe disabilities may be working on their own goals during class activities. It is important that these goals, however different, be regarded as meeting valued educational needs. Sean Miller, a high school biology teacher, says his biggest concern was how to grade the student with mild retardation in his class. He comments, "I didn't know what to do. The student was trying and doing her work, but it wasn't high school level. I wondered if I gave her a passing grade, was it fair to the other students? We (the special education staff and I) ended up sitting down and reviewing her goals and determining a grade based on that. I was comfortable with that idea."

A sheet that demonstrates the relationship between the IEP goals and the activities in the general education classroom helps everyone understand that individual goals can be met through classroom activities. One example, the IEP Goal–Activity Matrix shown in Figure 8.6 is for Manny, a second grade student with a moderate mental disability. Across the top of the matrix are the subjects and activities, with Manny's IEP goals down the side. Each indicates the logical time for Manny to work on his IEP goal during his school day.

Making Environmental Accommodations *Environmental accommodations* are changes made to the physical learning environment so that each student can participate successfully. These changes are often as simple as having a bean bag chair so that a student with cerebral palsy can be on the floor with peers during story time, or lifting the legs of a desk a few inches so that a wheelchair fits comfortably.

Team Teaching As you may recall from Chapter 4, team teaching involves two or more teachers (special and general education) cooperatively teaching a class or particular curriculum or thematic unit. The teachers often have different areas of expertise that build upon each other to make a successful lesson for all students. Team teaching reduces the teacher–student ratio, thereby making small group instruction more feasible.

Cooperative Learning Cooperative learning, also discussed in Chapter 4, it is an effective instructional method for including students with mental retardation and severe disabilities (Wilcox et al., 1987). In cooperative learning situations, the class is divided into groups for learning activities that have cooperative goals. Each student has a role, and it is important that each role is valued. Cooperative learning fosters interdependence and helps all involved to develop interpersonal skills. General education teachers need to be comfortable with the idea of having heterogeneous groups for cooperative learning. In a recently conducted study, Hunt, Staub, Alwell, and Goetz (1994) found that having a student with a severe disability in a cooperative group did not in any way hinder the progress of other members.

> Students with mental retardation and severe disabilities need to learn general work habits such as following directions, working with others, accepting feedback and supervision, asking for help, working steadily at a satisfactory rate, doing quality work, and completing the work (Kokaska & Brolin, 1985).

Accommodating Personal Learning Styles Accommodating learning styles involves letting students learn and demonstrate what they learn in ways that

FIGURE 8.6

IEP Goal–Activity Matrix

Student __Manny__   Semester __Fall 1997__

Grade __2nd grade__   Teachers __Ms. Nichols, Mr. O'Brian__

IEP Goals   **Subjects/Activities**

	Opening	Reading/ Language Arts	Recess	Math Their Way	Lunch	Science/ Social Studies
Writes name and functional words		X		X		X
One-to-one correspondence				X		X
Decision making	X	X	X	X	X	X
Initiating communication	X	X	X	X	X	X
Functional reading	X	X				X

reflect their individual strengths. Students may share their knowledge through an oral report instead of a written one, or by creating a collage about the topic being studied. High school teacher Lynn Blankenship, who teaches Independent Living Skills, says that because she encourages students to use various methods of demonstrating their knowl- edge, having Jessica, a student with moderate retar- dation, worked out well.

Providing Hands-On Instruction Hands-on or experientially based instruction relates learning to what students already know and uses real-life activities as teaching tools. This type of instruction provides greater opportunity for students with mental retardation and severe disabilities to be actively involved. The use of learning centers, math manipulatives, science projects, art projects, and computers are examples of hands-on activities that give students with mental retardation and severe disabilities the opportunity to participate.

Providing Opportunities for Functional Practice

In addition to hands-on activities, opportunities for **functional practice** are also important. When practice is relevant, students can easily see the connection between what they are practicing and its use in real life. For example, you can incorporate into reading instruction activities that stress reading for fun or to obtain information needed for daily life. Suggestions include:

- directions (e.g., for cooking, building a model, repairing an appliance)
- directional orientation and map reading
- menus
- labels on foods, medicines, clothing
- telephone book
- catalogs and advertisements (for selecting something to order)
- schedules (e.g., bus, train, television)
- signs
- adult and student newspapers and magazines

Writing activities also can be centered around daily activities, as follows:

- writing a message for a friend
- writing a letter to request something or complain
- writing a postcard or letter to a friend
- making a shopping list
- completing a job application or an application for a library card
- ordering something by filling out a form
- writing down a telephone message

Functional math activities include:

- making change
- counting money
- making a purchase
- using a checking account
- using a credit card
- budgeting money
- telling and estimating time
- reading a calendar
- reading a thermometer
- measuring
- determining weight and height

Students' success in functional activities can often predict the degree to which they will function successfully as adults.

Encouraging Parental Involvement Every teacher realizes the importance of parental involvement in a student's education. This involvement is especially important for a student with disabilities, whose parents play a key role in determining the student's educational program. Knowing the parents' goals for their child can help everyone work together as a team. The Research Brief presents parents' perspectives on inclusion and curriculum goals for children with severe disabilities.

RESEARCH BRIEF

PARENTS' PERCEPTIONS OF GOALS FOR STUDENTS WITH DISABILITIES

A frequently asked question is what types of goals students with mental retardation work on in the general education classroom. Parents are key members of the multidisciplinary team that determines what goals are important for the student. Knowing what parents think and feel is important information for school staff.

Hamre-Nietupski, Nietupski, & Strathe (1992) surveyed 68 parents of students (6–21 years old) with moderate or severe/profound disabilities to determine the relative value these parents placed on the following curricular areas: functional life skills (e.g., making simple meals), academic skills (e.g. addition), and development of friendships and social relationships (e.g., sharing games with peers). Parents of students with moderate disabilities ranked the areas' relative value in the following order: 1) functional life skills, (2) academic skills, and (3) friendship/social relationship development. Parents of students with severe/profound disabilities ranked the areas differently: (1) friendship/ social development, (2) functional life skills, and (3) academic skills.

What do parents of nondisabled children think about having a child with a severe disability in their child's class? Giangreco, Edelman, Cloninger, and Dennis (1993) surveyed 81 parents of nondisabled children (grades k–8) about their perceptions of their children having a classmate with a severe disability. The results showed that parents not only think that their children are comfortable interacting with a classmate with a severe disability and that this interaction has a positive effect on their children's social and emotional growth, but also that having a classmate with a severe disability has not interfered with their children's receiving a good education. Overall, the parents felt that having a classmate with a severe disability was a positive experience for their children.

When Anne Kiernan, a third grade teacher, learned that she was going to have a child with autism in her class, she insisted on sitting down with the parents before school started to learn more about the student's strengths and weaknesses. She said, "I wanted to know from John's parents what John was like, ... some of [his] habits ..., what works for them, what doesn't work, and what ... he like[s]. Not to find out negative things—just to talk with them. It was very helpful."

No one knows the student better than his or her family. The family's cultural background influences their perception and attitudes about disabil-ities. The Research Brief provides a brief summary of three cultural views of disabilities. An understanding of people's diverse views may be helpful to you before you meet with parents.

RESEARCH BRIEF

CULTURAL VIEWS OF DISABILITIES

Cultural beliefs can affect the manner in which a family accepts and adapts to a child with a disability. These beliefs can also determine the family's ability to request help and the level of trust they give professionals (Seligman, 1991). Before professionals attempt to provide help to families of diverse backgrounds, they should be aware of how that culture views disabilities, while also taking into account that every family is unique.

Latin American. When a child with a disability is born, the disability may be attributed to an external, nonmedical reason (Cheng, 1990). For example, several Latino mothers attributed their children's cleft palates to an eclipse during pregnancy. The disability may also be regarded as a punishment for the adults and as God's will, and be accepted as such. Although some families use extended support to help raise the child, other families may hide the child because of family pride. Individual family values related to the sex and status of the child may influence acceptance of the disability. The disability of a firstborn male might be harder to accept than that of a daughter (Lynch & Hanson, 1992).

African American. Some African Americans react with less distress than people of other cultures to having a child with a disability, because of family support and religious beliefs. Disability is often interpreted in either of two ways: as bad luck or misfortune, or less often as the result of "sins of the fathers." The perceived cause of the disability has no apparent effect on interactions with families who have a member with a disability or on how the family itself deals with the disability (Lynch & Hanson, 1992).

Native American. Native American families are likely to downplay the birth of a child with a disability. The birth of a child with a disability may be viewed as a "prenatal choice" by the infant, and consequently not be considered a negative event. Some tribes believe that a disability is the consequence of a transgression. The consequence is not seen as a punishment, but just the result (Ponchillia, 1993). Children with disabilities are for the most part accepted and taught to assume useful roles in the community.

As integration of students with mental retardation and severe disabilities into general education classrooms increases, it is important that you learn strategies for accommodating these students in your class. You may need to adapt the curriculum or have the students work on goals not specified in the curriculum. A key to successful integration is collaboration with and support from the specialists who work with these students. By making time for co-planning and ongoing communication, you can help ensure that students are successful and that you feel positive about the learning experiences of all the students in your class.

SUMMARY

- Students with mental retardation and severe disabilities represent a diverse group of individuals with varied learning needs and abilities.
- Although ability levels vary, difficulties often occur in four areas: intellectual functioning, and social, motor, and communication skills.
- The causes of mental retardation are unknown in 50 percent of the students with mental retardation, but it is known that many of the causes are preventable.
- An important part of students' success is participation in planning systems, such as the Planning Pyramid and MAPS.

- Functional assessment and discrepancy analysis are means of determining how students perform a skill and whether the skill should be taught or adapted.
- A change in teaching style to incorporate more hands-on and cooperative learning activities can help you include all students in classroom activities.
- Environmental accommodations, team teaching, cooperative learning, hands-on learning, providing practice in functional activities, and getting parents involved are all strategies to promote students' involvement and learning.

Key Terms and Concepts

adaptive behavior

autism

biased responding

communication board

deaf–blind

developmental period

discrepancy analysis

Down syndrome

dual sensory impairments

echolalia

ecological inventories

Fetal Alcohol Syndrome

functional assessment

functional practice

inclusion support teacher or specialist

intellectual functioning

McGill Action Planning System (MAPS)

mental retardation

multiple disabilities

partial participation

self-injurious behavior

severe disabilities

stereotypic behavior

systems of support

task analysis

Think and Apply

1. Think about Susie's role as an inclusion specialist in relation to your role as a classroom teacher. If one of Susie's students were to join your class, how would you plan, communicate, and work with Susie so that she could support both you and the student. List the questions you would want to ask Susie before the student joined your class.

2. Review AAMR's new definition for mental retardation, and think about two students with mental retardation. Decide which level of support they would need. Discuss with a classmate the pros and cons of this type of classification system.

3. Think about a classroom activity, then use the hierarchy of curriculum-modification questions to determine how a student with mental retardation and severe disabilities could participate in the activity.

4. ABLEDATA is a service with information about more than 20,000 assistive technology products and related services. Call 1-800-227-0216 or fax 301-587-1967 and ask one of the information specialists to research your area of interest. Report on what you learned.

5. Watch a student with a severe disability participate in a general education activity. Make a list of all the embedded skills you observe the student using (e.g., communicating, reaching).

Read More about It

1. *Changes in Attitudes, Changes in Latitudes* by Carol Tashie, Susan Shapiro-Barnard, Ann Donoghue Dillon, Mary Schuh, Cheryl Jorgensen, and Jan Nisbet. Durham, NH: University of New Hampshire, Institute on Disability.

   This colorful publication reviews the emerging role of inclusion facilitators and provides, with wit and wisdom, many stories about their experiences.

2. *Treasures: A Celebration of Inclusion* by Ann Donoghue Dillon, Carol Tashie, Mary Schuh, Cheryl Jorgensen, Susan Shapiro-Barnard, Beth Dixon, and Jan Nisbet. Durham, NH: University of New Hampshire, Institute on Disability.

   Second in the series, this thought-provoking, emotional photo essay on inclusive schooling is a celebration for all the families, students, and school personnel who have worked hard for inclusive schooling in New Hampshire.

3. *From Special to Regular, from Ordinary to Extraordinary* by Carol Tashie, Susan Shapiro-Barnard, Mary Schuh, Cheryl Jorgensen, Ann Donoghue Dillon, Beth Dixon, and Jan Nisbet. Durham, NH: University of New Hampshire, Institute on Disability.

   This third book, written to inspire and support families and professionals working toward inclusive schooling, includes strategies for beginning the inclusion process, meeting challenges along the way, and planning for success.

4. *Mental Retardation: A Life Cycle Approach* (6th edition) by Clifford Drew, Michael Hardman, and Donald Logan (1996).

   An overview of the field of mental retardation from an educational perspective.

5. The following articles provide general education teachers' perspectives about inclusion of students with mental retardation and severe disabilities:

   Ferguson, D. L., Meyer, G., Jeanchild, L., Juniper, L., & Zingo, J. (1992). Figuring out what to do with the grownups: How teachers make inclusion "work" for students with disabilities. *Journal for the Association for Persons with Severe Handicaps, 17*, 218–226.

   Giangreco, M. F., Dennis, R., Cloninger, C., Edelman, S., & Schattman, R. (1993). I've counted Jon: Transformational experiences of teachers educating students with disabilities. *Exceptional Children, 59*, 359–372.

   York, J., & Tundidor, M. (1995). Issues raised in the name of inclusion: Perspectives of educators, parents, and students. *Journal for the Association for Persons with Severe Handicaps, 20*, 31–44.

   York, J., Vandercook, T., MacDonald, C., Heise-Neff, C., & Caughey, E. (1992). Feedback about integrating middle-school students with severe disabilities in general education classes. *Exceptional Children, 58*, 244–258.

Teaching Students with Visual, Hearing, Physical, or Health Impairments

FOCUS QUESTIONS

1. How are visual and hearing impairments defined, both legally and functionally?

2. How are physical disabilities and health impairments defined?

3. How can you identify students with possible visual and hearing impairments?

4. What are some areas to assess when developing an education plan for students with physical disabilities or health impairments?

5. How can you modify instruction and the classroom environment to accommodate the needs of students' visual, hearing, physical, or health impairments?

6. How can you foster the acceptance and participation of students with vision, hearing, physical, and health impairments in your classroom?

7. What is the role of the orientation and mobility specialist, the interpreter, the physical or occupational therapist, and the adaptive physical education teacher?

Interview

Pat Childers and Diane Batson

Pat Childers, a middle school English teacher, teaches a combination seventh–eighth grade class of thirty students. One of Pat's students is Brandy Walters, an eighth grader who is totally blind and uses braille. Brandy is supported by Diane Batson, an itinerant teacher for students with visual impairments. Diane's diverse caseload includes students with visual impairments, students with multiple disabilities including visual impairments, and students who are both visually impaired and gifted. The vision of most of her students enables them to read print.

When Pat initially learned that Brandy would be a member of her classroom she had several concerns. First, she felt that students would be disrupted by having a second adult, Diane, in the room. Another concern was all the activities Pat believed Brandy would have difficulty doing. Pat's concern increased when Diane started bringing in Brandy's equipment, including a computer with a braille printer that (to Pat) sounded like a popcorn machine.

Because of all the equipment, Diane and Brandy took over a corner of the classroom, where Brandy had a table to herself. Pat found this arrangement unsatisfactory, in that Brandy was isolated from the rest of the class. Pat, who recognized that Brandy had social needs as well as academic needs, commented on her concerns, "Brandy could hide behind that computer and was off in the corner by herself. I moved her right in with the other kids so she'd be part of the classroom community. Then she started making friends with the other kids." At the end of the year Pat described Brandy's role in the class as,

. . . a part of the gang. The kids never excluded her. She followed the rules just like the rest of them.

One time, when Brandy did not follow a classroom rule, she had to pay the consequences just like the other students. In my room, students who break rules know they have to go out and run a lap around the track. When Brandy had to "do a lap," she took her long cane and used it to independently locate and travel around the track.

Pat and Diane both recognize the importance of working as a team. They learned to work together, noting that being flexible is what made it work. Diane says, "Sometimes Pat would change a lesson at the last minute. There was no way I could get the books, notes, and other written information brailled in time, so Pat would get a peer to read it to Brandy. Somehow, it would always work because Pat was flexible in her teaching."

Flexibility and organization, Pat learned, are equally important for the class to run smoothly. When she selected reading materials for the class or wrote a test, she shared the information with Diane, giving Diane time to prepare the materials in braille so that Brandy could participate in the activity. In fact, after working together for a year, both Pat and Diane commented that they continue to need to improve their co-planning and organization. For students with visual impairments (and the other types of impairments discussed in this chapter), the teachers' preparation prior to teaching is what often determines the degree to which the students can be included in the learning activities of the classroom.

Introduction

Although there are not many students with visual, hearing, physical, or health impairments, it is not unusual for these students to be educated in general education classrooms, particularly when they do not have multiple disabilities that include mental retardation. This chapter provides strategies for teaching and accommodating these students in your classroom. Because these students have different needs (based on their disabilities) and usually work with different specialists, this chapter is divided into three sections: *visual impairments* (VI), *hearing impairments* (HI), and *physical disabilities and health impairments* (PD/HI). When you work with these students, you will be part of a team that includes not only you, the parents, and the special education teacher who specializes in teaching students who are visually impaired, hearing impaired, or have physical or health impairments, but also such specialists as orientation and mobility specialists (VI), interpreters (HI), physical and occupational therapists, and adaptive physical education teachers.

Students with Visual Impairments

Both Pat and Diane have learned to modify materials and the environment to meet the needs of students who have visual impairments. This section's discussion of students with visual impairments focuses on instructional strategies you can use to assist these students in your classroom. So that you can better understand these students, the section begins with definitions and types of visual impairments, information about the characteristics, prevalence, and identification of students with visual impairments.

Definitions and Types of Visual Impairments

When glasses or contacts do not correct vision to within normal or near normal limits, students may be considered to have a visual impairment that may require special education services. Several definitions are used to describe visual impairments:

- **Partially sighted** individuals have (with best possible correction in the better eye) a measured visual acuity between 20/70 and 20/200.
- **Blind** individuals are unable to see, and therefore use tactual (touch) and auditory (hearing) abilities to access the environment.
- **Legal blindness** is a condition in which individuals (with the best possible correction in the better eye) have a measured visual acuity of 20/200 or worse, or a visual field restricted to 20 degrees or less.
- **Functional vision** is the amount of usable vision a person has with which to complete a task or interact with the environment.
- **Low vision** describes an individual who is either partially sighted or legally blind, and refers to the amount of functional vision a person has.

How clearly an individual can see a designated object at a distance of 20 feet is called **visual acuity**. How well an individual can see, using *peripheral* or side vision, is called **visual field**. Students with visual impairments may have limited visual acuity, visual field, or both.

The many causes of visual impairments are usually grouped in the following three areas:

- **diseases** (e.g., cataracts, glaucoma, retinopathy of prematurity)
- **trauma or injury** (e.g., car accidents, a blow to the head)
- **refractive errors** (e.g., myopia, hyperopia)

Although it is helpful to know the cause of a student's visual impairment, it is more important to know how the student uses vision functionally. When Eliosa Mendez was told that Amber, a student with cataracts, would be in her sixth grade classroom she was very nervous. Mrs. Mendez, whose grandmother had cataracts and was able to read only large print at a very slow pace, was surprised that Amber could see the blackboard (provided that she sat in the front row and Eliosa used white

> In the first five years of life, vision is responsible for between 80 to 90 percent of what we learn. Only 5 to 10 percent of people who are visually impaired can see nothing at all.

chalk). Amber could read regular print books, although she held them closer than the other students and sometimes used a hand magnifier to see details on maps and drawings. Eliosa quickly learned that although her grandmother and Amber both had the same eye disease, their functional vision varied considerably.

Characteristics of Students with Visual Impairments

Even though a student with a visual impairment is more like sighted peers than different from them, a visual impairment has an impact on all aspects of development. Its impact on each student varies considerably (Warren, 1994). Students may have difficulty learning concepts, especially those related to space (e.g., up–down, left–right) (Hall, 1982; Hill & Ponder, 1976). For young children, learning their way around the classroom may be challenging; it is important to help them learn landmarks and cues in their environment so that they can travel independently (Hill & Ponder, 1976). Some students may have difficulty with language skills; for example, they may engage in **echolalia** (inappropriately repeating words or phrases they hear) or they may ask many questions (Andersen et al., 1984; Elsner, 1983; Kitzinger, 1984). Motor development, especially eye–hand coordination, is another area of difficulty. For example, these students may have trouble with scissors, write illegibly, or spill liquids when pouring. Students with visual impairments often have significant problems in social development (Kekelis, 1988; Read, 1989; Sacks & Gaylord-Ross, 1992; Workman, 1986). The Research Brief gives examples and suggests strategies you can use to help students with visual impairments achieve social success in your classroom.

RESEARCH BRIEF

SOCIAL RELATIONSHIPS OF YOUNG STUDENTS WITH VISUAL IMPAIRMENTS

To learn how elementary-age children form and maintain social relationships, Linda Kekelis and Sharon Zell Sacks (1992) studied six kindergarten and first grade students with visual impairments in general education classrooms. For one school year, they observed the students for half a day each week and interviewed the classroom and special education teachers, the students, and their classmates.

Compared to sighted classmates, five of the six students with visual impairments showed lags in social development. These lags were influenced by the following four factors:

- student's ability to communicate with others, use social skills (especially the ability to initiate to peers), and travel independently in the classroom
- appropriateness of learning environment, including organization of materials, classroom rules, and behavior of sighted students
- degree to which teachers were involved with the students with visual impairments (including teacher's emphasis on social and academic growth, amount of student supervision provided, and amount of time special education teacher spent assisting and supporting the classroom teacher)
- classroom teachers' levels of acceptance and collaboration skills working with specialists.

The classroom teachers played an important role in the inclusion of students with visual impairments. Teachers who considered social growth as important as academic growth promoted social interaction by restricting group size and structuring activities. These modifications enabled the students with visual impairments to understand who was present in the immediate environment and what activities were appropriate and necessary. When visual information was required for success, teachers either modified the activity or assigned a sighted peer or adult to assist the student.

Often when we speak of success for students with disabilities in general education classrooms we think of academic success. The research of Kekelis and Sacks shows that social success is an equally important concern. You need to plan for social success when including students with visual impairments in general education classrooms.

Prevalence of Visual Impairments

Visual impairments are considered a low-incidence disability, which means that comparatively fewer students have visual impairments than high-incidence disabilities such as learning disabilities. According to the American Printing House for the Blind (1993), approximately 52,000 students with visual impairments (less than 1 percent of the school population) were counted in the United States in January, 1992. Of students with visual impairments, approximately half have some other disability (often mental retardation). Students with such multiple disabilities, including students who are deaf–blind, are discussed in Chapter 8.

It is estimated that about 25 percent of students with visual impairments are *visual* readers (use large print or some means of enlarging the print), 10 percent are *braille* readers (use braille for reading), and 9 percent are *auditory* readers (listen to tapes or others reading). The remaining students are either *prereaders* (young children) or *nonreaders* who, in addition to their visual impairment, have other disabilities (usually mental retardation) that interfere with their ability to read.

Identification and Assessment of Students with Visual Impairments

Certain signs may prevent or lessen the damage from a visual impairment or help you identify students to refer for evaluation. Following are common symptoms of visual impairments:

- red-rimmed, swollen, or encrusted eyes
- excessive blinking
- itchy eyes
- eyes that are tearing
- one or both eyes turn inward, outward, upward, or downward
- extreme sensitivity to light
- tilting or turning head to one side to see an object
- squinting or closing one eye to see an object
- covering one eye to view an object
- thrusting head forward to view an object
- headaches, fatigue, or dizziness after doing close work
- tripping, bumping into objects, or appearing disoriented
- recurring styes (i.e., inflamed swelling of gland at margin of the eyelid)

If you suspect that a student has a visual impairment, you should refer the student to the school nurse. To receive educational services from a special education teacher specializing in visual impairments, students must have a documented visual impairment. Written documentation in the form of an eye report is obtained from an ophthalmologist or optometrist.

After a student's visual impairment is identified, the special education teacher who specializes in visual impairments assesses the student's functional vision and compensatory skills (such as listening and orientation skills). Then the multidisciplinary team develops an IEP that addresses any necessary accommodations. **Compensatory skills** include skills needed for independence and include the use of braille, a slate and stylus, and an abacus. During assessment, the special education teacher observes the student in different activities and environments, including your classroom. The special education teacher examines lighting, colors, contrasts, optimal print size, seating preference, and visual features of the environment and suggests modifications and accommodations you can make for the student.

Heather Blair quickly realized that Winnie, a fourth grade student with low vision, relied on three **sensory channels** (modalities): visual, auditory, and tactile. Heather planned lessons and incorporated experiences that enabled Winnie to gain information through these three channels. All students learn through multiple channels. Students with visual impairments need to recognize their primary and secondary channels for learning. Koenig and Holbrook (1993) have designed a Learning Media Assessment procedure that teachers can use to determine a student's primary and secondary learning channels. The Learning Media Assessment involves observing the student in different situations to determine the manner in which the student attends to and accesses information. Figure 9.1 shows a portion of the Learning Media Assessment for Darren, a second grade student with low vision. Can you determine Darren's primary and secondary sensory channels for learning?

FIGURE 9.1

Learning Media Assessment Observation Form

USE OF SENSORY CHANNELS

Student _Darren_

Setting/Activity _Math Class_

Date _3 – 22_   Observer _S. Jones_

Observed Behavior	Sensory Channel		
teacher writing on board	[V]	T	A
Darren picks up pencil	V	(T)	A
Darren writes problem on paper	[V]	T	A
teacher calls on student who walks to board and	[V]	T	A
solves problem	V	T	A
Darren reaches in desk and pulls out eraser	V	(T)	A
Darren listens to teacher's directions	V	T	(A)
Darren turns page of book	[V]	(T)	A
Darren picks up pencil	V	(T)	A
Darren looks at book	[V]	T	A
Darren writes problem on paper	[V]	T	A
Darren raises hand	V	(T)	A
teacher calls on Darren	V	T	(A)
Darren states answer to problem	V	T	(A)
teacher tells class to do all problems on the page	V	T	(A)
Darren looks at book	[V]	T	A
Darren writes problem on page in notebook	[V]	T	A
	V	T	A
	V	T	A
	V	T	A
	V	T	A

☐ Probable Primary Channel: _Visual_

◯ Probable Secondary Channel(s): _Auditory_

Form reprinted with permission from Koenig, A., & Holbrook, M.G. (1993). *Learning media assessment of students with visual impairment: A resource guide for teachers.* Austin, TX: Texas School for the Blind and Visually Impaired.

Instructional Guidelines and Accommodations for Students with Visual Impairments

Some general education teachers feel overwhelmed when they see the materials and equipment that a student with visual impairments needs in the classroom. Ron Cross, a seventh grade science teacher, was awestruck the day before school started when Susan Brady, the itinerant special education teacher, carried into his classroom a tape recorder, the science textbook on audiotape and in braille (twelve volumes), and a brailler and braille paper (i.e., the machine and special paper used to write braille). During the year, Susan also provided tactual diagrams of cells and insects (i.e., diagrams that are raised and textured so that the features can be felt). Susan explained that the specialized equipment and materials would enable Josh, who for educational purposes is blind, to succeed in science class. She and Ron reviewed a list of accommodations and teaching suggestions she had prepared. Susan indicated that many of these accommodations, presented in Tips for Teachers 9.1, are also helpful for students who have some usable vision.

Using Braille and Braille Devices Some students, such as Josh, may have some usable vision but rely on tactual and auditory information gained by

TIPS FOR TEACHERS

9.1 Modifications of the Environment for Students with Visual Impairments

Physical Environment
- Announce your presence and identify yourself (e.g., "Hi girls, it's Mr. Johnson, May I join your science group to see how you are working together?"). Also announce your departure (e.g., "Thank you girls for letting me join you. I'm going to check in with Ryan's group now.").
- Leave doors fully opened or closed, and drawers closed, so that the student does not run into them.
- Describe the location of things, especially after rearranging the classroom. Start with the door and travel around the room systematically noting locations.
- Provide an extra desk or shelf space for the student to store materials.
- Provide access to an outlet for a tape recorder, lamp, or other electrical equipment.
- Offer early dismissal from class so that the student has time to travel to other classes.

Learning Environment
- Familiarize students with classroom materials (e.g., give them time to visually or tactually explore a globe before asking them to locate the longitude and latitude of a city).

- Have concrete examples students can touch (e.g., in science, have fossils, not just pictures of fossils).
- Provide lessons with tactual and auditory components, and adapt assignments so that students can participate by using alternative sensory channels.
- Consider lighting conditions. Some students do best with natural lighting, others do better with lamps. Backlighting reduces visibility, so avoid standing in front of a window when you present material to the class. Low contrast in materials and between backgrounds and foregrounds reduces visibility.
- Provide written copies of any materials you use on an overhead projector or chalkboard. When you use an overhead projector or chalkboard, say what you are writing as you do it.
- Allow a peer to take notes for the student, but check that the student is still paying attention and participating.
- Provide opportunities for students to work in groups, especially when the assignment has a visual component (e.g., conducting experiments in science class).
- Modify writing activities as necessary by allowing students to dictate into a tape recorder.

using these learning channels. These students use **braille**, a system of embossed or raised dots that can be read with the tips of the fingers. The basic unit of braille is a cell that contains six dots in two vertical rows of three dots each.

The Braille code was developed in France in 1829 by Louis Braille, who was blind.

Letters of the alphabet, numbers, punctuation marks, and contractions are formed by combining the dots. Contractions are used to save space. (For example, the entire word *understand* is written as ⠥⠝⠙⠑⠗⠎⠞⠁⠝⠙, whereas the contraction for *understand* takes up only four cells: ⠥⠝⠙⠺). When students learn braille, they learn to spell both the full and contracted forms. Figure 9.2 gives examples of braille forms. Young children exposed to braille before they start school are as ready to learn to read and write as their sighted peers (Rex et al., 1994).

There are several ways to write braille—by using a brailler (also called a *braillewriter*), by using a noiseless portable notetaker such as Braille 'n Speak, and by using a slate and stylus. The Tech Talk describes these and other high-tech solutions for students with visual impairments.

Using Orientation and Mobility Skills Students with visual impairments learn, from an orientation and mobility specialist, to travel indepen-

---

FIGURE 9.2

The Braille Alphabet, Numbers, and Punctuation

TECH TALK

High-Tech Solutions for Students with Visual Impairments

High tech equipment has made integrating the student with low vision or blindness into the general education classroom substantially easier. For example, computer screen magnification systems make print available to students with low vision. Systems can have other features as well, such as braille displays and printers. In the past, when you gave materials to a teacher specializing in visual impairments to put into braille, the task was performed manually on a braillewriter and often took several days. Today materials can be given to the teacher on disk, converted to braille with braille translation software, and can be printed and ready in a few hours. The computer and printer also make it easy to enlarge print on the screen and paper, and to enlarge and vary the fonts. The Kurzweil Reading Edge (Xerox Imaging System, 800-421-7323) is a specialized computer that scans print directly from a text and reads it aloud.

Special portable computers also facilitate the learning of students with visual impairments who use braille. For example, the Braille 'n Speak is a rechargeable computer, weighing less than a pound, which can serve as a word processor, stopwatch, calendar, and timer (Espinola, 1992). Other products are designed for people who read and write braille, for example, Power Braille and Braille Mate from TeleSensory (415-960-0920). The keys correspond to those on a brailler. An individual who is blind can braille on the Braille 'n Speak and, with the speech synthesizer, can hear the material that has been brailled—a letter, word, sentence, paragraph, or entire file at a time. Information can be transferred by connecting the device to an external braille printer, standard printer, modem, or another computer.

Courtesy of Xerox Imaging Systems.

Courtesy of TeleSensory.

---

dently in their environments. The goal is to enable the student to enter any environment, familiar or unfamiliar, and to function safely, efficiently, gracefully, and independently (Hill & Ponder, 1976). Consequently, it is not unusual for student and specialist to work not only in school but also in the community.

The student needs to develop both **orientation skills** (which include understanding one's own body, one's position in space, and abstract concepts such as the layout of a city block) and **mobility skills** (which include going up and down stairs, crossing streets, and using public transportation). The orientation and mobility specialist or the special education teacher who specializes in visual impairments can help you arrange your classroom to facilitate the student's mobility there.

Using Optical, Nonoptical, and Instructional Aids Students who have difficulty seeing street signs, building numbers, and bus signs might use a *monocular,* an optical aid that magnifies a distant object. Other optical aids include many types of magnifiers—hand held, lighted, or with a stand—as well as prescription lenses (glasses or contacts).

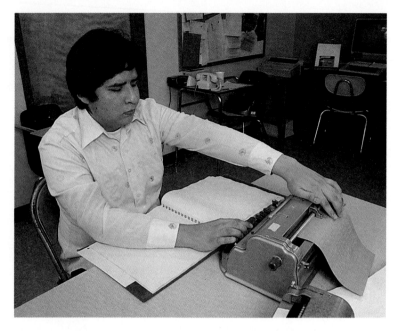

What low- and high-tech solutions available for students with vision impairments can students use in your classroom?

Large print is another option for students with visual impairments. Large print books are costly and difficult to store, however, and sometimes embarrass the students. Reading large print may also be tiring, in that it requires exaggerated head movements and adaptive seating positions. Optical aids, on the other hand, are more compact, less costly, and let students have access to all materials (Barraga & Erin, 1992). The key is to ask students what works for them.

Dog guides were first introduced in the United States in 1928. Today approximately 2 percent of individuals who are visually impaired travel with dog guides.

Some aspects to consider when selecting and preparing text is that it is clearly written, has adequate spacing between letters and words, and is on good quality paper. Reducing the amount of background patterns on the page or providing good contrast between the color of the print and the color of the page is important (Barraga & Erin, 1992).

Nonoptical aids also can help students to maximize visual potential. *Nonoptical aids* are devices that, although not prescribed by a doctor, promote efficient use of vision. Following are some examples of nonoptical aids:

- *lamp* (provides additional light). Lamps with adjustable necks help to minimize glare.
- *reading stand* (used to bring printed material closer to the eyes). Also reduces poor posture and fatigue.
- *bold line paper* (makes writing easier for students with visual impairments). The American Printing House for the Blind manufactures writing paper, graph paper, and large print paper with music staffs.
- *hats and visors* (can help reduce amount of light). Helpful for students who are sensitive to light (*photophobic*).
- *color acetate* (a plastic overlay that darkens print or increases contrast). Yellow is the color favored by many students with visual impairments.

Several nonoptical aids, available mainly from the American Printing House for the Blind, include the following:

TIPS FOR TEACHERS

9.2 Accommodations for Tests in the General Education Classroom

- Provide test materials in the student's primary learning medium (e.g., braille, large print, audiotape).
- Allow extra time to complete test items.
- Give students who read braille twice as much time as other students to complete a test.
- Give students who read regular or large print time and a half to complete a test (e.g., if the time limit is thirty minutes, given them forty-five minutes).

- Read written instructions to students with visual impairment to minimize the amount of reading they need to do (so as to reduce eye fatigue).
- Present test items orally.
- Allow students to write answers on the test material instead of a bubble sheet, or provide a large print bubble sheet.

- *Cranmer abacus,* an adapted device for the rapid computation of basic math functions, decimals, and fractions
- *raised line paper,* writing and graph paper with raised lines that can be followed tactually
- *writing guides,* rectangular templates designed to enable one to accurately place a signature, address an envelope, or write a check
- *measurement tools,* such as braille clocks, rulers, and measuring kits with raised marks

Testing Accommodations Classroom tests should be modified to make them accessible for students with visual impairments. Modifications may include assigning alternate items, orally reading sections of the test to the student, using large print or braille answer sheets, providing real objects for items shown in pictures, or coloring pictures to make them easier to see. The special education teacher who works with the student with visual impairments is an excellent resource for suggestions and help with the accommodations. Tips for Teachers 9.2 suggests several simple testing accommodations.

Students with Hearing Impairments

You may have the opportunity to teach a student who is deaf or hard of hearing. Nancy Shipka, a fifth grade math and science teacher who had that opportunity, worked with a special education teacher specializing in hearing impairments and an interpreter.. Nancy had no idea what to expect when two students who were deaf joined her math and science class. She was concerned not only that the students' academic performance would not measure up to that of the hearing students in her class, but also about working with a special education team in her classroom.

With the help of the special education team, Nancy worked with the students to determine where they could clearly see the interpreter, Nancy, the chalkboard, and the television monitor. She also learned to face the students directly when speaking and to vary her teaching methods, emphasizing hands-on activities and demonstrations. Nancy also learned that the role of the interpreter is one of facilitating communication. Nancy told the interpreter about difficult concepts ahead of time, and also provided written summaries and class notes so that the interpreter would be prepared to sign difficult or technical concepts.

During the year Nancy asked many questions and learned about students who are deaf or hard of hearing and how to accommodate them in her class. You also may have questions about working with these students. This section explains deafness, hearing loss, and accommodating students with hearing impairments.

Definition and Types of Hearing Impairments

Hearing loss, although often associated with aging, can occur at any time, including from birth. Hearing loss can occur as the result of several factors, including heredity, illness or disease, and excessive prolonged exposure to loud noises. Many of the causes of hearing loss in infants are unknown. Young children identified as having hearing losses before they learn language (two to three years old) are identified as prelingually deaf. This early loss of hearing significantly affects language development.

The degree of hearing loss is assessed by observing a person's responses to sounds. The *intensity* of a sound (loud versus quiet) is measured in decibels (dB); the *frequency* of the sound (high versus low) is measured in hertz (Hz). An audiologist tests and plots an individual's responses to sounds on a graph called an **audiogram,** a visual representation of an individual's ability to hear sound. Figure 9.3 shows a comparison of the frequency and intensity of various environmental and speech sounds, plotted on an audiogram.

> American Sign Language, the fourth most common language in the United States, is used also in parts of Canada. Other sign languages (that an ASL signer would not automatically understand) exist in other countries.

Characteristics of Students with Hearing Impairments

A person with normal hearing may have a loss of 0 to 15 decibels in one or both ears. As the loss increases, the amount of usable, or **residual hearing** decreases. Losses can be described as mild, moderate, severe, and profound:

- 15–40 dB = mild hearing loss
- 40–65 dB = moderate hearing loss
- 65–90 dB = severe hearing loss
- greater than 90 dB = profound hearing loss

A person with a mild to moderate loss is usually considered **hard of hearing**. Someone with a severe or profound loss is usually described as **deaf.**

Even a mild hearing loss can have significant educational effects if not recognized early in the student's life. Lauren Resnick, a first grade teacher, commented that she was surprised at the difference hearing aids made for Rider, a hard-of-hearing student in her class. When Rider was not wearing his hearing aids, he was often off task or seemed uninterested in class activities. With his hearing aids, however, he functioned like the other students in the class.

Hearing loss impacts normal speech and language development, which in turn impacts English-language reading development. Students who are deaf or hard of hearing and who do not learn English as their primary language may be significantly delayed in English vocabulary development and reading skills.

Students who are deaf use vision as their primary mode of communication and learning. Hard-of-hearing students, on the other hand, generally develop communication and learning skills based on speech rather than vision. Students with mild or moderate hearing losses do not hear all the sounds or words in their environment, and students with severe or profound losses may not hear any of the sounds in their language system. Thus, even though their vocal apparatuses function normally, they experience difficulty learning to produce the speech sounds because they do not get feedback from hearing the sounds they are producing.

Students who are deaf ordinarily use American Sign Language (ASL) as their primary mode of communication. Some hard-of-hearing students may use ASL, but many also use English as their primary mode of communication. **American Sign Language** is a visual, gestural language. (English is an aural, oral language.) ASL is not a visual representation of English, nor is it a simplified language or communication system. ASL is a full, complete language with its own unique grammar and usage.

FIGURE 9.3

Comparison of the Frequency and Intensity of Various Environment and Speed Sounds

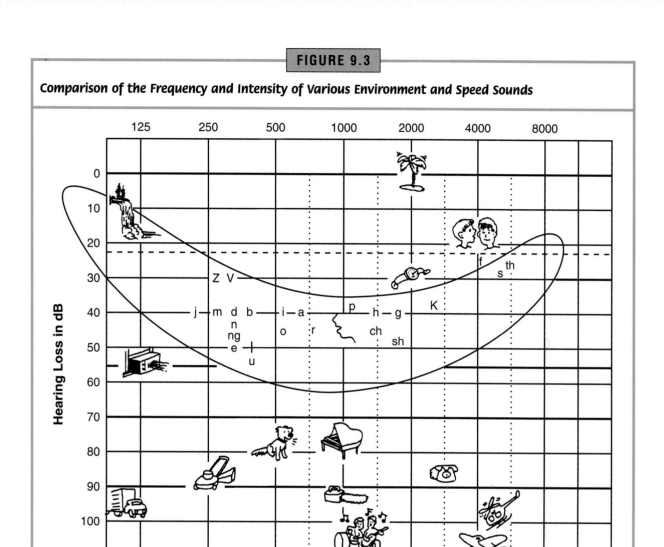

Reprinted with permission from Watkins, S. (Ed.) (1993). *Shy*HI resource manual* (p. G9). Logan, UT: H.O.P.E.

Finger spelling, on the other hand, is a system for representing the English alphabet manually. Finger spelling is used to "spell" names and proper nouns, as well as English words for which no ASL sign exists. Figure 9.4 shows the American finger-spelling alphabet.

Because many students and adults who are deaf speak a common language, ASL, and share similar backgrounds (in that they are deaf), they regard themselves as members of the Deaf culture.

Members of the Deaf culture view hearing loss not as a disability but as a common characteristic among their members (Christensen & Delgado, 1993). They share common stories and experiences and the desire to preserve their culture. This is one reason for the strong movement to keep special day and residential schools as a placement option for students who are deaf, and for the importance of ASL in the curricula in these schools.

FIGURE 9.4

American Finger-Spelling Alphabet

The manual alphabet as the receiver sees it:

The manual alphabet as the sender sees it:

Prevalence of Hearing Impairments

The annual survey from the Office of Demographic Studies at Gallaudet University reported that there were approximately 46,000 students who are deaf and hard-of-hearing in the United States in the 1993–1994 academic year (Schildroth & Hotto, 1995). This number includes approximately 60 percent of all students identified as deaf or hard of hearing (including children of preschool age). The majority of these students are hard of hearing rather than deaf.

Since the implementation of IDEA, public schools have served more students with hearing loss than have state residential schools. It has been reported that 54 percent of students who are deaf and hard of hearing are attending public academic classes with hearing peers (Schildroth & Hotto, 1993).

Identification and Assessment of Students with Hearing Impairments

Melanie Brooks, a kindergarten teacher, recalls her first experience identifying a student with a hearing loss. Chelsea had difficulty following directions, often asked that information be repeated, and had difficulty locating the speaker in group discussions. Melanie was also concerned about Chelsea's persistent colds, and she contacted the school nurse.

Together, the school nurse and Melanie began to identify ways to help Chelsea. They discovered that Chelsea had failed her kindergarten hearing screening and had incurred numerous ear infections as an infant and toddler. The district audiologist conducted further testing with Chelsea, discovering a mild-to-moderate hearing loss in both ears. Chelsea was fitted for aids. Melanie and the special education teacher specializing in hearing impairments worked with Chelsea to provide resources and adaptations to help her learn better. Melanie recalls her satisfaction at being able to make a difference in Chelsea's life.

Some losses, particularly mild to moderate ones, are first detected during kindergarten screening and by classroom teachers. By the time students are ready to attend school, most moderate, severe, and profound hearing losses have already been detected and identified. You should be aware of the following warning signs:

- daydreaming
- inattentive
- behavior problems—frustration
- lethargic
- failure to follow simple verbal commands
- verbal expressions of misunderstanding (e.g., "Huh?" and "I don't know")

- articulation errors
- limited speech or vocabulary
- inappropriate responses to questions
- difficulties with verbal tasks
- difficulty decoding phonetically
- voice quality (soft, nasal, high pitch, monotonous)
- mouth breathing
- persistent colds

Instructional Guidelines and Accommodations for Students with Hearing Impairments

When a student in your classroom is deaf or hard of hearing, you become an important member of a team that will make educational decisions for the student. In addition to you, the team can include a special education teacher specializing in hearing impairments, an interpreter, the student, the parents, a speech and language pathologist, an audiologist, and other resource people.

Using Amplification Amplification of sound is one common accommodation made for students with hearing impairments. Hearing aids are the most common form of amplification. Thanks to technological advances, hearing aids have improved and continue to do so. In classroom situations, however, even the best hearing aids have limitations. Because hearing aids amplify all sounds in the environment, the student may hear a lot of noise (background and reverberation) in addition to the desired signal (e.g., teacher's voice). In classroom situations, students often use **assistive listening devices** such as FM units. With an FM system, the teacher wears a wireless microphone and the student wears a wireless receiver incorporated with a hearing aid. The microphone allows the teacher's voice to be amplified twelve to fifteen decibels above the classroom noise and not be affected by distance.

Making Classroom Accommodations Accommodations for students who are deaf may differ from those for students who are hard of hearing. The following accommodations, however, benefit both types of students:

What are some advantages and disadvantages of amplification systems for students with hearing impairments? What communication alternatives are available for students who are deaf?

■ Use an overhead projector rather than a chalkboard, so that you can face student while you write.
■ Use natural gestures.
■ Use modeling to demonstrate how to do different procedures and tasks.
■ Use pictures, diagrams, and graphs.
■ Provide opportunities for experiential learning.

4. Maximize the use of visual media.
■ Provide closed-captioned television (see Tips for Teachers 9.3).
■ Provide access to computers.

5. Monitor student's understanding.
■ Ask student to repeat or rephrase important information or directions.
■ Reword statements for clarification.
■ Provide written instructions and summaries.

6. Promote cooperation and collaboration.
■ Use peer and classroom tutors and notetakers.
■ Identify speakers in a group discussion.
■ Inform interpreters of topics before class, and provide study guides or teaching notes.

1. Provide preferential seating.
■ Minimize strain of listening by having student sit near you and away from loud noises (high traffic areas, doors, air conditioning and heating units).
■ Make sure student can see you, the interpreter, and visual aids clearly.
■ Eliminate glare from windows or lights.

2. Minimize nonmeaningful environmental noise.
■ Use carpets, rugs, cork, and curtains to help absorb noise.
■ Avoid unnecessary background noise (music, hallway noise).

3. Use visual clues and demonstration.
■ Face student directly when you talk.

Using Interpreters and Notetakers Interpreters and notetakers are valuable resources in the classroom. Interpreters provide a communication link between students who are deaf and hearing individuals. Transliterators also provide such a link, but use an English-based sign system rather than ASL. It is important that students who use ASL or a sign language system have an interpreter in the educational setting. Although an interpreter facilitates communication between the teacher and the student who is deaf, he or she is not a substitute for you (the classroom teacher). Students who are deaf may at first rely on the interpreter for answers and guidance, but will learn to shift their confidence to you, their teacher.

To understand the information being presented, students who are deaf or hard of hearing need to be visually attentive to the speaker and the interpreter. By permitting these students to photocopy your lecture notes or a classmate's notes, or by providing carbon paper to a peer notetaker, you allow them to focus all their attention on you

TIPS FOR TEACHERS

9.3 Using Closed Captioning (CC)

Closed captioning is the process of encoding dialogue and sound effects from a program into readable text at the bottom of the television screen (similar to the subtitles in foreign films). *Decoders* are devices that enable you to view the words in a closed-captioning program.

In 1993, the federal Television Circuitry Decoder Act (passed in 1990) took effect. Thanks to this act all televisions marketed in the United States must be capable of decoding closed caption signals. With this development one does not need a special captioning machine to view closed captioned text.

Today, not only many television programs and specials, but also many films, videos, and educational resources are captioned and available for use in the classroom. When you order a film or video, find out whether you can order it captioned. For more information contact:

Captioned Films/Videos for the Deaf
Modern Talking Picture Service, Inc.
5000 Park Street North
St. Petersburg, FL 33709
(800-237-6213)

and the interpreter. Peer or adult notetakers and tutors can also help clarify and explain topics, pre-teach vocabulary, or review technical terms. Keep in mind that most students who are deaf and some students who are hard of hearing have limited English skills and need teaching techniques that support the development of concepts.

Students with Physical Disabilities and Health Impairments

Students with physical disabilities or health impairments are a small but diverse group. Disabilities can range from asthma, a comparatively mild condition, to cerebral palsy, which may involve neurological impairment that affects mobility and other functional skills.

One of Lanetta Bridgewater's second grade students, Emma, has cerebral palsy and is unable to speak, but understands what others are saying and is developing academic skills at a rate similar to her classmates. In planning and working with Emma, Lanetta worked closely with Susie Speel-

man, the inclusion support teacher you met in Chapter 8. Among the strategies Lanetta and Susie used to facilitate Emma's successful inclusion in Lanetta's classes were time to plan together, making the classroom more accessible for Emma and her wheelchair, use of technology (particularly of assistive devices to enable Emma to make choices and demonstrate her understanding), and reducing the amount of work (so that Emma has enough time to respond).

Definitions and Types of Physical Disabilities and Health Impairments

Most students with physical disabilities and health impairments may qualify for special education services under three IDEA categories: orthopedic impairment, other health impairment, and traumatic brain injury. IDEA defines **orthopedic impairment** as:

> a severe orthopedic impairment that adversely affects a child's educational performance. The term includes impairments caused by congenital anomaly (e.g., clubfoot, absence of some member, etc.), impairments caused by disease (e.g., poliomyelitis, bone tuberculosis, etc.),

and impairments from other causes (e.g., cerebral palsy, amputations, and fractures or burns that cause contractures) (*IDEA*, Section 300.7[7]).

Orthopedic impairments or physical disabilities may not only interfere with the students' coordination and mobility, but also affect their ability to communicate, learn, and adjust. Section 504 of the Vocational Rehabilitation Act of 1973 defines a *physical disability* as an impairment that substantially limits a person's participation in one or more life activities (home, school, or work activities) (Brimer, 1990). By this definition, a person whose impairment is controlled by medication is not considered physically disabled if he or she can participate in home, school, and work activities.

> Asthma is one of the most frequently cited reasons for students missing school. Another is head injury. One in 500 students is hospitalized each year for a head injury.

Other health impairment is defined as:

> having limited strength, vitality, or alertness, due to chronic or acute health problems such as heart condition, tuberculosis, rheumatic fever, nephritis, asthma, sickle cell anemia, hemophilia, epilepsy, lead poisoning, leukemia, or diabetes, that adversely affects a child's educational performance (*IDEA*, Section 300.7[8]).

With the 1990 amendments to IDEA, **traumatic brain injury** was identified as a category of disability and defined as:

> an acquired injury to the brain caused by an external physical force, resulting in total or partial functional disability or psychosocial impairment, or both, that adversely affects a child's education performance. The term applies to open or closed head injuries resulting in impairments in one or more areas, such as cognition; language; memory; attention; reasoning; abstract thinking; judgment; problem-solving; sensory, perceptual, and motor abilities; psychosocial behavior; physical functions; information processing; and speech. The term does not apply to brain injuries that are congenital or degenerative, or brain injuries induced by birth trauma (34.CRF, Sec. 300.7[6][12]).

Common causes of traumatic brain injuries are motorcycle, automobile, and off-road vehicle accidents; sports injuries; and accidents from violence, such as gunshot wounds and child abuse (Russo, 1991).

RESEARCH BRIEF

UNDERSTANDING CAUSES OF SPINAL CORD INJURY AND TRAUMATIC BRAIN INJURY

Spinal cord injuries in young children are most often caused by automobile accidents or child abuse. Automobile accidents, falls, gunshot wounds, and diving accidents cause most spinal cord injuries in adults and older children. Diseases and infections such as measles, polio, meningitis, and HIV can cause permanent damage to the central nervous system, therefore causing physical disabilities and health impairments. A lack of prenatal care and a mother's alcohol and substance abuse during pregnancy can also lead to physical disabilities and health impairments in children.

Over 50 percent of traumatic brain injuries in children and adolescents are caused by motor vehicle accidents, with falls causing another 21 percent. Sports and recreational injuries are the next major cause, follow by violence (Russo, 1991). Child abuse accounts for the majority of infant head injuries, and more than 75 percent of children under the age of three who are physically abused have a traumatic brain injury (Savage, 1993). Infants can also receive traumatic brain injury from being shaken (referred to as *shaken-impact syndrome*). In 10 to 25 percent of the cases, the child dies (Schroeder, 1993).

The following are typical behaviors associated with traumatic brain injuries:

■ lowered social inhibition and judgment; lowered impulse control

■ faulty reasoning

- lowered initiative and motivation
- overestimation of abilities
- depression
- flat affect with sudden outbursts
- agitation and irritability
- fatigue (Forness & Kavale, 1993; Tucker & Colson 1992; Tyler & Myles, 1990).

Physical disabilities and health impairments caused by traumatic brain injury and spinal cord injury are preventable. The case for prevention of traumatic head injuries is clear:

- 63 percent of all children involved in motor vehicle accidents were not wearing restraints.
- 99 percent of those injured in bicycle accidents were not wearing helmets.
- 70 percent of those injured in motorcycle accidents were not wearing helmets.
- 54 percent of those injured while riding on all-terrain and recreational vehicles did not use restraints (Medical Research and Training Center in Rehabilitation and Childhood Trauma, 1993).

The three general categories of physical disabilities and health impairments are: neurological impairments, neuromuscular diseases, and health impairments. A **neurological impairment** is an abnormal performance caused by a dysfunction of the brain, spinal cord, and nerves, thereby creating transmission of improper instructions, uncontrolled burst of instructions from the brain, or incorrect interpretation of feedback to the brain (Brimer, 1990). Some types of neurological impairment are seizure disorders, cerebral palsy, spina bifida, and traumatic brain injuries. **Neuromuscular diseases** involve both the nerves and muscles. They are neurological problems that affect the muscles. Muscular dystrophy, polio, and multiple sclerosis are examples of this type of physical disability. **Health impairments** include conditions such as asthma, cancer, cystic fibrosis, juvenile diabetes, prenatal substance abuse, fragile health, and communicable diseases like tuberculosis, cytomegalovirus, and HIV infection. As stated in the definition, the chronic or acute health problem must result in limited strength, vitality, or alertness.

Characteristics of Students with Physical Disabilities and Health Impairments

The following sections describe the characteristics of the most common neurological impairments, neuromuscular diseases, and health impairments. During your teaching career you undoubtedly will have students with these and other illnesses or conditions in your classroom.

Cerebral Palsy Students with cerebral palsy are one of the largest groups of children with physical disabilities (Heward, 1996). **Cerebral palsy** is caused by damage to the brain before or during birth. Conditions are classified according to the areas affected and the types of symptoms. The degree of severity varies and is often evidenced by lack of coordination, speech disorders, motor problems, and extreme weakness. Cerebral palsy generally has accompanying problems in such areas as learning, vision, hearing, cognitive functioning, and social–emotional growth (Meyen & Skrtic, 1995). The condition can interfere with head control, arm use, sitting positions, balance, posture, and mobility, and these problems can be exacerbated by fatigue and stress.

As a classroom teacher, you will want to be aware of the student's level of fatigue and stress. Paul Nichols, a high school math teacher, mentioned that his student, Allison, appeared stressed during tests, particularly if they were long or timed.

> I noticed that whenever we had a timed test with essays, Allison would have difficulty sitting up and holding up her head. At first I thought it was just a way for her to try and get out of the test so I tried to be firm with her. When I spoke to the physical therapist, he mentioned that she may be tired or stressed and then he taught her some relaxation techniques. She is doing better but it is still a difficult time for her. I did explain to her that the timed part was not as important as doing the work so now I give her extended time by allowing her to finish the test with the special education teacher during her resource period.

Spina Bifida Spina bifida, a birth defect that occurs when the spinal cord fails to close properly, often causes paralysis of parts of the body but seldom affects intellectual functioning. Most students with spina bifida walk with difficulty and lack complete bladder and bowel control. Some students need to use a catheter, which necessitates training in hygiene and extra time during the day to take care of the catheter. Generally, the school nurse or a special education teacher provides this training if it has not already been provided.

Epilepsy The most common neurological impairment in school-age children is convulsive disorders or epilepsy. **Epilepsy** is characterized by a tendency to have recurrent seizures—sudden, excessive, spontaneous, and abnormal discharges of neurons accompanied by alteration in motor function, sensory function, or consciousness (Coulter, 1993).

There are three major types of seizures. *Absence seizures (petit mal)* are characterized by short lapses in consciousness. Students may appear inattentive and often do not realize that they are having seizures. *Tonic-clonic seizures (grand mal)* are characterized by convulsions followed by loss of consciousness. Usually a tonic phase, in which the muscles are rigid, is followed by a clonic phase, in which the arms and legs jerk. Often the student loses consciousness and awakens disoriented and tired. Although these seizures usually last less than five minutes, they can be a frightening event for you and your students. Tips for Teachers 9.4 provides some pointers for handling

this type of seizure. If a student in your class has this type of seizure disorder, be sure to help the other students in the classroom understand the condition and respond appropriately to the student (Reisner, 1988).

During complex partial seizures the electrical discharge is limited to one area of the brain. With a psychomotor seizure, for example, the student seems to be in a dreamlike state and may make random movements such as picking at clothes or repeating phrases, whereas with a focal motor seizure, the student usually has sudden, jerky movements in one part of the body.

Muscular Dystrophy Muscular dystrophy is a chronic disorder characterized by the weakening and wasting of the body's muscles. Persons with muscular dystrophy progressively lose their ability to walk and effectively use their arms and hands (Brooke, 1986). There is no cure for muscular dystrophy at this time, and the only prevention is genetic counseling (the condition appears to run in families). Helping the student maintain independence through regular physical therapy, exercise, and necessary physical aids is important. School personnel need to be careful not to lift or pull a student with muscular dystrophy by his or her arms, because doing so may cause dislocation of limbs. Most students with muscular dystrophy

TIPS FOR TEACHERS

9.4 How to Respond to a Student with a Tonic–Clonic (Grand Mal) Seizure in the Classroom

- Ease student to the floor and clear the area around him or her.
- Put something soft under student's head to keep it from banging the floor.
- Do not interfere with the seizure. Turn student gently on his or her side, but do not put anything in the student's mouth and do not try to hold his or her tongue.

- Have someone stay with the student until he or she is fully awake.
- Allow the student to rest afterwards.
- Seek emergency assistance if seizure lasts longer than five minutes or if the student requests it.

need wheelchairs by the age of ten to fourteen, and teachers should be alert for signs of fatigue (Heward, 1996).

HIV and AIDS Human immunodeficiency virus (HIV) is a condition that infects and eventually destroys cells in the immune system that protect the body from disease (Colson & Carlson, 1993). A viral infection transmitted through bodily fluids, HIV is responsible for **acquired immunodeficiency syndrome** (**AIDS**). Students infected with HIV may eventually experience loss of stamina, developmental delays, motor problems, progressive neurological defects, repeated bacterial infections, psychological stresses, and death (Belman et al., 1988). HIV progresses through stages. In the latency stage, which generally lasts from two to ten years in children, there are no outward symptoms. As the disease progresses through the middle stages, individuals experience a general weakening of the immune system, which results in persistent fevers and infections. In the final stages, opportunistic infections increase in frequency and severity.

Most school districts have established policies regarding the inclusion of students with HIV in general education classrooms. If students in your classroom are identified as having HIV, consult with individuals knowledgeable about these policies, and work with the special education teacher and school nurse in planning for these students. One important question to ask is how the condition currently affects the student's health. Students whose frequent absences are due to recurrent infections may need a homebound teacher. In advanced stages, students may experience a loss of knowledge and skills due to brain degeneration and lack of vitality (Kelker et al., 1994).

By knowing and adjusting to the student's capabilities, you enable the student to participate more fully and successfully in classroom activities. For example, Shirley Meeder, an eighth grade social studies teacher, found that she could adapt assignments for Joey, a student in the middle stages of HIV, by reducing the amount of work required, giving him the option of listening to the textbook on tape, having a notetaker, and letting Joey take tests orally. These modifications helped Joey deal with his limited stamina. The special education teacher helped Shirley provide many of these accommodations. When Joey suffered from a prolonged infection, he received homebound instruction so that he could keep up with his classmates.

You may need to take some precautions with students with HIV. Casual contact among people in the classroom is not a problem, as this is not how HIV is transmitted (Wishom et al., 1989). But in situations in which you could come in contact with the blood or other bodily fluids of a student with HIV, then protective gloves should be worn (Kelker et al., 1994).

> At the beginning of 1992, 3,420 students under the age of thirteen had been diagnosed as having AIDS. About 80 percent of these children were infected by their mothers.

Prevalence of Physical Disabilities and Health Impairments

Approximately 52,000, or 1.1 percent of all students receiving special education services are categorized as having orthopedic impairments. Health impairments account for approximately 59,000, or 1.3 percent (U.S. Department of Education, 1993). It is important to remember that some students with physical disabilities and health impairments also have other disabilities and may be classified as having multiple disabilities.

Each year about 5,000,000 children receive head injuries, and of these about 200,000 are hospitalized (Rosman, 1994). About 2 to 5 percent of these children develop severe neurologic complications (Rudolph & Kamei, 1994). The occurrence of traumatic brain injuries increases dramatically during adolescence, with as many as 3 percent sustaining a head injury serious enough to cause school problems (Forness & Kavale, 1993). The following list of physical disabilities, health impairments, and related prevalence information is adapted from Turnbull et al. (1995):

Cerebral Palsy
- About 500,000 to 700,000 Americans have some degree of cerebral palsy, with about 5,000 to 7,000 infants born with cerebral palsy each year.
- 3 in 1,000 infants are born with cerebral palsy (Bigge, 1991).

Spina Bifida

- 0.5 to 1 in 1,000 infants are born with spina bifida (Bigge, 1991).
- If one child is born with spina bifida, the chances of the second child being born with spina bifida increase significantly.

Neuromuscular Diseases

- Considering the more than 40 neuromuscular diseases together, the rate of disabilities is about 1 in 1,000 (Ringel, 1987).

Seizure Disorders

- Approximately 1 percent of the American population, or about 2,000,000 individuals, have epilepsy (Epilepsy Foundation of America, 1987).

Asthma

- 4 million children under the age of 18, or about 6.1 percent, have asthma.
- Many do not require special education.

Cancer

- New cases of childhood cancer are estimated at 8,000 per year.

Diabetes

- Approximately 120,000 school-age children have juvenile diabetes.

HIV

- Approximately 310,000 adolescents and 5,000 children had AIDS in 1993.

Prenatal Substance Exposure

- An estimated 2 in 1,000 infants have fetal alcohol syndrome.
- In the United States, 100,000 infants per year are born drug-exposed.

Identification and Assessment of Students with Physical Disabilities and Health Impairments

Medical diagnosis usually provides the initial identification of physical disabilities and health impairments. Assessments are carefully designed to take into account that these students may have delayed motor skills or problems staying on task for long periods of time. Sirvis (1988) recommends assessments in the following areas:

- **Activities of daily living** (personal hygiene, eating, dressing, using public transportation)
- **Academic potential** (physical disabilities may or may not affect mental capabilities). Students with neurological damage may have problems with attention, concentration, initiation, or fatigue (Meyen & Skrtic, 1995).
- **Adaptations for learning** (academic and physical adaptations to help students achieve academic success and independence)
- **Communication** (students' ability to express and understand language)
- **Mobility** (students' current and potential range and mode of mobility)
- **Physical abilities and limitations** (positioning and necessary adaptive equipment and techniques that facilitate students' independence)
- **Psychosocial development** (effects of impairment on students' social and emotional functioning)
- **Transition skills** (skills needed for a successful transition into and from school, and between grade levels)

Remember—as a classroom teacher and a member of the education team, you are a valuable resource for information.

Instructional Guidelines and Accommodations for Students with Physical Disabilities and Health Impairments

Three basic principles can help you accommodate students with physical disabilities and health impairments in your classroom.

- **Use others as resources.** Call on the expertise of the student, parents, other school personnel, and others in health-related professions, as well as the student's classmates.
- **Be flexible in your planning.** Be willing to make last-minute changes in response to day to day changes in the student's condition and readiness to learn.
- **Be ingenious and creative.** One of the greatest rewards from working with students is helping them discover their strengths and ways to demonstrate them.

Transdisciplinary Teaming Because many students with physical disabilities or health impairments receive services from special education teachers, an occupational or physical therapist, an adaptive physical education teacher, and possibly a speech and language pathologist, effective teaming and communication are crucial. In **transdisciplinary teaming**, all members of the team work together and view the student as a whole, instead of working only on their specialty area (Downing & Bailey, 1990). All team members are aware of the student's goals, and observe each other as they work with the student so that they can share and generalize successful techniques and strategies.

Using Assistive Technology Recall that IDEA defines *assistive technology* as "any item, piece of equipment, or product system whether acquired commercially off the shelf, modified, or customized, that is used to increase, maintain, or improve functional capabilities of individuals with disabilities." Assistive technology devices are particularly useful for increasing mobility, communicating better, gaining access to computers, performing daily living skills, enhancing learning, and manipulating and controlling the environment (Lewis, 1993). By using such assistive technology as eye-gaze pointing, switch-controlled computing, and writing implements encased in plastic tubing or bicycle handle grips, for example, Lanetta's student, Emma, is able to participate more fully in classroom life. Check whether someone is responsible for assistive technology at the

As a classroom teacher, how will you assess and address the needs of a student with a serious health impairment?

district level in your school district, or work with an educational technology specialist.

Making Environmental Modifications In addition to the necessary accessibility modifications (wide aisle for wheelchairs, low drinking fountains, appropriate handles), other environmental modifications facilitate independence for students with physical disabilities and health impairments. Wright and Bigge (1991) discuss four types of environmental modifications:

- **changes in location of materials and equipment** (e.g., so that students in wheelchairs can reach items independently)
- **work surface modifications** (e.g., raising a desk so that a wheelchair fits under it)
- **object modifications** (e.g., attaching clips to a student's desk to secure papers)
- **manipulation aids** (e.g., using a page turner to reduce dependency on others)

Making a Difference provides more quick and easy ideas for helping students become more independent and successful.

Educating Classmates For students with health impairments and physical disabilities, some of the most important modifications relate to informing other students in the class. Classmates, particularly younger students with rare diseases or severe

As a classroom teacher, how can you help students with physical disabilities or health impairments in their psychosocial development and peer relations?

MAKING A DIFFERENCE

The 60-Second Lesson

Ways to Promote Independence in Students with Physical Disabilities or Health Impairments

- Retrace or enlarge print with a dark marker to help students see material more clearly.
- Schedule study buddies to help a student with disabilities gather learning materials.
- Assign a classmate or ask for a volunteer to take or copy notes for a student with disabilities.
- Ask students for whom writing is difficult whether they would prefer an oral assignment or test.
- Ask the special education teacher to provide (or advise you on acquiring) materials for securing small objects. Velcro and Dycem mat on a stu-

dent's desk prevent books, calculators, pencil boxes, and the like, from slipping off.
- Ask parents to provide a bandanna or sweat band, worn on the wrist, to help a student with limited control of facial muscles wipe off excess saliva.
- Arrange with the special education teacher for the assistance of a paraprofessional in moving a student from a wheelchair to a bean bag chair during floor activities, so that the student can be both supported physically and seated on the same level as peers.

---

disabilities, will most likely have limited knowledge and many questions. For example, Sexson and Madan-Swain (1993) found that students most often asked the following questions about a classmate with a health problem:

- What's wrong with the student?
- Is the disease contagious?
- Will (the student) die from it?
- Will he or she lose anything (such as limbs, hair)?
- Should we talk about the student's illness or ignore it?
- What will other students think if I'm still friends with this student?

Sexson and Madan-Swain (1993) suggest not only addressing these questions, but also talking about how the student may be different when he or she returns from a prolonged absence.

Dealing with Death During your teaching career you may have a student in your class who is dying. In this circumstance, counseling is indicated. Open communication with the student, parents, counselor, and other members of the education team becomes very important so that you can deal with the student's feelings and fears in a consistent and open manner. You may work directly with the

school counselor, but you need written permission from parents before you can contact a student's private counselor or psychologist.

Berner (1977) and others suggest that children go through stages as they move toward accepting death. Although not all children go through all stages, and some may be experienced simultaneously, knowledge of these stages can help you understand the behaviors and emotions that may be exhibited by a student who is dying. The stages include:

- shock and disbelief
- crying (sometimes hysterical)
- feelings of isolation and loneliness
- psychosomatic symptoms, which may distract the student from the fatal condition
- panic
- guilt that he or she is to blame
- hostility or resentment toward others
- resistance to usual routines and continuing to live
- reconciliation and beginning acceptance of the inevitability of death
- acceptance

Although the suggestions in Table 9.1 are from parents of children with cancer (Candlelighters Childhood Cancer Foundation, 1993),

---

TABLE 9.1

Parents' View: What Teachers Should and Should Not Do for a Student with Cancer

---

Helpful Teachers

✔ Take time to learn about the treatments and their effects on school performance.

✔ Demonstrate support for parents as well as student.

✔ Listen to parents' concerns and fears.

✔ Call or visit during absences.

✔ Encourage classmates to call or write during extended absences.

✔ Before re-entry, talk with the student about any fears or concerns.

✔ Adjust lessons and assignments based on students endurance.

✔ Follow parental and medical instructions regarding snacks, wearing a hat, bathroom visits.

✔ Treat the student as normally as possible and include the student in as many class activities as possible.

Less Helpful Teachers

✔ Fail to learn about the disease and its effects and treatments.

✔ Show fear about having the student in class.

✔ Allow other students to pity student.

✔ Fail to keep on-going communication with parents and student during absences.

✔ Ignore problems classmates have in adjusting to friend's disease.

✔ Before re-entry, fail to share information about the student and the disease with classmates.

✔ Do not give student the benefit of the doubt on assignments and homework.

✔ Make an issue of the student's differences in front of others.

✔ Do not give student opportunity to attempt what others are doing.

Adapted from The Candlelighters Childhood Cancer Foundation (1993). Advice to educators (adapted from a survey by A Wish with Wings). In *Educating the child with cancer* (pp. 21–22). Bethesda, MD: Author.

---

many apply also to children with other life-threatening illnesses, such as AIDS.

Providing Instruction of Motor Skills For students with physical disabilities and health impairments, working on motor skills is an important component of their education program. Many activities that support motor skills can be incorporated easily into daily classroom activities.

As you work with students who have visual, hearing, physical, or health impairments, your repertoire of teaching strategies and knowledge of classroom accommodations and assistive technology will grow. With the help of a number of specialists, who can assist both you and the student, you should feel confident of success in educating your students.

SUMMARY

- Students with visual impairment can be blind or partially sighted, depending on the degree and type of vision loss.

- It is important when planning for a student with visual impairments to consider the student's functional vision.

- Braille is the system of raised dots used for

reading and writing by students who cannot read print.

- It is important to make the classroom accessible for students who have visual impairments. These students may need instruction in orientation and mobility skills.

- High and low technology, including computers, have done much to help students who are visually impaired succeed in school.

- Hearing loss is measured by an audiologist, who plots the results of the hearing test on an audiogram.
- Although most children with significant hearing loss are identified prior to beginning school, it is important to watch for signs of mild hearing loss.
- American Sign Language is a sign and gestural language used by many individuals in North America who are deaf.
- Arranging the classroom to reduce background noise and to have the speaker's face visible when talking is important for students with hearing impairments.

- Interpreters and notetakers provide a means for students with hearing impairments to attend and learn from general education classes.
- The three main types of physical disabilities and health impairment are: neurological impairments, neuromuscular diseases, and health impairments.
- Assistive technology devices can enhance students' independence and learning. Devices range from low tech items such as handles to high tech devices such as computers.
- When working with students who have visual, hearing, physical, and health disabilities, you have a number of specialists with whom to collaborate.

Key Terms and Concept

acquired immunodeficiency syndrome (AIDS)

American Sign Language

assistive listening devices

audiogram

blind

braille

cerebral palsy

compensatory skills

deaf

echolalia

epilepsy

finger spelling

functional vision

hard of hearing

health impairments

human immunodeficiency virus (HIV)

legal blindness

low vision

mobility skills

muscular dystrophy

neurological impairments

neuromuscular diseases

orientation skills

orthopedic impairment

other health impairment

partially sighted

residual hearing

sensory channels

spina bifida

transdisciplinary teaming

traumatic brain injury

visual acuity

visual field

Think and Apply

1. In the opening interview, Pat Childers expressed that she lacked the knowledge and experience to work with students like Brandy. Other teachers, such as Nancy Shipka and Lanetta Bridgewater expressed the same concerns. What systems are in place to help these

teachers? Make a list of your questions, the persons you would ask, and the meetings or activities you would plan before a student with disabilities joins your class.

2. Interview and observe two or three of the specialists described in this chapter. Find out

about the students with whom they work, their roles and responsibilities, and how they team with general classroom teachers.

3. Develop a file of assistive technology resources in your state and local district. Visit the technology center or specialist and learn more about integrating assistive technology for students with disabilities.

4. Survey a classroom and school to determine accessibility for a student using a wheelchair. List modifications that you think would improve accessibility.

5. Interview several adolescents or young adults with a visual, hearing, physical, or health impairment. Ask the following questions:

- What impact does (the disability) have on your daily life?
- How do your routines differ because of (the disability)?
- How do others react to your disability?
- What advice would you give classroom teachers about helping other students with (the disability)?

Read More about It

Visual Impairments

1. Barraga, N. D., & Erin, J. N. (1992). *Visual handicaps and learning* (3rd ed.). Austin, TX: Pro-Ed.

   An introductory textbook with information on designing appropriate instructional settings and programs for students who are visually impaired.

2. Levack, N. (1994). *Low vision: A resource guide with adaptations for students with visual impairments* (2nd ed.). Austin, TX: Texas School for the Blind.

   This is a useful guide for parents and teachers who work with students with low vision. Includes information on teaching adaptations.

3. Torres, I., & Corn, A. L. (1990). *When you have a visually handicapped child in your classroom: Suggestions for teachers* (2nd ed.). New York: American Foundation for the Blind.

   A practical guide with many suggestions for integrating students with visual impairments into mainstream classes.

Hearing Impairments

1. Erting, C. (1994). *Deafness, communication, and social identity*. Washington, D.C.: Gallaudet University Press.

   A textbook about educating students with hearing impairments.

2. Kluwin, T. N., Moores, D. F. & Gaustad, M. G. (1992). *Toward effective public school programs for deaf students*. New York: Teachers College Press.

   A resource book for classroom teachers and specialists who work with students that have hearing impairments.

3. Luetke-Stahlman, B., & Luckner, J. (1991). *Effectively educating students with hearing impairments*. White Plains, NY: Longman.

   An introductory textbook on educating students with hearing impairments, includes ideas for teaching these students in general education classrooms.

Physical Disabilities and Health Impairments

1. Batshaw, M. L., & Perret, Y. M. (1992). *Children with disabilities: A medical primer* (3rd ed.). Baltimore: Brookes.

   An extensive overview of various types of physical disabilities and health impairments.

2. Bigge, J. L. (1991). *Teaching individuals with physical and multiple disabilities*. New York: Macmillan.

   A comprehensive textbook on physical and health impairments.

3. Moffitt, K., Nachahsi, J., & Reiss, J. (Eds.). (1993). *Special children, special care*. Tampa: University of South Florida.

   A practical guide for collaboration among professionals and families caring for children with complex health impairments.

4. Tyler, J. S. (1990). *Traumatic head injury in school-aged children: A training manual for educational personnel*. Kansas City: Children's Rehabilitation Unit, University of Kansas Medical Center.

   A resource book that provides guidelines for educators and information on traumatic brain injury.

Teaching Culturally and Linguistically Diverse Students

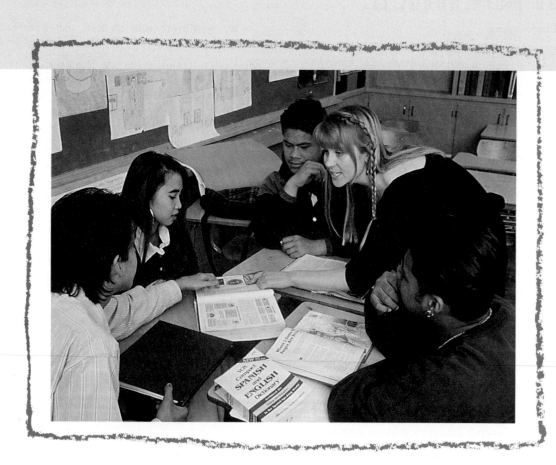

FOCUS QUESTIONS

1. How are the demographics of our schools changing?

2. What is the relationship between the macro-culture and the microcultures of culturally and linguistically diverse students?

3. As a classroom teacher, how can you learn about your culture and your students' cultures and communities?

4. What is multicultural education?

5. As a classroom teacher, how can you incorporate multicultural education and culturally relevant teaching into your curriculum?

6. What are five factors that affect second language acquisition, and how do they relate one to another?

7. What are the characteristics of Black Vernacular English (BVE) and how can you facilitate learning for students who use BVE?

8. As a classroom teacher, how can you promote second language acquisition in your classroom?

9. What accommodations can you make for students who are in the process of acquiring English as a second language?

Interview

Co-teachers at Mission Way School

Gloria Rodriguez is a fifth grade bilingual education teacher who co-teaches with Lidia Romo, a fourth grade bilingual education teacher at Mission Way Elementary School in southwest Arizona. Maria Chavez is the English as a second language (ESL) teacher for this K–5 elementary school. Most students at Mission Way speak Spanish or Spanish and Yaqui, a Native American language, as their first language(s). Although over 85 percent of these students qualify for free lunch, they come from rich cultural communities, such as the Mexican-American barrios or the Yaqui Reservation.

Two years ago, with the support of the principal, Gloria and Lidia decided to co-teach. They made this decision for several important reasons. First, by co-teaching they offer broader cultural and linguistic expertise. Gloria, whose background is Mexican American, grew up in the local barrios, attended a local university, and has been teaching at Mission Way for five years. In contrast, Lidia grew up on the Yaqui Reservation, went to a university in northern Arizona, and has been teaching three years at Mission Way. She has a rich knowledge of the Yaqui ways.

Second, by co-teaching they believe that they increase their ability to effectively use their approach to multicultural education. This approach, which uses the culture and community as the foundation on which learning and curriculum are built, provides students with the opportunity to learn about and respect their cultural and linguistic heritages. At the same time, the students are learning English and to assimilate into the mainstream of American life.

Third, by co-teaching Gloria and Lidia are able to group students flexibly while many of them make the transition from their first language(s) to English. As in other learning, not all students are ready to make the transition at the same time or at the same rate. The teachers believe that flexibility is important for students to succeed at becoming competent English speakers, readers, and writers. Lidia comments,

> The transition from first language to second language is one of the most complex aspects of bilingual education that we deal with. We often have a good sense for when students are ready to make this transition, but our curriculum and grouping doesn't allow us to meet the students'

needs. Team teaching with Gloria helps me better meet the needs of the students and make adjustments tailored to them.

Another reason that Gloria and Lidia decided to team teach is that it seems to give them more time to integrate the family and communities into the school and their classroom. Gloria comments,

> Fourth and fifth grades are often times when students are beginning to be pressured to join gangs. We feel that one reason our students are not as likely to join gangs is because they have a strong sense of respect for their own cultures. We feel that combining our cultural expertise and engaging the students in thematic units built on their cultures serves as a deterrent to joining gangs.

In contrast to Gloria and Lidia, the ESL teacher, Maria, grew up in Puerto Rico and New York City. She attended college in Puerto Rico and then taught for several years in a New York public school serving a Puerto Rican community. She started teaching ESL at Mission Way two years ago, when her husband was transferred to the Southwest. Maria has found that although both she and Gloria are considered Latinos or Hispanics, their cultural roots and heritage are different, in much the same way that the New Englanders differ from Southerners and Midwesterners.

In her teaching Maria works to broaden the students' knowledge of various cultures to include not only different Latino and Native American cultures, but also European American, African American, and Asian American cultures. In teaching ESL, Maria goes into the classroom or sometimes works with small groups of students in her resource room. On a regular basis, new students are enrolled in Mission Way who speak no English and have limited academic skills in their first language. Maria, whose job is to provide intensive support to these students and their teachers, sees herself also as a resource for the other teachers. She comments,

> I feel like one of my major job roles is that of a school-wide resource. I switch lunch periods during the week so that I have the opportunity to eat with different teachers and find out their needs and offer help. One of my concerns is how to be of assistance to more teachers. I think communication and time are the keys.

Introduction

Clearly, the cultural and linguistic diversity of Mission Way adds to the richness of the school community and the complexity of teaching. But compared to schools whose students come from many different cultural and linguistic backgrounds, Mission Way is relatively homogeneous.

This chapter focuses on the growing diversity of schools and students in the United States. It also presents the key concepts associated with multicultural education, linguistic diversity, second language learning, and bilingual education. Finally, it discusses instructional strategies for educating students who are culturally and linguistically diverse. As you read this chapter, think about how the ideas presented by Gloria, Lidia, and Maria create schools and classrooms that facilitate the successful education of culturally and linguistically diverse students.

Diversity in Classrooms and Schools

The United States is one of the most culturally diverse nations in the world. A Mexican immigrant commented, "Before I came to America I had dreams of life here. I thought about tall Anglos, big buildings, and houses with lawns. I was surprised when I arrived to see so many kinds of people— Black people, Asians. I found people from Korea and Cambodia and Mexico. In California I found not just America, I found the world" (Olsen, 1988). This diversity continues to increase as new immigrants relocate in the United States. By the year 2000, non-European Americans are expected to comprise more than one-third of the population, with the two largest minority groups—African Americans (currently over 30 million) and Latino Americans (currently over 22 million)—making up almost a third of the total school enrollment (Grossman, 1995). Asian Pacific Americans are the fastest growing "minority group" in the United States, numbering more than 7 million.

Approximately 30 percent of elementary school students are members of racial and ethnic minority groups (Snyder, 1993). Minorities constitute the majority of public school students in more than twenty of the country's largest school systems, including Miami, Philadelphia, Baltimore, and Los Angeles. Although many of these students do well in school, a substantial number of students come from homes in which families live in poverty and parents are unemployed or underemployed, have little education, few technical skills, and are not fluent in English. Furthermore, education practice oftentimes does not provide a good match with the students' cultures and the curriculum (Jordan, 1985). Tips for Teachers 10.1 has suggestions to help teachers learn about students' home communities.

The average achievement of African Americans, Native Americans, and Latino Americans is consistently lower than that of middle- and upper-class European Americans at every grade level (National Center for Educational Research, 1990). The dropout rates and the grade retention rates are also higher for these groups of students. It is estimated that 48 percent of Native American students, and 40 percent of Latino Americans, do not graduate from high school (Wyman, 1993). African Americans also have high dropout rates, with inner-city youth dropping out at a rate of 80 percent. The dropout rates for Asian Pacific Americans are lower, but when considering those Asian Pacific American students from developing countries only, the rate is high (Grossman, 1995).

Over 2 million people in the United States are Native Americans, representing over 500 tribal groups and speaking more than 200 languages. The largest tribes are Cherokee and Navajo. The largest populations of Native Americans are in California, Arizona, New Mexico, and Oklahoma.

A disproportionately high percentage of African Americans, Latin Americans, and Native Americans have been identified as having learning disabilities, mild mental retardation, and emotional or behavioral disorders (Drew et al., 1996). In contrast, a disproportionately low percentage of students from these cultural groups have been identified as gifted and talented (VanTassel-Baska et al., 1991).

The reasons for the limited success these students have in school are complex and interrelated, but several factors should be considered (Stephen et al., 1993). First, role models from minority groups are often limited in school, in that many teachers are European Americans and limited mentor programs are available for these students to connect with leaders in their communities. Second, discrimination against students from minority groups continues in assessment for and placement in advanced and gifted programs. Third, curriculum and educational practice is often not culturally responsive, with limited integration of information about different cultural groups into the curriculum (Erickson & Mohatt, 1982). Fourth, teaching styles may not match the learning styles of students from diverse cultures (Ladson-Billings, 1995).

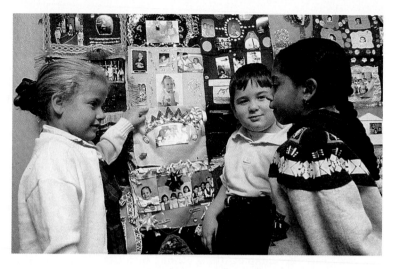

What is involved in the process of mediating among diverse cultures? What environmental and instructional measures can teachers take to help diverse students mediate between the microcultures of their homes and communities and the macrocultures of their nation and school?

Understanding Diverse Cultures

The United States is composed of a shared core culture and many subcultures (Banks, 1993a). Students in our schools are influenced by this core culture, sometimes referred to as the **macroculture.** The United States is such a complex and diverse nation that its core culture is somewhat difficult to describe, but Banks and Banks (1993) suggest the following key components:

- equality of opportunities for individuals in the society
- individualism and the notion that individual success is more important than the family, community, and nation–state
- social mobility through individual effort and hard work
- individualistic attitudes toward values and behaviors
- belief in the nation's superiority
- orientation toward materialism and exploitation of the natural environment

At the same time, students are influenced by their home cultures, or **microcultures.** Microcultures are often based on such factors as national origin, ethnicity, socioeconomic class, religion, gender, age, and disability (Gollnick & Chinn, 1990). Even geographical areas of the country (e.g., New England, Appalachia) can be considered microcultures because of differences in customs and mores.

Sometimes the core values of the macroculture and microcultures are relatively similar, but in other cases, the microculture values are quite different from those of the core culture (Banks, 1993a). For example, the emphasis on individuality is generally not as important in African American, Latino American, and Native American ethnic communities as it is in the European American macroculture. Instead, these communities place more importance on group and family values (Hale-Benson, 1986; Ramirez & Castaneda, 1974; Swisher & Deyhle, 1992). Hence, cooperative learning may be a better match than competitive learning for students from these ethnic backgrounds. In fact, cooperative learning activities that support equal status contact between majority and minority groups in pursuit of common goals have been shown to increase cross-ethnic friendships in classrooms (e.g., Kagan et al., 1985; Oishi et al., 1983). Another example of differences between the macroculture and various microcultures in the United States is the value given to personalized knowledge (e.g., knowledge that results from firsthand observation). Although the macroculture values knowledge based on objectivity, and educational institutions emphasize abstract "out-of-con-

TIPS FOR TEACHERS

10.1 Learning about the Funds of Knowledge in Students' Home Communities

Teachers may begin their teaching careers in schools in which the students' home communities are neither their home community nor similar to their home communities. Some ideas that help teachers learn about the students' home communities are:

- Learn about students' cultural backgrounds. Learn how the culture views the role of teachers and schools, and the role of parents in relation to schools.
- Locate at least one person in the community who can serve as your cultural guide or informant. This can often be a fellow staff member. Develop a relationship in which that person teaches you about the culture and community.

- Be a learner in the classroom. Discuss with students your interest in learning about their cultures, including community activities. Information that can help guide your learning includes: jobs of parents, their special skills and knowledge, special interests of students (at home and in the community), community activities, special occasions and holidays, family structure, family responsibilities and relationships.
- If appropriate and within school policy, visit students' homes and talk with parents and other family members. This is an ideal opportunity to learn more about the students, the households, and culture including interests of the family, the role of the extended family, the way in which jobs are shared, and the ways in which literacy is used in the home.

---

text" knowledge, research on woman's ways of knowing suggest that women value personalized knowledge (Belenky et al., 1986; Gilligan, 1982; Maher, 1987). Similarly, Ramirez and Castaneda (1974) found that Mexican-American students who were socialized within traditional Latino cultures also responded positively to knowledge presented in a personalized or story format.

When the core values in the macroculture and microculture are relatively different, teachers can help students understand and mediate differences between the cultures. To act as mediators, teachers need to learn about and incorporate the various microcultures and home communities into school life and the curriculum. For example, Luis Moll and his colleagues (e.g., Moll & Greenberg, 1990; Gonzales et al., 1995) have been working as participants and researchers in Tucson's barrio schools for a number of years. Moll's research and ethnographic methods of study provide strategies for teachers to integrate the home and school communities by building on the **funds of knowledge** found in the home community.

Learning about the funds of knowledge in the students' home community can help teachers to not overgeneralize characteristics that are often attributed to different cultural groups.

Cultural Characteristics

In learning about cultural influences there is a tendency to make generalizations based on common beliefs about a culture. As Lynch (1992) notes, however, "Culture is only one of the characteristics that determine individuals' and families' attitudes, values, beliefs, and ways of behaving ... Assuming that culture-specific information ... applies to all individuals from the cultural group is not only inaccurate but also dangerous—it can lead to stereotyping that diminishes rather than enhances cross-cultural competence" (p. 44). Still, having some knowledge of students' **cultural characteristics** serves as a starting point for understanding individual students' behaviors and learning styles.

Knowledge of cultural characteristics can keep teachers from misinterpreting students' actions. One example is the learning style of some Native American groups. Teachers typically encourage students to attempt tasks publicly or to answer questions, even though they are unsure of what to say or do, but the traditional learning styles of some Native American groups encourage learning privately and gaining competence before performing publicly. Learners repeatedly watch an activity and review it in their heads before attempting any kind of public performance (Appleton, 1983; Longstreet, 1978). For example, after watching a medicine man, an apprentice will collect a plant for a specific remedy. If the selection is not correct, the medicine man more than likely will walk to the correct plant and show and explain some characteristics that make it the appropriate plant. The same rich style of watching, modeling, and explaining is used for jewelry making, weaving, and classroom learning.

Werner and Begishe (1968) capture this contrast in learning by comparing the European American philosophy, "If at first you don't succeed, try, try, again" to the Native American philosophy, "If at first you don't think, and think again, don't bother trying." A teacher of Native American students comments, "The Indian students seem to need time to think about things before they take action on their assignment. It is almost like they have to make sure they can do it before they try . . . If I didn't know better, I could interpret this as they just do not care about doing their assignments" (Swisher & Deyhle, 1992, p. 82).

Díaz-Rico and Weed (1995) suggest that teachers learn about their students' cultural characteristics to understand the students' actions and help them to integrate the home and school cultures. Following are general areas and questions that teachers can use to guide their inquiry:

- **Time:** How do students perceive time? How is timeliness regarded in their cultures?
- **Space:** What personal distance do students use in interactions with other students and with adults? How does the culture determine the space allotted to boys and girls?
- **Dress and Food:** How does dress differ for age, gender, and social class? What clothing and accessories are considered acceptable? What foods are typical?
- **Rituals and Ceremonies:** What rituals do students use to show respect? What cele-

brations do students observe, and for what reasons? How and where do parents expect to be greeted when visiting the class?
- **Work:** What types of work are students expected to perform, and at what age, in the home and community? To what extent are students expected to work together?
- **Leisure:** What are the purposes for play? What typical activities are done for enjoyment in the home and community?
- **Gender Roles:** What tasks are performed by boys? By girls? What expectations do parents and students hold for boys' and girls' achievements, and how does this differ by subject areas?
- **Status:** What resources (e.g., study area and materials, study assistance from parents and siblings) are available at home and in the community? What power do parents have to obtain information about the school and to influence educational choices?
- **Goals:** What kinds of work are considered prestigious or desirable? What role does education play in achieving occupational goals? What education level does the family and student desire for the student?
- **Education:** What methods for teaching and learning are used in the home (e.g., modeling and imitation, didactic stories and proverbs, direct verbal instruction)?
- **Communication:** What roles do verbal and nonverbal language play in learning and teaching? What roles do conventions such as silence, questions, rhetorical questions, and discourse style play in communication? What types of literature (e.g., newspapers, books) are used in the home and in what language(s) are they written? How is writing used in the home (e.g., letters, lists, notes) and in what language(s)?
- **Interaction:** What roles do cooperation and competition play in learning? How are children expected to interact with teachers?

Common characteristics in a culture can serve initially to guide teacher inquiry. For example, Kitano (1973) and Cheng (1991) note several characteristics of Asian cultures that may help to explain parents' expectations and students' actions:

- Students are to be quiet and obedient, not calling attention to themselves in a group.

- Didactic methods of learning are common. Teachers are to teach by demonstrating or transmitting knowledge, skills, and strategies. Students are to study and learn.
- Teachers are to be respected and generally not to be challenged.
- In school, students respond when they have something important to share and do not engage easily in free discussion and brainstorming.

Based on these characteristics, a teacher would understand when students from Laos or Vietnam would not consider raising their hands and asking for clarification when a teacher is lecturing (Bliatout et al., 1988) or would not want to be singled out for attention or praise by teachers (Furey, 1986).

In many Native American cultures, the role of time is viewed differently. The time to begin is when people arrive for the gathering. Work is oriented toward the common good of the community rather than personal recognition and fame, and a deep respect for knowledge and wisdom of elders is evident (Pepper, 1976; Swisher & Deyhle, 1992). The role of silence is important, in that it communicates respect and thoughtfulness. Being comfortable with silence helped the counselor in the following scenario establish trust and rapport.

> Norman, a Paiute youth from Reno, Nevada, had an agonizing decision to make. At the age of 18, he had graduated from the Indian Youth Training Program in Tucson, Arizona, and was free to return home to live. Living at home would possibly jeopardize the hard-won habits of diligence and self-control that he had learned away from the home community, in which he had been arrested for juvenile delinquency. As the counselor in Norman's group home, I knew he could possibly benefit by talking over his decision. After school, I entered his room and sat on the chair by his bed, indicating that I was available to help him talk through his dilemma. One half hour of total silence elapsed. After thirty minutes he began to speak. Silence rather than language had achieved the rapport I sought" (Díaz-Rico & Weed, 1995, p. 246).

In African American cultures, interaction is more informal, with greater spontaneity and general participation in the discussion rather than the more focused question and answer format (Ratleff, 1989). In studying a small African American

community in the rural Carolinas, Heath (1983) noted that young children in "Trackton" were encouraged to use spontaneous verbal play, rich with metaphors and similes. The use of multiple modes of communication, particularly nonverbal expressions, plays an important role in understanding the meaning of the message.

In many Latin American cultures, the family and community are strongly valued, and time is more flexible. For example, "Adela, a Mexican-American first grade girl, arrived at school about twenty minutes late every day. Her teacher was at first irritated and gradually exasperated. In a parent conference, Adela's mother explained that braiding her daughter's hair each morning was an important time for the two of them to be together. This family time presented a value conflict with the school's time norm" (Díaz-Rico & Weed, 1995, p. 231). Just as family and community are valued, *interdependence* (rather than independence) is viewed as a strength. Decisions are made as a group, and those who are successful have responsibilities for others. Classrooms that foster learning through cooperation may help students extend their predisposition for interdependence (Díaz-Rico & Weed, 1995).

Ogbu (1978, 1992) has suggested that some cultural groups seem to cross cultural boundaries more easily than other groups. The case for this idea is built on the information presented in the Research Brief.

> Terminology for racial and ethnic groups changes, reflecting both cultural and political decisions and historical development (Nieto, 1996). Using the current preferred terms when referring to groups is important.

RESEARCH BRIEF

CROSSING CULTURAL BOUNDARIES

Teachers often ask why some cultural groups seem to cross cultural boundaries and succeed in school more easily than others do. Based on his comparative research, John Ogbu (1978; 1992) has put forth one explanation. In his work, he classified cultural groups as (a) autonomous minorities, (b) immigrant or voluntary minorities, and (c) caste-like or involuntary minorities.

- *Autonomous minorities* are considered minorities in a numerical sense, and include Jews, Mormons, and the Amish. In the United States, there are no non-White autonomous minorities.
- *Immigrant or voluntary minorities* are people who have moved to the new society or culture more or less voluntarily—because they desire greater economic opportunities and political freedom. The Chinese and Punjabi Indians are representative United States examples.
- *Castelike or involuntary minorities* are people who were brought to the United States or conquered against their will. Examples in the United States are African Americans, Native Americans, early Mexican Americans in the Southwest, and Native Hawaiians.

Ogbu (1992) suggests that voluntary groups experience initial (but not lingering) problems in school because of language and cultural differences. The involuntary minorities, on the other hand, usually experience greater, more persistent difficulties learning in school. This difficulty for involuntary minorities appears related to several factors:

- *Cultural inversion,* or the tendency to regard certain forms of behavior, events, symbols, and meanings as inappropriate because they are characteristic of European American culture.
- A *collective identity,* in opposition to the social identity of the dominant group, develops as the involuntary minorities are treated as subordinates by European Americans in economic, political, social, psychological, cultural, and language domains.

Hence, in an effort to retain their own identity and roots, students from involuntary minorities may be more oppositional and less motivated to learn in school. Ogbu (1992) explains, "They fear that by learning the White cultural frame of reference, they will cease to act like minorities and lose their identity as minorities and their sense of

community and self-worth" (p. 10). In contrast, because voluntary minorities do not feel the need to protect their cultural identity, they do not perceive learning the attitudes and behaviors required for school success as threatening to their own culture, language, and identities. Instead they interpret such learning as *additive,* that is, adding to what they already have (Chung, 1992).

It is important to note that these are generalized types that include groups who may more appropriately "fit" a different type. For example, Cubans who fled Cuba during the 1960s were an involuntary minority, yet many acculturated and became quite successful in the Miami community.

Cummins (1992) suggests that academic success of students from involuntary minority groups is related to the extent that schools reflect the following:

- Minority students' language and culture are incorporated into the school program.
- Minority community participation is encouraged as an integral component of children's education.
- Instruction (pedagogy) is used to motivate students to use language actively in order to generate their own knowledge.
- Professionals involved in student testing (assessment) become advocates for minority students by focusing primarily on ways in which students' academic difficulties are a function of interactions with and within the school context, instead of locating the problem within the students (p. 5).

Do not assume that cultural characteristics are common to all members of a cultural group. Rather, these characteristics serve as a starting point in your education about the cultural diversity of the students you teach. They also provide rich opportunities for students to learn about their cultural backgrounds, the focus of the next section.

Multicultural Education

Multicultural education is "an idea, an educational reform movement, and a process whose major goal is to change the structure of educational institutions so that male and female students, exceptional students, and students who are members of diverse racial, ethnic, and cultural groups will have an equal chance to achieve academically in school" (Banks, 1993a, p. 1). Multicultural education is closely linked to cultural diversity (Yee, 1991) and fosters pride in minority cultures, assists students in developing new insights into their cultures, reduces prejudice and stereotyping, and promotes intercultural understanding (Rubalcava, 1991).

Dimensions of Multicultural Education

Multicultural education is much more than a curriculum focused on learning about diverse cultures based on such parameters as gender, ethnicity, and race. It is a thread running through the total curriculum, not a subject to be taught (Tiedt & Tiedt, 1995). Banks (1991b) suggests that multicultural education has four dimensions: content integration, knowledge construction, an equity pedagogy, and an empowering school culture.

Content Integration Content integration focuses on using examples and content from a variety of cultures and groups to illustrate concepts, principles, generalizations, and theories. Ethnic and cultural content is infused into the subject areas in a natural, logical way (Banks, 1993a). For example, you can teach students about traditional dress and celebrations in many different cultures by discussing different holidays, the dress worn, and the reasons for the holidays and traditional dress. As a follow-up activity, students can interview their parents and other family members to learn about traditional dress and holidays celebrated by their families.

Knowledge Construction Knowledge construction refers to students learning about how implicit cultural assumptions, frames of reference, perspectives, and biases influence the ways that knowledge is constructed. For example, the discovery of America by Europeans has two very different frames of reference when presented from the perspectives of the Native Americans and the Europeans. Similarly, the power of the mind over the body is viewed differently by Asian and European cultures.

Equity Pedagogy With an **equity pedagogy**, the teacher attends to different teaching and learning styles and modifies teaching to facilitate the academic achievement of students from diverse cultures. Adjusting the learning process so that Native American students can learn in private, or encouraging the use of cooperative learning can accommodate cultural differences and promote academic learning.

Empowering School Culture An **empowering school culture** promotes gender, racial, and social-class equity. Establishing such a culture entails examining the school culture for biases and prejudices, developing strategies to alleviate them, and replacing them with opportunities that promote positive self-esteem for all students. An initial step in creating an empowering school culture is to have the staff share, learn about, and respect their own diversity.

A school's staff can learn about their school community through many of the activities used to help students learn about each other, such as sharing information about heritage, birthplace, family, traditional foods, and hobbies. For example, Stan Williams, the principal at an urban elementary school, takes time each year at the initial full-staff meeting for the staff to interview each other about their families, cultural backgrounds, areas of educational expertise, traditional foods, and hobbies. Then each interviewer uses the information garnered to introduce the interviewee to at least two other staff members. In the past, Stan has also displayed staff photos and profiles in the staff lounge. Stan comments, "When we take time [for] . . . this activity . . . , the staff immediately begins to learn . . . about each other and find common interests that are fostered throughout the school year. It helps to create a sense of equality across all . . . staff jobs (e.g., teachers, paraprofessionals, office staff, building maintenance staff)."

Multicultural education grew out of the civil rights movement of the 1960s, which called for curriculum reform to reflect the experiences, histories, cultures, and views of African Americans and other groups. Early responses included recognition of ethnic holidays and high school courses such as "Black Studies."

To implement multicultural education and integrate these four dimensions successfully, multicultural education should be conceptualized as much more than a curriculum or a subject to teach. Several leaders in the field have suggested that viewing the school as a social system and studying and reforming the major variables is necessary to create a learning environment in which students have an equal chance for school success (e.g., Banks, 1993a; Grant & Sleeter, 1993; Ladson-Billings, 1995; Ogbu, 1992). As a social system, Banks (1981) suggests that the following aspects of the school need to be considered:

How can school culture empower all students to succeed? What student outcomes lead to the goal of creating a learning community in which students understand and respect diversity and have equal opportunity for academic success?

- school policy and politics
- school staff: attitudes, perceptions, and actions
- school culture and hidden curriculum
- formalized curriculum and course of study
- assessment and testing procedures
- instructional materials
- learning styles for the school
- teaching styles and strategies
- language and dialects of the school
- counseling program
- community participation and input

As you study the schools in which you teach as social systems and teaching and learning communities, consider these variables and determine the degree to which they foster the overarching goals of multicultural education, that is, to create a learning community in which students not only have equal opportunities for academic success, but also an understanding of and respect for diversity.

Desired Student Outcomes

Given these dimensions of multicultural education and its overall goals, what are some desired student outcomes that lead to these goals? Tiedt and Tiedt (1995) suggest that students should be able to do the following:

- identify a strong sense of self-esteem, and express the need and right of others to similar feelings of self-esteem
- describe their own cultures, recognizing the influences that have shaped their thinking and behavior
- identify racial, ethnic, and religious groups represented in our pluralistic society
- identify needs and concerns universal to people of all cultures, and compare cultural variations
- recognize, understand, and critique examples of stereotypic thinking and social inequities in real life and literature, and develop solutions for altering their status
- discuss special gender-, ethnic-, age-, and disability-related concerns
- inquire multiculturally as they engage in broad thematic studies related to any field of study

Clearly, these outcomes call for learning curricula that highlight cultural diversity. The next section discusses curricula for multicultural education.

Multicultural Curricula

Banks (1993b) suggests that since multicultural education was introduced in the 1960s, curricular approaches to multicultural education have evolved, based on the degree to which diversity plays a central role in the curriculum. Banks (1993b) identifies four approaches—contributions, additive, transformation, and social action (see Table 10.1).

Contributions Approach The **contributions approach** is characterized by the insertion of ethnic heroes and discrete cultural artifacts into the curriculum—adding culturally diverse inventors and their inventions to a thematic unit on inventions, for example.

This approach is the easiest to use but has several serious limitations. First, because the heroes are usually presented in isolation, students do not gain an overall understanding of the role of ethnic and cultural groups in the United States. Second, this approach does not address issues such as oppression and discrimination. Instead, it reinforces the Horatio Alger myth in that ethnic heroes are presented with little attention paid to how they became heroes despite the barriers they encountered.

Additive Approach The **additive approach** is characterized by the addition of content, concepts, themes, and perspectives without changing the basic structure of the curriculum. Typical examples are adding books about different groups to the literature sets (e.g., Mildred Taylor's *Roll of Thunder, Hear My Cry*), adding a unit on Native Americans to an American history course, or adding a course on ethnic or gender studies to a high school curriculum. This approach offers better integration of multicultural perspectives than the contributions approach, but does not result in a restructured curriculum. For example, including a unit on the Plains Indians in a U.S. history class will increase students' understanding of Native Americans, but not as clearly as transforming the curriculum so that the movement to the West is viewed as both an expansion (from a European perspective) and an invasion (from a Native American perspective).

Transformation Approach In the **transformation approach**, the basic core of the curriculum is changed and the focus is on viewing events, concepts, and themes from multiple perspectives, based on diversity. Banks (1993b) suggests that, "When studying U.S. history, language, music, arts, science, and mathematics, the emphasis should not be on the ways that various ethnic and cultural groups have contributed to mainstream U.S. society and culture. The emphasis rather, should be on how the common U.S. culture and society emerged from a complex synthesis and interaction of the diverse cultural elements that originated within the various cultural, racial, ethnic, and religious groups that make up the U.S. society" (p. 204). In developing multicultural units, it is important to identify the key concept and generalizations associated with that concept. Specific activities can then be planned so that students have the evidence to draw the generalizations and understand the key concept. Table 10.2 provides an example of a unit for high school students on the key concept of social protest.

> Concern with gender equity in textbook publishing is an example of transformation and social action approaches in education. In 1972, Scott Foresman was the first to publish curriculum guidelines for recognizing women's achievement, treating girls and boys equally, and avoiding sex-role stereotypes and sexist language.

Social Action Approach The **social action approach** incorporates all the elements of the transformation approach and also includes a cultural critique. Teaching units that use this approach incorporate a problem-solving process in which students make decisions and take actions related to the concept, issue, or problem being studied, following these steps:

1. Identify the problem or question (e.g., discrimination in our school).
2. Collect data related to the problem or question (e.g., what is discrimination; what causes discrimination, what examples are evident in our school).
3. Conduct a value inquiry and analysis (i.e., students examine and reflect on their values, attitudes, and beliefs related to discrimination).

TABLE 10.1

Approaches for the Integration of Multicultural Content

Approach	Description	Examples	Strengths	Problems
Contributions	Heroes, cultural components, holidays, and other discrete elements related to ethnic groups are added to the curriculum on special days, occasions, and celebrations.	Famous Mexican Americans are studied only during the week of Cinco de Mayo (May 5). African Americans are studied during African American History Month in February but rarely during the rest of the year. Ethnic foods are studied in the first grade with little attention devoted to the cultures in which the foods are embedded.	Provides a quick and relatively easy way to put ethnic content into the curriculum. Gives ethnic heroes visibility in the curriculum alongside mainstream heroes. Is a popular approach among teachers and educators.	Results in a superficial understanding of ethnic cultures. Focuses on the life-styles and artifacts of ethnic groups and reinforces stereotypes and misconceptions. Mainstream criteria are used to select heroes and cultural elements for inclusion in the curriculum.
Additive	This approach consists of the addition of content, concepts, themes, and perspectives to the curriculum without changing its structure.	Adding the book *The Color Purple* to a literature unit without reconceptualizing the unit or giving the students the background knowledge to understand the book. Adding a unit on the Japanese American internment to a U.S. history course without treating the Japanese in any other unit. Leaving the core curriculum intact but adding an ethnic studies course, as an elective, that focuses on a specific ethnic group.	Makes it possible to add ethnic content to the curriculum without changing its structure, which requires substantial curriculum changes and staff development. Can be implemented within the existing curriculum structure.	Reinforces the idea that ethnic history and culture are not integral parts of U.S. mainstream culture. Students view ethnic groups from Anglocentric and Eurocentric perspectives. Fails to help students understand how the dominant culture and ethnic cultures are interconnected and interrelated.

Reprinted with permission from Banks, J.A. (1993b). Approaches to multicultural curriculum reform. In J.A. Banks (Ed.), *Multicultural education: Issues and perspectives* (2nd ed., pp. 208–209). Boston: Allyn & Bacon.

TABLE 10.1

Approaches for the Integration of Multicultural Content (continued)

Approach	Description	Examples	Strengths	Problems
Transformation	The basic goals, structure, and nature of the curriculum are changed to enable students to view concepts, events, issues, problems, and themes from the perspectives of diverse cultural, ethnic, and racial groups.	A unit on the American Revolution describes the meaning of the revolution to Anglo revolutionaries, Anglo loyalists, African Americans, Indians, and the British. A unit on 20th-century U.S. literature includes works by William Faulkner, Joyce Carol Oates, Langston Hughes, N. Scott Momoday, Saul Bellow, Maxine Hong Kingston, Rudolfo A. Anaya, and Piri Thomas.	Enables students to understand the complex ways in which diverse racial and cultural groups participated in the formation of U.S. society and culture. Helps reduce racial and ethnic encapsulation. Enables diverse ethnic, racial, and religious groups to see their cultures, ethos, and perspectives in the school curriculum. Gives students a balanced view of the nature and development of U.S. culture and society. Helps to empower victimized racial, ethnic, and cultural groups.	The implementation of this approach requires substantial curriculum revision, in-service training, and the identification and development of materials written from the perspectives of various racial and cultural groups. Staff development for the institutionalization of this approach must be continual and ongoing.
Social Action	In this approach, students identify important social problems and issues, gather pertinent data, clarify their values on the issues, make decisions, and take reflective actions to help resolve the issue or problem.	A class studies prejudice and discrimination in their school and decides to take actions to improve race relations in the school. A class studies the treatment of ethnic groups in a local newspaper and writes a letter to the newspaper publisher suggesting ways that the treatment of ethnic groups in the newspapers should be improved.	Enables students to improve their thinking, value analysis, decision-making, and social-action skills. Enables students to improve their data-gathering skills. Helps students develop a sense of political efficacy. Helps students improve their skills to work in groups.	Requires a considerable amount of curriculum planning and materials identification. May be longer in duration than more traditional teaching units. May focus on problems and issues considered controversial by some members of the school staff and citizens of the community. Students may be able to take few meaningful actions that contribute to the resolution of the social issue or problem.

TABLE 10.2

Key Ideas and Activities for a Unit on Social Protest

Key Ideas

Key Concept: Social Protest

Key Generalization: When individuals and groups are victims of oppression and discrimination, they tend to protest against their situation in various ways.

Intermediate-Level Generalization: Throughout their experiences in the United States, ethnic minorities have resisted discrimination and oppression in various ways.

Low-Level Generalization: Mexican Americans have resisted Anglo discrimination and oppression since Anglo-Americans conquered and occupied the Southwest

Activities

1. To give the students a general overview of Mexican-American history, show them a videotape, such as *Mexican People and Culture,* a videotape in *The Hispanic Culture Series* distributed by Zenqer Video. After showing the videotape, ask the students to discuss the questions:

   a. What major problems have Mexican Americans experienced in the United States?

   b. What actions have been taken by Mexican-American individuals and groups to eliminate the discrimination they have experienced?

2. Ask a group of students to prepare reports that reveal the ways in which the following men led organized resistance to Anglo-Americans in the 1800s:

   Juan N. Cortina
   Juan Jose Herrera
   Juan Patron

   The class should discuss these men when the reports are presented. A good reference for this activity is Rodolfo Acuña, *Occupied America: A History of Chicanos,* 3rd ed.

3. Ask a group of students to prepare a report to be presented in class that describes Chicano involvement in strikes and unions between 1900 and 1940. When this report is presented, the students should discuss ways in which strikes and union activities were forms of organized resistance.

4. Ask the students to research the goals, tactics, and strategies used by the following Mexican-American civil rights groups: Order of the Sons of America, League of United Latin-American Citizens, The Community Service Organization, The American G.I. Forum, Federal Alliance of Free Cities, and Crusade for Justice. Ask the students to write several generalizations about the activities of these groups.

5. Ask the students to research the following questions:

   a. How is the "Chicano" movement similar to other Mexican-American protest movements?

   b. How are its goals and strategies different?

   c. When did the movement emerge?

   d. What long-range effects do you think the movement will have? Why?

6. Ask the students to read and dramatize the epic poem of the Chicano movement, *I Am Joaquin,* by Rodolfo Gonzales.

7. Ask the students questions that will enable them to summarize and generalize about how Mexican Americans have resisted Anglo discrimination and oppression in both the past and in contemporary American society.

8. Conclude the unit by viewing and discussing the film *I Am Joaquin,* distributed by El Teatro Campesino, San Juan Bautista, CA.

Reprinted with permission from Banks, J.A. (1991a). *Teaching strategies for ethnic studies* (5th ed., pp. 491–492, 500). Boston: Allyn & Bacon.

TIPS FOR TEACHERS

10.2 Guidelines for Teaching Multicultural Content

- Take time to learn about your culture(s) and how it influences your beliefs and actions. Be sensitive to your attitudes and behaviors.
- To teach cultural content you need knowledge of cultural groups. Read at least several books that survey the histories of cultural groups in the United States. (See Read More about It for suggested books.)
- Make sure that your room conveys positive images of various cultural groups (through bulletin boards, posters, literature, software, and so on).
- Plan time in which you and your students can learn about each other's cultural backgrounds. (See Read More about It for reference books.)
- Be culturally conscious in selecting teaching materials. If the materials you use include stereotypes or present only one perspective, point out the limitation to the students.

- Use trade books, films, videotapes, and recordings to supplement the textbook and to present more varied perspectives.
- Use literature to enrich students' understanding of cultural pluralism.
- Be sensitive to the development levels of your students when you select concepts, content, and activities. Use concrete, specific concepts and activities for students in early elementary grades. As students develop, focus on more abstract concepts and problem solving.
- Use cooperative learning and group work to promote integration.
- Make sure that not only classroom but also school-wide activities (such as plays, sports, and clubs) are culturally integrated.

4. Make decisions and establish a plan of social action based on a synthesis of the knowledge obtained in step 2 and the values identified in step 3.

Robinson (1993) describes how a class of African-American middle-school students in Dallas used the social action approach. The important problem they identified was that their school was surrounded by liquor stores. Investigating further, they found that the city's zoning regulations made some areas dry but that their school was in a wet area. Further investigation revealed that schools serving White upper middle-class students were located in dry areas, whereas schools in poor communities were in wet areas. The students, assisted by their teacher, planned a strategy for exposing this inequity. By using mathematics, literacy, and social and political skills, the students proved their points with reports, editorials, charts, maps, and graphs. In this case the curriculum and the stu-

dents' learning became a form of cultural critique and social action.

As a teacher, you will undoubtedly use all four approaches to multicultural education, with the goal of primarily employing the transformational and social action approaches. Tips for Teachers 10.2 presents general strategies for integrating content about cultural groups into the school curriculum, and Tech Talk describes how to create a community video using videography. The curriculum should incorporate opportunities to foster student achievement and cultural competence as well as help students recognize, understand, and critique current social inequities (Ladson-Billings, 1995).

Linguistic Diversity and Second Language Acquisition

Linguistic diversity is not new in the United States, with its rich history of immigration. Today, as in

Using Videography to Create Community Videos

Creating videos of the home community integrates multicultural education and the students' home communities into the curriculum. This activity provides students the opportunity to learn about and celebrate their home communities and cultures while at the same time learning basic videography skills.

Even as simple a process as having students video typical scenes around the community and interview respected members of the community has opportunities for planning the video, developing storyboards, and writing and conducting interviews. If editing equipment is available, students can learn simple editing skills by piecing together the segments of videotape as they construct the community video.

Constructing a community video provides many opportunities to learn about the community's "funds of knowledge" and the people the community considers to be experts. These funds of knowledge can extend across many contexts including home life, traditions and celebrations, work, art, and politics. A community video can focus on one context or incorporate many different ones. For example, an upper elementary class might decide to focus on home life, traditions, and celebrations, whereas a high school American government class might select a political issue such as "illegal immigrants" for their community video.

Constructing a community video provides an ideal opportunity for students to learn basic videography skills, such as setting up the camera, focusing and adjusting the zoom, framing the subjects, and learning to use external microphones for interviews. It also provides opportunities for students to learn about the way a video is constructed to create interest, variety, and story. By using a story board to draw and describe the different parts of the video, students can plan and see the video before they begin to construct it on tape.

Planning and creating a community video also provides natural opportunities for meaningful language arts, art, and social studies activities. For example, students learn about their communities and cultural traditions, as well as who the good sources of this information are in the community.

Students write the interviews and practice their interviewing skills with each other. In most communities the arts—including dance, visual arts, theater and drama, and traditional dress—play an important role. As students construct a video, they usually integrate

scenes from the arts with their interviews to make the video interesting and to provide pictures of what is being described.

The finished video can be shared with many individuals. Copies can be placed in school and local libraries, and in the classroom, and a special showing for parents and the community can be held at the school.

Resources to help you plan a community video include the following:

1. Gross, L. S. & Ward, L. W. (1991). *Electronic movie-making.* Belmont, CA: Wadsworth. Describes how to make a movie, including preproduction activities (such as developing scripts and storyboards), production activities, and postproduction activities (such as editing).

2. Valmont, W. J. (1995). *Creating videos for school use.* Boston: Allyn & Bacon. Written for teachers; explains use of videos in schools; provides many examples of how to use video in class and how to teach basic videography skills.

3. Wigginton, E. (Ed.) *The Foxfire Series.* New York: Doubleday. An English teacher in an Appalachian community helped students publish their oral histories, starting with *The Foxfire Book* in 1972. Information about the Foxfire Teacher Networks is available from Foxfire Teacher Outreach, P.O. Box 541, Mountain City, GA 30562.

4. Zimmerman, W. (1988). *Instant oral biographies: How to tape record, video or film your life stories.* New York: Guarionex Press. Written for students in upper elementary and middle schools; describes how to make oral histories and includes sample interview forms.

the past, many students live in homes in which the language spoken is not English. This trend is increasing rather than decreasing. In 1992 a total of 32 million, or one in seven Americans above the age of five, spoke a language other than English at home—a 34 percent increase between 1980 and 1990. The number of Chinese speakers doubled during this period, and approximately 17 million Americans spoke Spanish in their homes in 1993 (Tiedt & Tiedt, 1995).

José is a good example of such a student. At the age of four, he immigrated with his parents and three siblings from a rural community in Mexico to an urban Spanish-speaking community in Texas. His parents spoke only Spanish when they arrived. Although José has some exposure to English and his father is taking a night course to learn English, he entered school at age five with Spanish as his first language and only a limited knowledge of his second language, English. This same scenario is true of children who immigrate from Central and South American countries, Asian and Pacific Island countries, and Eastern European countries. The U.S. Department of Education estimates that of the 40 million students in public and private schools, over 2 million have limited proficiency in English (Díaz-Rico & Weed, 1995).

The implications of this demography are that a growing number of students who enter school in the United States learn English as a second language in school. As a teacher, your knowledge of second language acquisition and general instructional guidelines can help make school a success for students like José.

Framework for Second Language Acquisition

Ellis (1985) provides a framework for second language acquisition that can guide you in making accommodations for students who first language is not English. Ellis suggests that five interrelated factors govern the acquisition of a second language. Figure 10.1 depicts the relationship among these factors.

Situational Factors Situational factors are related to the context or the situation (i.e., the learning environments) in which the second language learning occurs. Students learn the second lan-

guage in multiple learning environments—from relatives, friends, and neighbors who speak English, through ESL or bilingual education programs at school, and from peers in the classroom and on the playground.

Environments such as these can provide both formal teaching and more natural opportunities to acquire language. When José's uncle explains the concept "scientist" in Spanish and then pairs it with English, he is providing formal instruction. On the other hand, the instruction is much more natural when José and his uncle converse about what happened in school and his uncle provides José with words in English when José is searching for the English word. One goal of both bilingual education and English as a Second Language (ESL) instruction, is to create environments that are non-threatening and in which students are willing to take risks and play with the language. Maria, the ESL teacher interviewed at the beginning of this chapter, encourages students to play with the language by experimenting with sounds, words, and syntactic construction. She makes these opportunities for discovery by encouraging experimentation.

> Students whose first language is not English and who are not fluent in English are sometimes referred to as students with *limited English proficiency* (LEP).

Another situational factor that promotes second language acquisition is an environment in which the students' first language and culture are respected and valued. The research consistently demonstrates that valuing students' first language is an important factor for student success (Carter & Chatfield, 1986; Lucas et al., 1990). One important aspect of valuing the students' language is to learn about their community's funds of knowledge and language (refer to Tips for Teachers 10.1).

Linguistic Input Linguistic input refers to input received when listening to or reading a second language. Comprehensible input is a key factor for success (Krashen, 1985). Input is made more comprehensible by a number of strategies, including the following:

- selecting a topic of conversation familiar to students
- creating a context for what is being discussed

FIGURE 10.1

Framework for Second Language Acquisition

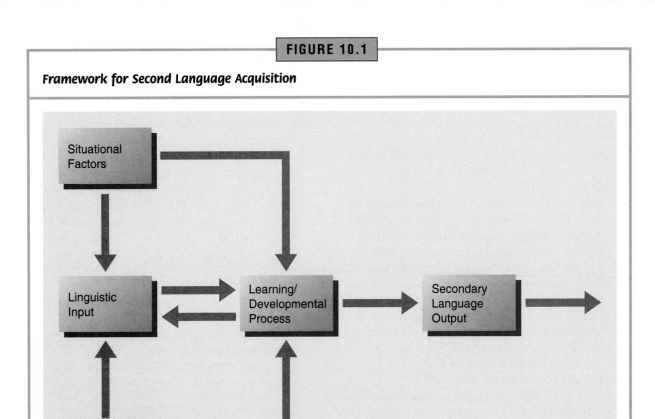

Adapted from Ellis, R. (1985). *Understanding second language acquisition.* Oxford: Oxford University Press.

- using simpler sentence construction
- repeating important phrases
- incorporating the students' first language into the instruction
- emphasizing key words to promote comprehensible input

When teaching linguistically diverse students, it is important to consider the linguistic input. Tips for Teachers 10.3 presents guidelines and ideas for making input more comprehensible.

Learner Characteristics The third factor affecting second-language acquisition or output are **learner characteristics**. Relevant learner characteristics include the age at which students learn a second language, their aptitude for learning language, their purposes and degree of motivation for learning the second language, their self-confidence in language learning, and their learning strategies.

Another important variable is the degree of acquisition or proficiency in the first language. Cummins (1991), in a review of research, concluded that the

Assessment used in screening for proficiency in English includes the Bilingual Syntax Measure (Burt et al., 1980), the IDEA Oral Language Proficiency Test (Ballard & Tighe, 1987), and the Language Assessment Scales (De Avila & Duncan, 1986).

TIPS FOR TEACHERS

10.3 Guidelines for Making Input More Comprehensible for Second Language Learners

- Begin teaching new concepts by working from the students' current knowledge and incorporating the funds of knowledge from the students' community.
- Use demonstrations and gestures to augment oral communication.
- To the degree possible, create the context in which the concepts occur. For example, when teaching about shellfish, visit an aquarium, watch a film, display shells in the classroom.
- Discuss connections between the concepts being taught and the students' home cultures.

- Encourage students to share the new vocabulary in their first language and incorporate the first language into instruction.
- If students share a common first language, pair more proficient second language learners with less proficient peers, and encourage students to discuss what they are learning.
- Highlight key words and phrases by repeating them and writing them.
- Use simple sentence constructions, particularly to present a new or difficult concept.

better developed the students' proficiency and conceptual foundation in the first language, the more likely they were to develop similarly high levels of proficiency and conceptual ability in the second language. He has referred to this as the **common underlying proficiency**, using the analogy of an iceberg to explain this hypothesis and relationship between first and second language acquisition (see Figure 10.2) and why proficiency in the first language complements proficiency in the second language (Cummins, 1981).

As shown in Figure 10.2, both languages have separate surface features, represented by separate icebergs. Below the surface and less visible, however, is the underlying proficiency common to both languages.

No matter which language the person is using, the thoughts that accompany the talking, reading, writing, and listening come from the same language core. One implication of this analogy is that individuals who are **balanced bilinguals** have an advantage over monolingual individuals in that they have greater cognitive flexibility and a greater understanding of language (see Research Brief).

RESEARCH BRIEF

RELATIONSHIP OF BILINGUALISM TO COGNITIVE DEVELOPMENT AND LEARNING

From the early nineteenth century to approximately the 1960s, dominant belief was that bilingualism was detrimental to cognitive development and academic learning. Diaz (1983) summarized the research performed prior to 1962, which built the case for bilingualism as a "language handicap." Researchers found that bilingual children had more limited vocabularies, deficient articulation, and more grammatical errors than monolingual students. One interpretation was that bilingualism caused "linguistic confusion," which affected students' cognitive ability and academic performance. This research overall had many flaws. Bilingual and monolingual groups were not matched for other important variables such as socioeconomic status, for example, and tests for intellectual functioning and learning of bilingual students generally were conducted in English, not in the first or more dominant language.

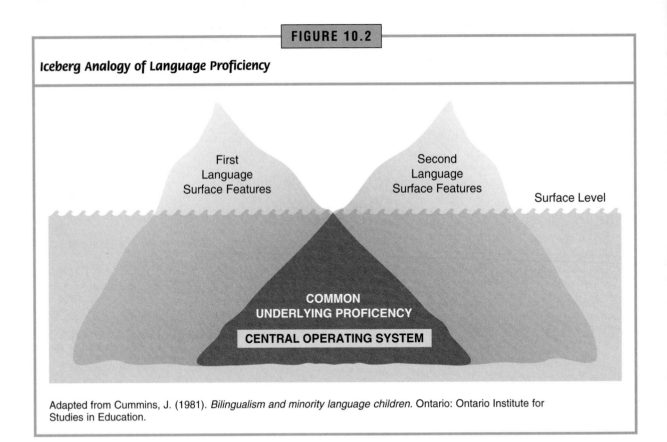

FIGURE 10.2

Iceberg Analogy of Language Proficiency

First Language Surface Features

Second Language Surface Features

Surface Level

COMMON UNDERLYING PROFICIENCY

CENTRAL OPERATING SYSTEM

Adapted from Cummins, J. (1981). *Bilingualism and minority language children.* Ontario: Ontario Institute for Studies in Education.

In 1962, Peal and Lambert published the study now considered the major turning point in the history of the relationship between bilingualism and cognition. This research broke new territory in two respects: it overcame many methodological deficiencies and, in addition, found that bilingualism leads to cognitive advantages over monolingualism. Peal and Lambert concluded that bilingualism provides greater cognitive flexibility, greater ability to think more abstractly, and greater ability in concept formation.

Subsequent research has shown that higher degrees of bilingualism are correlated with increased cognitive abilities in such areas as creativity, knowledge of how language works (*metalinguistics*), concept formation, and cognitive flexibility (Galambos & Goldin-Meadow, 1990; Skutnabb-Kangas, 1981).

The Learning and Developmental Process The fourth factor addresses the **learning and develop-**mental process of second language acquisition and learning. Cummins (1984) suggested that students generally acquire competency in the **basic interpersonal communication skills (BICS)** before becoming competent with **cognitive academic language proficiency (CALP)**. The BICS are the conversational competencies we develop with a second language—the greetings and "small talk" between peers, which generally do not require much cognitive effort or social problem solving. The CALP, on the other hand, refers to the more cognitively demanding language skills required for the new learning that occurs in school. In general, BICS develop in a second language prior to CALP. Cummins (1981) suggested that it takes from one to two years to develop BICS, but from five to seven years to develop competence in CALP.

Although these guidelines have been shown to vary widely, depending on situational factors, linguistic input, and learner characteristics, they do have implications for teachers in general education classrooms. You might assume that because students can converse easily with you in their second language, they are ready to learn new concepts, strategies, and skills in the second language. This is not necessarily the case. For example, when Hoang Hy Vinh entered Sarah Miles's third grade class, Sarah immediately noticed that he conversed easily with other students and with her. Vinh immigrated from Vietnam two years ago and began learning English through the school's ESL program. His parents, who take English in a night course, feel that learning English is important for their economic and personal success in America. Still, Vietnamese is the primary language spoken in the home.

As Sarah got to know Vinh, she realized that although his conversational skills were strong enough for him to be comfortable in the classroom community, he was not yet proficient in academic

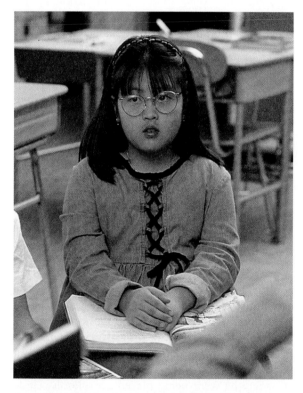

According to Ellis's framework for second language acquisition, what five factors will influence this student's acquisition of English? What kinds of programs for second language acquisition might you recommend for this student, based on effectiveness research?

tasks such as reading and writing in English. She also found that to teach new concepts in social studies and science, she needed to provide lots of context. Sarah incorporated an extended segment on farming communities into a thematic unit on California, for example, because Vinh and several other students came from other Asian and Mexican farming communities. From the school and public libraries, she checked out books and magazines about farming and rural life in Vietnam, Mexico, and other Asian countries. The students also visited a California market, as well as Asian and Mexican food markets. They compared the foods from the two markets, and learned how those foods were grown in the three communities. For Vinh and other students from other cultures who were in the process of acquiring English as a second language, providing the link to their cultures helped give them a context in which to build both their language and cognitive skills. This is an example of the **context-embedded communication and instruction** that Cummins (1981) and others (Chamot & O'Malley, 1994) recommend as facilitating second language learning.

> Giving students the opportunity to discuss a new concept in their first language helps to promote content learning for second language learners.

Secondary Language Output The fifth factor in the framework (Figure 10.1) is **secondary language output**. Students may understand a language (listening and reading), but not be proficient in producing the language (speaking and writing). An important part of developing speaking proficiency is the opportunity to engage in meaningful oral exchanges (in the classroom and the community) and to experiment with oral and written language in nonthreatening environments. Swain (1986) emphasized that not only **comprehensible input**, but also opportunities for students to develop **comprehensible output** by oral practice with the language are important for acquisition of a second language. Feedback from listeners and from self-monitoring enables second-language speakers to develop and fine tune their oral language.

Also important in a consideration of secondary language output is that receptive language skills typically develop before expressive language skills. It has been well documented that second-language learners experience a **silent or nonverbal period** (Ervin-Tripp, 1974; Hakuta, 1974), during which they are absorbing information and language that they cannot or do not yet feel comfortable demonstrating (Coelho, 1994). For example, Hakuta (1974) observed a five-year old Japanese girl, noting that it took from her arrival in October until the following April for her to begin speaking English. During that intervening period, she was attending kindergarten and played with neighborhood English-speaking friends, but did not speak English.

Language Variation and Dialect

Language variation, which refers to the fact that language varies from place to place and from group to group (Wolfram et al., in prep.), usually relates to the characteristics of groups of people (such as geographical region, social class, ethnic and cultural backgrounds, age, and gender). **Dialect** generally refers to language variations associated with a regional or social group of people (Wolfram et al., in prep.). All English speakers use a dialect or variation of the English language. Think for a moment. Do you use the term *pop, soda, soda pop, tonic* (or some other term) to label this popular type of drink? The answer depends on your dialect, which most likely relates to where you live and your cultural background. Dialect is also affected by age—use of the term *icebox,* rather than *refrigerator,* is more evident in older people in whose homes iceboxes were used.

Language variation or dialects vary in several ways. Regional dialects tend to be distinguished by pronunciation and vocabulary features, whereas social and cultural dialects show variation not only in these areas, but also in grammatical usage (Wolfram et al., in prep.). Dialects also reflect conversation patterns. In a good, satisfying conversation in some speech communities, for example, speakers overlap one another's talk. In other communities, the listener waits for a break to enter a conversation, and the speaker is likely to stop talking when someone else starts speaking.

Black Vernacular English (BVE) is a dialect used by some African Americans. It is the most prevalent native English vernacular dialect in the United States. (The word *vernacular* is included in the term to avoid the stereotype that all African Americans speak BVE.) Estimates based on socioeconomic demographics show about three-fourths of African Americans speak BVE. As with any other language or dialect, there is great language variation among speakers of BVE.

Because of African Americans' historical status as an oppressed and involuntary minority, there has been a tendency to consider BVE not as a valid language system, but rather as random errors (Labov et al., 1968). Like any other language, however, BVE has an internally consistent linguistic infrastructure and set of grammar rules. Table 10.3 on pages 296 and 297 presents some common grammatical contrasts between Black Vernacular English and Standard American English. In teaching about diversity, it is important that students study dialects and learn that BVE is a linguistic system. When teaching Standard American English to students who speak BVE, it is important to help them understand the systematic differences between the standard and vernacular forms. You can do so by using many of the strategies recommended for second language acquisition.

Historical Perspective on ESL Instruction and Bilingual Education

Bilingual education and English as a second language instruction for culturally and linguistically diverse students have evolved through the years. Figure 10.3 shows the chronology of this evolution in the United States.

What is interesting about this chronology is the way bilingualism has been tied to assimilation into American culture, and therefore linked to political policy. Bilingualism in our schools and communities dates back to the early colonies. It was common among both the working and educated classes that many official documents were published in German and French as well as English. By the late 1800s, however, language restrictions were being placed on schools. Under strong political pressures to assimilate immigrants, bilingual education was virtually eradicated by the 1930s. After World War II, students from minority cultures were described as "culturally deprived" and "linguistically disabled."

FIGURE 10.3

Recent Developments in Second Language and Bilingual Education in the United States

Prior to 1914 Many community schools existed to teach a specific language, such as German. Saturday classes were common.

1918 World War I brought about reactions against Germany and a resurgence of patriotic feeling; use of "English only" in schools legislated in many states.

1945 World War II led to realization of need for knowledge of foreign languages: teaching of foreign languages in schools encouraged.

1958 Soviet launching of *Sputnik* shocked United States' leaders, who then funded schools' efforts to promote key subject areas, including foreign languages.

1963 Dade County, Florida, initiated bilingual programs for Spanish-speaking Cuban children coming to Miami.

1964 Civil Rights Act forbade language-based discrimination.

1968 Bilingual Education Act: Title VII of Elementary and Secondary Education Act promoted bilingual programs in the schools.

1971 Massachusetts Bilingual Education Act: Law mandating bilingual education for non-English-speaking children; Massachusetts first state, other states followed.

1974 Bilingual Education Reform Act: Updated 1968 law; mandated language instruction; added study of history and culture in bilingual programs.

1974 U.S. Supreme Court Decision Lau v. Nichols gave non-English-speaking students the legal right to instruction that enables them to participate in education process, and to bilingual instruction, as part of "equal educational opportunity."

1975 United States Department of Education developed guidelines that specified approaches, methods, and procedures for educating students with limited proficiency in English. These Lau Remedies were not enacted.

1981 Senator S. I. Hayakawa first introduced a constitutional amendment to declare English the official language of the United States. (Defeated)

1981 Castenada vs. Pickard established a framework for determining whether school districts are in compliance with Lau vs. Nichols decision. The framework for compliance included:
Theory—Is the program based on sound theory?
Implementation—Does the district have an implementation plan?
Results—What kinds of results does the district have for implementing the program?

1984 California voters passed bill to publish ballots and other election material in English only.

1985 Secretary of Education William Bennett spoke out against federal bilingual education programs.

1994 Reauthorization of Bilingual Education Act (Title VII of the Improving American Schools Act, formerly Elementary and Secondary Education Act). In this reauthorization, bilingualism was reconceptualized as a valuable national resource. Bilingual programs are no longer defined by types: maintenance, transitional, and immersion.

1994 Reauthorization of Improving American Schools Act resulting in language minority students being eligible to receive Title I services, even if the source of disadvantage is determined to be language.

Adapted from Tiedt, P.L., & Tiedt, I.M. (1995). *Multicultural teaching: A handbook of activities, information, and resources* (p. 4). Boston: Allyn & Bacon.

TABLE 10.3

Grammatical Contrasts between Black Vernacular English and Standard American English

BVE Grammatical Structure	SAE Grammatical Structure
Possessive -'s Nonobligatory word where word position expresses possession.	Obligatory regardless of position.
Get *mother* coat. It be mother's.	Get *mother's* coat. It's mother's.
Plural -s Nonobligatory with numerical quantifier.	Obligatory regardless of numerical quantifier.
He got ten *dollar*. Look at the cats.	He has ten *dollars*. Look at the cats.
Regular past -ed Nonobligatory; reduced as consonant cluster.	Obligatory.
Yesterday, I *walk* to school.	Yesterday, I *walked* to school.
Irregular past Case by case, some verbs inflected, others not.	All irregular verbs inflected.
I *see* him last week.	I *saw* him last week.
Regular present tense third person singular -s Nonobligatory.	Obligatory.
She *eat* too much.	She *eats* too much.
Irregular present tense third person singular -s Nonobligatory.	Obligatory.
He *do* my job.	He *does* my job.
Indefinite *an* Use of indefinite *a*.	Use of indefinite *an*.
He ride in *a* airplane.	He rode in *an* airplane.
Pronouns Pronominal apposition: pronoun immediately follows noun.	Pronoun used elsewhere in sentence or in other sentence; not in apposition.
Momma *she* mad. She . . .	Momma is mad. *She* . . .
Future tense More frequent use of *be going to* (gonna).	More frequent use of *will*.
I *be going to* dance tonight. I *gonna* dance tonight.	I *will* dance tonight. I *am going to* dance tonight.
Omit *will* preceding *be*.	Obligatory use of *will*.
I *be* home later.	I *will* (I'll) *be* home later.
Negation Triple negative.	Absence of triple negative.
Nobody don't never like me.	*No* one ever likes me.
Modals Double modals for such forms as *might, could,* and *should*.	Single modal use.
I *might could* go.	I *might be able to* go.

TABLE 10.3

Grammatical Contrasts between Black Vernacular English and Standard American English (continued)

BVE Grammatical Structure	SAE Grammatical Structure
Questions	
Same form for direct and indirect.	Different forms for direct and indirect.
What *it is*?	What *is it*?
Do you know what *it is*?	Do you know what *it is*?
Relative pronouns	
Nonobligatory in most cases.	Nonobligatory with *that* only.
He the one stole it.	He's the one *who* stole it.
It the one you like.	It's the one (that) you like.
Conditional *if*	
Use of *do* for conditional *if*.	Use of *if*.
I ask *did* she go.	I asked *if* she went.
Perfect construction	
Been used for action in the distant past.	*Been* not used.
He *been* gone.	He left a long time ago.
Copula	
Nonobligatory when contractible.	Obligatory in contractible and noncontractible forms.
He sick.	He's sick.
Habitual or general state	
Marked with uninflected *be*.	Nonuse of *be*; verb inflected.
She *be* workin'.	She's working now.

Reprinted with permission from Owens, Jr., R.E. (1995). *Language disorders: A functional approach to assessment and intervention* (2nd ed. pp. A-8–A-9). Boston: Allyn & Bacon.

In the early 1960s, however, bilingual education was reborn in Dade County, Florida, as Cuban immigrants requested bilingual schooling for their children. Programs were developed throughout the United States, under the authority of the Bilingual Education Act passed (as Title VII of the Elementary and Secondary Education Act) in 1968. Based on the law, suits were brought to ensure better services for students with cultural and linguistic diversities. The most noted case is Lau vs. Nichols, in which the U.S. Supreme Court ruled that equal treatment is not merely providing students with the same facilities, textbooks, teachers, and curriculum, when students do not understand English.

Although the Bilingual Education Act and the Civil Rights Act and their rules and regulations have promoted equal access and bilingual education, recent political developments have moved the country back toward an assimilation philosophy. For example, in 1981, Senator S. I. Hayakawa introduced a constitutional amendment to declare English the official language of the United States. This amendment was defeated, but a growing number of states have passed what has been referred to as "English-only" legislation.

Instructional Guidelines and Accommodations for Culturally and Linguistically Diverse Students

As a teacher, you will have students from many cultures and students who are in the process of acquiring English as a second language or second dialect. You may or may not be familiar with the culture and language of these students, but it will be important for these students to feel comfortable in your class and to learn. To promote learning, you should incorporate their language and culture into the curriculum, demonstrate that you value their culture and language, have high expectations for these students, and make accommodations so that they can learn successfully. Research into the characteristics of effective teachers of students with cultural and linguistic diversities (Garcia, 1991; Ladson-Billings, 1995; Tikunoff, 1983) indicates that such teachers:

- have high expectations of their students and believe that all students are capable of academic success
- see themselves as members of the community and see teaching as a way to give back to the community
- display a sense of confidence in their ability to be successful with students who are culturally and linguistically diverse
- communicate clearly, pace lessons appropriately, involve students in decisions, monitor students' progress, and provide feedback
- through culturally relevant teaching, integrate the students' native language and dialect, culture, and community into classroom activities to make input more relevant and comprehensible, to build trust and self-esteem, and to promote cultural diversity and cultural pluralism
- use curriculum and teaching strategies that promote coherence, relevance, progression, and continuity

As you will learn from the next section, schools have developed specific programs to promote second language acquisition.

Programs for Promoting Second Language Acquisition

Two broad categories of programs have been used in schools in the United States to promote second language acquisition: English as a second language (ESL) instruction and bilingual education. English as a second language generally has as its goal the acquisition of English, whereas the goal of bilingual education is to promote bilingualism or proficiency in both the first and second languages.

Instruction in English as a Second Language
English as a Second Language (ESL) instruction uses English to teach students English as a second language, with limited emphasis on maintaining or developing proficiency in the student's first language. Instruction may be given during a specified instructional time (with students receiving the rest of their instruction in general education classrooms) or it may be integrated into content-area instruction (as is the case with Sheltered English). Sheltered English is a type of ESL instruction in which the goal is to teach English language skills at the same time that students are learning content area knowledge (Northcutt & Watson, 1986). Sheltered English techniques that you can use as a classroom teacher include the following:

- Increase wait time.
- Respond to the message, not to the correctness of the pronunciation or grammar.
- Simplify your language.
- Don't force reluctant students to speak.
- Demonstrate the concept; use manipulatives.
- Make use of all senses.
- Pair or group native speakers together.
- Adapt the materials, don't "water down" the content.
- Learn as much as you can about the language and culture of your students.
- Build on students' prior knowledge.
- Bring students' home language and culture into the classroom and curriculum (Sullivan, 1992; Towell & Wink, 1993).

Schools often use the ESL model when the non-English-speaking students are from several language groups or there are too few students from a common language group to support a bilingual education model. Many educators suggest that students should be encouraged to continue to develop proficiency in their first language, even if it is not formally supported through bilingual education (e.g., Cummins, 1989; Baker, 1993). To promote this, teachers can do the following:

- Encourage students to use their first language around school.
- Provide opportunities for students from the same language group to communicate with one another in their first language (e.g., in cooperative learning groups; during informal discussions).
- Recruit people who can tutor students in the first language.
- Provide, in classrooms and the school library, books written in various languages.
- Incorporate greetings and information in various languages in newsletters and other official school communications (Cummins, 1989).

The ESL teacher is usually considered a resource teacher, in that she works daily, or at least several times a week, with groups of students or whole classes of students for a specified instructional time. In addition, the ESL teacher is usually responsible for assessing the students' language proficiency in English and, depending on the language, in their first language.

When Maria, the ESL teacher inteviewed at the beginning of this chapter, was asked about her job and what she believed would make her most effective, she commented,

> I feel fairly comfortable teaching the ESL students. I use a model that requires active learning on the part of the students with lots of use of gestures, demonstrations, and playing with language integrated into the instruction. I also build the students' culture into the instruction and I encourage the students to use an inquiry model to learn more about their cultures and share them with the other class members. My greatest concern is my ability to serve as a resource for the classroom and bilingual teachers in the school. One way that I feel that I am more effective with classroom teachers is that I am doing more co-teaching. This allows me to demonstrate ESL techniques to the teachers, and I work with the teachers to plan ESL lessons that are relevant to the content being taught in class.

> Research indicates that academic and linguistic skills developed in a student's first language usually transfer easily to the second language (Lanauze & Snow, 1989).

The 60-Second Lesson

Teaching a Concept to Second Language Learners

When students do not understand a concept, use one or more of the following strategies:

- Draw a picture.
- Have students with the same first language explain it in that language.
- Re-explain, but simplify the language.

- Demonstrate it.
- Provide examples and, if necessary, nonexamples (i.e., use of nonexamples is typical language used in teaching concepts. Provide examples and show what the concept is not.)

Bilingual Education Bilingual education students usually spend the entire day in classrooms designated as *bilingual classrooms.* These students are learning English and may be receiving content instruction in their first language, in English, or in both, according to their level of development in English. Frequently, bilingual education approaches are described as *transitional* or *maintenance,* based on the degree to which the first language is developed and maintained.

The focus of **transitional bilingual education** is to help students shift from the home language to the dominant language. The time taken for this transition from the students' first language to English varies, depending on the program (Ramirez & Merino, 1990). In programs in which literacy is taught in the first language, with other content taught in English, students may make the transition in two years. In other transition programs, at least 40 percent of the instruction is in the first language—including reading, language arts, math, and sometimes social studies or science—and students usually remain in the programs through fifth or sixth grade (Ramirez, 1992).

Maintenance bilingual education fosters the students' first language and strengthens their sense of cultural identity while teaching the second language and culture. This model values bilingualism and sees the learning of a second language as a positive addition for the students' cognitive development and life success. This model also places a strong emphasis on incorporating the students' culture and heritage into the instruction. A particularly compelling use of the maintenance bilingual model is in the education of Native Americans (Díaz-Rico & Weed, 1995) in which the goal is to increase the number of speakers of Native American languages and preserve the cultural and linguistic heritage (Reyhner, 1992).

Recently, **two-way bilingual programs** have become an option for students learning English as a second language. In two-way programs, half the students are native speakers of English; the other half speak another language, usually Spanish. Instruction is in English half the time, and in Spanish the other half. The goal is for all students to become fully bilingual and biliterate. Although the number of programs in the United States is limited, estimated at under 200 programs (Willis, 1994), the long-term results from early established programs are promising (Collier, 1989), with most of the native English and Spanish speakers still bilingual and attending college, even though students were from poor, working class backgrounds. Results also indicate that the native English speakers have positive attitudes toward multicultural issues and are more sensitive toward students learning a second language.

When Gloria and Lidia, the bilingual education teachers team teaching at Mission Way, were asked about their model of bilingual education, they described it as best fitting the transition model, with a relatively late transition to English (fourth to fifth grade). One of the reasons Gloria and Lidia chose to team teach was to better meet the needs of their students as they made the transition from skill and content instruction in Spanish to English. Gloria comments,

> During grades four and five we transition the language of instruction to almost exclusively English. For us, the exception is reading and writing. In our literature-based reading program and writer's workshop, we continue to encourage the students to read some literature written in Spanish and to write some compositions in Spanish, although most instruction is in English. We also discuss the literature in Spanish. In this way students do not lose those Spanish literacy skills that they have developed in the bilingual programs. We feel that this is important not only for them to stay connected to their home community, but [also because] being bilingual and biliterate are highly desired job skills.

Promoting Language Learning during Content Instruction

Students who are acquiring English as a second language are focusing their attention not only on learning content and vocabulary, but also on learning English. Richard-Amato (1988) described

> When biliteracy is encouraged in second language learners, literacy skills transfer from one language to the other (Lanauze & Snow, 1989).

the following stages of second language development related to learning in content classes:

- **Low-Beginning:** Students depend on gestures, facial expressions, objects, pictures, a phrase dictionary, and often a translator to understand or be understood. Occasionally, students comprehend words or phrases.
- **Mid-Beginning:** Students begin to comprehend more, but only when the speaker provides gestural clues, speaks slowly, and uses concrete referents and repetitions. Students speak seldom and haltingly, show some recognition of written segments, and may be able to write short utterances.
- **High-Beginning to Low-Intermediate:** Students comprehend more, but with difficulty. Students speak in an attempt to meet basic needs but remain hesitant, and make frequent errors in grammar, vocabulary, and pronunciation. Students can read very simple text and can write a little (but writing is very restricted in grammatical structure and vocabulary).

TIPS FOR TEACHERS

10.4 Teaching Strategies for Promoting Content and Second Language Learning in General Education Classes

Beginning to Mid-Intermediate Proficiency Level

- Provide a supportive environment in which help is readily available to second language learners.
- Establish consistent patterns and routines in the classroom.
- Use gestures, visuals, and demonstrations to present concepts.
- Connect content to students' home cultures.
- Simplify grammar and vocabulary.
- Slow the pace of presentation, enunciate clearly, and emphasize key concepts through gesture, facial expression, intonation, and repetition.
- Record your lectures or talks on tape and make them available for students.
- Make copies of your notes, or have another student take notes, so that second language learners can concentrate on listening.

Beginning to Mid-Intermediate Proficiency Level

- Build in redundancy by restating the concept in a simpler form, providing examples, and giving direct definitions.

- Extend wait time so that second language learners have time to volunteer.
- Avoid forcing second language learners to speak.
- Arrange cooperative learning so that students with the same first language work together.
- Encourage students to use their second language in informal conversations.
- Whenever possible, use tutors who speak the native language of the second language learners.
- Alter criteria for grading.

High-Intermediate to Advanced Proficiency Level

- Add contextual support to your lesson (e.g., advance organizer, study guides, glossaries, videos/films).
- Take into account the linguistic demands of the content.
- Provide opportunities for students to write in the content area.
- Provide opportunities for second language learners to practice critical thinking skills.
- Coach second language learners in appropriate learning strategies for mastering content.

- **Mid-Intermediate:** Students may experience a dramatic increase in vocabulary recognition, but idioms and more advanced vocabulary remain difficult. Students often know what they want to say but grope for acceptable words and phrases. Errors in grammar, vocabulary, and pronunciation are frequent. Students can read text that is more difficult but still concrete, and can write with greater ease than before.
- **High-Intermediate to Low-Advanced:** Students begin to comprehend substantial parts of normal conversation but often require repetitions, particularly with academic discourse. Students are gaining confidence in speaking ability; errors are common but less frequent. Students can read and write text that contains more complex vocabulary and structures than before, but experience difficulty with abstract language.
- **Mid-Advanced:** Students comprehend much conversational and academic discourse spoken at normal rates, but sometimes require repetition. Speech is more fluent and meaning is generally clear, but occasional errors occur. Students read and write with less diffi-

culty materials commensurate with their cognitive development, but demonstrate some problems in grasping intended meaning.
- **High-Advanced:** Students comprehend normal conversation and academic discourse with little difficulty. Most idioms are understood. Students speak fluently in most situations with few errors. Students read and write both concrete and abstract materials and are able to manipulate the language with relative ease (Richard-Amato & Snow, 1992).

Based on this progression of second language development, Richard-Amato and Snow (1992) have developed strategies for general classroom teachers to use in teaching content (see Tips for Teachers 10.4 on page 301).

Although planning for culturally and linguistically diverse students takes some creative thinking and modifications of the curriculum, these students will broaden both your horizons and those of the class. In your planning, be sure to provide ample time for students to engage in meaningful conversations about topics related to language and culture.

SUMMARY

- The demographics of our nation and schools are changing, with the number of students with cultural and linguistic diversities increasing.
- In U.S. schools, the number of students whose first language is not English is increasing substantially.
- The macroculture represents the dominant culture of the United States, whereas the microcultures represent the students' home

cultures. Teachers can help students understand and mediate the macroculture.
- Learning about your students' home cultures and communities and integrating those cultures and communities into the curriculum is important.
- The goal of multicultural education is to change the structure of schools so that students from different cultural groups have an equal chance to achieve in school.

- Dimensions of multicultural education include content integration, knowledge construction, equity pedagogy, and an empowering school culture.
- Four basic approaches to multicultural education include the contributions, additive, transformation, and social action approaches.
- Five elements that affect second language acquisition are situational factors, linguistic input, learner characteristics, the learning and developmental process, and second language output.
- In considering language proficiency it is important to consider both the basic interpersonal communication skills (BICS) and cognitive academic language performance (CALP).
- Language varies from place to place and group to group and includes dialects such as Black Vernacular English (BVE).
- English as a second language instruction and bilingual education are two types of programs for educating second language learners.
- A number of strategies facilitate learning for students who are second language and dialect learners.

Key Terms and Concepts

additive approach
Black Vernacular English (BVE)
basic interpersonal communication skills (BICS)
bilingual education
cognitive academic language proficiency (CALP)
comprehensible input
comprehensible output
context-embedded communication and instruction
contributions approach
cultural characteristics
cultural inversion
dialect
English as a Second Language (ESL) instruction
funds of knowledge
language variation

learning and developmental process
learner characteristics
linguistic input
macroculture
maintenance bilingual education
microcultures
multicultural education
secondary language output
Sheltered English
silent or nonverbal period
situational factors
social action approach
transformation approach
transitional bilingual education
two-way bilingual programs

Think and Apply

1. Now that you have read Chapter 10, think about the interview with bilingual teachers Gloria Rodriguez and Lidia Romo, and with ESL teacher Maria Chavez. What questions do you have for them about strategies for working with students who are culturally and linguistically diverse? Make a list of the questions and then ask them of an ESL or bilingual education teacher.

2. Visit a school known for its positive emphasis on multicultural education. Watch for evidence of cultural integration and an empowering school culture. Observe a lesson to see how the teacher builds upon the students' cultural diversity.

3. To learn more about your own cultural background, answer the questions posed in the "Cultural Characteristics" section.

4. Select a unit you have taught or plan to teach. Review it for its focus on multicultural perspectives. Then, using one of the four approaches to multicultural education (contribution, additive, transformation, social action), modify the unit to include a stronger multicultural emphasis.

5. Select a unit you have taught or plan to teach, and review it to determine how you would modify it for second language or dialect learners.

Read More about It

1. Agar, M. H. (1980). *The professional stranger: An informal introduction to ethnography.* Orlando: Academic Press.

    A very readable book that provides information on strategies for learning about the home environment.

2. Banks, J. A. (1997). *Teaching strategies for ethnic studies* (6th ed.). Boston: Allyn & Bacon.

    An overview of ethnic studies for Native Americans, African Americans, European Americans, Hispanic Americans, and Asian Americans. This is an excellent resource for videotapes, films, children's literature, and trade books highlighting different ethnic groups.

3. Banks, J. A., and Banks, C. A. M. (Eds.) (1995). *Handbook of research on multicultural education.* New York: Macmillan.

    A reference work in which scholars report on multicultural education from a variety of disciplines and fields. A valuable resource for teachers.

4. Bennett, C. I. (1995). *Comprehensive multicultural education* (3rd ed.). Boston: Allyn & Bacon.

    Explores the impacts of individual and cultural differences on teaching and learning. Includes curriculum guidelines and lesson plans.

5. Block, C. C., & Zinke, J. A. (1995). *Creating a culturally enriched curriculum for grades K–6.* Boston: Allyn & Bacon.

    Provides activities and short units on different aspects of multicultural education. For each activity, children's literature (rated for difficulty) is provided.

6. Delpit, L. (1995). *Other people's children: Cultural conflict in the classroom.* New York: The New York Press.

    Collection of essays about effective ways to teach children from diverse racial, ethnic, and cultural groups.

7. Díaz-Rico, L., & Weed, K. Z. (1995). *The cross-cultural, language, and academic development handbook: A complete K–12 Reference Guide.* Boston: Allyn and Bacon.

    A very readable book about second language acquisition, bilingual education, culture and cultural diversity, and language policies, with many ideas for teaching.

8. Reyhner, J. (Ed.) (1992). *Teaching American Indian students*. Norman, OK: University of Oklahoma.

   Readings on strategies for teaching Native American students.

9. Siccone, F. (1995). *Celebrating diversity: Building self-esteem in today's multicultural classrooms*. Boston: Allyn & Bacon.

   Provides many multicultural activities to promote self-worth and confidence in students (grades K–8).

10. Sleeter, C. E., & Grant, C. A. (1993). *Making choices for multicultural education: Five approaches to race, class, and gender* (2nd ed.). New York: Merrill.

    Critically examines five alternative models of multicultural education that are used in Amercian schools and classrooms today.

11. Tiedt, P. L., & Tiedt, I. M. (1995). *Multicultural teaching: A handbook of activities, information, and resources* (4th ed.). Boston: Allyn & Bacon.

    Presents general strategies for multicultural education in addition to topical activities and units.

ELEVEN

Teaching Students at Risk

FOCUS QUESTIONS

1. How can you recognize whether a student in your classroom is at risk?

2. What conditions place students at risk? Are there conditions over which you as a teacher have some control? What are your responsibilities regarding conditions over which you have no control?

3. What programs are available to provide educational support for students at risk?

4. How can you create a positive, productive learning environment for students at risk?

5. What instructional practices can you implement to foster academic success for students in your classroom who are at risk?

Miriam Mades

Miriam Mades has taught kindergarten and first grade for over twenty years in Miami, Florida, with many students who might be considered to be at risk of school failure. Miriam has taught children who experience family poverty and live in neighborhoods where they are in daily contact with drugs and violence. Because of Miriam's success in the classroom, she has been appointed by the school district to visit other teachers' classrooms and demonstrate effective teaching strategies. Here is Miriam's advice for working with students who are at risk.

First, you love them. I know that this sounds pretty obvious, but it is the most vital component. Each one of my students is very special to me, and I let each one know it. My students know when they come to their classroom they are loved and they are safe.

Predictable classroom routines are also very important. Children who live in neighborhoods that are dangerous and unpredictable need to learn that some things in life are stable. For example, I set up their classroom in centers—a listening center, writing center, science center, and so on. At the beginning of the year I explain the center routine and children get it down pat. While students are working in independent centers, it gives me time to work with small groups of students on specific skills. The students know exactly what to do and what I expect of them. I really think they like the routine.

Many of the children I have taught over the years rarely have a chance to leave their neigh-borhoods. Their range of life experiences is limited to what they know about their little part of Miami. That's why I spend so much time planning hands-on activities and direct experiences. One of my favorites is when we bring an incubator to class and watch chicken eggs hatch. I have the children look through eggs using a candle and then try to predict what kind of bird is going to hatch, based on a scientific chart. After the chickens hatch, we plan a field trip to visit a farm. Field trips are very important for the children, so it is worth my time to think of ways to fund the trips. Local businesses have been particularly helpful.

Even though I have been teaching for some time, I think that it is important to constantly be on the lookout for new ideas. For example, I have recently moved away from same-ability groups in teaching reading. This was a big jump for me—I really thought that having high, medium, and low groups was the only way to go. Now I like more flexible grouping with different groups for different purposes—lots of mixed-ability groups. I find that this new arrangement is so much better for the social adjustment of low-ability readers. They don't feel set apart by being in the bottom group all the time. Trying out new strategies and methods helps me stay enthusiastic about my teaching. I get my ideas from reading teacher magazines and journals, from going to local and state conferences—but most of my ideas come from other teachers. Working with children at risk takes a great deal of energy. I get reenergized by trying out new ways of reaching my students.

Introduction

Every September three million 6-year-olds enter our nation's first grades. Most enter confident of doing well in school, highly motivated, and eager to learn. Just nine months later, many of these bright, enthusiastic youngsters have learned a hard lesson: they have failed first grade (Madden et al., 1991).

Many young people in our nation are led to believe, in some cases early on, that success in school is beyond their reach. Students who struggle to learn to read, write, compute, or master concepts in the content areas can get discouraged in the world of school and eventually squeak by without mastering basic skills, or drop out. The faces of students at risk are many, and the reasons for their lack of success in school are varied. But as Miriam Mades has learned, there are positive, productive ways for teachers to structure and support learning for students for whom learning (for whatever reason) is very difficult. In this chapter you'll read about students who are potentially at risk of school failure, promising programs for these young North Americans, and instructional practices for promoting student success.

Defining and Identifying Students at Risk

Who are students at risk? They are students like LeeAnn who is in fourth grade and doesn't know the alphabet or letter sounds. She still reads on a preprimer level. LeeAnn is the youngest of five children of a single mother. Because the mother works at night, LeeAnn spends evenings with her older siblings. LeeAnn said to her teacher, "Maybe if my mom could afford *Hooked On Phonics,* I could learn to read."

They are students like Henry who is in fifth grade, reads on a first-grade level, and has never had a grade higher than a D on a test. Henry goes to an urban school in which over 90 percent of the students qualify for free or reduced-price lunch. The school is overcrowded. Henry's class has thirty-five students. At the end of the school year Henry told his teacher, "I'm just tired of having a dumb brain."

They are students like Ryan who is in seventh grade and is failing three out of six subjects. Ryan's older brother and sister are excellent students, and both parents are college graduates. His teachers have identified Ryan as a gifted learner, but he doesn't seem to care about school and simply doesn't try. Ryan is candid about his position: "I can do the work if I want to. But I don't want to."

They are students like Javier who is in eighth grade and whose achievement test scores in reading and mathematics are extraordinarily low. Javier has attended more than a dozen schools. His parents, migrant workers, must move frequently to make a living. As Javier says, "I'd just like to stay put for awhile."

> Prior to the 1980s, terms such as "educationally disadvantaged" and "culturally deprived" were commonly used to describe students at risk.

The situations of LeeAnn, Henry, Ryan, and Javier are different, as are their reasons for having difficulty in school. What they do have in common is that they are all at risk of school failure.

Qualifications for At-Risk Status

The term *at risk* came into being on publication of the report, *A Nation at Risk,* from the National Commission on Excellence in Education (Gardner, 1983). This report indicated that quality of education in the United States was lacking, and that large numbers of students were in jeopardy of leaving school without the skills they need to help the United States compete in a world market. The commission's report ignited a rush of educational reform and made the term "at risk" part of everyday vocabulary. There are some who argue that the term now serves as a negative label and who would prefer a more upbeat term, such as "students at promise."

Slavin, Karweit, and Madden (1989) define **students at risk** by four areas that serve as qualifications for at-risk status: remediation, retention, dropping out, and substandard basic skills. Figure 11.1 shows the history of legislation that addresses the needs of students at risk.

Remediation Remediation refers to additional instruction for students who do not demonstrate

FIGURE 11.1

Selected Federal Laws for Equal Educational Opportunity for Students at Risk

1954   School Milk Program Act extended National School Lunch Act of 1946 to address basic needs of children in poverty.

1954   U.S. Supreme Court decision in Brown v. Board of Education of Topeka, Kansas, lead to laws requiring racial integration of schools to achieve equal educational opportunity.

1964   Economic Opportunities Act first provided federal funding for Head Start and other programs for students at risk.

1965   Public Law 89–313 funded educational support for children in hospitals and institutions.

1965   Elementary and Secondary Education Act (ESEA) established Title I programs for low-income learners, dropouts, vocational students, preschoolers, bilingual learners, and children of immigrant workers; provided funding for preservice and inservice teacher training for Title I programs; and defined *accountability*.

1966   National Upward Bound program established for low-income high school students who show potential for completing a postsecondary degree.

1968   Bilingual Education Act (Title VII) amended the Elementary and Secondary Education Act to require states to provide bilingual education programs.

1969   Public Law 91–230 recognized learning disabilities and giftedness as special-education categories.

1970   Drug Abuse Education Act provided first federal funding for anti-drug-abuse programs in schools.

1972   Women's Educational Equity Act (Title IX) amended the Elementary and Secondary Education Act to outlaw sex discrimination in schools.

1972   Public Law 92–424 amended the Elementary and Secondary Education Act to extend Head Start programs to children with disabilities.

1974   Juvenile Justice and Delinquency Prevention Act included federal funds for educational and school programs.

1975   Indian Self-Determination and Education Assistance Act extended the Indian Education Act of 1972 and gave Native Americans more control over their education.

1975   Indochina Migration and Refugee Assistance Act extended educational and other programs of the Migration and Refugee Assistance Act of 1962 to immigrants displaced by the Vietnam War.

1981   Education Improvement and Consolidation Act (ECIA) incorporated and amended key provisions of the Elementary and Secondary Education Act, renamed Title I programs as Chapter 1 programs, and gave states more control over funding the programs using one federal block grant.

1984   Public Law 98–377 added new science and mathematics programs, established magnet schools, and mandated equal access to public schools.

1987   Stewart B. McKinney Homeless Assistance Act was enacted, in part, to provide for educational needs of homeless children.

1988   The Hawkins-Stafford School Improvement Amendments made Chapter 1 schools more accountable for student achievement.

1994   As in 1984, public law continued federal funding for Head Start and Follow Through programs.

1995   Improving America's Schools Act (IASA) amended key provisions of the Elementary and Secondary Education Act, renamed Chapter 1 programs as Title I programs.

competency in basic skills in reading, writing, and mathematics at an expected rate. A third grade student who reads at kindergarten level may need remediation in letter and word recognition, for example. Or, a high school student who cannot add two-digit numbers may need remediation. Staggering numbers of students in the United States are in need of remediation. For example, according to the National Assessment of Education Progress (NAEP), 75 percent of students in Grade 4, 72 percent of students in Grade 8, and 63 percent of students in Grade 12 did not meet the standards set by The National Education Goals Panel (Sherman, 1994).

Why do students drop out of school? How does dropping out place students at further risk? What are some characteristics of successful dropout-prevention programs?

Retention The practice of having a student repeat a grade level because of low academic performance is referred to as **retention**. For example, a third grader who has not mastered the school district's reading and writing competencies may be required to repeat third grade, and a seventh grader who has received a failing grade in most academic subjects may be required to repeat seventh grade.

Retention policies vary considerably across the nation. Some school districts have lenient policies based on research indicating that retention does not have significant positive effects on student achievement and may even be harmful to students (Holmes & Matthews, 1984). Other school districts have more stringent criteria for passing from one grade to the next and contend that "social promotion" is an indication of lowered academic standards.

Dropping Out Students who do not complete high school are **dropouts**. School systems across the country have different systems for counting the number of students who leave school. In some districts, for example, marriage, death, entering college early, going to vocational school, entering the army, or taking a job qualifies as dropping out.

Therefore, a specific definition and the precise number of dropouts due to academic failure are difficult to determine. In 1994, the dropout rate was estimated at 16 percent of students.

Students who drop out of high school have limited employment opportunities and find it difficult to compete for a well-paid job. Typically, dropouts possess only low-level academic skills that limit employability, reduce opportunities for advancement, and reduce readiness for additional training (Rumberger, 1987). Lack of educational training and job preparation results in higher unemployment rates and lower pay among dropouts. The majority of individuals on welfare and in prison have not obtained a high school degree (National Education Goals Panel, 1994).

Substandard Basic Skills According to the National Education Goals Panel (1994), almost half the adults in the United States have substandard basic skills. They read, write, and compute at levels below those regarded as necessary for working in high-performance workplaces. It is estimated that 23 million adults are functionally illiterate (Thornburg et al., 1991).

HIDING OUT IN CLASSROOMS

How can someone graduate from high school and not know how to read? It seems impossible. One reason this can happen is that many young adults have developed a set of coping strategies to hide their inability to read. To examine how high school students "hide out" in classrooms, William Brozo (1990) spent a semester observing an eleventh grade class and also conducted interviews with the poorest readers in the class.

Brozo found that poor readers have the following strategies to avoid reading:

- avoid eye contact with teachers
- engage in disruptive behavior
- become good listeners
- rely on a "with it" classmate
- seek help from friends
- forget to bring books and materials to class
- engage in "apple polishing" to manipulate teachers and gain teachers' approval

To counteract students' reading avoidance, Brozo recommends that teachers use the following tactics:

- develop a personal rapport with students
- teach low readers to monitor their own reading performance
- provide instructional adaptations for low readers
- gain the help of the school's reading specialist

Characteristics of At-Risk Students

As a teacher you will have students who are at risk enrolled in your class. How will you recognize these students? Knapp and Turnbull (1991) argue against holding stereotypic notions about what to assume or expect of students at risk. For example, students who are at risk are not all from low-income families. The common characteristic of students at risk is that they are not achieving in school as they should be. Be aware of the following warning signals:

- *Poor academic performance.* Poor performance on standardized tests, failing grades on tests and assignments, and general difficulty in achieving competency in reading, writing, and mathematics are direct indicators that a student is having difficulty learning.
- *Counterproductive attitudes and behavior.* Some students do not value what they are learning, have a history of failure, and believe that they will be unsuccessful. Students who do not believe in themselves or do not see the purpose in schooling are not motivated to learn or achieve in school. Motivation problems can lead to distractibility, inattentiveness, no participation, and misbehavior.
- *Excessive absenteeism.* Students who are chronically tardy or absent may want to avoid school because they are not successful. For them, school is associated with failure.

Conditions That Place Students at Risk

In the 1930s and 1940s, educational researchers, psychologists, and physicians began to recognize that academic difficulties can be caused by a number of factors—social, psychological, physiological, and educational. A **multiple causation theory** emerged, suggesting that although some students may be at risk because of one primary condition, multiple conditions quite often interact to compound learning challenges. The theory applies to all areas of academic achievement and helps explain why students are at risk of failure in school.

Multiple conditions interact for most at-risk students. The bottom line is that these students have a hard time learning to read, write, and compute. Frymier (1992, p. 258) put it this way, "Children who hurt, hurt all over . . . Risk is pervasive. If a student is at risk in one area, that student is very likely to be at risk in every other area. The question then becomes, 'What are teachers and others in the schools doing to help students who are at risk?'"

The National Dropout Prevention Center, located at Clemson University, has compiled a list of variables related to being at risk of school failure. School districts can use the list (which is based on the research literature) with other variables that predict students at risk to develop screening instruments. Following are conditions (listed alphabetically) that can place students at risk:

- attendance
- educational level of parents
- family status (broken home, single parent family, family size)
- free and reduced-price lunch programs
- grade point average
- interest in school
- number of counseling referrals
- number of discipline referrals
- number of grade retentions
- number of school moves (transfers)
- number of suspensions
- participation in extracurricular activities
- pregnancy and teen parent
- reading and math scores
- standardized test composite scores

Many of these conditions are factors over which you as a classroom teacher have no control. For example, it is beyond your scope to change your students' economic level or living conditions. As Taylor, Harris, and Pearson (1988, p. 24) observed, "There is rarely a single causal factor for learning problems; even if teachers can identify a cause, eliminating the cause may be difficult, if not impossible." What teachers can do is be aware of conditions that explain why a student is at risk and "make the learning experience rich and rewarding in spite of the underlying cause." You can also be alert to other family, health and safety, and school conditions that potentially can put students at risk.

Family Conditions

There is no doubt that what happens in the home affects students' success or failure at school. Unsettling circumstances at home can affect student motivation and concentration both in and out of class. Sometimes these circumstances are temporary; at other times they are an ongoing part of the student's life. Home conditions that can potentially impact student academic performance include family poverty and family instability (Frymier, 1992).

Family Poverty Students whose families live in poverty often come to school without their basic needs of food, clothing, shelter, and health care being met. As Crosby (1993, p. 604) expressed it, "We certainly don't need a great deal of research to determine that a child of poverty is at risk and that poverty is harmful to one's mental and physical well being." The facts about poverty reported by the Children's Defense Fund (Sherman, 1994) are staggering:

- Over 14 million children in the United States (one out of every five) come from families living below the poverty level.
- Before age 16, approximately one out of every three students in the United States will experience poverty.
- The numbers of children in poverty is increasing, with more children in 1992 living in poverty than in any year since 1965.

Poverty knows no racial or ethnic boundaries. Although the greatest subgroup of poor children is white, the proportion of members of minority groups who are poor is higher. And poverty knows no geographic limits. Approximately 60 percent of poor students live in suburban or rural areas, and over 25 percent of children living in urban areas are living at or below the poverty level (Council for Exceptional Children, 1991).

The limitations poverty places on families are likely to impact students' performance in school. Families often cannot afford educational materials, home computers, and extended vacations or day trips that broaden horizons. Students may have extended work responsibilities, such as caring for siblings or contributing to the family income. A student's level of poverty does not automatically determine success or failure in school (Au, 1993), but disproportionate numbers of students from low-income families are less successful in school and eventually drop out (Kortering et al., 1992).

> The poverty rate among Native Americans (27.5 percent) is nearly twice the national average (Guy, 1991).

Family Instability Most families experience changes from time to time, but some changes in families are potentially hazardous to students'

TECH TALK

Improving Computer Equity

One of the realities of computers is that they are expensive. A home computer is simply not in the budget for many students from low-income families. Many schools in low-income areas, where additional money for computers (often donated by parent organizations) is not available, have fewer computers than schools in high-income areas.

Data also suggest that in schools with large numbers of at-risk students, computers are likely to be used for drill in basic skills, whereas in wealthier schools, computers are more likely to be used to teach programming (Maddux et al., 1992). In the twenty-first century, students without basic computer skills will be at a tremendous disadvantage in terms of employability. Thus, issues of **computer equity**—equal access to computers in the home and in the school—are a real concern (Maddux et al., 1992).

Here are some suggestions for improving computer equity:

- Structure opportunities for computer access before and after school. Consider starting a computer club.

- Include instruction in word processing, database management, spreadsheet usage, and computer programming, as well as opportunities to use software to improve basic skills.
- Select software that encourages problem solving and higher-order thinking.
- Select software that helps make connections between basic skills and real-life situations.

---

emotional and physical well-being and to their progress in school.

One of the most common jolts to family stability is divorce. Approximately 40 percent of students will experience parental divorce during their school years (Quay & Werry, 1986). Divorce can cause students to become depressed and angry, and can impact their desire to achieve in school (Wallerstein & Blakeslee, 1989).

Latchkey children (children who are home alone for long periods of time) may be more susceptible to psychological, behavioral, and academic problems (Garbarino, 1984).

In addition to its emotional impact, a divorce also causes inevitable changes in the home routine. For example, after a divorce children may have two homes instead of one, which can disrupt homework and study patterns, as well as such basic routines as getting dressed and ready for school.

Family mobility also can have a negative effect on schooling. Children of migrant workers who move from field to field face a multitude of problems. Regular attendance in school is limited, and students who might qualify for special services are not in one school long enough to go through the identification process. Another dilemma migrant students face is that if they are needed

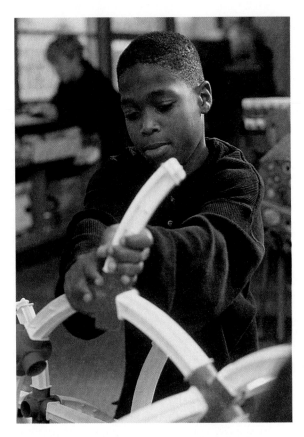

This student is in a school-based after-school program. What risk factors can before-school and after-school programs address?

Risks to Health and Safety

Every day we hear and read about risks to the health and safety of young people at home and at school. Consider the following statistics (Stevens & Price, 1992, p. 18):

■ Some 350,000 newborns each year are exposed prenatally to drugs, including alcohol.

■ Some three to four million children have been exposed to damaging levels of lead.

■ The incidence of pediatric infection with HIV (human immunodeficiency virus) has risen dramatically, affecting some 15,000 to 30,000 children.

■ Of the 37,000 babies born each year who weigh less than 3 1/2 pounds and live long enough to leave the hospital, many will face substantial learning problems as a result of prematurity and medical intervention.

Millions of young people face risks that not only inhibit learning but also can be life-threatening or can compromise normal growth and development. Poor nutrition, lack of adequate rest, lack of access to health care, exposure to harmful substances, and exposure to sexually transmitted diseases contribute to students' health problems. Another health issue of major consequence is adolescent pregnancy. Over one million teenage mothers parent children each year, which can result in physical, social, and emotional problems for both parent and child (Smith, 1994).

The National Coalition for the Homeless estimates that 57 percent of children who are homeless do not attend school (Rafferty & Rollins, 1989).

The sound bites we hear about safety issues are equally sobering. We hear about child abuse and neglect, and about domestic and neighborhood violence. Consider these facts about children in the United States, from the Children's Defense Fund (Sherman, 1994):

■ Every year, 2,695,010 children are reported abused or neglected.

■ Every four hours, a child commits suicide.

■ Every seven minutes, a child is arrested for a drug crime.

to help support the family, they must drop out (Prewitt-Diaz et al., 1990).

Lack of a permanent place to live is also a risk factor, with increasing numbers of students who are homeless. It is difficult to gauge exactly how many school-age children are homeless, but it is estimated that on any given day approximately 100,000 children in the United States are homeless (Sherman, 1994). The fastest growing segment of the homeless population (nearly 40 percent) is families with children (Council for Exceptional Children, 1991).

Many other situations can cause family instability. Although the educational impact (both short-term and long-term) of family instability varies from student to student, it is important that you, as a teacher, create a classroom atmosphere that is a safe haven from the unpredictable circumstances that impact your students' lives.

- Every four minutes, a child is arrested for an alcohol-related crime.
- Every two minutes, a child is murdered.

It is imperative that you, as a classroom teacher, become familiar with your school district's procedures for reporting cases of child abuse or neglect—a sensitive area. Certainly you would not want to accuse a parent or guardian unfairly; nonetheless, failure to report cases of suspected or confirmed abuse or neglect is a crime in some states.

Children who experience threats to their health, safety, and basic well-being are at risk of having academic and socioemotional problems at school, but appropriate assessment, instruction, and administrative planning can be provided. As Stevens and Price (1992, p. 23) wrote, "Strategies exist that schools can use to ameliorate the effects of the conditions described here and to give these children real opportunities to be successful learners."

At-Risk Schools

Some students are enrolled in schools that are ill-equipped, overcrowded, and in desperate need of renovation. Some teachers are not prepared to deal with students' individual needs, or suffer from burnout. Just as individual students can be at risk of school failure, so can schools be at risk when they do not provide an environment for learning. According to Waxman (1991, p. 5), at-risk schools:

- alienate students and teachers
- provide low standards and a low quality of education
- have lower expectations for some students
- have high student noncompletion rates for students
- are unresponsive to students
- have high truancy and disciplinary problems
- do not adequately prepare students for the future

At-risk schools also fail to ensure students' freedom from violence. The National School Safety Center reported the following data (Greenbaum, 1989):

- More than 28,000 students are physically attacked in secondary schools each month.

- Over 5,000 secondary school teachers are physically attacked each month.
- Approximately 8 percent of urban middle and high school students skip school at least one day a month because they are afraid to go to school.

As classroom teachers become more involved in the task of restructuring and revitalizing the American educational system, they are shifting their focus from children-who-have-failed-to-learn to children-we-have-failed-to-teach (Johnston & Allington, 1991). You, too, can assume the responsibility of becoming aware of programs available for at-risk students in your district and school, and creating a positive, productive learning environment in your own classroom. Professional collaboration should be part of this process.

The administrators, parents, and teachers of Magruder Elementary School in Newport News, Virginia, work together to restructure their school, following the school development model developed by James Comer (1980). Eighty percent of the 525 students in this school are considered to be potentially at risk of school failure. A planning team made up of key stakeholders developed a comprehensive plan for curriculum, staff development, hiring of a home–school coordinator, and keeping track of student progress. One feature of the plan is that teachers meet with administrators at the end of each grading period to report on individual student progress. One change is that teachers no longer use conditions that place students at risk as excuses for lack of achievement. Instead of saying, "This child's parent is incarcerated," the new mind-set is, "Yes, this child's parent is incarcerated, but can she read?" (Ramirez-Smith, 1995, p. 18). The focus now is on understanding and recognizing the dilemmas and hurdles that at-risk students face in their lives, and also on ways to structure education so that students will learn.

Programs for Students at Risk

Because a wide range of students with many different needs are at risk, a variety of programs and service-delivery models are needed to meet those needs. School districts across the country are developing programs to meet the needs of students at risk. Some programs are financed through federal funds, others by state or local governments or through private businesses and foundations. Programs for students at risk are both school-based and community-based, with most taking the forms of **compensatory education** (instruction designed to compensate for prior lack of educational opportunities), and intervention or prevention programs.

Compensatory Education

Schools with concentrations of students from low-income and immigrant families qualify for additional federal funding under Title I of the Elementary and Secondary Education Act (ESEA). **Title I** (formerly known as Chapter I), the core of the 1965 Elementary and Secondary Education

How might this Title I reading teacher coordinate her pull-out program with the classroom teacher's instructional efforts, and why is it important to do so? How can teachers ensure congruence between general education and remedial programs?

Act, provides funding for compensatory education for the most needy children in the United States, with funds used for additional teachers, paraprofessionals, and instructional materials for qualified students. The intent of the act is to provide local school systems that enroll large numbers of poor children with resources for intensive instruction in reading, writing, and mathematics. Most federal funds for compensatory education have been allocated to elementary schools.

> Congress allocates over 6 billion dollars a year to Title I of the Elementary and Secondary Education Act. Ninety percent of the school districts in the country receive Title I funds.

An important provision of Title I is the "supplement, not supplant" requirement (Miller, 1991); that is, Title I funds are designed to enhance, not to replace existing programs. The purpose of the funding is to provide something extra that would not normally be part of students' regular instruction. That something extra can be materials, lower student-to-teacher ratios, or additional time spent in intensive, direct instruction.

Today, implementation of Title I programs emphasizes coordination between Title I specialists and general education teachers of both procedural and instructional matters. If students in your class are assigned to a specialist for remedial services in reading, writing, or mathematics, your collaboration with the specialist will make a big difference for the children you teach. Tips for Teachers 11.1 provides suggestions for working with school-based specialists.

> Once a school qualifies for Title I funding, any low-achieving student in that school, regardless of socioeconomic status, is entitled to compensatory education. Identification of children for services within schools is based not on family income, but on academic achievement (Kennedy et al., 1986).

Compensatory education takes many forms, which the following sections explore.

Pull-Out Programs In elementary schools, compensatory education services typically are delivered in the resource room. Such services are

TIPS FOR TEACHERS

11.1 Working with Reading, Writing, and Mathematics Specialists in Your School

- Initiate contact early in the school year and schedule regular meetings throughout the year to discuss students' needs, plan instruction, and evaluate the program.
- Become familiar with each other's programs (philosophy, curriculum, instructional procedures, and materials).
- Discuss roles and decide on responsibilities. Clarify who will teach what skills, and how? Who will be accountable for grades and reporting to administrators and parents?
- Clarify procedures for placing students with the specialist and for making decisions to terminate student eligibility for special services.

- Discuss ways to support students in Title I classes. How can you reinforce each other's efforts?
- Start an information exchange, sharing with each other teaching tips and ideas that might be appropriate for specific children.
- Plan to attend conferences and professional workshops together, and discuss ways to incorporate new ideas into your program.
- Develop a system for handling irregularities in the schedule. What happens when one teacher is absent? How can you keep each other informed about special events, such as guest speakers and field trips?

---

called **pull-out programs** because children are literally pulled out of their general education classroom for supplemental instruction in basic skills. In middle schools and high schools, students who need special help in reading, writing, or mathematics are typically placed in a "remedial" class during regular school periods.

Caridad Ferrer, a Title I teacher in an urban elementary school, is responsible for providing supplementary reading instruction to seventy-five low-achieving third, fourth, and fifth grade students. She pulls out students in small groups for 30-minute lessons several times a week. Caridad is assigned a paraprofessional who supervises the children as they move between the classroom and the resource room and provides one-to-one instruction for children in the resource room, as necessary.

Caridad uses the same reading program the classroom teachers use, and keeps track of what teachers plan to cover in class each week. During the 30-minute Title I sessions, she gives students

individual reading assignments related to the skills they are learning in class.

The advantage to pull-out programs is that students who have difficulty keeping pace with regular classroom instruction can receive more individualized attention in a small group setting. Disadvantages develop when a lack of coordination of instruction exists between resource room and general education settings, when transitioning between settings is inefficient, and when pull-out programs interfere with a student's sense of belonging and peer relations.

It is important to communicate with remedial reading, writing, and mathematics teachers to know how best to work with the students who need most help. Walp and Walmsley (1989) suggest that both procedural and instructional congruence between general education and remedial programs must occur. **Procedural congruence** is needed to improve communication between classroom and remedial teachers, and time must be allocated for this to happen. For example, both teachers must have a common understanding of schedules and procedures.

One of the biggest issues related to elementary pull-out classes is, indeed, a procedural issue: movement from the general education classroom to the resource room and back. Transition from class to class takes time—not only to physically move from class to class, but also for students to "close up" one activity in one room and "settle into" activity in another room. Over a period of years this loss of instructional time can add up to staggering numbers. Make certain that your plan includes your ideas for the following procedures:

- moving from one room to the next
- communicating student absences to the specialist
- entering a room and settling into new activities
- closing up activities
- consequences for students' not following procedures

Instructional congruence at the elementary level is necessary to decide what type of remedial instruction is most appropriate for an individual student. Does the student need extra practice in skills taught in the general education classroom, or a totally different approach? At both elementary and secondary levels, instructional congruence is important to ensure that general education teachers are aware of the student's current level of functioning and how best to make instructional accommodations for the student in the general education setting.

In-Class Programs Because of the problems inherent in pull-out programs and the stigma that middle school and high school students often attach to remedial classes, many schools offer in-class programs as an alternative. As the name implies, the primary setting for **in-class programs**, sometimes called *pull-in* programs, is the general education classroom. The classroom teacher and reading or math specialist collaborate by planning for individual student needs, suggesting instructional adaptations, and demonstrating instructional strategies. Specialists can offer in-class tutoring that reinforces what the classroom teacher has presented. Specialists also can offer small-group

instruction to children with special needs while the general classroom teacher is working with other students.

Lisa Parker is a third grade teacher in a Title I elementary school. When the school administrator instituted a pull-in program for Title I, some teachers, including Lisa, were resistant to the idea of having another teacher in their class. Classroom teachers felt that they would lose autonomy in planning and instruction, and specialists were concerned about moving from class to class instead of working in their own resource room.

Collaborative planning time and administrative support for this change were in place, however. Lisa realized that the new arrangement would give her the opportunity to learn more about her students and their needs. She and the Title I teacher, Denise Pressman, made a commitment to planning, and decided that they were going to make the most of having two adults in the room for the 90-minute reading and language arts period. Denise and Lisa agreed to divide the class into two groups for reading instruction every day for 45 minutes, and that Denise would pull in individuals or small groups of students as necessary. Lisa and Denise also planned where in the room the groups would meet, and how groups would begin and end (to avoid disruptions). Both teachers became enthusiastic supporters of the pull-in program, as did the students. As one student said, "It's great to have two teachers. You can get more help and the teachers come up with more ideas. Two heads are better than one!"

Add-on Programs Services provided in time slots typically not allocated to regular instruction are called **add-on programs**. They include before- or after-school programs, year-round schools, and weekend or summer programs. Most public school sponsored add-on programs are located at the school site. The benefits of add-on programs are that the general education curriculum and routines remain intact, and the amount of instructional time is extended.

Bonnie Kohl is an eighth grade teacher who has been assigned to direct the after-school study hall—"The Homework Club." The goal of the Homework Club is to support students as they complete their homework and develop reading and math skills through recreational reading, games, and computers. When Bonnie agreed to take on this responsibility, she set up a system for regular communication with teachers to learn their systems for assigning homework. She also communicated with parents so that they would understand and support the Homework Club.

An example of a secondary-level add-on program is Upward Bound, a federally funded program that serves at-risk high school students whose parents have not attended college. Students attend Upward Bound sessions at a sponsoring college or university during the school year, then live on campus during the summer. Their sessions include classes in basic skills (reading, writing, mathematics), study skills, enrichment in content areas, tutoring, and counseling—personal, academic, and career.

Schoolwide Programs When the number of children qualifying for compensatory services is very high, **schoolwide programs** may be the answer. In schools in which more than 75 percent of the students are from low-income families, Title I funding can be used to improve instruction on a schoolwide basis (U.S. Department of Education, 1992). The advantage of schoolwide programs is that children are not singled out for special services.

For example, Tucker Elementary School in Coconut Grove (Miami), Florida, has a schoolwide program. Over 90 percent of the students receive free or reduced-price lunch and, for a variety of reasons, the number of students potentially at risk is high. Therefore, the faculty and administration decided to use their Title I funding to reduce class size and to purchase supplies for all classes, giving all classes the benefit of Title I funding.

Tracking The practice of placing students with similar needs together for extended periods of the school day is called **tracking**. Students may be assigned to classes on the basis of achievement test scores. At the middle school or high school level, low-achieving students may be placed together in basic or remedial tracks in a number of subject areas. The perceived advantages of tracking are to better serve students by reducing the range of academic diversity so that low achievers receive reme-

diation and high achievers are not slowed down. The disadvantages of tracking are well documented (see Research Brief).

RESEARCH BRIEF

NEGATIVE EFFECTS OF TRACKING

Research (Oakes, 1985; 1990) has suggested that students placed in low tracks have limited access to information and are likely to be exposed to a limited curriculum. Also, the quality of instruction in low-track classes is generally inferior because teachers spend instructional time on discipline, use methods and materials that do not foster higher-order or critical thinking, and often speak in demeaning ways to students. Students often suffer from lowered self-esteem and become decreasingly disinterested in academics and other school-related activities.

Tracking also tends to reinforce social inequality. Low-income and minority students are overrepresented in lower tracks, thus stratifying the educational system by class and race. Placement of students in tracks tends to become permanent. A student labeled as low-achieving is likely to wear that label throughout the school experience.

Early Intervention Programs

Research on programs for students at risk has indicated that the most fruitful time to provide remediation is during the preprimary and early primary grades (Kennedy et al., 1986). The trend is to implement **early intervention programs**. Two early intervention programs—Reading Recovery and Success for All—have received a great deal of national exposure for their success in early prevention of failure in reading. The premise of both programs is that early, intensive intervention, although costly, saves the higher cost of later remediation, retention, and dropouts.

Reading Recovery Reading Recovery is an early intervention program based on the work of Marie Clay of New Zealand (Clay, 1985; Pinnell, Fried, & Estice, 1990). The first extensive Reading Recovery program in the United States was launched at Ohio State University, but school districts throughout the country now implement this program (Pinnell, 1990). Reading Recovery involves individual tutoring of low-achieving first grade students for thirty minutes a day. Students continue with the program until they are reading at a level comparable to average-achieving students in their class or until they have completed a certain number of tutoring sessions. Teachers who have received training in Reading Recovery procedures conduct the tutoring sessions with eight or so students a day. Lessons involve both reading and writing activities. The reading books are storybooks that one could find in the library, but are carefully selected for their natural language and predictable text.

A typical session involves the following activities:

1. child rereading a familiar book
2. teacher analyzing the reading by keeping a running record
3. letter identification activities, if necessary
4. child writing a story, with emphasis on hearing the sounds of words
5. putting together a cut-up story
6. child becoming acquainted with and reading a new book

Reading Recovery is not a packaged program in that very few materials are required—pencil, paper, and books that are appropriate for the student's reading level, and have good stories. Reading Recovery's success is based on the teacher (Pinnell, 1990), who commits to intensive teacher development to learn how to conduct ongoing assessment of student needs during the tutoring sessions and how to respond appropriately to those needs.

Success for All The Center for Research on Effective Schooling for Disadvantaged Students, housed at Johns Hopkins University, sponsors **Success for All** (Madden et al., 1991), a program being adopted in schools across the United States. Success for All targets children in grades K–3 and involves a high degree of collaboration between remedial and general educators and parents. The program includes the following components:

- a family-support team (including a social worker and a parent liaison)
- reading tutoring for students with particular problems, for as long as necessary
- an innovative curriculum that integrates reading and writing instruction in meaningful contexts
- regrouping of students across grades for reading instruction

All students in Success for All participate in a 90-minute instructional reading period, during which time additional tutors participate to reduce class size. During reading periods students go from their grade-level classes to a reading group of ten to twenty students who read at about the same level. For example, a beginning Grade 2 class might include students from first, second, or third grades—all reading at approximately a Grade 2 level. The curriculum, which is consistent in both general education classes and in individual tutoring sessions, includes instruction in phonics, reading comprehension, and listening comprehension. Typical tutoring sessions include reading of familiar stories, drill on letter sounds, reading of stories with controlled vocabulary, and writing activities.

Slavin and his colleagues have adapted the reading and mathematics programs developed for Success for All into a new program called **Roots and Wings**. Roots and Wings adds guidelines for an integrated approach to other content areas, such as science and social studies. Roots and Wings has two objectives. The first (the *roots*) is to guarantee that every child, regardless of family background or disability, will successfully complete elementary school, achieving the highest standards in basic skills such as reading and writing, as well as in mathematics, science, history, and geography. The program's second objective (the *wings*) is to engage students in activities that enable them to apply everything they learn so that they can see the usefulness and interconnectedness of knowledge (Slavin et al., 1994).

During a 90-minute integrated learning period (called *WorldLab*), students work in cooperative learning groups to learn about a particular theme in science and social studies topics. A variety of materials (e.g., videos and newspapers) and instructional activities (e.g., role playing, field trips, experiments) are used. The emphasis is on making the learning true to life. For example, one Roots and Wings class studied the Chesapeake Bay, its history, geography, and related scientific issues such as pollution, tides, and wildlife. Then the class visited the bay and drafted letters to legislators about preserving the estuary.

School–Community Prevention Programs

The conditions that place students at risk are so pervasive that schools alone cannot alleviate or compensate for the problems that interfere with student success. Throughout the country, school–community partnerships are coordinating efforts to prevent problems and improve the quality of education. Many innovative school–community partnerships are being developed by individual teachers. As a teacher you will want to discover the programs and resources available in your own school and community.

Parent Involvement The assumption that parents of students at risk do not care about their children's progress in school and are not capable of making substantive contributions to their children's education is unwarranted. Increasingly, school personnel are not only exploring ways to involve parents in making decisions about their children's education, but also providing parents with resources for promoting learning in the home. The process of involving parents can be difficult. Some parents do not have a phone, cannot take time away from work to come to school. Some parents may be illiterate or may not know English. And some parents are intimidated by schools and teachers because of cultural differences or lack of personal success as a student. Don't assume that parents who don't attend school functions or respond to your notes do not care. Many parents want to help but are not sure what they can do.

Terry Bradford has been particularly effective in involving parents in her classroom. Terry teaches third grade at an inner city school with many students from low-income families. Many of her students are children of single, teenage mothers.

Two of her students live in foster homes, and three others are being raised by grandparents. Terry describes her parent-involvement program as follows:

> Each year I identify three or four parents who are willing to serve on a parent committee. The role of the parent committee is to help me brainstorm about topics for parent workshops, ways of getting information home, and ways of involving parents as volunteers. Parents know their neighbors and know their community much better than I do. They are the experts.
>
> I work with my students to develop a monthly newsletter for parents. The newsletter contains headlines about what we are studying in class. I try to make sure that *every* student's name is mentioned at least once in the newsletter. Also, the newsletter includes a homework and special events calendar for the month. It also includes a list of ways that parents can get involved, developed by the parent committee. Some of the ideas are things that working parents can do at home to help out the class—for example, preparing materials for art projects. This all takes a great deal of work and planning, but it pays off.

Full-Service Schools A **full-service school** serves as a hub for educational, psychological, physical, financial, social, and health-related services for a community (Dryfoos, 1994). The school houses health centers, social service and employment agencies, and adult education organizations. Mobile health care units and other such temporary services can be brought on site and advertised to the community. Full-service schools can also organize services for basic family needs, including distribution of food and clothing, child care, and transportation. At a single facility, families can have dental work, workshops on parenting skills, financial counseling, and crisis management.

Frequently, low-income families have difficulty finding transportation from one agency to another, have limited access to telephones during work hours, and often do not have the luxury of taking off a day from work to take family members to the doctor. Full-service schools provide for the integration and coordination of health, educational, and social services. By making access to these services more convenient for parents, many of the barriers that keep students from learning can be overcome.

Funding for full-service schools is often multifaceted, with support coming from federal, state, and local sources. Businesses, church groups, and private foundations also are frequently involved, to fund personnel (such as nurses or social workers), donate equipment, underwrite special events or programs, or to enlist and train volunteers.

Volunteer Programs Another growing area of community–school partnering is the use of volunteers. Volunteer tutors can offer students a service that is sometimes difficult for classroom teachers to provide: sustained one-on-one assistance with academics. As Tips for Teachers 11.2 indicates, however, volunteer tutors need training and monitoring. A volunteer might know how to read, but not how to teach someone to read.

Mentoring programs are volunteer efforts that structure partnerships between a student and an adult who can offer guidance and support. In some mentoring programs adults from the community provide general guidance for students who need to talk with a positive role model for staying in school or for achieving a successful career. In other programs students who are going through a personal or academic crisis are paired with someone who has overcome a similar difficulty. In Dade County, Florida, the Committee of 100 is a community group of successful African-American males who volunteer to mentor students at risk in the public schools. Members of the Committee visit the schools and meet one-on-one with students to listen, talk, and encourage.

Students at risk also benefit from participating in volunteer activities. By helping someone else, students learn responsibility and compassion. Cross-age tutoring, which involves pairing an older student (tutor) with a younger student (learner), is one of the most popular ways to involve students in volunteer activities. The tutor typically receives training in tutoring basics (developing rapport, conducting a tutoring session, giving positive feedback) and in tutoring techniques (how to read aloud to a learner, how to respond to the learner's writing, how to help learners solve math problems).

Business–School Partnerships Private corporations are becoming more responsive to the needs of communities through sponsorship of school programs and activities. Business involvement comes in many forms. The Pizza Hut Book-It (reading

TIPS FOR TEACHERS

11.2 Working with Volunteers

- *Decide why you need volunteers.* Possible jobs include clerical tasks, working with individual students, reading aloud to students, and planning and implementing special events.
- *Conduct a volunteer-recruitment campaign.* Begin by contacting your school or district volunteer coordinator, or try a sign-up table at school events and PTA meetings. Also, contact local retirement communities, and check high schools and universities, especially those that require students to complete service learning hours.

- *Train volunteers in their roles and responsibilities.* Include where to find equipment and materials, what school rules to enforce, and how to report to you when they will be absent.
- *Have a system for monitoring volunteers.* Make certain that they feel comfortable with their duties and have no questions or concerns.
- *Have a plan for recognizing and thanking volunteers.* You and your students might plan a party or send a thank-you letter. Be sure to let volunteers know that their time and energy are appreciated.

incentive) Program and grants from IBM and Apple for computer equipment are examples. On the local level, many businesses are making large commitments to schools through Adopt-A-School programs. In such cases businesses make financial contributions, organize apprenticeship programs (in which students spend time working at the business), or recruit volunteers for the school from among their personnel.

You may want to apply for a corporate-sponsored grant or to solicit funds for a specific project or piece of equipment for your class. In arranging a business sponsorship, you should first clear your request with your school principal.

Instructional Guidelines and Accommodations

The purpose of this section is to provide you with practical suggestions for teaching students at risk. The emphasis is on helping students earn passing grades and become successful in their work at school. Instructional guidelines and accommodations address the following areas:

■ communicating high expectations
■ creating a positive classroom climate

■ enhancing motivation
■ using authentic learning tasks

Communicating High Expectations

Remind yourself that all students are capable learners, and keep your expectations high. For students to be able to accomplish what you expect, you must communicate your expectations clearly, explicitly, and repeatedly. Be especially definite about your expectations in the following areas:

■ classroom rules and routines
■ students' roles and responsibilities
■ what they will learn
■ following directions for completing assignments
■ quantity and quality of process and product

You communicate your expectations to students daily through ongoing conversations and lessons. Research has indicated that many teachers have fewer instructional encounters and more disciplinary ones with low-achieving students than with students' higher-achieving peers. Teachers also have a tendency to "talk down" to low achievers. These practices must be avoided. You can show students that you respect them by treat-

TIPS FOR TEACHERS

11.3 Treating Low-Achieving Students Equitably

- Give all students ample time to answer questions.
- Call on low-achieving students as often as you call on other students.
- Avoid calling on other students to constantly correct errors made by lower-achieving students.
- Give all students the opportunity to answer difficult and higher-order questions.
- Give lower-achieving students as informative feedback about their answers as you would other students.

- Accept the ideas of all students and respect their ideas as valuable.
- Interact with low-achieving students on instructional matters as frequently as with other students.
- Avoid differentiating curriculum, materials, and instructional methods to the degree that these accommodations publicly reinforce the idea that students are low-achieving.

ing them equitably. Tips for Teachers 11.3, which provides hints for avoiding bias in your interactions with low-achieving students, is based on the work of Good and Brophy (1994).

Creating a Positive Classroom Climate

Teachers who are successful in working with students at risk develop a classroom atmosphere that is both compassionate and productive. Two key factors are critical to creating such a climate: caring and order.

Communicate that you care about each of your students and want them to be successful. One way to show that you care is to get to know your students' names the first day of class. After that, keep trying to learn as much as possible about each student's interests, strengths, and learning challenges. Some teachers find it helpful to keep a log with a page for each student and to record notes about the student and how best to teach him or her. By identifying their interests you can engage students in personally meaningful ways. By knowing their strengths you can give each student the opportunity to be an expert and to share expertise with classmates.

The second factor, order, is important because students cannot learn when the classroom is chaotic and the rules change daily. Whether you prefer an active classroom in which students talk and interact with each other to accomplish tasks, or a quiet classroom with students working individually at their desks, you can be a successful teacher. The key point is that you need to let students know routines, boundaries, and expectations.

An orderly, businesslike classroom environment that focuses on productivity is especially helpful to students at risk. Knapp et al. (1991) explain that classroom environments that enable students to learn have the following common characteristics:

- minimal disruptions
- pacing of instruction appropriate for the topic and for students
- consistent classroom routines
- regular systems for giving feedback to students
- systematic ways to keep students accountable for their work

- planning of instructional assignments and tasks appropriate for students' level of learning

Enhancing Motivation

Keeping at-risk students motivated and willing to learn can be challenging. You are the one who can provide the structure and strategies to make students willing to be actively involved in learning. But how can you get low-achieving students to focus less on their inability to learn and more on effort? How can you get students to value learning enough to be willing to invest the effort it might take to complete a learning task? Tips for Teachers 11.4 provides suggestions for improving motivation.

Keep in mind that different students are likely to become motivated in different ways. Some students might be motivated by a pat on the back or a smile, others might like completing a project and then showing it to classmates, other students might be encouraged to learn through group work, still others might become more engaged in hands-on learning. Try to attend to each of your students and note what seems to work best for each one.

Sometimes, rewards such as food, extra time on the computer, or working with a friend may be appropriate. When you do give rewards, reward *improvement,* emphasizing the student's hard work and effort and why the accomplishment is important. In addition, make a clear connection between the reward and the accomplishment, and make certain that the reward is something the student values (McIntyre, 1992). For example, after students learn in math class how to make change, you may decide to award a certificate to take home. When you award the certificate you might say, "Todd, I know how hard you worked to learn how to make change. You completed six homework assignments and participated in our practice activities with money in class. Making change is an important skill to know—not only as a worker, but also as a customer. You'll know that you're not being shortchanged by a cashier."

Students can be motivated to learn through the type of praise you offer for effort and for a job well done. Brophy (1981) suggests that praise is effective when it is

TIPS FOR TEACHERS

11.4 *Helping Students Improve Motivation to Learn*

- *Create an orderly, safe learning community.* Avoid practices that tend to isolate, stigmatize, or disfavor at-risk students.
- *Set clear purposes for learning.* Let students know their academic mission and the importance of what they are learning.
- *Have high present expectations for academic achievement,* allowing students gradually to develop high expectations for future achievement.
- *Choose tasks and materials at an appropriate level of difficulty,* so that students can be successful without too much or too little effort.
- *Encourage and reward effort and improvement,* making students feel special when they are high achievers. Explain how effort contributed to their success.
- *Base assessment of student performance on improvement.*

- *Provide a comfortable atmosphere* in which students are not afraid to take risks or ask for help.
- *Give immediate substantive feedback* to reinforce the idea that completing assignments and participating in class are important.
- *Attribute students' successes and failures to effort and perseverance (or lack thereof) and other intrinsic qualities that students can control.* Teach students to make appropriate attributions in explaining their successes and failures.
- *Develop activities that call for individual effort or cooperation rather than competition.* Enable every student to feel like a winner.
- *Integrate into curriculum and instruction opportunities for students to build self-esteem and a sense of what they can accomplish.*
- *Present lessons and assign learning activities that are fun.* Develop interesting ways for students to apply basic skills instruction.

- for a specific accomplishment
- specific about the aspects of the accomplishment that were particularly well done
- guided to help students appreciate their task-related behavior
- focused on particularly difficult tasks
- acknowledged that the student's effort led to the success
- recognized that this success can lead to success with similar tasks in the future

Another important way to motivate students is to involve them in setting their own learning goals, which helps them become more independent. For example, a student who is learning multiplication tables might set goals for mastering each table in a certain period of time.

Using Authentic Learning Tasks

When is learning authentic? **Authentic learning** takes place when students can do the following:

- construct meaning by connecting new information to what they already know and have experienced
- recognize the value of what they are learning (beyond grades and success in school)
- connect what they learn in school to the "real world"

Newmann and Wehlage (1992–93) identified five standards of instruction for authentic learning: higher-order thinking, depth of knowledge, connectedness to the world beyond the classroom,

How does this authentic learning activity stimulate higher-order thinking and provide social support for student learning? How will these students' learning connect to the world beyond the classroom?

topic before all students have understood or (because they lack depth of knowledge) been able to successfully apply what they have learned to new situations. Rapid pacing can be especially devastating for students at risk.

By planning, you can help students acquire depth of knowledge and still keep a reasonable pace of instruction. The Planning Pyramid (refer to Chapter 2) can help you select which topics to cover comprehensively so that students gain a deeper understanding.

substantive conversation, and social support for student achievement.

Higher-order Thinking One common stereotype about students who are low achievers and students at risk is that their thinking is basic and concrete. Students at risk are capable learners, however, and capable of higher-order thinking. **Higher-order thinking** involves problem solving, decision making, creative thinking, critical thinking, and investigation. Instructional methods for at-risk students should not be limited to mindless recitation, skill, and drill. Make certain that students have opportunities to apply skills to solve real-life problems, make decisions, or complete meaningful projects. For example, after a lesson on angles, you might ask the students, "How might our classroom look if there were no right angles?" Students might draw diagrams to demonstrate their answers.

Depth of Knowledge In most school systems, teachers are under pressure to cover content. This pressure impels teachers to increase the pace of instruction and, frequently, to move on to the next

Connectedness to the World beyond the Classroom

Learning becomes meaningful when it is connected to reality—to the world beyond the classroom. You can help students make connections by making links between their own worlds and what they are learning, and by providing opportunities to expand their worlds through rich examples and direct experiences.

Students come to school with knowledge about their own language, culture, communities, and customs. Take the time to get to know your students and then design instructional tasks and select examples that are meaningful to them and apply to real-life situations in their own worlds. For example, reading materials that reflect students' interests, experiences, and background help them to realize that their culture and heritage are to be valued.

For secondary students in particular, learning must be relevant to their future. Poor academic performance and dropping out of school can result when students do not see the relevance of what they are learning to their occupational goals (Natriello, McDill, & Pallas, 1990). Two ways to connect the worlds of school and work are to bring in guest speakers from the community who represent various occupations, and to develop apprenticeship programs in local businesses.

Clearly, people remember and learn best what they experience directly. Direct experiences can help students broaden their world and transfer their learning. In 1969, Edgar Dale proposed what is now considered a classic model for providing direct experiences in the classroom. Figure 11.2 presents Dale's **cone of experience**, which classifies experience on a scale from concrete to abstract, and from action to observation to representation.

Direct experiences such as some examples in Dale's cone of experience can be difficult to engineer. Fantasy, role playing, and simulation can help. For example, elementary students can create a pretend grocery store in the classroom to learn about money and product labels. High school students might assume the roles of historical figures deciding turning points in history. Involvement in contemporary real-life problems also can help build interest in learning. For example, science or social studies classes might become interested in local environmental or social issues.

Teachers can be as frustrated when students try and fail as when students do not try, or come to school with problems that interfere with their learning. The conditions that place students at risk and the educational needs of these students vary. Instructional tactics must address their individual needs. Miriam Mades offers this general advice for teachers working with children who are difficult to teach: "I think to myself that I need to be *positive*—I keep on believing that they will learn and I structure learning activities to make them believe it too. I need to be *persistent*—I don't give up and I won't let them give up either. I need to be *patient*—sometimes children just have a different schedule for learning and it is my role to keep on encouraging them to do their best."

MAKING A DIFFERENCE
The 60-Second Lesson

Helping Students Make Book Choices

Library visits are prime time for 60-Second Lessons on research skills or for just incidental enrichment of vocabulary and concepts as students browse through the stacks. While students search for books, you have the opportunity to circulate and meet with them individually. Students who are poor or reluctant readers frequently have a tough time choosing books. The following procedure is one way to help students find books:

1. Identify a topic of interest to the student (you may have to do some probing to get an area of interest or genre: "What is your favorite TV show?" "What new skills would you like to learn?" "Where would you like to go for your dream vacation?")
2. Find three or four books on the topic.
3. Read a few lines from each book.
4. Have the student select one of the books.
5. Make a point to follow up to see whether the student has started reading the book, and schedule a "book talk."

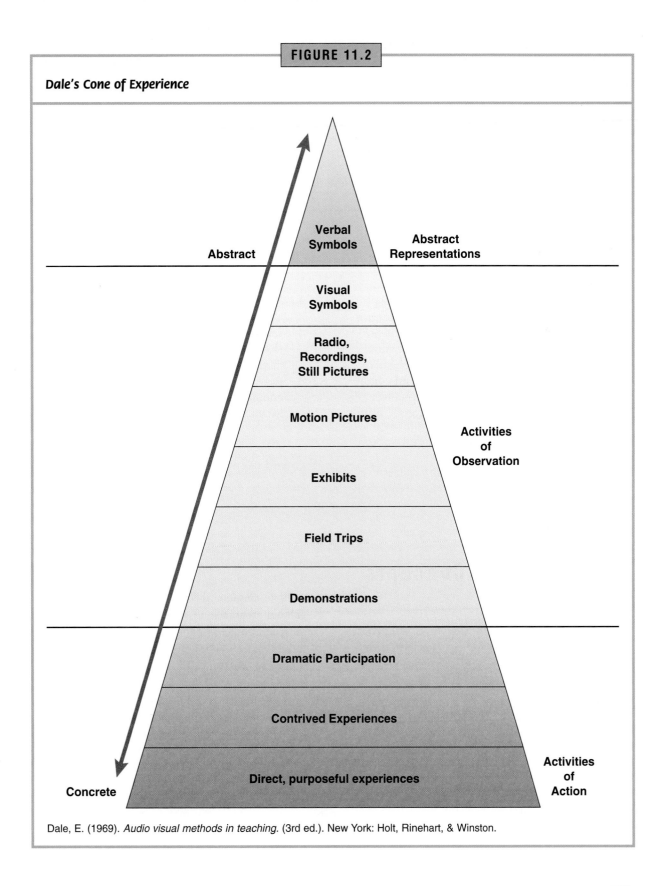

FIGURE 11.2

Dale's Cone of Experience

Abstract

Verbal
Symbols

Abstract
Representations

Visual
Symbols

Radio,
Recordings,
Still Pictures

Motion Pictures

Exhibits

Activities
of
Observation

Field Trips

Demonstrations

Dramatic Participation

Contrived Experiences

Direct, purposeful experiences

Concrete

Activities
of
Action

Dale, E. (1969). *Audio visual methods in teaching.* (3rd ed.). New York: Holt, Rinehart, & Winston.

SUMMARY

- Students at risk are those who, for whatever reason, are in jeopardy of qualifying for remediation or for retention, dropping out of school, or having substandard basic skills.
- Students who are at risk may exhibit poor academic performance, develop negative attitudes toward school, misbehave, and be chronically tardy or absent.
- The conditions that place students at risk vary, and include family conditions (including poverty and instability), risks to health and safety, and at-risk schools.
- A variety of local, state, and federal programs (including Title I) are available to provide funding for educating students at risk.
- Federal compensatory education programs are designed to compensate for the negative effects that poverty and adverse social conditions may have on academic performance.
- Remediation for students at risk can be provided through many forms and contexts, including pull-out, in-class, add-on, school-wide, and tracking models.

- Two early intervention programs—Reading Recovery and Success for All—have received national recognition for their success in early prevention of literacy problems.
- Throughout the United States, school–community partnerships are being developed (through parent involvement, full-service schools, volunteer programs, and business–school partnerships) in a coordinated effort to prevent problems that lead to academic failure and to improve the quality of life and education for students at risk.
- Many of the instructional guidelines and accommodations for students at risk represent quality teaching for all students. Those that are particularly important for students at risk include communicating high expectations, creating a positive classroom climate, enhancing motivation, and using authentic learning tasks.

Key Terms and Concepts

add-on programs
authentic learning
compensatory education
computer equity
cone of experience
dropouts
early intervention programs
full-service school
in-class programs
instructional congruence
higher-order thinking
mentoring programs

multiple causation theory
pull-out programs
procedural congruence
Reading Recovery
Roots and Wings
remediation
retention
schoolwide programs
students at risk
Success for All
Title I
tracking

Think and Apply

1. Review the interview at the beginning of this chapter, and Miriam Mades's advice. How does this teacher provide love and establish trust? How does she create a positive classroom climate? What authentic learning experiences does she provide, and how does she use a school–community partnership to enhance authentic learning? How does Miriam build social support for all students' learning?

2. Interview Title I teachers involved in "pull-out" and "pull-in" programs. Ask them to identify the strengths and weaknesses of the two service-delivery models, and explain why the particular model was determined in their situation.

3. After reading about tracking, think about your own position on the subject and draft a position paper providing a rationale for your stance.

4. Develop a script illustrating a substantive instructional conversation with a small group of students in a subject area you plan to teach. Collaborate with classmates to role-play scripts, and discuss the qualities that make conversations authentic.

5. Develop a plan for ways you intend to use volunteers in your classroom. Include in your plan ways to recruit, train, monitor, and recognize volunteers.

6. For your content area, plan a lesson that focuses on "authentic" learning.

7. Using the updated version of Dale's cone of experience, identify learning activities in your content area for each segment of the cone.

8. What questions would you ask of experienced teachers concerning effective practices for teaching students at risk? Develop a list of questions, keep it in your teaching portfolio, and take advantage of opportunities to systematically answer those questions or to add new ones.

Read More about It

1. Anthony, P., & Jacobson, S. L. (1992). *Helping at-risk students: What are the educational and financial costs?* Newbury Park, CA: Corwin Press.

   Includes descriptions of federal and state programs and policies for students at risk, including students from low-income families, students with limited English proficiency, and Native American students.

2. Barr, R. D., & Parrett, W. H. (1995). *Hope at last for at-risk youth.* Boston: Allyn & Bacon.

   Describes school-based programs and strategies that have proven effective for different grade levels.

3. Dryfoos, J. G. (1994). *Full-service schools: A revolution in health and social services for children, youth, and families.* San Francisco: Jossey-Bass.

   A comprehensive overview of full-service schools. Includes descriptions of how full-service schools are organized, funded, and staffed.

4. Harman, M. (1994). *Inspiring active learning: A handbook for teachers.* Alexandria, VA: Association for Supervision and Curriculum Development.

   A dynamic book that provides specific suggestions for actively involving students in learning. Suggestions that are particularly helpful for students at risk include strategies for raising student motivation, organizing the classroom, producing meaningful learning, and stimulating thinking.

5. Hiebert, E. H., & Taylor, B. M. (Eds.) (1994). *Getting reading right from the start.* Boston: Allyn & Bacon.

   Includes descriptions of effective early intervention programs for teaching reading to students at risk, including Reading Recovery, Success for All, and others.

6. Johnson, L. A. (1993). *My posse don't do homework.* New York: St. Martin's Press.

   One teacher's success story about working with high school students at risk of school failure.

7. Sherman, A. (1994). *Wasting America's future: The Children's Defense Fund report on the costs of child poverty.* Boston: Beacon Press.

   A brief yet powerful summary of the state of poverty in the United States.

CHAPTER

TWELVE

Teaching Students Who Are Gifted and Talented

FOCUS QUESTIONS

1. What are the key components of different definitions of gifted and talented? How can these definitions impact who receives special services?

2. What are the characteristics of students who are gifted and talented?

3. How can you identify students who are gifted and talented in your classroom and refer them for special programs?

4. What are the main approaches to the content of instruction and administrative arrangements for students who are gifted and talented?

5. How can you adapt curriculum and instruction for your students who are gifted and talented?

Interview

Lawanzer Ellis

Lawanzer Ellis is a fourth grade teacher at South Miami Heights Elementary School in Miami, Florida. Students at South Miami Heights Elementary are among the most ethnically and linguistically diverse in Dade County Public Schools. Of the thirty-four students assigned to Lawanzer this year, seventeen were identified by the school district as qualifying for special services for the gifted and talented. To simplify scheduling, the principal decided to place all fourth grade gifted and talented students in one general education classroom. Two days a week the seventeen students go to a resource room to work with a teacher trained in gifted education. On those two days, Lawanzer teaches the other seventeen children—a group representing a wide range of achievement levels.

Lawanzer has succeeded in creating a classroom climate that enables all her students to get excited about learning and to feel affirmed about themselves as learners. She attributes her success to four factors:

> This classroom seems to work for a number of reasons. First, I think that the physical appearance and arrangement of the classroom sets the tone for learning. The classroom really is set up as a workplace, with work stations or centers all around the room. The writing center, the computer center, and the art center are used every day. Even though it is almost the end of the school year, my class is still very neat and well ordered. That's because the students take responsibility for their work environment very seriously. The students have helped me plan bulletin boards and centers all year long. I really believe that they feel a sense of ownership about the classroom.
>
> A second reason that things have gone well this year is that every student feels good about his or her own gifts and talents. Sometimes this is really difficult for me to accomplish. I work hard to recognize everyone as being special and as having something important to contribute to our classroom community.
>
> A third reason is that I have high expectations for all my students, and I communicate those expectations to my students and to their parents. Mostly I expect everyone to do his or her best and to stay on task. I give very detailed instructions about what to do and how to do it. We don't have much wasted time around here. Don't get me wrong, I don't over-pressure them. But I do expect them to work hard. I know each student's strengths and areas of need very, very well. They know that they can get help if they need it.
>
> Finally, things go well around here because I'm a good planner. Some teachers get frustrated because the gifted kids get pulled out and miss so much of what is taught in the regular class. I just plan carefully. Other teachers get upset because the gifted teacher is off doing her own thing—I'm lucky we plan together. Some teachers never know what to do to keep the gifted kids busy—they finish their work so fast. Look around this room—there's always something to learn around here. It just takes coordination and planning.

Introduction

Lawanzer Ellis is a "planful" teacher. She knows her students and realizes the importance of a well-structured learning environment. She also realizes that a child's learning environment extends beyond her own classroom. Thus, having learned to think about each student's "whole day," she plans with the gifted resource teacher and communicates with parents regularly. Her careful planning has enabled her to circumvent some of the potential pitfalls of a classroom with a full range of academic diversity, including students identified as gifted and talented.

Lawanzer is concerned about the academic and social progress of all of her students. She finds, as do many teachers, that planning for and teaching students with extraordinary potential for high performance (either academically or creatively) or who have exceptional talent in specific areas (e.g., music, leadership, art) pose special challenges. Consider the following quotation:

> Of all the students you are teaching in a given class, which group do you think will probably learn the least this year? It may surprise you to find that in a class that has a range of abilities (and which class doesn't?), it is the most able, rather than the least able, who will learn less new material than any other group (Winebrenner, 1992, p. 1).

How can this occur?

Think about Henry, a fifth grade student, who knows all the spelling words at the beginning of the week. He gets a grade of 100% on the spelling test, but has he learned anything?

Think about Rohan, a sixth grade student, who is a voracious reader and is particularly interested in astronomy. He skims the chapter in his general science textbook, quickly gets its gist, and realizes that the content is basic and boring. The class lecture does not go beyond answering the end-of-chapter questions. Rohan does not have the opportunity to share what he really knows and "tunes out" during class discussion. He gets a grade of 70% on a chapter test, because he simply doesn't care about "proving" what he knows.

Think about Carolina, an eighth grade student, who has known all about the eight parts of speech since third grade. Even if she had forgotten the eight parts of speech in third grade, it wouldn't have mattered because they were also taught in fourth, fifth, sixth, and seventh grades. She gets a grade of 100% on a grammar unit test, but has she learned anything?

Think about Thaddeus. Thaddeus loves to draw and does so constantly—at home and at school. Unfortunately, he'd rather draw than do anything else, and his teacher frequently reprimands him for "doodling" rather than completing assignments. The once-a-week art class does not provide Thaddeus with the instruction he needs to develop his talent.

You've got the picture. Frequently, students identified as gifted or talented and other high-achieving students already know the material being covered in the general curriculum. Can you imagine spending seven hours a day, five days a week, school year after school year, reviewing information you already know? Can you imagine having genuine artistic talent and not having the opportunity to develop that talent or to share with others?

Providing for the needs of all students can be difficult, but (as Lawanzer Ellis has demonstrated) with careful planning, it can be done! This chapter provides information about gifted education and about your responsibilities, as a classroom teacher, in meeting the needs of children who are identified as gifted and talented. Included here are both background information, and specific strategies to help you teach children who are gifted and talented as you meet the instructional needs of all children in your classroom.

Historical Perspective on Gifted Education

For decades gifted education has been shrouded in controversy. There are educators, parents, and politicians who argue that gifted and talented students are among the most neglected in our educational system. Proponents of special programs for qualified students contend that by ignoring this valuable resource we not only fail to nurture the brain power our country will need to survive in a competitive international marketplace, but also fail to provide appropriate education for these students, regardless of their potential contribution to society. On the other hand, there are educators and members of the general public who maintain that providing special services for an elite subset of our population is undemocratic and therefore unnecessary. They maintain that all children have exceptional gifts and should have the opportunity to have those gifts recognized and developed. Even when critics agree that services should be provided, however, the questions of who should receive those services and how services should be delivered are also topics for debate.

As a classroom teacher you may find yourself at the center of this controversy. For example, parents of students identified as gifted and talented may expect you to provide their children with increasingly advanced work. Or parents of students not identified as gifted and talented may pressure you to nominate their children for special services. How can you provide children who excel academically, socially, or artistically with the instructional challenges they need while trying to meet the needs of all students in your class?

To guide your thinking about the controversy surrounding gifted education, this section provides a brief historical overview of gifted education in the United States, which can be divided into two periods: pre- and post-Sputnik. Prior to the launching of the Soviet satellite, *Sputnik*, on October 4, 1957, enthusiasm for students with exceptional ability was random at best. The Soviet accomplishment—embarrassing to the educational system in the United States—ignited a careful examination of how we might cultivate superior students.

Rear Admiral H. G. Rickover, the first commander of the nuclear submarine *Nautilus* during the Cold War, said that identifying and educating talented youth was in the national interest, because the United States needed highly skilled workers to compete with the Soviet Union.

The Pre-Sputnik Period

School systems in the United States were slow to make provisions for academically gifted students. In the early years, these students typically were promoted through the grades ("skipping" grades); junior and senior high school students typically took extra courses. These practices were not without critics, however, who warned of potential social and physical problems associated with rapid movements through the grades (Hollingworth, 1926).

Prior to 1958, few programs for gifted students existed, and those few were largely confined to urban areas (Trimble, 1955). In the 1800s, two school systems started ability-group tracks to accommodate gifted children: St. Louis, Missouri, in 1867, and Elizabeth, New Jersey, in 1886 (Sumpton & Leuking, 1960). In the early 1900s, New York City and Baltimore, Maryland, started special schools for the gifted. The emphasis in these schools was rapid acceleration through the curriculum.

By 1920, other large school systems began taking a different approach in their designs for separate programs specifically for gifted students. The emphasis of these programs was on **enrichment** (breadth and depth of the curriculum) rather than on rapid promotion through the grades or **acceleration** through the curriculum (Gossard, 1940; Sumpton & Leuking, 1960). Los Angeles, California, and Cleveland, Ohio, were among the school systems that experimented with programs designed to offer gifted students a more challenging, enriched curriculum (Davis & Rimm, 1989).

The Post-Sputnik Period

After the launch of *Sputnik,* educators scrambled to establish programs and curricula to nurture future scientists, engineers, and critical thinkers (McDaniel, 1993). Ability grouping and tracking at elementary and secondary levels became prevalent. Advanced math and science curricula were developed, and college-level courses were offered to qualifying students at the high school level. Peak interest in gifted education was short-lived, however (Davis & Rimm, 1989). Moreover, critics recognized that the national talent search for the brightest and best was narrow in its interpretation of exceptional abilities. Because of testing instruments that were culturally biased, few minority students became eligible for special services.

After the initial *Sputnik* frenzy, interest in the education of the gifted was erratic. In the early 1970s, under the administration of United States Commissioner of Education Sydney Marland, a task force was formed to study educational services for the gifted. The report of the task force, the "Marland Report," brought attention to the inadequacies of educational services for the gifted (Feldhusen et al., 1989). Perhaps the most significant contribution of the task force was to offer a broadened view of who might be available for special services.

A major growth of interest in gifted education began in the early 1980s, with strong interest continuing to the present. In 1988, Congress passed the Jacob Javits Gifted and Talented Act. This act permitted the reopening of an office for gifted and talented (which had closed inexplicably in 1981) in the Department of Education, and the funding of the National Research Center on the Gifted and Talented, led by Joseph S. Renzulli at the University of Connecticut. One of the most significant aspects of the Javits Act was the direction of funds for research on the identification of gifted individuals in typically overlooked populations (e.g., minorities, disadvantaged) (Harrington-Lueker, 1991).

Currently, approximately half the states in our country mandate services for the gifted and talented; the other half have legislative support for such services (Harrington-Lueker, 1991). Services to rural and minority students continue to be a challenge (Benbow, 1992). Also, the nature and quality of programs, and the criteria for selection of students vary from state to state, school district to school district, and school to school (Cox et al., 1985).

In some areas, particularly in states not having mandated programs, gifted programs are being closed because of budget cutbacks (Harrington-Lueker, 1991). In other areas, movements toward grouping students of mixed achievement levels, cooperative learning programs, and inclusive service delivery models are causing a careful examination of whether separate programs for the gifted are necessary (Benbow, 1992). The *National Excellence: A Case for Developing America's Talent* (Ross, 1993) report was an effort to offset what appears to be an "antigifted" movement. This movement toward the elimination of special programs for the gifted is caus-

ing a great deal of controversy among educators and parents of the gifted. At issue is whether the needs of gifted students can be adequately met in the general education setting (Gallagher, 1993).

Definitions of Giftedness

Defining "giftedness" is a task that has challenged parents, educators, theoreticians, and researchers for decades (Borland, 1989). Some definitions assume that intelligence is innate and fixed—in other words, you are born with a certain capacity for learning. Other definitions assume that intelligence can be developed and shaped by a nurturing environment. Some definitions are based on the notion that intelligence is a **unidimensional trait**, whereas others assume that intelligence is characterized by **multidimensional traits**.

Traditional definitions of giftedness, which tend to emphasize the stability of intelligence, underlie the practice of gauging student eligibility for gifted programs strictly on scores on an intelligence (IQ) test. For example, a student might need to achieve a cutoff score of 130 on an intelligence test such as the Wechsler Intelligence Scale-Revised (WISC-R) to be eligible for a school district gifted program. This practice is still common in some areas of the country despite the fact that intelligence tests (which emphasize language and

How are giftedness and talent defined? How does the theory of multiple intelligences overcome the limitations of assessment procedures that identify students who are gifted on the basis of IQ?

logical skills) are inappropriate (culturally and lin-guistically) for some students and are not designed to identify extraordinary ability in many areas (e.g., art, music, leadership).

Although a federal definition approved by the United States Congress has been adopted by most states and school districts, no single definition is endorsed uniformly. Nonetheless, definitions are important because they determine how giftedness is to be measured, what programs will be offered, and ultimately who will receive services. This section presents both federal and alternative definitions of gifted and talented, as well as information about prevalence of gifted and talented students in the United States.

Federal Definitions of Gifted and Talented

In the early 1970s, the previously mentioned "Marland Report" brought attention to the inadequacies of educational services and to the resentment of such programs among some school personnel (Feldhusen et al., 1989). Perhaps the most significant contribution of the Marland task force was a definition of the gifted that offered a broadened view of who might be available for special services. This definition (Marland, 1972) has been criticized for its lack of specificity and inability to translate easily into practice (especially in respect to identification of students), but its spirit of defining giftedness beyond intelligence-test performance is important:

> Gifted and Talented children are those identified by professionally qualified persons who by virtue of outstanding abilities, are capable of high performance. These are children who require differentiated educational programs and/or services beyond those normally provided by the regular school program in order to realize their contribution to self and society. Children capable of high performance include those with demonstrated achievement and . . . potential ability in the following areas:
>
> - general intellectual ability
> - specific academic aptitude
> - creative or productive thinking
> - leadership ability
> - visual or performing arts
> - psychomotor ability

The 1988 definition of giftedness approved by the U.S. Congress—the most recent in a series of revisions of the Marland Report definition—is a definition commonly used in designing state and local programs for the gifted:

> The term "gifted and talented students" means children and youth who give evidence of high performance capability in areas such as intellectual, creative, artistic, or leadership capacity, or in specific academic fields, and who require services or activities not ordinarily provided by the school in order to fully develop such capabilities" (P.L. 100–297, Sec. 4103. Definitions).

Alternative Definitions of Gifted and Talented

Some definitions of giftedness make a distinction between being *gifted* (i.e., having extraordinary intellectual ability and creativity) and being *talented* (i.e., having exceptional skills and ability in a specific area such as art, music, science, language, and so on) (e.g., Cohn, 1981; Gagne, 1991). The following is an example of such a definition:

> In general, giftedness is characterized by above average intellectual ability, which may be accompanied by superior academic achievement and creative capability. Talented individuals, in contrast, excel in one or more specific areas of endeavor: drama, art, music, leadership, and so on (Lewis & Doorlag, 1995, p. 447).

More recent, although not uniformly adopted, definitions of giftedness also include a reference to commitment to task (i.e., motivation and task completion). The idea is that gifted behavior is an interaction among ability, creativity, and task commitment (Renzulli & Delcourt, 1986). The following is an example:

> Giftedness refers to cognitive (intellectual) superiority (not necessarily of genius caliber), creativity, and motivation in combination and of sufficient magnitude to set the child apart from the vast majority of age-mates and make it possible for him or her to contribute something of particular value to society and to be identified for special services (Gallagher, 1993).

The limitations of definitions of giftedness and the practice of using intelligence test scores alone as indicators of giftedness have long been recognized. The work of Howard Gardner has offered an alternative that makes sense to parents, teachers, administrators, and researchers. In his book *Frames of Mind* (1983), Gardner proposes the theory of **multiple intelligences**. Gardner suggests that human beings are capable of exhibiting intelligence in seven domains: linguistic, logical–mathematical, spatial, musical, bodily–kinesthetic, interpersonal (i.e., discerning and responding to the needs of others), and intrapersonal (i.e., having detailed and accurate self-knowledge). Traditional intelligence tests tap only linguistic and logical–mathematical intelligence. Gardner advocates a revamping of assessment procedures to tap all seven areas in ways that are sensitive to culture, age, gender, and social class (Gardner & Hatch, 1989).

Characteristics of Students Who Are Gifted and Talented

There are two common (and conflicting) misconceptions about individuals who are gifted (Hallahan & Kauffman, 1991). One is that gifted individuals are intellectually advanced but physically, socially, and emotionally behind. The other misconception is that gifted individuals are "superhuman" and exceptional in every way. The longitudinal research initiated by Terman has made a major contribution to dispelling these misconceptions (see Research Brief). The reality is that gifted persons are human beings with special gifts in certain areas—areas that differ considerably depending on the individual.

RESEARCH BRIEF

FACTORS THAT INFLUENCE LATER ACHIEVEMENT

In 1921, 1,528 middle-class twelve-year-olds from California schools were identified as intellectually gifted, based on their performances on the Stanford-Binet intelligence test (each with an IQ measured at over 135). Researchers asked the following questions: What childhood traits are associated with high IQ? To what extent do those childhood traits persist into adulthood? How does high IQ relate to factors that affect achievements later in life? (Terman & Oden, 1951).

Finding the answers to these questions required long-term study. By deciding to study the identified students as they grew up, Lewis Terman began the now famous Stanford Project, ongoing since 1921 (even after Terman's death in 1959). The most recent data were collected in 1992. The Stanford Project is slated to end in 2020, but we don't have to wait until then to begin to frame answers to the questions.

The Project's progress reports and related studies of the "Termites" (nickname for the subject) suggest that high IQ is associated with the following childhood traits: extraordinary prowess in reading, arithmetical reasoning, science, and the arts; varied interests and hobbies; superior general health; and high trustworthiness and emotional stability. These traits generally persisted into adulthood. As Terman (1954, p. 227) put it, "So far, no one has developed post-adolescent stupidity!" Moreover, when compared to the general public this group experienced superior achievement patterns. For example, 95 percent of the men were in the top two Census career categories (Holahan, 1995). Similarly, considering the role of women in society during the subjects' life span, an extraordinary number of the women graduated from college (Sears & Barbee, 1977).

Perhaps the major contribution of the Terman studies is that findings have helped dispel the myths about individuals with high intelligence. To read more about this extraordinary longitudinal study, you may want to read:

Holahan, C. K., R. R. (1995). *The gifted group in later maturity*. Stanford, CA: Stanford University Press.

As a classroom teacher, you'll need to get beyond these misconceptions and stereotypes to recognize the characteristics of students with extraordinary gifts and talents so that you can help identify students for special services and provide appropriate instruction for gifted students who are members of your class. This section describes the cognitive and affective characteristics of the intellectually gifted and creatively gifted or talented.

Intellectually Gifted

Students who are **intellectually gifted** are exceptional learners. They tend to excel both in the classroom and on standardized tests, but they are not homogeneous in their thinking strategies. Some are *convergent thinkers* who approach tasks in a sequenced, linear fashion. Others are *divergent thinkers* who employ creativity and innovation to express ideas. Concrete thinkers exhibit a wealth of specific information, whereas abstract thinkers have the ability to understand complex ideas and create mental structures of concepts that may be vague to their understanding (Berger, 1994).

Students who are intellectually gifted usually respond more quickly and appropriately to questions than their peers. Given several alternatives, these students will usually select the best course of action, the preferred outcome, or the most accurate response. They are usually very curious and ask numerous questions about the topic or subject under discussion. During discussions, and also in their writing, the intellectually gifted demonstrate the ability to make applications and abstractions from their knowledge. They tend to perform in a goal-related manner and can clearly define the final goal or outcome of an activity or project.

There are downsides to these seemingly desirable student behaviors in general education classrooms. The gifted student's insatiable curiosity can interfere with the teacher's lesson, taking the lesson off track and in directions far beyond the other students' level of understanding. Gifted students' high verbal ability can lead to domination of class discussions. Usually understanding general principles, gifted students may become impatient when the teacher focuses on specific steps or details in a procedure for the benefit of other students in the class. They may become frustrated or bored when others are not able to understand a concept quickly. Intellectually gifted students sometimes focus on their personal educational goals and ignore those set by the teacher, thus causing misperceptions that the child is stubborn or self-centered (Tuttle et al., 1988).

Creatively Gifted or Talented

Creatively gifted or talented students display their unique abilities within the framework of the visual or performing arts. They demonstrate a superior ability to express ideas through various forms of communication (drawing, music, singing, writing, and acting). Significant factors in talent development are early and ongoing parental support, early commitment followed by intense and continuous work in the specific area, opportunities for interaction with a peer group of similar interests and abilities, opportunities for out-of-school learning, and motivation to be superior at a talent (Durden & Tangherlini, 1993).

Students with artistic talent are enthusiastic about expressing themselves and enjoy participating in art activities that allow incorporation of different media. They display unusual and creative solutions to artistic challenges. Students with musical ability display a lifelong interest in music and look for opportunities to listen to and create music. They can hear small differences in musical tones and can remember and reproduce these tones easily and accurately. Students with dramatic talent effectively incorporate gestures, facial expressions, body language, and voice to communicate feelings and to express meaning. They can hold the attention of others when they tell a story or perform. Students who are talented writers are able to make their point clearly, and to revise and edit without losing the essence of their ideas (Renzulli & Smith, 1979).

Talented students who don't have an outlet for their gifts can run into problems in the general education class. They can become totally focused on their area of interest and exclude the tasks set forth in the curriculum. Teachers of talented students need to find ways to incorporate their interests and talents into the daily routines.

Figure 12.1 provides an overview of characteristics of gifted and talented students. As you can see, some characteristics relate to academic factors, others refer to social and emotional factors, and some characteristics are positive, whereas others are negative. Note that not all students identified as gifted or talented demonstrate every one of these characteristics.

As you might expect, there is a wide range of individual differences in the physical, academic,

FIGURE 12.1

Characteristics of Gifted And Talented Students

✔ Advanced vocabulary for chronological age

✔ Outstanding memory; possesses lots of information

✔ Curious; asks endless questions ("why?" "and then what?")

✔ Has many interests, hobbies, and collections

✔ May have a "passionate interest" that has lasted for many years (example: dinosaurs)

✔ Intense; gets totally absorbed in activities and thoughts

✔ Strongly motivated to do things of interest; may be unwilling to work on other activities

✔ Operates on higher levels of thinking than same-age peers; is comfortable with abstract thinking

✔ Perceives subtle cause-and-effect relationships

✔ Prefers complex and challenging tasks to "basic" work

✔ May be able to "track" two or more things simultaneously (example: a teacher's daydreams and words)

✔ Catches on quickly, then resists doing work, or works in a sloppy, careless manner

✔ Comes up with "better ways" for doing things; suggests them to peers, teachers, and other adults

✔ Sensitive to beauty and other people's feelings and emotions

✔ Advanced sense of justice and fairness

✔ Aware of global issues that are uninteresting to many age-level peers

✔ Sophisticated sense of humor; may be "class clown"

Source: Winebrenner, S. (1992). *Teaching gifted kids in the regular classroom.* Minneapolis: Free Spirit Publishing.

social, and behavioral traits of students who are gifted.

The "Invisible Gifted"

In the late 1970s, Congresswoman Shirley Chisholm brought the issue of underrepresentation of minority students in gifted and talented programs in schools in the United States to the attention of Congress and the general public. Chisholm argued that traditional methods for recognizing the unique gifts and talent of individuals are inappropriate for minority populations. Since

that time, others have continued to recognize underidentified groups—or as Davis and Rimm (1989, p. 277) put it—"the **invisible gifted.**"

The unfortunate consequence of being among the "invisible" is that such students are not identified for special services and tend to become underachievers. **Underachievers** are individuals with high academic or creative potential but low academic or creative performance. These students are a source of frustration for parents and teachers because they fail to "live up" to their ability. Underachievement can be caused by a number of different factors in the home, school, or community. Students who are underachievers often exhibit low self-esteem, poor work habits, and negative attitudes toward academic tasks.

Who are the invisible gifted? Some of the most frequently cited groups are the following:

- *Minorities.* Students who are members of cultural or linguistic minorities have been underrepresented among programs for the gifted and talented. This underrepresentation is frequently attributed to assessment tools and procedures that are largely insensitive to diverse cultural values and abilities, or to tests developed on norming populations that do not include minorities (Masten, 1981).

- *Disabled.* Students with physical or learning disabilities are among the invisible gifted. Quite often parents and teachers attend more to the educational and social implications of students' disabilities than to their unique cognitive and creative gifts.

- *Females.* Although the gap between numbers of girls and boys identified for gifted programs has narrowed over the years, at least two lingering concerns remain. First, girls tend to score lower than boys on mathematical-ability assessments. Second, the early achievement of girls who have been identified as gifted appears to diminish during adolescence and beyond.

RESEARCH BRIEF

STUDENTS WHO ARE GIFTED AND LEARNING DISABLED: WHAT DO WE KNOW?

Perhaps one of the most perplexing special populations is gifted and learning disabled—students who are gifted, but have a learning difficulty that inhibits academic achievement. In a comprehensive review of the literature on the gifted and learning disabled, Vaughn (1989) found a great deal of confusion over the definition of gifted and learning disabled. Coben and Vaughn (1994) updated the literature review and concluded that interventions for meeting the needs of gifted students with learning disabilities have not been systematically examined through research. Should these students be served in programs for the learning disabled, for the gifted, in both programs, or in programs especially designed for their needs?

Another group of particular interest to many general education teachers is that of high-achieving students who are not identified for special programs. Frequently, teachers will notice a child with extraordinary talents and abilities who may not, however, meet state or school district criteria to qualify for a special program. It becomes the general education teacher's responsibility to provide such children with the support, encouragement, and stimulation they need to feel productive and successful.

What determines the number of individuals in the student population who are identified as academically or creatively exceptional? What groups tend to be underidentified and why?

The predicament of how best to identify gift-edness among historically marginalized groups continues to perplex school districts throughout the United States. Similarly, research examining how best to provide programs for members of these populations is in its infancy. Therefore, it is imperative that classroom teachers not only keep abreast of current trends and developments, but also continue to recognize the special gifts and talents of all students and find opportunities to strengthen and develop those gifts in a nurturing classroom environment.

Identifying Students Who Are Gifted and Talented

The number of individuals in the population of students identified as either academically or creatively exceptional depends largely on which definition of giftedness is used to identify students for special services. Perhaps the simplest (and most restrictive) way of determining prevalence is through students' scores on standardized intelligence tests. With this approach, students who score highest on the test (roughly 3 to 5 percent) are identified for gifted education services (Davis & Rimm, 1989).

The United States Department of Education accumulates records of the number of students enrolled in both public and private schools across the nation. These records, which are compiled each year at the National Center for Educational Statistics, include the number of students participating in programs for the gifted and talented. As of August 1995, approximately 6 percent of the public school population and 5 percent of the private school population receive special services.

Some have argued that multiple measures of giftedness should be used, primarily because intelligence tests are inappropriate for students with cultural and linguistic differences and because such tests cannot gauge such areas as artistic talent and leadership skills. The **talent pool approach** developed by Renzulli and Reis (1991) is a frequently used procedure that represents this more inclusive point of view. Using both test and nontest criteria, 15 to 20 percent of the school population qualifies for special services. The broadened criteria included in the talent pool approach avoid the danger of overlooking students with exceptional talents and abilities who might not be identified solely through a single intelligence test or teacher nominations.

According to a survey of state educational consultants (Adderholdt-Elliot et al., 1991), most states currently employ multiple measures to identify students who are gifted and talented. These measures can include tests of individual and group academic prowess and creativity, as well as samples of student work. In addition, teachers (past and present), parents, peers, school counselors, and principals may also complete rating scales and checklists about the candidates (Davis & Rimm, 1989). These data sources typically are compiled and reviewed by a screening committee to determine eligibility, after which the results are discussed with the student's parents (Gearheart et al., 1993).

> The number of students receiving services as gifted or talented is second only to one other exceptionality—learning disabilities (Ysseldyke & Algozzine, 1990).

Although general education teachers generally are not responsible for determining a student's eligibility for gifted programs, teachers nonetheless play an important role in the identification process. What is the role of the general education teacher? Mike Hamasaki, a beginning fourth grade teacher, learned about his role in the identification process during the first open house of the school year. Mike describes it this way:

> Open house went really well. Parents of all but three of my students showed up. I especially enjoyed circulating around the room and talking with parents as they looked over their kid's work. My only trouble was that two different sets of parents cornered me. In both cases the parents thought that their children were bored and not challenged enough in my class. They wanted their children tested for giftedness. Their children are bright, but I'm not certain that they're "gifted." At least two other children in my class seem to have more outstanding vocabularies and catch on to new ideas more quickly. I'm not sure what the process is for getting them tested, but I promised the parents that I'd find out.

The next day, Mike met with the school guidance counselor, Maria Plaza, who provided an orientation to the school district's referral process. He learned that, in his district, nominations could be initiated by teachers or parents. In either case, he would be responsible for completing several checklists, providing examples of representative work, and attending a school-based referral meeting for each of the nominated students. Maria gave Mike a sample of the nomination form used by their school district (see Figure 12.2).

Maria Plaza also gave Mike the following suggestions:

■ *Realize that teachers are on the front line.* Parents frequently come to the teacher first. The parents of other children who could possibly qualify for special services may not speak out in their behalf. In such cases, it is the teacher's responsibility to document observations and initiate the referral. In fact, teacher nomination is the most frequent pathway to student referral (Davis & Rimm, 1991).

FIGURE 12.2

Nomination Form for Gifted Education

Student's Name _____   Grade _____

Teacher's Name _____   Date _____

1. In what areas do you feel this student has special talents or abilities?

2. What makes you feel that this student's educational needs are not being met in the general education classroom?

3. Has this student had any problems in your class as a result of high ability? Explain.

4. Describe briefly the student's work habits.

5. Rate the student's academic levels in various school subjects on a 1 to 5 scale (1 = low, 5 = high):

   Language Arts _____

   Math   _____

   Art   _____

   Music   _____

   Social Studies _____

   Science   _____

6. What is the student's most outstanding academic area? If possible, include sample of exceptional work.

7. What are the student's major interests, activities, and hobbies?

8. Describe this student's involvement in any special projects.

9. List any particular traits that you feel differentiate this student from others of the same age.

10. List any additional information about this student that you feel is relevant to potential placement in a gifted program.

- *Understand state and school district criteria.* Guidelines for qualification for programs for the gifted and talented differ from place to place. It is important to find out what the guidelines are and then to be constantly on the lookout for students who might meet those guidelines.
- *Document student behavior.* If you think one of your students has the potential to qualify for special services, gather information to document your impressions. Documentation can include samples of student work and anecdotal records of student performance in class. Present the documentation to the person responsible at your school for initiating the referral process.
- *Go beyond academic performance.* Your state and school district definition of giftedness and identification criteria provide structure for observing your students. Nonetheless, in considering students for referral, do not limit yourself to grades and achievement test scores. Traditional measures of performance may not be sensitive to the potential of students who are culturally different, who have not had the experiential and economic advantages of other students, or who are not motivated to complete tasks that seem boring or repetitive. Develop a sensitivity to students who think critically and creatively, have powerful concentration, and who have large vocabularies.
- *Listen to parents.* Parents have the opportunity to observe their children in environments other than the classroom. They see their children during play and in community-related activities, and witness involvement in academic and creative activities beyond the more restrictive setting of the classroom. The information parents gather about their children is information that may not be readily apparent to the classroom teacher, and is extraordinarily valuable in the referral process. A common myth—that *all* parents think their children are gifted and entitled to special services—is not the case (Feldhusen et al.). Many parents do take action, however, when they feel the school is not meeting the educational needs of their child (Feldhusen et al., 1989).
- *Understand the politics.* Identification of students for programs for the gifted and talented is not without controversy. Some argue that identification procedures are elitist and favor teachers' children or the children of parents in a position of power in the community. Some say that identification procedures are biased toward students from minority populations, yet others contend that minority students are underrepresented. It is important that you understand the politics involved, but that you do not let the politics inhibit your judgment about what is fair and appropriate for your students.

Mike's situation is not unusual. Frequently, teachers learn about the referral process only when the need arises, and often need to network with other professionals to learn what to do and how to do it. As you might expect, the referral process for gifted and talented students varies from state to state and even from district to district within a state. Tips for Teachers 12.1 outlines generic steps in the referral process.

Programs for Students Who Are Gifted and Talented

As discussed earlier, individual states and school districts vary tremendously in their policies toward education of gifted individuals. Similarly, individual states and school districts offer a wide array of service delivery models for education of these students. Although there are many possible combinations and variations, programs can be classified by approach to the content of instruction and by administrative arrangement (Hallahan & Kauffman, 1991).

Approaches to Content of Instruction

As you may recall, the earliest procedure for educating gifted students was to accelerate them quickly through the grades. Since those early years, gifted education programs in the United States have varied in their emphasis on acceleration or enrichment. In some cases, programs in general education have elected to incorporate elements of both. Research concerning effective practices with

TIPS FOR TEACHERS

12.1 Referral Process for Gifted and Talented

The referral process for gifted and talented will vary among states and communities, but, in general, these are the steps taken to qualify a student for a program.

Screening: The process of screening is the initial identification of students who demonstrate unusual ability. Students can be screened using one or more of the following criteria.

- academic achievement, as indicated by standardized test scores or course-work grades
- unusual creative output in artistic, literary, scientific, or mathematic endeavors
- very rapid learning rate or unusually insightful conclusions
- multiple nominations from teachers or staff who perceive unusual talent
- parental reports of unusual developmental behavior, such as early reading and verbal precocity or evidence of mechanical aptitude
- outstanding academic, creative, or leadership abilities—self-reported or reported by peers or adults

Referral: school contact person or guidance counselor submits referrals to the district office responsible for Exceptional Student Education. The following items usually are submitted as part of the referral packet:

- standardized test scores
- copy of academic transcript
- referral forms or checklists
- student questionnaire providing information on nonacademic performance

After the completed referrals are submitted to the district teacher or advisor coordinating the program, the district arranges for psychological evaluation of the student.

Determining Eligibility: if district criteria are met, the student is recommended for placement and an Education Plan is developed.

Source: Jeanne Bergeron, University of Miami.

---

gifted and talented students (Coleman & Gallagher, 1995; Ormrod, 1995; Van Tassel-Baska, 1992) corresponds with the strategies Lawanzer Ellis uses in her general education classroom. Lawanzer's class is an appropriate learning environment for all students, including those who are gifted and talented. Lawanzer's approach to teaching is as a facilitator of learning, rather than a disseminator of knowledge. She extends learning beyond the textbook and insists on high standards for everyone in her class, including herself. She also realizes that excellence for all students does not necessarily mean that all students are doing the same thing. Her ideas for classroom strategies and adaptations are provided in Tips for Teachers 12.2.

Acceleration Gallagher and Gallagher (1994) make a distinction between two types of acceleration. **Student acceleration** is the rapid movement of students through their years of schooling. An

example of this type of acceleration is the 16-year-old who's been admitted to medical school. Student acceleration can be accomplished through home schooling, grade skipping, college courses in high school, or early admission to college.

Content acceleration, on the other hand, is the practice of rapid movement through the curriculum, "to speed up the delivery of content, to deliver more content, to examine content in greater depth, or to deal with more complex and higher levels of subject matter" (Feldhusen et al., 1989, p. 106). An example of content acceleration is a fifth grade student learning introductory algebra in a fifth grade class. In short, content acceleration is the process of providing students with advanced work beyond their current grade placement or age.

Enrichment The intent of enrichment programs is to provide students with supplementary learning opportunities that help them branch beyond the

TIPS FOR TEACHERS

12.2 Classroom Strategies and Adaptations for Gifted Students

Research concerning effective practices with gifted and talented students (Coleman & Gallagher, 1995; Ormrod, 1995; Van Tassel-Baska, 1992) corresponds with the strategies that Lawanzer Ellis uses in her general education classroom. Lawanzer's class is an appropriate learning environment for all students, including those who are gifted and talented. Lawanzer's approach to teaching is as a facilitator of learning, rather than a disseminator of knowledge. She extends learning beyond the textbook and insists on high standards for everyone in her class, including herself. She also realizes that excellence for all students does not necessarily mean all students are doing the same thing.

Several strategies and adaptations are incorporated into the daily activities to ensure that all students maximize their potential. The strategies that Lawanzer uses include:

- an exploratory, interdisciplinary curriculum
- emphasis on thinking strategies, problem-solving, creative solutions, and decision-making within the context of specific subject areas
- open-ended, self-paced assignments
- students set their own high, yet realistic, outcomes for assignments that vary in complexity for each student
- centers, where students select topics and work together on projects that require several types or levels of skills
- interest-group assignments that enable gifted students to work together
- use of outside resources to help students develop their talents

Source: Jeanne Bergeron, University of Miami.

---

basic curriculum presented in the general classroom. Enrichment activities offer students the opportunity to explore topics in depth or breadth and can include extended reading, creative research and art projects, community service projects, and field trips. For example, if your class is studying the environment, gifted students might be assigned enrichment activities such as writing poetry about the environment, developing position statements about environmental policies, or planning a service project for cleaning debris from a local river bank.

Administrative Arrangements

School districts throughout the nation have devised a full range of administrative arrangements for the education of the gifted and talented. As a general education teacher, you may be involved in referring students for participation in a variety of special programs, as well as in planning collaboratively with other professionals when the students you teach are placed in gifted programs housed in your school. The general administrative arrangements for programs are resource, self-contained, and inclusion.

Resource Programs In *resource programs,* students are grouped homogeneously with other gifted and talented students for part of their educational program. The most frequently used resource model at the elementary level is the pull-out program, in which students are "pulled out" of the general education program for several hours, usually once or twice per week, for special services. In some elementary schools, pull-out services are provided at the individual school site by a resident teacher of the gifted. In some cases an itinerant teacher services a number of elementary schools, whereas in other cases students from several schools are transported to a gifted center for the resource program.

Resource programs at the elementary and secondary level can also include weekend, after-school,

TECH TALK

High-Tech Alternatives for Gifted Learners

Gifted students need access to contemporary tools that bring incredible amounts of information to their fingertips in an instant (Trotter, 1991). Emerging technologies include personal computers, CD-ROM, super-computers, laser disc players, and telecommunications networks. Interactive videodiscs, such as *The National Gallery of Art* (Voyager Company, 1-800-446-2001), can bring the world of art to your students. Access to online services such as America Online (1-800-227-6364) and Prodigy (1-800-284-5933) can help students retrieve information and communicate with others through the Internet.

Technology allows gifted students to increase their productivity. Using computers, students can do more work in a given amount of time (Morgan, 1993). Students can use the time saved to do more involved research into topics of interest. Ways to incorporate productivity tools into gifted programs include using CD-ROMs for literature searches and developing multimedia presentations for school (Morgan, 1993).

With another technological advance—telecommunications—students in a social studies class, for example, can communicate with other students from around the world (Morgan, 1993). Gifted and talented students

need to feel comfortable communicating through worldwide networks to be prepared for the future.

Gifted students can use graphing calculators and equation-processing software to take care of many mathematical calculations. These tools allow students to think more about mathematical concepts than procedures (Morgan, 1993).

By using new technologies, all learners, including gifted students, can take a creative, active role in their education, stretching beyond the walls of the classroom.

---

and summer programs for gifted and talented students. Workshops, institutes, and individualized mentoring or supervised independent study programs may be sponsored by local or state educational agencies and are frequently centered around a particular theme or academic or artistic area.

Self-Contained Programs *Self-contained programs* are those in which homogenous groups of gifted and talented students receive all their instruction. In some areas of the country, individual elementary schools place students who have been identified for special services in a self-contained class for gifted students. At the secondary level, gifted students are placed in an honors track and assigned to classes composed primarily of children with exceptional academic abilities. Many

large school districts designate specific elementary and secondary schools as centers (or **magnet schools**) for the education of gifted and talented students. Students from throughout the district who are identified as gifted or talented are assigned to the target school, which frequently focuses on a theme (such as performing arts or particular academic subjects). In a few states, gifted and talented high school students are invited to attend full-time residential programs at sites that are much like college campuses (Kollott, 1991, in press).

Inclusion Programs Many states and school districts have inclusionary models in which children of all achievement levels are educated in heterogeneous general education classrooms. Inclusion programs may be instituted by default (lack of funding for special programs) or by design (a recognition of the benefits, for all students, of learning in mixed-ability groups). *Inclusion by default* is simply the placement of gifted and talented students in general education classrooms, with no systematic plan for attending to their special needs or for helping teachers with ways to develop expertise in working effectively with these students. *Inclusion by design* represents a comprehensive district wide or school-wide effort to meet the needs of gifted and talented students in general education settings. In such cases, general education teachers may receive extra training through professional development workshops, are assisted with their planning through collaboration with a gifted education specialist, and may co-teach with a gifted education specialist in the general education classroom for all or part of the school day.

Another approach to inclusionary schooling is the **Schoolwide Enrichment Model**, in which a large portion of the school population is given the opportunity to participate in enrichment activities (Olenckak & Renzulli, 1989; Renzulli & Reis, 1991). School personnel engage in ongoing assessment of student abilities, interests, and needs to identify individual "talent pool" students who would profit by engaging in more advanced independent research and art enrichment activities. This pool includes up to 15 percent more students than would normally be serviced by gifted programs (Renzulli & Reis, 1991). Enrichment activities include research projects, learning study and research skills, individual and small-group problem solving, and communication skills (Renzulli & Reis, 1991). When appropriate, these activities are incorporated into the general education curriculum. As you might expect, staff development is necessary to get the Schoolwide Enrichment Model up and running, which also requires ongoing attention to program implementation and evaluation by a Schoolwide Enrichment Team.

Instructional Guidelines and Accommodations for Students Who Are Gifted and Talented

The suggestions in this section are frequently recommended for teaching gifted and talented students and other high-achieving students in general education settings. Keep in mind that this group of students is diverse, and that deciding on the most appropriate instruction is complicated. Moreover, your class is likely to include students who have not been formally identified as gifted, talented, creative, or high achieving but who may benefit from the instructional practices described here. As a classroom teacher, you need to get to know the traits and needs of each of your students so that you can make instructional decisions.

Planning

Without careful planning for students who need to be challenged, instruction can become random and stress producing. Imagine having to think up activities to keep a student busy whenever he or she finished an assignment early. Quite frankly, you'd be exhausted and the student would not receive the benefits of a well-structured, well-conceptualized instructional plan. Planning takes time, but ultimately avoids hassle!

At the beginning of the school year, work with the parents, the student (and the gifted education teacher, if applicable) to set long-range goals. These can be either acceleration or enrichment goals, depending on the needs and interests of the student. Work collaboratively to determine how these goals will be met: determine activities, structure a time for completing activities, and agree on a system for evaluating work and reporting to parents. Include guidelines for handing in assignments, doing independent projects, and for work habits when completing in-class enrichment or acceleration activities. The consequences for not following the guidelines should be clear and enforced consistently.

One of the most common problems in elementary programs is the issue of making up work covered in the general education classroom while gifted students are pulled out into resource programs.

Similar problems can arise in secondary programs when students enrolled in gifted programs are involved in extended field trips or other activities that cause them to miss general education classes. Be sure to include in your long-range planning a system for making up work assigned while students are out of your room. For example, you might provide all students with homework and class assignments on a handout at the beginning of each week.

Using the Planning Pyramid as a framework for your unit and lesson planning can be particularly helpful as you think about students who are gifted and talented. As you plan a unit or lesson, think about enrichment and acceleration activities for the top of the Pyramid—"What a few students will learn." These activities may be appropriate not only for students who are gifted, talented, or high achieving, but also for other students in your class who want to stretch with a topic.

In your weekly planning, include activities for what to do when there's nothing to do. In other words, plan meaningful learning tasks for all students who finish their work early. At the beginning of each week, communicate your plan to your students. Many students who excel academically will finish their work early, and you need to be prepared for this. The activities can be related to what you have planned from the top of the Pyramid, and can also focus on holidays, birthdays of famous individuals, and historical events. Also, make certain that students always have a library book for personal reading, as well as writing projects in progress that they can work on between other activities.

> Curriculum compacting strategies include allowing students to identify content they already know or to "test out" of a unit and move on to more advanced or more in-depth materials for that unit.

Sometimes students are reluctant to complete additional activities because they are "just extra work" or because they "don't count for a grade." When assignments are purposeful, meaningful, and challenging, these complaints are likely to diminish. Moreover, teachers whose classrooms are productive workplaces expect students to be actively engaged in learning tasks.

Assessing Prior Knowledge

Some of your students will have exceptionally large vocabularies, a wide information base, and will remember skills and concepts taught in previous grades. When appropriate, pretests or mastery tests can be used to permit students to "test out" of previously learned material (Treffinger, 1982). Pretests can be administered to the whole class or to volunteers willing to take the risk to test out.

One way to assess prior knowledge (a way that takes little preplanning) is "most difficult first" (Winebrenner, 1992). In a list of tasks organized by relative difficulty, identify the most difficult tasks and have students who are willing to take the challenge do them first. Allow students who demonstrate mastery to go on to a self-selected task. Students who are gifted or high achieving frequently get bored with undue repetition and practice. "Most difficult first" can help circumvent this problem.

Renzulli, Smith, and Reis (1982) suggest that general education teachers work cooperatively with teachers in gifted programs to "compact" the general education curriculum for gifted students. **Curriculum compacting** provides students with the opportunity to demonstrate what they already know about a subject. Teachers can then eliminate content that is repetitive or review for students, replacing it with advanced learning experiences.

Promoting Inquiry and Independent Learning

Many students like—and indeed crave—**independent learning**. Students who learn how to work independently not only gain a great deal of knowledge and personal satisfaction by exploring topics in breadth and depth, but also develop strategies for inquiry and knowledge acquisition that will help them become lifelong learners.

Winebrenner (1992) offered some general procedural tips for teachers and students working on individual activities. Specific planning for independent learning can be tricky, and should include behavioral guidelines for students (see Tips for Teachers 12.3). Also worth noting are routines some general education teachers have found effective for independent learning.

Gail Hargrave, a third grade teacher, has found that several of her students need to work ahead in mathematics. With the help of a self-management sheet (see Figure 12.3), Gail structures independent activities to promote acceleration through the curriculum. This self-pacing of instruction allows students to move ahead independently, but also makes provisions for instructional episodes as well.

Fifth grade teacher Marina Alvarez likes to provide her students with opportunities for more extensive independent library and scientific

TIPS FOR TEACHERS

12.3 Working Conditions for Alternative Activities

1. Stay "on task" at all times with the alternative activities you have chosen.
2. Don't interrupt the teacher while he or she is teaching.
3. When you need help, and the teacher is busy, ask someone else who is also working on the alternative activities.
4. If no one else can help you, continue to try the activity yourself until the teacher is available, or move on to another activity until the teacher is free.
5. Use "6-inch voices" (voices that can be heard no more than six inches away) for talking to each other about the alternative activities.

6. Never brag about your opportunities to work on the alternative activities.
7. If you must go in and out of the room, do so soundlessly.
8. If you are going to work in another location, stay on task there, and follow the directions of the adult in charge.
9. Don't bother anyone else.
10. Don't call attention to yourself.

Source: Winebrenner, S. (1992). *Teaching gifted kids in the regular classroom*. Minneapolis: Free Spirit Publishing.

research, or art projects for independent study. Marina's experience with such projects has taught her that students should be held accountable for a product and should have the opportunity to share their product with an audience (either peers or an audience beyond the classroom). She has also learned that although some students are able to set personal goals and accomplish tasks

---

FIGURE 12.3

Self-Management Sheet

Student's Name <u>Manny Garcia</u>   Grade <u>3</u>

Teacher's Name <u>Gail Hargrave</u>   Date <u>03/22/96</u>

Textbook: Mathematics and You

Page	Instructions	Complete	Required Correct	If Not
98	Read Sec. A	Evens 2–22	9	Odds 1–21
100	See teacher	Evens 2–16	6	Odds 1–15
101	Read Carefully	10–15	4	1–9

---

autonomously, others need more guidance and structure, especially with particularly ambitious projects. Marina uses a project planning sheet (see Figure 12.4) and research paper checklist (see Figure 12.5) as formats for initiating planning of independent projects.

Teaching Thinking Skills

Throughout the school day, opportunities exist for teaching students processes for thinking. Here's an example. Lawanzer Ellis (the teacher interviewed at the beginning of the chapter) was annoyed that

---

MAKING A DIFFERENCE

The 60-Second Lesson

Instant Enrichment

During Writer's Workshop in her fourth grade class, Lawanzer Ellis is giving a whole-class lesson on how to edit. As she explains how writing is marked for deletion, insertion, paragraph indentation, and the like, she writes some symbols and examples on the board. Lawanzer mentions that even authors of books and magazine articles have their work improved through the help of professional editors, and that professional editors use similar marks. Robert, an intellectually gifted high achiever who is very interested in creative writing, looks up from the limerick he has been drafting. On his own he has already practiced applying carets to insert words in his poem. Now he wants to know more about editorial marks and the work of professional editors. Lawanzer acknowledges him before his urgent arm waving and enthusiastic bouncing-in-place disrupt the lesson.

Robert: Are the ways you are showing us to edit our work the same as professional editors?

Lawanzer: Professional editors have a much more complex system for marking changes. We're just looking at a few of the most common ways.

Robert points to the symbols on the board.

Robert: Are those the right ones? How many marks are there? Is there a mark for every kind of change you could think of?

Lawanzer: I don't know.

Robert: Does everyone use the same marks? In that case it would be like a language. Is it like the periodic table? Everyone in the whole world knows that He stands for Helium.

Lawanzer heads for the reference dictionary. Other students are beginning to respond to Robert with

groans and stray remarks ("What's a periodic table?" "That's what we need here—helium, for balloons.") Lawanzer knows the dictionary has a page on editors' and proofreaders' marks.

Lawanzer: Class, let's think about what Robert said just now. If all professional editors everywhere used the same marks for editing, would that be like a language?

Some students answer yes, others no, but small discussions start up in the room. To students answering yes, Lawanzer asks, "Why?" To those answering no, she asks, "Why not?" Meanwhile, she places the dictionary on Robert's desk and speaks quietly to him, one-on-one:

Lawanzer: I think you'll find the answers to some of your questions in here, Robert. I see you're already using editorial marks in your poetry—good for you. I wonder if you would mind preparing a poster that shows *all* the editorial marks, for students who are interested. We could keep it in the Writing Workshop.

Lawanzer moves back to the front of the class, leaving Robert dazzled with possibilities and therefore temporarily content. She calls on students to answer Robert's question, accepts the first answer suggesting that editorial marks are like a language for editors, and moves on. Amazingly, only a minute has passed, but she has managed to take advantage of an opportunity to provide enrichment for both Robert and his classmates while still accomplishing her instructional goals. She has ideas for following up with Robert, such as helping him set up communication with a professional editor on the Internet.

FIGURE 12.4

Project Planning Sheet

---

1. Decide on a project theme.　　　　　　　　　**Date Done** _____

2. Have the theme approved by your teacher.　　**Date Done** _____

Theme: _____

3. Make a list of things you need to do to complete your project. Rank them in the order they should be completed.

    Will Need Help With:　　　　　　　　　　**Who Will Help Me:**

4. Set deadlines for finishing each part of your project. Write the deadline dates on your calendar.

    Task　　　　　　　**Date Due**　　　　**Date Done**　　　　**Person Responsible**

5. Make a list of materials you will need. Estimate how much they will cost.

    Item　　　　　　　　　　　　　　　　**Cost**

6. Send away for resource materials.

    Resource Material　　　　　　　　　　**Date Requested**　　**Date Received**

7. Contact community resources.

    Community Resource　　　　　　　　　**Date Contacted**　　**Result(s)**

8. Visit the library.

    Purpose of Visit　　　　　　　　　　　**Date of Visit**

9. Complete your project on schedule.

    Date Turned In: _____　　　　**Grade:** _____

Source: Schumm, J. S., & Radencich, M. (1992). *School power.* Minneapolis: Free Spirit Publishing.

FIGURE 12.5

Research Paper Checklist

Assignment: To write a term paper on _____

Due Date: _____

Requirements:

My paper will need: It should be:

_____ title page   _____ typed

_____ table of contents   _____ doublespaced

_____ bibliography   _____ handwritten OK.

_____ graphics

What kind of graphics? _____

Steps	Date Due	Date Done
_____ 1. Choose a topic.	_____	_____
_____ 2. Write a thesis sentence. Have it approved by the teacher.	_____	_____
_____ 3. Do library research. *Sources:*	_____	_____
_____ 4. Contact community resources for information. *Names of resources:*	_____	_____
_____ 5. Write letter to request information from national sources. *Wrote letter to:*	_____	_____
_____ 6. Take notes. *Took notes from these sources:*	_____	_____
_____ 7. Make a writing plan.	_____	_____
_____ 8. Write a rough draft.	_____	_____
_____ 9. Revise and edit rough draft; make corrections.	_____	_____
_____ 10. Write the final draft.	_____	_____
_____ 11. Turn the final draft in on time.	_____	_____

Source: Schumm, J. S.., & Radencich, M. (1992). *School power.* Minneapolis: Free Spirit Publishing.

her students were writing on their desks—essentially defacing school property. She presented the problem to the class (including a discussion about school property and how that property was funded through local taxes) and asked them to brainstorm about the situation. The discussion continued, addressing issues related to graffiti and litter on public building and highways.

After some deliberation, the class came up with a solution—to put a strip of wide masking tape around the perimeter of their desks, and write on the tape, not on the desk itself. The students further refined their idea, deciding to call the strips of tape "reference borders" and to use these borders to record frequently misspelled words and ideas that students wanted to remember. Soon realizing that the reference borders could serve as opportunities to cheat on tests, the students set up class rules for use and misuse of reference borders. The ideas worked! There was a real problem, and the class worked together to solve it.

It is important that you, as a teacher, structure activities that help students get beyond simple memorization of facts or mastery of skills, enabling them to think critically and creatively, and helping them identify and solve problems. Thinking skills are important for all students. We live in an information age. All students must learn how to access information, evaluate it, and make decisions about or act upon that information. Students must also have opportunities to create new products, come up with fresh ideas, and synthesize the ideas of others in an innovative way. For students with excep-

tional talent for higher level thinking, this aspect of education is vital (Davis & Rimm, 1989).

As Lawanzer's experience indicates, thinking skills can be taught indirectly. Throughout the school day and in all subject areas, you can initiate critical thinking and problem solving related to subject matter or to issues in and beyond the classroom. You can also increase students' awareness of and appreciation for creative people and creative ideas by talking about them and—most important—by involving students in creative activities.

In recent years, emphasis on thinking and problem-solving skills has increased. Although a detailed description of curriculum in this area is beyond the scope of this chapter, Table 12.1 lists the components typically included in a thinking skills curriculum.

You can teach these skills directly, using a curriculum specifically designed to focus on creative or critical thinking or problem solving. (For information about a number of commercial thinking skills programs, see the Read More About It section of this chapter.) In selecting a commercial program, you may want to consider the following:

- make certain that you have adequate training for implementing the program
- evaluate whether the program is attractive, enjoyable, and appropriate for your students
- determine whether the skills taught seem applicable to real-life situations
- decide whether the program's content seems worthwhile in light of everything you need to teach during the school year

Adapting Assessment for Gifted Learners

There is a great deal of pressure on gifted students to earn good grades for all their work, but the criteria used to assign grades to gifted students are often unclear. Often, students are not only given a more rigorous curriculum as part of a gifted program, but also evaluated by a more rigorous grading system. This may cause gifted students to resent their participation in advanced work, and they may request to be excused from such assignments. They may not see the advantages of working harder on extra assignments for the grades they receive (Hoctor & Kaplan, 1989). Tips for

Why might this and similar activities engage a student who is gifted? What kinds of instructional strategies and learning activities can be vital to students with exceptional talent for higher-level thinking?

TABLE 12.1

List of Core Thinking Skills

Skill	Description
Analyzing	Examining the parts of an idea or task, organizing the parts and seeing relationships among the parts
Synthesizing	The process of creating a new thought, idea, or product after analysis
Evaluating	Judging a thought, idea, or product by subjecting it to a set of predetermined criteria
Recalling	Remembering specific words, facts, or other information after sensory input
Translating	Transforming information coming in through the senses into one's own words
Interpreting	Recognizing and giving meaning to information (thoughts, ideas, concepts, etc.)
Extrapolating	Using present or past information, experiences, and so on to predict future or sequential events
Applying Information	Using information to accomplish a task, solve a problem, or create additional or new knowledge
Classifying	Categorizing and labeling objects, ideas, phenomena, and so on, according to similar characteristics; the ability to differentiate examples from nonexamples
Defining	Identifying words, phrases, or expressions that connote the essential nature of a person, thing, and so on
Describing	Using words or graphic symbols to express the characteristics of a given thing or experience
Identifying the Main Idea	Deciding the central theme or notion presented by or connected with a given experience or story line, speech, or paragraph
Drawing Conclusions	Deciding on an appropriate consequence or reasoned judgment based upon prior examination of one or more related propositions taken as premises
Identifying	Examining characteristics of an object, idea, phenomenon, recognizing which label best fits the datum, and so labeling it
Justifying	Using facts, principles, theories, passages, to support one's answers or ideas
Recalling Details	Remembering specific facts, words, information
Seeing Relationships	Recognizing how one variable or set of variables is related to others
Sequencing	Recognizing the chronology of happenings, operations, and so on
Explaining	Using words, concepts, or other information to make an idea clear and understandable
Summarizing	Covering the main points of an idea in a presentation, article, speech, and so on
Imagining	Forming a mental picture of something not presently available to the senses
Cause and Effect	Recognizing how one or more variables has a direct or indirect effect upon other variables
Inferring	Making logical guesses; concluding from examination of ideas or relationships among things, experiences, and so on
Comparing	Identifying similarities between two or more things
Contrasting	Identifying differences between two or more things
Elaborating	Expanding on an idea by adding details, examples, or relevant information
Hypothesizing	A formal prediction based on reference to facts and other information
Observing	Noticing the attributes of things

Source: Hannemann, C. (1995). List of thinking skills. Unpublished manuscript.

TIPS FOR TEACHERS

12.4 Grading Strategies for Gifted Students

1. Formally evaluate grade-level assignments but not enrichment activity products. Treat enrichment activities as opportunities to explore personal interests.
2. Give credit for learning behavior associated with an enrichment activity, such as staying on task, adhering to alternative working condition rules, persisting with frustrating tasks, or sharing what was learned with classmates.
3. Provide incentives for undertaking more challenging learning tasks on a contractual basis by offering an automatic high minimum grade if the terms of the contract are met.
4. Use alternative holistic methods of assessment that include student's self-evaluation on the basis of predetermined criteria.

Teachers 12.4 suggests effective grading strategies for gifted students (Winebrenner, 1992).

One suggestion for avoiding these negative feelings is to formally evaluate students on grade-level assignments only. Enrichment activities should not be graded at all; they should serve as an opportunity for students to explore topics of interest and share what they have learned with their classmates (Winebrenner, 1992). If a student wants credit for an enrichment activity, "credit may be earned staying on task with alternate activities, adhering to the working conditions, persisting with frustrating tasks, or sharing what was learned with the class" (Winebrenner, 1992, p. 112). Another grading strategy for gifted students is to give them an incentive to participate in more challenging tasks—e.g., telling them that "the lowest

grade their work can earn is a 'B,' assuming that they complete the terms of the contract they negotiate with the teacher" (Winebrenner, 1992, p. 112). Teachers can also use alternative or holistic methods of assessment, leading students to develop the ability to evaluate their own work according to a set of predetermined criteria. The teacher can discuss with students the objectives they must meet in an assignment in order to earn a B, and those required to earn an A.

Research has shown that some parents of gifted students feel that they had *not* received adequate information regarding the standards used to determine their children's grades (Collins & Goldinher, 1984). Whatever grading methods you decide upon, it is important to discuss your rationale for grading with the parents.

SUMMARY

- The history of education for gifted and talented students can be divided into two periods: pre- and post-*Sputnik*. The Soviet launch of *Sputnik* accelerated interest in special programs for students with extraordinary abilities. Since that time, interest in education for the gifted and talented has waxed and waned, and controversy about the nature of

- special services and who should receive those services continue.
- The way in which students are identified for special services for the gifted or talent depends largely on the definition used and the measures employed, consistent with the definition.
- Definitions have varied throughout the history of gifted education in the United States,

and continue to differ from state to state and even school district to school district.

- Not all students identified as gifted or talented exhibit the same characteristics—a wide range of extraordinary characteristics exists, with marked individual differences in respect to physical, academic, social, and behavioral traits.
- Planning for students who are high achieving, gifted, and talented should include both acceleration activities (i.e., opportunities to advance through the curriculum at an appropriate rate) and enrichment activities (e.g., experiments, independent projects, field trips).
- Administrative arrangements for gifted and talented students include resource programs, self-contained programs, and inclusion programs.
- As a classroom teacher, your responsibilities toward students who are gifted and talented lie primarily in referral and in providing adequate instruction for such students in your classroom.
- Typical instructional suggestions for gifted, talented, and high-achieving students include assessing prior knowledge, promoting inquiry and independent learning, and teaching thinking skills.
- Adaptations in pacing of instruction, curriculum, and assessment may be necessary for students who are gifted, talented, or high achieving.

Key Terms and Concepts

acceleration
creatively gifted or talented
content acceleration
curriculum compacting
enrichment
giftedness

independent learning
intellectually gifted
invisible gifted
magnet schools
mentorship
multidimensional traits

multiple intelligences
Schoolwide Enrichment Model
student acceleration
talent pool approach
underachievers
unidimensional traits

Think and Apply

1. Now that you have read Chapter 12, review Lawanzer's list of critical factors for a successful classroom. What other factors might you add to this list, particularly as you consider how to meet the needs of gifted, talented, and high-achieving students?
2. Interview a teacher of the gifted in your school district. Ask about state and school-district definitions of gifted and talented, identification and assessment procedures, and predominant service-delivery models.
3. You have read about enrichment and acceleration approaches to gifted education. What do you think are the pros and cons of each? Be

prepared to discuss the pros and cons with your classmates.
4. Using the Unit Planning Pyramid form, plan a unit that you are going to teach and include acceleration opportunities for students who have mastered the material previously.
5. Using the Lesson Planning Pyramid form, plan a lesson that you are going to teach to provide enrichment opportunities for students who need to expand their understanding of the topic.
6. Develop a list of meaningful, engaging activities that students who finish early can accomplish. Include a system for keeping students accountable for their work.

7. Work with a fellow student to role-play the following situation: an irate parent calls a conference with you. The parent's complaint is that his child is bored and is simply not getting enough academic stimulation in your class. What is your response?

8. Contact the following organizations to find out what services they provide for parents and teachers of students who are gifted and talented, and for students themselves:

American Association for Gifted Children (AAGC)
P.O. Box 40077, Durham, NC 27706-007

The Association for the Gifted (TAG).
A Division of The Council for Exceptional Children
1920 Association Drive, Reston, VA 20091

Association for Gifted and Talented Students (AGTS)
Northwestern State University
Natchitoches, LA 71302

National Association for Gifted Children
1155 15th Street N.W., Washington, D.C. 20005

Read More about It

1. Chaffee, J. (1987). *Thinking critically.* Boston: Houghton-Mifflin.

   Describes methods of teaching students to think critically, with particular emphasis on applying problem-solving skills to real-life situations.

2. Colangelo, N., & Davis, G. A. (1991). *Handbook of gifted education.* Boston: Allyn & Bacon.

   In this book, designed primarily as a "scholarly handbook," with chapters written by thirty-seven experts in the field of gifted education, the sections on instructional models and practices, and creativity and thinking skills are of particular interest to practitioners.

3. DeBono, E. (1986). *CoRT thinking teacher's notes.* New York: Pergamon Press.

   Describes *CoRT* (Cognitive Research Trust), a system for direct teaching of thinking skills in gifted or general education classrooms. Includes lessons in three areas: basic thinking skills, creative thinking, and critical and interactive thinking.

4. Gallagher, J. J., & Gallagher, S. A. (1994). *Teaching the gifted child* (4th ed.). Boston: Allyn & Bacon.

   This comprehensive book provides detailed information about curriculum and instruction for gifted and talented students, including specific suggestions for modifying content in mathematics, science, social studies, language arts, and visual and performing arts.

5. Gardner, H. (1985). *Frames of mind.* New York: Basic Books.

   Presentation of Gardner's theory of multiple intelligence. Includes a description of the seven types of intelligence, as well as an introduction to applications of this model.

6. Hannemann, C. E., & Potter, R. L. (1993). Brainstorm 1000, 2000, 3000: *Cooperative learning case studies in critical thinking.* Austin, TX: Steck-Vaughn.

   A curriculum for direct teaching of critical thinking skills for middle school students. Combines teaching of critical thinking with cooperative learning.

7. Micklus, S. (1986). *OM program handbook.* Glassboro, NJ: OM Association.

   Describes the *Odyssey of the Mind*, a creative problem-solving program for students in grades K–12 that emphasizes teamwork and communication skills as students work collaboratively to solve short- and long-term problems.

8. Parker, B. N. (1989). *Gifted students in regular classrooms.* Boston: Allyn & Bacon.

   Contains practical suggestions for adjusting the pace and varying the depth of learning, accommodating interests, and modifying the curriculum. Includes suggestions for program planning and classroom management as they pertain to students who are gifted and talented.

9. Schmitz, C. C., & Galbraith, J. (1985). *Managing the social and emotional needs of the gifted.* Minneapolis: Free Spirit.

   A practical guide to coping positively, for teachers and parents of gifted students.

10. Winebrenner, S. (1992). *Teaching gifted kids in the regular classroom.* Minneapolis: Free Spirit Publishing.

    This compact book provides numerous practice suggestions for general education teachers. The forms for learning contracts and suggestions for classroom activities are particularly helpful.

THIRTEEN

Facilitating Reading

FOCUS QUESTIONS

1. What are current trends and issues in reading curriculum and instruction, and how might they impact your planning for reading instruction in your classroom?

2. What is the reading process, and what learning difficulties in the reading process are you likely to encounter among the students you teach?

3. What are principles of effective reading instruction for all learners?

4. What specific strategies can you implement for students who have difficulty with phonological awareness and word recognition?

5. What are some activities you can use to help your students become more fluent readers?

6. What strategies can you use to help improve students' comprehension before, during, and after they read?

nterview

Ines Lezcano

Ines Lezcano is a third grade teacher at Flamingo Elementary School in Miami, Florida. Of the thirty-one students in her inclusion classroom, four are children with *learning disabilities* (LD) and are in her class full-time. Ines works with the special education teacher, Joyce Duryea, to plan for the reading and writing instruction of these four students. Joyce, whose responsibilities are to co-teach lessons and to make necessary adaptations for the students with LD, comes to Ines's class each day during the reading and language arts block.

Ines considers herself to be a whole-language teacher (defined and described later in this chapter). Her undergraduate training focused on whole language and her principal has encouraged teachers to implement whole language. Ines uses the school district curriculum guide to plan her reading program. She uses a basal reader from time to time, but only as one set of materials in addition to different trade books, magazines, and so on. Ines talks about ways in which her reading program meets the needs of special learners.

> I've been teaching in an inclusion classroom for two years now. Even though I received a lot of support from Joyce, I was still concerned about whether or not the academic needs of the students with learning disabilities could be met in my classroom. What I've learned is that it can be done, but I've had to rethink my teaching style—especially for reading. There are a few of my students who have reading skills that are far below the other students in my class. I keep on having to think, "How can I meet their needs and still keep things going for everyone else in the classroom?" I've figured out how to do this through multilevel activities and adaptations during regular activities.
>
> Multilevel activities are just great. They are activities that all of my students can plug into—whatever their skill level in reading. They are

activities designed so that everyone can learn and everyone can succeed. My favorite multilevel activity is Classwide Peer Tutoring. During Classwide Peer Tutoring everyone is reading to a partner. I like it because the students really get involved and learn how to give each other help with their reading.

Some assignments that I give in class are for the whole class—I can't individualize or include multilevel activities all the time. When I do give whole-class assignments in reading that I think are going to be hard for the students with reading problems, that's when I have to plan for adaptations. For example, sometimes we read a story from the basal reader. I have a listening station set up in my room so that my lowest readers can listen to an audiotape of the story. The audiotapes are made by volunteer readers from the sixth grade class. It's important to try to keep in mind how to give kids the support they need to do well.

Most of my students are pretty solid with their word-recognition skills, but [I] do have a few that need intensive instruction in sight words and phonics. I can hit these areas through multilevel activities such as Word Wall and Making Words, but some kids just need more. Joyce typically meets with these students daily in a small group or sometimes individually. She set up a program for each one based on their IEP. We're really starting to see some progress.

The reading [and] language arts block is my favorite time of the day. It's fun to see my students get excited about reading. It is also rewarding to watch their progress and to see how much more fluent and competent they're becoming with their reading. It's a challenge to think about what each one needs, but I'm getting better at observing them and thinking of ways to help them out. I feel that during reading [and] language arts time I'm giving them the tools they need to be successful learners in all of their subjects.

Introduction

Ines takes a multipronged approach to meeting the needs of special learners during reading instruction. In her two years as an inclusion teacher she has learned to value the help and support of her partner, the special education teacher, but she has also been on the lookout for strategies and procedures that can make all students successful learners. Ines has also developed ways to observe students' progress in reading on an ongoing basis and respond to their individual needs. This chapter focuses on what general education teachers can do to provide appropriate instruction for students with reading problems who spend all or part of the school day in general education classrooms.

Current Trends in Reading Programs

For decades, reading instruction in general education classrooms remained remarkably unchanged. From the time of "Dick and Jane," teachers relied on **basal reading programs** (graded reading materials) to structure reading programs. The most substantive challenge to traditional basal reading programs has been the **whole-language** movement, with its emphasis on teacher and student empowerment and of authenticity of reading materials. Basal reading programs, whole-language programs, and **eclectic programs** that merge the two are in place in classrooms throughout the United States.

Traditional Basal Reading Programs

The books used in traditional basal reading programs are graded readers (grades K–8) containing stories with carefully controlled sentence length and vocabulary. Supplemental materials (e.g., workbooks, worksheets, instructional charts) help teachers teach word recognition and reading comprehension. The main difference between the basal readers of various publishing companies is their approach to word-recognition instruction—some have a stronger emphasis on phonics instruction than others.

Teachers whose approach is more traditional use a separate spelling book and a language arts book in addition to the basal readers. In these classes, the schedule includes separate time slots for reading, spelling, and language arts. Because traditional reading programs center on materials, the scope and sequence of instruction is virtually mapped out for teachers.

Fourth grade teacher Okhee Moon uses a traditional basal reading program. Okhee uses a placement test provided by the basal publisher to determine which of three groups best suits each student: Group A uses a third grade basal; Group B, a fourth grade basal; and Group C, fifth grade basal. During the 60-minute reading period, Okhee meets with one group at a time for skills lessons. While she is working with one group, the other groups complete workbook activities or read stories in the basal. All skill activities and tests are included with the series. Okhee teaches spelling and writing at a different time, using different books.

One of the advantages of basal reading programs is that teachers' planning time—particularly the time spent planning activities and selecting materials—is streamlined. Another advantage is that reading skills are clearly delineated, and that instruction and assessment are clearly linked to these skills. In traditional programs, instruction is systematic in a class and across classes in a school.

Critics of traditional basal programs (e.g., Goodman, 1986; Goodman et al., 1988) challenge traditional basal instruction on the following grounds:

- Materials-centered programs disempower teachers and students, and keep teachers from planning and implementing a relevant, meaningful curriculum.
- Basal programs isolate the instruction of reading, writing, speaking, and listening.
- In basal programs emphasis is greater on isolated skills than on making meaning.
- Instructional activities such as workbook exercises do not give students the opportunity to engage in genuine reading and writing tasks.

> Dick and Jane were the main characters in a basal reading program that was popular during the 1950s and 1960s. Basals now include characters who represent the cultural diversity of the United States.

- The language in basal reading stories is stilted and unnatural, and does not represent the best of children's literature.

For students with reading problems, these criticisms are even more acute. Observations of students in special education resource rooms, Title I pull-out programs, and in low reading groups taught in traditional "skills" programs indicate that less-proficient readers not only receive even more instruction in isolated skills than their more-proficient peers, but also get less specific instruction about how to transfer these skills to other reading tasks. They also have very little opportunity to read genuine, connected text (Allington, 1983; Bean et al., 1991; Hiebert, 1983). In short, students who have problems learning how to read are afforded few opportunities to engage in personally meaningful, purposeful reading. See Tips for Teachers 13.1 for ideas on making the most of basal readers.

Whole-Language Programs

Whole-language programs with a strong emphasis on reading for meaning are an alternative to traditional basal reading programs. Although whole-language historians trace the roots of whole-language programs to Rousseau and Dewey (see Goodman et al., 1991, for fascinating historical vignettes), the work of Kenneth and Yetta Goodman, beginning in the late 1970s, launched the whole-language movement (which gained momentum in the 1980s and 1990s). A number of definitions of whole language have been presented in the literature. After examining sixty-four definitions, Bergeron (1990) offered the following:

> *Whole language* is a concept that embodies both a philosophy of language development as well as the instructional approaches embedded within, and supportive of, that philosophy. This concept includes the use of real literature and writing in the context of meaningful, functional, and cooperative experience in order to develop in students motivation and interest in the process of learning (p. 319).

What does reading instruction in whole-language classrooms look like? The curriculum in these classrooms is organized around themes (such as space, the environment, or the animal kingdom), which can be determined by state or school

TIPS FOR TEACHERS

13.1 Making the Most of Basal Readers

Wiggins (1994) offers these suggestions for the effective use of basal readers:
- Consider the basal as one tool for teaching reading. Use other materials as you see fit.
- Make direct connections between the skills students are learning from their basal reader and their recreational reading and reading in the content areas.
- Use flexible grouping strategies to teach skill lessons. Use supplementary basal assessment materials (and your own judgment) to decide who needs to be in what group for what purpose.
- Make use of centers for students to obtain additional practice in critical areas.

- You do not have to use every worksheet or skill-pack page. If a particular activity is not well constructed, eliminate it or write your own.
- You do not have to read every story. Some stories may be poorly written or inappropriate for your students. Feel free to substitute trade books or other reading material when necessary.
- Emphasize reading beyond the basal. Encourage all students to read trade books, magazines, and other materials.

Adapted from Wiggins, R. A. (1994). Large group lesson/small group follow-up: Flexible grouping in a basal reading program. *The Reading Teacher, 47,* 450–460. Copyright by the International Reading Association. Adapted with permission.

district curriculum objectives or by teacher or student interests. Teachers and students are highly engaged in the planning and implementation of instruction in whole-language classrooms. Integrated oral language, reading, and writing instruction is embedded in authentic language and literacy activities based on the designated theme (Cousin et al., 1991). Strong emphasis is placed on the use of trade books, magazines, and other authentic reading materials. Skill instruction (including instruction in phonics) is provided, but more on an incidental, as-needed basis. Thus, whole language is intended to center on teachers and students rather than on materials.

Tom Hill's seventh grade reading and language arts class is based on a whole-language philosophy. Tom does not use a basal reader, nor does he schedule separate times for reading and writing instruction. Visitors to Tom's class see students busily engaged in reading and writing activities. Tom organizes his class around the themes of literary genres (e.g., biographies, mysteries, and so on). Students are required to select a book and write a story or composition related to the theme. Whole-class and small-group discussions are related to the theme, but students are encouraged to select and engage in other reading and writing as well. Grammar, spelling, reading, and other skills are taught incidentally. When Tom notices that an individual or small group needs to learn a particular skill, he teaches it.

The advantages of whole language—teacher and student empowerment, integration of the language arts, emphasis on making meaning, use of genuine reading and writing tasks, and use of the best of children's literature—are a stark contrast to the disadvantages of traditional basal instruction. Most significant for students with reading and learning difficulties is the emphasis on their areas of competence as language learners. "Children who have trouble in reading and writing do have strengths—making sense of language is natural for people" (Goodman, 1986, p. 56).

As a survey of whole-language teachers revealed, however, there are problems associated with this philosophy of reading instruction (Walmsley & Adams, 1993). The New York teachers surveyed indicated that whole language is all of the following:

- *demanding*—in respect to teacher planning time
- *alienating and dividing*—in respect to different points of view among administrators, faculty, and parents
- *cumbersome*—in respect to classroom implementation
- *confusing*—in respect to definitional issues and to its incompatibility with traditional assessment, such as standardized tests

The most persistent concern about whole-language programs for teaching reading to students with severe reading problems is the lack of consistent, systematic instruction in word identification and comprehension (Gersten & Dimino, 1993; Pressley, 1994). Many people recognize the positive impact of whole-language programs on students' attitudes about reading, but there is concern about whether these programs can provide the intensive instruction that students with reading problems need (Pressley, 1994; Stahl et al., 1994).

These students are working with print from authentic contexts. How will skill instruction in reading be provided? What are some advantages and disadvantages of learning to read in a whole-language classroom?

Eclectic Programs

As you have already detected, traditional and whole-language programs represent very different approaches to reading instruction, and debate has been heated between adherents of each position. After a comprehensive review of the research comparing traditional and whole-language programs, Stahl et al. (1994, p. 182) offered a "plea for eclecticism."

Overattention to reading subskills and isolated tasks does not offer students the opportunity to develop a rich, rewarding, and purposeful sense of what reading is all about. Attention to meaning and positive attitudes about reading can help some students who have problems with word recognition and comprehension "feel" good about themselves as readers—even if they can't read very well.

> Many teachers and researchers recommend a balance in reading programs. The International Reading Association now has a special-interest group called Balanced Reading Instruction.

This is how Stahl et al. (1994, p. 182) describe an eclectic program:

> Such a program might include a great deal of attention to decoding, especially in the early grades, but would give greater emphasis to the reading of interesting and motivating texts. Such a program might include open-ended tasks and discussion about literature but also might include some specific instruction in comprehension strategies. Such a program might include student choice of reading materials part of the time, but teachers would choose materials that challenge their students both in terms of readability and intellectual challenge. In short, such a program would incorporate much from whole language but include more teacher-directed instruction, especially in terms of decoding and comprehension strategies.

In response to the criticisms of traditional basal reading programs issued by whole-language advocates, many basal reading programs have made drastic changes (Hoffman et al., 1994). Newer literature-based basal readers include more stories from children's literature, more language arts connections, and suggestions for more authentic reading and writing activities. Specific suggestions and materials for skills instruction are incorporated in these newer books. Morrow (1992) found that a merger of basal instruction with whole-language activities had positive effects in the reading comprehension of students from minority backgrounds.

In recent years many educators have advocated using only one grade-level basal for a whole class. In other words, every student in a fourth grade class would be in a fourth grade basal—whether or not every student reads on a fourth grade level. Advocates of this procedure recommend whole-class instruction with flexible grouping based on individual needs (Radencich & McKay, 1995; Wiggins, 1994). It is also recommended that teachers use **two-tiered instruction** for students with reading problems. Tier one uses grade-level material (the basal) with adaptations, so that all students feel like members of the class. Tier two materials are "comfort-level" materials on a more appropriate reading level for the student (Radencich & McKay, 1995).

In a second type of eclectic program, explicit, systematic word-identification instruction is included in a whole-language program (Mather, 1992). For example, Uhry and Shepherd (1990) included a traditional phonics-based spelling instruction in a whole-language program. Cunningham, Hall, and Defee (1991) developed what they called a "balanced approach" to teaching reading that included writing, phonics, directed reading activities, and self-selected reading.

What type of general education reading program is best for all students? The answer to this question is what educators, parents, and students have known for a long time—it is not the program that makes the difference, it is the teacher who makes the difference (Bond & Dykstra, 1967; McKenna et al., 1994). Students have learned to read with teachers who have (or have not) used basals, who have (or have not) used whole language, and with teachers who have taken a more eclectic approach. The secret—especially for students from whom learning to read is very difficult—is to be attentive to the individual needs of your students and to respond to those needs systematically and intensively.

RESEARCH BRIEF

PERSPECTIVE ON PHONICS INSTRUCTION

Marilyn Jager Adams conducted a systematic review of the research on how individuals learn to read. Her review, printed in the form of a book, *Beginning to Read: Thinking and Learning about Print* (1990), is considered to be the most comprehensive summary of the topic since Jeanne Chall's 1967 classic, *Learning to Read: The Great Debate.*

In respect to phonics instruction, Adams made the following recommendations, based on her review:

- Phonics instruction is helpful in teaching reading and spelling.
- Invented spellings should be encouraged, in that they help students develop the necessary phonological awareness skills for reading and spelling.
- Teaching of some phonics rules and generalizations can be helpful if they bring attention to word patterns. But learning rules is no substitute for practicing with word patterns.
- Teaching of onsets, rhymes, and blending is particularly important in reading programs.

Learning Difficulties in the Process of Reading

"Reading is the process of constructing meaning from written texts. It is a complex skill requiring the coordination of a number of interrelated sources of information" (Anderson et al., 1985, p. 7). Because reading is a complex process, there are many areas of potential difficulties. As Figure 13.1 indicates, many factors influence whether students experience success in learning how to read.

As you know, reading problems typically are caused by a number of interrelated factors. Stanovich (1986) refers to this combination of factors as **reciprocal causation**—essentially a domino effect, in which an initial problem with reading leads to a second problem, and then to a third. For exam-

ple, a child who is not read to in the home may not have the opportunity to become familiar with the alphabet and letter sounds, which then leads to frustration in learning how to decode, which then leads to problems in motivation to read, which results in limited learning of vocabulary and new concepts. As a classroom teacher, you must be sensitive to the factors that influence reading and to the individual needs of your students in their attempts to tackle this complex process.

Think about what it takes to read a chapter of a book. You need to:

- look at and decode the individual words
- think about the meaning of each word
- think about the meaning of each sentence and its relationship to the sentences that precede and follow it
- pick up on the meaning of each paragraph and the way it relates to the meaning of the entire text

Because you are a mature reader, this all happens rapidly. If you can't pronounce a word, figure out the meaning of a word or sentence, or summarize a passage, you have strategies for overcoming those difficulties. You have mastered the individual subprocesses of reading (e.g., recognizing letters, matching letters with sounds, activating the meanings of words), and can quickly coordinate all these subprocesses to make meaning.

Bos and Vaughn (1994) have identified five important concepts that describe reading as a process. In the next section you'll read about these concepts and difficulties each may pose for students with reading problems.

Reading Is an Interactive Process

Three cue systems—grapho-phonic cues, syntactic cues, and semantic cues—are available to readers. **Grapho-phonic cues** have to do with written symbols of language and their relationships to the sound system of language. Written English is based on an **alphabetic principle**; that is, we use letters of the alphabet to form words. In an alphabetic system, letters represent sounds. The understanding of how to listen to and produce sounds is called **phonological** (or phonemic) **awareness**.

FIGURE 13.1

Factors That Influence Reading

Cognitive Factors
intelligence
memory
attention span
cognitive learning
    strategies

Communication Factors
listening abilities
speaking abilities
language abilities

Neurophysiological Factors
auditory acuity
visual acuity
brain development
brain function

FACTORS THAT INFLUENCE READING

Personality Factors
motivation
sense of personal
    competence
ability to work in groups
consistency in behavior
willingness to ask for help

Educational Factors
opportunity for
    appropriate instruction
exposure to print
quality of early reading
    instruction
early intervention of
    reading problems

Textual Factors
print type
clarity of writing style
vocabulary
sentence structure
format and design

Sources: Stanovich, 1986; McCormick, 1995; Taylor, Harris, & Pearson, 1988; Johnston & Allington, 1991; Hiebert & Taylor, 1994.

Syntactic cues relate to the grammatical structure of language, and **semantic cues** relate to the reader's understanding of the meaning of concepts and their interrelationships.

Good readers are proficient at using all three cue systems interactively (Stanovich, 1980). When one cue system breaks down, good readers know how to access the others.

Although students who have difficulty reading may have problems with any one of the cue sys-

tems, difficulties with phonological awareness are the most debilitating, and are highly pervasive among students with reading and learning disabilities. The ability to perform phonological awareness tasks is the best predictor of early reading (Adams, 1990; Stanovich & Siegal, 1994).

Students with reading problems may also have difficulty using all three cue systems interactively, such that their reading becomes halted and disconnected. When students have difficulty with fluency (reading quickly and smoothly), it is difficult to understand what is being read because so much effort is spent just on figuring out the words.

Reading Is a Strategic Process

Reading requires a variety of thinking strategies, including those for recognizing words—sometimes called **decoding** or **word identification** strategies. Readers also need strategies for monitoring ongoing understanding, for recognizing when understanding is not happening, and for activating fix-up strategies, such as rereading or looking up a word in a dictionary, when needed. Knowing about these strategies and when to use them is called **metacognition**. Students with reading problems may have difficulty with metacognitive skills, including processing words (Mann, 1991; Torgesen, 1985) and monitoring comprehension (Wong, 1980, 1987; Zabrucky & Ratner, 1992).

Reading Is an Active Search for Meaning

Reading is more than just figuring out the words—it is an active search for meaning. **Reading comprehension** involves being able to understand individual words, phrases and clauses, sentences, paragraphs, and larger units of text. It includes summarizing the literal message of a text as well as being able to make inferences and judgments about what was read. Students who are passive (Ryan et al., 1986) or unmotivated (Licht & Kistner, 1986) learners may not become actively involved in an active search for meaning from their reading.

Reading Is the Process of Constructing Meaning

When people read, they actively try to make a connection between what the author presents and their own personal background knowledge and experience. Students with reading problems may have difficulty not only in activating prior knowledge but also in linking what they already know to new information (Daneman, 1991). Bear in mind also that students' developmental level, language culture, personal experiences, and interests all affect the way students construct meaning, and be prepared to deal with individual differences in meaning construction.

Reading Is a Socially Mediated Language-Learning Activity

Because reading is a mode of communication, learning to read, like learning to listen, speak, and write, is socially mediated (Vygotsky, 1978). When students and teachers talk about what they are reading, they share what they already know about the topic and integrate their knowledge with that of the text. When students and teachers talk about the reading process, they share the strategies they use to construct meaning from semantic, syntactic, and grapho-phonic cues. The social (Pearl et al., 1986) and attentional (Krupski, 1986) problems of some students can interfere with learning to read.

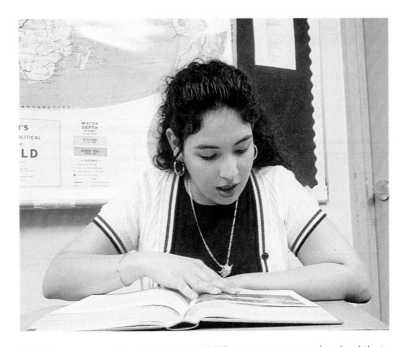

What happens as this student reads? What processes are involved that students with disabilities might find difficult?

Effective Reading Instruction for All Learners

Roma McCormick is an elementary school reading resource specialist. Roma's job is to coordinate the reading program throughout the school—for general and special education—and to provide support for teachers who need help in planning and implementing reading instruction for all learners. Roma has developed basic guidelines for effective reading instruction, based on her understanding of the research in teaching reading to special learners and her experience in working with students in classrooms and in resource rooms. The following sections describe the guidelines Roma uses as she works with the reading teachers in her school.

Establish an Environment That Promotes Reading

Research has documented the importance of exposure to books, magazines, and other forms of print for vocabulary and conceptual development (Cunningham & Stanovich, 1991; Stanovich & Siegal, 1994). Fortunately, the teachers in Roma's school agree that when students enter their classrooms the physical environment should communicate, "This is a place where we read!"

Jane Saunders' room is a good example of a **print-rich environment**. When her second graders walk into the classroom on the first day of school, they feel right at home. There are curtains on the windows, a basket for writing supplies at the center of each cluster of four student desks, and a reading center with a couch, lounge chair, and carpet for informal reading. The writing center has materials for making books. The library center is well stocked with reading materials (e.g., newspapers, magazines, catalogs, brochures) and organized with books color-coded according to genre and alphabetized by author. Jane involves students in planning and organizing their entire classroom, including bulletin boards and learning centers, as a place to read.

The social environment for reading is also critical. Jane plans times when students can engage in recreational reading. She also models reading by reading aloud to students daily, reading silently when they do, and talking about books she has read. Parents, grandparents, school personnel, and community leaders frequently visit Jane's class to read to students and to listen to students read. Reading is valued, reading is emphasized—reading happens!

Establish Appropriate Goals

In establishing appropriate goals, Roma recommends that teachers consider Duffy and Roehler's (1989) three goals of reading instruction. **Attitude goals** refer to an individual's attitudes about reading in general and about himself or herself as a reader. **Process goals** refer to the individual's knowledge of how the reading process works. Process goals include not only the skills you expect your students to learn to become proficient readers (e.g., phonological awareness, word recognition, reading comprehension), but also metacognitive strategies that empower individuals to reflect about understanding. **Content goals** relate to the application of the reading process in reconstructing an author's intended meaning. Understanding how reading works as a process is a means to achieving content goals (Duffy & Roehler, 1989). Exposure to and familiarity with a variety of genres influences an individual's ability to apply the reading process to different reading tasks.

Provide Early Intervention

Early intervention programs address students' reading difficulties as soon as they become apparent. At Roma's school, first graders who do not make immediate progress in learning to read and write are enrolled in the school's Reading Recovery program. Title I teachers in Roma's school provide intensive, one-on-one instruction 30 minutes a day for identified students. Tips for Teachers 13.2 provides strategies for working with students who reverse words.

For grades 2 through 5, Roma asks teachers early in the school year to identify any students who are displaying signs of difficulty with grade-level reading material. Roma confers with teachers to decide whether the needs of individual students would best be served in the general education classroom or in other settings.

TIPS FOR TEACHERS

13.2. What Should I Do About Reversals?

Some students reverse letters when they read (saying *was* for *saw*) or when they write (writing *b* for *d*). As a teacher, when should you worry about such reversals being a symptom of dyslexia? Many children make reversals in their reading and writing up to the age of seven, and these reversals should not be a cause for concern. A few students, however, may continue to make reversals and may need some help. Here are some tips:

1. Letter-tracing activities can help students get in touch with the features of letters. Trace a letter and talk about the characteristics of the letter. Ask the student to follow your model.
2. Work with the student to develop a mnemonic picture device to help remember the direction of the letter. With the letter *p*, for example, you can say, "What letter does the word *pie* begin with? It begins with a *p*. Here is a straight line. This is me

before I eat my pie. Now here is a circle that is my swollen stomach after I eat the pie. Think about the line and the swollen stomach and that will help you remember how the letter *p* goes."

3. Put easily confused words in sentences and ask students to read the sentences to see whether they make sense. For example, with *was* and *saw* you could use the following sentences:

   I *saw* the snake.
   I *was* very upset.

4. Create cloze exercises, and have students fill in the missing words.
5. Provide opportunities for students to read easily confused words in meaningful text.
6. Provide opportunities for repeated readings of sentences that contain commonly reversed words.

Provide Appropriate Intensive Instruction

For students with special learning needs in reading, whole-class instruction can be treacherous. Therefore, Roma works with teachers to find ways to provide instruction that is both appropriate for meeting individual student's needs and intensive enough for progress to occur.

Reading instruction is appropriate when students have the following:

- a clear understanding of teacher expectations and the goals of instruction
- a match between their instructional needs and the instruction provided
- appropriate instructional groups
- ample opportunity to read material of a comfortable reading level
- support from teachers and peers, when necessary

Teachers frequently ask, "What skills do I teach?" and "How do I decide what students to put in a particular skills group?" Suggestions in Tips for Teachers 13.3 are based on the work of Paratore (1995).

Reading instruction is intensive when students receive:

- direct instruction in the skills they need to become proficient readers
- direct instruction in strategies that will help them become more independent learners
- opportunities to be actively involved during lessons and seatwork
- systematic and ongoing evaluation of their progress in reading

Provide Appropriate Assessment

As a reading resource specialist, Roma is under pressure to improve test scores on the standardized

TIPS FOR TEACHERS

13.3 Flexible Grouping Strategies for Reading Instruction

- At the beginning of the school year, decide on the critical skills and strategies you want all students to learn by the end of the school year. Make a checklist of these skills and place the list in each student's assessment portfolio. Keep a master list in your planbook or gradebook.
- Base skills and strategies on your textbook series, school district curricular guides, and your own goals for reading and writing instruction.
- Schedule a regular time to meet with skill groups. Skill lessons can be whole-class, small-group, or for individual students, depending on student needs.

- Keep the membership of skill groups flexible. You may have a permanent group of low achievers that you meet with regularly, but include them as members of other groups as well.
- Do not limit skill and strategy lessons to low-achieving students only. Average and high-achieving students also need this instruction.
- Focus on a few skills or strategies each week, allowing some time in your schedule to teach skill lessons based on student requests and needs that arise from your daily observation of student work.
- Keep a record of the skill lessons you teach and which students participate in each lesson.

FIGURE 13.2

Standards for the Assessment of Reading and Writing

GOALS

- The interests of the student are paramount in assessment.
- The primary purpose of assessment is to improve teaching and learning.
- Assessment must reflect and allow for critical inquiry into curriculum and instruction.
- Assessments must recognize and reflect the intellectually and socially complex nature of reading and writing and the important roles of school, home, and society in literacy development.
- Assessment must be fair and equitable.
- The consequences of an assessment procedure are the first, and most important, consideration in establishing the validity of the assessment.

IMPLEMENTATION

- The teacher is the most important agent of assessment.
- The assessment process should involve multiple perspectives and sources of data.
- Assessment must be based in the school community.
- All members of the educational community—students, parents, teachers, administrators, policy makers, and the public—must have a voice in the development, interpretation, and reporting of assessment.
- Parents must be involved as active, essential participants in the assessment process.

Source: International Reading Association and National Council of Teachers of English, 1994. Prepared by the IRA/NCTE Joint Task Force on Assessment.

test the school district administers each spring. She encourages teachers to help prepare students for "high-stakes tests" by teaching them test-taking strategies and familiarizing them with exercises similar to those on the test. Standardized test scores can provide valuable general information about students' vocabulary and their ability to recognize words, and to answer explicit and implicit questions. Standardized tests have been criticized, however, for trivializing the reading process and lacking relevance to authentic reading tasks (Calfee & Hiebert, 1991).

Because standardized tests focus on the "product" of reading and ignore many salient factors that influence success or failure in literacy development (such as motivation, repertoire of reading strategies, and exposure to print), Roma encourages teachers to think about a balanced approach to assessment. Ongoing, informal assessment is powerful in guiding instruction and in helping teachers plan for flexible grouping. Roma also encourages teachers to keep in mind the goals for assessment issued by The International Reading Association and the National Council of Teachers of English (see Figure 13.2).

Strategies for Helping All Students with Phonological Awareness and Word Identification

Good readers can identify words quickly, so quickly that they do not depend on semantic or syntactic cues for word identification (Stanovich, 1980). Rapid, context-free word identification is the hallmark of a good reader.

Although word recognition is laborious for many students with reading problems, they should not spend most of the school day drilling on words in isolation. Rather, students should understand that reading is for meaning and always have ample opportunities to read text that's relevant to their lives. Students with reading difficulties do need systematic word-identification instruction, however, with lots of practice. Because of the whole-language movement, many teachers are

reluctant to return to phonics workbooks. Yet, recognizing that students who have difficulty learning to read need intensive instruction in word identification, teachers are searching for alternative methods that can provide intensive instruction but motivate students.

Teaching Phonological Awareness and Phonics

As stated earlier, recent research has indicated the importance of phonological awareness in learning to read. A **phoneme** is the smallest unit of speech sound. Phonological awareness involves being in tune with and knowing how to manipulate the sounds of language. Phonological awareness includes the following skills:

- **rhyming** (identifying similarities and differences in word endings)
- **alliteration** (identifying similarities and differences in word beginnings)
- **blending** (putting sounds or phonemes together to form words)
- **segmentation** (dividing ideas into words, and words into syllables and individual phonemes)

Children who are successful readers can rhyme by age four (Maclean et al., 1987) and blend and segment by the end of first grade (Perfetti et al., 1987). Even at the end of second grade and beyond, however, some students with reading problems will not have mastered these skills (Vellutino & Scanlon, 1987). Some children seem to develop phonological awareness naturally and independently; others need instruction and guided practice. Research with students (with and without learning disabilities) has demonstrated that phonological awareness

> Children who develop phonological awareness early in life begin to read earlier, read more books, and develop a larger vocabulary and store of knowledge than other children. Stanovich (1986) call this the "Matthew Effect" in reading, based on the Matt. 25:29 (commonly known as the Bible's "rich get richer" passage).

Computerized Curriculum-Based Measurement

Lynn and Doug Fuchs and their colleagues at Vanderbilt University have been working with classroom teachers for a number of years on developing strategies for improving the academic performance of students with learning and behavior problems in the general education elementary classroom (e.g., Fuchs et al., 1994; Phillips et al., 1995; Phillips et al., 1993). They have utilized a computer-based, curriculum-based measurement system (CBM) to provide teachers and students with feedback on student performance. Each week students work at the computer, taking assessments in reading and math that take between 1.5 and 6 minutes, depending on the grade level. Every two weeks the students and teachers receive computer-generated performance feedback on individual students, and each teacher receives a class report. Students are taught to ask themselves such questions as, "Are my scores going up?", "Are my boxes getting darker?", and "Which skills can I work harder on next time to get darker boxes?"

Teacher interviews indicated that when 19 to 20 teachers compared their instruction prior to participation in the curriculum-based assessment (paired with peer tutoring), they reported that the model not only increased their students' academic performance but also improved students' maintenance of skills and test-taking skills (Phillips, et al., 1994).

activities can improve both reading and spelling (Bradley & Bryant, 1983; Hohn & Ehri, 1983; Lundberg et al., 1988). Fortunately, playing with letter sounds can be fun! Particularly in the early grades, multilevel activities can be planned for the whole class.

Phonological awareness training is the foundation for **phonics instruction**—the systematic teaching of the alphabetic principle and the way spelling patterns relate to sound patterns (Stahl, 1992). Stahl suggested the following nine guidelines for exemplary phonics instruction:

- builds on a child's rich concept of how print functions
- builds on a foundation of phonological awareness
- is clear and direct
- is integrated in the total reading program
- focuses on reading words, not learning rules
- may include alliteration and rhymes
- may include invented spelling practice
- develops independent word-recognition strategies focusing on the internal structure of words

- develops automatic word-recognition skills so that students can devote their attention to comprehension, not words

If your memory of phonics workbooks and phonics drills is less than positive, don't worry. Stahl also suggests that phonics instruction can be fun! Here are some suggestions for phonological awareness and phonics instruction.

Phonemic Pairs Phonemic Pairs is a strategy designed to help students learn how to read and spell words (Gordon et al., 1993). Pairs of students work together to analyze words, looking at alliteration and rhyme. They also practice segmentation and blending skills. Partners are trained to use the strategy in a whole-class or small-group setting. Procedures for Phonemic Pairs are presented in Figure 13.3.

Making Words Cunningham, Hall, and DeFee (1991) have worked in classrooms in North Carolina to develop teacher- and student-friendly procedures for intensive, systematic instruction in word identification. **Making Words** (Cunningham & Cunningham, 1992) is a whole-class guided activity that helps students develop phonological awareness and become more sensitive to common

spelling patterns. Although initially developed for students in the primary grades, Making Words can also be used with upper elementary or middle school students who need to work on common spelling patterns, prefixes, and suffixes.

Making Words is being considered as one component of a multimethod, multilevel reading-instruction program. The initial feedback is very encouraging:

- Teachers find the practice effective and an efficient way to organize for reading instruction (Cunningham, 1991)
- Students find the practice "fun" and helpful in learning to recognize word patterns (Cunningham & Cunningham, 1992)
- The practice is effective for poorer readers, but does not hinder the progress of better readers (Cunningham et al., 1991)
- The practice allowed poorer readers to be full participants in classroom activities and to develop friendships that cut across ability group lines (Cunningham et al., 1991)

Cunningham and Cunningham (1992) suggested two steps to a Making Words lesson. Schumm and Vaughn (1995) added a third step to pick up the pace for some students. Figure 13.4 provides an overview of the three revised steps: (1) Making Words Slowly, (2) Word Sorting, and (3) Making Words Quickly. The whole sequence (including distribution of materials) takes about 30 minutes.

What are the characteristics of a good phonics program? How can phonics instruction be enhanced through strategies for teaching phonemic awareness?

Using the DISSECT Strategy As students become more advanced in their reading, they begin to use structural analysis to identify words. **Structural analysis** involves the use of root words, prefixes, and suffixes to determine the pronunciation and meaning of a word, including multisyllable words and merged words such as compounds (buttermilk, pancake) and contractions (don't, can't).

Lenz, Schumaker, Deshler, and Beals (1984) developed a strategy for secondary students with learning disabilities to approach a multisyllable word in a strategic way. This strategy, known by

FIGURE 13.3

Procedures for Phonemic Pairs

Introduction: "Today we are going to play several games to learn three spelling words."

Complete the following steps for each word (3 per day):

1. **Look at the word:** "First we are going to look at the word. Let's look at the word _____." Show the model and say the word.

2. **Oral alliteration:** "The first game we are going to play is related to the beginning sound of the word. The beginning sound of the word _____ is /_____/. I will say four words and I want you to show me with thumbs up or thumbs down (demonstrate) if the word begins like _____." If the student misses any one example, correct the error and have the student provide a correct example. "You said _____ begins with a /_____/ sound, but it begins with /_____/ which is different. Can you give me a word that begins like _____?" On the word list, use a plus to indicate a correct response and a minus to indicate an incorrect response.

3. **Written alliteration:** "Now we are going to play another beginning sound game, but this time you are going to write the beginning sound of the word. I want you to write the beginning sound of the word _____." If the student hesitates or makes an error, compare the model which is still on the table with the blank and say, "This is the word _____, you need to fill in the beginning sound of the word."

4. **Oral rhyme:** "The second game we are going to play is related to rhyme. Rhyming words are words that end with the same sound. In the word _____, the rhyme is _____. I will say four words and I want you to show me with thumbs up or thumbs down (demonstrate) if the word rhymes with _____." If the student misses any one example, "You said _____ rhymes with _____, but _____ ends with /_____/ which is different. Can you give me a word that rhymes with _____?" On the word list, use a plus to indicate a correct response; use a minus to indicate an incorrect response.

5. **Written rhyme:** "Now we are going to play another rhyming game, but this time you are going to write the rhyme of the word. I want you to write the rhyme of the word _____." If the child hesitates or makes an error, compare the model which is still on the table and the blank and say, "This is the word _____. You need to fill in the rhyme of _____."

6. **Segmentation and blending:** "In the last game we are going to look at the different sounds that make up the word. First I want you to listen as I read the sounds of the word slowly and then read the word." Say the sounds while pointing to the dots under each phoneme on the model. Read the word. "Now I want you to say the word slowly like I just did, by naming the sounds that make up the word as I point to the dots, and then read the word." The student should say the sounds and read the word. If the student hesitates or makes an error, model the sounds and read the word again.

7. **Write the word:** "Now I want you to write the word without looking." Remove the model and have the student write the word on a blank card. If the student is unsuccessful, repeat steps 1–6 and indicate on the word list the number of times needed to complete step 7 successfully.

Adapted from: Gordon, J., Schumm, J.S., & Vaughn, S. (1993). *The effects of phonemic training on the spelling performance of elementary students with learning disabilities.* Unpublished manuscript, University of Miami, Coral Gables, FL.

FIGURE 13.4

Steps in Making Words

STEP 1. **Making Words Slowly (about 15 minutes)**

Students make 12 to 15 words, using a set of individual laminated letters. The teacher guides students through the lesson by directing them to spell words with their letters. The last word includes all the letters a student has been given that day. For example, a student might be given the letters "eudhnrt." The teacher would direct them to spell words such as: *red, Ted, Ned, her, hut, rut, under,* etc. The final word would be *thunder.* After the students spell the words with their own letters, the teacher or a student shows the correct spelling, using large letters and a sentence strip chart in the front of the room. Students correct their own work.

STEP 2. **Word Sorting (about 10 minutes)**

The teacher puts up on the sentence strip board word cards with all the words spelled that day. Students are then asked how some of the words are alike. A volunteer sorts the words on the sentence strip board by putting all like words together (e.g., *fat, rat, sat*). The other students in the class then guess why those words are grouped together, which helps students focus on word patterns.

STEP 3. **Making Words Quickly (about two minutes)**

Students write as many words as they can using the day's letters, writing the words in a Making Words Log. Students take one minute to write the date and the day's letters at the top of the page; when the teacher says, "Go," they write words for two minutes. This activity helps build fluency. Because each lesson starts with easy words and ends with more difficult words, all students in the class can participate.

the acronym **DISSECT**, includes the following steps:

1. Discover the word's context.
2. Isolate the prefix. Students look at the beginning of the word to see whether the initial letters of the word match a prefix they know. If they do recognize a prefix, they isolate it, e.g., *pre/heat.* If students do not recognize a prefix, they proceed to step 3.
3. Separate the suffix. Students look at the end of the word to see if the letters match a suffix they know. If they do recognize a suffix, they separate it; if not, they go on to the next step.
4. Say the stem.
5. Examine the stem. Students dissect the stem into easy-to-pronounce parts, two or three letters at a time. When they can pronounce the whole word, students reread the whole sentence to check their understanding. If students still cannot figure out the word, they go on to the last steps.
6. Check with someone.
7. Try the dictionary.

DISSECT can be taught to your whole class. Students can then practice using the strategy in small groups or pairs. You may also want to put the steps for DISSECT on a poster in front of your room and remind students regularly about the steps.

In the upper elementary grades, middle school, and high school, reading instruction focuses more on comprehension and reading for learning in the content areas. Even so, it is not unusual for students who decode at a third grade level or below to be members of heterogeneous classes. What can you do when only a few students are nonreaders? Tips for Teachers 13.4 presents some other strategies for teaching older students to read.

TIPS FOR TEACHERS

Teaching Sight Words

Some students have difficulty with automatic recognition of words in print. This is especially problematic when students have difficulty with **high-frequency words**—words such as *the, you, and,* and *was*—that serve as the basic glue of our language. According to Fry, Fountoukidis, and Polk (1985) about 50 percent of written language contains 100 high-frequency words, such as those presented in Table 13.1.

Because these words occur so often, it is inefficient for students to have to slowly decode the words each time they see them in print. LaBerge and Samuels (1974) argue that it is important for students to develop **automaticity** with high-frequency words—that is, to recognize them on sight. You can choose from the basal reader, literature, or content-area textbook high-frequency words that you really want students to learn. You can also choose words from graded word lists (see Table 13.1).

Word Wall The Word Wall is a whole-class, multilevel activity for sight word instruction. The Word Wall (Cunningham, 1995) is a large, permanent bulletin board to which five words are added each week in alphabetical order. When a new word is added, the teacher and students talk about its meaning, use the word in a sentence, and determine whether its spelling follows a regular or irregular pattern. The words remain on the Wall throughout the school year. Students can use these words to help them spell words they are writing, and eventually learn to read and spell the words through repeated practice.

Cunningham (1995) suggests that some students might need portable Word Walls, especially if they move from classroom to resource room. A portable Word Wall is a file folder with one square for each letter of the alphabet. Each week the five new Word Wall words are added to the Wall and to the student's folder.

The Sight Word Association Procedure The Sight Word Association Procedure (SWAP) (Bradley, 1975) is a way to help students associate spoken words with their printed forms. SWAP can be used individually, with pairs of students, or with small groups. Working as reading partners or directed by the teacher, students follow these steps:

1. Select five to ten words, and introduce each word as you do with Word Wall.

TABLE 13.1

The Instant (Sight) Words

THE FIRST 100 WORDS (approximately first grade)					THE SECOND 100 WORDS (approximately second grade)			
Group 1a	Group 1b	Group 1c	Group 1d		Group 2a	Group 2b	Group 2c	Group 2d
the	he	go	who		saw	big	may	ran
a	I	see	an		home	where	let	five
is	they	then	there		soon	am	use	read
you	one	us	she		stand	ball	these	over
to	good	no	new		box	morning	right	such
and	me	him	said		upon	live	present	way
we	about	by	did		first	four	tell	too
that	had	was	boy		came	last	next	shall
in	if	come	three		girl	color	please	own
not	some	get	down		house	away	leave	most
for	up	or	work		find	red	hand	sure
at	her	two	put		because	friend	more	thing
with	do	man	were		made	pretty	why	only
it	when	little	before		could	eat	better	near
on	so	has	just		book	want	under	than
can	my	them	long		look	year	while	open
will	very	how	here		mother	white	should	kind
are	all	like	other		run	got	never	must
of	would	our	old		school	play	each	high
this	any	what	take		people	found	best	far
your	been	know	cat		night	left	another	both
as	out	make	again		into	men	seem	end
but	there	which	give		say	bring	tree	also
be	from	much	after		think	wish	name	until
have	day	his	many		back	black	dear	call

Reprinted with permission; Edward Fry, author.

2. Flash the words to students, one card at a time for five seconds, with you or the reading partner saying the word twice.

3. Shuffle the cards and have the student read each word. Provide corrective feedback by verifying the correctly identified words, giving the correct word for any word miscalled, and saying the word if the student does not respond in five seconds.

4. Present all the words again, using the same format given in step 2.

5. Have the student identify each word, using the same format as in step 3. Repeat this step at least two more times, or until students can automatically recognize all the words.

6. After initially teaching the words, review them for several days to see whether students remember the words.

7. If a student has difficulty recognizing a word after the seventh exposure to the word, switch from a recall task to a recognition task. To do this, place several word cards on the table and have learners point to each word as you say it. If the student still has difficulty with the words, use a different technique such as writing the word in a sentence on the back of the card or having the student draw a picture representing the word on the back of the card.

Strategies for Helping All Students Develop Fluency

Students are fluent in reading when they can recognize printed words quickly and effortlessly (LaBerge & Samuels, 1974). With automaticity, students' reading comprehension is improved (Rasinski, 1990). Reading fluency takes practice. The suggestions in this section focus on how you can help students become more fluent readers.

Repeated Reading Children have a natural tendency to enjoy hearing familiar stories over and over again. Eventually, as you sit with them and read a book, they automatically begin to read along with you. At first, they join in on some of the words and phrases. Eventually, they are reading with you for most of the book. With repeated reading of a story, children become so familiar with the text that their memory helps them become fluent readers.

Repeated reading consists of reading short, meaningful passages several times until a satisfactory level of fluency is reached. The procedure is then repeated with a new passage. The general format for this reading procedure is to have the student repeatedly read short passages (from 50 to 200 words long) until they reach a fluent reading rate (about 85 words per minute) and adequate accuracy (about 90 percent word recognition).

In general education classrooms, repeated reading can be incorporated into whole-class or small-group routines. For younger children, **Big Books**, books with large pictures and words that can be seen by the whole class, are ideal for repeated reading in groups. Students can also be grouped in pairs to read to each other. One way to motivate students to read a story over and over again is to have them read stories they have written themselves! Ongoing, informal assessment of repeated reading can help you gauge student progress and make decisions about future instruction. Tips

TIPS FOR TEACHERS

13.5 Reading Aloud for a Variety of Purposes

When it's time to read aloud in class, what should you do about students who cannot read very well? Many teachers are getting away from *round-robin reading* (taking turns reading passages in class) because students often lose their place, lose interest, or become impatient with slower readers. Also, reading aloud in class can be embarrassing for students with reading problems.

Johns, VanLeirsburg, and Davis (1994) recommend that you think about oral reading for different purposes: assessment, performance, information, and personal sharing:

1. For assessment, use oral reading to learn about students' reading strengths and challenges. On a one-to-one basis, use informal checklists and assessment tools such as informal reading inventories to check on student progress.
2. For performance, use oral reading to give students a chance to share the joy of reading with each other. Students can read their own writing, short stories, jokes, riddles, plays, or do choral reading. Give students a chance to practice before reading to a larger group.
3. For information, use oral reading to help students learn from the textbook or other resources. Select important parts of the chapter you want to share and discuss with the whole class, and assign those parts to students for oral reading. Assign selections to all students, not just the best readers. Involve parents so that students can practice reading in advance at home.
4. For personal sharing, use oral reading between two people. Schedule time for students to read to you, one-to-one to you, focusing on enjoyment and sharing. Also schedule time for students to read aloud with partners, using favorite poems, favorite parts of a story, or favorite characters.

for Teachers 13.5 offers suggestions for having students read aloud for a variety of purposes.

Classwide Peer Tutoring In Classwide Peer Tutoring (CWPT), students of different reading levels, one average or high, one low, are paired. The reading material for the tutoring sessions can be a basal reader, trade book, or magazine—what is important is that the least able reader in the pair can read it easily. During CWPT sessions, which last approximately 30 minutes, the pairs work through a sequence of structured activities in which partners read orally, share story retelling, and summarize what was read. Students earn points as they work through the series of activities.

CWPT has been researched extensively in various school settings (e.g., Delquadri et al., 1986; Greenwood et al., 1989; Mathes et al., 1994; Mathes & Fuchs, 1993). Results indicate that when the procedure is implemented consistently (three times a week over a period of sixteen weeks), the amount of reading practice time increases substantially and students of all ability levels improve in fluency and comprehension. CWPT is particularly helpful for students with learning disabilities who have reading problems.

Strategies for Helping All Students Improve Reading Comprehension

Understanding is the ultimate goal of reading. For many students, however, reading the words is not enough to make understanding happen. Students with reading difficulties need to learn specific ways to get ready for reading, to understand what they're reading while they read it, and to summarize and reflect about what they have read. In other words, students need **comprehension strategies** (designed to improve students' understanding of text) to use before, during, and after reading. Students also need to learn strategies for dealing with both *narrative* and *expository* text (stories and informational writing, respectively). Dole, Duffy, Roehler, and Pearson (1991) identified five learning goals to strive for when you teach reading comprehension: determining importance, summarizing information, drawing inferences, generating questions, and monitoring comprehension.

Each of the instructional strategies in this section focuses on one or more of these goals.

Collaborative Strategic Reading By adding a cooperative learning component to reciprocal teaching, which was designed to be used with small, teacher-facilitated, homogeneous groups (see Research Brief), Klingner, Vaughn, and Schumm (in review) developed Collaborative Strategic Reading, a way to help students read content-area textbooks more efficiently and effectively. In Collaborative Strategic Reading, students in large, heterogeneous classrooms work together in small groups, helping each other understand text. A well-structured learning environment seems to be key to the success of Collaborative Strategic Reading. Students learn procedures and practice well-defined roles. In a group of five students, for example, each might assume one of the following roles:

- *Encourager*—lets everyone know when they're doing a good job and gets everyone to participate.
- *Timer*—keeps group on-time and on-task.
- *Strategy Monitor*—moves group through the stage of the strategy.
- *Recorder*—keeps notes on strategy sheet.
- *Reader*—reads aloud sections of text, as necessary.

RESEARCH BRIEF

RECIPROCAL TEACHING

Reciprocal teaching (Palincsar & Brown, 1984, 1986) is a comprehensive approach to teaching reading comprehension and helping students construct meaning from a text. Teachers first introduce each strategy, modeling its use while reading through a passage. Teachers then guide students through the process and provide scaffolds as necessary. When students become efficient in predicting, summarizing, generating questions, and clarification they take over the role of teacher in work with peers. One of the strongest features of reciprocal teaching is the social context. Students are working together to monitor their understanding.

Reciprocal teaching has been researched extensively by Palinscar and colleagues and by others (Rosenshine & Meister, 1994). The research indicates that reciprocal teaching helps students who can decode, but cannot comprehend construct meaning from text (e.g., Palincsar & Brown, 1984). It has been used successfully with elementary and middle school students with and without learning disabilities (Lysynchuk et al., 1990; Klingner & Vaughn, 1996).

Collaborative strategic reading involves four steps. First, working in groups, students preview a content-area reading assignment. Then, after reading short segments of the text, students "click and clunk" words and ideas that they do or do not understand. (When reading is going well the information seems to *click* in the student's mind; however, when comprehension difficulties occur, the information *clunks*.) Student groups work together to formulate explanations for the confusing words or ideas. Next, after click and clunk strategies are used, students collaborate to "get the gist" by saying what they think is important and what it means. Finally, having finished all segments of a passage, students complete a wrap up, summarizing what they learned and formulating questions that they anticipate might be asked on a test. Figure 13.5 provides a cue sheet for collaborative strategic reading.

Question–Answer Relationships Strategy (QAR)
Teachers' manuals and students' workbooks, readers, and textbooks contain many comprehension questions. There are different kinds of questions that can be asked about reading, and different ways of classifying these questions. Pearson and Johnson (1978) developed a way to classify questions based on the relationship between the question and the location of its answer. From this classification system a strategy for teaching students how to answer different types of questions was also developed. This strategy, called the **Question–Answer Relationships Strategy (QAR)** (Raphael, 1982, 1984, 1986), helps students realize that, when answering questions, they need to not only consider both the text and their prior knowledge but also use strategic behavior to adjust the use of each of these sources.

The four question–answer relationships are based on the source of information and the types of reasoning involved:

1. *Right There.* Words used to create the question and words used for the answer are in the same sentence.
2. *Think and Search.* The answer is in the text, but words used to create the question and those used for an appropriate answer are not in the same sentence.
3. *Author and Me.* The answer is implied in the author's language, style, and tone.
4. *On My Own.* The answer is not found in the text but in one's head on the basis of personal experience.

Teaching the question–answer relationships (QARs) involves having students learn first to differentiate between the two sources of information and then between the four question–answer relationships. Students also learn how to identify the type of questions they are trying to answer. Figure 13.6 presents a cue card students can use during instruction.

Adapted from Raphael (1986), the following are procedures for introducing the QAR strategy to students:

1. The first day, introduce students to the concept of question–answer relationships (QARs), using the two major source categories. Read several short passages to demonstrate the relationships. Provide practice by asking students to identify the type of QAR, the answer to the question, and the strategy they used for finding the answer. The progression for teaching should be from highly supportive to independent:

   Most Supportive: Provide text, questions, answers, QAR label for each question, and reasons the label is appropriate.

   Most Independent: Have students generate their own questions, QAR labels, and reasons for their choices.

2. When students have a clear picture of the difference between "In My Head" and "In the Book," teach the next level of differentiation for each of the major categories. First, work on In the Book, then go to In My Head. The key distinction between the two In My Head subcategories is "whether or not

FIGURE 13.5

Q Sheet for Collaborative Strategic Reading

S: Say to the group.
R: Read to yourself.

Preview (Before You Read):
S: Before we start reading, let's figure out what the topic is. Who would like to read the title and say what the topic is?
R: Call on someone to say what the topic is.
S: OK, what do we already know about the topic? The recorder is going to write this down where it says "Preview—What We Already Know."
R: Encourage everyone to think of something they already know about the topic.
S: What do you think we'll learn about the topic when we read this passage? The recorder is going to write this down where it says "Preview—What We Predict We Will Learn."
R: Wait until everyone has an answer, and then go around the group and have each student give an answer.

Read:
S: Who would like to read the first two paragraphs?
R: Call on someone to read.

Click and Clunk:
S: Were there any clunks? The recorder will write down any clunks where it says "Clunks."
R: If someone does not understand a word, the group should try to explain it to the person. If no one in the group knows what the word means, have someone reread the sentence before the word, and the sentence after the word. Try to figure out what the word means. If no one can figure it out, ask for help.

Get the Gist:
S: What is the most important idea we have learned about the topic so far? The recorder is going to write down our gists where it says, "Get the Gist."
R: Wait until everyone has an answer, and then ask two people what they think. When someone can't think of a gist, the group should try to help the person.
S: Keep repeating Click and Clunk, Get the Gist, and Read until the group has finished the passage.

Wrap Up (After You Read):
S: Now let's think of some questions, to make sure we understood what we read. The recorder is going to write down questions where it says "Wrap Up—Questions."
R: Wait until everyone has a question. Call on two people to ask their questions. Have the group answer the questions.
S: Let's think about what we learned from reading this passage. The recorder is going to write down what we learned where it says, "Wrap Up—What We Learned."
R: Wait about a minute, then go around the group, asking each person to tell something they learned. Encourage everyone to be good listeners. If an answer is repeated, encourage the person to think of another response.

Compliments and Suggestions:
S: Everyone think of a compliment to give the person to your right about how that person did in today's activity.
R: Go around the group and share compliments.
S: What might help us do even better next time?
R: Wait until everyone has a suggestion, and then ask two people what they think.

FIGURE 13.6

Question–Answer Relationships (QARs)

IN THE BOOK QARS

Right There

The answer is in the text, usually easy to find. The words used to make up the question and words used to answer the question are **Right There** in the same sentence.

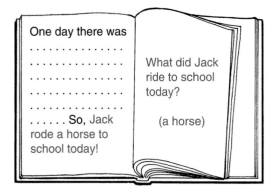

Think and Search (Putting It Together)

The answer is in the story, but you need to put together different story parts to find it. Words for the question and words for the answer are not found in the same sentence. They come from different parts of the text.

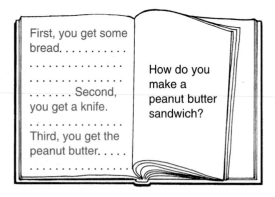

IN MY HEAD QARS

Author and You

The answer is not in the story. You need to think about what you already know, what the author tells you in the text, and how it fits together.

On My Own

The answer is not in the story. You can even answer the question without reading the story. You need to use your own experience.

Source: Adapted from T. E. Raphael, "Teaching Question–Answer Relationships, Revisited," *The Reading Teacher, 39*(6) (1986):519

the reader needs to read the text for the questions to make sense" (Raphael, 1986, p. 519). When the information must come from the reader, but in connection with the information presented by the author, then the QAR is Author and You.

3. When students can use the QAR strategy effectively in short passages, gradually increase the length of the passages and the variety of reading materials. Review the strategy, model its use on the first question, then have students use the strategy on the rest of the questions.

4. When students are proficient, use expanded or alternative QAR activities:

- Have students work in pairs or cooperative learning groups, using QAR to answer comprehension questions.
- Ask students to write stories with questions; have other students determine the answer to each question and what kind of question it is.
- Play a detective game in which students answer questions in their search for clues to solve the case, and must cite the source for their evidence.
- Divide students into teams and have the teacher read a short passage, followed by questions. The teams earn points by answering questions and determining the QAR labels.

[These procedures are] adapted from Raphael, Taffy E. (1986, February). Teaching question answer relationships, revisited. *The Reading Teacher, 39*(6), 516–522. Copyright by International Reading Association.)

Story Retelling Story retelling actively involves students in the reconstruction of stories they have read or heard. Retelling stories not only enhances comprehension but also has the following benefits (Morrow, 1985; Pellegrini & Galda, 1982):

- Students acquire a sense of story structure.
- Recall of details is enhanced.
- Oral language is improved.
- Vocabulary is improved.
- Peer interaction and student involvement are promoted.

It is important to establish conditions that make students willing and eager to participate in a story retelling session. The following guidelines are helpful:

- Select a story your students would enjoy having you read to them. Read to them with all the enthusiasm and animation you can muster.
- Explain why it is important to share stories with friends.
- With the same enthusiasm and animation, model the retelling process. Be sure to include a description of characters and setting, key plot elements, problems, and resolution to the problems. Demonstrate how to use prompts such as puppets, pictures, toys, and real objects.
- Help students find stories to share.
- Discuss with students how to be enthusiastic and animated when retelling stories.
- Ask students to retell the story as if talking to a friend.
- Ask students questions that bring out the characters, setting, plot, problem, and resolution.
- Use prompts if students have difficulty in the beginning of the retelling.
- Prompt the correct sequence when necessary.
- Prompt students to continue when necessary.

What strategies might these students use to increase their reading comprehension? How can they learn those strategies? Why are strategies such as repeated reading, questioning, and story retelling helpful for students with reading difficulties?

Provide a variety of audiences, such as younger children from other classes, or parents, so that students can get plenty of practice. From time to time during the school year, you may want to have each student retell you a story so that you can gauge their progress and provide appropriate instruction and practice.

Summarization Strategy Summarization requires the student to generate the main idea and important details from a text. Based on an analysis of informational texts, Brown and Day (1983) generated the following five rules for writing summaries:

- Delete irrelevant or trivial information.
- Delete redundant information.
- Select topic sentences.
- Substitute a more general term or event for a list of terms or actions (e.g., fruit instead of apples, oranges, or bananas).
- Invent topic sentences when none are provided by the author.

Gajria and Salvia (1992) used these same rules to teach sixth through ninth grade students with learning disabilities how to summarize expository passages by generating oral summaries. At the end of training, performance of these students on questions was significantly better than that of an untrained control group of students with learning disabilities, and similar to that of an untrained group of average-achieving students. Students who participated in the strategy instruction also generalized these skills.

To teach the **summarization strategy**, use sets of short paragraphs, with each set highlighting a different rule. In this way, the rules can be explained, modeled, and practiced individually. Then apply the rules to information passages. As students learn the rules and their application, give them greater responsibility for practicing the rules and checking that each rule has been applied.

The K–W–L Strategy K–W–L is a strategy to help students become actively engaged in comprehension before, during, and after reading (Ogle, 1986, 1989). The **K–W–L strategy** is based on research that underscores the importance of activating prior knowledge before reading (e.g., Anderson, 1977; Anderson et al., 1977), and consists of three basic steps:

- accessing what I **K**now
- determining what I **W**ant to learn
- recalling what I did **L**earn

FIGURE 13.7

K–W–L Strategy Sheet

K—What we know	W—What we want to find out	L—What we learned and still need to learn
Whales are mammals.	What do whales have in common with other mammals?	Whales give birth to live young. Baby whales drink milk from the mother. What else?

Source: Adapted from Ogle, Donna M. (1986, February). K–W–L: A teaching model that develops active reading of expository text. *The Reading Teacher, 39*(6), 564–570.

During the Know step, teachers and students engage in a discussion about what they already know about a topic, such as volcanoes, to be read. During the Want-to-learn step, teachers and students describe what they hope to learn from reading about the topic. Finally, during the Learned stage, teacher and students discuss what they learned and what information the passage did not provide. As with many reading comprehension strategies, K–W–L can also be used as a listening comprehension strategy before and after lectures. Figure 13.7 shows a K–W–L worksheet you can use to help students learn this strategy.

Putting It All Together

As you may recall from the beginning of this chapter, Ines's plan for teaching reading includes instruction in word identification, fluency, and comprehension. Because planning for reading instruction includes so many components and because the range of student reading levels in a general education classroom can be broad, learning about what other teachers do can often help you put together the puzzle pieces. In this section you'll read about two elementary teachers' reading programs. Their stories focus on how they schedule their reading instruction. Similar program plans can be developed for middle school reading and language arts classes.

Putting It Together in a Basal Program

Yvette Schatz teaches third grade at a large, urban elementary school. Yvette's school has adopted a basal reading program. The basal authors recommend whole-class instruction, using one basal for the whole class, coupled with flexible grouping. Yvette feels comfortable with the basal and uses the basal readers as well as the supplementary workbooks and instructional charts. She teaches a 90-minute reading and language arts block daily.

In her more than twenty years of experience, Yvette has learned that pull-outs are inevitable, but that when students are in her class, appropriate instruction must be planned. Three of Yvette's students are new immigrants who are pulled out for intensive English instruction during part of the reading and language arts block. All three of these students need to work on English vocabulary and fluency. Although they get direct instruction in reading from their ESL teacher, Yvette plans opportunities for them to improve their vocabulary and fluency through whole-class lessons and Classwide Peer Tutoring at the beginning of the reading and language arts block (while they are still in the room).

One of her students, Rolando, has been identified by the school district as having a learning disability. Although he leaves the classroom daily for a pull-out special education resource room, Rolando returns to Yvette's classroom for the last half hour of reading and language arts. Because his main difficulty in reading is word identification, Yvette plans her small-group word identification lessons while Rolando is present. Once a month Yvette meets with the special education teacher to share an overview of her plans and to discuss Rolando's special needs.

Sometimes the word-identification lessons are whole class; at other times they are with small groups of students who need instruction in a specific skill area. Yvette uses the skill tests provided with the basal series to decide who needs additional help in small groups. While Yvette meets with a small group, the rest of the class completes other suitable reading and writing activities related to the basal story. Figure 13.8 presents Yvette's weekly schedule.

Putting It Together in a Whole-Language Program

Debbie Greenspan teaches second grade in a school that has adopted the whole-language philosophy. The faculty has elected not to purchase basal readers; instead, funds are allocated for the purchase of trade books for each classroom. Debbie plans around thematic units. The art and music specialists in her school do not have separate classes. Rather, they help Debbie set up music and art centers and activities related to her thematic unit, and at least twice a week they come to Debbie's class to work with students during center time.

Figure 13.9 outlines Debbie's daily schedule. Debbie likes to include plenty of time for independent reading and writing activities, and for sharing activities. Debbie allots time for whole-class instruction in reading, writing, and mathematics. She

FIGURE 13.8

Yvette's Weekly Reading and Language Arts Schedule

Monday

Whole Class
9:00–9:30   Classwide Peer Tutoring
9:30–10:05   Introduction to basal vocabulary and spelling words
10:05–10:30   Lesson on word identification or comprehension skill

Tuesday

Whole Class
9:00–9:30   Self-selected reading
                 Journal writing
9:30–10:05   Prestory discussion

Seatwork and Centers
10:05–10:30   Centers focus on additional practice with vocabulary, spelling, and skill
                 lesson of week
                 Teacher meets with small groups of students who need extra help
                 with target skills
                 Some students with reading problems listen to a tape recording of a basal story

Wednesday

Whole Class
9:00–9:30   Classwide Peer Tutoring
9:30–10:05   Directed silent reading of story. Some students continue to listen to
                 audiotape of story

Seatwork
10:05–10:30   Workbook questions related to story

Thursday

Whole Class
9:00–9:30   Self-selected reading
                 Journal writing
9:30–10:05   Continued discussion of story
                 Discussion of workbook questions finished previous day

Seatwork and Centers
10:05–10:30   Writing centers have follow-up activities related to story
                 Teacher meets with small groups for skill lessons

Friday

Whole Class
9:00–9:30   Classwide Peer Tutoring
9:30–10:05   Spelling Test
                 Basal Comprehension and Skills Tests

Seatwork and Centers
10:05–10:30   Reteaching of skills in small groups as needed

FIGURE 13.9

Debbie's Daily Schedule

8:30–9:00	Arrival, journal writing, self-selected reading. Morning "Sharation"—time for news of the day, sharing of great books read and great stories written by students, singing.
9:00–9:20	Word Wall Activities
9:20–9:50	Making Words (Monday and Wednesday) Classwide Peer Tutoring (Tuesday and Thursday) Comprehension Strategy Lessons (Friday)
9:50–10:30	Writer's Workshop
10:30–11:30	Math
11:30–12:00	Lunch
12:00–12:20	Teacher Read Aloud
12:20–1:00	Whole Class Science/Social Studies Lesson. (Using Reading Comprehension Strategies such as Collaborative Strategic Reading and K–W–L as needed when text is used)
1:00–1:45	Time in reading, writing, science, social studies, music, and math centers related to thematic units.
1:45–2:15	Physical Education
2:15–2:45	Independent reading and writing, conferences, mini-lessons.
2:45–3:00	Afternoon "Sharation," review of the day, story retelling, singing.

also plans regular minilessons for small groups of students, and provides individual and small-group minilessons as necessary. During writing period, for example, Debbie might pull a small group of students for a minilesson on consonant blends while other students work on independent reading. Debbie uses her school district's curricular objectives as a framework for planning minilessons. During the school year she carefully observes each student's reading and writing, and keeps anecdotal records of evidence of their progress in meeting each objective. She also keeps folders that include examples of their work, and checklists of curricular objectives on which she records when a student masters an objective. This ongoing informal assessment helps Debbie decide who to pull for individual or small-group minilessons.

SUMMARY

- The most substantive challenge to traditional basal reading programs has been the whole-language instruction movement, with its emphasis on teacher and student empowerment and of authenticity of reading materials.
- The most persistent concern about whole-language programs for teaching reading to students with reading problems is the lack of consistent, systematic instruction in word identification and comprehension.
- Newer literature-based basal readers include more stories from children's literature, more language arts connections, and suggestions for more authentic reading and writing activities.

- *Eclectic* programs—programs that merge whole language with intensive, systematic approaches to word recognition and comprehension instruction—are beginning to emerge.
- Five important concepts describe reading as a process. Reading is *interactive, strategic,* an *active search for meaning, construction of meaning,* and *socially mediated.*
- Because reading is a complex process, it includes not only many areas of potential difficulty for students, but also many factors that influence whether students will learn to read.
- The key principles of effective reading instruction for all learners include: establishing an environment that promotes reading, establishing appropriate goals, and providing appropriate instruction and assessment.
- Students—especially those with reading and learning problems—need systematic instruction in word identification, which includes lots of practice with words in context and with words in isolation.
- Research has indicated the importance of phonological awareness in learning to read.

Training in phonological awareness (which involves being in tune with the sounds of language and how to manipulate them) is the backbone of phonics instruction.
- Some students have difficulty automatically recognizing words in print, and need specific instruction with sight words.
- Students are fluent in reading when they can recognize printed words quickly and effortlessly. When students read with automaticity, their reading comprehension is improved. Reading fluency takes practice; when teaching fluency, it is recommended that techniques for word identification and comprehension be taught simultaneously.
- The ultimate goal of reading is understanding. For many students, however, just reading the words does not mean that they understand the words. Students frequently need to learn specific ways to get ready for reading, to activate understanding during reading, and to summarize and reflect about what they have read.

Key Terms and Concepts

alliteration
alphabetic principle
attitude goals
automaticity
basal reading program
Big Books
blending
Classwide Peer Tutoring (CWPT)
content goals
comprehension strategies
decoding
DISSECT
eclectic programs
fluency
grapho-phonic cues

high-frequency words
K–W–L strategy
Making Words
metacognition
phoneme
Phonemic Pairs
phonics instruction
phonological awareness
print-rich environment
process goals
Question–Answer Relationships Strategy (QAR)
reading comprehension
reciprocal causation

reciprocal teaching
repeated reading
rhyming
segmentation
semantic cues
story retelling
structural analysis
summarization strategy
Sight Word Association Procedure (SWAP)
syntactic cues
two-tiered instruction
whole-language
word identification

Think and Apply

1. Now that you have read Chapter 13, reread the interview with Ines. What strategies does she use to teach word identification, fluency, and comprehension to her third grade students? What procedures does she use that you would or would not incorporate into your own reading program?

2. Make a list of pros and cons of basal reading programs for students with reading and learning disabilities. Make a list of pros and cons of whole-language programs for students with reading and learning disabilities. Then write a position statement indicating your personal resolution.

3. Think about your own experience learning to read. What instructional methods were most helpful in mastering the process of reading? What instructional methods were least helpful?

4. Think about several students you have taught or are currently teaching who are not experiencing success in learning to read. Which components of the reading process pose the most problems for each student?

5. Plan a whole-class lesson to teach phonological awareness, phonics, sight words, fluency, and comprehension.

6. Plan a small-group activity to teach phonological awareness, phonics, sight words, fluency, and comprehension.

7. Interview three teachers about how they plan their reading and language arts program. Specifically ask about how they plan for students with reading and learning disabilities.

8. Review the last main section in this chapter. How would you change Yvette's and Debbie's schedules if you were to teach in a basal or whole-language program?

Read More about It

1. Cunningham, P., & Allington, R. (1994). *Classrooms that work: They can all read and write.* New York: HarperCollins.

   An excellent resource for planning effective, multi-level reading instruction in diverse classrooms.

2. Cunningham, P. M. (1995). *Phonics they use: Words for reading and writing* (2nd ed.). New York: HarperCollins.

   A short, power-packed manual of instructional strategies for teaching word recognition.

3. Duffy, G. G. (Ed.). *Reading in the middle school* (2nd ed.). Newark, DE: International Reading Association.

   Contains excellent suggestions for reading assessment and instruction in the middle school.

4. Edelsky, C., Altwerger, B., & Flores, B. (1991). *Whole language: What's the difference?* Portsmouth, NH: Heinemann.

5. Irwin, J. W., & Baker, I. (1989). *Promoting active reading comprehension strategies: A resource book for teachers.* Englewood Cliffs, NJ: Prentice-Hall.

   A virtual cookbook of ideas for teaching and assessing reading comprehension.

   A brief overview of the whole-language philosophy, with history and descriptions of whole-language classrooms.

6. Morrow, L. M. (1993). *Literacy development in the early years: Helping children read and write.* Boston: Allyn & Bacon.

   An excellent tool for planning reading programs for preschool through the primary grades.

7. Stahl, S. A., Osborn, J., & Lehr, F. (1990). *Beginning to read: Thinking and learning about print, a summary.* Urbana-Champaign, IL: Center for the Study of Reading.

   A monograph summarizing the book authored by Marilyn Adams and printed by MIT Press (commissioned by the United States government).

8. Tierney, R. J., Readence, J. E., & Dishner, E. K. (1990). *Reading strategies and practices: A compendium* (3rd ed.). Boston: Allyn & Bacon.

   A collection of detailed strategies for word identification, fluency, and comprehension, includes underlying research as well as cautions and comments.

MAKING A DIFFERENCE
through Action Teaching

Reading Activities for All Learners

Phonological Awareness Songs

Objective: To teach sound matching, isolation, blending and segmentation.

Grades: Kindergarten to Third grade.

Materials: Song sheets or poster with words to songs.

Teaching Procedure:
1. For younger students, the singing and rhyming may occur only as a listening activity.
2. For older students, words and letters could be added using song sheets or posters with words to the songs.

Yopp-Troyer Song Sheet

Sound Matching Activity
(To the tune of "Jimmy Cracked Corn and I Don't Care")

Teacher: Who has an /m/ word to share with us?
           Who has an /m/ word to share with us?
           Who has an /m/ word to share with us?
           It must start with the /m/ sound.

Child: Man is a word that starts with /m/
           Man is a word that starts with /m/
           Man is a word that starts with /m/
           Man starts with the /m/ sound.

Sound Isolation Activity
(To the tune of "Old MacDonald Had a Farm")

What's the sound that starts these words:
Turtle, time, and teeth? (wait for a response)
T is the sound that starts these words:
Turtle, time, and teeth.
with a /t/, /t/ here, and a /t/, /t/ there,
Here a /t/, there a /t/, everywhere a /t/, /t/.
T is the sound that starts these words:
Turtle, time, and teeth.
(This can be used with medial and final sounds as well).

Blending Activity
(To the tune of "If You're Happy and You Know It, Clap Your Hands")

If you think you know this word, shout it out!
If you think you know this word, shout it out!
If you think you know this word,
Then tell me what you've heard,
If you think you know this word, shout it out!
(Sound out a word slowly such as /m/–/a/–/n/ and have students blend the sounds to make a word)

Segmentation Activity
(To the tune of "Twinkle, Twinkle, Little Star")

Listen, listen
To my word

Then tell me all the sounds you heard: cape
(slowly)
/k/ is one sound
/a/ is two
/p/ is last in cape
It's true.
Thanks for listening
To my words
And telling all the sounds you heard!

Yopp, H. (1992). Developing phonemic awareness in young children. *The Reading Teacher, 45,* 696–703.

Sound Magic Game

Objective: To improve phonological awareness of beginning, medial, and ending sounds.

Grades: Primary.

Materials: List of one syllable words.

Teaching Procedure:
1. Decide if you want to play Sound Magic with the whole class or with small groups of students.
2. Place all participating students in a circle.
3. Begin by introducing a one syllable word.
4. Explain that you play the game by moving the word around the circle from person to person. To move the word you make a new word by changing the beginning, middle, or middle sound and say the new word out loud. For example, you might start out with the word "sit." The first child might form the new word "hit," next child "hat," and next child "mat" and so on.
5. If a child can't think of a word in a reasonable period of time, the child can pass.
6. Keep going until there are three passes in a row.
7. Start again with a new word and with the next child.
8. The object of the game is to make words out of one word and to break the group's record.

Compound Concentration

Objective: To give the students practice in identifying compound words and to illustrate how words may be combined to form compound words.

Grades: Intermediate and secondary

Materials: 36 index cards (3" × 5") on which the two parts of 18 compound words have been written. Make sure each part can only be joined with one other part.

Reading Activities for All Learners (continued)

Teaching Procedure: Explain the game. Have the students shuffle the cards and place them face down in six rows with six cards each. Each player takes a turn at turning over two cards. The student then decides whether the two words make a compound word. If they do not, the cards are again turned face down and the next player takes a turn. If the words make a compound word, the player gets the two cards and turns over two more cards. The student continues playing until two cards are turned over that do not make a compound word. The game is over when all the cards are matched. The player with the most cards wins.

Adaptations: Students can match synonyms, antonyms, prefixes, suffixes, initial or final consonants, categories, and sight words.

Bos, C., & Vaughn, S. (1994). *Strategies for students with learning and behavior problems* (3rd ed.). Boston: Allyn & Bacon.

How Short Can You Make It?

Objective: To improve summarizing skills.

Grades: Intermediate grades and above.

Materials: Any reading material.

Teaching Procedure:
1. Decide whether to play this game as a whole class or small group activity.
2. Have students read a sentence or paragraph aloud or silently.
3. Give students time to think how to reduce the sentence or paragraph to its most important ideas, write down their reduction, and make edits as needed.
4. Have students "bid" on how short they can make it. For example, one student might say, "I can reduce it to six words," another might say, "I can reduce it to four words."
5. The lowest bidder then reads his or her reduction. If the group agrees that it maintains all key ideas, then the lowest bidder gets to conduct the next round of bidding. If not, then necessary revisions are made and the teacher runs the next round of bidding.

WH-Game

Objective: To provide students practice in answering who, what, when, where, why, and how questions.

Grades: All grades.

Materials: (1) Generic gameboard, spinner, or die, and markers. (2) WH Cards: cards with "WH-Game" written on one side and one of these written on the other: Who, What, When, Where, Why, How. (3) Sets of Story and Article Cards: copies of short stories and articles mounted on cards. There should be one set for each player. Select topics of interest for the students' age level.

Teaching Procedure: Explain the game to students or have them read the directions. First, the players set up the game. Next, they select a set of Story or Article Cards. All players read the card and place it face down. Each player then takes a turn by throwing the die or spinning and selecting a WH-Card. The player must make up a question using the WH word and answer it correctly to move his or her marker the indicated number of spaces. If another player questions the validity of a player's question or answer, the players may look at the Story or Article card. Otherwise, these cards should remain face down during play. After ten questions have been asked using one Story or Article card, another set is selected. The students read this card and the game continues. The first player to arrive at the finish wins.

Adaptations: Students may also work in pairs, with one person on the team making up the question and the other person answering it.

Bos, C., & Vaughn, S. (1994). *Strategies for students with learning and behavior problems* (3rd ed.). Boston: Allyn & Bacon.

Comp Checks

Objective: To help students learn to monitor their own comprehension.

Grades: All grades.

Materials: Paper strips (2" × 8"). Assigned reading.

Teaching Procedure:
1. As you prepare a reading assignment, think about the characteristics of the text, your purpose for having students read the assignment, and your goals for learning about students response to the text.
2. Identify key comprehension monitoring goals. For example, you may want to know during a social studies reading assignment when a student is bored or confused, when a student thinks an idea is important, and when a student encounters a surprising new fact.
3. Brainstorm with students to create a code. For example, Bored = ^, Confused = ?, Important idea = *, Surprising fact = !
4. While students read, have them record page numbers and codes on paper strips.
5. After reading, focus the discussion on what students found to be boring, confusing, new, and surprising.

Facilitating Writing

FOCUS QUESTIONS

1. What are current trends in writing curriculum and instruction, and how might they impact your planning for writing instruction in your classroom?

2. What are areas of potential difficulty in writing for students with disabilities?

3. What are principles of effective writing instruction for all learners?

4. What strategies can you implement for students who have difficulties with composition?

5. What strategies can you implement for students who have difficulties writing stories?

6. What strategies can you implement for students who have difficulties with informational writing?

7. What strategies can you implement to help all students develop spelling skills?

8. What strategies can you implement to help all students develop handwriting skills?

Interview

Gina Terry

Gina Terry is a fourth grade teacher at South Miami Heights Elementary in Miami, Florida. The special education teacher, Galia Pennecamp, is assigned full-time to Gina's inclusion classroom of thirty-two students, twelve of whom are students with learning disabilities.

In Florida, all fourth grade students are required to take a statewide writing assessment test, *Florida Writes.* Here's what Gina says about writing instruction:

When I first heard about the *Florida Writes* test, I panicked. I really didn't learn too much about writing instruction in my undergraduate program. Even when I was in elementary school, we didn't write much and what I remember about it wasn't too motivating. All I remember is a lot of red ink! I kept wondering, "How am I going to prepare them for this test—and keep it fun?"

Two events in my life helped changed my attitude about writing. The first is that Nina Zaragoza, a professor at Florida International University, taught a workshop about writing at our school. While she was giving the workshop, she talked about different stages of writing—brainstorming, drafting, editing, and publishing—but frankly, I didn't think my students would have the patience for all that. Nina agreed to spend a day in my class to show me how to get it going. I was amazed—the students were excited about writing for the first time. They really felt like authors and started taking pride in their written work. Nina showed me that it could be done. The students with problems with writing didn't necessarily publish as much as some other children, but they worked hard on their stories. It was not unusual for students to say, "Can we write today?" They actually asked to write! Best of all, Nina taught me how to build spelling, handwriting, and composition skills required by the school district curriculum objectives into the students real writing. I began to realize that students could spend more time on their writing, less time on worksheets. Through whole-class and small-group minilessons, they could still learn their basic language arts skills. Galia, my special education partner, is most helpful here. While students write their books and stories, she zeros in on the students with learning disabilities and gives them the support they need to feel successful as authors.

The second event that changed my mind about writing was attending the Zelda Glazer Writing Workshop sponsored by Dade County Public Schools and the University of Miami. Each school in Dade County is allowed to nominate one teacher . . . to go to this week-long summer event. During that week I learned strategies to spark student writing even more. Probably the most helpful thing I learned was how to give students feedback about their writing in positive, constructive ways.

We do what we call Writing Workshop in our class three or four times a week. You should see it—it really looks like a writer's studio. The children are busy brainstorming about stories with their friends, drafting, editing each other's drafts, or working in the publishing center making covers or illustrating their books. Their favorite time is when we share stories together as a whole class.

You should also know that writing is not limited to Writing Workshop time. Writing is integrated with our thematic units and with the literature that we read together and individually. Each student has a personal journal and makes daily entries in the journal. Each student also has a pen pal. My college roommate teaches fourth grade in Ohio, so we send letters to our Ohio pen pals every other week. It's safe to say that we write all day long.

Introduction

Like many teachers, Gina has discovered that writing instruction can be dynamic and exciting. Throughout the country students are beginning to realize that they are authors—writing to real audiences for real purposes. Recently, for example, one of the authors of this book met Sara, a second grader, who asked, "What do you do?" When told, "I am a writer," Sara said, "I am an author too. I've written six books." Her mother proudly concurred. Sara's six books are part of the family's home library and will be saved to share with Sara's children and grandchildren some day. They are a family treasure. This chapter focuses on ways to bring the joy of writing to all students.

Current Trends in Writing Curriculum and Instruction

Gina's experience is similar to that of many teachers over the past decade. Over a period of two years Gina—already aware of the current trend toward integration of the language arts (reading, writing, speaking, and listening)—gradually picked up on other major trends in writing instruction:

- movement toward a student-centered model of writing instruction
- importance of early writing experiences
- greater allotment of time to writing instruction

A Student-Centered Model of Writing Instruction

In recent years, the growing trend has been toward a **student-centered model** of instruction for English and the language arts. The emphasis in this model is on giving students ample opportunity to find personal meaning in what they are reading and writing. Skills (rather than being taught in isolation, as they are in more traditional models) are part of connected, meaningful experiences in communication.

The work of Donald Graves (1983) is a major contribution to the understanding of writing as a student-centered activity. His observations of children as they write reveal that even young children go through an **authoring cycle** of prewriting, composing (drafting), and post-writing (revising, editing, and publishing). Graves and others (Atwell, 1987; Calkins, 1991; Hansen, 1985; Routman, 1991) have provided educators with procedures for implementing this authoring cycle in the classroom and for helping students and teachers realize the importance of authorship and audience.

Charles Schwartz teaches eighth grade language arts, using a student-centered model. Charles—who uses no textbooks—integrates reading, writing, speaking, and listening activities in his language arts program. To document students' progress in writing, Charles uses writing samples, self- and peer evaluations, and teacher-observation checklists. His classroom looks like a writer's workshop—daily, students are busy prewriting, writing, post-writing, and thinking of new and creative ways to share their work in the classroom and beyond. Charles says that his role is to serve as a writing coach providing not only encouragement, but also direct skills instruction.

> Two, three, and four year olds scribble and sometimes mix their scribble with letters and pictures. For young writers scribble has meaning (Heald-Taylor, 1984).

Although the student-centered model promotes creativity and student productivity, critics claim that teaching of skills is incidental, inconsistent, and not intensive enough for students with problems in learning to write. This chapter provides specific suggestions for making a student-centered model work for all students in your classroom.

Early Writing Experiences

Until recently, traditional thinking was that students needed to learn to read before they could learn to write. As a matter of fact, not only was writing instruction delayed until students learned to read, but composition was not encouraged until students learned to form letters and spell in a conventional manner. The work of Read (1971) and Chomsky (1979) indicates that reading and writing develop simultaneously and that children's **invented spelling** (i.e., their early attempts to spell in their own way) can reveal a great deal about their phonological awareness.

Thus, the current trend is to encourage students—as early as possible—to write. Even if they can't form conventional letters or spell standard English, it is important to try to get their ideas down in any way possible: pictures, scribble, pretend letters, or invented spelling. These early forms of writing create a natural sequence for learning to write, and should be encouraged.

More Instructional Time for Writing

In response to national concern about the quality of writing among students in the United States, the amount of time allotted to writing instruction has increased in recent years (Graham et al., 1991). Fifteen years ago, when Alice Newell started teaching eleventh grade English, she gave her students one writing assignment every other week. At the end of the year, students had to spend about one month writing a research paper on some aspect of U. S. history.

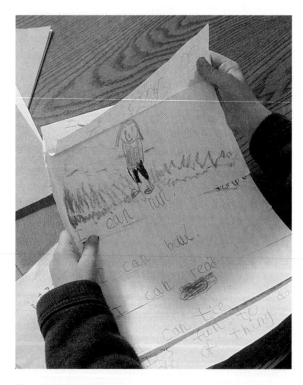

Should children be encouraged to write before they can read or spell? Why or why not?

Three years ago, when her school district mandated daily writing assignments, Alice was upset—daily assignments, when she was overwhelmed by having to grade *weekly* assignments for her 135 students? Since that time Alice has learned that students can be taught to provide constructive peer review of each other's writing. She has learned also that although students write daily, they might work on the same piece (revising, editing, etc.) for several days—or several weeks. And she has learned that the teacher does not need to be the only audience for student work—there are other ways for students to share what they have written.

The trend toward allotting more time to writing extends to other content areas at all grade levels. For example, secondary teachers are assigning both informal (e.g., journals, diaries) and formal (e.g., essays, reflection papers) writing in their classes (Ellis, 1994; Healy & Barr, 1991).

Teaching of Writing as a Process

Think about some of your recent experiences as a writer. Perhaps you were writing a research paper for school. You might have been writing a letter or an e-mail message to a friend. Maybe you were carefully crafting a letter to apply for a job. Think about the process. To compose, you needed to:

- formulate your message in your head
- organize your ideas in a logical fashion
- think about the reader, and how he or she might understand and react to the message
- choose words carefully to make the flow of language, the syntax, smooth
- select individual words to convey your meaning succinctly
- attend to your spelling, capitalization, and punctuation
- consider the appearance of the final product (legibility of your handwriting, typing, or word processing)

Like reading, writing is a complex process. Difficulties can occur at any point in the process. Tips for Teachers 14.1 offers general guidelines for teaching writing to students who have difficulty.

TIPS FOR TEACHERS

14.1 Guidelines for Teaching Writing to Students with Learning Disabilities

1. *Allocate adequate time for writing.* Adequate time is a necessary criterion for improving the writing skills of special learners. Students need a minimum of thirty minutes a day for writing.
2. *Provide a range of writing tasks.* Students should select topics and write about what they know. After students' skills improve, the range of writing tasks should broaden to include problem solving, writing games, and other assignments.
3. *Create a social climate that promotes and encourages writing.* Teachers set the tone through acceptance and encouragement. Conferences between students, students and teachers, and students and other people in the school are conducted to provide constructive feedback and audiences with whom to share writing.
4. *Integrate writing with other academic subjects.* Writing can be integrated with every subject. Use writing as a means of expression in content areas such as social studies and science.
5. *Focus on the processes central to writing.* These processes include prewriting activities, writing, and rewriting activities.
6. *Focus on composing, and attend to spelling and punctuation after the writing is complete.*

Mechanics interfere with some students' ability to get ideas down on paper successfully. Focus first on basic elements to facilitate the writing process.

7. *Teach characteristics of good writing.* Implicit knowledge about writing needs to be made explicit. For example, discuss different genres and their characteristics.
8. *Teach skills that aid composing.* Skills include conferencing, brainstorming, sentence writing, and evaluating the effectiveness of the written piece.
9. *Ask students to identify goals for improving their writing.* Students can set realistic goals regarding their progress in writing. Goals can focus on prewriting, writing, and rewriting. Students and teacher can provide feedback on how well the goals are realized.
10. *Avoid using instructional practices that do not improve writing.* Such practices include grammar instruction, diagramming sentences, and overemphasis on students' errors.

Source: Graham, S., & Harris, K. R. (1988). Instructional recommendations for teaching writing to exceptional students, *Exceptional Children, 54*(6), 506–512. Copyright 1988 by The Council for Exceptional Children. Reprinted with permission.

Writing Is an Interactive Process

As readers use graphophonic, syntactic, and semantic cue systems to decode and understand text, writers use the sounds, grammar, and meaning of our language system to **encode** and to communicate a message to the reader. And in writing as in reading, students may have problems with any aspect of the language system—with using language interactively, and with using it fluently. In addition, students may have problems with the physical act of writing.

For example, Grant Ellsworth, a fifth grader with learning disabilities, loves to tell stories—especially about fishing with his father—but is reluctant when asked to write them. Grant is a poor speller and for some reason cannot get the hang of capitalization and punctuation rules. In addition, his handwriting is illegible and he doesn't have the patience to learn to use a keyboard. Writing a single sentence takes Grant so long that he soon loses his story and its intended meaning. Even though Grant can tell stories in a most entertaining way, he cannot get them on paper.

Writing Is a Strategic Process

Because writing is such a complex task, successful writers need a strategy or plan to communicate ideas clearly. It is important to have systematic procedures for being successful and productive at each stage of the authoring cycle. Students, especially those with learning and behavior problems, often have difficulty not only planning their writing, but also monitoring and regulating themselves while they write. Since the 1980s, researchers have worked to develop ways to teach students to become strategic writers (Graham et al., 1991). Students should find a checklist like the one in Tips for Teachers 14.2 helpful for monitoring their writing.

Writing Is an Active Attempt to Convey Meaning

The purpose of writing is to communicate a message. If you ask a student with good writing skills, "What is writing?" the response might be, "Writing is communication of thoughts and ideas," or "Writing is sharing a good story." Some students, however, assume that the purpose of writing is to conform to the conventions of writing (Graham et al., 1991). Asked the same question, students with writing problems might respond, "Writing is spelling all the words right," or "Writing is making a very neat paper."

How can students arrive at such a misconception about writing? Consider the example of Jim Reed, a seventh grade student with learning disabilities who has been assigned to the special education resource room since third grade. In all that time, the focus of his instruction in writing has been on mechanics—spelling, capitalization, and punctuation. He has had worksheet after worksheet for more than four years, and still can't get it right. Jim's case is not unusual. In an examination of writing instruction in ten urban schools, Christenson, Thurlow, Ysseldyke, and McVicar (1989) found that the majority of writing instruction for students with learning disabilities was related to mechanics rather than to composing for genuine audiences.

Writing Is a Process of Constructing Meaning

When a writer composes, he or she needs to keep potential readers in mind. Readers need to have background information and specific links (such as examples, and definitions of new terms) to help them connect the new information with what they already know. In short, the writer needs to take responsibility for helping readers to construct meaning. Students with writing difficulties may not understand the role of audience or potential readers, or how to help readers construct meaning by providing background knowledge and using predictable story or informational writing structures.

For example, Terry Macinello wrote a story about a recent trip but did not indicate where or why he went on his trip, and only gave sketchy details of one event. In his narrative, which had no distinguishable beginning, middle, or end, he referred to family members without letting the reader know who they were. Terry doesn't realize that when he writes a story, it is for someone to read, and that he needs to fill in some gaps so that readers can understand and enjoy his story.

RESEARCH BRIEF

EFFECTIVENESS OF THE WRITING PROCESS WITH STUDENTS WITH LEARNING DISABILITIES

How do students with disabilities progress as writers in a general education Writer's Workshop? Zaragoza and Vaughn (1992) conducted three year-long case studies (with students identified as gifted, low-achieving, and learning disabled) in which they examined the students' progress in writing and writing-related skills (e.g., capitalization, spelling, punctuation). Single case studies have revealed that students in all achievement groups benefit from participating in the writing process. For example, one student with learning disabilities was very hesitant about writing. He asked for constant teacher assistance and would not write unless a teacher worked closely with him. He wrote slowly and neatly, even on first drafts. His first piece of writing was untitled and incomplete. He was insecure about working with

TIPS FOR TEACHERS

14.2 Helping Students Monitor Their Writing

_____ I found a quiet place to work.

_____ I set up a schedule for when I would work on this paper.

_____ I read or listened to the teacher's directions carefully.

_____ I thought about who would read my paper.

_____ I thought about what I wanted my paper to accomplish.

_____ I started planning my paper before I actually started writing it.

_____ I tried to remember everything I already knew about the topic before I started to write.

_____ I got all the information I needed before starting to write.

_____ I organized my information before starting to write.

_____ I thought about the reader as I wrote.

_____ I thought about what I wanted to accomplish as I wrote.

_____ I continued to develop my plans as I wrote.

_____ I revised the first draft of my paper.

_____ I checked what I wrote to make sure that the reader would understand it.

_____ I checked to make sure that I accomplished my goals.

_____ I reread my paper before turning it in.

_____ I asked other students, the teacher, or my parents when I needed help.

_____ I rewarded myself when I finished my paper.

Source: Harris, K. R., & Graham, S. (1992). _Helping young writers master the craft: Strategy instruction and self-regulation in the writing process._ Boston: Brookline Books. Reprinted by permission.

---

other students and never volunteered to share his writing. His piece, entitled "Disneyworld," demonstrated an understanding that you can write down what you really think. He included his own dog in a Disneyworld theme ("Goofy is a dog I like to play with but Goofy is not better than my dog.") The other students loved this story, and asked him to read it over and over.

Subsequently, he frequently volunteered to share his writing with the class. He had a flair for good endings and became the class expert on developing endings. For example, in "The Spooky Halloween," he ended with "Halloween is nothing to play with." "Freddy Is in My Room" ended with "Give it up." This student and many others demonstrated gains on standardized writing measures, as well as increased confidence and skills in their daily writing.

Writing Is a Socially Mediated Language-Learning Activity

To become more proficient writers, students must have social interaction with others to move forward (Vygotsky, 1978). Students who have experienced failure learning to write may be reluctant to share their writing with teachers and peers because they are embarrassed about their lack of skill in writing mechanics. It is important, however, that students have the opportunity not only to share their writing, but also to have that sharing

Shared writing (writing with a teacher, student partner, or group of students) can help some reluctant writers get started and feel more confident about authorship (Mather & Lackowicz, 1992).

focus on the intended meaning rather than on how many words are misspelled. It is also important for young writers to have time to talk with the teacher about composing strategies (Bereiter & Scardamalia, 1982).

Strategies for Establishing an Environment That Promotes Writing

From what you have already read about current trends and effective writing instruction, you can imagine the importance of planning the environment in which writing is taught. You may recall that Gina (a general education teacher) and her teaching partner Galia (a special education teacher) have created a classroom environment that encourages students to write. Gina and Galia have learned that the classroom's physical and social environment both need to be considered when you establish a writing community.

Physical Environment

As they planned the physical arrangement of their classroom at the beginning of the year, Gina and Galia had a vision of creating a writer's studio. According to Graves (1983), the classroom setting should create a work atmosphere similar to that of a studio, which promotes independence and in which students can easily interact. Gina and Galia felt that structuring their classroom as a studio was especially important for students who had already experienced failure in writing. The message they wanted to convey from day one was, "This is a place for writers and all of us are writers. Enjoy!" Figure 14.1 shows how Gina and Galia arranged the room to create such an atmosphere.

A publishing center is set up for making books. Writing materials and supplies are plentiful and readily available to students. At the beginning of the year, Gina and Galia explain guidelines for using materials in responsible ways. In addition to individual writing folders for ongoing writing projects, each student also has an assessment portfolio that serves as a record of his or her progress in writing. Individual folders and portfolios are located in a permanent place in the classroom—ready

for student or parent conferences. Gina and Galia wanted the room arranged so that students could work together or individually. They planned spaces for writing conferences of small groups of students, teacher and student, and student and student.

Social Environment

Realizing that for students to write well, an environment of mutual trust and respect is essential, Gina and Galia have posted the Writing Workshop's student guidelines (see Figure 14.2) in their classroom.

Writers must also be able to depend on the predictability of the classroom structure. Most important, Gina and Galia have read that the tone for writing is set by what the teacher does (Graves, 1983). The guidelines these teachers follow to establish a social environment for a productive writing community are presented in Tips for Teachers 14.3.

Strategies for Conducting a Writing Workshop

If you were to visit Gina and Galia's classroom during their Writing Workshop, the first thing you would notice is variety of activities. Some students would be working individually on a writing project, others would be working in small groups or pairs, generating ideas for a book or putting the final touches on a story. You would also observe that the teachers are very busy. You might see Gina **conferencing** with a student or Galia teaching a minilesson on punctuation to a small group. You would discover that students choose not only their own topics but also their own writing format (e.g., letter to a pen pal, story biography) and that many have two or three writing projects in progress at a time. Some students have even elected to co-author with a classmate. You would also note that amid all this activity, there is routine. Students seem to know exactly what to do and how to get help if they need it.

What is involved in the writing process? In **prewriting**, a writer collects information about a topic by observing, remembering, interviewing, and reading. In **composing** (or **drafting**), the author

FIGURE 14.1

Room Diagram

Writing Rules

Carrels

Carrels

Room Rules

Computer

Reference & Trade Books

Writing Supplies

Individual Folders

Bos, C. S., & Vaughn, S. (1994). *Strategies for teaching students with learning and behavior problems* (3rd ed.). Boston, MA: Allyn & Bacon.

attempts to get ideas on paper in the form of a draft. The drafting process tells the author what he or she knows or does not know. In **post-writing,** the author revises, edits, and publishes the work.

During **revising,** the focus is on meaning—points are explored further, ideas are elaborated, and further connections are made. When the author is satisfied with the content, **editing** takes place as the

FIGURE 14.2

Writing Workshop

Writing Workshop

1. Write three first drafts.
2. Pick one draft to publish.
3. Self-edit your draft.
4. Have a friend edit your draft.
5. Take your draft to an adult to edit.
6. Publish your draft.
7. Read over your final copy and make corrections.
8. Give a friend your final copy to make corrections.
9. Give an adult your final copy to make corrections.
10. Put your final copy in a cover.
11. Share, help others, go back to step 1.

Our Rights

- We have the right to use the things in our classroom.
- We have the right to receive caring from our teachers.
- We have the right to be listened to by our teachers and friends.
- We have the right to call our families in cases of emergency.
- We have the right to be decision makers in our classroom.

Our Responsibilities

- We have the responsibility to encourage and be caring toward our friends and teachers.
- We have the responsibility to treat all things in our classroom carefully.
- We have the responsibility to participate in all activities and help our community to become strong and positive.
- We have the responsibility to help others to meet their responsibilities successfully.

Classroom Rules

- We try our best.
- We listen and look when others talk.
- We are kind and helpful to others.
- We help others remember the rules.

Rewards

- We feel proud.
- We have parties and free time.
- We call, tell, write our family.

Consequences

- We feel sad and disappointed.
- We lose parties and free time.
- We call, tell, write our family.

Zaragoza, N., & Vaughn, S. (1995). *Writing Workshop Manual.* Unpublished manuscript.

author reviews the piece line by line to determine that each word is necessary. Punctuation, spelling, and other mechanical processes are checked. The final element is **publishing**. If the author considers the piece a good one, it is published.

Students with writing problems differ in the degree to which components of the writing process are difficult for them (Stires, 1983; Zaragoza & Vaughn, 1992). Many students with writing problems experience significant difficulty

TIPS FOR TEACHERS

14.3 Establishing a Social Environment for Productive Writing

1. *Write every day for at least thirty minutes.* Students need time to think, write, discuss, rewrite, confer, revise, talk, read, and write some more. Good writing takes time.
2. *Encourage students to develop areas of expertise.* At first, students will write broadly about what they know. With encouragement, however, they can become class experts in a particular area, subject, or writing form. Take the time to help students discover their own writing "turf."
3. *The teacher writes.* Write with students in the classroom. Using an overhead or easel, teachers may share how they compose.
4. *Share writing.* Include in the writing time an opportunity for the whole class to meet to read their writing to others and to exchange comments and questions.

5. *Read to the students.* Share and discuss books, poems, and other readings. Young authors can learn from the writing of others.
6. *Expand the writing community outside the classroom.* Place books published by your students in the library so that other students can use them and so that students can share their writing with other classes. Encourage authors from other classrooms to visit and read their writing.
7. *Develop students' capacity to evaluate their own work.* Students need to develop their own goals and document their progress toward them. By conferring with the teacher, they will learn methods for evaluating their own work.
8. *Slow the pace.* Graves (1985) says, "Teachers need to slow down so kids can hurry up." When teachers ask questions, they need to be patient, giving students time to answer.

---

in editing and writing final copies because they have difficulty with mechanics. These students often produce well-developed stories that are hard to read because of the mechanical errors. Other students with writing problems have difficulty organizing during the composing stage and need to rethink the sequencing during revision. Following are descriptions of each of the elements of the writing process.

Prewriting: Getting Started

"What should I write about?" As a teacher, it's easy to say, "Write about what you did during your summer vacation," but Graves (1983) emphasizes that the key to engaging students as writers is to have them select topics. Saying to students, "Just write about anything," isn't enough. The following section shows how to help students approach topic selection. Here's how.

Selecting Topics Give each student (and yourself) a piece of paper. Say to them, "You know lots of things about yourself, about your family, and about your friends. You have hobbies and activities that you like to do. You have stories about things that have happened to you and to people you know. You have lots of things to share with others. I want you to make a list of things you would like to share with others through writing. Do not put them in any specific order—just write them down as you think of them. You will not have to write on all of these topics. The purpose of this exercise is to think of as many topics as you can. I will give you about ten minutes. Begin."

Model the process by writing as many topics as you can think of during the assigned time. When time is up, tell the students to pick a partner and share their topics. They may add any new topics they think of at this time. Then share your list with the entire group and comment on topics you are looking forward to writing about. Ask for volunteers to read their topic lists to the entire group. Have students select the three topics they are most interested in writing about and place their topic lists in their writing folders as resources for future writing. Finally, ask students to select one of their top three topics and begin writing.

Topics should be selected by students (not by teachers with story starters, picture cues, and other stimuli). Every student knows things and has stories to tell. We need to have confidence in them and give them an opportunity to discover what they know.

What characteristics of a learning environment promote writing? How can teacher and students effectively conduct a Writing Workshop?

Problems in Topic Selection Maintaining a supply of writing topics is difficult for some students. When students tell you stories, ask them whether the story generates a topic they might want to write about. When students read or you read to them, ask whether the reading has given them ideas for their own writing. If they were going to write the end of the story, how would they do it? If they were going to continue this story, what would happen? If they were going to add characters to the story, what type of characters would they add? Would they change the setting?

> One way to model brainstorming for a topic is to use an overhead projector. On the transparency write a list of things you do very well—in which you're an expert. Then select one item from the list to write about. Have your students develop their own "expert list" and add it to their writing folder (Routman, 1991).

You can also facilitate topic selection by presenting a range of writing genres, including stories, factual descriptions, mysteries, poems, and observations. Students often begin by telling personal experiences. Through your writing and the writing of other authors, students can be introduced to different experiences that can generate topics.

Some students want to repeat the same topic. Students with writing problems may find security in repeating a topic or theme in their writing.

Before suggesting that students change topics, check whether their stories are changing in other ways (through development of vocabulary, concept, story, or character). Students may be learning a great deal about writing, even though the topic is the same.

Planning Prewriting also includes developing a plan for writing. Planning for writing includes the following steps:

1. *Identify the intended audience.* To make a writing project meaningful, it is important that the writer identify the audience. Who will be the reader? The audience might be family, friends, business people, politicians, teachers, potential employers—or one's self.
2. *State a purpose for writing.* The purpose for writing may be to inform, entertain, or persuade. An example of a purpose statement might be, "I am writing this imaginary story about my pet shark Gums to entertain my friends."
3. *Decide on a format.* Before writing begins it's good to have a general idea of how the piece will be structured. Although the structure may change during drafting and revision, at the prewriting stage it's good to have an initial road map.

Some students are limited in text-organization skills because they have difficulty categorizing ideas related to a specific topic, providing advance organizers for the topic, and relating and extending ideas about the topic (Englert & Raphael, 1988). As you teach the thought that goes into a piece of writing, you can model your own thinking as you move from topic selection to planning for audience, purpose, and format to drafting. During whole-class sharing time you can also encourage students to tell how they generated topics and planned for their own writing.

Composing

The purpose of the composing stage is to develop an initial draft that will be refined later. Some teachers call this a *sloppy copy*. Many students with learning and behavior problems think of a topic and, without much planning, begin writing. Composing is also difficult for students who lack fluency in the mechanics of writing or in the physical act of writing. During composing it is important that you assume the role of coach and encourage students to concentrate on getting their ideas on paper (Graham, 1992).

Revising and Editing

The purpose of revision is to make certain that the meaning is clear and that the message can be understood by others. Editing focuses mainly on mechanics, such as proofreading. After the students and teacher are happy with the content, it is time to correct spelling, capitalization, punctuation, and language. During editing, students circle words whose spelling they are not sure of, put boxes where they are unsure of punctuation, and underline sentences in which they feel the language may not be correct. Students are not expected to correct all errors, but are expected to correct known errors.

Revising and editing are difficult tasks for all writers, especially beginning writers and students for whom writing is difficult. Getting the entire message down on paper the first time is difficult enough; making changes so that the piece is at its best and can be understood by others is a most formidable task.

Most students with learning and behavior problems have difficulty revising and editing. Teachers often find it best initially to let students move to publication without much revision, then gradually show them the benefits of revision and editing.

The AOK Strategy The AOK strategy, which stands for all OK, (Schumm, 1987) is a way to help students learn to read and reread for different purposes during revision and editing: for meaning, paragraphs, sentences, words, and neatness. For students with learning and behavior problems, concentrate on one aspect of the AOK strategy at a time and build gradually. The strategy consists of evaluating five areas, as follows:

> *Revising,* which means attending to meaning, is an ongoing process. You need to tell your students that they may need to revise once, twice, or more until they feel that their intended meaning is expressed clearly and completely.

- **MOK** (Is the meaning OK?) This stage involves reading for revision, to determine whether the message is communicated to the reader. After "MOKing," many authors need to obtain more information or to confer with others to find out what parts of the piece are going over well and what parts need additional work. It is also at this stage that some authors abandon the piece and start again with a new idea.
- **POK** (Is each paragraph OK?) "POKing" is reading to see whether paragraphs are logically organized and made up of sentences that are all related to each other.
- **SOK** (Is each sentence OK?) "SOKing" is reading to determine whether sentences are well constructed and punctuated correctly.
- **WOK** (Is each word OK?) "WOKing" is reading to determine whether words are spelled, capitalized, and used correctly.
- **NOK** (Is the neatness OK?) "NOKing," the final stage, refers to getting the piece ready for publication.

The AOK strategy can be adapted to meet curriculum objectives at any grade level (see Table 14.1).

Peer Editing In addition to revising and editing their own work, students can serve as editors for

| **TABLE 14.1** |

AOK Sample Questions

FIRST GRADE	SIXTH GRADE
MOK (Is the meaning OK?) 1. Did I say what I wanted to say? 2. Does it make sense? 3. Are my facts correct?	**MOK** (Is the meaning OK?) 1. Are ideas expressed clearly? 2. Are ideas expressed concisely? 3. Are ideas expressed completely? 4. Are ideas expressed correctly?
	POK (Is each paragraph OK?) 1. Is each paragraph indented? 2. Do paragraphs consist of sentences related to one topic sentence? 3. Is each paragraph connected logically with paragraphs that come before and after?
SOK (Is each sentence OK?) 1. Is there a period or question mark at the end of each sentence? 2. Is the first word capitalized? 3. Does each sentence make sense?	**SOK** (Is each sentence OK?) 1. Is there a period, question mark, or exclamation mark at the end of each sentence? 2. Is the first word capitalized? 3. Does each sentence make sense? 4. Does each sentence express a complete thought? 5. Is the sentence a fragment or a run-on? 6. Do the subject and verb agree? 7. Are commas used correctly? 8. Are direct quotations capitalized and punctuated correctly?
WOK (Is each word OK?) 1. Is each word spelled correctly? 2. Are the names of people capitalized?	**WOK** (Is each word OK?) 1. Is each word spelled correctly? 2. Is each word capitalized correctly? 3. Is each word correct the way it is used in the sentence? 4. Are slang words used? 5. Are pronoun referents clear? 6. Are any words over-used? 7. Is each word the BEST word or could a more effective synonym be substituted?
NOK (Is the neatness OK?) 1. Are the size and shape of each letter OK? 2. Are words and letters spaced correctly? 3. Are the margins even? 4. Is the heading correct?	**NOK** (Is the neatness OK?) 1. Are the size, shape, and slant or letters OK? 2. Are words and letters spaced correctly? 3. Are the margins even? 4. Is the format correct?

Source: Schumm, J. S. (1987). A-OK: A reading for revision strategy. *Reading: Exploration and Discovery, 10* (1), 26–34.

the work of their peers. This **peer editing** can work several ways. One way is to have students edit their own work first and then ask a friend to edit it. Another way is to establish a class editor responsible for reading the material and finding mechanical errors. The role of class editor can rotate so that every student has an opportunity to serve in that capacity.

Using Microcomputers for Word Processing

Word processing on microcomputers holds great promise not only for students with writing disabilities, but also for students who have problems composing, spelling, or with handwriting. Using word processing software, students can revise and edit text more easily and can publish a neat, legible final product. Reviewing research on the use of microcomputers with students with writing disabilities, Majsterek (1990) observed that research in this area is in its infancy and has yielded mixed findings. Nonetheless, based on the current research, Majsterek made the following initial recommendations about using microcomputers with students with writing disabilities:

- Select computer software that emphasizes a process approach to writing (i.e., prewriting, composing, revising, editing, publishing). Examples are *The Ultimate Writing and Creativity Center* and *Student Writing and Research Center* (The Learning Company, 800-852-2255) *The Writing Workshop* (Milliken Publishing, 1-800-643-0008), and *Kidsworks,* by Davidson & Associates (800-545-7677).
- Select computer software that uses a sequence of menus rather than complicated Control keys or multistep commands.
- Make certain that students are familiar with the writing process before you introduce them to computer software.
- Review the software manual and either adapt for students with reading problems or develop cue sheets to simplify procedures.
- Keep in mind that, for many students, concurrently learning keyboarding, machine skills, and writing software commands can be a demanding task. Teach basic keyboarding and machine skills before you introduce writing-process software.
- Keep a balance between writing with and without a word processor so that students will work on handwriting, spelling, and composition skills in both modes.

Courtesy of The Learning Company.

Courtesy of Davidson & Associates, Inc.

It is important that students not be too critical while revising and editing each other's work. You can communicate that the purpose of revising and editing is to support the author in developing a finished piece. You can also model acceptable ways to give feedback.

Publishing

Not all student writing is published; often only one in five or six pieces is published. *Publishing* means preparing a piece so that others can read it. Publication is often in the form of books with cardboard bindings decorated with contact paper or scraps of wallpaper. Books can include a picture of the author, a description of the author, and a list of books published by the author. Young children writing short pieces may publish every two weeks, whereas older students who spend more time composing and revising publish less frequently.

Publishing is a way to confirm a student's hard work and share the piece with others. Publishing is also a way to involve others in school and at home with the students' writing. It is important for all students to publish, not just the best authors.

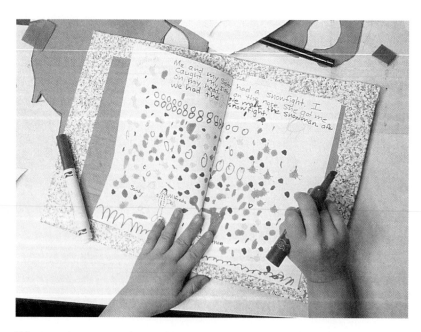

What are the stages of the writing process? What are some effective strategies for teaching each stage to students?

Sharing

Sharing work with others is important during all stages of the writing process. The "author's chair" (Graves & Hansen, 1983) is a formal opportunity to share writing. When Romain, a student who recently moved from Haiti to the United States, signed up for "author's chair" early in the school year, Galia and Gina were surprised. Romain, the most reluctant writer in their class, was also extremely self-conscious about not being able to spell. During "author's chair" Romain sat on a special stool in a circle of peers and read his letter to an imaginary pen pal in Haiti. He described life in Miami and ended with a wish, "I hope that you are happy and have enough food to eat." It turned out that most of Romain's story wasn't written at all—he held a paper in front of him and made up the letter as he spoke. But because Romain got a positive response from his audience about how well he communicated his ideas, he was encouraged to become a writer. The "author's chair" experience was his launching point.

Teachers often need to set rules for students' behavior when a classmate is sharing work in the "author's chair." Such rules might include raising your hand, asking a question, making a positive comment, and giving feedback when asked. A simple but powerful framework for students to give each other feedback about their writing is called TAG (Zaragoza, 1987):

Tell what you like.
Ask questions.
Give suggestions.

After an author has read his or her writing, the author leads the class in a TAG session, asking class members the three questions: "What did you like?" "Do you have any questions?" "Do you have any suggestions?" Three or four responses are usually allowed for each question. TAG sessions give authors valuable feedback about their writing as well as a chance to lead class discussion.

Conferencing The heart of the Writing Workshop—the student–teacher writing conference—is ongoing. The student comes to the writing conference prepared to read his or her piece, to describe problem areas, and to respond to questions. Students know that the teacher will listen and respond, and that they will be asked challenging questions about their work. Questions should be carefully selected, with enough time allotted for the student to respond. Even though you may see many problems with the piece of writing, try to focus on only one or two specific areas. Some key points about conferencing with students are presented in Tips for Teachers 14.4.

Teaching Writing Skills A question frequently asked about Writing Workshop is, "When do I teach skills?" This question is especially important for teachers whose students have poor writing skills to begin with. Prolific writing without help from a teacher will not lead to improvement (Graham, 1992).

Skills lessons can be taught using flexible grouping practices. Skills lessons, or minilessons, should be brief (five to fifteen minutes), and the topics for these lessons should be based on the students' needs. Ideas for topics can come from your observations of student writing, requests for help, and data from writing conferences. After teaching a skill and providing ample opportunities to practice it, help students to generalize and apply the skill in their daily writing. As Graham (1992, p. 140) recommended for students with writing problems, skills are best taught in the context of "real" writing and have most impact when they bring the greatest rewards in writing improvement.

Strategies for Teaching Narrative Writing

In the elementary grades and in middle school, students typically practice **narrative writing** (writing stories). For many students, story writing is not a problem. Through hearing and reading stories they have learned the basic elements of a story and can incorporate those elements into their own storytelling and writing. According to Montague and Graves (1993), students with writing problems may be aware of story elements, but may not incorporate them into their writing in a systematic way. Students with writing problems

> In addition to student–teacher writing conferences, students can learn (with some preparation) to have writing conferences with each other. Guidelines for giving and receiving feedback need to be clearly defined.

TIPS FOR TEACHERS

14.4 Guidelines for Conducting a Writing Conference

1. *Follow the student's lead during the conference.* Avoid imposing your ideas about the topic or the way you would write the story.
2. *Listen to and accept what the student says.* When you talk more than the writer does during conferences, you are being too directive.
3. *Ask questions the student can answer.*

4. *Make conferences frequent and brief.* Although conferences can range from thirty seconds to ten minutes, most last two to three minutes.
5. *Listen to what students have written and tell them what you hear.* Nancy Atwell (1985) suggests that students should retain the right to reject the teacher's advice.

may also exhibit the following problems when they compose stories:

- lack of organization
- lack of unity and coherence
- lack of character development
- incomplete use of story elements

Story webbing and direct instruction on the development of story elements are effective ways to address these difficulties.

Using Story Webs to Plan Story webs, or *maps*, were originally developed as visual displays to help students understand the structure of the sto-

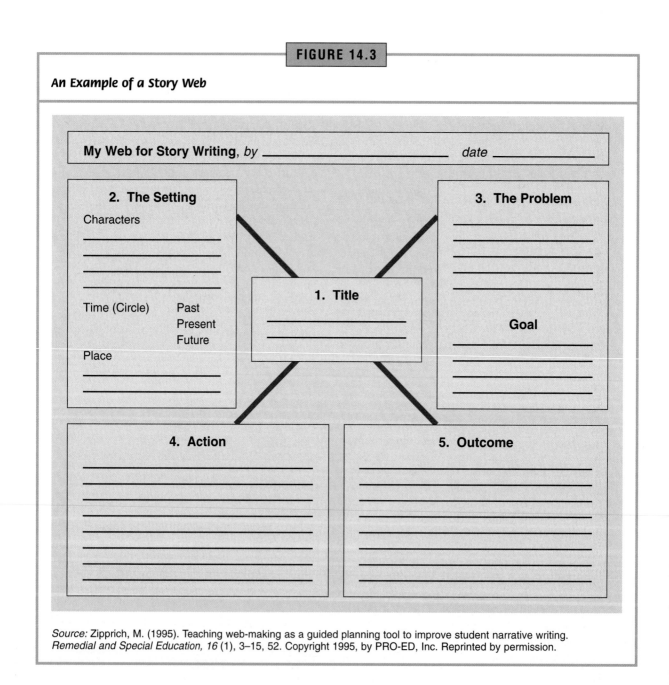

FIGURE 14.3

An Example of a Story Web

My Web for Story Writing, *by* _____ *date* _____

2. The Setting

Characters
_____
_____
_____

Time (Circle)　　Past
　　　　　　　　Present
　　　　　　　　Future

Place
_____
_____

1. Title
_____
_____

3. The Problem
_____
_____
_____

Goal
_____
_____

4. Action
_____
_____
_____
_____
_____
_____

5. Outcome
_____
_____
_____
_____
_____
_____

Source: Zipprich, M. (1995). Teaching web-making as a guided planning tool to improve student narrative writing. *Remedial and Special Education, 16* (1), 3–15, 52. Copyright 1995, by PRO-ED, Inc. Reprinted by permission.

TIPS FOR TEACHERS

14.5 Teaching Characterization in Story Development

1. In discussing stories students have read or heard, talk about how authors develop characters.
2. Provide explicit instruction in character development by conducting minilessons on describing physical appearance, speech, actions, thoughts, and emotions.
3. Have students brainstorm examples of vivid words for physical appearance, speech, actions, thoughts, and emotions.

4. Teach students to evaluate character development in their own stories and to use feedback to improve their writing.
5. Provide a cue sheet to help students monitor character development as they plan and write.

Adapted from: Leavell, A. & Ioannides, A. (1993). Using character development to improve story writing. *Teaching Exceptional Children, 25,* 41–45.

---

ries they read (Beck & McKeown, 1981; Bos, 1987; Idol, 1987). Stories are composed of predictable elements and have a characteristic narrative structure or story grammar. Elements of stories include the setting, characters, problem statement, the goal, event sequence or episodes, and the resolution or ending (Mandler & Johnson, 1977; Stein & Glenn, 1979). Using story webs such as the one shown in Figure 14.3, students can trace these elements when they read, plan, or write a story.

You can conduct minilessons on webbing with your whole class or just with students who need help with story planning. To introduce the web, first talk about its components and model its use in planning a story. You may want to have students work together in small, mixed-ability groups to plan a group story.

Instruction in Story Development As previously stated, some students might include a story element, such as a main character, in their stories but fail to develop the element fully. Leavell and Ioannides (1993) provided some recommendations for helping students improve character development in their stories (see Tips for Teachers 14.5). Graves and Hauge (1993) developed the cue sheet shown in Figure 14.4 to help students improve their story writing.

FIGURE 14.4

Story Check

Source: Graves, A. & Hauge, R. (1993). Using cues and prompts to improve story writing. *Teaching Exceptional Children, 25 (4),* 38–45. Copyright 1993 by The Council for Exceptional Children. Reprinted with permission.

Strategies for Teaching Expository Writing

Expository writing, or informational writing, once reserved for middle and upper grades, is now being included in the curriculum for even very young students. Expository writing poses particular problems to students with writing problems who may be unaware of the purpose of informational writing (Englert et al., 1988). Graham and Harris (1989) reported that the informational writing of students with learning disabilities often contains irrelevant information and inappropriate conclusions.

Paragraph Writing Students with writing problems often have difficulty developing coherent, logical paragraphs. The **PLEASE strategy** (Welch, 1992; Welch & Link, 1989) was developed to provide students with a step-by-step procedure for paragraph writing:

> Pick the topic, audience, and paragraph type (cause/effect, compare/contrast, etc.)
> List information about the topic.
> Evaluate whether the list is complete and also determine how to order items in the list.
> Activate your writing by starting with a topic sentence.
> Supply supporting or detail sentences, using items from the list.
> End with a strong concluding sentence, and evaluate the paragraph by revising and editing.

Essay Writing As students mature and move through the grades, they must progress from writing paragraphs to writing well-developed essays. Graham and Harris (1989) developed a three-step strategy for helping students learn to write essays:

Step 1. Think about the audience and purpose for writing the essay.

Step 2. Plan the essay, using the TREE method:

> T write a Topic sentence
> R think of Reasons to support the topic sentence
> E Examine your reasons
> E think of an Ending or conclusion

Step 3. Write the essay.

Typically, essays written to persuade or convince others are included in school curricula and state writing-assessment tests. Atwell (1987) suggests the following procedure for helping students learn to write persuasive essays:

1. *Make a list of arguments.* State your arguments in positive terms. Be convincing.
2. *Start with a purpose statement,* and explain why you are presenting the argument.
3. *Organize the list of arguments* into points to be made.
4. *Write one paragraph to elaborate each point.*
5. *Use transition words* (e.g., *moreover, in addition*) to aid coherence and logic.
6. *End with a strong closing statement* that summarizes the argument and suggests future action.

Strategies for Helping All Students Acquire Spelling Skills

Even in the age of computers and word processors with spell check programs, learning how to spell is important. If a writer is bogged down with the spelling of even commonly used words, progress in writing is stymied. Many students with reading and learning disabilities are poor spellers (Johnson & Myklebust, 1967). Spelling, like reading, involves phonological awareness. Research by Gentry (1982) on the stages of spelling development clearly points to the role of phonological awareness in learning to spell standard English (see Figure 14.5).

Without specific instruction, some students (because of their problems with phonological awareness) can easily get "stuck" in the early stages of spelling development. You will discover also that even very good readers can be poor spellers (Carpenter & Miller, 1982; Frith, 1980). The English language contains many irregular forms and is not as regular phonemically as other written languages, such as Spanish. Irregularities can stump even the most phonemically aware.

Spelling instruction is important for all students, but the students in your class are likely to differ in terms of their stages of development, the

FIGURE 14.5

Characteristics of Learners in Five Stages of Development

Stage 1: Precommunicative Spelling
- Uses scribbles, letter-like forms, letters, and sometimes numbers to represent a message.
- May write from left-to-right, right-to-left, top-to-bottom, or randomly on the page.
- Shows no understanding of phoneme-grapheme correspondences.
- May repeat a few letters again and again or use most of the letters of the alphabet.
- Frequently mixes upper- and lowercase letters but shows a preference for uppercase letters.

Stage 2: Semiphonetic Spelling
- Becomes aware of the alphabetic principle that letters are used to represent sounds.
- Uses abbreviated one-, two-, or three-letter spelling to represent an entire word.
- Uses letter-name strategy to spell words (e.g., U for you).

Stage 3: Phonetic Spelling
- Represents all essential sound features of a word in spelling.
- Develops particular spellings for long and short vowels, plural and past tense markers, and other aspects of spelling.
- Chooses letters on the basis of sound, without regard for English letter sequences or other conventions.

Stage 4: Transitional Spelling
- Adheres to basic conventions of English orthography.
- Begins to use morphological and visual information in addition to phonetic information.
- May include all appropriate letters in a word but reverse some of them.
- Uses alternate spellings for the same sound in different words, but only partially understands the conditions governing their use.
- Uses a high percentage of correctly spelled words.

Stage 5: Correct Spelling
- Applies the basic rules of the English orthographic system.
- Extends knowledge of word structure, including the spelling of affixes, contractions, compound words, and homonyms.
- Demonstrates growing accuracy in using silent consonants and doubling consonants before adding suffixes.
- Recognizes when a word doesn't "look right" and can consider alternate spellings for the same sound.
- Learns irregular spelling patterns.
- Learns consonant and vowel alternations, and other morphological structures.
- Knows how to spell a large number of words.

Source: Gentry, J. R. (1982). An analysis of developmental spelling in GYNS at WRK. *The Reading Teacher, 36,* 192–200. Copyright by the International Reading Association.

types of errors they make, and what they need to learn in spelling to become more fluent writers. What instructional methods can you use to teach all your students to spell?

Traditional Spelling Instruction

Mary Jacobs uses a traditional spelling-instruction model in her third grade class. All students in the class have the same third grade spelling book.

Each lesson in the speller focuses on a particular pattern (e.g., long vowels, short vowels, vowel plus *r*, prefixes). On Monday Mary gives a spelling pretest on the fifteen new words, and for homework students write (five times) each word they missed. On Tuesday and Wednesday nights students are assigned exercises in the spelling book. On Thursday night they write one sentence for each word on the list. On Friday during class Mary gives students a spelling test on the fifteen words. Some teachers vary this traditional pattern by selecting words from the basal reader or from the current science or social studies unit.

Spelling Instruction for Students with Problems Learning How to Spell

How appropriate is the traditional approach for classrooms that include students of different academic levels? Many students who are good spellers know all the words at the beginning of the week and so have no real challenge. For students with learning difficulties, fifteen words may be too many to learn, feedback about their errors may be ineffective, and the amount of practice insufficient. In addition, traditional spelling instruction does not teach for transfer to new situations. Students often learn words from their speller, get 100% on the test, but misspell those same words in their compositions.

RESEARCH BRIEF

SPELLING INSTRUCTION FOR STUDENTS WITH LEARNING DISABILITIES

Gordon, Vaughn, and Schumm (1993), in a search for empirically based instructional practices for improving the spelling skills of students with learning disabilities, reviewed fifteen studies on spelling acquisition, dating from 1978 to the present, in which the research focused on students with learning disabilities. Findings from the studies can be grouped into six areas of instructional practice:

- error imitation and modeling
- unit size
- modality
- computer-assisted instruction (CAI)
- peer tutoring
- study techniques

Error imitation and modeling. Students with learning disabilities need to compare each incorrectly spelled word with the correct spelling. The teacher copies the incorrect spelling and then writes the word correctly, calling attention to features in the word that will help students remember the correct spelling.

Unit Size. Students with learning tend to become overloaded and have difficulty when they have to study several words at once. These students can learn to spell if the unit size of their assigned list is reduced to three words a day and if effective instruction is offered for those three words.

Modality. When studying words, students with learning disabilities learned equally by (1) writing the words, (2) arranging and tracing letter shapes or tiles, and (3) typing the words at a computer. Most students preferred to practice their spelling words at a computer.

Computer-Assisted Instruction (CAI). Computer-assisted instruction (CAI) has been shown to be effective in improving the spelling skills of students with learning disabilities. CAI software programs for spelling improvement often emphasize awareness of word structure and spelling strategies and make use of time delay, voice simulation, and sound effects.

Peer Tutoring. A teacher's individual help is preferable, but structured peer tutoring can be a viable alternative. In a study conducted by Harper and colleagues (1991), daily peer tutoring was extended classwide by using a team game format. Tutored by their peers, students with learning disabilities achieved 100 percent mastery of their weekly spelling words.

Study Techniques. Study techniques provide a format and a standard procedure that help students with learning disabilities organize their study of spelling.

Meredith Millan is a third grade teacher whose three students with learning disabilities are in a pull-out program for special education services. Meredith and the special education teacher have agreed that Meredith will assign students their weekly spelling words. Meredith has worked hard to integrate spelling instruction into her ongoing writing program. She likes the idea of having weekly spelling tests but knows that the range of student spelling levels in her class is too broad for all students to benefit from having the same words, and the same number of words to learn. The following section describes the way Meredith has structured her spelling program.

Selecting Words Meredith follows Routman's (1991, p. 240) suggestions for selection of words. Meredith chooses words students misspell, words they ask for, words she knows they need, and words relevant to a topic or theme.

Each student in Meredith's class has a spelling log, a running list of words. At the beginning of the week students select words from the log for the Friday spelling test and write the words on their homework sheet. Meredith and each student agree in advance on the number of words. Some students have five or six words, others as many as twenty. Meredith also assigns all students two to three words from the thematic unit they are studying at the time.

Words that students misspell are taken from the edited drafts of their compositions. During a writing conference, Meredith not only discusses the words a student should add to his or her spelling log, but also asks, "Are there other words you really would like to learn to spell?" and adds them to the log.

Providing Instruction and Practice Meredith provides spelling instruction and practice in four ways—through minilessons, student pairs, parental involvement, and collaboration with the special education teacher.

Each week, Meredith provides minilessons on spelling patterns. For example, she noticed that about twenty students were using *-ing* words in their writing and spelling them incorrectly. Meredith met with this group for two weeks, gave them minilessons on adding *-ing,* and included *-ing* words on their spelling tests.

Early in the school year Meredith figured out that ten of her students needed more practice preparing for spelling tests. She decided to have these students work in pairs, and taught them the following spelling strategy (Graham & Freeman, 1986):

1. Say the word.
2. Write and say the word.
3. Check the word.
4. Trace and say the word.
5. Write the word from memory.
6. Check the word.
7. If incorrect, repeat steps 1–5.

The pairs meet for fifteen minutes, three times a week, usually while other students are composing during Writing Workshop.

Meredith involves parents in the spelling program in two ways. First, at the beginning of the year she writes parents a letter about the spelling program and ways parents can help their child study for spelling tests. Second, she invites parents to add one or two words to the spelling list each week. Parents observe their children's writing at home and can pick up on important misspellings.

Two of the students with learning disabilities, Kara and Mitchell, need additional help learning their words. In collaboration with Meredith, the special education teacher helps Kara and Mitchell learn and maintain new words by using individualized, multisensory methods.

Keeping Track of Student Progress All students take their Friday spelling test during the same class period. Because it is not possible to give thirty-six students an individual spelling test based on the words in their spelling logs, Meredith pairs the students to test each other. Students follow these strict guidelines during the test period:

- You can talk only to your partner and only about the test.
- You cannot give or receive information about how to spell words.
- You must take your test in ink—no erasing allowed.

Meredith monitors the test process, collects and grades papers, and adds words missed to next week's spelling list.

Principles of Effective Spelling Instruction

The following sections describe principles of effective spelling instruction that Meredith observes. Any spelling approach used with students who have spelling problems should include these principles.

Teach Spelling Patterns Cunningham and Cunningham (1992) have written that the human brain remembers patterns of words better than rules. In other words, teaching students common **spelling patterns** may be more advantageous than teaching them rules. According to Graham and Miller (1979) students should have frequent exposures to common word patterns such as base words, prefixes, suffixes, consonants, consonant blends, digraphs, and vowel sound-symbol associations.

Teach in Small Units Teach students with spelling problems three words a day rather than four or five. In one study, students with learning disabilities who were assigned three words a day performed better than a control group of students with learning disabilities who were assigned four or five words (Bryant et al., 1981).

Provide Sufficient Practice and Feedback Give students opportunities to practice words each day, with feedback. Many teachers do this by having students work with spelling partners who ask them words and provide immediate feedback. Try the following procedure for self-correction and practice:

1. Fold a paper into five columns, and write the correctly spelled words in the first column.
2. The student studies one word, folds the column back, and writes the word in the second column. The student then checks his or her spelling against the correctly spelled word in column one.
3. Folding columns one and two back, the student writes the word in the third column. When the word is spelled correctly three times, the student moves on to the next word. The student continues until each word is spelled correctly from memory three times in a row.

Select Appropriate Words The most important strategy for teaching spelling is to make sure that students know how to read the word and already know its meaning. Selection of spelling words should be based on students' existing vocabularies.

Maintain Previously Learned Words For students to be able to remember how to spell words, you must frequently assign (for review) words they've already learned, along with new words. Previously learned words must be reviewed frequently to be maintained.

Teach for Transfer of Learning After spelling words have been mastered, provide opportunities for students to see and use the words in different contexts.

Motivate Students to Spell Correctly Using games and activities, selecting meaningful words, and providing examples of the use and need for correct spelling are strategies that help motivate students and give them a positive attitude about spelling (Graham & Miller, 1979).

Include Dictionary Training Dictionary training (which includes alphabetizing, identifying target words, and locating the correct definition when several are provided) should be developed as part of the spelling program.

Strategies for Helping All Students Develop Handwriting Skills

Before typewriters, legible handwriting was a must. Even though we now have typewriters and word processors, learning how to write legibly is still a must for students who are physically able. For most students, learning how to write legibly and fluently is a key to success in school.

Traditional Handwriting Instruction

In traditional handwriting instruction in the United States, students learn **manuscript writing** (printing) in the early grades and move to **cursive writing** (script) in third grade (Hodges, 1991).

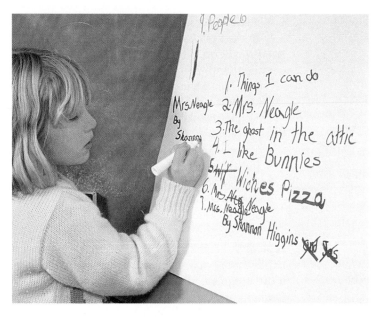

What strategies work with students who have difficulty learning to spell? How can you help students who have difficulty with handwriting?

early on and maintained. Students who can make the transition to cursive should have the opportunity to do so.

Students with Difficulty in Handwriting

Students with dysgraphia have severe problems learning to write. Hamstra-Bletz and Blote (1993, p. 690) define dysgraphia as follows:

> *Dysgraphia* is a written-language disorder that concerns the mechanical writing skill. It manifests itself in poor writing performance in children of at least average intelligence who do not have a distinct neurological disability and/or and overt perceptual-motor handicap.... Furthermore, dysgraphia is regarded as a disability that can or cannot occur in the presence of other disabilities, like dyslexia or dyscalculia.

Clare Whiting teaches handwriting as a whole-class activity. To plan her lessons, she uses a commercial handwriting program that includes individual student booklets and extra worksheets to serve as models. As a third grade teacher, Clare begins the school year by reviewing manuscript writing, then introduces the cursive alphabet after the first grading period. Clare assigns grades based on her judgment of the legibility of students' handwriting.

Critics of traditional handwriting instruction say that spending valuable class time on developing legible handwriting is time not well spent, and that time could be better spent teaching students to keyboard. Some critics maintain that handwriting should be taught during composition rather than whole-class instruction (Graves, 1994). Others argue against teaching two handwriting systems, with some arguing for manuscript and others for cursive (see Table 14.2). Frose (1981) proposes that both systems be maintained, with students deciding individually which form is most comfortable for them. The controversy over manuscript and cursive handwriting adds to the problems of students who have difficulties learning to write. In general, manuscript should be taught

---

TABLE 14.2

Manuscript versus Cursive

Manuscript
1. It more closely resembles print and facilitates learning to read.
2. It is easier for young children to learn.
3. It is more legible than cursive.
4. Many students write manuscript at the same rate as cursive and this rate can be significantly influenced through direct instruction.
5. It is better for students with learning disabilities to learn one writing process well than to attempt to learn two.

Cursive
1. Many students want to learn to write cursive.
2. Many students write cursive faster.
3. Many adults object to students using manuscript beyond the primary grades.

Source: Bos, C. S., & Vaughn, S. (1994). *Strategies for teaching students with learning and behavior problems* (3rd ed.). Boston, MA: Allyn & Bacon.

Poor handwriting, whether of students with dysgraphia or others, may include any of the following characteristics:

- poor letter formation
- letters that are too large, too small, or inconsistent in size
- incorrect use of capital and lowercase letters
- letters that are crowded and cramped
- inconsistent spacing between letters
- incorrect alignment (letters do not rest on a base line)
- incorrect or inconsistent slant of cursive letters
- lack of fluency in writing

Fortunately, with direct instruction and regular practice, most of these problems can be handled and corrected.

Principles for Effective Handwriting Instruction

The following instructional principles (Hagin, 1983) are suggested for any effective handwriting program:

- use direct instruction
- use individualized instruction
- use a variety of techniques and methods, matching the students' individual needs
- teach handwriting frequently, several times a week
- teach brief handwriting lessons within the context of students' writing
- teach handwriting skills separately and then encourage students to use them
- have students evaluate their own handwriting and, when appropriate, the handwriting of others
- present your handwriting as a model for the students to follow
- teach handwriting not as only a visual or a motor task, but as both

To teach handwriting you must focus on two major components—legibility and fluency—that can be improved when students have correct posture, pencil grip, and paper position:

- *Posture.* Hips touch the back of the chair and feet rest on the floor. The torso leans forward slightly in a straight line. Both forearms rest on the desk, with elbows slightly extended.
- *Pencil grip.* The pencil is held lightly between the thumb and first two fingers, about one inch above the point. The first finger rests on top of the pencil. The end of the pencil points toward the shoulder.
- *Paper position.* For manuscript writing, the paper is held straight in front of the writer, and the nonwriting hand holds the paper in place. For cursive writing, the paper is slanted counterclockwise for a right-hander, or clockwise for a left-hander.

Legibility Legibility is the most important goal of handwriting, and incorrect letter formation is the most frequent obstacle to reaching that goal. Graham and Miller (1980) suggest the following procedures for teaching letter formation:

- Point out critical attributes by comparing and contrasting letters.
- Use physical prompts and cues—move the student's hand, or provide indicators such as arrows or colored dots.
- Provide specific reinforcement for letters or parts of letters formed correctly, and corrective feedback for letters that need work.
- Teach *self-verbalization* (saying aloud the letter formation, and then saying it to oneself while writing).

Hanover (1983) provided a system for teaching cursive writing based on the similarities of letters or letter families. Because students learn letters in groups with similar strokes, learning to write letters is easier. Letter families in the **Hanover method** (Hanover, 1983) are shown here in the order recommended for teaching them:

e family	e, l, h, f, b, k
handle family	b, o, v, w
hump-shaped family	n, s, y
c family	c, a, d, o, q, g
hump family	n, m, v, y, x
back-tail family	f, q
front-tail family	g, p, y, z

One of the most effective ways to develop legibility is to provide a **moving model**. Modeling how to form letters and words is more helpful to students than simply having them copy letters and words (Wright & Wright, 1980). To provide a moving model, sit next to the student. As you form a letter or word, talk the student through the motions you are making. If the child writes with a different hand than you, have another child, a volunteer, or another teacher who writes with that hand provide the model. If you decide to have whole-class handwriting lessons, first provide a model by using the chalkboard or overhead projector; then circulate around the room, providing an individual moving model for students who seem to need the extra support.

Fluency After students begin to master basic letter forms, and their writing becomes more legible, the next goal is to learn to write quickly and with ease. Tom Reynolds helps students in his class improve their fluency through timed writings and journal writing.

Tom has three students in his fifth grade class who have improved the legibility of their writing considerably during the school year, but who still need to learn to write more quickly. He decided to group the three students together for timed writings. (In a timed writing, students copy a fifty-word passage and record the number of minutes the process takes.) When the group met for the first time, Tom showed them how to conduct a timed writing and keep records. For each student, he set up a folder with a collection of passages and a chart for recording progress. During this first meeting Tom also explained that the idea is to work toward personal improvement, not to compete, and he talked about ways they could encourage each other. In time the students could see that each was becoming a more fluent writer.

The daily fifteen-minute journal-writing activity Tom plans for all his students is a good way to enhance fluency. Because students know that their journals will not be graded for spelling or handwriting, they take risks and write more. Tom encourages students to evaluate their own journal writing. Tom makes certain that students with fluency problems evaluate how much they write.

At the beginning of the year, Tom talked with the first grade teacher, Helen Byers, and they decided to initiate a *dialogue journal* activity (Atwell, 1984; Bode, 1989; Gambrell, 1985). A **dialogue journal** is actually an ongoing written conversation between two students (or in some cases between a student and an adult). Each of Tom's fifth graders was paired with one of Helen's first graders. Once a week the fifth graders visit the first grade class and tell or read aloud a story to their first grade partners. Then the pairs spend some time writing in a dialogue journal.

SUMMARY

- In recent years, the growing trend has been toward a student-centered model of instruction for English and the language arts.
- Reading and writing develop simultaneously, and children's invented spelling can reveal a great deal about their phonological awareness. Thus, a current trend is to encourage students to write as early as possible.
- In response to national concern about the quality of writing among students in the United States, the amount of time allotted to writing instruction has increased.
- As a process, writing (like reading) is (1) interactive, (2) strategic, (3) an active attempt to convey meaning, (4) constructing meaning, and (5) socially mediated.

- Writing is a complex process with many areas of potential difficulty for students. In addition to extra time for writing, students who have difficulty need direct instruction in composing, spelling, and handwriting.
- The elements of the authoring cycle include prewriting, composing, revising, editing, and publishing.
- Skills lessons can be taught in conjunction with students' ongoing writing, using flexible grouping practices. The topics of skills lessons can be based on observations of student writing, requests for help, and data collected from writing conferences.
- Although students with writing problems may be aware of the elements of a story, they do not necessarily incorporate these elements into their writing. Students need direct instruction in narrative writing.
- Students need instruction in expository writing, including typical informational writing patterns and strategic planning for composing informational text.
- Spelling is an important tool for writers. Effective instruction for students with spelling problems includes teaching spelling patterns, teaching in small units, providing feedback and practice, selecting appropriate words, and maintaining previously learned words.
- Because handwriting is still necessary for success in school, students need specific instruction in how to write legibly and fluently.

Key Terms and Concepts

AOK strategy
authoring cycle
composing
conferencing
cursive writing
dialogue journal
drafting
editing
encode
expository writing
Hanover method
invented spelling
manuscript writing

moving model
narrative writing
peer editing
PLEASE strategy
prewriting
post-writing
publishing
revising
spelling patterns
story webs
student-centered model
TAG

Think and Apply

1. Now that you have read Chapter 14, reread the interview with Gina. What strategies does she use to teach writing to her students? What changes might you make to her writing program?

2. What are the pros and cons of competency and student-centered models of writing instruction? Which is most consistent with your own way of thinking about teaching of writing?

3. Think about your own experience in developing your writing skills. What instructional methods and procedures were most helpful? Least helpful?

4. Develop a personal writing portfolio to share with your students. In your portfolio include samples of your own writing from different phases of the authoring cycle. If possible, include some samples of your writing (and perhaps pictures of yourself) as a child. The portfolio will demonstrate to your students that you are a writer and illustrate your progress as a writer.

5. Interview ten students from several grade levels to get their perceptions of writing. Ask them, "What is a writer?" and "Are you a writer?" Also ask them, "What kinds of writing do you do at school?" and "What kinds of writing do you do at home?"

6. If you were conducting Writing Workshop in your classroom, how would you identify students who need minilessons? How would you keep track of what students are learning?

7. Plan the following activities: story writing, informational writing, spelling, and handwriting minilessons.

Read More about It

1. Atwell, N. (1987). *In the middle: Writing, reading, and learning with adolescents.* Portsmouth, NH: Boynton/Cook.

   A middle school teacher's inspirational, informative story about initiating writing and reading workshops in the classroom.

2. Graves, D. H. (1983). *Writing: Teachers and children at work.* Portsmouth, NH: Heinemann.

   A classic introduction to the writing process, with suggestions for implementing the writing process in the classroom.

3. Graves, D. H. (1994). *A fresh look at writing.* Portsmouth, NH: Heinemann.

   An excellent resource for implementing the writing process, with sections on using portfolios to assess writing, engaging parents in the writing process, and introducing students to different genres.

4. Moffett, J., & Wagner, B. J. (1992). *Student-centered language arts, K–12* (4th ed.). Portsmouth, NH: Boynton/Cook.

   Nine objectives for discourse and specific instructional suggestions for helping students learn to send and receive oral and written messages.

5. Routman, R. (1991). *Invitations: Changing as teachers and learners K–12.* Portsmouth, NH: Heinemann.

   A comprehensive guide to whole-language teaching, with excellent chapters on setting authentic contexts, journal writing, and spelling instruction. A chapter on students with learning disabilities includes case studies and suggestions for reading and writing instruction.

through Action Teaching

Writing Activities for All Learners

Interview a Classmate

Objective: To give students practice in developing and using questions as a means for obtaining more information for the piece they are writing.

Grades: Adapted for all levels.

Materials: Writing materials and a writing topic; a list of possible questions; a tape recorder (optional).

Teaching Procedures: Using the format of a radio or television interview, demonstrate and role-play "mock" interviews with sport, movie, music, and political celebrities. Give the students opportunities to play both roles.

Discuss what types of questions allow the interviewee to give elaborate responses (e.g., open questions), and what types of questions do not allow the interviewee to give a very expanded answer (e.g., closed questions). Practice asking open questions.

Use a piece that you are writing as an example, and discuss who you might interview to obtain more information. For example, "In writing a piece about what it might be like to go to the New York World's Fair in 1964, I might interview my grandfather, who was there, to obtain more information."

Ask the students to select an appropriate person to interview for their writing piece and to write possible questions. In pairs, the students refine their questions for the actual interview. The students then conduct the interviews and later discuss how information from the interview assisted them in writing their piece.

Bos, C., & Vaughn, S. (1994). *Strategies for students with learning and behavior problems* (3rd ed.). Boston: Allyn & Bacon.

Flashwriting

Objective: To improve writing fluency

Grades: Intermediate and above

Materials: Paper and pencil; timer

Teaching Procedures:

1. Give students one or two minutes to think of a topic.
2. Start the timer and give students five to ten minutes to flashwrite about the topic.
3. The goals is to keep writing about the topic. If ideas don't come, just write, "I can't think of what to write," until an idea pops up.

4. At the end of the designated time, have pairs of students share their writing.
5. Have the pairs circle key ideas that might be worth developing during extended writing periods.

Sentence Stretching

Objective: To help students learn to elaborate simple sentences

Grades: Intermediate, middle school

Materials: Paper and pencil

Teaching Procedures:

1. On the board, write a simple sentence of two to four words—for example, "The king fell."
2. Have students expand the sentence by adding words and phrases.
3. If you choose, have students illustrate their expanded sentences and share with the class.

Up in the Air for a Topic

Objective: To provide support to students with problems with topic selection

Grades: Primary and intermediate

Materials: Poster with suggestions for topic selection; paper and pencil

Teaching Procedures:

1. During Writing Workshop, discuss topic selection and ask students what they do when they are "stuck" for a topic.
2. Present the following suggestions on a poster:

   - Check your folder and reread your idea list.
   - Ask a friend to help you brainstorm ideas.
   - Listen to others' ideas.
   - Write about what you know: your experiences.
   - Write a make-believe story.
   - Write about a special interest or hobby.
   - Write about how to do something.
   - Think about how you got your last idea.

3. Model or solicit examples for each suggestion, add students' other suggestions, and post the chart in the room for students to consult whenever they are "stuck" for a topic.

through Action Teaching

Writing Activities for All Learners (continued)

Finding the Topic by Using the Goldilocks Rule

Objective: To help students brainstorm for expository writing topics

Grades: Intermediate and above

Materials: Timer; paper and pencil

Teaching Procedures:
1. Describe the "Goldilocks procedure."
   - Brainstorm as many ideas as possible in five minutes.
   - Write down all ideas. Don't stop to read or judge them.
   - Stop when timer goes off.
   - Organize ideas into categories with the Goldilocks Rule:

     Too broad
     Too narrow
     Just right

   - Choose a topic from the Just Right category.
2. Model the use of the Goldilocks procedure.
3. Try out the procedure as a whole-class activity.
4. Have students try out the procedure independently and then share their topics in small groups.

Source: Schumm, J. S., & Radencich, M. (1992). *School power.* Minneapolis: Free Spirit Publishing.

Tell It Again

Objective: To help students learn story elements

Grades: Primary, intermediate

Materials: Paper, pencil, crayons, markers

Teaching Procedures: Story retellings are a good way to determine which elements of a story are familiar (and unfamiliar) to your students. To help students "Tell It Again," follow these steps:

1. *Provide a story for your students.* It might be a story you read, that they read independently or with a partner, or a story they hear on TV or on a video.
2. *Decide on a retelling format.* Students can retell the story by drawing pictures of major events (making a wordless picture book), rewriting and illustrating the story, dramatizing the story, or by orally retelling the story to you or to a friend.
3. Keep tabs on the story elements your students include in their retellings. If a story element (such as setting, character, plot) is missing, provide instruction (either individually, in small groups, or with the class as a whole) about one element at a time. Monitor that element in subsequent retelling assignments.

The RAFT Technique

Objective: To help students learn to vary their writing in respect to writer's role, audience, format, and topic

Grades: Intermediate and above

Materials: Paper and pencil

Teaching Procedures: The RAFT technique was developed by Santa (1988) to help secondary students write in the content areas. RAFT provides a framework for thinking about how to write for different purposes by varying the writer's role, audience, format, and topic. Here's how to teach it:
1. Explain the components of RAFT:

   Role of the writer. Who are you? A professor? A volcano? An ancient Egyptian?
   Audience. Who will be your reader? A friend? A famous athlete? A lawyer?
   Format. What form will your writing take? A brochure? A letter? A newspaper article?
   Topic. What topic have you chosen? Hazards of smoking? Need for gun control? How cheese is made?

2. Write R–A–F–T on the board or on a transparency. Brainstorm with students about possible roles, audiences, formats, and topics. Following is an example:

   R—Role = a liver
   A—Audience = alcoholic
   F—Format = script for TV commercial
   T—Topic = the ill effects of drinking

3. Have students work in cooperative groups to generate other RAFT ideas.
4. Have students work independently to complete a RAFT assignment.

Helping All Students Succeed in Mathematics

FOCUS QUESTIONS

1. What are some of the reasons students with learning problems have difficulty with traditional mathematics curricula?

2. What are the recommended changes to traditional mathematics curricula, and the implications of such changes for students with learning problems?

3. Which factors, in addition to knowledge of mathematics, can affect students' mathematical ability?

4. What curriculum resources are especially helpful for students with learning problems?

5. How can teachers check that students understand the meaning of a mathematical operation and not just the answer to the problem?

nterview

One Student's Experience

Paul is a freshman at the University of Miami, but unlike most freshman he is twenty-one years old, not eighteen. Since Paul was very little, his parents have known he was not like the other children in the family or other children they knew. He was extraordinary in many ways and had problems in other ways. These problems were apparent when Paul started school. Although few subjects were easy for him, all subjects were easier than math.

Through elementary and high school, Paul received poor grades in mathematics, but not because of a lack of effort on his part. Paul says, "No matter how much I studied, I just did not get it. When I say I can't do math, I mean it's not that I'm not trying, it's that it just really doesn't make any sense to me." Paul also recalls that teachers made few accommodations to help him improve his mathematical abilities. He explains it this way, "I was mainstreamed in a public school and there were twenty-nine other students in the class. I think the attitude towards students, especially students with learning disabilities is, 'why should I change my teaching style just for you?'" In addition, Paul characterizes his teachers in elementary and high school as "unknowledgeable about learning disabili-

ties," and therefore, unsure about how to accommodate their instructional practices and class assignments to better meet his particular learning needs. Paul describes his years in school this way, "It's like somebody saying we are going to make you do this even though you don't know how, you can't do it, and they are going to make you do it. It was so hard and frustrating all of the time."

In high school, Paul began to advocate for himself and seek out assistance with his courses, but again he describes the school as being uninformed, "I felt I had to fight every day in high school to get what I needed. And a lot of that was because I am LD; the school thought it was an excuse, and never understood what the label really means."

Paul's experiences with mathematics have been so negative that he currently goes to great strides to exclude math from his life. "I don't take math. I switched my major so I won't have to take math. Math is just not a part of my life." As a student with learning disabilities, what advice would Paul give teachers? "The reason a student is coming to you with a problem, and saying that they're LD is not because they want to give you more problems in your life, it's because they want you to help them."

Introduction

The purpose of this chapter is to introduce procedures for effectively instructing students like Paul who have extraordinary problems learning mathematics.

Think about how you felt about mathematics instruction. Was it a subject you looked forward to, or did you dread it? What do you think were some of the factors that influenced how you felt about mathematics instruction? Surely, the teachers you had and the way mathematics was taught had a great deal of influence on how you feel about the subject today. Unfortunately, far too few students think about mathematics as an exciting subject (Mercer et al., 1994).

Current Trends in Mathematics Curriculum and Instruction

A central topic in education is mathematics instruction. This issue has been paramount for students with learning difficulties. There is growing national concern that students across all achievement groups are not faring well in mathematics, compared with students in countries such as Belgium, Canada, England, Finland, Hungary, Japan, New Zealand, Scotland, and Sweden. Some think that the mathematics performance of students in the United States is related to the way mathematics is taught. For example, in Japan mathematics is taught with a greater emphasis on conceptual problem solving rather than rote facts (McKnight et al., 1987).

Mathematics instruction has been in a state of change over the past thirty years. Perhaps the most influential advocate for mathematics instructional practices is the National Council of Teachers of Mathematics (NCTM). This group has prepared curriculum standards for the development and implementation of mathematics curricula (National Council of Teachers of Mathematics, 1989). Standards for the teaching of mathematics are summarized in Figure 15.1.

Implication of Trends for Students with Special Needs

Think about your own mathematics instruction when you were in school. Was the emphasis on worksheets and learning computation or was it on problem solving and activities? Math educators suggest that the emphasis in mathematics instruction should be on problem solving and activity-based learning. The argument made by many math educators is that too much time has been spent in the mathematics curricula on skill and drill and too little time on teaching students to think and discover mathematically (Romberg, 1993). The goal is to increase the emphasis on teaching students to solve problems effectively.

The authors of the **NCTM standards** state:

> We are convinced that if students are exposed to the kinds of experiences outlined in the *Standards,* they will gain *mathematical power.* This term denotes an individual's abilities to explore, conjecture, and reason logically, as well as the ability to use a variety of mathematical methods effectively to solve nonroutine problems. This notion is based on the recognition of mathematics as more than a collection of concepts and skills to be mastered; it includes methods of investigating and reasoning, means of communication, and notions of context. In addition, for each individual, mathematical power involves the development of personal self-confidence. (NCTM, 1989, p. 5)

Despite this plea for additional emphasis on problem solving, computation is still an essential component of the mathematics curriculum. Some feel that students with learning problems potentially have the most to lose as the curriculum shifts away from computation and toward an emphasis on problem solving and teaching students to think mathematically (Hofmeister, 1993). The concern is that because students with learning problems need to learn basic math facts, and because a lack of knowledge of these facts is a common impediment to learning higher-level math, students with learning problems may learn neither math computation nor higher-order mathematics. NCTM (1989) recommendations on mathematics instruction for students with learning problems are provided in Figure 15.2.

FIGURE 15.1

Standards for Teaching Mathematics

1. Students should be engaged in worthwhile mathematics tasks that reflect students' experiences and interests and that:

   ✔ call for problem solving, reasoning, and problem formulation.

   ✔ respond to the diverse interests and backgrounds of students.

   ✔ promote students' understanding of mathematics, connections between ideas, and promote communication about mathematics.

2. Students should be engaged in mathematical discourse by teachers who:

   ✔ listen to their ideas.

   ✔ pose questions that challenge and engage them in thinking.

   ✔ require students to clarify and justify their ideas both orally and in writing.

   ✔ assist students by attaching mathematical language and ideas to their notions.

   ✔ encourage students to participate and motivate them to learn.

3. Students' role in discourse should be to:

   ✔ question, respond to, and listen to each other and the teacher.

   ✔ solve problems, communicate, reason, and think mathematically through the use of a variety of tools.

   ✔ provide solutions to problems, initiate problems, and develop and pursue answers to questions.

   ✔ explore answers by developing examples and counter examples.

   ✔ use mathematical evidence and argument to determine validity, convince themselves and others of responses, solutions, and answers.

4. Teachers should encourage the use of:

   ✔ computers, calculators, and other technology.

   ✔ concrete materials, pictures, diagrams, tables, and graphs.

   ✔ terms and symbols.

   ✔ oral and written explanations, arguments, and presentations.

5. The learning environment for mathematics shall:

   ✔ provide and structure the time necessary to grapple with ideas and problems.

   ✔ provide adequate space and materials.

   ✔ provide a context that respects and values students responses, ideas, and progress.

   ✔ provides for intellectual discussion regarding mathematics that includes validating and supporting ideas with mathematical arguments.

6. Ongoing analysis of teaching and learning should be displayed by:

   ✔ observing, listening, and gathering information about students' learning.

   ✔ challenging, extending, adapting, and changing activities while teaching.

   ✔ planning both long and short range.

   ✔ ensuring that every student is learning and developing a positive attitude about mathematics.

Adapted from: National Council of Teachers of Mathematics. (1991). *Professional standards for teaching mathematics.* Reston, VA: Author.

FIGURE 15.2

The National Council of Teachers of Mathematics Recommendations

★ Do not alter curricular goals to differentiate students; change the type and speed of instruction.

★ Make mathematics education student-oriented, not an authoritarian model that is teacher-focused.

★ Encourage students to explore, verbalize ideas, and understand that mathematics is part of their life.

★ Provide opportunities on a daily basis for students to apply mathematics and to work problems that are related to their daily lives. Relate what they are learning to real life experiences.

★ Teach mathematics so that students understand when they can estimate an answer and when they need to compute an exact answer.

★ Teach problem solving, computer application, and calculators to all students.

★ Teach students to understand probability, data analysis and statistics as they relate to daily decision making, model building, operations, research, and application to computers.

★ Shift from relying primarily on paper-and-pencil activities to use of calculators, computers, and other applied materials.

Students with learning problems are slower, but not necessarily less accurate, when it comes to doing and learning math facts (Garnett, 1992). When you teach mathematics in your classroom, consider that students with learning problems may need more time and additional practice to learn math facts and mathematics computations because they often lack the "automatization" to perform math computation effectively and efficiently (Garnett & Fleischner, 1983). It will be important for you to monitor their progress in these areas because they are less likely than the other students in your classroom to learn these skills incidentally (through the process of problem solving).

Difficulties in Learning Mathematics

Not surprisingly, students with behavior disorders, mental retardation, learning disabilities, and attention problems typically score below their same-aged peers on measures of math achieve-ment (Scruggs & Mastropieri, 1986; Zentall & Smith, 1993). Some of their difficulties in mathematics relate to understanding the problem. In other instances, they lack the computation skills to adequately complete the problem. Interestingly, not all of their difficulties in mathematics relate to their knowledge of math.

RESEARCH BRIEF

MATHEMATICS AND MEMORY

There is increasing evidence that students who display mathematics difficulties do so because of their poor use of working memory to execute or retrieve information to aid in solving problems (Geary et al., 1991). A primary factor that contributes to an early learning problem in mathematics is difficulty in the retrieval of basic information from long-term memory (Goldman et al., 1988; Svenson & Broquist, 1975). The reason students continue to use counting strategies beyond the point at which they are helpful is that they are unable to retrieve basic facts from long-term memory. This difficulty in memory inhibits their progress in mathematics. What is unknown is the extent to which students have difficulty learning the information; thus, it is never stored in long term memory, or whether students have difficulty accessing the information. Children with mathematics difficulties also appear to have relatively poor working memory resources which may lead to frequent use of verbal counting strategies that in turn may lead to computational errors.

According to Kosc (1981), four variables—cognitive, educational, and personality factors, and neuropsychological patterns—influence the mathematics ability of all students.

Cognitive Factors Intelligence, cognitive ability, distractibility, and cognitive learning strategies influence students' thinking and therefore their skills in math.

Educational Factors Learning is influenced directly by the quality and amount of instructional intervention across the range of areas of mathematics (e.g., computation, measurement, time, and problem solving).

Personality Factors Persistence, self-concept, and attitudes toward mathematics influence students' motivation and performance. As with all learning, the extent to which we are interested in a topic and motivated to learn influences our performance. Many math educators are convinced that students' judgments about math relay the message that "you have to be a genius to do it," and that such judgments stem, at least in part, from faulty instruction (Mtetwa & Garofalo, 1989).

Neuropsychological Patterns Perception, memory, and neurological trauma influence students' abilities to effectively solve mathematical problems. Students with learning problems often have difficulty with spatial relationships, distance, size, and sequencing. These difficulties interfere with

such math skills as measurement, estimation, problem solving, and geometry. Students with special learning needs also display memory problems that interfere with their progress in math (Geary et al., 1991). You can assist students with memory problems by reducing the amount of new information they are required to learn, and by giving them opportunities to verbalize and demonstrate the new material.

After you consider these factors, it is not difficult to determine why many students with learning and behavior problems would have difficulty with mathematics. Although most students with learning and behavior problems have average or above-average intelligence, they often demonstrate difficulties in cognitive functioning that influence their learning. Furthermore, they are often characterized as passive learners who are less likely than other students to actively use their cognitive abilities. Because the focus of much of their everyday math instruction has been on computation, largely on activities that require students to complete problems and turn in worksheets, these students have had many negative experiences with math. They have had few opportunities to engage in problem solving or learning the language and reasoning of mathematics. Most of these students have had few opportunities to apply computation skills to the problems of daily life.

RESEARCH BRIEF

COMPUTATION AND CALCULATORS

There is a preponderance of evidence that calculators assist in the acquisition of mathematics achievement for students with learning problems. Reviews of the calculator research have drawn the following conclusions:

1. Calculators for instructional purposes do not impede the acquisition of basic skills. In fact, calculators can increase skill acquisition.
2. The advantages of using calculators are more obvious for problems that include computation rather than for problem solving.

What is the most appropriate use of calculators in math instruction? When and how are calculators especially helpful for students with disabilities?

3. Students who use calculators on criterion tests produce higher achievement scores than students who do not.

4. Studies indicate that students do not develop a negative attitude towards math because of calculator use. In fact, calculators improve students' attitudes towards mathematics.

5. It is appropriate to introduce calculators at the same time that the paper and pencil methods are taught.

6. Students can develop their own complex problems and then solve them with use of the calculator. This also serves to increase their self-concept about math skills.

Developmental Arithmetic Disorder

Developmental arithmetic disorder refers to students who have significant difficulties learning arithmetic—difficulties that are unexpected given the students' overall cognitive functioning and academic performance in other subject areas. For example, Paul, the student introduced at the beginning of this chapter, demonstrated significant arithmetic disorder. His performance in arithmetic was unexpectedly low, given his overall cognitive performance. His difficulty in mathematics was also long lasting, not related to an area of mathematics or a particular teacher. Good teaching is likely to help students with developmental arith-

metic disorder, but probably not enough to ensure grade-level performance.

Nonverbal Math Difficulties

Johnson and Myklebust (1967) were the first to introduce the notion of **nonverbal math disabilities**. They were referring to a small group of students who displayed good reading and verbal expression but extreme difficulty with mathematics. Other problems associated with students who display nonverbal mathematics problems include the following:

- social immaturity
- disorientation
- deficits in visual, motor, and self-help skills
- problems estimating distance and time

Research supporting the social deficits associated with individuals who have good reading and poor math skills has been confirmed by others (Badian & Ghublikian, 1983; Rourke, 1993).

Saje, a third grade student who read at grade level but had difficulties in mathematics, was really a puzzle to his teacher. She could not figure out why, despite Saje's high verbal expression and good vocabulary, he continually mixed up old and new rules. He not only had problems in math, but also was frequently inattentive, disorganized, and avoided responsibility. No matter how often she

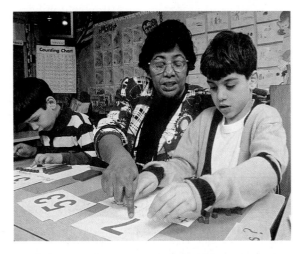

What kinds of difficulties in mathematics do students with disabilities have? How can teachers help students with these kinds of difficulties?

TIPS FOR TEACHERS

15.1 How to Help Students with Nonverbal Math Difficulties

1. *Teach one mathematical principle until mastery.* Allow time for knowledge or a skill to become routine before introducing another.
2. *Take advantage of students' language skills to teach mathematics.* Use rhyming, word games, and songs to teach math facts. For example, sing the addition facts to a commonly known song and count objects by number to reinforce math facts (e.g., 4, 8, 12, 16, 20, 24, 28, 32, 36).
3. *Provide organizational helpers* (e.g., graph paper with large boxes in which to write numbers) to students who need neater papers. Students can often correct mistakes if they can read and write numbers neatly and accurately.
4. *Provide alternative methods* for students to record and perform mathematics. For example, computers and tape recorders are effective devices for improving mathematics skills.

---

reminded Saje to keep his math paper neat, the papers he turned in had frayed edges, numbers all over the place (instead of problems written in neat columns), and were covered with eraser marks and holes. She asked the special education teacher how to help Saje. The special education teacher worked with Saje, administered some tests, and explained to Saje's classroom teacher that he had a nonverbal math difficulty. Although math would always be challenging for Saje, she could do some things to help him (see Tips for Teachers 15.1).

According to a survey of teachers of students with learning disabilities conducted by McLeod and Armstrong (1982), the following mathematics deficits were the ones most often reported: upper-level skills of division of whole numbers; basic operations involving fractions, decimals, percent fraction terminology; and multiplication of whole numbers.

Effective Math Instruction for All Learners

Students display poor math performance for several reasons. The one that can be most readily corrected is the inappropriate or inadequate instruction in mathematics that many students receive. Many professionals feel that the math difficulties of students with learning problems are compounded by ineffective instruction (e.g., Carnine, 1991; Cawley et al, 1987). Most teachers know the simple algorithms for solving mathematics computation problems, but do not know alternative algorithms. Few teachers have procedures for using concrete approaches and manipulatives to teach computation. Figure 15.3 provides a summary of guidelines for adequate math instruction.

Evaluating Mathematics Curricula

Traditional math curricula have not worked very well for students with learning problems, for the following reasons (Blankenship, 1984; Carnine, 1990):

1. *Students have difficulty reading the information provided.* Because the reading vocabulary is too difficult and the reading level is too high, students with math difficulties are able to learn very little by reading their math books. All the information in the book must be taught directly to them.

   Max Diamond, a tenth grade math teacher, assigned several pages of reading in the math textbook as homework. Realizing that several of his students would not be able

FIGURE 15.3

Summary of Guidelines for Adequate Math Instruction

1. Select appropriate, comprehensive math content.

2. Select goals that establish high expectations.

3. Provide systematic and explicit instruction.

4. Teach students to understand math concepts.

5. Monitor the progress of students.

6. Teach to mastery.

7. Promote a positive attitude toward math.

8. Teach students to generalize the math skills they learn.

---

to adequately read and understand the text, Max had these pages read into a tape recorder and made the tapes and recorders available to all students in his class.

2. *Math concepts are often presented poorly.* Multiple concepts are introduced at one time, and information is often presented in a scattered fashion.

For this reason, Dawn McQueen reorganizes the information in the math text so that she can teach computation skills to mastery rather than skipping around teaching many new ideas in two weeks. Dawn introduces only one concept at a time, teaching that concept until *all* students in her class (not just those with learning problems) learn it. Then she moves on to the next concept. Although Dawn follows a sequence of pages different from that presented in the book, she feels her efforts are worth it because her students seem to understand better.

3. *There are insufficient problems covering any one concept or operation, and too few opportunities for application of knowledge learned.* The problems are not presented in enough different situations for students to learn and transfer what they know.

Janice Kauffman, a sixth grade teacher, addresses this problem by developing her own supportive materials to supplement the book. She also provides practice with problem solving, reasoning, and real-life application that help students transfer their knowledge to real-life settings.

4. *Students often do not have the necessary prerequisite skills assumed by the text* (thus, the next level is too difficult).

As Margaret Gardner plans each math unit she teaches, she spends considerable time considering the prerequisite skills students need to master the concept or operation she is teaching. After identifying these prerequisite skills, she tells students directly that she is looking to see whether they know them. She prepares activities and exercises so that she knows which students do and which do not possess the skills needed to move on to the next math concept or operation.

5. The pages and organizational format of the text vary considerably and make learning from text difficult.

Linda Saumell, recognizing this problem, "walks students through the text section by section," explaining the format to them.

Considering this mismatch between most mathematics curricula and the learning needs of all students, particularly students with learning problems, teachers need to adapt traditional math curricula to best meet the learning needs of students in their classrooms.

Adapting Basal Materials for Students with Special Needs

Teachers need to do several things to adapt basal materials. One is to select appropriate math content. There is considerable concern that poor math content is a result of the **spiral curriculum**, which occurs when the same skills (e.g., mathematics skills) are woven into every year of school and students continually "relearn" the same skills in the same area. Jason, an eighth grade student, said it this way, "It seems every year we start with multiplication and then go to division and then we learn something about fractions and then we stop. Then the next year, we do it all over again." One approach to teaching mathematics, the Corrective Mathematics Program (Englemann & Carnine, 1982) described later in this chapter, is designed to avoid the problems of the spiral curriculum and provide satisfactory pacing of instruction.

A key aspect of selecting the appropriate curriculum is that it be comprehensive. Gary Lancelotta reflected, "I know my curriculum should be more comprehensive than just the facts and computation, but I'm not sure what else I should teach. Also, the students seem to really need the time to learn computation." Working on other skills in mathematics does not mean that computation is left behind; in fact, computation can often be enhanced while other components of math are taught. Students need to be taught and involved in a full range of mathematics skills that include: basic facts, computation, word problems, operations, problem solving, mathematical reasoning, time, measurement, fractions, and math application.

> Students who select their own math goals improve their performance on math tasks over time more than those students whose math goals are assigned to them by a teacher (Fuchs et al., 1988).

Using Curricular Programs for Students with Math Difficulties

Other than the basal curriculum books, math workbooks, and the curriculum guidebooks published by many state Departments of Education, what curriculum resources are available to teachers? This section provides brief descriptions of some resources that are helpful for students who have difficulty learning math.

Project Math Project Math is a math curriculum designed specifically for students with mild disabilities (Cawley et al, 1976). The program—which includes work on sets, patterns, numbers, operations, fractions, geometry, measurement, and lab activities—has eliminated many problems commonly associated with typical math curricula. Project Math reduces the reading level, provides a direct link between assessment and instruction, establishes procedures that encourage teaching to mastery, and provides for individualized instruction.

DISTAR Arithmetic Program DISTAR Arithmetic Program stresses direct instruction through a highly sequenced format that provides immediate feedback to students (Englemann & Carnine, 1972, 1975, 1976). The DISTAR arithmetic kits come with a detailed teacher's guide, workbooks, teaching book, and take-home sheets for homework and parent involvement. The entire program is based on behavioral principles of learning and provides explicit instructions for the teacher.

Computational Arithmetic Program Computational Arithmetic Program provides 314 worksheets for teaching basic math skills to students in grades one through six (Smith & Lovitt, 1982).

Corrective Mathematics Program Corrective Mathematics Program provides remedial math for students in grades three through twelve. This math program requires only minimal reading skills (Englemann & Carnine, 1982).

Structural Arithmetic Structural Arithmetic involves students in kindergarten through third grade in making, discovering, and learning math concepts and facts (Stern, 1965). The emphasis is on the use of materials to promote discovery learning.

Milliken Wordmath Milliken Wordmath uses computer programs to teach problem-solving strategies within the mathematics curriculum to children in fourth grade and up who have been unsuccessful in adequately learning problem-solving skills (Coffland & Baldwin, 1985).

Real-Life Math Program Real-Life Math Program focuses on teaching students with learning difficulties the mathematics skills they need for daily living (Schwartz, 1977). The content for teaching functional math includes: consumer skills, homemaking skills, health care, auto care, home care, and vocational needs. The focus is on older individuals, ages thirteen to eighteen, who need to learn appropriate math skills for daily life.

Touch Math Touch Math is a program for teaching students math skills through math strategies that include touch-point, count-on, count-off, and count by strategies (Bullock, 1991). Touch math focuses on teaching the basic math facts in addition, subtraction, multiplication, and division.

Key Math Teach and Practice Key Math Teach and Practice is designed to provide remedial practice in, and diagnosis of math difficulties (Connolly, 1985). Materials include a teacher's guide, a student progress chart, and a sequence chart, as well as activities and worksheets.

> Computer-assisted instruction is a sound way to provide large amounts of effective practice for students with learning problems, particularly in automating math skills (Okolo, 1992). Instructional computer games can improve the basic skill and automaticity of students with learning disabilities.

Establishing Appropriate Goals

Goals can be selected by the teacher, student, or both together. Expectations for meeting the goals should be clearly established. There is growing support for the premise that the goals and expectations teachers set for students with learning problems are too low. They need to challenge students and provide support so that students can meet the challenges.

Marie Fernandez realized that she often responded to students' low self-image by setting goals too low for them. Several of the students with learning problems in her class would indicate that the work was too difficult or that there was too much work and she would respond without considering what they could do if they jointly set goals.

Student Goal Setting and Self-Monitoring In the goal-setting process, students are asked to set realistic goals for how much work they can complete and how many problems they can solve. Students can also set computational fluency goals. Students

who set their own goals outperform students who do not.

Strategies designed to teach students to instruct themselves and monitor their own progress have been shown to work well with students who have difficulty learning mathematics. Leon and Pepe (1983) used the following sequence to teach students how to teach themselves:

1. *The teacher models and verbalizes the procedure for the student:* "First I read the numbers out loud and estimate how much it will be. Let's see—86 plus 22 is going to be more than 100, but not much more. Now I start on the right and add the column. Now I add the column on the left. The total is 108."

2. *The teacher guides the student through the verbalization of the problem computation and solves the problem with the student.* Thanks to the teacher's prompts and guidance, the student does not have to work through the verbalization alone. When the student has difficulty, the teacher fills in.

3. *The student verbalizes the procedure independently while the teacher monitors his or her progress.* In this step the verbalization should be done almost solely by the student, with minimal support and assistance.

4. *The student whispers the procedure to himself or herself.* Now the teacher lets the student work independently. When a new mathematical concept or procedure is introduced or the student is having difficulty, the teacher and the student return to step one.

Cooperative Instructional Practices Peer tutoring is an extremely effective way for students with arithmetic problems to learn computation skills (Beirne-Smith, 1991). Peer tutoring is effective not only for the student who is tutored, but also for the student who does the tutoring. Remember that students with mathematical difficulties frequently receive help from their classmates, and be sure to provide them with opportunities to be the tutor, as well. Teaching not only helps enhance their self-concept, but also helps them learn a great deal.

Cooperative learning occurs when the teacher divides the class into small groups (ordinarily three or four students per group), usually not based on ability, and asks these groups to work together to solve problems. Maheady, Harper, and Sacca

Video Discs and CD-ROMS Help Teach Fractions

Kelly, Carnine, Gersten, and Grossen (1987) compared interactive video disk programs with traditional basal mathematics programs for teaching fractions to students and found that the interactive video programs outscored basal programs on both the post-test and the maintenance checks. The researchers ascribed the success of interactive video disks to the following attributes:

1. They systematically reviewed previously taught skills.
2. There were discrimination practices among the different strategies.
3. Numerous examples were provided.
4. The terms *numerator* and *denominator* were taught separately.
5. The programs explicitly taught different strategies for problem solving.

Interactive computer applications also help students visualize information, which fosters problem solving. Shiah, Mastropieri, Scruggs, and Fulk (1994) taught students with learning disabilities to do mathematical word-problem solving on the computer. Students made substantial gains and reported that the pictorial information helped them with word problems.

From Stickeybear's Mathtown by Optimum Resource, Inc.

From Math Blaster by Davidson & Associates, Inc.

(1988) conducted a cooperative-learning math instruction program for ninth and tenth grade students with mild disabilities. The study showed that students who participated in the cooperative teams performed better in mathematics and received higher grades than those who did not.

Slavin, Madden and Leavey (1984) designed **Team-Assisted Individualization** (TAI), in which individualized instruction is provided in a cooperative learning model. Each of the four or five students in the heterogeneous learning team is assigned individualized mathematics material at his or her own level. Students on the same team help each other with problems and also manage checking and record keeping for the individualized math materials. Students work independently, but teachers teach skills to groups of students who are at the same level by pulling them from various teams.

Providing Appropriate Instruction

Christenson, Ysseldyke, and Thurlow (1989) discussed four elements that contribute to systematic and explicit instruction:

- A teaching routine that includes demonstration–prompt–practice enhances a student's outcome (See Tips for Teachers 15.2).

- Explicit instruction that not only involves highly organized step-by-step presentations related to the specific target skill, but that also provides information about why learning this skill facilitates student learning.
- Assurance that students understand the directions and the task demands. Periodic checks are necessary to determine whether students understand the directions, and the teacher must monitor students' progress.
- The systematic use of learning principles. This refers to maintaining and using positive reinforcement, providing varied practice, and ensuring motivation.

In their review of intervention studies in mathematics for students with learning disabilities, Mastropieri, Scruggs, and Shiah (1991) identify three major types of interventions. One is behavioral, the second is cognitive, and the third is alternative instructional delivery systems (including cooperative learning, computer-assisted instruction, and interactive video disks). According to the authors, "Although these interventions seem varied, the general perspective on mathematics instruction—involving direct teacher explanations, strategy instruction, relevant practice with worksheets, peers, or computer-assisted instruction,

TIPS FOR TEACHERS

15.2 Strategies for Cueing Students during Feedback

Ferrara (1987) provides the following hint-sequence scheme for cueing students when giving them feedback.

1. *Give simple negative feedback.* In this case the student is told that the solution is not quite right and is encouraged to try again.
2. *Refresh working memory.* Repeat parts of the problem verbatim and discuss the known quantities.
3. *Use numerals as memory aids.* Ask students to write down the quantities they know, based on information provided in the text.

4. *Provide a transfer hint.* Ask students to think about a similar problem they have done. Students provide the example of the similar problem.
5. *Provide a demonstration and rationale.* Provide all the information to solve the problem and an explanation or rationale for it.
6. *Give a strategic-orientation hint.* Encourage the students to apply the information they have just learned to other types of problems.

direct measurement, and feedback and reinforcement—represents a view of instruction that is currently well supported in special education" (p. 97).

Math Manipulatives Learning the language of mathematics is an important skill for all students. Peterson, Mercer, and O'Shea (1988) examined the effectiveness of a three-stage teaching sequence on students' abilities to learn place value. The sequence included going from concrete to semiconcrete and then to abstract teaching strategies. In the *concrete* stage, the mathematical concept was taught by using manipulative objects such as pegs. In the *semiconcrete* stage, pictorial representations were used for instruction. In the *abstract* stage, only numbers were used. Students who used this three-step process for learning place values significantly outperformed a control group. Tips for Teachers 15.3

> Students who were taught to do mathematical word-problem solving on the computer made substantial gains in mathematics word-problem solving and enjoyed working on the computer (Shiah et al., 1994). Students also felt that the pictorial information assisted them in solving the word problems.

shows another way to help students move from the concrete to the abstract.

As a teacher, the most important thing for you to remember is to begin with the concrete and then move to the abstract when you are teaching new math concepts or when a student is having difficulty learning a math concept. Because all students have had opportunities to interact with objects, the process makes sense to them. By using examples from the manipulation to develop problems and to write them numerically, you bridge the gap between the abstractness of mathematics and students' needs to learn the information concretely.

Teaching for Comprehension Teach students to understand math concepts. Most instruction is provided to ensure that the answer is correct, the math computation has been accurately completed, or that the math fact is memorized. Additional emphasis on ensuring that students understand the math process needs to be included in the math curriculum. Jan Hughes, a third grade teacher, continually asked students to say in their own words what she had just said. During math problem solving, she often asked students to work in groups of three to write story problems that went along with an operation she had just taught. She continually

TIPS FOR TEACHERS

15.3 Helping Students Move from Concrete to Abstract Learning

1. *Concrete.* Provide manipulative and interactive opportunities to integrate the new mathematical concept. Encourage students to use both oral and written language to relate to the new mathematical vocabulary and concept.
2. *Pictorial.* Represent the mathematics problem with pictures. Provide the problem and have students interpret it and draw pictures to represent it.
3. *Linking.* Encourage students to talk about what they have learned and to explain it to others. By recording or demonstrating what they have learned

in meaningful ways, they can link their language to the mathematical algorithm.
4. *Symbolic.* Have students demonstrate knowledge about the symbols by talking about them and demonstrating through drawing, pointing, or replicating the meaning of the symbol or algorithm.
5. *Abstract.* Have students teach the steps for computing or problem-solving with alternative solutions, and then solve problems in new and creative ways without using concrete or pictorial representation.

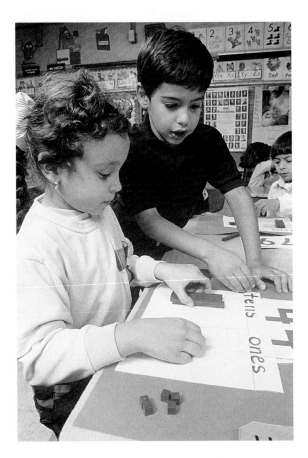

What procedures can teachers develop for using concrete approaches and manipulatives in mathematics instruction? What instructional strategies work for helping students move from the concrete to the abstract?

lem with pictures of flowers, this is what Trinette drew:

Trinette demonstrated that she did not understand the problem, although she had successfully memorized the answer and her facts.

The following drawing illustrates how rows of chips can be used to illustrate multiplication. For example, ask, "How many fours make twenty?" "Fours are placed on the board _____ times." $4 \times$ _____ $= 20$

thought about ways to make the mathematics she was teaching "real" to students.

The following section describes ways to check for comprehension in math instruction.

Checking for Comprehension: The Case of Trinette
Be certain that students understand the *meaning* of an operation, not just the answer. Students who have memorized the facts by rote often operate with little understanding of what they are doing. For example, Trinette was asked to write the answer to the following math problem:

$$3 \times 2 =$$

Answering correctly, she wrote 6. But when Trinette's teacher asked her to illustrate the prob-

Other ways to check for comprehension include having students "talk aloud" what is involved in solving a problem. Instead of letting them merely *read* the problem, ask them to *explain* what it means. For example, 63 – 27 could mean that someone had 63 pieces of gum and gave 27 pieces to a friend. Another strategy is to have one student explain the process to another student by using block manipulatives. For example, 24 + 31 is the same as adding 4 one-block pieces to 1 one-block piece and 2 ten-block pieces to 3 ten-block pieces. Some teachers use vocalization or have students close their eyes and use noises to illustrate operations. To illustrate multiplication, for example, the teacher and student might tap to indicate groups of six.

Constant Time Delay Procedure
Constant time delay is a procedure for teaching math facts that provides for the systematic introduction of teacher assistance. This near errorless technique employs a controlling prompt to ensure the successful per-

formance of the student (Gast et al., 1988; Stevens & Schuster, 1988). In general, the procedure involves presentation of a stimulus (e.g., a word or math fact), after which the student is allowed a specific amount of time (e.g., three seconds) to provide the correct answer (e.g., read the word or answer the fact). If the student does not respond within the time allowed, a controlling prompt (typically a teacher modeling the correct response) is provided. The controlling prompt is a cue which ensures that the student will respond correctly (e.g., the word name or the answer to the problem is modeled). The student then repeats the teacher's model. Although correct responses before and after the prompt are reinforced, only correct responses given before the prompt count toward the criterion. The effectiveness of the constant time delay procedure has been demonstrated with a variety of academic skills, students, and instructional arrangements (Mattingly & Bott, 1990; Schuster et al, 1990; Stevens & Schuster, 1987; Wolery et al, 1991).

Correction and Feedback Immediate correction and feedback are essential to the success of students with math difficulties. Saying, "Orlando, the first six problems are correct and then the third row is all wrong. Please redo them," is an example of insufficient feedback. Teachers often tell students which problems are correct and which are wrong, and hope that this feedback is adequate. For students with learning problems it is not. They need more sustained interaction to help them acquire not only the skills for identifying what they did wrong, but also the procedures for how to do it differently. The teacher must analyze the problem and also obtain sufficient information from the student to determine why the problem was not done correctly. A better model for correction and feedback follows:

"Orlando, point to the problems you think are correct. Think about each problem before you point." (Teacher positively reinforces Orlando as he points to problems that are right.) "Yes, those are all correct. You did an excellent job with those. You started on the right, added them correctly, carried numbers when you needed to." When students are first learning a math concept or operation, teachers need to provide a great deal of assistance to ensure that students perform cor-

rectly. Over time, teachers need to systematically reduce the amount of help they give students.

Providing Practice

Practice is important if students are to exhibit high levels of accuracy consistently and across multiple problem types. **Mastery** occurs when students meet expectations for accuracy and speed in different types of problems. In operations, mastery refers to the ability to use multiple algorithms to solve an operation, so that students truly learn (rather than memorize). Denise, a ninth grade student, expresses her frustration this way: "I never seem to be able to really learn anything. Just when I feel like I'm starting to get it, we move on to a different thing. I wish I could just stay with something until I really get it."

Counting by Numbers Students are taught to "count by" numbers, beginning with two, ten, and five, then three, four, six, seven, eight, and nine (Lloyd et al., 1981). This is done by group counting, singing the numbers in sequence, writing the numbers, erasing some numbers in the sequence and having students fill them in, and having students work on worksheets with the count by sequences.

After students have learned to count by numbers they can apply the strategy to multiplication by using the following steps:

1. Point to the number you can count by.
2. Make hash marks to represent the other number.
3. When you count by the number, point to each of the hash marks. The last number said when you reach the end of the hash marks is the answer to the problem.

Games Games can be an important way for students to learn mathematics skills. Larson and Slaughter (1984) provide the following suggestions for using games in mathematics instruction:

1. *Choose games that reinforce present instruction.* Be sure that the selected game reinforces much of what students already know.
2. *Consider the complexity of the game* so that students do not spend more time learning the

game's procedures and rules than they spend learning the math-related material.

3. *Foresee potential problems associated with games*, such as disruptive behavior, shouting out, and so on.
4. *Provide an answer key if an adult is not available.*
5. *Play at least one round of the game with students* to ensure that they understand the rules and procedures and are acquiring the mathematics skills desired.
6. *Use aides or parent helpers to monitor the games.*

Monitoring and Communicating Progress

Carefully and systematically monitor the progress of students, checking their academic work frequently. More is involved in the monitoring process than simply determining whether students are doing the problem correctly or incorrectly. Effective math instruction involves checking students' work frequently and providing feedback. Student progress needs to be assessed, and if students are not progressing adequately, procedures should be altered.

Students in Alex Chinn's fifth grade class were asked to complete a worksheet to practice a new skill he taught them for using dollar signs and decimal points in subtraction problems. Alex told the students to complete only the first problem. After they completed the problem they were to consider whether the answer made sense and whether dollar signs and decimal points were used correctly. If so, they were to place a C next to the problem. If they were not sure whether the problem was correct, they were to mark it with a ?, and if they thought the problem was wrong, they were to use a star (*). Alex moved quickly from student to student, checking the first problem and providing them with feedback and reinforcement: "Jacob, you were right, you did have the problem correct. Maxine, what are you unsure about? Now, look at it again. What do you think? Yes, that's right it's correct. Beth, let's do this problem together."

Being a Model in Math Most of the time, a positive attitude towards math comes from effective instruction and the interest the teacher shows in mathematics. Tips for Teachers 15.4 offers suggestions for promoting positive attitudes toward math.

TIPS FOR TEACHERS

15.4 Promoting Positive Attitudes toward Math

1. Involve students in setting attainable goals that are challenging and require their participation and effort.
2. Provide opportunities for success. Failure should be infrequent.
3. Use progress charts that students can maintain to keep track of their progress, with the process of charting their progress serving as reinforcement.
4. Discuss the relevance of math to real-life situations. Remind and demonstrate that math is useful and necessary for success in the real world.

5. Model an enthusiastic, positive attitude toward mathematics and its application.
6. Give students positive reinforcement for their efforts and progress.
7. Link students' efforts to their achievement. Remind students that they performed the task well because they worked hard, persisted, reread, rethought, visualized, modeled, and so on.

Adapted from: Mercer, C. D., & Mercer, A. R. (1993). *Teaching students with learning problems* (4th ed.). New York: Merrill/Macmillan.

Strategies for Helping All Students Acquire Basic Math Skills

Mathematics instruction used to focus on the acquisition of the basic math skills, saving problem solving for later in the math curriculum. We now realize that teaching basic skills and problem solving must be coordinated from the beginning of math instruction.

Key components of basic math skills include:

- prenumber
- numeration
- place value
- fractions

These skills, and related subcomponents, are presented next.

Prenumber Skills

Many students with learning problems come to school without certain basic prenumber skills necessary for initial success in mathematics. Sonya Perez, a first grade teacher, described Malcolm in this way: "When he came to my class he knew how to count to ten but he didn't know what he was doing. He didn't know what the numbers meant. As far as he knew he could have been saying his ABCs." She realized that he first needed to learn one-to-one correspondence.

One-to-One Correspondence One-to-one correspondence occurs when the student understands that each object corresponds to another object. For example, when a student puts out cereal bowls for himself, his sister, and his mother he learns that each bowl represents one person. Early man used one-to-one correspondence to keep track of his accounts. He would put a rock in a bucket to represent each bag of grain he gave to a neighbor. The following activities can be used to teach one-to-one correspondence:

1. *Use everyday events to teach one-to-one correspondence.* Allow students with difficulties in this area to pass out materials. "Allison, please get one pair of scissors for each student in your group." "Naja, you need to have a chair for each member of your group. How many chairs are there? How many more do you need?"
2. *Use objects to work with small groups of students who need help with one-to-one correspondence.* Give each student ten small blocks. Place three blocks in the center. Say, "I want you to place a block next to each one in the center. As you place a block I want you to say the number. I will do the first one and then you do what I did."
3. *Give students a set of cards with pictures on each card.* Ask students to put the correct number of objects (e.g., pegs) on top of each number card. Reverse the task by giving objects to students and asking them to put the correct picture card next to the objects.

Classification Classification, the ability to group or sort objects based on one or more common properties, is an important prenumber skill because it focuses students, making them attend to the common properties of objects and reduce large numbers of objects to smaller groups. Classification can be by size, color, shape, texture, or design. Fortunately, most students are naturally interested in sorting and think that activities related to this prenumber skill are fun. Examples of such activities follow:

1. Provide students with a bag of miscellaneous articles that vary in size, shape, and color. Ask students to sort the articles any way they like into an empty egg carton or into empty plastic containers. After they finish, ask them to tell you the rules for sorting their articles. After they have had a chance to listen to others, give them a chance to sort the articles again, and to explain their rules for sorting.
2. Provide students with an empty egg carton and a box of small articles. Ask students to sort the articles by a single property, such as color. Now ask them whether there is another way in which they might be able to sort the articles. For example, ask them to consider size, texture, and so on.
3. Ask students to work in small groups, and provide them with a bag of articles. Ask one student to sort several of the articles by a property. Then ask other students in the

group to guess the property that qualifies the articles for the group.

4. Use pictures for sorting tasks. Good pictures include ones that represent animals, foods, plants, and toys.

5. Board games and Bingo games can be played by sorting or classifying shapes, colors, and pictures.

Seriation Seriation, the ability to rank objects according to the degree to which they possess a certain common characteristic, is similar to classification in that it depends on the recognition of common attributes of objects, but differs from classification in that the order in which objects are placed depends on the extent to which each object possesses the attribute. For example, seriation can occur by length, height, color, or weight. Sample activities for teaching seriation follow:

1. Give students a long piece of string. Ask them to cut the pieces into various lengths. Now ask them to put the lengths in order from shortest to longest. Now ask students to work in groups of three. Using those same piles of string, create one long seriation, from shortest to longest. Continue to ask students to work in different groups and sort the string sizes.

2. Ask students to work in groups of eight. In these groups, ask them to put themselves in order from shortest to tallest. Now ask them to put themselves in order from longest to shortest hair. Continue asking students to put themselves in seriation based on different attributes.

3. Using a peg with various sizes of rings, put the rings on the peg from largest to smallest.

4. Fill jars of the same size with different amounts of sand or water and ask students to put them in order.

Working with Numeration

Numeration is the understanding of numbers and their manipulations. Do not assume that because students can count or identify numbers they understand the value and the meaning of the numbers. This is a mistake that many teachers and parents make. Understanding numerals is an extremely important basic concept, one that throws many children into mathematical confusion early. A good example is Michelle, whose early experiences with math were positive. She learned to say, read, and write numbers with little or no difficulty. In first and second grade, she began to work with math addition and subtraction facts, and did these problems easily. When Michelle was asked to do problems that involved addition with regrouping, however, her lack of knowledge of numerals and their meaning became quickly evident. Following are examples of the way Michelle did some problems:

$$1)\ 27 + 15 = \qquad 2)\ 49 + 36 =$$
$$312 \qquad\qquad 715$$

As you can see from Michelle's answers, she remembered her math facts but did not understand what the numbers meant.

Understanding numeration and place value is necessary for progress in computation. Like Michelle, many students fail to make adequate progress in math because they do not understand the meaning of the numerals and the place value with which they are working. For example, students who understand the meaning of the numerals 25 and 17 would be less likely to make the following conceptual error:

$$25 - 17 = 12$$

Estimating Many students with learning difficulties in math do not have a sense of how much a certain amount really is—what it means to have five dollars, for example, or how many eggs are in a dozen, or about what 15 and 15, added together, should equal. These students cannot check their answers to determine how far off they are because they do not have a good idea of what an answer that made sense would be.

Estimating is something that can be done throughout the day and throughout the curriculum. For example, start the day by asking students to estimate how many children are absent. Estimation can be included in subject matters as well. You can use estimation in science, social studies, and even with art projects.

Students who do not understand the real meaning of numerals have difficulty applying computation to everyday problems. For example, when Michelle's teacher posed the following problem, she did not understand how to begin to find the answer. "Let's pretend that you had three one dollar bills and you were going to McDonald's to buy lunch. Let's pretend that your hamburger cost 89 cents, your French fries cost 74 cents, and your medium-sized coke cost 69 cents. How much money would you have left to spend?"

Mistakes occur when students attempt problems that are entirely too difficult for them or when they do not understand the "idea" behind the problem. In such cases the solutions students provide are totally unreasonable, given the problem. One of the best ways to help students who demonstrate this problem is to continually ask them to think about the problem and estimate what their answer probably will be. When students are taught to consider what a reasonable answer should be, they are better able to catch their mistakes.

Why is extra practice in estimation and other basic math skills important for students with math difficulties? How can instruction in those skills be modified for students with learning problems?

Understanding Regrouping Regrouping errors are less likely to occur when students understand numeration. Following are examples of regrouping errors:

$$39 + 27 = 516$$
$$56 - 18 = 42$$
$$41 - 24 = 23$$

Examine the errors students make and use the information to provide instruction.

Understanding Zero Students need to understand that zero is a number and means more than *nothing*. In the number *30,* for example, students need to understand that the number zero is a place holder. In the number *306,* students need to understand that there are 0 tens and that zero is serving as a place holder.

Understanding Place Value

Before students can understand place value, they must understand numeration. Students who know the meaning of numbers will have far less difficulty understanding place value. For example, if a student knows what *56* actually means, then when someone talks about the tens place equaling 50, the student will not be confused. When someone talks about the ones place equaling 6 ones, the student will understand what is meant.

Grouping by Ones and Tens To teach grouping, start with manipulatives (buttons, sticks, and blocks are useful), then pictures, and then numbers. Ask students to practice grouping by ones and tens. Students can also develop a table to record their answers, as follows:

Hundreds	Tens	Ones	Numerals
1	3	1	131
1	2	3	123
1	4	5	145

Use "ten blocks" and "single blocks" to represent numerals. For example, *35* can be represented as follows:

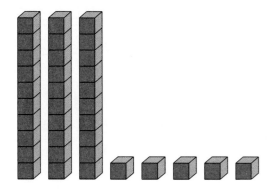

Naming Tens Teach students to identify numerals by the number of tens. For example, six tens is 60, four tens is 40, eight tens is 80, and so on. Give students opportunities to count by tens and then name the number. For example, "Count by tens three times." "Ten, twenty, thirty." "Count by tens seven times." "Ten, twenty, thirty, forty, fifty, sixty, seventy." Also, give students opportunities to draw picture diagrams that represent the place values of tens and ones, and to identify the number.

Place Value beyond Two Digits When students can accurately group and identify numbers at the two-digit level, introduce them to three- and four-digit numbers. It is a good idea to be certain that

students have mastered the concept of two-digit place value before you introduce numerals and place value. Give students plenty of opportunity to group, orally name, and sequence three- and four-digit place values.

Because place value is a skill taught during the primary grades, older students who have not adequately learned the skill will have difficulty with computation and word problems, and may have little opportunity to learn place value. Many of the games and activities designed to teach place value are aimed at young children and are less appropriate for older students. Tips for Teachers 15.5 provides sources of numbers that may be useful for teaching place value to older students.

Learning Fractions

Although often thought of as one of the more difficult mathematical skills, fractions are actually introduced early in the mathematics curriculum. Children between the ages of three and five discover fractions when they begin to cook. "Pour in 1/2 cup of milk and 1/3 cup of raisins" is often a youngster's introduction to fractions. Sharing—as in, "Give 1/2 of your cookie to your sister"—is also a good way for children to discover fractions.

The teaching of fractions—mirroring that of other computations—proceeds from concrete to abstract. Many manipulative aids can be used to teach fractions: colored rods, cardboard strips and squares, blocks, fractional circle wheels, cooking

TIPS FOR TEACHERS

15.5 Sources of Numbers for Teaching Place Value to Older Students

- an odometer
- numbers from students' science or social studies texts
- numbers from school population (e.g., number of

freshmen, sophomores, juniors, seniors, and so on)
- population data from town, county, state, or country
- financial data page from the newspaper

utensils such as measuring cups and spoons, and any unit divider (e.g., egg cartons and muffin pans).

Students with learning problems are unlikely to learn fractions, however, unless they are taught directly and systematically (Kelly et al., 1990). Such teaching includes:

■ *Systematic practice in discrimination among different problem types.* Students with learning disabilities and behavior problems often confuse algorithms when they compute fractions. For example, they learn to compute the denominator and then use this procedure when adding, subtracting, multiplying, and dividing.
■ *Separation of confusing elements and terminology.* Because much of the language of learning fractions is unfamiliar and confusing, students are more likely to learn fractions successfully when the language and concepts are clearly explained and illustrated.
■ *Use of a wide range of elements to illustrate each concept.* Students have a difficult time generalizing beyond the number of examples provided by the teacher; thus, by providing many different examples you help students understand.

The teaching sequence for fractions, which ensures that each student can do certain work, follows:

1. *Manipulates concrete models.* Refers to student's success at using fraction blocks and pegs, and using instruments that require understanding of fractions (such as measuring cups, spoons, and rulers).
2. *Matches fractional models* (e.g., matching halves, thirds, fourths).
3. *Points to fractional model when name is stated by another* (e.g., teacher says, "half" and student selects a model of "half" from several distracters).
4. *Names fractional units when selected by another* (e.g., teacher points to a fractional unit such as a "fourth," and student names it).
5. *Draws diagrams or uses manipulatives to represent fractional units* (e.g., teacher says or writes fractional units such as "whole,"

"half," and "third," and student uses manipulative drawings to represent these units).
6. *Writes fraction names when given fractional drawings.*
7. *Uses fractions to solve problems* (e.g., 1/2 cup of sugar in a bowl).

Strategies for Helping All Learners Acquire and Use Computation Skills

The emphasis on problem solving from NCTM (1989) does not mean that students do not need to learn math computation. In fact, students will be unsuccessful problem solvers if they spend too little time on math computation. You can help students with special needs, who often have difficulty with math computation.

Patterns of Common Computation Errors

The computation errors that students make fit certain patterns. Rourke (1993) identifies common types of mechanical arithmetic errors, described in the following sections. Tips for Teachers 15.6 has suggestions for helping students learn computational techniques.

Spatial Organization Mistakes in **spatial organization** are those that occur because students misalign numbers in columns. These mistakes can occur when students copy problems incorrectly or as they solve problems. One way to help students correct misaligned numbers is to tell them to draw vertical lines through their numbers to ensure that ones, tens, and hundreds are all in the right place. Another way to help is to provide graph paper with large squares so that students can write the numbers in boxes and more easily align them.

Visual Detail Mistakes involving **visual detail** occur when students misread one aspect of the arithmetic problem—misreading a minus sign as a plus sign, for example, or disregarding a dollar sign. Because many of the problems that occur in

TIPS FOR TEACHERS

15.6 Teaching Students Computational Strategies

1. *Use doubles.* Students know that $2 + 2 = 4$, $3 + 3 = 6$, and $5 + 5 = 10$. With this basic information, they can easily compute related facts. For example, if $3 + 3 = 6$ what is $3 + 4$? Yes, it is one more.

2. *Count-on.* Students do not need to resort to counting from one to solve math facts. They can learn to count on from the largest numeral in an addition fact. For example, $8 + 3$ means counting on 3 more from 8, for a sum of 11. Students learn to count on three more from eight: "nine, ten, eleven." The answer is the last number they say after they have counted on the correct number. Students can use this same principle for subtraction. For example, when asked to solve the following problem:

$$8 - 3 = \underline{\qquad}$$

   they now count backward from eight, "seven, six, five." Again, the last number is the answer.

3. *Use the commutative idea.* With addition and multiplication, the order of the numbers does not matter—it always yields the same answer. For example, $3 + 4 = 7$ and $4 + 3 = 7$. With multiplication this is also true: $4 \times 6 = 24$ and $6 \times 4 = 24$. Give students many opportunities to use this principle, to be sure they understand and apply it.

4. *Think one more or one less than a known fact.* When students know a math fact, teach them that they also know related math facts. For example, Guido knew that $6 + 7 = 13$. When he was faced with the problem $6 + 8 = \underline{\qquad}$, he panicked. When his teacher told him that eight is one more than seven, thus the answer is one more than $6 + 7 = 13$, he was able to solve the problem quickly. Pictures such as the following can help to illustrate the principle:

   $5 + 5 = 10$ ♥♥   ♥♥
               ♥♥ + ♥♥ =
               ♥   ♥

   $5 + 6 =$ ♥♥   ♥♥
             ♥♥ + ♥♥ =
             ♥   ♥♥

   $5 + 4 =$ ♥♥   ♥♥
             ♥♥ + ♥ =
             ♥   ♥

5. *Using tens.* Students can learn that $10 +$ any single-digit number merely changes the 0 in the 10 to the number they are adding to it, as in the following examples:

$$10 + 4 = 14$$
$$10 + 8 = 18$$

6. *Using nines.* There are two strategies students can apply to addition facts that involve nines. First, they can think of the 9 as a 10 and then subtract 1 from the answer. In the following example, the student is taught to "think" of the 9 as a 10:

      9   10
   $\underline{+ 6}$ think $\underline{+ 6}$
                   $16 - 1 = 15$

   Second, students can think that whenever there is a 9 in an addition problem, the answer in the ones column is always one less than the number they are adding to the 9. For example:

      9   8   9
   $\underline{+ 4}$ $\underline{+ 9}$ $\underline{+ 6}$
     13   17   15

7. *Counting by twos, threes, fours, fives, and tens.* Beginning with 10, teach students to count by the number. This may be done with individual students or with a small group. It is sometimes helpful to develop a rhythm to the counting sequence:

$$10–20–30–40–50–60–70–80–90–100$$

   After students can count by tens to 100, ask them to count aloud by ten from two points other than 10 and 100. For example, "Count aloud from 20 to 80." After students have learned to count by tens, they should be taught to count by fives and then by twos, threes, and fours. Being able to count by multiples helps in addition, multiplication, and division. Multiplication facts can be taught by interpreting $3 - 4$ as counting by threes four times. Division facts, such as 8 divided by 2, can be interpreted as, "How many times do you count by twos before you reach 8?"

8. *Relationship between addition and subtraction, and multiplication and division.* After students learn addition facts, they can be shown the relationship between the addition fact and subtraction. For example, students who know $7 + 6 = 13$ can learn the relationships between the known addition fact and the subtraction fact, $13 - 7 = \underline{\qquad}$. Whenever possible, reinforce this principle as students are working, "You know $8 + 4 = 12$, so $12 - 4 =$ must be $\underline{\qquad}$." Give students known facts and ask them to form subtraction problems. These sample relationships can be used to teach multiplication and division facts.

Adapted from: Thornton, C. A., & Toohey, M. A. (1985). Basic math facts: Guidelines for teaching and learning. *Learning Disabilities Focus, 1,* 44–57; and Thornton, C. A., Tucker, B. F., Dossey, J. A., & Brazik, E. F. (1983). *Teaching mathematics to children with special needs.* Menlo Park, CA: Addison-Wesley.

mathematics can easily be corrected by the student, teach students to stop and reread the problem and their answers before they go to the next problem, to be sure that they neither misread nor omitted something.

Procedural Error Procedural error occurs when students misapply a procedure from one arithmetic operation to another. For example, a student learns that $5 \times 5 = 25$ and misapplies this information to a problem in which 5 and 5 should be added.

Failure to Shift Operations A failure to shift operations occurs when students fail to move to one operation after completing another operation. For example, when the problem involves both subtraction and addition, the student fails to move to addition after completing the subtraction portion of the problem. To help students who demonstrate this problem, ask them to reread the problem and tell you whether more than one operation is involved. Ask them to identify the types of operations involved and to provide an example of each one. Ask them to tell you how they will monitor their process and to determine how they will ensure accuracy in switching from one operation to the next.

Motoric Problems Mistakes resulting from motoric problems can occur when the students' writing is so difficult to read that it leads to errors in arithmetic. Many students with learning problems demonstrate such poor writing ability that it interferes with their ability to successfully perform arithmetic computations. These students have difficulty not only writing their numbers but also reading them. They often mistake their fives for threes, their twos for threes, and so on. Thus, their calculations may be accurate, based on their interpretation of the number, but the answers are wrong because they have mistaken the number.

Memory Problems Mistakes resulting from memory problems occur when students forget or misremember a fact that leads to an error in arithmetic calculation. As a teacher, you can help students with learning problems by providing them

with adequate time and frequent opportunities to rehearse and learn arithmetic facts.

Difficulty with Zero Difficulty with zero can lead to mistakes that occur when students do not understand the multiple meanings and uses of zero. Many students with learning problems learn that zero means nothing, and never really understand that zero is a number or the role of zero as a place holder. The best way to help students who have difficulty with zero is to ensure that they understand how zero can be used as a place holder. You can teach a minilesson to a small group of students who demonstrate difficulty with this concept, to facilitate their understanding and adequate use of zero.

RESEARCH BRIEF

MATH PROBLEM SOLVING

Hofmeister (1989) provides a summary of the research on math problem solving:

- Problem-solving skills can and should be taught.
- Some generalization of problem-solving skills should be planned for and systematically taught. This generalization is most likely to occur across problems without a domain. Transfer across domains will depend on the similarity of the problem.
- It may be unreasonable to expect the majority of specific problem-solving strategies in one domain, such as ratio-based word problems, to transfer to another domain, such as geometry proofs.
- The development of practical problem-solving skills will require a considerable investment of time and explicitly taught strategies and practices.
- Teaching of problem-solving strategies should be integrated with the teaching of other content in the domain, such as computational and factual knowledge.

Strategies for Helping All Students Develop Problem-Solving Skills

Another component of effective math instruction is problem solving, which has several unifying components that include the following:

- a mathematics knowledge base
- an application of knowledge to new and unfamiliar situations
- an ability to actively engage in thinking processes and apply this knowledge base to problems

Problem solving is increasingly visible in mathematics textbooks and curricula in regular education. Few programs are designed to instruct students with learning problems in problem solving (Cawley et al., 1987; Geary, 1993). Secondary students with learning problems often demonstrate extreme difficulty in problem solving because of the poor instruction they have received (Cawley et al., 1987).

Problem-Solving Strategies

Mercer and Miller (1992) have developed a procedure called FAST DRAW to teach the concrete-representational-abstract teaching principle advocated in mathematics instruction. The Strategic Math Series is the name of their program. Following is an explanation of the **FAST DRAW** strategy:

Find what you're solving for.
Ask yourself, "What are the parts of the problem?"
Set up the numbers.
Tie down the sign.

Discover the sign.
Read the problem.
Answer or draw a conceptual representation of the problem, using lines and tallies, and check.
Write the answer.

At the secondary level, Montague and Bos (1986) provided instruction in word-problem solving for six students. Five of the six students improved after the cognitive strategy training. Subsequent work in cognitive problem solving has yielded positive outcomes for students with learning problems (Montague, 1992). Their strategy included an eight-step process, as follows:

1. Read the problem aloud.
2. Paraphrase the problem.
3. Visualize what the problem is about.
4. State the problem in your own words.
5. Hypothesize.
6. Estimate.
7. Calculate.
8. Self-check.

Hutchinson (1993) also implemented a strategy for teaching adolescents with learning problems to solve algebra word problems. She taught them to ask themselves questions (self-question), to think aloud, to provide guided practice, and to use graphs to monitor their progress. Students displayed increased abilities to solve problems and transferred their skills to other settings. The self-questions Hutchinson used included the following:

1. Have I read and understood the sentence?
2. Do I have the whole picture, a representation, for this problem?
3. Have I written the representation on the worksheet?

In summary, when teaching story problems to students with learning and behavior problems, keep the following guidelines in mind (Bos & Vaughn, 1994):

- Be certain the students can perform the arithmetic computation before introducing the computation in story problems.
- Develop a range of story problems that contain the type of problem you want students to learn to solve.
- Instruct with one type of problem until mastery is attained.
- Teach students to read through the word problem and visualize the situation. Ask them to read the story aloud and tell what it is about.
- Ask students to reread the story—this time to get the facts.
- Identify the key question. In the beginning stages of problem solving, students should write the key question so that it can be referred to when computation is complete.

- Identify extraneous information. Tell students to note that this information will not be used.
- Reread the story problem and attempt to state the situation in a mathematical sentence. The teacher plays an important role in this step by asking the students questions and guiding them in formulating the arithmetic problem.
- Tell students to write the arithmetic problem and compute the answer. Students can compute some problems in their heads without completing this step.
- Tell students to reread the key questions and be sure they have completed the problem correctly.
- Ask students whether their answer is likely, based on their estimate.

Tips for Teachers 15.7 should be helpful as you design and implement problem-solving activities for students with learning problems.

Designing Math Problem-Solving Activities for Students with Special Needs

What should teachers consider when they design math problem-solving activities for students with special needs? To what extent will these designs benefit other students? The instructional practices that we recommend for teaching problem solving will benefit all students.

Integrating Math Problem Solving into the Curriculum

Problem solving does not have to occur only during math time. It is an interesting and fun activity to integrate into the rest of the curriculum. Math story problems are especially easy to integrate into the reading curriculum. How? Take stories that children are reading or books that you are reading to the entire class, and change the stories so that they include numbers and problems the students need to answer.

TIPS FOR TEACHERS

15.7 Designing Math Problem-Solving Activities for Students with Learning Difficulties

1. Begin problem solving as part of the initial mathematics program. Do not wait.
2. Make problem solving the reason for computation.
3. Develop a long-term perspective on the development of programs to teach problem solving.
4. Conduct problem solving as a multimodel activity.
5. Assist students with what they cannot do so that they can solve problems. If a student cannot read the problem, rewrite it. If the computation is too complex, make it simpler.
6. Ask students to write their own problems and to modify existing problems.
7. Differentiate between process and knowledge.
8. Prepare problems in such a way that students must act upon the information. Prepare a set of problems in which all problems have the same questions.
9. Use familiar subject matter as the content for the problems.
10. Monitor progress and modify problems to fit the students' weaknesses and progress.

Adapted from: Cawley, J. F., Miller, J. H., & School, B. A. (1987). A brief inquiry of arithmetic word-problem-solving among learning disabled secondary students. *Learning Disabilities Focus*, 2(2), 87–93.

For example, Joan Lindquist asked students the following questions about a story they were reading in class. "How many friends has Marcia told us about? How many friends does Linda have? All together, how many friends do they have? How many more friends does Linda have than Marcia?" Teachers can also add information to the stories and then ask children to solve word problems based on the additional information provided. It is also educational and fun to ask students to work in pairs to write their own word problems from the stories they are reading. Then have them read their word problems to the entire class, so that the class can solve them.

Word problems can be easily integrated into the social studies curriculum also. When dates are discussed, ask students to compute how many years ago the event occurred. Ask students word problems about the age of central figures in the social studies lesson. Add numbers and information to the lesson and construct word problems. Cawley (1984) identifies the integration of math into other content areas as an important means of promoting generalization of math concepts.

Return to the interview at the beginning of this chapter where you met Paul, a college student with learning disabilities who had extreme difficulty with math. What questions would you want to ask him? If Paul were in your class, how would you implement the suggestions in this chapter to ensure that his experiences in mathematics would be as positive as possible? Remember, you *can* make a difference in students' lives.

SUMMARY

- The current trend in mathematics instruction is to emphasize effective problem solving, and to promote positive attitudes toward a broad view of mathematics than toward rote memorization.
- Difficulties in mathematical problem solving may originate from cognitive factors, educational factors, personality factors, and neuropsychological patterns.
- Several curriculum resources are available to teachers of students who have difficulty learning math.
- Teachers tend to lower their expectations of students who have difficulty in mathematics, but lower expectations do not solve the problem. Instead, teachers should instruct students to develop their own goals, help them develop joint (teacher–student) goals , and then provide the type of instruction that will maximize students' strengths.
- Appropriate and specific feedback can help students better understand their mistakes in mathematics, promote student self-monitoring, and boost student self-concept.
- Just as basic skills must be mastered before higher-order problems can be taught and understood, mathematics instruction should begin at a concrete level and gradually move to increasingly abstract levels.

Key Terms and Concepts

classification

Computational Arithmetic Program

constant time delay

Corrective Mathematics Program

developmental arithmetic disorder

difficulty with zero

DISTAR Arithmetic Program

failure to shift operations

FAST DRAW

Key Math Teach and Practice

mastery

memory problems

Milliken Wordmath

motoric problems

one-to-one correspondence

NCTM standards

procedural error

nonverbal math disabilities

Project Math

Real-Life Math Program

spatial organization

spiral curriculum

Structural Arithmetic

Team-Assisted Individualization

Touch Math

visual detail

Think and Apply

1. Reread Paul's description, at the beginning of the chapter, of his experience with math. Think of three things you would do if Paul were a student in your elementary math class. Be sure to consider how you might motivate Paul, what your attitude toward Paul would be, and what instructional practices you would consider implementing.

2. Make a copy of the summary of the NCTM guidelines. Show them to three special education teachers and ask for their opinions of the application of these standards to the special education students they teach. Be sure to ask them to identify the types of needs their students have and the extent to which the needs of their students relate to the requirements of the guidelines.

3. Write to two publishing companies that provide educational materials for students with special needs (e.g., PRO-ED, 8700 Shoal Creek Blvd., Austin, TX 78757–6897) and ask them to send you a copy of their materials catalog. In the catalog, examine the materials designed to teach mathematics to students with special needs. Consider the following questions: (a) Are more materials available to teach language arts or mathematics? (b) Of the materials available to teach mathematics, what proportion are designed for elementary students and what proportion are designed for secondary students? (c) Make a list of the skills that the materials indicate they cover. What skills are frequently not included?

4. A considerable amount of software is available for instruction in mathematics. Identify two software programs that you think would be effective for teaching mathematics to young children (ages 5–8). Identify two software programs that you think would be effective for teaching mathematics to intermediate-age children (ages 9–12).

Read More about It

1. Bley, N. S., & Thornton, C. A. (1995). *Teaching mathematics to students with learning disabilities* (3rd ed.). Austin: PRO-ED.

   Describes the relationship between learning disabilities and mathematical performance, discusses different areas in mathematics (e.g., money and time, number and place value), describes the most common errors made in each area by students with learning disabilities, and provides instructional techniques for improving students' mathematical performance in each area.

2. Cawley, J. F., Fitzmaurice-Hayes, A. M., & Shaw, R. A. (1988). *Mathematics for the mildly handicapped.* Boston: Allyn and Bacon.

   Aims at developing a long-term, comprehensive curriculum for teaching mathematics to students with mild disabilities. Emphasis is on determining which area of mathematics to teach, when and for how long to teach this component.

3. Cuevas, G., & Driscoll, M. (Eds.). (1993). *Reaching all students with mathematics.* Reston, VA: National Council of Teachers of Mathematics.

   Discusses current trends in mathematics instruction, emphasizing ways to capitalize on increasingly diverse classrooms, and describes recent programs aimed at improving the mathematics instruction and outcome performance of special student populations.

4. Helton, S. M. (1991). *Math activities for every month of the school year.* West Nyack: NY: Simon & Schuster.

   Activities (appropriate for grades 3–6) for twelve basic math concepts are related to events (e.g., holidays, seasonal changes) in a particular month. Includes ideas for classroom displays, as well as reproducible activity sheets.

MAKING A DIFFERENCE

through Action Teaching

Mathematics Activities for All Learners

Cake for Four—No, Make that Six!

Objective: Developing students' concept of fractions by having them partition an object into equal parts.

Grades: Second through fourth grade (possibly higher)

Materials: For each student: (1) a 6-inch paper circle; (2) 5 strips construction paper, 1/4-inch wide by 8 inches long, in a contrasting color to the paper circle; and (3) 8 Teddy Grahams (or other small cookies), placed in a small sandwich bag.

Teaching Procedures:

1. Students move desks together so that each has a partner with whom to compare his or her work. Materials are distributed. Teacher introduces the lesson as a *Let's Pretend* activity in which students will learn that when they eat a piece of cake that has been divided into equal parts, they are eating a fraction of the cake.

2. Students are asked to imagine that they have just helped bake their favorite kind of cake for supper. To feed the four people in their pretend family, they need to divide the cake into four equal pieces. They are asked to think of the paper circle on their desk as the top of the cake, and to show the teacher (and their partners) how—using the strips of paper—they would divide the cake into four equal parts. When each student has successfully demonstrated this partitioning task, they are asked what fraction of the whole cake each piece is, and how that fraction is written.

3. Next, students are asked to imagine that their grandmother and grandfather have arrived unexpectedly and have accepted the family's invitation to stay for supper. Now, because students certainly want to share the cake with the grandparents also, into how many pieces will they divide it?

   The teacher makes sure that each student shows six equal portions and understands that each piece of cake is now 1/6 of the whole—just enough for the six people at the dinner table.

4. Before the cake is served, however, Uncle Bob and Aunt Doris arrive! Now the cake will be divided into how many equal pieces?

5. Finally, the time comes to decorate the cake with the Teddy Grahams, cut it, and serve it. (As a reward for all their good thinking, students now get to eat the decorations, 1/8 at a time!)

Students enjoy the story associated with this activity, and they enjoy comparing their partitioned cakes with those of their peers. (This is a good example of cooperative learning.) They especially enjoy eating their cookies at the end of this activity.

Reprinted with permission: Bos, C., & Vaughn, S. (1994). *Strategies for teaching students with learning and behavior problems* (3rd ed.). Boston: Allyn and Bacon.

Bingo Clock Reading

Objective: To give students practice in associating the time on a clock face, its written form on a game board, and its spoken form.

Grades: Primary

Materials: (1) Cards that show times on a standard clock; (2) large game boards with sixteen squares and with times written at the bottom of each square; (3) sixteen "clock" chips (made by placing gummed labels on game-board chips and drawing a clock on the face of the label); (4) markers.

Teaching Procedure:

1. A caller holds up a clock face. Players must decide whether the time shown by that clock is on their game board. If it is, players place a marker in the square that contains the written form. The winner is the first person who completes a row in any direction and reads the time in each winning square.

Reprinted with permission: Bos, C., & Vaughn, S. (1994). *Strategies for teaching students with learning and behavior problems* (3rd ed.). Boston: Allyn and Bacon.

Mathematics Activities for All Learners (continued)

Slap It!!!

Objective: To provide practice in responding quickly to math.

Grades: Second through eighth grade

Materials: A set of 4-inch by 6-inch cards on which the answers to math facts are written. Cards can be established as answers to addition, subtraction, multiplication, or division facts.

Teaching Procedures:

1. Students and teacher stand around a small table (preferably round), and teacher shows students the cards, each with a number (the answer to a math fact). Teacher spreads the cards (approximately 10) on the table, with the number side up.
2. Students are told to keep both hands on the table until the teacher says, "Go." Students who lift either hand prior to the "go" signal are eliminated from that round of competition.
3. The teacher says a computation problem, followed by the word *go*. For example, "6 × 7 = (go)."
4. Students slap the card that has the correct answer. The first hand on the card gets to keep the card. The student with the most cards gets to be the teacher.

Adaptations:

1. Teachers can use the same game with word problems.
2. Teachers can use more than one computation during the game.

Measurement

Objective: To reinforce understanding of perimeter and area

Grades: Third grade and above

Materials: 1-inch graph paper, scissors, teacher-made table worksheet

Teaching Procedures:

1. Have students cut out squares of graph paper of different sizes: a 1-inch square, a 2-inch square, a 3-inch square, a 4-inch square, and a 5-inch square.
2. Measure the number of small squares in each large cutout square, and complete the following table:

edges	1	2	3	4	5	6
perimeter						
area						

3. Ask, "What happens to the perimeter and area each time the edges are doubled?"
4. Have students experiment with different-size squares and then complete the table.

Reprinted with permission of the publisher, *Teaching K–8,* Norwalk, CT 06854. From the April 1993 issue of *Teaching K–8.*

Subtraction with Money

Objective: To introduce the concept of subtraction of three-digit numbers with regrouping, using play money.

Grades: Third grade and above

Materials: Play money (20 one-dollar bills, 20 dimes, and 20 pennies for each student), place-value board for each student.

Teaching Procedures:

1. Review 100 pennies = 1 dollar
   10 pennies = 1 dime
   10 dimes = 1 dollar
2. Write example on the board: $5.36
   − 1.27
3. Student makes $5.36 on place-value board.
4. Teacher begins questioning, "You have 6 pennies, you have to give me 7 pennies. Do you have enough pennies?" "Can you trade something?" "That's right. 1 dime = 10 pennies. Take 1 dime from your dimes place and trade it for 10 pennies from your bank. Put the 10 pennies in the pennies place." "Now, how many pennies do you have?" "Can you take 7 pennies away? How many are left?" (Teacher writes 9 in the ones column.) "Can you take 1 dollar away? How many are left?" (Teacher writes 3 in the hundreds place.)
5. Give students ample guided practice with one trade before giving them independent practice in pairs. Encourage students to self-question while completing each step.

Modifications: When students become proficient in subtracting with one trade, provide examples of problems involving two trades.

Teaching in the Content Areas

FOCUS QUESTIONS

1. What are some critical issues that content area teachers face when promoting learning for all students?

2. What difficulties do students face in content area learning?

3. What steps can you take to prepare student-friendly demonstrations?

4. How can you promote student participation through questioning and classroom discussion?

5. What procedures can you use to learn the strengths and weaknesses of your textbook?

6. How can you adapt textbooks for students with reading difficulties?

7. How can you promote success in homework, class assignments, and tests for all learners?

8. How can you plan interdisciplinary thematic units to integrate the content areas?

nterview

Nancy Brice

Nancy Brice is a social studies teacher at South Miami Middle School, a suburban school that is among the most ethnically mixed in the city of Miami, Florida. She teaches approximately one hundred fifty seventh and eighth graders in six different classes (five civics and one geography). Fifteen of her students have been school-identified as having learning disabilities, seven have been identified as gifted, and two as vision-impaired. Thus, Nancy's classroom has a range of cultural, linguistic, and academic diversity coupled with an extraordinary range of individual needs.

Nancy puts a lot of energy into her teaching. She is feisty and highly interactive with students. She is constantly on her feet, frequently moving around the room, working with small groups of students, and checking in with individual students. Nancy is positive, upbeat, and full of energy. A visit to her classroom gives you the feeling that she is ready to teach. Despite the challenge of large classes and frequent interruptions during the day, learning happens in her class. Here's Nancy's explanation:

> I try to make my class interesting and entertaining. When I was teaching "supply and demand" I made up a game where all students were given play money when they came into class and had to buy their desks. I made up a relay race when it was time to review for a test. When I plan I try to think, "How can I make it fun?"

> My particular challenge this year is my geography class. First of all, it is the first time I've taught it. I don't even have a textbook that I like. The real problem is that it is an elective and only one out of three students actually signed up for it. The rest didn't get their first choice for an elective and so were just dumped in this class.

Many of the students with disabilities are placed in this class. To make this class work I really have to do some careful planning and be ready to make adaptations to meet their needs.

With one hundred fifty students, I can't make individual plans for each student with special needs. On a day-to-day basis I don't sit down and plan for Rudy, for example.

But I do spend a great deal of time planning each lesson, and I plan for adaptations. I meet with the special education and gifted teachers at the beginning of the school year so that I am aware of individual student needs. I discuss their IEPs and brainstorm with these resource teachers about how I can adapt curriculum. For example, [I give] students with learning disabilities . . . extra time to take tests. In book work we do a lot of cooperative learning so they can work back and forth with each other. When I lecture, I show them how to take notes.

Even though I have too many students, I get to know each one by name. I think my relationship with the kids is excellent. I like to joke and laugh with the students, and I help them see that we're a family in here. But at the same time, I'm pretty strict. There are rules they must follow in the class, but they know I'm fair.

The kids also know that in my class, they have to think and they have to think about their thinking. We have debates, discussions, you name it. I even demonstrate how to think. I'll say something like, "I'm sorry it's taking me so long to think, but it's a tough problem." Then I talk through my thinking to show them how to solve problems. I also make them answer their own questions through research. I'll say, "Find out, do you think I'm the encyclopedia of knowledge?" and then I show them how to find out.

Introduction

How does Nancy Brice ensure that learning takes place in her social studies classes? How does Nancy attend to the needs of special learners while teaching one hundred fifty students in a content area in which students with special learning needs are most often mainstreamed, creating the greatest possible academic diversity?

This chapter begins with a discussion of critical issues in content area instruction and the learning difficulties students experience in content area classes. The focus is on teaching strategies you can use to promote learning in your content area classes.

Current Trends in Content Area Instruction

Tony Valenti teaches ninth grade world history in an urban high school. His teaching responsibilities include six classes a day, with approximately thirty-five students per class. The textbook is Tony's primary tool for planning. Content coverage is his main concern.

> I have thirty-eight chapters to cover in thirty-six weeks. We really have only thirty weeks, when you consider pep rallies and things like that. My biggest problem is trying to fit everything in. My assistant principal, who supervises curriculum and instruction, would like me to teach study skills and to make adaptations for kids who can't read, but frankly I don't see how to cram it into an already impossible schedule.

Tony took a course on making adaptations for students with special learning needs. He enrolled for the class because he felt that what he learned would help him work with the many students at risk he teaches. His classroom teaching was videotaped and a graduate student served as a peer coach to help him resolve his concerns

about content coverage. As he watched the videotape, Tony realized that he was flooding students with information. There was little time for students to ask questions, process the information, or distinguish what information was most important. His overheads were difficult to read, and he had difficulty being specific about what he wanted students to learn. As Tony put it, "I was an information machine gun."

Peer-coaching sessions focused on how Tony could present information more clearly to students and teach them note- and test-taking skills. At the end of the course Tony acknowledged, "I have all the same challenges, but I am more considerate and better at recognizing the scope of special needs. The time spent on process has made me more focused and has made the students more focused."

Balancing Content and Process

Tony is faced with a common problem of many content area teachers—the **content and process dilemma.** Vacca and Vacca (1989, p. 9) put it this way, "Teachers who are wedded to a discipline walk a tightrope between content and process. It's a balancing act every time the attempt is made to influence what is learned (content) and how it should be learned (process)." Teachers are often

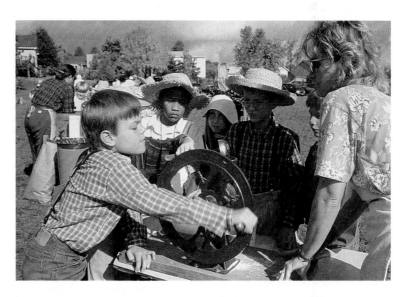

These students are participating in a community-based activity as part of their integrated thematic unit on colonial life. Why are collaborative and integrative curricula desirable in content area learning?

pressured to complete a textbook during a semester or to cover a set of objectives determined by state or school district curriculum guides. This pressure to cover content causes teachers to move steadily through material, even though some students have not had the opportunity to learn how to learn it.

The current trend is to strive for balance between content coverage (subject-centered) and process (student-centered) (Readence et al., 1992). Process includes teacher-directed instructional activities that help students understand material. For example, by teaching key vocabulary before reading you can help students zero in on key ideas while they read. Process also includes student-implemented study skills.

Balancing Text-driven and Activities-driven Instruction

Sara Hood teaches social studies to one hundred ninety sixth grade students in their first year of middle school. To prepare for lessons, Sara examines the whole unit in the book and chooses the fundamental ideas that she wants students to learn. She then thinks of ways to give them background information and to teach key vocabulary. Sara uses the state-adopted social studies textbook as the basis of her planning. One major concern in planning is to find activities that will keep her middle school students involved in learning and thus help her maintain control of the class. As Sara commented, "My college professors encouraged us to use activities-based learning for social studies, but frankly every time I try something 'hands-on,' they freak out!" Consequently, Sara relies heavily on routines such as guided textbook reading and answering the questions at the end of the chapter.

Like Tony, Sara attended the university course on making adaptations for students with special needs. She had a peer coach, and her teaching was videotaped. After watching her first videotaped lesson, Sara realized that her students were not as engaged as she thought. As she watched the tape she commented, "When I was going through the lesson it seemed to be going well. But now that I'm looking at it on the tape, I'm bored to tears. If I'm bored, they must really be bored."

Sara and her peer coach talked about planning in terms of the Planning Pyramid (refer to Chapter 2) and co-constructed plans. They brainstormed about teaching and learning strategies that would encourage involvement and provide alternatives to the "read the chapter, answer the questions" routines. They talked about how she could incorporate cooperative learning groups into her planning, and discussed how to place students with different talents and needs together in groups so that they could provide support for each other.

Sara used the Planning Pyramid to plan a 2-and-1/2-week unit on Latin American countries. She planned to divide the classes into mixed-ability cooperative learning groups that would select a country and present what they learned to the rest of the class. The bottom of the Pyramid (see Figure 16.1) listed topics that all groups

These students are giving a group presentation. What decisions did their social studies teacher need to make on the content/process dilemma? How might this presentation reflect an effort to balance text-driven and activities-driven instruction in a content area?

FIGURE 16.1

Planning Pyramid for a Unit on Latin American Countries

How
present
day
government
operates

Currency rate of exchange

Anything I haven't thought of!!!

Nobel Prize winners

20th century rulers

Topography

Capital; major cities

Latitude; longitude

Famous persons

Birth; death rate

Currency used

Historical highlights

Major bodies of water

Natural resources
and industry

Food

would research and on which all students would be tested. The middle and top of the Pyramid listed student-selected material.

The unit was successful, and Sara began using cooperative learning groups regularly. Students were actively engaged in helping each other and were learning to respect each other's talents. Sara found that students are more engaged in learning when textbook assignments are balanced with other activities.

Sara's experience is not unusual. In social studies and science courses the trend is toward activities-oriented learning that emphasizes real-world, hands-on experiences. The benefits of activities-oriented learning include increased student engagement in learning and increased opportunities for students who do not read and write well to be actively involved.

Activities-oriented instruction, coupled with effective content area reading methods, can enable all students to become effective learners.

RESEARCH BRIEF

TEXTBOOK OR ACTIVITY APPROACH: WHAT WORKS FOR STUDENTS WITH LEARNING DISABILITIES?

For decades, science educators have debated the relative merits of textbook versus activity approaches to science instruction. Some say a textbook approach prepares students for the rigors of college reading and standardized achievement tests. Others prefer hands-on science instruction, on the premise that students learn by doing. This debate is particularly salient for middle school students with learning disabilities who have difficulty reading and learning from text.

Thomas Scruggs, Margo Mastropieri, and their colleagues (1993) conducted a carefully controlled investigation that compared both approaches for twenty-six students with learning disabilities in four middle school special education classrooms. The textbook approach consisted of guided reading coupled with paper-and-pencil vocabulary and comprehension tasks. The activity approach engaged students in experiments and recording observations. All twenty-six students were exposed to both approaches.

Outcomes were better in the activity approach than in the textbook approach in measures of vocabulary, factual recall, and application of concepts. Moreover, these middle schools students overwhelmingly preferred the activity approach, commenting that it helped them learn more and was more enjoyable.

Coordinating Content Area Teaching and Learning Strategies

Another current trend in instruction is to emphasize professional collaboration. One way that professionals collaborate is to teach learning strategies. Teachers agree on a core group of learning strategies that will be reinforced from grade to grade and from course to course.

Al Fabre was able to initiate such a coordinated program at his school, the Louisiana State University Laboratory School. The program was called the Learning Environment and Attitude Program (LEAP) for Success (Cowart & Fabre, 1986). All teachers in the middle school agreed to implement four strategies (note taking, test taking, textbook reading, and vocabulary study). Teachers participated in workshops to learn how to teach the strategies, students took a minicourse to learn how to use the strategies, and parents were introduced to the strategies at open house and through a parent handbook.

Integrating the Curriculum

Vern Glidden is a sixth grade science teacher at a large inner-city middle school that is organized by teams. One teacher from each subject area is assigned to a team, and the same cohort of students rotates from teacher to teacher during the day. The team includes several specialists (e.g., English as a second language teacher, special education teacher, gifted education teacher) who serve students in the cohort. Vern chairs his team, which meets daily to coordinate planning and to discuss individual student needs. The principal charged each team to set professional development goals for the next two school years. After much deliberation, Vern's team decided on two goals. Their Year 1 goal was to learn more about how to incorporate all language processes (reading, writing, listening, and speaking) in content area instruction. Their Year 2 goal was to learn how to plan collaboratively across their content areas to develop interdisciplinary thematic units.

The goals set by Vern's team represent two important trends in content area learning. The first trend is toward integration of all language processes in the content areas. Content area classes require students to use the basic skills of reading and writing, and to speak and listen. Conley (1995, p. 9) suggests that content area teachers take a **communication approach** by "teaching the student how to (1) communicate with oneself and others and (2) integrate reading with other language skills including writing, speaking, and listening."

The second trend is toward integrating subject areas through **interdisciplinary thematic units**—teaching several subject areas around a central theme. For example, in high school the teaching of marine science, history, geography, and American literature could be centered around a theme of whales (*Moby Dick*).

Learning Difficulties in the Content Areas

Why do students have difficulty learning in the content areas? The question is so broad that you might as well ask, "Why do students have difficulty learning?" You could answer that question by summarizing all you have learned about different students, but typical content area classes pose particular problems for students. These problems include the following:

- Not all subjects are uniformly interesting to all students.
- Not all subjects are consistent with students' cultural backgrounds and prior knowledge.
- Learning in some content areas requires basic skills in reading, writing, and mathematics that some students do not possess.
- The pace of instruction in some content areas is too fast for some students.
- The level of conceptual complexity and density in some content areas is overwhelming for some students.
- Textbooks in content area classes can be dull and encyclopedic.
- Content area classes require both regular homework and assignments and long-term projects.
- Taking tests is a required component of many content area classes.

The suggestions in this chapter focus on how to give students who have difficulties in these areas the support they need to succeed in your content area class.

Effective Content Area Instruction for All Learners

Faimon Roberts is a seventh and eighth grade science teacher at Louisiana State University Laboratory School. Although Faimon recognizes that his primary responsibility is to teach science, he also understands his responsibility includes teaching students how to learn in science classes. In Faimon's more than twenty years of teaching experience, he has learned that students need to get ready to listen and to read. Their minds are on a million different things, and prelearning activities help them focus. In addition, Faimon has learned that setting a purpose for learning is essential, especially for students who tend to get lost when they read science textbooks or hear a lecture. Also, Faimon says, some students need to be told, "Here is the structure that the author of your textbook uses to organize the material. Watch for this structure."

This section describes ways that teachers like Faimon Roberts provide effective content area instruction for all learners, including ways to develop prelearning activities, to structure classroom presentations, and to promote student participation.

Utilizing Prelearning Activities

Prelearning activities are strategies teachers use to activate students' prior knowledge and to preteach vocabulary and concepts—essentially, to prepare students to learn. Faimon typically uses purpose-setting activities, semantic maps, and concept diagrams to help students prepare to learn new information.

Purpose Setting **Purpose-setting activities** provide students with a reason for completing a reading assignment or for listening to a lecture. For a few students, getting a good grade on a test is reason enough. Other students set their own purposes for reading and listening. For example, a chapter entitled "The Stormy Sixties" might get a student to think, "I really want to know what life was like when my parents were my age." Setting a purpose for learning helps guide the reading and listening process and helps students to improve the depth of their comprehension. Purpose-setting activities are important for all learners, but particularly for students with motivational and attentional problems. Tips for Teachers 16.1 provides guidelines for setting a purpose before you give a lecture or a reading assignment.

Common misconceptions: (a) students learned to read in elementary school, (b) reading and comprehending content area textbooks is no different from reading and comprehending basal readers, and (c) remedial reading classes will ensure the necessary skills for reading in the content areas (Readence, Bean, & Baldwin, 1992).

Semantic Maps Providing students with visual representations of concepts and vocabulary to be learned is a powerful prelearning tool, particularly for special learners. One visual tool commonly used in prelearning activities is a **semantic map** (Pearson & Johnson, 1978), a visual aid that helps

16.1 Setting a Purpose for a Lesson

- Keep the purpose brief, but make it powerful. Students become more actively involved in listening, reading, or participating in a classroom activity when they have a reason for doing so.
- Set a single purpose. When students are given too many purposes, they can lose their focus.
- Make certain that the purpose statement is not too narrow in scope and that it does not reveal too much content, which can actually inhibit comprehension.
- Have a regular purpose-setting routine. For example, write the purpose for learning on the board or demonstrate how the purpose was set.

- After reading, begin discussion with a reiteration of the purpose for reading.
- Help students learn how to set their own purposes. Talk about the importance of setting a purpose and how to develop purpose statements.
- Keep the written purpose statement in full view of students while they are participating in a class activity. Some students may need to be reminded about the purpose of the lesson.

Blanton, W. E., Wood, K. D., and Moorman, G. B. (1990). The role of purpose in reading instruction. *The Reading Teacher, 43*(7), 486–493.

---

students see how ideas are related to each other and to what students already know.

Lists of words prepared in advance by the teacher or generated by students through teacher-guided brainstorming are placed on the board. After discussing the words' meanings, the class discusses how to cluster the words and works together to develop a map to represent visually the relationships that exist among the ideas.

For example, Figure 16.2 shows a semantic map for the following words for a chapter on Egypt:

Nile	mummy
Cairo	hieroglyphics
Great Pyramids	obelisk
papyrus	Valley of the Kings
lotus flower	kartoush
Red Sea	Mediterranean Sea
Suez Canal	King Tut
Luxor	chariot
Karnak	Aswan Dam
Sphinx	Rosetta Stone
pharaohs	Alexandria
Sahara Desert	

Students can use the map as a listening or reading guide. The map can also serve as a framework for post-listening and reading discussions and an aid for studying for tests or quizzes.

Concept Diagrams Concept diagrams (Bulgren et al., 1988) are another way to introduce a lecture or reading assignment. A **concept diagram** (see Figure 16.3) is similar to a semantic map, but also helps students determine the definitions, characteristics, examples, and nonexamples of a concept.

To create and use a concept diagram, follow these steps:

1. Identify major concepts to teach.
2. List important characteristics of the concepts. Think about whether each characteristic is "always present," "sometimes present," or "never present."
3. Locate examples and nonexamples of the concept.
4. Construct a definition of the concept by naming the superordinate concept, its characteristics, and the relationship among characteristics.

FIGURE 16.2

Example of a Semantic Map

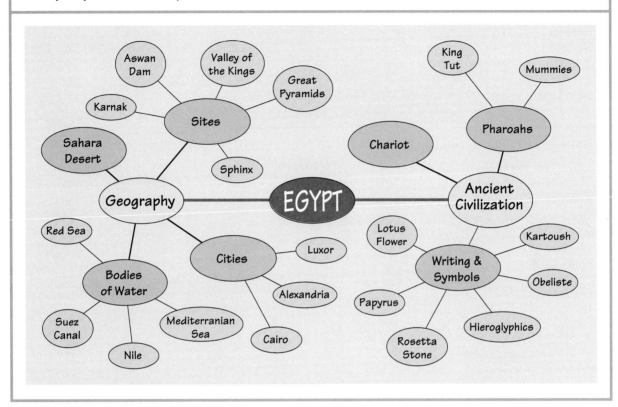

5. Introduce the concept diagram to students, using an advance organizer.
6. Elicit a list of key words or ideas that relate to the concept.
7. Explain or review the parts of the concept diagram and their intended use.
8. With students, name and define the concept.
9. Discuss characteristics that are always present, sometimes present, and never present in the meaning of the concept.
10. Discuss examples and nonexamples of the concept.
11. Link the examples and nonexamples to the characteristics.

Concept diagramming is time consuming. Select concepts with care. Choose those that are pivotal to the curriculum and that students need to understand thoroughly.

Developing Classroom Presentations

The goal of classroom presentations is to enhance student understanding. One key to enhancing understanding is **instructional clarity**—the clear, direct, explicit presentation of information. McCaleb and White (1980) list the following five components of instructional clarity:

- *understanding*—connecting new information with what students already know
- *structuring*—providing a clear format for the presentation, one that students can follow easily
- *sequencing*—arranging a presentation in a logical order
- *explaining*—defining key terms and providing examples, as necessary
- *presenting*—delivering material in an articulate and lively manner with correct pacing, and using visual aids, as necessary

FIGURE 16.3

Concept Diagram

Concept Name:	fossils

Definitions:	Fossils are remains or prints of plants or animals who lived thousands of years ago which have been preserved in the earth.

Characteristics Present in the Concept:

Always	Sometimes	Never
remains or prints	frozen in ice	still alive
plants or animals	trapped in tar	still decaying
thousands of years old	crushed by water	
preserved in the earth	in volcanic ash	

Example:		Nonexample:
tigers in La Brea tar pits		your pet cat
Siberian mammoth		elephant in Africa today
petrified forest in Arizona		tree limbs and leaves in your yard
fish skeleton in limestone layers		fish in supermarket

From C. S. Bos & S. Vaughn, *Strategies for Teaching Students with Learning and Behavior Problems, 3e.* Copyright 1994 by Allyn & Bacon. Reprinted by permission.

In all classroom presentations, clarity should be your goal. Clarity is important for all students, but particularly for students who have poor organizational skills, poor language skills, or little prior knowledge of a topic.

Instructional clarity is particularly important during lectures. Lectures are often necessary to generate interest in a topic, provide information not included in textbooks, or to clarify or embellish textbook information. Although lectures tend

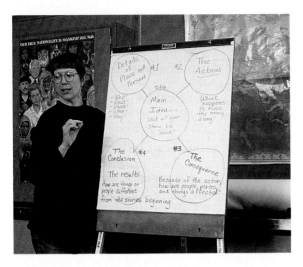

What steps did this presenter follow to develop an effective concept diagram? What other prelearning activities can teachers use to increase success for all learners in the classroom?

to be overused, used properly they can be an effective way to teach. By improving your lectures you help students to improve their note taking.

Giving Demonstrations

Demonstrations can be used to show students how to perform a skill, complete a task, or solve a problem. Demonstrations can be for the whole class, small groups, or individual students. They can be preplanned or can occur on-the-spot as part of interactive planning when students need more explanation. The key to demonstrations is that they must engage students, especially passive learners who will watch your demonstration and then forget every step of it. The important thing is to get students involved and thinking about what you are doing.

As with any lesson, before you give a demonstration be sure to set a purpose, define key vocabulary, and provide an overview or advance organizer of the presentation, including key things to observe (Good & Brophy, 1994). Also, provide guidelines for student participation during the presentation. Should they take notes? Should they ask questions before, during, or after? (Good & Brophy, 1994).

After the demonstration, ask students to summarize the steps, or have one or two students

repeat the demonstration for the class. Rivera and Deutsch-Smith (1988) offer an additional strategy for giving demonstrations to students with learning problems—the **demonstration plus model strategy**. To use this strategy, after completing your demonstration by following the steps outlined in the preceding paragraph, you would add these two steps:

- after viewing the demonstration, have a student perform each step, verbalizing each step as you did
- have all students complete additional practice exercises independently, using the steps

You can also improve a demonstration by describing your thinking as you move through the demonstration. Teacher **think alouds** are a way to model how to think and learn. Davey (1983, p. 45) listed the following five powerful uses of think alouds:

- making predictions or showing students how to develop hypotheses
- describing your visual images
- sharing an analogy or showing how prior knowledge applies
- verbalizing confusing points or showing how you monitor developing understanding
- demonstrating fix-up strategies

Facilitating Student Participation

As you have seen, student engagement can be fostered through cooperative learning groups and involvement in hands-on learning activities. This section includes additional suggestions for facilitating participation of all students in your class through two common content area practices: questioning and discussion.

Questioning Suellen Cannon teaches fifth grade. To the principal and to her school's special education teacher, Suellen is exemplary in the way she promotes learning for students in her class who have learning and behavior problems. During graduate school Suellen read a research article by Allington (1983), which reported that instruction for low-achieving students tends to focus on low-level questioning. This article made Suellen rethink her questioning practices in her own class:

I began to realize that not only did I tend to ask more questions of higher achieving students, but when I did ask questions of lower achieving students the questions were low level and didn't make them think very much. Frankly, I just didn't want to embarrass them and put them on the spot. Since that time I've set six goals for myself:

1. *Distribute questions evenly among all my students.* To get myself started with this I put a check by a student's name on a class list when I asked him or her a question. I don't need to do that any more, now that I'm in the habit of spreading the questions around.
2. *Make certain that my questions are clearly stated.* Sometimes my questions are clear to me, but ambiguous to students. If students seem confused, I try to reword the question so that it comes out right. I've learned that it's OK to say, "Oops, let me try to word that again."
3. *Ask all kinds of students all kinds of questions.* This was really hard to do at first. I want all students to succeed and I want to make certain that they shine in front of the class. I've found that if I give students enough time to think through an answer, they come up with something that I can build on with follow-up questions and probes.
4. *Give students feedback about their answer.* I let them know when an answer is right and why it is right. I let them know when an answer is wrong and why it is wrong. The trick is trying to do this in positive and constructive ways and to use sensitive language. I'm getting better at this.
5. *Let students explain why an answer is right.* If a student gets an answer right, sometimes I let him or her explain how the answer was determined. This gives everyone a chance to learn how to answer that kind of question the next time.
6. *Let students explain their thinking when they get an answer wrong.* I let my students know that it is OK to make a mistake. When they do, then the important thing is to learn from the mistakes. Sometimes when a student gets an answer wrong I ask them to tell me how they arrived at the answer. I then say, "I can understand how you were thinking that way. Here's another way to look at it."

Suellen had been under the impression that the best thing to do with low-achieving students and students with disabilities was to leave them alone. She didn't want them to expose what they didn't know to the rest of the class. Suellen has learned to work at involving all students in classroom questioning.

Classroom Discussions One way to involve students is through **vibrant discussions** (Bean, 1985) in which student participation is high, students' thinking is stimulated, and students have opportunities to connect what they are learning to their personal knowledge and experience. Vibrant discussions help students learn how to express ideas, justify positions, listen to the ideas of others, and ask for clarification when they don't understand (Kauchak & Eggen, 1993).

RESEARCH BRIEF

CLASSROOM DISCUSSIONS: TEACHERS' BELIEFS AND PRACTICES

Alvermann, O'Brien, and Dillon (1990) asked middle school teachers to define discussion to determine their beliefs and attitudes about this essential component of content area teaching. Teachers said that in effective discussions, "students are active participants and thoughtful sharers of information" (p. 306). What did subsequent classroom observations and teacher interviews indicate?

Of the twenty-four classroom discussions observed, the researchers classified eleven as *recitation* (consisting of activities such as answering textbook questions), six as *lecture and recitation* (which included long segments of teacher talk), and seven as *open forum discussions* with exchanges on a variety of issues. Discussions that best matched teachers' definitions of the ideal were not textbook-bound. The research also showed that teacher concerns about maintaining control, using class time, and covering content affected the quality of classroom discussion.

TIPS FOR TEACHERS

16.2 Techniques for Stimulating Discussion without Asking Questions

- *Declarative statements.* Provide information to which students can respond or react.
- *Declarative restatements.* Summarize student comments.
- *Indirect questions.* Ask questions that begin "I wonder" or "What would happen if. . ."

- *Imperatives.* Make statements that encourage students to tell more about what they were thinking or to provide examples.
- *Student questions.* Invite students to ask questions of each other.
- *Deliberate silence.* Give everyone time to think and to gather their thoughts.

Your role in a discussion is that of moderator and encourager. As a moderator you help the group to establish a focus and stay on the topic. As an encourager you engage reluctant participants and make certain that students are free to express their points of view. For vibrant discussions, try the alternatives to traditional questioning in Tips for Teachers 16.2 (Dillon, 1979).

The **discussion web** (Alvermann, 1991) is a graphic aid to help students prepare for classroom discussions in content area classes. As Figure 16.4 shows, the discussion web is designed to help students examine both sides of an issue. It is appropriate for elementary and secondary students, and can be used before and after lectures.

Alvermann suggests the following procedure for implementing the discussion web:

- Prepare students for reading or listening by introducing key vocabulary, activating prior knowledge, and setting a purpose for reading.
- After students have read a selection or listened to a lecture, introduce the discussion web with a provocative ques-

tion. For example, after giving a lecture about the First Amendment, you could ask, "Should rap music be censored?" Students discuss the pros and cons of the issue in pairs and complete the discussion web as a team. Students take turns filling in as many Yes and No statements as the team can generate.

- Pairs are regrouped into teams of four students who then compare their discussion

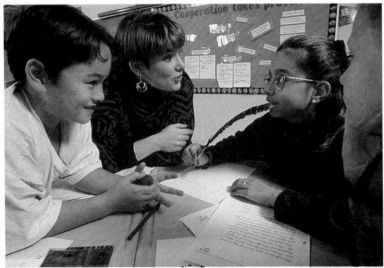

What qualities are present in a vibrant discussion group? How can discussion skills be directly taught? What are other ways to facilitate student participation in content area learning?

FIGURE 16.4

A Discussion Web

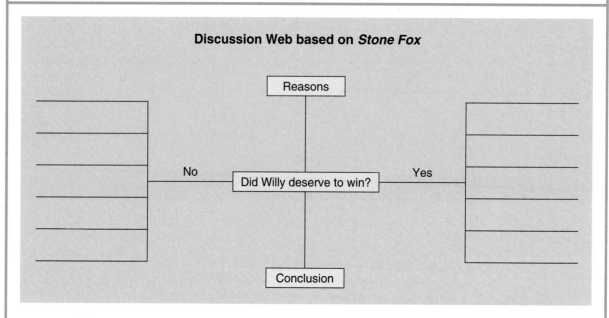

Discussion Web based on *Stone Fox*

Reasons

No | Did Willy deserve to win? | Yes

Conclusion

Alvermann, D. E. (1991). The discussion web: A graphic aid for learning across the curriculum. *The Reading Teacher, 45*(2), 92–99. Copyright by the International Reading Association.

webs and build consensus on an answer to the question.

- The group selects and records the strongest argument and the reason for their choice.
- A spokesperson from each group takes three minutes to report the results, and individual students with dissenting or unrepresented points of view are given an opportunity to state their positions.
- As an individual activity, students write a position statement about their point of view on the issue.

Searfoss and Readence (1989) refer to the typical exchange that goes on in a classroom as *ping pong discussion*. The teacher asks questions and students answer, back and forth. When teachers "serve the ball" only to students who are most capable of supplying the answer, other students become mere spectators.

The discussion web provides a structure for *critical thinking*—examining both sides of an issue carefully before making a judgment.

Effective Content Area Reading Instruction for All Learners

Many content area teachers continue to rely on the textbook as a primary medium of instruction (Alvermann & Moore, 1991; Muther, 1985; Woodward & Elliott, 1990). This section shows you how to become familiar not only with the strengths and weaknesses of your textbook, but also with the ways in which students interact with and respond to the text. This section also contains effective strategies for making textbook adaptations for special learners and planning content area reading lessons.

Familiarizing Yourself with the Textbook

As a classroom teacher you may not have the opportunity to select the textbook used in your content area classroom. Typically, state selection committees decide on a limited number of "state-adopted" textbooks from which school districts can choose. At the district level, the list is shortened by a district committee. At the school level, grade- or committee-level teams frequently choose the textbook. Chances are that like Nancy Brice, the teacher interviewed in this chapter, you will inherit a textbook that someone else has chosen for you.

To familiarize yourself with your textbook you need to consider the same five factors that textbook-selection committees consider: subject matter content, social content, instructional design, readability level, and level of considerateness. You will also need to consider ways to go beyond the textbook.

Subject Matter Content The **subject matter content** refers to comprehensiveness of content coverage and the currency and accuracy of information (Young & Riegeluth, 1988). Ask the following guiding questions: What is being taught? Is the content current, accurate, and up-to-date? Is the content consistent with our state and district curriculum guides? If the textbook is lacking in any of these areas, you will need to supplement the textbook with other materials.

Social Content The values represented in a textbook are part of its **social content**, which also includes the textbook's portrayal of ethnic groups, genders, age groups, and individuals with disabilities. Young and Riegeluth (1988) suggest that curricular materials be examined closely and systematically to detect subtle biases. If the textbook lacks social content, it is your responsibility as a teacher to supplement the text.

Instructional Design The way content is taught—how skills and concepts are introduced, developed, and reinforced—reflects the **instructional design**. Suggestions in the teacher's edition, and supplemental materials (such as worksheets, workbooks, sample tests, transparencies, audiovisual aids, and computer software) also are part of instructional design. You may need to create or collect additional or alternative instructional materials. You may also need to adapt textbook materials for special learners; as an example, you might need to add graphic organizers to help students learn important concepts (Chambliss, 1994).

Readability Level Traditionally, a textbook's level of difficulty is gauged by its **readability level**, expressed as a grade level. For example, you might hear a teacher say, "This history book is a sixth grade book, but the readability level is seventh grade." Readability levels are determined by applying to the text one or more readability formulas (e.g., Dale & Chall, 1948; Fry, 1977; Raygor, 1977). Such formulas are based on sentence complexity (measured by sentence length) and word difficulty (measured by word length and frequency).

Textbook publishers typically supply readability information. Software programs that calculate the readability level of the text you type are available, as are word processing programs, such as Microsoft Word, that analyze readability. People who use readability formulas must understand not only that these formulas measure only two of the many factors that affect the difficulty of a text, but also that they are not exact Different formulas yield different grade levels. Finally, the typical standard error of measurement for readability formulas is plus or minus approximately 1.5 grade levels (Singer & Donlan, 1989). For example, a text with readability predicted at grade 6.5 ranges by chance from grades 5.0 to 8.0.

> "Students who are behind their peers in textbook reading do not need 'watered down' textbooks, nor do they need 'different' or 'slower' instruction. Rather, they need instructors to help them discover how to gain or regain the confidence in their abilities and control of their learning lost through years of an accumulation of academic frustration and failure." (Ciborowski, 1995, p. 90).

Some textbooks are written to match a readability formula by using shorter sentences and simpler words. Simplified texts do not always convey ideas meaningfully, however, and force the reader to make connections that words normally provide.

Friendliness Friendly or **considerate text is** written and formatted in such a way that information can be extracted easily, and support is available when the reader does not understand (Armbruster & Anderson, 1988; Singer, 1986). The degree to which text is considered friendly or considerate to the reader is determined by the number of features that promote learning (such as headings and subheadings, vocabulary in boldface type, and chapter summaries) included in text.

Familiarize yourself with the textbook you plan to use, and learn to recognize friendly text features that support student learning as well as areas in which you will need to intervene. Friendly text has the following characteristics:

- **organization**—how the author orders information in the text. Organization includes general structure of the text as well as consistency and connectedness of ideas.
- **explication**—how the author explains ideas and teaches the reader. Explication includes necessary background information and examples.
- **conceptual density**—the number of new vocabulary terms or concepts the author introduces.
- **metadiscourse**—the degree to which the author "talks" to the reader. Metadiscourse includes direct explanations of how to learn from the text and how to connect ideas from one part of the text to another.
- **instructional devices**—the number of learning tools the author provides. Examples of learning tools include a table of contents, marginal annotations, and a glossary.

Understanding How Students Interact with and Respond to Text

Your examination of the textbook helps you anticipate how you will need to supplement it. The ultimate judge of the readability and friendliness of a textbook is the reader. The **FLIP chart strategy** helps students learn to evaluate text on their own (Schumm & Mangrum, 1991). (FLIP stands for Friendliness, Language, Interest, Prior knowledge.) By filling out charts like the one shown in Figure 16.5, students learn what is comfortable for them individually as readers. After students have completed the FLIP chart you can learn (through class discussions and individual conferences) about what is difficult for them in terms of text friendliness, language, interest, and prior knowledge. Students with reading and learning problems especially need to learn how to talk about the textbook and any problems they have with it. Classroom discussions based on the FLIP chart strategy also help students think as a group about effective strategies for coping with text they find difficult.

Making Textbook Adaptations

Suppose you learn that the textbook is too difficult for some of your students. What will you do? Research indicates most content area teachers seldom implement many adaptations for a number of reasons (Schumm & Vaughn, 1992; Schumm et al., 1992). First, adapting textbooks takes time, and teachers' time for planning and preparing for instruction is already limited. Second, textbook adaptations often slow down instruction, and teachers cannot cover as much material as they would like. Third, some teachers think that making adaptations for the few students who need them is not fair to the higher achieving students who are ready to work at a faster pace.

Despite these concerns, however, research indicates that students at all achievement levels feel that they need textbook adaptations and are not getting the adaptations they need (Schumm et al., 1992). Also, adaptations can be helpful to all students and thus are worth your planning time. Tips for Teachers 16.3 lists textbook adaptations you might consider, three of which are discussed here in greater depth.

Study Guides Study guides are tools teachers can use to lead students through a reading assignment. A typical study guide is a series of questions or activities that students complete while they read a selection. As Wood, Lapp, and Flood (1992, p. 1) put it, "Study guides are designed to accompany

FIGURE 16.5

The FLIP Chart

Title of assignment _____

Number of pages _____

General directions: Rate each of the four FLIP categories on a 1–5 scale (5 = high). Then determine your purpose for reading and appropriate reading rate, and budget your reading/study time.

F = Friendliness: How friendly is my reading assignment?

Directions: Examine your assignment to see if it includes the friendly elements listed below.

Friendly text features

Table of contents	Index	Glossary
Chapter introductions	Headings	Subheadings
Margin notes	Study questions	Chapter summary
Key terms highlighted	Graphs	Charts
Pictures	Signal words	Lists of key facts

1 ———————— 2 ———————— 3 ———————— 4 ———————— 5

No friendly text features   Some friendly text features   Many friendly text features

Friendliness rating _____

L = Language: How difficult is the language in my reading assignment?

Directions: Skim the chapter quickly to determine the number of new terms. Read 3 random paragraphs to get a feel for the vocabulary level and number of long, complicated sentences.

1 ———————— 2 ———————— 3 ———————— 4 ———————— 5

Many new words;   Some new words;   No new words;
complicated sentences   somewhat complicated sentences   clear sentences

Language rating _____

I = Interest: How interesting is my reading assignment?

Directions: Read the title, introduction, headings/subheadings, and summary. Examine the pictures and graphics included.

1 ———————— 2 ———————— 3 ———————— 4 ———————— 5

Boring   Somewhat interesting   Very interesting

Interest rating _____

P = Prior knowledge: What do I already know about the material covered in my reading assignment?

Directions: Think about the title, introduction, headings/subheadings, and summary.

1 ———————— 2 ———————— 3 ———————— 4 ———————— 5

Mostly new information   Some new information   Mostly familiar information

Prior knowledge rating _____

Overall, this reading assignment appears to be at:
☐ a comfortable reading level for me
☐ a somewhat comfortable reading level for me
☐ an uncomfortable reading level for me

Schumm, J. S., & Mangrum, C. T. (1991). FLIP: A framework for textbook thinking. *Journal of Reading, 35,* 120–124. Copyright by the International Reading Association.

TIPS FOR TEACHERS

16.3 Guidelines for Adapting Content Area Textbooks

Substitute the Textbook for students who have severe word-recognition problems:
- Audiotape textbook content.
- Read textbook aloud to students.
- Pair students to master textbook content.
- Use direct experiences, films, videotapes, recorders, and computer programs as substitutes for textbook reading.
- Work with students individually or in small groups to master textbook material.

Simplify the Textbook for students whose reading level is far below that of the textbook used in class:
- Construct abridged versions of the textbook content or use the publisher's abridged version.
- Provide students with chapter outlines or summaries.
- Use a multilevel, multimaterial approach.

Highlight Key Concepts for students who have difficulty comprehending textbook material:
- Preview reading assignments with students to orient them to the topic and provide guidelines for budgeting reading and study time.
- Provide students with a purpose for reading.
- Provide an overview of an assignment before reading.
- Structure opportunities for students to activate prior knowledge before starting a reading assignment.

- Introduce key vocabulary before assigning reading.
- Develop a study guide to direct learning.
- Summarize or reduce textbook information to guide classroom discussions and independent reading.
- Color-code or highlight textbooks.
- Reduce length of assignments.
- Slow down the pace of reading assignments.
- Provide assistance in answering text-based questions.
- Demonstrate or model effective reading strategies.
- Place students in cooperative learning groups to master textbook content.
- Teach comprehension-monitoring techniques to improve ongoing understanding of text material.
- Teach students to use graphic aids to understand textbook information.

Increase Idea Retention for students who have difficulty with long-term memory.
- Structure postreading activities to increase retention of content.
- Teach reading strategies to improve retention.
- Teach students to record key concepts and terms for study purposes.
- Teach memory strategies to improve retention of text material.

reading, not follow it." Study guides help direct students to the key points to be learned. They also provide structure for students to reflect about what they are reading and to engage in higher-order thinking. In short, study guides can help "tutor" a student through a chapter.

Commercially prepared study guides can be purchased as supplements to some textbooks. For example, with a chemistry text you may be able to purchase a blackline master book or individual workbooks for students that include study guides for each chapter. The advantage of commercially prepared study guides is that they are already done. Real time savers! The disadvantage is that the publisher does not know your style of teaching, your emphasis, or your school district's requirements. Moreover, the publisher does not know your students. Many teachers elect to construct their own study guides.

Study guides are appealing to all students, but particularly to students with learning and behavior problems (Hudson et al., 1994). The guides help students to stay focused on what they need to learn. Students can use study guides independently or in conjunction with cooperative learning activities.

Many types of study guides exist. Some are designed to help students activate prior knowledge, others to help students understand literal or inferential information in the textbook, others to foster peer interaction and discussion, and still others to help students recognize meaning patterns in text (e.g., cause and effect, compare and contrast). Following are some general suggestions for developing study guides (Wood, Lapp, & Flood, 1992):

- *Decide whether a guide is needed.* Is textbook information particularly dense? Are there few considerate features? Will student with special needs need support and guidance to get through the chapter and to grasp the most important ideas?
- *Analyze the chapter.* Can some parts be omitted? Are some parts easier to understand than others? What skills will your students need to read and understand this material?
- *Decide how you want to structure your study guide.* Create one that includes the suggested components.

All study guides should also include the following components, Hudson et al. (1994):

- specific information about the reading assignment (page numbers, title)
- learning objectives of the assignment
- purpose statement for the assignment
- introduction of key terms or vocabulary
- activities for students to complete
- questions for students to answer as they read

Text Highlighting Students with comprehension problems have difficulty sifting out important information. Underlining or highlighting key points in the textbooks can help students attend to the most salient information (Wood & Wooley, 1986).

As you read the textbook, highlight the information you think is most important. Then student or adult volunteers can use your book as a guide to highlight the same information in books for students with reading and learning disabilities. Keep in mind that this is an intermediate step. Students should also be taught how to highlight and identify key information on their own.

Using Alternative Reading Materials After you and your students have taken a careful look at your textbook, you may realize that you will need to go beyond the textbook to provide your students with alternative reading material. Here's how Steve Beaumont, a fifth grade teacher, selects reading material for his science and social studies classes:

> My textbook is actually very good and I use it regularly, but I find that there are such marvelous reading materials out there that I feel a strong responsibility to expose my students to materials beyond the textbook. My three students who are nonreaders need to have exposure to text and they simply can't read the textbook. I have some other students who are ready for more challenging material. So I use a lot of informational trade books. I find that the quality of writing and the illustrations of these books are fabulous. My local public library lets teachers check out twenty-five books at a time. When I start a new unit, on astronomy for example, I load up with books from the library. I make certain that books represent a range of reading levels. I find picture books and books written in easy text for students who have trouble reading.
>
> I have also started using novels and biographies in teaching science and social studies. Students often get tired with the informational style of writing in the textbook. Novels and biographies make science, history, and geography come alive.
>
> Finally, I collect articles from the newspaper and magazines related to whatever I'm teaching in science and social studies. My students collect articles as well! These articles usually have catchy titles, summarize information clearly, and are written in an engaging style. The pictures in magazines are also appealing. I've found that articles are a good way to "hook" my reluctant readers.

Audiotaping Content Area Textbooks

Students who have low reading skills or vision impairments can listen to chapters that have been audiotaped by classmates or volunteers. Recordings for the Blind & Dyslexic (800-221-4792) is a nonprofit organization that records trade books and textbooks for individuals who are blind, have low vision, or have learning disabilities. This organization provides on-loan recorded books at all academic levels.

Audiotaped books are increasingly popular and acceptable to students. Students can listen to the tapes in a listening center in elementary classrooms, resource rooms, school libraries, or at home. Here are some suggestions for audiotaping reading assignments:

- Instead of recording an entire chapter verbatim, read the key sections and paraphrase the less important sections.
- Code the text so that readers or listeners will know whether the person on the tape is reading or paraphrasing.
- Provide a short advanced organizer on the tape to help students get ready to read and listen.
- Insert questions that readers or listeners can stop and think about.
- Remind readers or listeners to stop periodically and think about what they have read.
- Use a natural tone of voice and a comfortable rate.
- Have students experiment with taped texts to see whether they comprehend better with or without the text.

Effective Content Area Assignments, Homework, and Tests for All Learners

Students' success or failure in a content area class is often based on their performance on assignments, homework, and tests. But what about students with learning and behavior problems? Should they have the same assignments and tests as everyone else? What if a student cannot read? What if a student cannot work under timed conditions?

Interestingly, as mentioned previously, teacher surveys, interviews, and classroom observations indicate that teachers of all grade levels (elementary through high school) do not often make individual adaptations in homework, assignments, and tests (Schumm & Vaughn, 1991; Schumm & Vaughn,

TIPS FOR TEACHERS

16.4 A Strategy for Giving Assignments

1. Explain the purpose of the assignment. Stress what you expect students to learn and why learning the skill or concept is important. Connect the skill or concept to real-life applications.
2. Explain in detail the procedures for completing the assignment. Ask one or two students to summarize the procedures, to check for understanding.
3. Get students started by modeling one or two problems or by providing an example.
4. Describe the equipment and materials needed to complete the assignment.
5. Anticipate trouble spots and ask students how they might tackle difficult parts in the assignment.
6. Explain when the assignment is due.
7. Explain how the assignment will be graded and how it will impact students' grades.
8. Describe appropriate ways to get help or support in completing the assignment.
9. For an in-class assignment, explain your expectations for student behavior while they complete the assignment, and what students who finish early should do.
10. Address student questions.

1992; Schumm et al., 1995). Constructing individual assignments and tests may not be feasible on a day-to-day basis, and may not even be necessary. In this section you'll learn about ways to prepare effective assignments, homework, and tests for all students.

Making and Adapting Class Assignments and Homework

After conducting a comprehensive review of the literature, Cooper and Nye (1994) concluded that homework assignments for students with disabilities should be brief, focused on reinforcement rather than new material, monitored carefully, and supported through parental involvement.

The most important aspect of making assignments is to give complete information. You need to let students know why the assignment is important, when it is due, what support they will have for completing the task, and the steps necessary for getting the job done. Having complete information helps to motivate students. The procedure in Tips for Teachers 16.4 can help you provide students with a complete set of directions.

Class assignments and homework can be adapted for special learners so that they can experience success without undue attention being brought to their learning difficulties. The key to success is to make assignments appropriate in content, length, time required to complete, and skill level needed to accomplish the task. It is also important that students know how and where to get help when they get stuck.

> In a survey of students in grades 6–8 (forty-eight with learning disabilities and forty-eight without), the students with learning disabilities had greater difficulty completing homework assignments because of problems with attention, motivation, and study skills (Gajria & Salend, 1995).

Constructing and Adapting Tests

Tests are a way to find out what students have learned. The best way to discover what students have learned is to construct student-friendly tests, adapt test administration and scoring as necessary, consider alternatives to testing (such as assessment portfolios), and teach test-taking skills.

Student-friendly tests are considerate to the test taker in content and format. The content has been covered in class or assigned readings, and students have been told explicitly that they are responsible for learning it. The format is clear and easy to understand.

In one study of middle and high school content area teachers, test scores, including those for students with disabilities, represented about half of the students' grade (45.9 percent). The percentage was lower (37.3 percent) for English classes, higher for mathematics (53.6 percent) (Putnam, 1992).

To construct student-friendly tests, you must first decide what skills and concepts to include. The lesson- and unit-Planning Pyramids can be particularly helpful here—to complete them you decided which concepts are most important and prioritized those concepts for instructional purposes. You know what you want all, most, and some of your students to know and you have told them your expectations. You can cover those skills and concepts on the test.

In test format, directions should be clear and unambiguous, and items should be legible and properly spaced. Students should have sufficient room to place their answers, and specific guidelines if answers are to be written on a separate sheet (Salend, 1994). Attention to format is important for all students, but particularly for those who have difficulty reading and taking tests and who are very anxious about test taking.

Even with student-friendly tests, students with learning problems may have difficulty reading tests, working within time constraints, or resisting distractions during a test. Other special learners may have physical needs (they may tire easily, for example) that inhibit performance on a test. Tips for Teachers 16.5 suggests adaptations in test administration and scoring. As you decide which, if any, adaptations to use, consider the material to be covered by the test, the test's task requirements (e.g., reading, taking dictation), and the particular needs of special learners. Consult with the special education teacher and other specialists in your school to get advice about the most appropriate adaptations for individual students.

TIPS FOR TEACHERS

16.5 Testing Adaptations

- Teach students test-taking skills.
- Give frequent quizzes rather than only exams.
- Give take-home tests.
- Test on less content than rest of the class.
- Change type of questions (e.g., essay to multiple choice).
- Use tests with enlarged print.
- Use black-and-white copies (versus dittos).
- Highlight key words in questions.
- Provide extra space on tests for answering.
- Simplify wording of test questions.
- Allow students to answer fewer questions.
- Give extra help preparing for tests.
- Give the actual test as a study guide.
- Give practice questions as a study guide.
- Give open-book and note tests.

- Give tests to small groups.
- Give extended time to finish tests.
- Read test questions to students.
- Allow use of learning aids during tests (e.g., calculators).
- Give individual help with directions during tests.
- Allow oral instead of written answers (e.g., tape recorders).
- Allow answers in outline format.
- Allow word processors.
- Give feedback to individual students during test.

Jayanthi, M., Epstein, M. H., Polloway, E. A., & Bursuck, W. D. (in press). Testing adaptions: A national survey of the testing practices of general education teachers. *Journal of Special Education.*

TIPS FOR TEACHERS

16.6 Development of Assessment Portfolios

- Develop a portfolio plan consistent with your purposes for the assignment.
- Clarify what work will go into portfolios.
- Start with only a couple of different kinds of entries and expand gradually.
- Compare notes with other teachers as you experiment with portfolios.
- Have as a long-term goal the inclusion of a variety of assessments that address content, process, and attitude goals across the curriculum.
- Make portfolios accessible in the classroom. Students and teachers should be able to add to the collection quickly and easily.
- Develop summary sheets or graphs that help to describe a body of information (e.g., "I can do" lists, lists of books read, or pieces of writing completed). Let students record these data when possible.

- Work with the student to choose a few representative samples that demonstrate the student's progress.
- Review portfolios with students periodically (at least four times during the school year). The review should be a time to celebrate progress and to set future goals.
- Encourage students to review portfolios with a classmate before reviewing with the teacher. Students should help make decisions about what to keep.
- In preparation for a parent conference, have students develop a table of contents for the portfolio.

From Radencich, M. C., Beers, P. C., & Schumm, J. S. (1993) *A handbook for the K–12 reading resource specialist.* Boston: Allyn & Bacon, pp. 119–120.

In addition to or instead of tests, consider using portfolios as an assessment tool. **Assessment portfolios** are collections of work samples that document a student's progress in a content area. You can use portfolios to provide tangible evidence of student performance over a period of time. Portfolios can include writing samples of all stages of the writing process in all genres. Suggestions for developing assessment portfolios are included in Tips for Teachers 16.6.

Examples of items you can include in a portfolio are as follows (Radencich et al., 1993):

student interviews
self-assessments
audiotapes
videotapes
diagnostic tests
achievement tests
teacher-made tests
pages from journals
awards

personal reading and writing records
peer assessments
interest and attitude inventories
photographs
copies of passages read fluently
contributions from parents
report cards
list of accomplishments
observation checklists

Planning Interdisciplinary Thematic Units

As you may recall, increasing numbers of educators are planning interdisciplinary thematic units as a way to provide more holistic instruction (see Figure 16.6). Meinbach, Rothlein, and Fredericks (1995, p. 5) describe a **thematic interdisciplinary approach,** as follows:

FIGURE 16.6

Interdisciplinary Thematic Unit Planning Form

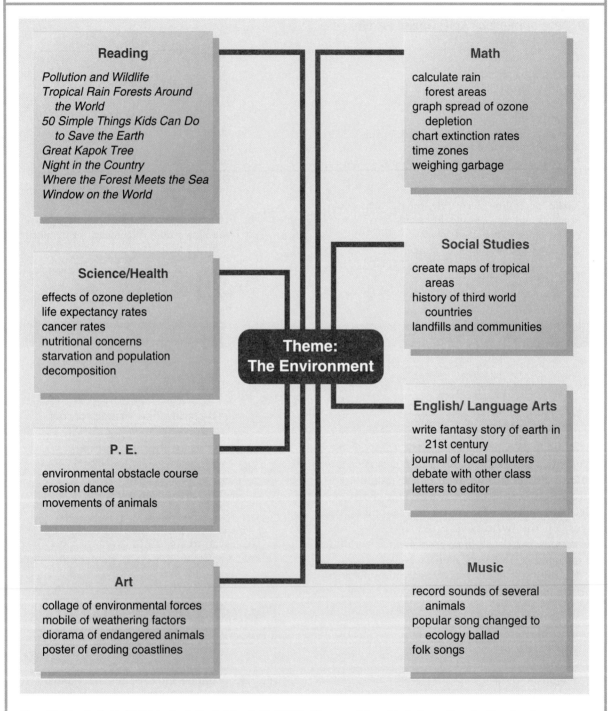

Reading

Pollution and Wildlife
Tropical Rain Forests Around
the World
50 Simple Things Kids Can Do
to Save the Earth
Great Kapok Tree
Night in the Country
Where the Forest Meets the Sea
Window on the World

Math

calculate rain
forest areas
graph spread of ozone
depletion
chart extinction rates
time zones
weighing garbage

Science/Health

effects of ozone depletion
life expectancy rates
cancer rates
nutritional concerns
starvation and population
decomposition

Social Studies

create maps of tropical
areas
history of third world
countries
landfills and communities

**Theme:
The Environment**

English/ Language Arts

write fantasy story of earth in
21st century
journal of local polluters
debate with other class
letters to editor

P. E.

environmental obstacle course
erosion dance
movements of animals

Art

collage of environmental forces
mobile of weathering factors
diorama of endangered animals
poster of eroding coastlines

Music

record sounds of several
animals
popular song changed to
ecology ballad
folk songs

From Meinbach, A. M., Rothlein, L., & Fredericks, A. D. (1995). *The complete guide to thematic units: Creating the integrated curriculum,* p. 15. Norwood, MA: Christopher-Gordon. Used with permission of publisher.

A thematic approach to learning combines structured, sequential, and well-organized strategies, activities, children's literature, and materials used to expand a particular concept. A thematic unit is multidisciplinary and multi-dimensional; it knows no boundaries. It is responsive to the interests, abilities, and needs of children and is respectful of their developing aptitudes and attitudes. In essence, a thematic approach to learning offers students a realistic arena in which they can pursue learning using a host of contexts and a panorama of literature.

Thematic units are increasingly popular in elementary and secondary settings because they help students explore topics in depth, see connections between subject areas, and see the connection between what they learn in school and real life. They are particularly appropriate for diverse classrooms because the emphasis is on providing a variety of learning activities. Thematic units also help consolidate areas in a crowded curriculum and make the teaching of curriculum more efficient (Shanahan et al., 1995).

A thematic unit can last for a few days or for weeks. The unit can involve a single classroom teacher, multiple grades, or several teachers in a grade. In any case, interdisciplinary units take careful planning and organization to avoid confusion and chaos. Meinbach, Rothlein, and Fredericks (1995) identified the following five steps in planning a thematic unit:

1. *Selecting the Theme:* a theme can be derived from curricular objectives, current events and issues, special events or holidays, and student interests.
2. *Organizing the Theme:* a theme web can be used to show what content areas will be represented and what objectives and activities will be associated with each content area.
3. *Gathering Materials and Resources:* thematic units extend beyond a single textbook. Both print and nonprint resources are used to make the unit come alive. A variety of reading levels of materials should be included as well as multisensory resources. Students and parents can become actively involved in gathering materials.

4. *Designing Activities and Projects:* to avoid making a thematic unit no more than a set of isolated activities around a single theme; activities must be selected that are purposeful and lead to an integrated experience.
5. *Implementing the Unit:* decide how long the unit will last and how it will be merged with your ongoing curriculum plans. Figure 16.6 shows the sample thematic unit plan in these five steps.

When teachers are working as a team to plan an interdisciplinary unit, trying to come up with a theme can be a challenge. Fogarty (1994) suggested the following strategy, organized around the acronym THEMES, for deciding on a theme:

- *Think of themes.* Brainstorm twenty to fifty themes.
- *Hone the list.* Divide the list into three groups—topics, concepts, and problems. Have each group member select one "champion theme" from each group. Agree on a final three.
- *Extrapolate criteria.* Think of why the final three were chosen and record those reasons for future thinking. Decide on the final theme.
- *Manipulate the theme.* Generate as many questions as you can about the theme to give it further depth and direction.
- *Expand into activities.* List activities that can be planned to teach skills and introduce concepts.
- *Select valued outcomes.* Decide what outcomes are desired. How will these outcomes be observed and recorded?

The last step is particularly important. With thematic units, it is easy to get caught up in the activity and forget what student outcomes were desired. This is especially true for students with learning problems. It is important not only to identify valued concepts using the Planning Pyramid, but also to communicate those outcomes to students and to monitor student progress in meeting those outcomes during the implementation of the unit.

SUMMARY

- Critical issues faced by content area teachers as they try to promote learning for all students include balancing content and process, balancing text-driven and activities-driven instruction, coordinating content area teaching and learning strategies, and integrating the curriculum.

- Students can have difficulty learning in content classrooms because not all subjects are uniformly interesting or consistent with students' cultural background and prior knowledge. To learn in some content areas, students need basic skills they do not have. The pacing and conceptual load of some subjects is cumbersome, and learning tasks such as textbook reading, assignments, and tests are overwhelming for some students.

- Content area teachers can use prelearning activities such as purpose setting and semantic mapping to improve students' comprehension and depth of learning.

- Student participation in class can be improved through the planning and implementation of well-structured questions and vibrant discussions.

- You can become familiar with the strengths and weaknesses of your textbook by evaluating its subject-matter content, social content, instructional design, readability level, and friendliness level.

- One way to learn how your students interact and respond to the textbook is to use the FLIP Chart.

- Textbook adaptations include study guides, highlighting, and alternative reading materials.

- As you construct class assignments, homework, and tests for students with learning and behavior problems, be sure to consider the following factors: clarity of assignments, appropriateness of assignments and tests, student-friendliness of tests, and adaptations for administration and scoring of tests.

- Interdisciplinary thematic units can be used to integrate the curriculum. For students with learning and behavior problems, however, care must be taken to identify desired student outcomes, to communicate those outcomes to students, and to monitor student progress during the implementation of the unit.

Key Terms and Concepts

assessment portfolios
communication approach
concept diagram
conceptual density
considerate text
content and process dilemma
demonstration plus model strategy
discussion web
explication
FLIP chart strategy

friendly text
instructional clarity
instructional design
instructional devices
interdisciplinary thematic units
metadiscourse
organization (of text)
ping pong discussion
prelearning activities

purpose-setting activities
readability level
semantic map
social content
study guides
think alouds
thematic interdisciplinary approach
THEMES
vibrant discussions

Think and Apply

1. Now that you have read Chapter 16, think about how Nancy Brice planned and made adaptations for special learners in her classroom. What practices did she use? What additional strategies would you use in your own class?
2. Plan a lesson, using a prelearning activity. What would you plan as a follow up?
3. Plan and deliver a demonstration, using the suggestions provided in this chapter.
4. Lead a class discussion or questioning session, using one of the formats provided in this chapter.
5. Familiarize yourself with a content area textbook. Include in your analysis an evaluation of subject matter content, social content, instructional design, readability level, and considerateness level. What are the strengths of the textbook? How friendly is the textbook? What adaptations would you need to plan for students who are nonreaders or low-level readers?
6. Construct a student-friendly test for a lesson or unit. What adaptations would you need to plan for students with learning or behavior problems?

Read More about It

1. Alvermann, D. E., Dillon, D. R., & O'Brien, D. G. (1987). *Using discussion to promote reading comprehension.* Newark, DE: International Reading Association.

   This monograph provides examples of ways to implement vibrant discussions in your classroom.

2. Anders, P. L., & Guzzetti. B. J. (1996). *Literacy instruction in the content areas.* Fort Worth, TX: Harcourt Brace.

   An excellent resource for helping teachers plan and implement reading and writing instruction in the content areas.

3. Farr, R., & Tone, B. (1994). *Portfolio performance and assessment.* Fort Worth, TX: Harcourt Brace.

   This extensive, user-friendly guide to portfolio assessment includes detailed explanations of portfolio conferences and scoring systems.

4. Meinbach, A. M., Rothlein, L., & Fredericks, A. D. (1995). *The complete guide to thematic units: Creating the integrated curriculum.* Norwood, MA: Christopher-Gordon.

   A brief but comprehensive guide to planning and implementing thematic units.

5. Moore, D. W., Readence, J. E., & Rickelman R. J. (1988). *Prereading activities for content area reading and learning* (2nd ed.). Newark, DE: International Reading Association.

   This monograph provides an excellent collection of prereading and prelistening activities.

6. Readence, J. E., Bean, T. W., & Baldwin R. S. (1992). *Content area reading: An integrated approach* (4th ed.). Dubuque, IA: Kendall/Hunt.

   This comprehensive book includes excellent suggestions for determining the appropriateness of textbooks for your students, as well as instructional activities for learning technical vocabulary and for helping students comprehend content area textbooks.

7. Wood, K. D., Lapp, D., & Flood, J. (1992). *Guiding readers through text: A review of study guides.* Newark, DE: International Reading Association.

   Explains fourteen types of study guides, with examples and suggested applications.

MAKING A DIFFERENCE
through Action Teaching

Content Area Instructional Activities for All Learners

Interview a Classmate

Objective: To give students practice in developing and using questions as a means for obtaining more information for the piece they are writing.

Grades: Adapted for all levels.

Materials: (1) Writing materials and a writing topic. (2) A list of possible questions. (3) A tape recorder (optional).

Teaching Procedures: Using the format of a radio or television interview, demonstrate and role-play "mock" interviews with sport, movie, music, and political celebrities. Give the students opportunities to play both roles.

Discuss what types of questions allow the interviewee to give elaborate responses (e.g., open questions), and what types of questions do not allow the interviewee to give a very expanded answer (e.g., closed questions). Practice asking open questions.

Use a piece that you are writing as an example, and discuss who you might interview to obtain more information. For example, "In writing a piece about what it might be like to go to the St. Louis World's Fair in 1904, I might interview my grandfather, who was there, to obtain more information."

Ask students to select an appropriate person to interview for their writing piece and to write possible questions. In pairs, the students refine their questions for the actual interview. The students then conduct the interviews and later discuss how information from the interview assisted them in writing their piece.

Bos, C., & Vaughn, S. (1994). *Strategies for students with learning and behavior problems* (3rd ed.). Boston: Allyn & Bacon.

Conversational Discussion Groups

Objective: To help students become comfortable in classroom discussions.

Grades: Intermediate and above.

Teaching Procedures: The idea behind Conversational Discussion Groups is that discourse about reading assignments and lectures should be more like conversations—the type of conversation two friends might have about a book or movie (O'Flahavan, 1989). Discussion Groups can be held after reading a book or other selection, listening to a lecture, hearing a guest speaker, or viewing a video in class. There are three steps to implementing Conversational Discussion Groups:

1. *Introduce/review rules.* Before dividing students into conversation groups, either introduce or review rules. You'll need to determine rules in advance or perhaps have the group generate rules related to etiquette for speaking in a group, participation, staying on task, and behavior.
2. *Lines of thought.* During the discussion time the teacher presents students with three questions— one at a time. When students finish with one question, the teacher goes to the group to hear and respond to their answer and then gives a second question. Questions are related to background knowledge, summarizing the story or lecture, and making personal reactions or reflections.
3. *Debriefing.* Students then spend some time to reflect and evaluate their experiences in the Conversational Discussion Group. The reflection is guided by three questions: (a) How did we go about getting our answers today? (b) How did we do? (c) What can we do to improve next time?

Depending on the group of students, they may need more or less teacher direction and modeling in how to discuss what they have read or heard. The real goal of Conversational Discussion Groups is to get beyond a formalized structure and to encourage students to have productive, personally meaningful discussions with their peer.

Content Area Instructional Activities for All Learners (continued)

Jig Saw Puzzle Method

Objective: To help students work cooperatively to learn content area material (Aronson, Stephan, Sikes, Blaney, & Snapp, 1978).

Grades: Intermediate and up.

Materials: Expert sheets.

Teaching Procedures:

1. Select a unit of material for students to learn that can be broken up into four sections. For example, a social studies chapter on Italy might be broken up into : imports and exports, natural resources, famous sights, and native foods.

2. Assign students to four different "expert" groups. The members of each group are responsible for learning the material in their assigned section—they must become experts.

3. Allow expert groups enough time to complete "expert sheets." Expert sheets are handouts you have prepared for students to record important information that they have learned.

4. Prepare a quiz (2 or 3 questions) that each group member must pass to truly become an "expert." Students who do not pass the test can work with you or with group mates to learn the information. You can decide whether or not students can use their expert sheets to take the quiz.

5. Move the students into their Jig Saw groups. A Jig Saw Group consists of one expert from each of the four different groups.

6. Each expert then teaches the content he or she learned to members of the Jig Saw Group.

Library Scavenger Hunts

Objective: To help improve research skills.

Grades: Intermediate and above.

Materials: Scavenger hunt lists.

Teaching Procedures:

1. Divide students into groups of 3 or 4 students. Assign students to groups so that each group has a mixture of students in respect to research skills.

2. Provide each group with a list of questions to answer by finding information in the library. You may want to include hints or clues about where the items might be located. Make certain that a variety of research resources are used.

3. Discuss rules for the scavenger hunt. For example: talk only to your team members and only about the hunt, use soft voices, and answer the question and document your sources.

4. Give a time limit for the hunt.

5. At the end of the time limit, collect all documentation from the groups.

6. At the next opportunity, discuss what information was found and how it was found.

Eventually individuals or groups of students in your class may want to write scavenger hunt lists for other classmates.

Send a Problem

Objective: To help students learn content area material.

Grades: Intermediate and above.

Materials: Index cards.

Teaching Procedures:

1. Students work individually to generate questions about a reading assignment or lecture.

2. Questions are recorded on the front of an index card; answers are recorded on the back of the same card.

3. Students are assigned to work in groups of 3 or 4 students to review the questions and answers for accuracy of the answers. Answers are revised if needed.

4. The stack of question cards is then passed to another group of students. Members of the group take turns asking and answering questions.

5. The process of passing continues until time is up or until all groups have had the opportunity to review the cards of every group.

APPENDIX

Making a Difference through Action Learning: Teaching Study Skills, Learning Strategies and Self-Advocacy

Introduction

As a middle or high school teacher, one of your major challenges is to balance teaching content (e.g., American government, chemistry, earth science, English, history) with teaching learning strategies and study skills. Teachers are pressured to complete the textbook or cover a set of objectives specified in state or district curriculums, but many students with disabilities and those who are at risk need to be taught how to study and learn more effectively. This appendix describes activities you can integrate into content area classes. The activities are grouped in the following areas:

■ effective time management
■ organizing your studying
■ setting goals, self-monitoring, and self-advocacy
■ listening and taking notes
■ remembering information
■ studying and taking tests

When you teach learning strategies and study skills, keep in mind several general principles or stages of teaching. By using these principles (Deshler et al., 1996), you help ensure that students become proficient in using the skill or strategy and that they generalize its use to different situations.

■ *Develop the rationale for learning the study skill or learning strategy.* With students, establish why learning to use the skill or strategy is worthwhile.
■ *Analyze the skill or strategy, and if possible determine the steps students can use to develop the skill or strategy.*
■ *Develop a memory device, such as an acronym, to help students remember the steps in the skill or strategy.* For editing written work, for example, use COPS—for Capitalization, Organization, Punctuation, and Spelling (Schumaker et al., 1985).
■ *Demonstrate or model each step in the skill or strategy. Use "thinking aloud" to model*

what you are thinking. It is important to demonstrate not only what you are doing but also what you are thinking. Cue students with a phrase such as, "When I do (describe action), what I am thinking is (describe thinking)."

- *Help students memorize the steps in the skill or strategy.* Use of a memory device can be quite helpful in memorizing the strategy.
- *Provide ample opportunity for students to practice the skills or strategy.* Start by applying the skill or strategy to easy tasks, then to more difficult ones.
- *Cue students to use the skill or strategy.*
- *Throughout the teaching process, discuss when, where, and how the skill or strategy can be used in different situations, such as different classes, tasks, and settings (school and job).* This principle is important for students to generalize the skill or strategy.
- *Have students monitor their success in using the skill or strategy and the way it affects their learning.*

The approach you use to teach study skills and learning strategies can vary. You can present the skill or strategy and its steps, or you can have students develop their own steps in cooperative groups, through class discussion, or independently. Whatever your approach, an important key to success is to use the preceding principles.

Resources: For more information about teaching study skills, learning strategies, and self-advocacy, see the following books:

- Bos, C. S., & Vaughn, S. (1994). *Teaching students with learning and behavior problems* (3rd ed.). Boston: Allyn and Bacon.
- Bragstad, B. J., & Stumpf, S. M. (1982). *A guidebook for teaching study skills and motivation.* Boston: Allyn and Bacon.
- Deshler, D. D., Ellis, E. S., & Lenz, B. K. (1996). *Teaching adolescents with learning disabilities* (2nd ed.). Denver: Love.
- Ellis, D. B. (1985). *Becoming a master student* (5th ed.). Rapid City, SD: College Survival, Inc.
- Lenz, B. K., Ellis, E. S., & Scanlon, D. (1996). *Teaching learning strategies to ado-
lescents and adults with learning disabilities.* Austin, Tex.: Pro-Ed.
- Strichart, S. S., & Mangrum, C. T., II. (1993). *Teaching study strategies to students with learning disabilities.* Boston: Allyn and Bacon.

Action Learning Area: Effective Time Management

Time management is the organization and monitoring of time so that tasks can be scheduled and completed in an efficient and timely manner. Effective time management includes the following steps:

- identifying the tasks to be completed
- estimating the time needed to complete the tasks
- prioritizing tasks and estimating time
- scheduling the time
- working toward meeting deadlines
- monitoring progress and adjusting deadlines or tasks
- reviewing deadlines after task completion and adjusting schedules and priorities based on past performance

Use the following four activities to teach effective time management.

Interviewing Others About Time Management

Objective: To help students learn the importance of managing their time.

Grades: Middle school, high school, and postsecondary classes

Teaching Procedures: Have students interview a parent and one other adult they consider a successful manager of time, asking questions such as:

- Describe your schedule or what you do for two typical days during the week and one typical weekend day.
- What strategies do you use to schedule your time so that your tasks get completed?

- What strategies do you use to help you remember what you have to do?
- Do you think that managing your time is important? Why?

Have students work in cooperative groups to compile lists of strategies for scheduling and monitoring schedules. Also have them compile a list of reasons for managing time, such as the following (Bragstad & Stumpf, 1982), making sure that they add their own ideas:

Why Bother with a Schedule?

- Parents will "get off your back" when you have regular study times.
- Writing down what you have to do gives you less to remember.
- When you give yourself a set amount of time to do an assignment, you concentrate more.
- With a schedule you are less likely to extend your breaks longer than scheduled.
- You feel more satisfied when your are in control of your life and know what you plan to do when.
- Organizing your time helps you come to class prepared.
- Scheduling your time is the smart way to operate if you want to have more time for fun and friends.

Content Class Integration: A unit on time management is easily integrated into any class. It can be the first unit of the year in a math class emphasizing time use and computation of time. It can be integrated into an economics class emphasizing how time relates to productivity, or into a life skills class.

Determining How You Spend Your Time

Objective: Students determine how they currently spend their time and how much time it takes to complete usual activities.

Grades: Middle school and above

Teaching Procedures: Have student groups identify usual activities and estimate the time it takes to complete them. Distribute a schedule form (see Figure A) to students, and have them use the form to keep track of their activities for one week. Also have students list each school assignment and note whether they had "too much time" (+), "the right amount of time" (x), or "too little time (-) to complete it.

At the end of the week, have student groups review their schedules and compare how much time they spent on different activities such as sleeping, eating, studying, attending class, and so on. Also have students compare their estimates with the actual time it took to complete the activities. Usually students underestimate their time by about 50 percent.

Planning a Schedule

Objective: To have students plan their weekly schedules and develop To-Do lists.

Grades: Middle school and above

Teaching Procedures: Have students list due dates for assignments, tests, and other important projects. Help them divide complex tasks or projects into smaller tasks and determine the due dates for each smaller task. Next, have students make a To-Do list for each day (refer to Figure A) so that they can see how they need to plan their time, particularly their study time.

Have students plan their weekly schedules, using the following guidelines (Bos & Vaughn, 1994):

- Plan regular study times with at least one-hour blocks.
- Use daytime or early evening for studying, if possible.
- When studying for longer than an hour, plan breaks and stick to the time allowed.
- Determine which assignments you are going to work on.
- For each assignment, take a few minutes to review what you have done and learned, and to plan what you are going to accomplish.
- Work on your more difficult assignments when you are most alert (usually first).
- Distribute your study time for a test, instead of cramming for it.
- Plan time for recreational activities.

Sample Weekly Schedule and To-Do List

Name: _____   Week of: _____

Time	Monday	Tuesday	Wednesday	Thursday	Friday	Saturday	Sunday
6 – 7 AM							
7 – 8 AM							
8 – 9 AM							
9 – 10 AM							
10 – 11 AM							
11 – 12							
12 – 1 PM							
1 – 2 PM							
2 – 3 PM							
3 – 4 PM							
4 – 5 PM							
5 – 6 PM							
6 – 7 PM							
7 – 8 PM							
8 – 9 PM							
9 – 10 PM							

To Do List						
Monday	Tuesday	Wednesday	Thursday	Friday	Saturday	Sunday

Adapted with permission from Bos, C. S., & Vaughn, S. (1994). *Teaching students with learning and behavior problems* (3rd ed.) (p. 284). Boston: Allyn and Bacon.

- Reward yourself by crossing off items on your To-Do list when you complete them.

Monitoring Your Schedule

Objective: To have students monitor their schedules and task completion, and adjust their schedules.

Grades: Middle school and above

Teaching Procedure: Monitoring task completion is the key to successful use of schedules and To-Do lists. Following are some suggestions for monitoring:

- Have students spend about five minutes during the class period to update their schedules and cross off tasks they have completed. This can be done at the beginning of class when you are taking roll.
- Meet with students, as necessary, to review their schedules and their monitoring.

- Have students adjust their schedules as necessary.

Action Learning Area: Organizing Your Studying

In addition to organizing and using a schedule, students need to organize their study environment and notebook, and develop positive study habits. The three activities in this section can help students get organized. All the activities can be integrated as a first unit in any content area class.

Organizing Your Study Environment

Objective: To have students assess their study environment at home and modify it to promote studying.

Grades: Middle school and above

FIGURE B

Study Environment Checklist

Name _____ Date _____

Evaluate each statement by checking the column that describes the place where you study.

Statement	Rarely	Generally	Almost Always
1. I study in a consistent place.			
2. The place I study is quiet.			
3. It has good light.			
4. There are no visual distractions.			
5. There are a comfortable desk/table and a chair.			
6. The materials I need are at my desk.			
7. The study area is available when I need it.			
8. A computer is available.			

Adapted with permission from Strichart, S. S., & Mangrum, C. T. II, (1993). *Teaching study strategies to students with learning disabilities* (p. 356). Boston: Allyn and Bacon.

Teaching Procedures: Let parents know that students will be assessing and thinking about modifying their home study environment to promote studying. After students complete a study environment checklist (see Figure B), have them meet in groups to discuss the results and their ideas for modifying their study environments.

Meet with each student individually to summarize the results and to write one to three goals for improving the study environment if warranted. Have students report on their progress toward meeting their goals.

Shaping Up Your Study Habits

Objective: To help students assess their study habits and modify them to promote studying.

Grades: Middle school and above

Teaching Procedures: Let parents know that students will be assessing and thinking about modifying their study habits to promote studying. After students complete a study habits checklist like the one shown in Figure C, have them meet in groups

---

FIGURE C

Study Habits Checklist

Name _____   Date _____

Evaluate each statement by checking the column that describes your study habits.

Statement	Rarely	Generally	Almost Always
1. I set aside a regular time to study.			
2. I do not take calls or allow interruptions during study time.			
3. I take short breaks when I get tired, but return to work.			
4. I take a few minutes at the beginning to organize my study time.			
5. I begin with the hardest assignments.			
6. I finish one assignment before going on to the next one.			
7. I break long projects down into short tasks and work on the tasks over time.			
8. I begin studying for a test at least three days before the test.			
9. I have someone I can contact when I get stuck.			
10. I write down questions I need to ask the teacher.			

Adapted with permission from Strichart, S. S., & Mangrum, C. T. II, (1993). *Teaching study strategies to students with learning disabilities* (p. 356). Boston: Allyn and Bacon.

to discuss the results and their ideas for changing their study habits to promote studying at home.

Next, meet with each student individually to summarize the results and to write from one to three goals for improving study habits. Finally, have students report on their progress toward meeting their goals.

Organizing Your Notebook

Objective: To teach students to organize their notebooks so that materials and information are easy to retrieve and use.

Grades: Middle school and above

Teaching Procedures: Alert parents that students will be reviewing their notebooks for organization, and send home a list of recommended materials, including the following:

- three-ring notebook, so that pages can be added easily
- supply pouch and school supplies such as pens, pencils, erasers, computer disks, calculator, hole punch, package of file cards, ruler
- labeled dividers—one for each class, plus others labeled "Schedules and Calendar," "Reference Information," "Notebook Dictionary," "Personal Word List," "Notebook Paper," "Graph Paper," "Computer Paper"

Have students look at their notebooks to determine how they have organized information for each class, their assignments, schedules, and materials. Work with students to organize their notebooks, using the following suggestions:

- Include a semester calendar, weekly schedules, and To-Do lists in the section on schedules and calendar.
- After the divider for each class, organize materials for that class (starting with class outline or syllabus).
- Date notes and place them in order.
- In the personal word list, alphabetically list frequently misspelled words.

Action Learning Area: Goal Setting, Self-Monitoring, and Self-Advocacy

One way to get students actively involved in learning is to plan activities in which students learn to set goals, monitor their accomplishments, and advocate for what they want and need. The two activities in this section set the stage for active learning.

Goal Setting and Self-Monitoring

Objective: Students learn to set, plan, and monitor their goals.

Grades: Middle school and above

Teaching Objectives: Whether you are working on finishing a term paper or saving enough money to buy a car, it is important to set goals, make a plan to accomplish the goals, and monitor your progress. Van Reusen and Bos (1992) developed a strategy that students can use for setting goals and monitoring progress. The strategy uses the acronym *MARKER* (it gives students a *mark* to work toward and is a *marker* of their progress), and includes the following steps:

> **M**ake a list of goals, set the order, set the dates.
> **A**rrange a plan for each goal and predict your success.
> **R**un your plan for each goal and adjust if necessary.
> **K**eep records of your progress.
> **E**valuate your progress toward each goal.
> **R**eward yourself when you reach a goal, and set a new goal.

For each goal, students use a Goal Planning Sheet (see Figure D) to answer the following questions:

- Can I describe my goal?
- What is the reason or purpose for the goal?
- Where am I going to work on and complete this goal?
- How much time do I have to complete the goal?

Goal Planning and Monitoring Sheet

Name: _____ Class: _____ Date: _____

1. Goal: _____

2. Reason(s) for working on goal: _____

   _____

3. Goal will be worked on at: _____

4. Date to reach goal (due date): _____

5. Materials needed: _____

   _____

6. Steps used to reach the goal: _____

   _____

7. Progress toward the goal: Record in each box the date and progress rating.

   3—Goal reached   2—Good progress made   1—Some progress made   0—No progress made

Date / Rating				
Date / Rating				
Date / Rating				

8. Reward for reaching goal: _____

Adapted from Van Reusen, A. K., & Bos, C. S. (1992). *Use of the goal-regulation strategy to improve the goal attainment of students with learning disabilities* (Final Report). Tucson, Ariz.: University of Arizona.

■ What materials do I need to complete the goal?

■ Can I divide the goal into steps or parts? If so, in what order should I complete each step or part?

■ How am I going to keep records of my progress?

■ How will I reward myself for reaching my goal?

Students usually work on one to three goals at one time, keeping progress data on each goal.

Content Class Integration: This strategy can be taught as a unit in almost any class, but is particularly appropriate for social studies and life skills classes. When Van Reusen and Bos (1992) used this strategy with middle and high school students with learning disabilities and behavior disorders, they found that students accomplished more goals and gained a more informed perspective on their educational and personal goals.

Resources: For more information, see:

■ Lenz, B. K., Ehren, B. J., & Smiley, L. (1991). A goal attainment approach to improve completion of project-type assignments by adolescents with learning disabilities. *Learning Disabilities Research and Practice, 6,* 166–176.

■ Van Reusen, A. K., & Bos, C. S. (1992). *Use of the goal-regulation strategy to improve the goal attainment of students with learning disabilities* (Final Report). Tucson, AZ: University of Arizona.

Self-Advocacy

Objective: To help students inventory their learning strengths, weaknesses they need to improve, goals, and interests, and then advocate for themselves with key adults (e.g., parents, teachers, counselors).

Grades: Middle school and above

Teaching Procedures: *Self-advocacy* occurs when individuals effectively communicate and negotiate for their interests, desires, needs, and rights. It involves making informed decisions and taking responsibility for those decisions (Van Reusen et al., 1994). The I PLAN self-advocacy strategy is one way to help students develop their advocacy skills.

During the first (Inventory) step, students (working in instructional groups) develop their own personal inventories. Each student examines the following items:

■ strengths
■ areas to improve or learn
■ goals
■ choice for learning or accommodations

If the emphasis is on career and transition planning, students also think about areas related to jobs and adult life. The major components of an education inventory and a transition inventory are presented in Table A.1.

TABLE A.1	
Components of Education and Transition Inventories	
Strengths	Reading
	Writing
	Math
	Study Skills
	Social Skills
	Career & Employment Skills
	Independent Living Skills
	Leisure & Recreation Skills
Areas to Improve or Learn	Based on learning strengths and needs
Goals	Academic
	Social
	Extracurricular/Recreation
	Career/Employment
	Independent Living
Choices for Learning	Helpful Activities
	Learning Preferences
	Helpful Materials
	Testing Preferences
Accommodations	Changes that need to be made so that student can succeed

Adapted from Van Reusen, A. K., Bos, C. S., Schumaker, J. B., & Deshler, D. D. (1994). *The self-advocacy strategy for education and transition planning.* Lawrence, KS: Edge Enterprises.

The remaining four steps in the strategy focus on the communication skills needed to present the information and advocate with teachers, parents, counselors, and others. These steps are presented, discussed, and then practiced through simulations:

Provide your inventory information
Listen and respond
Ask questions
Name your goals

Students also learn the following SHARE behaviors to promote positive communication:

Sit up straight
Have a pleasant tone of voice
Activate your thinking

- Tell yourself to pay attention
- Tell yourself to participate
- Tell yourself to compare ideas

Relax
- Don't look uptight
- Tell yourself to stay calm

Engage in eye communication

Content Class Integration: This activity can be integrated into most content classes, but is particularly suited for social studies and life skills classes.

Resources: For additional information, see *The self-advocacy strategy for education and transition planning,* by A. K. Van Reusen, C. S. Bos, J. B. Schumaker, and D. D. Deshler, published (1994) by Edge Enterprises, Lawrence, Kansas.

Action Learning Area: Listening and Taking Notes

Listening to lectures, asking questions, and taking notes are skills critical for success in school. Teachers generally are more willing to accommodate students who actively participate in class, and these students tend to be more successful academically (Schumm & Vaughn, 1991). The six activities in this section can be used to promote active listening, note taking, and class participation.

Creating Rationales for Effective Note Taking

Objective: To teach students how to develop rationales for taking notes.

Grade: Upper elementary and above

Teaching Procedures: On the average, teachers in secondary settings spend at least half their class time presenting information through lectures, and base a significant number of items on

tests on information presented in class discussion and lectures (Putnam et al., 1993). Note taking is one of the most efficient ways to record this information.

Using class discussion or cooperative groups, have students generate a rationale for the importance of taking notes to success in school. If students do not mention the following reasons, make sure that you do:

- Note taking increases attention.
- Note taking requires a deeper level of thinking than just listening, because students must make sense of the information and write the ideas.
- Because students must process information on a deeper level, note taking makes learning and remembering information easier.

With class discussion or cooperative groups, have students create a list of requirements for effective note taking. If the following items are not part of the list, be sure to mention them:

- paying attention
- writing fast and legibly
- using abbreviations
- deciding what to write
- spelling
- making sense of notes after the lecture

Finally, through class discussion or cooperative groups, develop a list of ideas for accommodations for each requirement in the list (e.g., for "spelling," teacher could write difficult words on board, transparency, or handout).

Post the three lists so that students can review them.

Content Class Integration: Completing a unit on listening and note taking can be valuable in any content class. Such a unit not only improves students' note taking, but also makes them aware of your style of presenting information.

Using Listener-Friendly Lectures

Objective: To use strategies that make it easier for students to understand and take notes on the information you present during lectures.

Grades: Upper elementary and above

Teaching Procedures: As you plan your teaching, the following guidelines can make your lectures "*listener-friendly*":

- Use advance organizers.
- Use cue words or phrases to let students know what information is important (e.g., "It is important that you know ...," "The key information to remember is ...," "In summary ...").
- Repeat important information.
- Write important information on board, transparency, and handout.
- Stress key points by varying the tone and quality of your voice.
- Number ideas or points (e.g., first, second, next, then, finally).
- Write technical words or words that are difficult to spell.
- Use a study guide that lists the major concepts, with space for students to add other information.
- Use pictures, diagrams, and semantic maps to show relationships among ideas.
- Provide examples and nonexamples of the concepts you are discussing.
- Ask questions or encourage discussion that requires students to relate the new information to ideas they already know (from their own background or your previous lectures).
- Stop frequently and have students work with partners and discuss what they have learned.
- Allow time at the end of a lecture for students to look over their notes, summarize, and ask questions.

By using these guidelines you will naturally incorporate cues that indicate what information is important.

Content Class Integration: Whenever you give a lecture in any content course, make sure it is "listener-friendly."

Pause Procedure

Objective: To give students frequent opportunities to review notes, check for understanding, and ask questions.

Grades: Upper elementary and above

Teaching Procedures: The pause procedure is a technique that helps students learn more from lectures. During logical breaks in a lecture (approximately every ten minutes), the teacher pauses for two minutes. During that time, pairs of students compare their notes to make certain that key concepts have been recorded. Students also ask each other questions to check for understanding.

At the end of the two minutes, ask students whether they have any questions or concepts that need further discussion or clarification. Then resume lecturing.

Resources: For additional information, see the following publications:

- Ruhl, K. L., Hughes, C. A., & Gajar, A. H. (1990). Efficacy of the pause procedure for enhancing learning disabled and nondisabled college students' long- and short-term recall of facts presented through lecture. *Learning Disability Quarterly, 13,* 55–64.
- Ruhl, K. L., Hughes, C. A., & Schloss, P. J. (1987). Using the pause procedure to enhance lecture recall. *Teacher Education and Special Education, 10,* 14–18.

Teaching Note Taking

Objective: To help students evaluate their notes and improve their note-taking strategies.

Grades: Middle school and above

Teaching Procedures: Teaching note-taking skills to students in your class is a good investment of time and effort. As you teach a content unit you can use the following procedure to evaluate your students' note-taking skills and to introduce and teach alternative ways to take notes:

1. *Have students evaluate the effectiveness of their current note-taking skills.* Give a lecture from the content unit and have students take notes as usual. The next day, give students a quiz. Have them evaluate the completeness, format, and legibility of their notes, as well as their ease of use for review.

2. *Use videotaped lectures to teach students to listen effectively and take notes.* Use a videotape of your lecture so that students can listen and watch for cues you give to note important information. When students notice a cue, stop the videotape and replay it so that all the students can hear and see it.

3. *Control the difficulty of the lectures.* Select the first unit of the year to teach note taking. This unit usually contains simple information that was presented the previous year.

4. *Discuss with students ways to record notes* (i.e., record key ideas, not sentences; use consistent abbreviations; use an outline format; spell a word the way it looks or sounds). As a class, have students develop a set of abbreviations to be posted on a wall chart.

5. *Teach students how to review their notes,* add missing information, and clarify information that is unclear. Have students, working as partners or cooperative groups, use their notes to study for tests. Teach students how to use their notes to create questions and then check to see that they can answer them.

6. *Have students monitor their note taking.* Have them keep track of how often they use their note-taking skills in your class (and others), and record how they are doing on tests and assignments (and the effect of their improved note-taking skills).

Content Class Integration: You can integrate teaching how to take notes into any content class. Teaching these skills early in the year improves the atmosphere and student learning throughout the year.

Using Cues When Listening to Lectures

Objective: To help students learn to listen and watch for cues during lectures, and to record important information.

Grades: Middle school and above

Teaching Procedures: Use the following list of cues to help students learn how to listen and watch for important information:

Type of Cue	Examples
Organizational Cues	
	Today, we will be discussing ...
	The topic I want to cover today ...
	There are (number) points I want you to be sure to learn. ...
	The important relationship is ...
	The main point of this discussion is ...
	Any statement that signals a number or position (e.g., first, last, next, then)
	To review/summarize/recap ...
Emphasis Cues	
Verbal	You need to know/understand/remember ...
	This is important/key/basic/critical ...
	Let me repeat this, ...
	Let me check, now do you understand ...
	Any statement repeated.
	Words are emphasized.
	Teacher speaks more slowly, loudly, or with more emphasis.
	Teacher stresses certain words.
	Teacher spells words.
	Teacher asks rhetorical question.
Nonverbal	Information written on overhead or board.
	Information handed out in study guide.
	Teacher emphasizes point by using gestures.

Encourage students to listen and watch for additional cues and add them to the list.

Content Class Integration:

When integrating a content unit with a unit on note taking, the information presented in this activity can be placed on a handout and posted on a wall chart.

Resources: For more information, see:

- Suritsky, S. K., & Hughes, C. A. (1996). Notetaking strategy instruction. In D. D. Deshler, E. S. Ellis, & B. K. Lenz (Authors), *Teaching adolescents with learning disabilities* (2nd ed.), pp. 267–312. Denver: Love.

Guidelines for Effective Note Taking

Objective: To teach students to use a note-taking system that is effective for recording and studying information.

Grades: Middle school and above

Teaching Procedures: Teach the specifics of note taking, using the following guidelines:

- Use a two- or three-column system for taking notes, with one column for recording key concepts and questions (see Figure E).
- Date and number each page of notes, and label the topic.
- Use a modified outline format, leaving space in which to add information when notes are reviewed.
- Write key ideas or phrases. (Paraphrase; do not write complete sentences.)
- Use pictures and diagrams to relate ideas.
- Use consistent abbreviations.
- Record information that the lecturer writes on the board or transparency.

- Underline, highlight, or use asterisks to mark key information.
- If you miss information, draw a blank and fill it in later.
- If you cannot spell a word, spell it the way you think it looks or sounds.
- As soon as possible, review your notes and fill in missing information. Check with your teacher or other students if you have questions.

Action Learning Area: Remembering Information

Using memory strategies to remember information is critical for success in school. Students, particularly students with disabilities and those who are at risk, often have difficulty memorizing information. Sometimes students do not understand the information, but in other cases students' may not perform well because they have difficulties retrieving information or because they do not use deliberate

---

FIGURE E

Sample Two-Column Note-taking Format

Date: _____   Page: _____

Topic: _____

Key Concepts/Questions	Notes

memory strategies. This section highlights two activities you can use to teach memory strategies.

Guidelines for Remembering Information

Objective: To use general guidelines to increase the amount of information students remember.

Grades: Upper elementary and above

Teaching Procedures: When you present information, make it easier to remember by following these guidelines:

- Cue students when important information is being presented.
- Activate prior knowledge and help students make connections between old and new knowledge.
- Use visual aids such as semantic maps and diagrams to make the information more memorable.
- Limit the amount of information presented; group related ideas.
- Control the rate at which information is presented.
- Provide time to review, rehearse, and elaborate on the information.
- Teach students how to use and apply memory strategies and devices.
- Provide opportunities for distributed review of information and encourage over-learning.

Generating Acronyms and Acrostics

Objective: To teach students to generate acronyms and acrostics that help them remember information.

Grades: Middle school and above

Teaching Procedures: *Mnemonics* are memory-triggering devices that help us remember and retrieve information by forming associations that do not exist naturally in the content. Two types of mnemonics are acronyms and acrostics. *Acronyms* are words created by joining the first letters of a series of words. Examples are *radar* (**ra**dio detecting and ranging), *scuba* (self-contained under-water breathing apparatus), and *laser* (light amplification by stimulated emission of radiation). *Acrostics* are sentences created by words that begin with the first letters of a series of words. A popular example of an acrostic is "Every good boy does fine," which represents the notes on the lines of the treble clef staff: E, G, B, D, F. By teaching students to construct acronyms and acrostics, sharing them in class, and then cueing students to use them when they study and take tests, you help them to learn and retrieve information.

The FIRST-letter mnemonic strategy is one strategy you can teach to help students construct lists of information to memorize and develop an acronym or acrostic for learning and remembering the information. The strategy includes an overall strategy (LISTS) and a substrategy for making the mnemonic device (FIRST). The steps in the overall strategy include the following:

Look for clues. (In class notes and textbooks, look for lists of information that are important to learn. Name or give a heading to each list.)
Investigate the items. (Decide which items should be included in the list.)
Select a mnemonic device, using FIRST. (Use the FIRST substrategy, explained shortly, to construct a mnemonic.)
Transfer the information to a card. (Write the mnemonic and the list on one side of a card and the name of the list on the other side of the card.)
Self-test. (Study by looking at the heading using the mnemonic to recall the list.)

To complete the Select step, students use the FIRST substrategy to design an acronym or acrostic:

Form a word. Using uppercase letters, write the first letter of each word in the list; see whether an acronym—a recognizable word or nonsense word—can be made.
Insert a letter(s). Insert letter(s) to see whether a word can be made. (Be sure to use lowercase letters so that you know they do not represent an item on the list—BACk, for example.)
Rearrange the letters. Rearrange the letters to see whether a word can be made.

Shape a sentence. Using the first letter of each word in the list, try to construct a sentence (an acrostic).

Try combinations. Try combinations of these above steps to generate the mnemonic.

Content Class Integration: This strategy can be taught in any content class but is particularly effective in science and social studies classes in which lists of information are to be learned. The strategy provides a systematic method for students to review text and class notes, construct lists, and develop acronyms and acrostics that help them remember and retrieve information.

Resources: For more information, read *The FIRST-letter mnemonic strategy* (Learning Strategies Curriculum), by B. R. Nagel, J. B. Schumaker, and D. D. Deshler, (1986), published by Edge Enterprises, Lawrence, Kansas.

Action Learning Area: Studying and Taking Tests

Tests are the primary means that teachers use to determine whether students have learned new concepts and can apply them. If your goal in testing is to measure what students have learned (and not test-taking skills), then teaching test-taking strategies as part of the curriculum is important. This section contains five activities for teaching strategies for studying and taking tests.

Guidelines for Studying for Tests

Objective: To help students use general strategies when studying for tests.

Grades: Middle school and above

Teaching Procedures: Teach the following general guidelines to help students develop positive study habits when studying for tests.

■ *Manage your study time.* Keep up with assignments and do daily and weekly reviews. Plan five minutes each day for students to review the material. On Monday, take an extra five minutes and have students review the previous week's material. Use partners, cooperative groups, and whole-class discussion to review.

■ *Create study aids.* Create a semantic map, study guide, mnemonic, and other study aids to help students remember key information. Use an ongoing map or study guide that students add to daily.

■ *Create flashcards.* Teach students how to create and use flashcards. When students are learning vocabulary, have them put the word on one side and the definition and an example on the other. For other information, have students put the question on one side and the answer on the other. In math or science, have students put a formula on one side and examples of its use on the other. Have students keep index cards in their notebooks and on their desks during class. Cue students to make a card when they learn about a key concept or idea.

■ *Use flashcards to review.* One advantage of flashcards is that each item or piece of information is on a separate card. Have students sort cards into categories, arrange the cards in a semantic map, or review them in random order.

■ *Learn about the test.* Rather than telling students about the test, have them learn about it by asking questions. Start the discussion with, "Let's talk about the test. What do you want to ask me?" Use the following checklist to guide the students' questioning:

■ Format of test; types of questions
■ Date of test
■ Time allotted for test
■ Whether books and notes are allowed
■ How much test counts toward the class grade
■ Information covered
■ Teacher's recommendations for how to study
■ Teacher's recommendations for what to study

■ *Predict questions.* Show students how they can predict what questions will be asked. Have students predict questions by using what they know about the teacher's testing style, class notes and textbook, and study aids. Two days before a test, have students—working as partners or in cooperative groups—write (and then answer) the questions they think will be on the test.

- *Think positive.* Help students develop a positive attitude by asking the following questions during each day's review:

  - What have you learned today?
  - How does it relate to what you already know?
  - What will you be working on tomorrow?
  - How well have you learned the information?

  Have students rate how well they think they will do on the test and think about what they can do to improve their ratings.

- *Review test-taking strategies and visualize success.* Just before a test, review test-taking strategies and have students visualize themselves being successful as they take the test.

Content Class Integration: Guidelines for studying for tests are easily taught in any content class. Students learn not only about effective ways to study in general, but also about your views on developing, studying for, and giving tests.

Guidelines for Taking Tests

Objective: To teach students general strategies for taking tests.

Grades: Middle school and above

Teaching Procedures: Teach students the following general guidelines for taking tests:

- Bring the necessary materials.
- Be on time and sit where you will not be disturbed.
- Survey the test.
- Read the directions carefully and make sure that you understand them. If not, ask for assistance.
- Schedule your time.
- Be sure you understand the scoring system (i.e., is guessing penalized?).

- If you have memorized specific outlines, formulas, mnemonics, and so on, write that information before you forget it.
- When answering questions, place a mark in the margin next to questions about which you are unsure or that you want to review.
- Avoid changing answers arbitrarily.
- Review your answers and proofread written responses.

Using a Test-Taking Strategy

Objective: To teach students to use a test-taking strategy.

Grades: Middle school and above

Teaching Procedures: Some students may profit from learning a specific test-taking strategy that they can use when taking objective tests. Introduce the PIRATES strategy, letting students know that its use generally improves test scores by from 10 to 30 percent. Then model the steps in the strategy:

1. Prepare to succeed
   Put your name and the word PIRATES on the test.
   Allot time and order the sections.
   Say affirmations.
   Start within two minutes.
2. Inspect the instructions
   Read instructions carefully.
   Underline what to do and where to respond.
   Notice special requirements.
3. Read, remember, reduce
   Read the whole question.
   Remember what you studied.
   Reduce your choices.
4. Answer or abandon
   Answer the question.
   Abandon the question for the moment.
5. Turn back
6. Estimate your answer
   Avoid absolutes.
   Choose the longest or most detailed choice.
   Eliminate similar choices.
7. Survey
   Survey to ensure all questions are answered.
   Switch an answer only if you're sure.

Tell students that to repeat the second, third, and fourth steps (i.e., Inspect the instructions; Read, remember, reduce; Answer or abandon) for each section of the test.

Give students the opportunity to learn the mnemonic (PIRATES) and the steps in the strategy, as well as the opportunity for practice. Cue students to use the strategy and discuss when, where, and how it can be used. Have students monitor their success in using the strategy and how it affects their test scores.

Content Class Integration: Teaching a test-taking strategy takes time but is worthwhile if you use objective tests as the major way to grade students.

Resources: For more information, see the following publications:

- Hughes, C. A., & Schumaker, J. B. (1991). Test-taking strategy instruction for adolescents with learning disabilities. *Exceptionality, 2*, 205–221.
- Hughes, C. A., Schumaker, J. B., Deshler, D. D., & Mercer, C. D. (1988). *The test-taking strategy.* Lawrence, Kans.: Edge Enterprises.

Tips for Answering Objective Questions

Objective: To teach students tips for answering objective questions.

Grades: Middle school and above

Teaching Procedures: Discuss the following tips with students and give them a handout. In your discussion, include ideas that you and the students generate. Allow students to use the handout when they answer objective questions.

True-False Questions
- Remember, *everything* in a true statement must be true. One false detail makes it false.
- Look for qualifying words that tend to make statements false, such as: *all, always, everyone, everybody, never, no, none, no one, only.*
- Look for qualifying words that tend to make statements true, such as: *generally, most, often, probably, some, sometimes, usually.*

- Simplify questions that contain double negatives by crossing out both negatives and then determining whether the statement is true or false.
- Don't change an answer unless you have a good reason to. Usually your first impression is correct.

Matching Questions
- Read directions carefully. Determine whether each column contains an equal number of items and whether items can be used more than once.
- Read both columns before you start matching, to get a sense of the items.
- Focus on each item in one column and look for its match in the other column.
- If you can use items only once, cross out each item as you use it.

Multiple-Choice Questions
- Determine whether you are penalized for guessing.
- Answer the questions you know, putting a check in the margin next to items you want to return to later.
- Read all possible options, even when you are pretty sure of the right answer.
- See whether multiple options are available (e.g., c. A and B; d. All of the above).
- Minimize the risk of guessing by reading the stem with each option to see which option is most logical.
- Use a process of elimination, crossing out options you know are wrong.
- When you do not know the answer and you are not penalized for guessing, use the following signals to help you select the right option:

  - The longest option is often correct.
  - The most complete answer is often correct.
  - The first time the option "all of the above" or "none of the above" is used, it is usually correct.
  - The option in the middle, particularly if it is the longest, is often correct.
  - Answers with qualifiers such as *generally, probably, sometimes,* and *usually* are frequently correct.

Completion Questions

- Determine whether more than one word can be put in one blank.
- If blanks are of different lengths, use length as a clue for the length of the answer.
- Read the question to yourself so that you can hear what is being asked.
- If more than one answer comes to mind, write them down; then reread the question with each answer to see which one fits best.
- Makes sure that the answer you provide fits grammatically and logically.

Content Class Integration: In any content class, you can teach students to use tips for taking objective tests. You may want to modify the list to better match the type of objective tests you give in your class.

Resources: For more information, read J. Lagan's *Reading and study skills* (2nd ed.), 1982, published by McGraw-Hill, New York.

Using Instruction Cue Words for Answering Essay Questions

Objective: To help students learn and apply the meaning of instruction cue words when they answer essay questions.

Grades: Middle school and above

Teaching Procedures: When you teach strategies for answering essay questions, discuss the meanings of different instruction cue words such as those in Table A.2. In your discussion, add other

---

TABLE A.2

Instruction Cue Words for Answering Essay Questions

Cue	Meaning	Cue	Meaning
Analyze	Break into parts and examine each part.	Interpret	Explain and share your own judgment.
Apply	Discuss how the principles would apply to a situation.	Justify	Provide reasons for your statements or conclusion.
Compare	Discuss differences and similarities.	List	Provide a numbered list of items or points.
Contrast	Discuss differences and similarities, stressing the differences.	Outline	Organize your answer into main points and supporting details. If appropriate, use outline format.
Critique	Analyze and evaluate, using criteria.	Prove	Provide factual evidence to support your logic or position.
Define	Provide a clear, concise statement that explains the concept.	Relate	Show the connection among ideas.
Describe	Give a detailed account, listing characteristics, qualities, and components as appropriate.	Review	Provide a critical summary in which you summarize and present your comments.
Diagram	Provide a drawing.	State	Explain precisely.
Discuss	Provide an in-depth explanation. Be analytical.	Summarize	Provide a synopsis that does not include your comments.
Explain	Give a logical development that discusses reasons or causes.	Trace	Describe the development or progress of the idea.
Illustrate	Use examples or, when appropriate, provide a diagram or picture.		

Add your own Instruction Cue Words and definitions!!!

Adapted from Bos, C. S., & Vaughn, S. (1994). *Teaching students with learning and behavior problems* (3rd ed.) (p. 303). Boston: Allyn and Bacon.

---

cue words and meanings generated by you and the students. Develop a handout and have students use it when they answer essay questions. Ask students to underline the instruction cue words in each essay question.

Content Class Integration: This activity gives students an opportunity to learn how instruction cue words determine what information to include in an answer. For example, as a social studies teacher you can demonstrate how taking one concept, such as *democracy,* and using different instruction cue words (*define* versus *illustrate*) will change the answer.

GLOSSARY

Acceleration. Rapid promotion of a student through grade levels

Acquired Immunodeficiency Syndrome (AIDS). A viral infection transmitted through bodily fluids that may eventually cause a loss of stamina, developmental delays, motor problems, progressive neurological defects, repeated bacterial infections, psychological stresses, and death

Adaptive behavior. Refers to the effectiveness or degree with which individuals meet the standards of personal independence and social responsibility expected for age and cultural group

Additive approach. A strategy characterized by the addition of content, concepts, themes, and perspectives without changing the basic structure of the curriculum

Add-on programs. Services provided in time slots typically not allocated to regular instruction

Advance organizer. Information presented in advance of and at a higher level of generality, inclusiveness, and abstraction than the learning task itself

Advocacy. One of the primary characteristics of the Individuals with Disabilities Education Act, which involves the assignment of representatives (advocates) for individuals with disabilities who lack parents or guardians

African American Vernacular English. (Also called Black English) A dialect used by some African Americans, and the most prevalent native English vernacular dialect used in the United States

Age. The ages, defined by law, during which children with disabilities must be educated (and which exceed those stipulated for nondisabled students)

Alliteration. Identification of similarities or differences in word beginnings

Alphabetic principle. The use of the letters of the alphabet to form words

American Sign Language. A visual, gestural language

Anxiety-withdrawal. A type of problem behavior involving extreme worry, anxiousness, or depression

AOK Strategy. A way to help students learn to read and reread for different purposes during revising and editing for meaning, paragraphs, sentences, words, and neatness

Articulation disorders. Occur when students are unable to produce the sounds and sound combinations of language

Assessment portfolios. Collections of work samples that document student progress in one or more subject areas

ASSET. A social skills program for adolescents, designed to effectively teach students strategies to enhance their social functioning

Assistive listening devices. Tools that aid in the process of hearing

Attention deficit disorder (ADD). A disorder consisting of two subtypes of behavior: inattention and hyperactivity-impulsivity

Audiogram. A visual representation of an individual's ability to hear sound

Augmentative communication. Systems that attempt to facilitate and compensate, temporarily or permanently, for the impairment and disability patterns of individuals with severe expressive and/or language comprehension disorders

Authentic learning. Takes place when students can construct meaning by connecting new information to what they already know and have experienced, recognize the value of what they are learning beyond grades and success in school, and connect what they learn in school to the "real world"

Authoring cycle. A cycle of prewriting, composing (drafting), and post-writing (revising, editing, and publishing)

Autism. A developmental disability characterized by extreme withdrawal and communication difficulties

Balanced bilingual. Characterized by fluency in two languages

Basal Reading Program. A reading program that consists of graded readers (grades K–8) containing stories with carefully controlled sentence length and vocabulary, accompanied by supplemental materials (e.g., workbooks, worksheets, instructional charts) that help teachers provide instruction in word recognition and reading comprehension

Basic interpersonal communication skills. Refer to the conversational competencies that develop with a second language

Biased responding. The tendency of students to respond with "yes," due to their desire to please the teacher or in an effort to hide their confusion

Big Books. Books with large pictures and words that can be seen by a whole class and used for shared reading activities

Bilingual education. An educational program involving instruction in two languages, with the goal being to promote *bilingualism* (proficiency in both languages)

Black Vernacular English (BVE). Articulation used by some African Americans that reflects the complex racial and economic history of the African American in the United States

Blending. Putting sounds or phonemes together to form words

Blind. Describes an individual who is unable to see and therefore, uses tactual (touch) and auditory (hearing) abilities to access the environment

Braille. A system of embossed or raised dots that can be read with the tips of the fingers

Cerebral palsy. Results from damage to the brain before or during birth; conditions are classified according to the areas affected and the types of symptoms

Child Find. A requirement that each state identify and track the number of students with disabilities, and plan for their educational needs

Class meetings. Meetings that include all students in the class, as well as the teacher; used to foster students' involvement in the management of their classes

Classification. The ability to group or sort objects by one or more common properties

Classwide Peer Tutoring. Students of different reading levels (one average or high, and one low) are paired and read materials that can be easily read by the least able reader in the pair

Cloze procedure. An informal method of measuring reading level and comprehension

Cognitive academic language performance. Refers to the more cognitively demanding language skills required for the new learning that is characteristic of school settings

Cognitive strategies. Thinking processes used by students to complete their academic work

Collaboration. A style for direct interaction between at least two co-equal parties voluntarily engaged in shared decision making as they work toward a common goal

Collaborative open-note tests. Tests given after students have had an opportunity to compare and further develop their notes in collaborative groups; students have the opportunity to answer test questions as a collaborative group

Common underlying proficiency. The phenomenon that the better developed the students' first language proficiency and conceptual foundation, the more likely they are to develop similarly high levels of proficiency and conceptual ability in the second language

Communication approach. Teaching the student how to (1) communicate with oneself and others and (2) integrate reading with other language skills including writing, speaking, and listening

Communication board. An example of augmentative communication that includes the "board" itself and symbols or pictures

Communication disorders. Difficulties with the transfer of knowledge, ideas, opinions, and feelings

Compensatory education. Instruction designed to compensate (make up) for prior lack of educational opportunities, and intervention or prevention programs

Compensatory skills. Skills, needed for independence, that may include the use of braille, a slate and stylus, and an abacus

Composing. Process in which the author attempts to get ideas on paper in the form of a draft

Comprehensible input. Refers to input received and made understandable when listening to or reading in a second language

Comprehensible output. Refers to output transmitted and made understandable when speaking

Comprehension. A person's ability to understand what is being communicated

Comprehension strategies. Techniques designed to improve students' understanding of text

Computational Arithmetic Program. Provides 314 worksheets to teach basic math skills in grades one through six

Computer-assisted instruction (CAI). Involves learning through the use of computers and/or multimedia systems

Computer equity. Equal access to computers in the home and in the school

Concept diagram. A way to introduce a lecture or reading assignment (similar to a semantic map) that also helps students determine the definitions, characteristics, examples, and nonexamples of a concept

Conceptual density. The number of new vocabulary terms or concepts the author introduces

Conduct disorder. Includes behaviors such as hitting, fighting, throwing, temper tantrums, acting defiant or disobedient, and being irritable or over-active, difficult to get along with, uncooperative, inconsiderate, resistive, jealous, quarrelsome, distractible, teasing, irresponsible, and inattentive

Cone of experience. Classifies experience on a scale from concrete to abstract, from action to observation to representation

Confidentiality of records. The Individuals with Disabilities Education Act requires that all records and documents regarding students with disabilities remain undisclosed to the public, but accessible to parents

Conflict resolution. A strategy for resolving conflicts between students and between students and teachers

Consequences. The ramifications of not following classroom guidelines

Considerate text. Text that is written and formatted in such a way that information can be extracted easily, with support available when the reader does not understand

Constant time delay. A procedure for teaching math facts that provides for the systematic introduction of teacher assistance

Consultation model. An interactive process that enables people with diverse expertise to generate creative solutions to mutually defined problems

Content. The semantics of language

Content acceleration. The practice of rapid movement through the curriculum

Content goals. Relates to the application of the reading process in reconstructing an author's intended meaning

Content integration. Focused use of examples and content from different cultures and groups to illustrate concepts, principles, generalizations, and theories

Content/process dilemma. The conflict between covering sufficient material (content) or altering instruction so that students with special needs master the learning process (sometimes by covering less material)

Context embedded communication and instruction. Providing a link between students' culture, and the instruction they receive, and the mode in which they receive it

Continuum of services. A full range of service options for students with disabilities, provided by the school system

Contributions approach. Characterized by the insertion of ethnic heroes and discrete cultural artifacts into the curriculum

Cooperative learning groups. Groups of students work together toward a common goal, usually to help one another learn academic material

Cooperative teaching. General and special education teachers work together to coordinate curriculum and instruction and teach heterogeneous groups of students in the general education classroom setting

Co-planning. General and special education teachers work together to plan activities for students

Co-Teaching. (See *cooperative teaching*)

Corrective Mathematics Program. A math program that requires only minimal reading skills and provides remedial math for students in grades three through twelve

Course Planning Routine. A long-range planning guide for classrooms with diverse learners; includes procedures for setting goals for the course, getting the course off on the right foot, monitoring and managing the course during the year, and closing the course

Creatively gifted or talented. Describes students who display their unique abilities within the framework of the visual or performing arts and who usually demonstrate a superior ability to express ideas through various forms of communication (drawing, music, singing, writing, and acting)

Cross-age pairing. A method of pairing older students with younger students for reading instruction

Cross-categorical approach. Accommodations for exceptional learners are discussed in terms of students' shared needs rather than in terms of their identification as members of a disability category

Cultural characteristics. Traits or aspects that characterize a particular culture

Cultural inversion. The tendency to regard certain forms of behavior, events, symbols, and meanings as inappropriate because they are characteristic of European–American culture

Curriculum compacting. Provides students with the opportunity to demonstrate what they already know about a subject by eliminating repetitive or review content and replacing it with advanced learning experiences

Cursive writing. Script writing

Deaf. Describes a person with a severe or profound loss of hearing

Deafness–blindness. Also known as *dual sensory impairment*; involves impairments in the two main channels (auditory and visual) of receptive communication and learning

Decoding. A strategy for recognizing words

Degrees of Learning. This primary component of the Planning Pyramid is based on the premise that although all students are capable of learning, not all students will learn all the covered content

Demonstration-plus-model strategy. A strategy for giving demonstrations to students with learning problems that includes completion of the demonstration, having a student perform each step, verbalizing each step as you did, and having all students complete additional practice exercises independently, using the steps

Developmental Arithmetic Disorder. Refers to students who have significant difficulties learning arithmetic (difficulties that are unexpected, given the students' overall cognitive functioning and/or academic performance in other subject areas)

Developmental pathways. The etiologies associated with specific disorders

Developmental period. A period, prior to the age of 18 years, during which the bulk of human development occurs

Diagnostic and Statistical Manual of Mental Disorders (DSM). A reference book published by the American Psychiatric Association

Dialect. Refers to language variations associated with a regional or social group of people

Difficulty with zero. Refers to students' misunderstanding of the multiple meanings and uses of zero that causes errors in arithmetic

Discrepancy analysis. A review of each specific step or skill and determination of how a student does the step or skill compared to what is expected

Discussion web. A graphic aid to help students prepare for classroom discussions in content area classes

DISSECT. A learning strategy for secondary students with learning disabilities to approach a multisyllable word in a strategic way

DISTAR Arithmetic Program. Stresses direct instruction through a highly sequenced format that provides immediate feedback to students

Down syndrome. One of the most common chromosomal disorders, usually associated with mental retardation

Drafting. (See *composing*)

DRAW. An acronym for teaching the concrete-representational-abstract principle advocated in mathematics instruction

Dropouts. Students who do not complete high school

Dual sensory impairments. Refers to impairments in the two main channels (auditory and visual) of receptive communication and learning

Due process. Ensures that everyone with a stake in the student's educational success has a voice; also addresses written notification to parents for referral and testing for special education, parental consent, and guidelines for appeals and record keeping

Dyads. Pairs of students who work together

Dyscalculia. Severe disability in learning mathematical concepts and computation

Dysgraphia. Severe difficulty learning to write (including handwriting)

Dyslexia. Severe difficulty learning to read, particularly as it relates to decoding

Early intervention programs. Special learning programs provided during the preprimary and early primary grades

Early intervention services. Comprehensive services that incorporate goals in education, health care, and social services

Echolalia. A repetition of what was said without necessarily understanding the meaning

Eclectic programs. Reading programs that balance traditional and whole-language instruction

Ecological inventories. Analyses of the different skills a student needs in relation to his or her specific environments

Editing. Takes place as the author reviews the written work line by line to determine whether the overall content is appropriate and the mechanics are correct

Educational interventions. Special strategies for meeting the diverse needs of students

Educational placement. The type of educational setting in which a particular student is instructed; examples include general education classrooms, resource rooms, special schools, and other types of settings

Effective listening. Requires hearing the message being sent, and often requires asking questions to clarify the true message being sent

Elaboration. Process of building upon the content of the student's language and providing additional information on a topic

Emotional or behavioral disorders. Behavior that falls considerably outside the norm

Empowering school culture. Promotes gender, racial, and social-class equity

Encode. To change written language to symbols; to write

English as a Second Language (ESL) instruction. Students are taught English as a second language, with limited emphasis on maintaining or developing proficiency in their first language

Enrichment. Adding breadth and depth to the traditional curriculum

Environment-related factors. Factors that pertain to the context in which one teaches (including state, local, and class factors) and which can influence the planning process

Epilepsy. A condition characterized by the tendency to have recurrent seizures that are sudden, excessive, spontaneous, and abnormal discharges of neurons accompanied by alteration in motor function, and/or sensory function, and/or consciousness

Equity pedagogy. The teacher attends to different teaching and learning styles and modifies teaching to facilitate the academic achievement of students from diverse cultures

Exceptionalities. Refers to students who represent a range of disability categories (e.g., students with emotional disorders, learning disabilities, physical impairments, and students who are gifted)

Expansion. A technique used to facilitate the development of more complex language form and content

Explication. How the author explains ideas and teaches the reader, including the provision of background information and examples

Expository text. Text that is designed to teach or inform the reader

Expository writing. Informational writing

Expressive language. A person's ability to convey the intended message

Externalizing behaviors. Behaviors such as aggression, hitting, and shouting that are readily observable and tend to impact others

Extinction. The elimination of a student's undesirable behavior by removing reinforcers

Failure to shift operations. Occurs when the student fails to move to the next operation after completing a previous operation

Family adjustment. A family's changes in response to having a child with severe disabilities, mental retardation, or physical disabilities

FAST. A strategy designed to teach students to consider problems, identify alternatives, and evaluate consequences to their interpersonal problems

Fetal alcohol syndrome (FAS). Refers to a spectrum of birth defects caused by the mother drinking during pregnancy

Figurative language. Represents abstract concepts and usually requires an inferential rather than literal interpretation

Finger spelling. A system for manually representing the English alphabet

Flexible grouping. The use of different student grouping patterns that vary in composition, size, and frequency of meetings

FLIP Chart Strategy. Helps students learn to evaluate the difficulty of text on their own by examining text friendliness and language as well as their interest in and prior knowledge of the topic

Flow of the Planning Process Model. A model that indicates the sequence and relation among three types of planning and the factors that influence planning

Fluency. The ability to recognize printed words quickly

Fluency disorders. Refers to difficulty with the rate and flow of speech

Form. The phonology, morphology, and syntax of language

Free and appropriate public education (FAPE). Mandatory legislation provides that all children with disabilities be given a free and appropriate public education

Friendly text. A text that features elements that support student learning

Full inclusion. A movement that advocates educating all students with disabilities in the general education classroom full-time

Full-service schools. Schools that serve as hubs for educational, psychological, physical, financial, social, and health-related services for communities by housing health centers, social service and employment agencies, and adult education organizations

Functional assessment. Involves analyses of the skills needed to complete a particular activity or task

Functional practice. Relevant practice that helps students to easily see the connection between what they are practicing and its use in real life

Funds of knowledge. The information and resources available in the student's home community

Gangs. Groups of individuals working to unlawful or antisocial ends

Giftedness. Evidence of high performance capability in areas such as intelligence, creativity, art, or leadership, or in specific academic fields, that requires services or activities not ordinarily provided by the school in order to more fully develop these capabilities

Graphic organizers. Adaptations to textbook materials that help students better learn important concepts

Grapho-phonic cues. Cues that have to do with written symbols of language and their relationships to the sound system of language

Group behavior. Behaviors displayed in the presence of other group members

Hanover method. A system for teaching cursive writing, based on the similarities of letters or letter families

Hard of hearing. Describes a person with a mild to moderate loss of hearing

Heterogeneous grouping. The practice of putting students with a range of achievement levels together for instruction (also called *mixed-ability grouping*)

Higher order thinking. Involves problem solving, decision making, creative thinking, critical thinking, and investigation

High-frequency words. Words that occur frequently in spoken language and in written text

Homogeneous grouping. The practice of putting students at approximately the same achievement level together for instruction (also called *same-ability grouping*)

Human Immunodeficiency Virus (HIV). A condition that infects and eventually destroys cells in the immune system that protect the body from disease

Hyperactivity. Refers to a group of behaviors associated with restlessness and excess motor activity

Ignoring on purpose. A method of eliminating a student's undesirable behavior by purposely removing the teacher's and other students' attention to that behavior

Immaturity. Behaviors that include lack of perseverance, failure to finish tasks, short attention span, poor concentration, and frequent day dreaming or preoccupation

Impulsivity. Refers to a group of behaviors associated with an inability to control one's own actions

Inattention. Refers to difficulty sustaining attention

In-class programs. Programs that use the general education classroom as the primary setting for instruction (sometimes called *pull-in programs*)

Inclusion. The situation in which students with disabilities are educated with their nondisabled peers, with special education supports and services provided as needed

Inclusion support teacher. A teacher whose responsibilities include supporting students with disabilities (e.g., mental retardation, severe disabilities, physical disabilities, visual impairments) in general education classrooms

Independent learning. Occurs when students work and learn without assistance from others

Individualized education program (IEP). A written plan, developed to meet the special learning needs of each student with disabilities

Individualized family service plan (IFSP). A plan, for children from birth to 3 years of age, developed to meet not only the special needs of each student with disabilities but also those of his or her family

Individuals with Disabilities Education Act (IDEA). Legislation designed to ensure that all children with disabilities receive an appropriate education through special education and related services

Informal member checks. A form of monitoring student understanding that involves frequent, quick observations by teachers to determine whether students are comprehending the current lesson

Instructional clarity. The clear, direct, and explicit presentation of information

Instructional congruence. Occurs between general education and remedial programs and is necessary for determining what type of remedial instruction is most appropriate for an individual student

Instructional conversations. Discussions that make visible the thinking processes needed for understanding

Instructional design. The way the content is taught—how skills and concepts are introduced, developed, and reinforced

Instructional devices. The number of learning tools an author provides (examples include a table of contents, marginal annotations, and a glossary)

Instructional unit. A series of lessons related to the same topic

Intellectual functioning. An individual's overall mental abilities

Intellectually gifted. Students who are exceptional learners and tend to excel both in the classroom and on standardized tests, but are not homogeneous in their thinking strategies

Interactive planning. Involves monitoring students' learning and making adaptations in response to their needs

Interdisciplinary thematic units. The teaching of several subject areas around a central theme

Internalizing behaviors. Behaviors such as shyness, withdrawal, or depression that tend to be less readily observable that impact negatively the individual exhibiting the behaviors

Interpersonal problem solving. A strategy for teaching students to identify their problems, goals, and a wide range of alternatives for effectively solving their problems

Invented spelling. Children's early attempts to spell in their own way

Job developer. An individual who coordinates transition services (e.g., the transition into a job or career), usually for older students with disabilities

Key Math Teach and Practice. A program designed to provide remedial practice in, and diagnosis of, math difficulties

K–W–L strategy. A strategy (based on research underscoring the importance of activating prior knowledge before reading) to help students become actively engaged in comprehension before, during, and after reading

Language disorders. A major area of communication disorders

Language use. The pragmatics of language.

Language variation. Refers to the fact that language varies from place to place and from group to group

Learner characteristics. The third factor affecting second language acquisition or output: includes the age at which students learn a second language, their aptitude for learning language, their purposes and degree of motivation for learning the second language, their self-confidence in language learning, and the learning strategies they have for learning language

Least restrictive environment (LRE). The instructional setting most like that of nondisabled peers that also meets the educational needs of each student with disabilities

Legal blindness. Describes an individual who with the best possible correction in the better eye has a measured visual acuity of 20/200 or worse, or a visual field restricted to 20 degrees or less

Lesson Planning Pyramid. A framework for lesson planning that helps teachers consider individual student needs within the context of planning for the class as a whole

Linguistic input. Refers to the type of input received when listening or reading in a second language

Long-term planning. Planning for the term or the entire school year

Low vision. Describes an individual who is either partially sighted or legally blind

Macroculture. The core culture in a school

Magnet schools. Designated elementary or secondary schools that serve as centers for the education of gifted and talented students

Mainstream Assistance Team. A prescriptive approach to problem solving in which a specialist (e.g., the special education teacher) serves as consultant and the classroom teacher as the consultee

Mainstreaming. The participation of students with disabilities in general education classrooms to the extent appropriate for meeting their needs

Maintenance bilingual education. Attempts to foster the students' first language and strengthen their sense of cultural identity

Making Words. A whole-class guided activity that helps students develop phonological awareness and become more sensitive to common spelling patterns

Manuscript writing. Print writing

Mastery. Occurs when accuracy, speed, and knowledge have met expectations

McGill Action Planning System (MAPS). A planning activity that fosters relationships in order to improve the quality of life for persons with severe disabilities while facilitating participation in inclusive settings

Memory problems. Occur when students forget or misremember a fact; lead to errors in arithmetic calculation and other areas

Memory strategies. Mental techniques for increasing students' abilities to memorize information and utilize information in memory

Mental retardation. Characterizes individuals who have limited intellectual functioning that affects their learning

Mentoring programs. Volunteer efforts that structure partnerships between a student and an adult who can offer guidance and support

Mentorship. Process in which one individual uses his or her experience and knowledge to guide another individual or group of individuals

Metacognition. Knowing about thinking strategies and when to use them

Metadiscourse. The degree to which the author "talks" to the reader; includes direct explanations of how to learn from the text and how to connect ideas from one part of the text to another

Metalinguistics. Involves thinking about, analyzing, and reflecting upon language as an object in much the same way one reflects on tables or friends

Microcultures. Home cultures based on such factors as national origin, ethnicity, socioeconomic class, religion, gender, age, and disability

Milliken Wordmath. Uses computer programs to teach problem-solving strategies within the mathematics curriculum to students in fourth grade and up who have been unsuccessful in adequately learning problem-solving skills

Mistaken goal. Evidenced when students display inappropriate behavior because they believe it will get them the recognition and acceptance they desire

Mixed-ability grouping. (See *heterogeneous grouping*)

Mobility skills. Skills such as going up and down stairs, crossing streets, and using public transportation

Modeling. A technique for teaching language that involves following examples illustrated by others

Monitoring. A form of checking-in with students that helps teachers keep in touch with what students are learning and sensitive to students' difficulties

Morpheme. The smallest unit of language that conveys meaning

Morphology. Focuses on the rule system that governs the structure of words and word forms

Motor excess. Students who display restless, overactive behavior; also referred to as *hyperactivity*

Moving model. Modeling to students how to form letters and words in order to develop their legibility

Multicultural education. An educational reform movement whose major goal is to change the structure of educational institutions so that male and female students, exceptional students, and students who are members of diverse racial, ethnic, and cultural groups have an equal chance to achieve in school

Multidimensional traits. The concept that a variety of individual characteristics and traits define intelligence

Multidisciplinary team (MDT). This group of individuals usually includes a representative of the local education agency, the classroom teacher, the special education teacher, parents or guardians and, when appropriate, the student, who together develop and implement the IEP

Multiple causation theory. Suggests that although some students may be at risk due to one primary condition, quite often multiple conditions interact to compound learning challenges

Multiple disabilities. Describes individuals who have severe or profound mental retardation and one or more significant motor or sensory impairments and/or special health needs

Multiple intelligences. Theory that human beings are capable of exhibiting intelligence in seven domains: linguistic, logical-mathematical, spatial, musical, bodily-kinesthetic, interpersonal (i.e., discerning and responding to the needs of others), and intrapersonal (i.e., having detailed and accurate self-knowledge)

Multiple meanings. Applies to words that have more than one meaning

Muscular dystrophy (MD). A chronic disorder characterized by the weakening and wasting of the body's muscles

Mutual Interest Discovery. A strategy for increasing peer acceptance of students with special needs in the general education classroom by pairing students who do not know each other so that they have a structured opportunity to discover things they have in common

Narrative writing. Writing stories

NCTM standards. Recommended changes to the mathematics curriculum and suggestions for mathematics instruction

Negative reinforcement. The removal of a stimulus to increase responding

Neurological impairment. A disability caused by a dysfunction of the brain, spinal cord, and nerves, thereby creating transmission of improper instructions, uncontrolled bursts of instructions from the brain, or incorrect interpretation of feedback to the brain

Neuromuscular diseases. Disorders that involve both the nerves and muscles

Noncompliance. Failure to comply with the law; the Individuals with Disabilities Act requires that states mandate consequences for noncompliance

Nondiscriminatory evaluation. An evaluation that does not discriminate on the basis of language, culture, and student's background; must be provided for each individual assessed for special education

Nonverbal math disabilities. Students who display good reading and verbal expression but who have extreme difficulty with mathematics

One-to-one correspondence. Situation in which each object corresponds to another object

Open question. A question that allows a full range of responses and discourages short "yes" or "no" answers

Organization (of text). How the author orders information in the text; includes general structure of the text as well as the consistency and connectedness of ideas

Orientation skills. Includes understanding one's own body, one's position in space, and abstract concepts such as the layout of a city block

Orthopedic impairment. Includes deficits caused by congenital anomaly (e.g., clubfoot, absence of some member), impairments caused by disease (e.g., poliomyelitis, bone tuberculosis), and impairments from other causes (e.g., cerebral palsy, amputations, and fractures or burns that cause contractures)

Other health impairments (OHI). Limited strength, vitality, or alertness (caused by chronic or acute health problems such as heart condition, tuberculosis, rheumatic fever, nephritis, asthma, sickle cell anemia, hemophilia, epilepsy, lead poisoning, leukemia, or diabetes), that adversely affects a student's educational performance

Parallel talk. A process in which the teacher describes what students are doing or thinking

Parent participation. Involvement of parents in all aspects of identifying and evaluating students with disabilities, including decision making

Partial participation. A concept that assumes an individual has the right to participate, to the extent possible, in all activities

Partially sighted. Describes an individual who with best possible correction in the better eye has a measured visual acuity between 20/70 and 20/200

Peer Collaboration Model. Developed to help classroom teachers solve problems by providing time and structure to do so

Peer editing. Students revise and edit each other's work

Peer tutoring. One student in a pair acts as a teacher for the other student

Pervasive developmental disorder. Characterized by students who express far-fetched, unusual, or unbelievable ideas

Phoneme. The smallest unit of speech sound

Phonemic awareness. The understanding of how to listen to and produce sounds

Phonemic Pairs. A strategy designed to help students learn to read and spell words; pairs of students work together to analyze words by looking at alliteration and rhyme

Phonics instruction. The systematic teaching of the alphabetic principle and the way spelling patterns relate to sound patterns

Phonological awareness. Possession of skills such as rhyming, alliteration, blending, and segmentation

Phonology. Focuses on the sounds of language and the rules that determine how the sounds fit together

Ping pong discussion. The typical back-and-forth exchange in which a teacher asks a question and a student answers

Planning Pyramid. A framework for unit planning, aimed at meeting diverse student needs

PLEASE. A strategy developed to provide students with a step-by-step procedure for paragraph writing

Positive reinforcement. The presentation of a stimulus (verbal response, physical response such as touching, or tangible response such as a reward) following the target behavior to maintain or increase the target behavior

Postplanning. Follow-up planning that comes at the end of a lesson and allows teachers to reflect about how students performed and to use this information to guide their planning for subsequent instruction

Post-writing. Process in which authors revise, edit, and publish their written work

Pragmatics. Refers to the purposes or functions of communication or how we use language to communicate

Prelearning activities. Strategies teachers use to activate students' prior knowledge and to preteach vocabulary and concepts—essentially, to prepare students to learn

Premack principle. Provides the opportunity for behaviors that are desirable to both teachers and students to serve as reinforcers for other behaviors that are more desirable to teachers than students

Preplanning. Advanced preparation that involves decisions about what to teach and how to teach it

Prereferral assistance team (PAT). A group of teachers from the same school who meet regularly to discuss the specific progress of students brought to their attention by other teachers in the school

Prewriting. Process in which a writer collects information about a topic through observing, remembering, interviewing, and reading

Print-rich environment. The physical environment of the classroom communicates to students that the classroom is a place to read

Procedural congruence. A common understanding of the schedules and policies between classroom and remedial teachers that allows for improved communication

Procedural error. Occurs when a student misapplies a procedure from one arithmetic operation to another

Process goals. Goals that incorporate not only the skills students are expected to learn to become proficient readers (e.g., phonological awareness, word recognition, reading comprehension), but also metacognitive strategies that empower individuals to reflect about understanding

Production. A person's ability to convey the intended message

Project Math. A math curriculum designed specifically for students with mild disabilities

Public Law 94–142. This legislation, designed to ensure that all children with disabilities receive an appropriate education through special education and related services, was originally referred to as the Education for All Handicapped Children Act, enacted in 1975, and later reauthorized and expanded as the Individuals with Disabilities Education Act (IDEA)

Publishing. Preparing a written work in a way that enables others to read it

Pull-out programs. Programs in which children are literally pulled out of their general education classroom for supplemental instruction in basic skills

Punishment. The opposite of reinforcement, in that it follows a behavior and decreases the strength of the behavior or the likelihood the behavior will continue to occur

Purpose-setting activities. Give students a reason to complete a reading assignment or listen to a lecture

Question-Answering Relationships Strategy. A strategy for teaching students how to answer different types of comprehension questions

Readability level. The level of difficulty of a textbook

Reading comprehension. The ability to understand individual words, phrases and clauses, sentences, paragraphs, and larger units of text

Reading Recovery. An early intervention program based on the work of Marie Clay, of New Zealand; involves individual tutoring of low-achieving first grade students for thirty minutes a day

Real content. The main idea or key information that someone wants to convey

Real Life Math Program. Focuses on teaching students with learning difficulties the mathematics skills they need for daily life

Receptive language. A person's ability to understand what is being communicated

Reciprocal causation. The combination of factors related to a student's reading problems

Reciprocal Teaching. A strategy for reading comprehension, designed to be used with small, teacher-facilitated groups

Register. A language style the speaker uses to communicate to meet the needs or expectations of the speaker. Includes such features as choice of words, sentences, intonation, and formality.

Regular Education Initiative (REI). A concept that promotes coordination of services between regular and special education

Related services. The types of services to which students with disabilities are entitled, including: speech therapy, audiology, psychological services, physical therapy, occupational therapy, recreation, early identification and assessment, counseling, medical services for diagnostic or evaluation purposes, school health services, transportation, and social work services

Remediation. Additional instruction for students who do not demonstrate, at an expected rate, competency in basic skills in reading, writing, and mathematics

Repeated readings. Process of reading passages over and over again to develop fluency in reading

Residual hearing. Usable hearing

Retention. The practice of having a student repeat a grade level because of low academic performance

Revising. Stage of writing during which points are explored further, ideas are elaborated, and further connections are made

Rhyming. Identifying similarities and differences in word endings

Roots and Wings. A learning program that adds guidelines for an integrated approach to other content areas, such as science and social studies

Same-ability grouping. (See *homogeneous grouping*)

Scaffolding instruction. Instruction that involves successively more difficult content and process levels

Schoolwide Enrichment Model. Learning strategy in which a large portion of the school population is given the opportunity to participate in enrichment activities

School-wide programs. Policies that affect every classroom and student in a school

Secondary language output. The level of proficiency in producing (speaking and writing) a language

Segmentation. Process of dividing ideas into words, and words into syllables and individual phonemes

Self-injurious behavior. A behavior that may consist of head banging, scratching, or biting oneself

Self-management. Skills that enable students to be more aware of their own behaviors and to govern the reinforcers for their behaviors

Self-questioning. A learning strategy in which students are first taught the concept of a main idea

Self-recording. A form of self-monitoring for improving students' academic performance

Self-talk. A technique in which the teacher describes what he or she is doing or thinking

Semantic cues. Relate to readers' understanding of the meaning of concepts and their interrelationships

Semantic feature analysis. A vocabulary-enhancement procedure that involves the placement of categories or critical features along one axis and the specific vocabulary along the other axis

Semantic mapping. A prelearning activity for increasing students' comprehension

Semantics. The content of language

Sensory channels. The means through which individuals perceive stimuli

Severe disabilities. Conditions that significantly affect typical life activities

Sheltered English. A type of ESL instruction in which the goal is to teach English language skills at the same time that students are learning content area information

Sight Word Association Procedure. A learning technique that helps students associate spoken words with their printed forms

Silent or nonverbal period. A time during which children are absorbing information and language that they cannot or do not yet feel comfortable demonstrating

Situational factors. Factors related to the context or situation in which the second language learning occurs

SLAM. A strategy for teaching students to act and respond appropriately to negative feedback from others

SMARTER. The acronym used to remember the six steps of the Course Planning Routine

Social action approach. Incorporates all the elements of the transformation approach, but also includes cultural critique and problem solving that requires students to make decisions and take actions related to the concept, issue, or problem being studied

Social competence. Those responses that prove effective in a given situation or, in other words, maximize the probability of producing, maintaining, or enhancing positive effects for the interactor

Social content. The values represented in a textbook

Social learning. Involves observing and modeling or imitating the behavior of others

Socialized-aggression. Refers to students who routinely engage in antisocial behavior

Special education resource room. A placement outside the general education classroom where students with disabilities receive specialized, individualized, and intensive instruction to meet their needs

Specific learning disabilities. Represents a heterogeneous group of students who, despite adequate cognitive functioning and the ability to learn some skills and strategies quickly and easily, have great difficulty learning other skills and strategies

Speech disorders. Disorders that involve unintelligible or unpleasant communication

Spelling patterns. Common word patterns such as base words, prefixes, suffixes, consonants, consonant blends, digraphs, and vowel sound-symbol associations

Spina bifida. A birth defect that occurs when the spinal cord fails to close properly

Spiral curriculum. Occurs when the same skills (e.g., mathematics skills) are woven into every year of school and students continually repeat knowledge acquisition in the same area

Stereotypic behavior. Behaviors that characterize a disorder or condition such as rocking, flapping fingers, twirling or spinning objects, and grinding teeth

Stimulant medications. Medications frequently used in the treatment of ADD

Stimulus. Something that incites activity or attention

Story retellings. Technique that actively involves students in the oral or written reconstruction of stories they have read or heard

Story webs. Developed as visual displays to help students understand the structure of the stories they read

Structural analysis. Involves the use of root words, prefixes, and suffixes to determine the pronunciation and meaning of a word, including multisyllable words and merged words such as compounds (buttermilk, pancake) and contractions (don't, can't)

Structural Arithmetic. Involves students in kindergarten through third grade in discovering and learning math concepts and facts

Structured overviews. The provision of an organized overview of material before reading

Student acceleration. The rapid movement of students through their years of schooling

Student-centered model. An educational model in which students have ample opportunity to create personal meaning from what they are reading and writing

Student-related factors. Factors (which can and should influence the planning process) that pertain to who individual students are, how they learn, and how they respond to instruction—both academically and socially

Students at risk. Students who fail to succeed academically and who require additional instruction

Study guides. Tools teachers can use to lead students through a reading assignment

Stuttering. The most common fluency disorder, involving an interruption of the forward flow of speech

Success for All. A program that targets children in grades K–3 and involves a high degree of collaboration between remedial and general educators and parents

Summarization Strategy. Requires the student to generate the main idea and important details from a text

Syntactic cues. Relate to the grammatical structure of language

Syntax. Focuses on the rules that govern the order of words in sentences

Systems of support. Refers to the coordinated set of services and accommodations matched to the student's needs

TAG. A strategy for students to provide each other with feedback about their writing

Talent pool approach. Procedure used to avoid overlooking students with exceptional talents and abilities who might not be identified through IQ tests or teacher nominations alone

Task analysis. A breakdown of each individual step or skill, with the necessary adaptations, that will be used as a guide for teaching the step or skill to the student

Teacher assistance team (TAT). A group of teachers who provide initial strategies and support for fellow classroom teachers prior to referring a student for assessment for special education services

Teacher-related factors. Factors that pertain to teachers as planners for their classes as a whole, as well as for students with special needs

Team-Assisted Individualization. Provision of individualized instruction within a cooperative learning model

Thematic interdisciplinary approach. Combines structured, sequential, and well-organized strategies, activities, children's literature, and materials to expand a particular concept

Think alouds. A way to model how to think and learn

Think-pair-share. A method that can be used during monitoring activities and that yields high student involvement and verbal interaction

Time-out. Time during which the student is removed from the opportunity to receive reinforcement

Title I. A law that provides funds for additional teachers, paraprofessionals, and instructional materials for qualified students

Token system. A system in which students receive tokens in exchange for meeting classroom objectives and can exchange the tokens for rewards

Topic-related factors. Factors that directly concern the topic of instruction

Touch Math. A program for teaching students math skills through math strategies (including the touch-point, counting-on, count-off, and count-by strategies)

Tracking. The practice of placing students with similar needs together for extended periods of the school day

Transdisciplinary teaming. Refers to a group of experts working together and viewing the student as a whole instead of working independently in a single specialty area

Transformation approach. The basic core of the curriculum is changed, and goals focus on viewing events, concepts, and themes from multiple perspectives, based on diversity

Transitional bilingual education. Helps students shift from the home language to the dominant language

Traumatic brain injury. An injury to the brain, caused by an external physical force, that causes total or partial functional disability or psychosocial impairment, or both, which adversely affects a student's educational performance

Tutoring. A systematic plan for supplementing the student's educational program

Two-tiered instruction. A method of teaching reading in which all students use grade-level material for some instruction (Tier 1), and comfort-level materials (Tier 2) for some instruction

Two-way bilingual programs. A program in which half the students are native speakers of English and the other half speak another language, usually Spanish. Instruction is delivered in English half the time, and in the other language the other half

Underachievers. Individuals who have high academic or creative potential but low academic or creative performance

Unidimensional traits. The concept that human intelligence is made up of a unitary element

Unit Planning Pyramid. A flexible framework that teachers can adjust to their personal style of planning and teaching, and that enhances the learning of all students (see Lesson Planning Pyramid)

Vibrant discussions. Discussions in which student participation is high, students' thinking is stimulated, and students have opportunities to connect what they are learning to their personal knowledge and experience

Visual acuity. The clarity with which an individual can see an object from a distance of 20 feet

Visual detail. Ability to perceive details in the visual field. Difficulties in this area may lead to academic problems such as misreading an aspect of an arithmetic problem.

Visual field. How well an individual can see using peripheral or side vision

Vocabulary. An individual's working knowledge of words

Vocational Rehabilitation Act. This act (Public Law 93–112), prevents any private organization that uses federal funds, or any local or state organization, from discriminating against persons with disabilities solely on the basis of those disabilities

Voice disorders. Disorders that relate to the quality of the voice itself

Whole-class grouping. A grouping strategy in which the group comprises all students in the class

Whole language. A philosophy of reading instruction that emphasizes teacher and student empowerment and authenticity of reading materials

Within-class same-ability grouping. Occurs when students with the same abilities and from the same classroom are placed together for instruction

Word identification. A strategy for recognizing words involved in reading

Word retrieval. Finding words from memory

Zero reject. An element of IDEA which states that no child with disabilities can be excluded from receiving a free and appropriate education

REFERENCES

Accardo, P., Blondis, T., & Whitman, B. (1991). *Attentional deficit disorders and hyperactivity in children.* New York: Marcel Dekker.

Achenbach, T. M., & Edelbrock, C. S. (1981). Behavior problems and competencies reported by parents of normal and disturbed children aged four through sixteen. *Monographs of the Society for Research in Child Development, 46* (1 Serial No. 188).

Adams, M. J. (1990). *Beginning to read: Thinking and learning about print.* Cambridge, MA: MIT Press.

Adams, A., Carnine, D., & Gersten, R. (1982). Instructional strategies for studying content area texts in the intermediate grades. *Reading Research Quarterly, 18,* 27–55.

Adderholdt-Eliot, M., Algozzine, K., Algozzine, B., & Haney, K. (1991). Current state practices in educating students who are gifted and talented. *Roeper Review, 14* (1), 20–23.

Agar, M. H. (1980). *The professional stranger: An informal introduction to ethnography.* Orlando: Academic Press.

Allan, S. D. (1991). Ability-grouping research reviews: What do they say about grouping and the gifted? *Educational Leadership, 48* (6), 60–65.

Allington, R. L. (1983). The reading instruction provided readers of differing ability. *Elementary School Journal, 83,* 548–559.

Alvermann, D. E. (1991). The discussion web: A graphic aid for learning across the curriculum. *The Reading Teacher, 45* (2), 92–99.

Alvermann, D. E., Dillon, D. R., & O'Brien, D. G. (1987). *Using discussion to promote reading comprehension.* Newark, DE: International Reading Association.

Alverman, D. E., O'Brien, D. G., & Dillon, D. R. (1989). What teachers do when they say they're having discussion of content reading assignments: A qualitative analysis. *Research Reading Quarterly, 25,* 296–322.

Alvermann, D. E., & Moore, D. W. (1991). Secondary school reading. In R. Barr, M. L. Kamil, P. B. Mosenthal, and P. D. Pearson (Eds.), *Handbook of reading research Vol. 2.* (pp. 951–983). New York: Longman.

American Association on Mental Retardation. (1992). *Mental retardation: Definition, classification, and systems of supports* (9th ed.). Washington, DC: Author.

American Printing House for the Blind. (1993). *Annual report of the American Printing House for the Blind, Inc.: July, 1992–June 30, 1993.* Louisville, KY: American Printing House for the Blind.

American Psychiatric Association. (1994). *Diagnostic and statistical manual of mental disorders* (4th ed.). Washington, DC: Author.

American Speech-Language-Hearing Association. (1993). Definitions: Communicative disorders and variations, *ASHA, 35* (Suppl. 10), 40–41.

American Speech-Language-Hearing Association Committee on Prevention of Speech-Language and Hearing Problems. (1984). Prevention: A challenge for the profession. *ASHA, 26,* 35–37.

Amish, P. L., Gesten, E. L., Smith, J. K., Clark, H. B., & Stark, C. (1988). Social problem-solving training for severely emotionally and behaviorally disturbed children. *Behavioral Disorders, 13* (3), 175–186.

Anders, P. L., & Guzzetti, B. J. (1996). *Literacy instruction in the content areas.* Fort Worth, TX: Harcourt Brace.

Andersen, E., Dunlea, A., & Kekelis, L. S. (1984). Blind children's language: Resolving some differences. *Journal of Student Language, 11* (3), 645–664.

Anderson, R. C. (1977). The notion of schemata and the educational enterprise. In R. C. Anderson, R. J. Spiro, & W. E. Montague (Eds.), *Schooling and the acquisition of knowledge* (pp. 415–431). Hillsdale, NJ: Erlbaum.

Anderson, R. C., Hiebert, E. H., Scott, J. A., & Wilkinson, I. A. (1985). *Becoming a nation of readers. The report of the commission on reading* (pp.7). Washington, DC: National Institute of Education.

Anderson, R. C., Reynolds, R. E., Schallert, D. L., & Goetz, E. T. (1977). Frameworks for comprehending discourse. *American Educational Research Journal, 14,* 367–382.

Anderson, T. H., & Armbruster, B. B. (1986). *The value of taking notes* (Reading Education Report No. 374). Champaign, IL: University of Illinois, Center for the Study of Reading.

Anthony, P., & Jacobson, S. L. (1992). *Helping at-risk students: What are the educational and financial costs?* Newbury Park, CA: Corwin Press.

Appleton, N. (1983). *Cultural pluralism in edcuation.* New York: Longman.

Armbruster, B. B., & Anderson, T. H. (1988). On selecting "considerate" content area textbooks. *Remedial and Special Education, 9,* 47–52.

Aronson, E., Stephan, C., Sikes, J., Blaney, N., and Snapp, M. (1978). *The jigsaw classroom.* Beverly Hills, CA: Sage.

Atwell, N. (1984). Writing and reading literature from the inside out. *Language Arts, 61,* 240–252.

Atwell, N. (1985). Writing and reading from the inside out. In J. Hansen, T. Newkirk, & D. Graves (Eds.), *Breaking ground: Teachers relate reading and writing in the elementary school.* (pp. 147–168). Portsmouth, NH: Heinemann.

Atwell, N. (1987). *In the middle: Writing, reading, and learning with adolescents.* Portsmouth, NH: Boynton/ Cook.

Au, K. (1993). *Literacy instruction in multicultural settings.* Fort Worth, TX: Harcourt Brace Jovanovich.

Ausubel, D. P., & Robinson, F. G. (1969). *School learning: An introduction to educational psychology.* New York: Holt, Rinehart and Winston.

Babad, E., Bernieri, F., & Rosenthal, R. (1991). Students as judges of teachers' verbal and nonverbal behavior. *American Educational Research Journal, 28,* 211–234.

Badian, N. A., & Ghublikian, M. (1983). The personal-social characteristics of children with poor mathematical computation skills. *Journal of Learning Disabilities, 16* (3), 154–157.

Baker, C. (1993). *Foundations of bilingual education and bilingualism.* Clevedon, England: Multilingual Matters.

Baker, J. M., & Zigmond, N. (1990). Are regular education classes equipped to accommodate students with learning disabilities? *Exceptional Children, 56,* 515–526.

Balla, D. A., & Zigler, E. (1979). Personality development in retarded persons. In N. R. Ellis (Ed.). *Handbook of mental deficiency: Psychological theory and research* (2nd ed., pp. 154–168). Hillsdale, NJ: Erlbaum.

Ballard, W. S., & Tighe, P. L. (Eds.). (1987). *Idea language proficiency test* (Level I & II). Brea, CA: Ballard & Tighe, Inc.

Bandura, A. (1971). *Psychological modeling.* Chicago: Aldine/Atherton.

Bandura, A. (1973). *Agression: A social learning analysis.* Englewood Cliffs, NJ: Prentice-Hall.

Bangert-Drowns, R. L. (1993). The word processor as an instructional tool: A meta-analysis of word processing in writing instruction. *Review of Education Research, 63,* 69–93.

Banks, J. A. (1981). (Ed.) *Education in the 80s: Multiethnic education.* Washington, DC: National Education Association.

Banks, J. A. (1991a). *Teaching strategies for ethnic studies* (5th ed.). Boston: Allyn & Bacon.

Banks, J. A. (1991b). The dimensions of multicultural education. *Multicultural Leader, 1,* 4.

Banks, J. A. (1993a). Multicultural education: Characteristics and goals. In J. A. Banks and C. A. Banks (Eds.), *Multicultural education: Issues and perspectives* (2nd ed., pp. 1–28). Boston: Allyn & Bacon.

Banks, J. A. (1993b). Approaches to multicultural curriculum reform. In J. A. Banks and C. A. Banks (Eds.), *Multicultural education: Issues and perspectives* (2nd ed., pp. 195–214). Boston: Allyn & Bacon.

Banks, J. A., & Banks, C. A. M. (Eds.) (1995). *Handbook of research on multicultural education.* New York: Macmillan.

Barkley, R. A. (1990). *Attention deficit hyperactivity disorder: A handbook for diagnosis and treatment.* New York: Guilford.

Baroody, A., & Ginsburg, H. (1991). A cognitive approach to assessing the mathematical difficulties of children labeled "learning disabled." In H. L. Swanson (Ed.), *Handbook on the assessment of learning disabilities* (pp. 117–228). Austin: Pro-Ed.

Barr, R. (1995). What research says about grouping in the past and present and what it suggests about the future. In M. C. Radencich & L. J. McKay (Eds.), *Flexible grouping for literacy in the elementary grades* (pp. 1–24). Boston: Allyn & Bacon.

Barr, R., & Dreeben, R. (1991). Grouping students for reading instruction. In R. Barr, M. Kamil, P. Mosenthal, & P. D. Pearson (Eds.), *Handbook of reading research: Vol. 2. Literacy and schooling* (pp. 885–910). New York: Longman.

Barr, R. D., & Parrett, W. H. (1995). *Hope at last for at-risk youth.* Boston: Allyn & Bacon.

Barraga, N. C., & Erin, J. N. (1992). *Visual handicaps and learning* (3rd ed.). Austin, TX: Pro Ed.

Bauwens, J., Hourcade, J. J., & Friend, M. (1989). Cooperative teaching: A model for general and special education integration. *Remedial and Special Education, 10* (2), 17–22.

Bean, T. W. (1985). Classroom questioning: Directions for applied research. In A. C. Graesser & J. Black (Eds.), *Psychology of questions* (pp. 335–358). Hilsdale, NJ: Erlbaum.

Bean, R. M., Cooley, W. W., Eichelberger, R. T., Lazar, M. K., & Zigmond, N. (1991). Inclass or pullout: Effects of setting on the remedial reading program. *Journal of Reading Behavior, 23* (4), 425–444.

Beck, I., & McKeown, M. G. (1981). Developing questions that promote comprehension: The story map. *Language Arts, 58,* 913–918.

Beirne-Smith, M. (1991). Peer tutoring in arithmetic for children with learning disabilities. *Exceptional Children, 57* (4). 330–337.

Beirne-Smith, M., Patton, J., & Ittenbach, R. (1994). *Mental retardation.* (4th. ed.). New York: MacMillan College Publishing.

Belenky, M. F., Clinchy, B. M., Goldberger, N. R., Tarule, J. M. (1986). *Women's ways of knowing: The development of self, voice, and mind.* New York: Basic Books.

Belman, A., Diamond, G., Dickson, D., Horoupian, D., Llena, J., & Rubinstein, A. (1988). Pediatric acquired immunodeficiency syndrome: Neurological syndromes. *American Journal of Diseases of Children, 142,* 29–35.

Benbow, C. P. (1992). Meeting the needs of the gifted in rural areas through acceleration. *Gifted Child Today, 15* (2), 15–19.

Bennett, C. I. (1995). *Comprehensive multicultural education: Theory and practice* (3rd ed.). Boston: Allyn & Bacon.

Bereiter, C., & Scardamalia, M. (1982). From conversation to composition. In R. Glaser (Eds.), *Advances in instructional psychology: Volume 2.* Hillsdale, NJ: Erlbaum.

Berger, S. L. (1994) *College planning for gifted students.* Reston, VA: Council for Exceptional Children.

Bergeron, B. (1990). What does the term whole language mean? Constructing a definition from the literature. *Journal of Reading Behavior, 22,* 301–329.

Berler, E. S., Gross, A. M., & Drabman, R. S. (1982). Social skills training with children: Proceed with caution. *Journal of Applied Behavior Analysis, 15,* 41–53.

Berliner, D. C., & Casanova, U. (1993). *Putting research to work in your school.* New York: Scholastic.

Berner, R. (1977). What parents and teachers should know about death education. *DOPHHH Journal, 3,* 17–21.

Bernstein, D. K., & Tiegerman, E. (1993). *Language and communication disorders in children* (3rd. ed.). New York: MacMillan.

Bierman, K. L., & Furman, W. (1984). The effects of social skills training and peer involvement on the social adjustment of preadolescents. *Child Development, 55,* 151–162.

Bigge, J. L. (1991). *Teaching individuals with physical and multiple disabilities* (3rd ed.). New York: Macmillan.

Bishop, D. V. M., & Adams, C. (1992). Comprehension problems in children with specific language impairments: Literal and inferential meaning. *Journal of Speech and Hearing Research, 35,* 119–129.

Blachman, B. A. (1989). Phonological awareness and word recognition: Assessment and intervention. In A. G. Kamhi & H. W. Catts (Eds.), *Reading disabilities: A developmental perspective.* San Diego: College-Hill.

Blankenship, T. (1984). Update: These school systems swear by the four-day school week because students work harder and face fewer distractions. *American School Board Journal, 171* (8), 32–33.

Blanton, W. E., Wood, K. D., & Moorman, G. B. (1990). *The role of purpose in reading instruction. The Reading Teacher, 43* (7), 486–493.

Bley, N. S., & Thornton, C. A. (1995). *Teaching mathematics to students with learning disabilities* (3rd ed.). Austin: Pro-Ed.

Bliatout, B., Downing, B., Lewis, J., & Yang, D. (1988). *Handbook for teaching Hmong-speaking students.* Folsom, CA; Folsom Cordova Unified School District, Southeast Asia Community Resource Center.

Bliss, C. (1965). *Semantography.* Sydney, AUS: Semantography Publications.

Block, C. C., & Zinke, J. A. (1995). *Creating a culturally enriched curriculum for grades K–6.* Boston: Allyn & Bacon.

Bloom, L., & Lahey, M. (1978). *Language development and language disorders.* New York: John Wiley.

Bloom, L., Miller, P., & Hood, L. (1975). Variation and reduction as aspects of competence in language development. In A. Pick (Ed.), *Minnesota symposium on child psychology* (Vol. 9). Minneapolis: University of Minnesota.

Boatner, M. T., Gates, J. E., & Makkai, A. (1975). *A dictionary of American idioms* (rev. ed.). Woodbury, NJ: Barron's.

Bode, B. A. (1989). Dialogue journal writing. *The Reading Teacher, 42,* 568–571.

Bond, G., & Dykstra, R. (1967). The cooperative research program in first-grade research instruction. *Reading Research Quarterly, 2,* 5–142.

Borkowski, J. G., Estrada, M. T., Milstead, M., & Hale, C. A. (1989). General problem-solving skills: Relations between metacognition and strategic processing. *Learning Disability Quarterly, 12,* 57–70.

Borkowski, J. G., Turner, L. A. (1990). Transsitutational characteristics of metacognition. In W. Schneider & F. E. Weinert (Eds.), *Interactions among aptitudes, strategies, and knowledge in cognitive performance* (pp. 159–176). New York: Springer-Verlag.

Borland, J. H. (1989). *Planning and implementing programs for the gifted.* New York: Teachers College Press.

Bos, C. S. (1987). *Promoting story comprehension using a story retelling strategy.* Paper presented at the annual meeting of the Arizona Association for Children with Learning Disabilities Conference, Phoenix.

Bos, C. S., & Anders, P. L. (1990). Effects of interactive vocabulary instruction on the vocabulary learning and reading comprehension of junior-high learning disabled students. *Learning Disability Quarterly, 13,* 31–42.

Bos, C. S., & Anders, P. L. (1990). Interactive teaching and learning: Instructional practices for teaching content and strategic knowledge. In T. E. Scruggs & B. Y. L. Wong (Eds.) *Intervention research in learning disabilities* (pp. 116–185). New York: Springer Verlag.

Bos, C. S., & Anders, P. L. (1992). A theory-driven interactive instructional model for text comprehension and content learning. In B. Y. L. Wong (Ed.), *Contemporary intervention research in learning disabilities: An international perspective.* (pp.81–95). New York: Springer-Verlag.

Bos, C. S., & Anders, P. L. (1992). Using interactive teaching and learning strategies to promote text comprehension and content learning for students with learning disabilities. *International Journal of Disability, Development, and Education, 39,* 225–238.

Bos, C. S., & Filip, D. (1984). Comprehension monitoring in learning disabled and average students. *Journal of Learning Disabilities, 17,* 229–233.

Bos, C. S., & Vaughn, S. (1994). *Strategies for teaching students with learning and behavior problems* (3rd ed.). Boston: Allyn & Bacon.

Bos, C. S., & Vaughn, S. (1994). *Teaching students with learning and behavior problems* (3rd ed.). Boston: Allyn & Bacon.

Bradley, J. M. (1975). *Sight word association procedure.* Unpublished manuscript, College of Education, University of Arizona, Tucson.

Bradley, L., & Bryant, P. E. (1983). Categorizing sounds and learning to read: A causal connection. *Nature, 301,* 419–421.

Bradley, L., & Bryant, P. E. (1985). *Rhyme and reason in reading and spelling.* IARLD Monograph No. 1. Ann Arbor: University of Michigan Press.

Bragstad, B. J., & Stumpf, S. M. (1982). *A guidebook for teaching study skills and motivation.* Boston: Allyn & Bacon.

Brandenburg, N. A., Friedman, R. M., & Silver, S. E. (1990). The epidemiology of childhood psychiatric disorders: Prevalence findings from recent studies. *Journal of the American Academy of Child and Adolescent Psychiatry, 29,* 76–83.

Brigance, A. H. (1981). *Brigance Diagnostic Inventory of Essential Skills.* North Billerica, MA: Curriculum Associates.

Brimer, R. W. (1990). *Students with severe disabilities: Current perspectives and practices.* Mountain View, CA: Mayfield Publishing.

Brooke, M. H. (1986). *A clinician's view of neuromuscular diseases* (2nd ed). Baltimore: Williams & Wilkins.

Brooks, G. (1985). The study of maturational timing effects in adolescence. *Journal of Youth and Adolescence, 14* (3), 149–161.

Brophy, J. (1981). Teacher praise: A functional analysis. *Review of Educational Research, 51,* 5–32.

Brophy, J. (1988). Educating teachers about managing classrooms and students. *Teacher and Teacher Education, 4,* 1–18.

Brown, A. L., & Day, J. D. (1983). Macrorules for summarizing texts: The development of expertise. *Journal of Verbal Learning and Verbal Behavior, 22,* 1–14.

Brozo, W. G. (1990). Hiding out in the secondary classroom: Coping strategies of unsuccessful readers. *Journal of Reading, 33,* 324–328.

Brunk, G. L. (1990). *Supporting the growth of the self-advocacy movement: What we can learn from its history and activists.* Unpublished manuscript, University of Kansas, Beach Center on Families and Disabilities.

Bryan, T., Pearl, R., & Herzog, A. (1989). Learning disabled adolescents' vulnerability to crime: Attitudes, anxieties, experiences. *Learning Disability Quarterly, 5,* 51–60.

Bryant, N. D., Drabin, I. R., & Gettinger, M. (1981). Effects of varying unit size on spelling achievement in learning disabled children. *Journal of Learning Disabilities, 14* (4), 200–203.

Bulgren, J., Schumaker, J. B., & Deshler, D. D. (1988). Effectiveness of a concept teaching routine in enhancing the performance of LD students in secondary-level mainstream classes. *Learning Disabilities Quarterly, 11,* 3–17.

Bullis, M., & Walker, H. M. (1994). *Comprehensive school-based systems for troubled youth.* Eugene, OR: University of Oregon, Center on Human Development.

Bullock, J. (1991). *Touch Math.* Colorado Springs: Innovative Learning Concepts.

Burke, J. C. (1992). *Decreasing classroom behavior problems: Practical guidelines for teachers.* San Diego, Ca: Singular.

Burt, , M., Dulay, H., & Hernández-Chávez, E. (1975, 1980). *Bilingual syntax measure* (Level I & II). San Antonio, TX: The Psychological Corporation.

Button, H. W., & Provenzo, E. F. (1983). *History of education and culture in America.* Englewood Cliffs, NJ: Prentice Hall.

Calfee, R., & Hiebert, E. (1991). Classroom assessment of reading. In R. Barr, M. L. Kamil, P. Mosenthal, & P. D. Pearson (Eds.), *Handbook of Reading Research: Vol. 2* (pp. 281–309). New York: Longman.

California Deaf–Blind Services (1992). *How to interact with individuals with dual sensory impairments* (Fact Sheet). California: Author.

Calkins, L. M. (1991). *Living between the lines.* Portsmouth, NH: Heinemann.

The Candlelighters Childhood Cancer Foundation. (1993). Advice to educators (adapted from a survey by A wish with Wings). In *Educating the child with cancer* (pp. 21–22). Bethesda, MD: Author.

Canfield, J., & Wells, H. C. (1994). *100 ways to enhance self-concept in the classroom.* Boston: Allyn & Bacon.

Cantwell, D.P., & Baker, I., (1987). *Developmental speech and language disorders.* New York: Guilford.

Carlson, R. (1984). *Picsyms categorical dictionary.* Lawrence, KS: Baggeboda Press.

Carnine, D. (1990). New research on the brain: Implications for instruction. *Phi-Delta-Kappan, 71* (5), 372–377.

Carnine, D. (1991). Curricular interventions for teaching higher order thinking to all students: Introduction to the special series. *Journal of Learning Disabilities, 24* (5), 261–269.

Carpenter, D., & Miller, L. J. (1982). Spelling ability of reading disabled LD students and able readers. *Learning Disabilities Quarterly, 5,* 65–70.

Carroll, J. (1964). *Language and thought.* Englewood Cliffs, NJ: Prentice-Hall.

Carter, J. F. (1993). Self-management: Education's ultimate goal. *Teaching Exceptional Children, 25* (3), 28–32.

Carter, T. P., & Chatfield, M. L. (1986). Effective bilingual schools: Implications for policy and practice. *American Journal of Education, 5* (1), 200–234.

Cartwright, G. P., Cartwright, C. A., & Ward, M. E. (1995). *Educating Special Learners.* Belmont, CA: Wadsworth.

Cawley, J. F. (1984). Selection, adaptation and development of curriculum and instructional materials. In J. F. Cawley (Ed.), *Developmental teaching of mathematics for the learning disabled* (pp. 227–251). Austin, TX: Pro-Ed.

Cawley, J. F., Fitzmaurice, A. M., Sedlak, R., & Althaus, V. (1976). *Project Math.* Tulsa: Educational Progress.

Cawley, J. F., Miller, J. H., & School, B. A. (1987). A brief inquiry of arithmetic word-problem-solving among learning disabled secondary students. *Learning Disabilities Focus, 2* (2), 87–93.

Cawley, J. F., Fitzmaurice-Hayes, A. M., & Shaw, R. A. (1988). *Mathematics for the mildly handicapped.* Boston: Allyn and Bacon.

Ceci, S. (1985). A developmental study of learning disabilities and memory. *Journal of Experimental Child Psychology, 39,* 202–221.

Chaffee, J. (1987). *Thinking critically.* Boston: Houghton-Mifflin.

Chalfant, J. C., & Pysh, M. V. (1989). Teacher assistance teams: Five descriptive studies on 96 teams. *Remedial and Special Education, 10* (6), 49–58.

Chalfant, J. C., & Pysh, M. V. (1993). Teacher assistance teams: Implications for the gifted. In C. J. Maker (Ed.), *Critical issues in gifted education: Vol III—gifted students in the regular classroom* (pp. 32–48). Austin, TX: Pro-Ed.

Chalfant, J. C., Pysh, M. V., & Moultrie, R. (1979). Teacher assistance teams: A model for within—building problem solving. *Learning Disability Quarterly, 2,* 85–96.

Chambliss, M. J. (1994). Evaluating the quality of textbooks for diverse learners. *Remedial and Special Education, 15* (6), 348–362.

Chamot, A., & O'Malley, J.M. (1994). *The CALLA handbook: Implementing the cognitive academic language learning approach.* Reading, MA: Addison-Wesley.

Chappell, G. (1985). Description and assessment of language disabilities of junior high school students. In Simon, C. (Ed.), *Communication skills and classroom success: Assessment of language-learning disabled students.* San Diego, CA: College-Hill.

Charles, C. M. (1989). *Building classroom discipline: From models to practice.* White Plains, NY: Longman.

Cheng, L. L. (1990). Asian American cultural perspectives on birth defects: Focus on cleft palate. *The Cleft Palate Journal, 27,* 294–299.

Cheng, L. L. (1991). *Assessing Asian language performance.* Oceanside, CA: Academic Communication Associates.

Children and Adults with Attention Deficit Disorders. (1988). *Attention deficit disorders: A guide for teachers.* Plantation, FL: Author.

Children and Adults with Attention Deficit Disorders. (1992). Testimony to the Senate and U.S. House of Representatives Subcommittee on Appropriations. *CH.A.D.D.ER, 6* (2), 24.

Chomsky, C. (1976). After decoding: What? *Language Arts, 53,* 288–296.

Chomsky, C. (1979). Approaching reading through invented spelling. In L. Resnick & P. Weaver (Eds.), *Theory and practice of early reading, Vol. 2* (pp. 43–65). Hillsdale, NJ: Erlbaum.

Christensen, K. M., & Delgado, G. L. (Eds.) (1993). *Multicultural issues in deafness.* White Plains, NY: Longman.

Christenson, S., Thurlow, M., Ysseldyke, J., & McVicar, R. (1989). Written language instruction for students with mild handicaps: Is there enough quantity to ensure quality. *Learning Disability Quarterly, 12,* 219–229.

Christenson, S. L., Ysseldyke, J. E., & Thurlow, M. L. (1989). Critical instruction factors for students with mild handicaps: An integrative review. *Remedial and Special Education, 10* (5), 21–31.

Chung, J. P-L. (1992). *The out-of-class language and social experience of a clique of Chinese immigrant students: An ethnography of a process of social identify information.* Unpublished doctoral dissertation, State University of New York at Buffalo.

Ciborowski, J. (1995). Using textbooks with students who cannot read them. *Remedial and Special Education, 16* (2), 90–101.

Clarizio, H. F., & McCoy, G. F. (1983). *Behavior disorders in children.* New York: Crowell.

Clark, J.O. (1990). *Harrup's dictionary of English idioms.* London: Harrup.

Clay, M. (1985). *Early detection of reading difficulties.* Portsmouth, NH: Heinemann.

Coben, S. S., & Vaughn, S. (1994). Gifted students with learning disabilities: What does the research say? *Learning Disabilities Quarterly, 5,* 87–94.

Cochran-Smith, M. (1991). Word processing and writing in elementary classrooms: A critical review of related literature. *Review of Educational Research, 61,* 107–155.

Coelho, E. (1994). Social integration of immigrant and refugee children. In F. Genesee (Ed.), *Educating second language children: The whole child, the whole curriculum, the whole community* (pp. 301–328). Cambridge: Cambridge University Press.

Coffland, J. A., & Baldwin, R. S. (1985). *Milliken Wordmath.* St. Louis: Milliken.

Cohen, E. (1994). *Designing groupwork: Strategies for the heterogeneous classroom* (2nd ed.). New York: Teachers College Press.

Cohen, E., Conway, R., & Gow, L. (1988). Mainstreaming special class students with mild handicaps through group instruction. *Remedial and Special Education, 9* (5), 34–41.

Cohn, S. J. (1981). What is giftedness? A multidimensional approach. In A. H. Karmer (Ed.). *Gifted children: Challenging their potential.* New York: Trillium.

Colangelo, N., & Davis, G. A. (1991). *Handbook of gifted education.* Boston: Allyn & Bacon.

Coleman, M. R., & Gallagher, J. J. (1995). The successful blending of gifted education with middle schools and cooperative learning: Two studies. *Journal for the Education of the Gifted, 18* (4), 363–384.

Collier, V. P. (1989, April). *Academic achievement, attitudes, and occupations among graduates of two-way bilingual classes.* Paper presented at the annual meeting of the American Education Research Association, San Francisco.

Collins, R. A., & Goldinher, M. R. (1984). *Evaluative Summary of the Dade County Public Schools Elementary Gifted Program.*

Collis, B., & Heeren, E. (1993, August). Tele-Collaboration and groupware. *The Computing Teacher,* 36–39.

Colson, S. E., & Carlson, J. K. (1993). HIV/AIDS education for students with special needs. *Intervention in School and Clinic, 28* (5), 262–274.

Comer, J. P. (1980). *School power.* New York: The Free Press.

Conley, M. W. (1995). *Content reading instruction: A communication approach* (2nd ed.). New York: McGraw-Hill, Inc.

Connolly, A. J. (1985). *Key Math Teach and Practice.* Circle Pines, MN: American Guidance Service.

Cooper, H. (1989). *Homework.* White Plains, NY: Longman.

Cooper, H., & Nye, B. (1994). Homework for students with learning disabilities: The implications of research for policy and practice. *Journal of Learning Disabilities, 27* (8), 470–479.

Cortes, C. E. (1978). Chicano culture, experience and learning. In L. Morris, G. Sather & S. Schull (Eds.), *Extracting learning styles from social/cultural diversity: A study of five American minorities.* Norman, OK: Southwest Teachers Corps Network.

Coulter, D. L. (Ed.) (1993). Special Issue: Epilepsy and mental retardation. *American Journal of Mental Retardation, 98* (supplement), 1–62.

Council for Exceptional Children. (1991). Some statistical clues to today's realities and tomorrow's trends. *Teaching Exceptional Children (24),* 80.

Cousin, P. T., Prentice, L., Aragon, E., Leonard, C., Rose, L. S., & Weekley, T. (1991). Redefining our roles as special educators: Understandings gained from whole language. In S. Stires (Ed.), *With Promise: Redefining reading and writing for "special students"* (pp. 165–171). Portsmouth, NH: Heineman.

Cowart, D., & Fabre, A. (1986, March). *LEAP for success.* Paper presented at the meeting of the National Association of Laboratory Schools, New Orleans.

Cox, J., Daniel, N., & Boston, B. (1985). *Educating able learners.* Austin, TX: University of Texas Press.

Crosby, E. A. (1993). The 'at risk' decade. *Phi Delta Kappan, 74* (8), 598–604.

Cruickshank, W., Bentzen, F., Ratzeburgh, F., & Tannhauser, M. (1961). *A teaching method for brain-injured and hyperactive children.* Syracuse, NY: Syracuse University Press.

Cuevas, G., & Driscoll, M. (Eds.). (1993). *Reaching all students with mathematics.* Reston, VA: National Council of Teachers of Mathematics.

Cummins, J. (1992). The empowerment of Indian students. In J. Reyhner (Ed.), *Teaching American Indian students* (pp. 1–12). Norman, OK: University of Oklahoma Press.

Cummins, J. (1991). Interdependence of first- and second-language proficiency in bilingual children. In E. Bialystok (Ed.).

Language processing in bilingual children. Cambridge, England: Cambridge University Press.

Cummins, J. (1989). A theoretical framework for bilingual special education. *Exceptional Children, 56,* 111–119.

Cummins, J. (1984). *Bilingualism and special education: Issues in assessment and pedagogy.* Clevedon, England: Multilingual Matters.

Cummins, J. (1981). *Bilingualism and minority language children.* Ontario: Institute for Studies in Education.

Cunningham, A. E., & Stanovich, K. E. (1991). Tracking the unique effects of print exposure in children: Associations with vocabulary, general knowledge, and spelling. *Journal of Educational Psychology, 83,* 264–274.

Cunningham, P. M. (1991). *Phonics they use: Words for reading and writing.* New York: Harper Collins.

Cunningham, P. M. (1995). *Phonics they use: Words for reading and writing* (2nd ed.). New York: Harper Collins.

Cunningham, P. M., & Allington, R. L. (1994). *Classrooms that work: They can all read and write.* New York: Harper Collins.

Cunningham, P. M., & Cunningham, J. W. (1992). Making words: Enhancing the invented spelling-decoding connection. *The Reading Teacher, 46* (2), 106–115.

Cunningham, P. M., Hall, D. P., & Defee, M. (1991). Non-ability-grouped, multilevel instruction: A year in a first grade classroom. *The Reading Teacher, 44,* 566–571.

Dale, E. (1969). *Audio Visual Methods in Teaching* (3rd ed.). New York: Holt, Rinehart, & Winston.

Dale, E., & Chall, J. (1948). A formula for predicting readability. *Educational Research Bulletin, 27,* 37–54.

Daneman, M. (1991). Individual differences in reading skills. In R. Barr, M. L. Kamil, P. Mosenthal, & P. D. Pearson (Eds.), *Handbook of Reading Research: Vol. 2* (pp. 512–538). New York: Longman.

Davey, B. (1983). Think-aloud—modeling the cognitive processes of reading comprehension. *Journal of Reading, 27,* 44–47.

Davis, G. A., & Rimm, S. B. (1989). *Education of the gifted and talented* (2nd ed.). Englewood Cliffs, New Jersey: Prentice Hall.

De Avila, E., & Duncan, S. E. (1986). *Language assessment scales* (Includes PreLAS). Monterey, CA: McGraw-Hill.

DeBono, E. (1986). *CoRT thinking teacher's notes.* New York: Pergamon Press.

Delpit, L.; (1995). *Other People's Children: Cultural Conflict in the Classroom.* New York: The New Press.

Delquadri, J., Greenwood, C. R., Whorton, D., Carta, J. J., & Hall, R. V. (1986). Classwide peer tutoring. *Exceptional Children, 52* (6), 535–542.

Deshler, D. D., Ellis, E. S., & Lenz, B. K. (1996). *Teaching adolescents with learning disablties* (2nd ed.). Denver: Love.

Dettmer, P., Thurston, L. P., & Dyck, N. (1993). *Consultation, collaboration, and teamwork for students with special needs.* Boston: Allyn & Bacon.

Diaz, R. (1983). Thought and two languages: The impact of bilingualism on cognitive development. *Review of Research in Education, 10,* 23–34.

Díaz-Rico, L. & Weed, K. Z. (1995). *The crosscultural, language, and academic development handbook: A complete K–12 Reference Guide.* Boston: Allyn & Bacon.

Dillon, J. (1979). Alternatives to questioning. *High School Journal, 62,* 217–222.

Di Vesta, F. J., & Smith, D. A. (1979). The pausing principle: Increasing the efficiency of memory for ongoing events. *Contemporary Educational Psychology, 4,* 288–296.

Dixon, M. E. (1983). *Questioning strategy instruction: Participation and reading comprehension of learning disabled students.* Unpublished doctoral dissertation, University of Arizona, Tucson.

Dole, J. A., Duffy, G. G., Roehler, L. R., & Pearson, P. D. (1991). Moving from the old to the new: Research on reading comprehension instruction. *Review of Educational Research, 61* (2), 239–264.

Dowhower, S. L. (1987). Effects of repeated reading on second-grade transitional readers' fluency and comprehension. *Reading Research Quarterly, 22,* 389–406.

Downing, J., & Bailey, B. R. (1990). Sharing the responsibility: Using a transdisciplinary team approach to enhance the learning of students with severe disabilities. *Journal of Educational and Psychological Consultation, 1,* 259–278.

Dreikurs, R., & Cassel, P. (1972). *Discipline without tears.* New York: Hawthorn.

Dreikurs, R., Grunwalk, B., & Pepper, F. (1982). *Maintaining sanity in the classroom.* New York: Harper & Row.

Drew, C. J., Hardman, M. L., & Logan, D. R. (1996). *Mental retardation: A life cycle approach* (6th ed.). Englewood Cliffs: Merrill/Prentice-Hall.

Dryfoos, J. G. (1994). *Full-service schools: A revolution in health and social services for children, youth, and families.* San Francisco: Josey-Bass.

Duffy, G. G. (Ed.). *Reading in the middle school* (2nd ed). Newark, DE: International Reading Association.

Duffy, G. G., & Roehler, L. R. (1989). *Improving classroom reading instruction: A decision making approach* (2nd ed.). New York: Random House.

Dunn, L. (1968). Special educationfor the mildly retarded: Is much of it justifiable? *Exceptional Children, 35,* 5–22.

Durden, W. G., Tangherlini, A. E. (1993). *Smart Kids: How academic talents are developed and nurtured in America.* Kirkland, WA; Hogrefe & Huber Publishers. p. 133–134.

Durkin, D. D. (1978–79). What classroom observations reveal about reading comprehension instruction. *Reading Research Quarterly, 14,* 481–533.

Dusek, J. B., & Joseph, G. (1983). The bases of teacher expectancies: A meta-analysis. *Journal of Educational Psychology, 75* (3), 327–346.

Echevarria, J. (1995). Interactive reading instruction: A comparison of proximal and distal effects of instructional conversations. *Exceptional Children, 61* (6), 536–552

Edelsky, C., Altwerger, B., & Flores, B. (1991). *Whole language what's the difference?* Portsmouth, NH: Heinemann.

Eden, G. R., Stein, J. F., Wood, M. H., & Wood, F. B. (1995). Verbal and visual problems in reading disability. *Journal of Learning Disability, 28,* 272–290.

Eggen, P. D., & Kauchak, D. (1992). *Educational psychology: Classroom connections.* New York: Macmillan.

Eiserman, W. D. (1988). Three types of peer tutoring: Effects on the attitudes of students with learning disabilities and their regular class peers. *Journal of Learning Disabilities, 21* (4), 249–252.

Elam, S. M., & Gallup, A. M. (1989). The 21st annual Gallup poll of the public's attitudes toward the public schools. *Phi Delta Kappan, 71,* 41–54.

Elbaum, B. E., Schumm, J. S., & Vaughn, S. (1995). *Students' perceptions of grouping formats for reading instruction.* Paper presented at the American Educational Research Association Conference, San Francisco.

Ellis, D. B. (1985). *Becoming a master student* (5th ed.). Rapid City, SD: College Survival, Inc.

Ellis, E. (1991). *SLANT: A starter strategy for participation.* Lawrence, KS: Edge Enterprises.

Ellis, E. S. (1994). Integrating writing strategy instruction with content-area instruction: Part II—writing process. *Intervention in School and Clinic, 29,* 219–228.

Ellis, R. (1985). *Understanding second language acquisition.* Oxford: Oxford University Press.

Elsner, W. (1983). Abnormalities in the verbal communication of visually-impaired children. In A. E. Mills (Ed.), *Language acquisition in the blind child: Normal and deficient.* San Diego: College Hill Press.

Emmer, E. T., Evertson, C. M., Sanford, J. P., Clements, B. S., & Worsham, M. E. (1989). *Classroom management for secondary teachers* (2nd ed.). Englewood Cliffs, NJ: Prentice-Hall.

Englemann, S., & Carnine, D. (1972). *DISTAR: Arithmetic Level III.* Chicago: Science Research Associates.

Englemann, S., & Carnine, D. (1975). *DISTAR: Arithmetic Level I*. Chicago: Science Research Associates.

Englemann, S., & Carnine, D. (1976). *DISTAR: Arithmetic Level II*. Chicago: Science Research Associates.

Englemann, S., & Carnine, D. (1982). *Corrective Mathematics Program*. Chicago: Science Research Associates.

Englert, C. S. (1992). Writing instruction from a sociocultural perspective: The holistic, dialogic, and social enterprise of writing. *Journal of Learning Disabilities, 25*, 153–172.

Englert, C. S., & Raphael, T. E. (1988). Constructive well-formed prose: Process, structure, and metacognitive knowledge. *Exceptional Children, 54*, 513–520.

Englert, C. S., Raphael, T. E., Anderson, L. M., Anthony, H. M., Fear, K. L., & Gregg, D. D. (1988). A case for writing intervention: Strategies for writing informational text. *Learning Disabilities Focus, 3* (2), 98–113.

Englert, C. S., Raphael, T. E., Anderson, L. M., Anthony, H. M., & Stevens, D. D. (1991). Making writing strategies and self-talk visible: Cognitive strategy instruction in regular and special education classrooms. *American Educational Research Journal, 28*, 337–372.

Englert, C. S., Raphael, R. E., & Mariage, T. V. (1994). Developing a school-based discourse for literacy learning: A principled search for understanding. *Learning Disability Quarterly, 17*, 2–32.

Epilepsy Foundation of America. (1983). *Preventing epilepsy*. Landover, MD: Author.

Epstein, J. L., & Becker, J. H. (1982). Teacher practices of parent involvement. *The Elementary School Journal, 83*, 103–113.

Erickson, F., & Mohatt, G. (1982). Cultural organization and participation structures in two classrooms of Indian students. In G. Spindler (Ed.), *Doing the ethnography of schooling* (pp. 141–174). New York: Holt, Rinehart & Winston.

Ervin-Tripp, S. (1974). Is second language learning like the first? *TESOL Quarterly, 8* (June), 111–127.

Espinola, O. (1992). *A user's guide to Braille 'n Speak*. Forest Hill, MD: Blazie Engineering.

Evers, R. B., & Bursuck, W. D. (1995). Helping students succeed in technical classes: Using learning strategies and study skills. *Teaching Exceptional Children, 27* (4), 22–27.

Falvey, M. A. (1995). *Inclusive and heterogeneous schooling: Assessment, curriculum, and instruction*. Baltimore: Brookes.

Farr, R. & Tone, B. (1994). *Portfolio and performance assessment: Helping students evaluate their progress as readers and writers*. New York: Harcourt Brace & Company.

Fasold, R. W., & Wolfram, W. (1970). Some linguistic features of Negro dialect. In R. Fasold & R. Shuy (Eds.), *Teaching standard English in the inner city* (pp. 41–86). Washington, DC: Center for Applied Linguistics.

Feldhusen, J., Van Tassel-Baska, J., & Seeley, K. (1989). *Excellence in educating the gifted*. Denver, Colorado: Love Publishing Company.

Ferguson, D. L. & Baumgart, D. (1991). Partial participation revisited. *Journal for the Association for Persons with Severe Handicaps, 16*, 218–227.

Ferrara, R. A. (1987). *Learning mathematics in the zone of proximal development: The importance of flexible use of knowledge*. Unpublished doctoral dissertation, University of Illinois, Urbana-Champaign.

Fettler, F., & Tokar, E. (1982). Getting a handle on teacher stress. *Educational Leadership, 39*, 456–457.

Fimian, M. J., Zoback, M. S., & D'Alonzo, B. J. (1983). Classroom organization and synthesization. In B. J. D'Alonzo (Ed.), *Educating adolescents with learning and behavior problems* (pp. 123–151). Rockville, MD: Aspen.

Fiore, T. A., Becker, E. A., & Nero, R. C. (1993). Educational interventions for students with attention deficit disorder. *Exceptional Children, 60* (2), 163–173.

Flood, J., Lapp, D., Flood, S., & Nagal, G. (1992). Am I allowed to group? Using flexible patterns for effective instruction. *The Reading Teacher,45* (8), 608–616.

Flores, D. M., Schloss, P. J., & Alper, S. (1995). The use of a daily calendar to increase responsibilities fulfilled by secondary students with special needs. *Remedial and Special Education, 16* (1), 38–43.

Floyd, C. (1954). Meeting children's reading needs in the middle grades: A preliminary report. *Elementary School Journal, 55*, 99–103.

Fogarty, R. (1994). Thinking about themes: Hundreds of themes. *Middle School Journal, 25* (4), 30–31.

Ford, D. Y. (1992). An American achievement ideology and achievement differentials among preadolescent gifted and nongifted African American males and females. *Journal of Negro Education, 61*, 45–64.

Forest, M., & Lusthaus, E. (1989). Promoting educational equality for all students: Circles and maps. In S. Stainback, W. Stainback, and M. Forest (Eds.), *Educating all students in the mainstream of regular education* (pp. 45–57). Baltimore: Brookes.

Forness, S. R. (1973). The reinforcement hierarchy. *Psychology in the Schools, 10* (2), 168–177.

Forness, S. R. (1988). School characteristics of children and adolescents with depression. In R. B. Rutherford, C. M. Nelson & S. R. Forness (Eds.), *Bases of severe behavioral disorders of children and youth*. Boston: Little Brown.

Forness, S. R., & Kavale, K. A., (1993). The Balkanization of special education: Proliferation of categories and sub-categories for "new" disorders. *The Oregon Conference Monograph, 5*, ix–xii.

Forness, S. R., & Knitzer, J. (1992). A new proposed definition and terminology to replace "serious emotional disturbance" in Individuals with Disabilities Education Act. *School Psychology Review, 21*, 12–20.

Foster, S. L., & Ritchey, W. L. (1979). Issues in assessment of social competence in children. *Journal of Applied Behavior Analysis, 12*, 625–638.

Fowler, M. (1992). *CH.A.D.D. educators manual: An in-depth look at attention deficit disorders from an educational perspective*. Plantation, FL: Children and Adults With Attention Deficit Disorders.

Fowler, S. A., Schwartz, I., & Atwater, J. (1991). Perspective on the transition from preschool to kindergarten for children with disabilities and their families. *Exceptional Children, 58*, 136–145.

Fox, C. (1989). Peer acceptance of learning disabled children in the regular classroom. *Exceptional Children, 56*, 50–57.

Friend, M., & Cook, L. (1992). *Interactions: Collaboration skills for school professionals*. White Plains, NY: Longman.

Frisbee, K., & Libby, J. (1992). *All together now*. Concord, NH: Chubb Life America.

Frith, U. (1980). *Cognitive processes in spelling*. London: Academic Press.

Frith, U., & Frith, C. (1980). Relationships between reading and spelling. In J. Kavanagh & R. Venezky (Eds.), *Orthography, reading and dyslexia* (pp. 287–295). Baltimore, MD: University Park Press.

Frose, V. (1981). Handwriting: Practice, pragmatism, and progress. In V. Frose & S. B. Straw (Eds.), *Research in the language arts: Language and schooling* (pp. 227–243). Baltimore, MD: University Park Press.

Fry, E. B. (1977). Fry's readability graph: Clarifications, validity, and extension to level 17. *Journal of Reading, 21*, 242–252.

Fry, E. B., Fountoukidis, D. L., & Polk, J. L. (1985). *The new reading teacher's book of lists*. Englewood Cliffs, NJ: Prentice-Hall.

Frymier, J. (1992). *Children who hurt, children who fail. Phi Delta Kappan, 74* (3), 257–259.

Fuchs, L. S., Bahr, C. M., & Reith, H. J. (1988). *Effects of goal structures and performance contingencies on the math performance of adolescents with learning disabilities*. Paper presented at the annual meeting of the American Association of Educational Research, New Orleans, LA.

Fuchs, D., & Fuchs, L. S. (1988). Mainstream assistance teams to accommodate difficult to teach students in general education. In J. L. Graden, J. E. Zins & M. J. Curtis (Eds.), *Alternative educational delivery systems: Enhancing instructional options for all students* (pp. 49–70). Washington, DC: National Association of School Psychologists.

Fuchs, D., & Fuchs, L. S. (1994). Inclusive school movement and radicalization of special education reform. *Exceptional Children, 60,* 294–309.

Fuchs, D., Fuchs, L. S., & Bahr, M. W. (1990). Mainstream Assistance Teams: A scientific basis for the art of consultation. *Exceptional Children, 57* (2), 128–139.

Fuchs, L. S., Fuchs, D., Hamlett, C. L., Phillips, N. B., & Bentz, J. (1994). Classwide curriculum-based assessment: Helping general educators meet the challenge of student diversity. *Exceptional Children, 60,* 518–537.

Fugate, D. J., Clarizio, H. F., & Phillips, S. E. (1993). Referral-to-placement ratio: A finding in need of reassessment? *Journal of Learning Disabilities, 26,* 413–416.

Furey, P. (1986). A framework for cross-cultural analysis of teaching methods. In P. Byrd (Ed.), *Teaching across cultures in the university ESL program.* Washington, DC: National Association of Foreign Student Advisors.

Gagne, F. (1991). Toward a differentiated model of giftedness and talent. In N. Colangelo & G. A. Davis (Eds.). *Handbook of gifted education* (pp. 65–80). Boston: Allyn & Bacon.

Gajria, M., & Salend, S. J. (1995). Homework practices of students with and without learning disabilities: A comparison. *Journal of Learning Disabilities, 28* (5), 291–296.

Gajria, M., & Salvia, J. (1992). The effects of summarization instruction on text comprehension of students with learning disabilities. *Exceptional Children, 58,* 508–516.

Galambos, S., & Goldin-Meadow, S. (1990). The effects of learning two languages on metalinguistic development. *Cognition, 34,* 1–56.

Gallagher, J. (1993). *Gifted education policy studies program: cooperative learning as perceived by educators of gifted students.* Chapel Hill, NC: University of North Carolina at Chapel Hill.

Gallagher, J. J., & Gallagher, S. A. (1994). *Teaching the gifted child* (4th ed). Boston: Allyn & Bacon.

Gambrell, L. B. (1985). Dialogue journals: Reading-writing interaction. *The Reading Teacher, 38,* 512–515.

Garbarino, J. (1984). *Can American families afford the luxury of childhood?* Unpublished manuscript. University Park: Pennsylvania State University, College of Human Development.

Garcia, E. E. (1991). Effective instruction for language minority students: The teacher. *Journal of Education, 173* (2), 130–141.

Gardner, D. P. (1983). *A nation at risk: The imperative for education reform.* Washington, DC: United States Department of Education.

Gardner, H. (1985). *Frames of mind.* New York: Basic Books.

Gardner, H., & Hatch, T. (1989). Multiple intelligences go to school: Educational implications of the theory of multiple intelligences. *Educational Researcher, 18* (8), 4–9.

Garnett, K. (1992). Developing fluency with basic number facts: Intervention for students with learning disabilities. *Learning Disabilities Research and Practice, 7* (4), 210–216.

Garnett, K., & Fleischner, J. E. (1983). Automatization and basic fact performance of normal and learning disabled children. *Learning Disability Quarterly, 6* (2), 223–230.

Gast, D., Ault, M., Wolery, M., Doyle, P., & Belanger, S. (1988). Comparison of constant time delay and the system of least prompts in teaching sight word reading to students with moderate retardation. *Education and Training in Mental Retardation, 23,* 117–128.

Gearheart, B. R., Mullen, R. C., & Gearheart, C. J. (1993). *Exceptional individuals: An introduction.* Pacific Grove, CA: Brooks/Cole.

Geary, D. C. (1993). Mathematical disabilities: Cognitive neuropsychological, and genetic components. *Psychological Bulletin, 114,* 345–362.

Geary, D. C., Brown, S. C., & Samaranayake, V. A. (1991). Cognitive addition: A short longitudinal study of strategy choice and speed-of-processing differences in normal and mathematically disabled children. *Developmental Psychology, 27* (5), 787–797.

Gentry, J. R. (1982). An analysis of developmental spellings in Gnys at wrk. *The Reading Teacher, 36,* 192–200.

Gerber, A. (1993). *Language related learning disabilities: Their nature and treatment.* Baltimore: Brookes.

Gerber, R. J., Ginsberg, R., & Reiff, H. B. (1992). Identifying alterable patterns in employment success for highly successful adults with learning disabilities. *Journal of Learning Disabilities, 25,* 475–487.

German, D. J. (1992). Word-finding intervention for children and adolescents. *Topics in Language Disorders, 13* (1), 33–50.

Gerstan, R., & Dimino, J. (1993). Visions and revisions: A special education perspective on the whole language controversy. *Remedial and Special Education, 14* (4), 5–13.

Giangreco, M. F., Dennis, R., Cloninger, C., Edelman, S., & Schattman, R. (1993). I've counted Jon: Transformational experiences of teachers educating students with disabilities. *Exceptional Children, 59,* 359–372.

Giangreco, M. F., Edelman, S., Cloninger, C. & Dennis, R. (1993). My child has a classmate with severe disabilities: What parents on nondisabled children think about full inclusion. *Developmental Disabilities Bulletin, 21* (1), 77–91.

Gibbs, R. W. (1987). Linguistic factors in children's understanding of idioms. *Journal for Child Language, 14,* 569–586.

Gilligan, C. (1982). *In a different voice: Psychological theory and women's development.* Cambridge, MA: Harvard University Press.

Glatthorn, A. A. (1990). Cooperative professional development: Facilitating the growth of the special education teacher and the classroom teacher. *Remedial and Special Education, 11* (3), 29–34, 50.

Glennen, S. (1992). Augmentative and alternative communication. In G. Church & S. Glennen (Eds.), *The handbook of assistive technology* (pp. 93–122). San Diego: Singular Publishing Group.

Gold, M., & Mann, D. (1972). Delinquency as a defense. *American Journal of Orthopsychiatry, 42,* 463–479.

Goldenberg, C. (1992–1993). Instructional conversations: Promoting comprehension through discussion. *The Reading Teacher, 16* (4), 316–326.

Goldman, S. R., Pellegrino, J. W., & Mertz, D. L. (1988). Extended practice of basic addition facts: Strategy changes in learning disabled students. *Cognition & Instruction, 5,* 223–265.

Goldstein, S., & Goldstein, M. (1990). *Managing attention disorders in children.* New York: Wiley.

Goldstein, A. P., & Huff, C. R. (1993). *The gang intervention handbook.* Champagne, IL: Research Press.

Goldstein, H., & Kaczmarek, L. (1992). Promoting communicative interaction among children in integrated intervention settings. In S.F. Warren & J.Reichle (Eds.), *Causes and effects in communication and language intervention* (pp. 81–112). Baltimore: Brookes.

Gollnick, D. M., & Chinn, P. C. (1990). *Multicultural education in a pluralistic society* (3rd ed.). New York: Merrill.

Gonzalez, N., Moll, L. C., Floyd-Tenery, M. Rivera, A., Rendón, P., Gonzales, R., & Amati, C. (1995) Teacher research on funds of knowledge: Learning from households. *Urban Education, 29,* 443–470.

Good, T. L., & Brophy, J. E. (1994). *Looking in classrooms* (6th ed.). New York: Harper Collins College Publishers.

Goodlad, J. I. (1984). *A place called school.* New York: McGraw-Hill.

Goodman, K. (1986). Basal readers: A call for action. *Language Arts, 63,* 359–363.

Goodman, K. (1986). *What's whole in whole language?* (pp. 56). Portsmouth, NH: Heinemann.

Goodman, K. S., Bird, L. B., & Goodman, Y. M. (1991). *The whole language catalog.* Santa Rosa, CA: American School Publishers, Macmillan/McGraw-Hill.

Goodman, K., Shannon, P., Freeman, Y., & Murphy, S. (1988). *Report card on basal readers.* New York: Richard C. Owen.

Goor, M. B., & Schwenn, J. O. (1993). Accommodating diversity and disability with cooperative learning. *Intervention in School and Clinic, 29* (1), 6–16.

Gordon, J., Schumm, J. S., & Vaughn, S. (1993). *The effects of phonemic training on the spelling performance of elementary students with learning disabilities.* Unpublished manuscript, University of Miami, Miami.

Gordon, J., Vaughn, S., & Schumm, J. S. (1993). Spelling interventions: A review of literature and implications for instruction for students with learning disabilities. Learning *Disabilities Research & Practice, 8* (3), 175–181.

Gossard, A. P. (1940). *Superior and backward children in public schools.* Chicago: University of Chicago Press.

Goswami, U., & Bryant, P. (1990). *Phonological skills and learning to read.* East Sussex, UK: Erlbaum.

Graham, S. (1992). Helping students with LD progress as writers. *Intervention in School and Clinic, 27,* 134–144.

Graham, S. & Freeman, S. (1986). Strategy training and teacher vs student-controlled study conditions: Effects on LD students' spelling performance. *Learning Disability Quarterly, 9,* 15–22.

Graham, S., & Harris, K. R. (1988). Instructional recommendations for teaching writing to exceptional students, *Exceptional Children, 54* (6), 506–512.

Graham, S., & Harris, K. (1989). Cognitive training: Implications for written language. In J. Hughes & R. Hall (Eds.), *Cognitive behavioral psychology in the schools: A comprehensive handbook* (pp. 247–279). New York: Guilford Publishing.

Graham, S., & Harris, K. R. (1989). Improving learning disabled students' skills at composing essays: Self-instructional strategy training. *Exceptional Children, 56,* 201–214.

Graham, S., Harris, K. R., MacArthur, C. A., & Schwartz, S. (1991). Writing and writing instruction for students with learning disabilities: Review of a research program. *Learning Disabilities Quarterly, 19,* 2–89.

Graham, S., & Miller, L. (1979). Spelling research and practice: A unified approach. *Focus on Exceptional Children, 13* (2), 1–16.

Graham, S., & Miller, L. (1980). Handwriting research and practice: A univied approach. *Focus on Exceptional Children, 13* (2), 1–16.

Graham, S., Schwartz, S., & MacArthur, C. (1991). *Learning disabled and normally achieving students' knowledge of the writing process, attitudes toward writing and self-efficacy.* Manuscript submitted for publication.

Grant, C. A., & Sleeter, C. E. (1993). Race, class, gender, and disability in the classroom. In J. A. Banks and C. A. Banks (Eds.), *Multicultural education: Issues and perspectives* (2nd ed., pp. 48–67). Boston: Allyn & Bacon.

Graves, A. & Hauge, R. (1993). Using cues and prompts to improve story writing. *Teaching Exceptional Children, 25* (4), 38–40.

Graves, D. H. (1983). *Writing: Teachers and children at work.* Portsmouth, N.H.: Heinemann Educational Books.

Graves, D. H. (1985). All children can write. *Learning Disability Focus, 1* (1), 36–43.

Graves, D. H. (1994). *A fresh look at writing.* Portsmouth, NH: Heinemann.

Graves, D. H., & Hansen, J. (1983). The author's chair. *Language Arts, 60,* 176–183.

Greenbaum, S. (1989). *Set straight on bullies.* Encino, CA: National School Safety Center.

Greenwood, C. R., Delquadri, J. C., & Hall, R. V. (1989). Longitudinal effects of classwide peer tutoring. *Journal of Educational Psychology, 81,* 317–383.

Gross, L. S. & Ward, L. W. (1991). *Electronic movie making.* Belmont, CA: Wadsworth.

Grossman, H. J. (1983). *Classification in mental retardation.* Washington, D.C.: American Association on Mental Deficiency (now Retardation).

Grossman, H. (1995). *Special education in a diverse society.* Boston: Allyn & Bacon.

Gulland, D. M., & Hinds-Howell, D. G. (1986). *The Penguin dictionary of English idioms.* London: Penguin.

Guy, E. (1991). Vocational rehabilitation services for American Indians. *OSERS News in Print, 3* (4) 10–15.

Haager, D., & Vaughn, S. (1995). Parent, teacher, peer, and self-reports of the social competence of students with learning disabilities. *Journal of Learning Disabilities, 28* (4), 205–215.

Hagin, R. A. (1983). Write right or left: A practical approach to handwriting. *Journal of Learning Disabilities, 16,* 266–271.

Hakuta, K. (1974). A report on the development of grammatical morphemes in a Japanese girl learning English as a second language. *Working Papers in Bilingualism,* (Vol. 4, pp. 18–44). Toronto: OISE Press.

Hale-Benson, J. E. (1986). *Black children: Their roots, culture, and learning styles* (rev. ed.). Baltimore: Johns Hopkins University Press.

Hall, A. (1982). Teaching specific concepts to visually handicapped students. In S. S. Mangold (Ed.), *A teachers' guide to the special educational needs of blind and visually handicapped children.* New York: American Foundation for the Blind.

Hallahan, D. P. (1992). Some thoughts on why the prevalence of learning disabilities has increased. *Journal of Learning Disabilities, 25* (8), 523–528.

Hallahan, D. P., & Kauffman, J. M. (1991). *Exceptional children: Introduction to special education* (5th ed.). Englewood Cliffs, NJ: Prentice Hall.

Hallenbeck, B. A., & Kauffman, J. A. (1995). How does observational learning affect the behavior of students with emotional or behavioral disorders? A review of research. *The Journal of Special Education, 29,* 45–71.

Hallinan, M. T., & Sorensen, A. B. (1985). Ability grouping and student friendships. *American Educational Research Journal, 22* (4), 485–499.

Hallowell, E. M., & Ratey, J. J. (1995). *Driven to distraction: Recognizing and coping with attention deficit disorder from childhood through adulthood.* New York: Touchstone.

Halvorsen, A. T., & Sailor, W. (1990). Integration of students with severe and profound disabilities: A review of research. In R. Gaylord-Ross (Ed.), *Issues and research in special education* (pp. 110–172). New York: Teachers College Press.

Hamre-Nietupski, Nietupski, & Strathe, J. (1992). Functional life skills, academic skills, and friendship/social relationship development: What do parents of students with moderate/severe/profound disabilities value? *Journal for the Association for Persons with Severe Handicaps, 17,* 53–58.

Hamstra-Bletz, L., & Blote, A. W. (1993). A longitudinal study on dysgraphic handwriting in primary school. *Journal of Learning Disabilities, 26,* 689–699.

Hanline, M. F., & Knowlton, A. (1988). A collaborative model for providing support to parents during their child's transition from infant intervention to preschool special education public school programs. *Journal of the Division for Early Childhood, 12,* 116–125.

Hannemann, C. E. & Potter, R. L. (1993). *Brainstorm 1000, 2000, 3000: Cooperative learning case studies in critical thinking.* Austin, TX: Steck-Vaughn.

Hanover, S. (1983). Handwriting comes naturally? *Academic Therapy, 18,* 407–412.

Hansen, J. (1985). Skills. In J. Hansen, T. Newkirk, and D. Graves (Eds.), *Breaking ground: Teachers relate reading and writing in the elementary school.* (pp. 147–168). Portsmouth, NH: Heinemann.

Hanson, M. J., & Lynch, E. W. (1989). *Early intervention.* Austin, TX: Pro-Ed.

Harman, M. (1994). *Inspiring active learning: A handbook for teachers*. Alexandria, VA: Association for Supervision and Curriculum Development.

Harper, G. F., Mallete, B., & Moore, J. (1991). Peer-mediated instruction: Teaching spelling to primary school children with mild disabilities. *Reading, Writing and Learning Disabilities, 7*, 137–151.

Harrington-Lueker, D. (1991). Empty promises. *Executive Educator, 13* (11), 18–25.

Harris, K. R., & Graham, S. (1992). *Helping young writers master the craft: Strategy instruction and self-regulation in the writing process*. Boston, MA: Brookline Books.

Harris, K. R., Graham, S., Reid, R., McElroy, K, & Hamby R. S. (1994). Self-monitoring of attention versus self-monitoring of performance: Replication and cross-task comparison studies. *Learning Disability Quarterly, 17*, 121–139.

Harris, L., & Associates. (1994). *National Organization on Disability/Harris Survey of Americans with Disabilities*. New York: Author.

Harris, A. J., & Sipay, E. R. (1980). *How to increase reading ability* (7th ed.). New York: Longman.

Harry, B., Allen, N., & McLaughlin, M. (1995). Communication versus compliance: African-American parents' involvement in special education. *Exceptional Children, 6* (4), 364–377.

Hasazi, S. B., Johnson, R. E., Hasazi, J., Gordon, L. R., & Hull, M. (1989). A statewide follow-up of high school exiters: A comparison of former students with and without handicaps. *Journal of Special Education, 23*, 243–255.

Haynes, W. O., Moran, M. J., & Rindzola, R. H. (1990). *Communication disorders in the classroom*. Dubuque, IA: Kendall/Hunt.

Hazel, J. S., Schumaker, J. B., Sherman, J. A., & Sheldon-Wildgen, J. (1982). Group training for social skills: A program for court-adjudicated, probationary youths. *Criminal Justice and Behavior, 9*, 35–53.

Heacox, D. (1991). *Up from under-achievement*. Minneapolis, MN: Free Spirit Publishing.

Heald-Taylor, B. G. (1984). Scribble in first grade writing. *The Reading Teacher*, 4–9.

Healy, M. K., & Barr, M. (1991). Language across the curriculum. In J. Flood, J. M. Jensen, D. Lapp, & J. R. Squire (Eds.) *Handbook of research on teaching the English language arts* (pp. 820–826). New York: Macmillan.

Heath, S. B. (1983). *Ways with words*. Cambridge: Cambridge University Press.

Hechtman, L., Weiss, G., & Perlman, T. (1980). Hyperactives as young adults: Self-esteem and social skills. *Canadian Journal of Psychiatry, 25* (6), 478–483.

Helmstetter, E., & Durand, V. M. (1991). Nonaversive interventions for severe behavior problems. In L. Meyer, C. Peck, & L. Brown (Eds.), *Critical issues in the lives of people with severe disabilities* (pp. 559–600). Baltimore: Brookes.

Helton, S. M. (1991). *Math activities for every month of the school year*. West Nyack, NY: Simon & Schuster.

Henley, M., Ramsey, R. S., & Algozzine, R. (1993). *Characteristics of and strategies for teaching students with mild disabilities*. Boston: Allyn & Bacon.

Herr, S. S. (1983). *Rights and advocacy for retarded people*. Lexington, MA: Lexington Books.

Heward, W. L. (1996). *Exceptional children: An introduction to special education* (6th ed.). Englewood Cliffs, NJ: Prentice Hall.

Hiebert, E. H. (1983). An examination of ability grouping for reading instruction. *Reading Research Quarterly, 18*, 231–235.

Hiebert, E. H., & Taylor, B. M. (Eds.). (1994). *Getting reading right from the start*. Boston: Allyn & Bacon.

Higgins, K., & Boone, R. (1993). Technology as a tutor, tool, and agent for reading. *Journal of Special Education Technology, 12*, 28–37.

Hildreth, B. L., Macke, R. A., & Carter, M. L. (1995). The comprehensive calendar: An organizational tool for college students with learning disabilities. *Intervention in School and Clinic, 30*, 306–308.

Hill, E. W., & Ponder, P. (1976). *Orientation and mobility techniques*. New York: American Foundation for the Blind.

Hill, S., & Haynes, W. (1992). Language performance in low-achieving elementary school students. *Language, Speech, and Hearing services in Schools, 23*, 169–175.

Hoctor, M., & Kaplan, S. (1989). *Developing Policies for a Gifted/Talented Program: A Handbook*. California Association of the Gifted.

Hodges, R. E. (1991). The conventions of writing. In J. Flood, J. M. Jensen, D. Lapp, & J. R. Squire (Eds.) *Handbook of research on teaching the English language arts* (pp. 775–786). New York: Macmillan.

Hoffman, J. V. (1994). So what's new in the new basals? A focus in first grade. *Journal of Reading Behavior, 26*, 47–73.

Hofmeister, A. M. (1989). Teaching problem-solving skills with technology. *Educational Technology, 29* (9), 26–29.

Hofmeister, A. M. (1993). Elitism and reform in school mathematics. *Remedial and Special Education, 14* (6), 8–13.

Hohn, W., & Ehri, L. (1983). Do alphabetic letters help prereaders acquire phonemic segmentation skill? *Journal of Educational Psychology, 75*, 752–762.

Holahan, C. K. (1995). *The gifted group in later maturity*. Stanford, CA: Stanford University Press.

Hollingworth, L. S. (1926). *Gifted children: Their nature and nurture*. New York: Macmillan.

Holmes, C. T., & Matthews, K. M. (1984). The effects of non-promotion on elementary and junior high school pupils: A meta-analysis. *Review of Educational Research, 54*, 225–236.

Hoover, J. J., & Patton, J. R. (1995). *Teaching students with learning problems to use study skills: A teacher's guide*. Austin, TX: Pro-Ed.

Howe, M. L., Brainerd, C. J., & Kingman, J. (1985) Storage-retrieval process of normal and learning disabled children: A state-of-learning analysis of picture-word effects. *Child Development, 56*, 1120–1133.

Hudson, F., Ormsbee, C. K., & Myles, B. S. (1994). Study guides: An instructional tool for equalizing student achievement. *Intervention in School and Clinic, 30* (2), 99–102.

Hughes, C. A. (1991). Studying for and taking tests: Self-reported difficulties and strategies for university students with learning disabilities. *Learning Disabilities, 2*, 65–71.

Hughes, C. A. (1996). Memory and test-taking strategies. In D. D. Deshler, E. S. Ellis, & B. K. Lenz (Authors), *Teaching adolescents with learning disabilities* (2nd ed.), p. 208–266. Denver: Love.

Hughes, C. A., & Schumaker, J. B. (1991). Test-taking strategy instruction for adolescents with learning disabilities. *Exceptionality, 2*, 205–221.

Hughes, C. A., Schumaker, J. B., Deshler, D. D., & Mercer, C. D. (1988). *The test-taking strategy*. Lawrence, KS: Edge Enterprises.

Hughes, M. E. T. (1995). *Parental involvement in literacy instruction: Perceptions and practices of Hispanic parents of children with learning disabilities*. Unpublished doctoral dissertation, University of Miami, Coral Gables.

Hulit, L. M. & Howard, M. R. (1993). *Born to talk*. New York: Macmillan.

Hull, R. H., & Dilka, K. L. (1984). *The hearing-impaired child in school*. Orlando: Grune & Stratton.

Hunt, P., Staub, D., Alwell, M., & Goetz, L. (1994). Achievement by all students within the context of cooperative learning groups. *Journal for the Association for Persons with Severe Handicaps, 19*, 290–301.

Hunter, M. (1982). *Mastery teaching*. El Segundo, CA: TIP.

Huntington, D. D., & Bender, W. N. (1993). Adolescents with learning disabilities at risk? Emotional well-being, depression, suicide. *Journal of Learning Disabilities, 26* (3), 159–166.

Hutchinson, N. L. (1993). Effects of cognitive strategy instruction on algebra problem solving of adolescents with learning disabilities. *Learning Disability Quarterly, 16*, 34–63.

Idol, L. (1987). Group story mapping: A comprehension strategy for both skilled an unskilled readers. Journal of *Learning Disabilities, 20*, 196–205.

Idol, L., Paolucci-Whitcomb, P., & Nevin, A. (1986). *Collaborative consultation.* Rockville, MD: Aspen.

Individuals with Disabilities Education Act. (1991). Washington, DC: U.S. Government Printing Office.

Individuals with Disabilities Education Act (1992 Amendments). Washington, DC: U.S. Printing Office.

Irvine, J. J. (1991). *Black students and school failure: Policies, practices, and prescriptions.* New York: Praeger.

Irwin, J. W., & Baker, I. (1989). *Promoting active reading comprehension strategies: A resource book for teachers.* Englewood Cliffs, NJ: Prentice Hall.

Jacobs, D. H. (1994). Environmental failure: Opresion is the only cause of psychopathology. *Journal of Mind and Behavior, 15* (1–2), 1–18.

Jankowski, M. S. (1991). *Islands in the street: Gangs and American urban society.* Berkeley, CA: University of California Press.

Janney, R. E., Snell, M. E., Beers, M. K., & Raynes, M. (1995). Integrating students with moderate and severe disabilities into general education classes. *Exceptional Children, 61* (5), 425–439.

Jayanthi, M., Bursuck, W. D., Epstein, M. H., & Cumblad, C. (1992). [School reform: Impact of homework, testing, and grading on students with disabilities and their families]. Unpublished raw data.

Johns, J. L., VanLeirsburg, P., & Davis, S. J. (1994). *Improving reading: A handbook of strategies.* Dubuque, IA: Kendall/Hunt.

Johnson, L. A. (1993). *My posse don't do homework.* New York: St. Martin's Press.

Johnson, D. J., & Myklebust, H. R. (1967). *Learning disabilities: Educational principles and practices* (Report No. EC–001–107). New York: Grune & Stratton, Inc. (ERIC Document Reproduction Service No. ED 021 352)

Johnson, D. W., & Johnson, R. T. (1991). *Learning together and alone: Cooperative, competitive, and individualistic learning* (3rd ed.). Boston: Allyn & Bacon.

Johnson, L. J., & Pugach, M. C. (1991). Peer collaboration: Accommodating students with mild learning and behavior problems. *Exceptional Children, 57* (5), 454–461.

Johnson, R. (1985). *The picture communication symbols: Book II.* Solana Beach, CA: Mayer-Johnson.

Johnson, T. E., Chandler, L. K., Kerns, G. M., & Fowler, S. A. (1986). What are parents saying about family involvement in school transitions: A retrospective transition interview. *Journal of the Division for Early Childhood, 11,* 10–17.

Johnston, D. (1985). *Core picture vocabulary.* Wauconda, IL: Don Johnston Developmental Equipment.

Johnston, P., & Allington, R. (1991). Remediation. In R. Barr, M. L. Kamil, P. Mosenthal, & P. D. Pearson (Eds.), *Handbook of reading research: Volume II* (pp. 984–1012). New York: Longman.

Jordan, C. (1985). Translating culture: From ethnographic information to educational program. *Anthropology and Education Quarterly, 16,* 105–123.

Kagan, S., Zahn, G. L., Widaman, K. F., Schwarzwald, J., & Tyrell, G. (1985). Classroom structural bias: Impact of cooperative and competitive classroom structures on cooperative and competitive individuals and groups. In R. E. Slavin, S. Sharan, S. Kagan, R. Hertz-Lazarowitz, C. Webb, and R. Schmuck (Eds.), *Learning to cooperative, cooperating to learn* (pp. 177–209). New York: Plenum.

Kameenui, E. J., & Simmons, D. C. (1990). *Designing instructional strategies: The prevention of academic learning problems.* Columbus, OH: Merrill.

Kamhi, A. G. (1987). Metalinguistic abilities in language-impaired children. *Topics in Language Disorders, 7* (2), 1–12.

Kamhi, A. G., & Catts, H. W. (1989). Language and reading: Convergence, divergences, and development. In A. G. Kamhi & H. W. Catts (Eds.), *Reading disorders: A developmental language perspective* (pp. 1–34). San Diego: College-Hill.

Kauchak, D. P., & Eggen, P. D. (1993). *Learning and teaching: Research-based methods* (2nd ed.). Boston: Allyn & Bacon.

Kauffman, J. M. (1989). *Characteristics of children's behavior disorders* (4th ed.). Columbus, OH: Merrill.

Kauffman, J. M. (1993). *Characteristics of emotional and behavioral disorders of children and youth* (5th ed.). Columbus, OH: Merrill/Macmillan.

Kazdin, A. (1993). Treatment of conduct disorder: Progress and directions in psychotherapy research. *Development and Psychopathology, 5* (1/2), 277–310.

Keilitz, I., & Dunivant, N. (1986). The relationship between learning disability and juvenile delinquency: Current state of knowledge. *Remedial and Special Education, 7* (3), 18–26.

Kekelis, L. (1988). Increasing positive social interactions between a blind child and sighted kindergartners. In S. Sacks, L. Kekelis, & R. Gaylord-Ross (Eds.), *The social development of visually impaired children.* San Francisco: San Francisco State University.

Kekelis, L. S., & Sacks, S. Z. (1992). The effects of visual impairment on children's social interaction in regular education programs. In S. Sacks, L. Kekelis, & R. Gaylord-Ross (Eds.), *The development of social skills by bind and visually impaired students.* New York: American Foundation for the Blind.

Kelker, K., Hecimovic, A., & LeRoy, C. H. (1994). Designing a classroom and school environment for students with AIDS: A checklist for teachers. *Teaching Exceptional Children, 26* (4), 52–55.

Kelly, M. (1990). *School-home notes: Promoting children's classroom success.* New York: Guilford press.

Kelly, B., Carnine, D., Gersten, R., & Grossen, B. (1987). The effectiveness of videodisc instruction in teaching fractions to learning handicapped and remedial high school students. *Journal of Special Education Technology, 8* (2), 5–17.

Kelly, B., Gersten, R., & Carnine, D. (1990). Student error patterns as a function of curriculum design: Teaching fractions to remedial high school students and high school students with learning disabilities. *Journal of Learning Disabilities, 23,* 23–29.

Kennedy, M. M., Birman, B. F., & Demaline, R. E. (1986). *The Effectiveness of Chapter I services.* Washington, DC: U.S. Government Printing Office.

Kennedy, M. M., Jung, R. K., & Orland M. E. (1986). *Poverty, Achievement and the Distribution of Compensatory Education Services.* Washington, DC: U.S. Government Printing Office.

Keogh, B. K. (1993). Linking purpose and practice: Social-political and developmental perspectives on classification. In G. R. Lyon, D. B. Gray, J. R. Kavanagh, & N. A. Krasnegor (Eds.), *Better understanding learning disabilities* (pp. 311–323). Baltimore: Paul H. Brookes.

Kiewra, K. A. (1985). Investigating notetaking and review: A depth of processing alternative. *Educational Psychologist, 20,* 23–32.

King, R. T. (1982). *Learning from a PAL. Reading Teacher, 35* (6), 682–685.

King-Sears, M. E., Mercer, C. D., & Sindelar, P. T. (1992). Toward independence with keyword mnemonic: A strategy for science vocabulary instruction. *Remedial and Special Education 13,* 22–33.

Kirkpatrick, E. M., & Schwarz, C. M. (Eds.). (1982). *Chambers idioms.* Edinburgh, Scotland: Chambers.

Kirstein, I., & Bernstein, C. (1981). *Oakland schools picture dictionary.* Pontiac, MI: Oakland Schools Communication Enhancement Center.

Kitano, M. K. (1973). Highlights of Institute on Language and Culture: Asian component. In L. A. Bransford, L. M. Baca, & K. Lane (Eds.), *Cultural diversity and the exceptional child* (pp. 14–15). Reston, VA: Council for Exceptional Children.

Kitzinger, M. (1984). The role of repeated and echoed utterances in communication with a blind child. *British Journal of Disorders of Communication, 19,* 135–146.

Klein, R. G., & Last, C. G. (1989). *Anxiety disorders in children.* Newbury Park, CA: Sage.

Klingner, J. K., & Vaughn, S. (1996). Reciprocal teaching of reading comprehension strategies for students with learning disabilities who use English as a second language. *The Elementary School Journal, 96,* 275–293.

Klingner, J. K., Vaughn, S., & Schumm, J. S. (in review). *Using scaffolded instruction for teaching reading comprehension in heterogeneous elementary schools.*

Kluwin, T. N., Moores, D. F. & Gaustad, M. G. (1992). *Toward effective public school programs for deaf students.* New York: Teachers College Press.

Knapp, M. S., & Turnbull, B. J. (1991). Alternatives to conventional wisdom. In M. S. Knapp & P. M. Shields (Eds.), *Better Schooling for the Children of Poverty: Alternatives to conventional wisdom* (pp. 329–353). California: McCutchan Publishing Corporation.

Knapp, M. S., Turnbull, B. J., & Shields, P. M. (1990). New directions for educating the children of poverty. *Educational Leadership, 49* (1), 4–8.

Knitzer, J., Steinberg, Z., & Fleisch, B. (1990). *At the schoolhouse door.* New York: Bank Street College of Education.

Knowlton, E. K. (1982). *Secondary teacher's expectations of learning disabled students* (Research Report No. 75.). Lawrence, KS: University of Kansas, Center for Research on Learning.

Koenig, A. & Holbrook, M. C. (1993). *Learning media assessment of students with visual impairment: A resource guide for teachers.* Austin, TX: Texas School for the Blind and Visually Impaired.

Kokaska, C. J., & Brolin, D. E. (1985). *Career education for handicapped individuals* (2nd ed.). New York: Merrill/Macmillan.

Kollott, P. B. (1991). Special residential high schools. In N. Colangelo & G. A. Davis (Eds.), *Handbook of gifted education.* Boston: Allyn & Bacon.

Kortering, L., Haring, N., & Klockars, A. (1992). The identification of high-school dropouts identified as learning disabled: Evaluating the utility of a discriminant analysis function. *Exceptional Children, 58* (2), 422–435.

Kosc, D. (1981). Neuropsychological implications of and treatment of mathematical learning disabilities. *Topics in Learning and Learning Disabilities, 1* (3), 19–30.

Koskinen, P. S., & Blum, I. H. (1985). Paired repeated reading: A classroom strategy for developing fluent reading. *The Reading Teacher, 40,* 70–75.

Kosma, C., & Stock, J. S. (1993). What is mental retardation? In R. Smith (Ed.), *Children with Mental Retardation* (pp. 1–49). Rockville, MD: Woodbine House.

Kovacs, M., Paulauskas, S., Gatsonis, C., & Richards, C. (1988). Depressive disorders in childhood: A longitudinal study of comorbidity with and risk for conduct disorders. *Journal of Affective Disorders, 15,* 205–217.

Koziol, S. (1973). The development of noun plural rules during the primary grades. *Research in the Teaching of English, 7,* 30–50.

Krashen, S. (1985) *The input hypothesis: Issues and implications.* London: Longman.

Kreviski, J., & Linfield, J. L. (1974). *Bad speller's dictionary.* New York: Random House.

Krupski, A. (1986). Attention problems in youngsters with learning handicaps. In J. K. Torgesen and B. Y. L. Wong (Eds.), *Psychological and Educational Perspectives on Learning Disabilities* (pp. 161–192). Orlando, FL: Academic Press.

LaBerge, D., & Samuels, S. J. (1974). Toward a theory of automatic information processing in reading. *Cognitive Psychology, 6,* 293–323.

LaBlance, G. R., Steckol, K. F., & Smith, V. L. (1994). Stuttering: The role of the classroom teacher. *Teaching Exceptional Children, 26* (2), 10–12.

Labov, W., Cohen, P., Robins, C., & Lewis, J. (1968). *A study of the non-standard English of Negro and Puerto Rican speakers in New York City* (Rept. on Cooperative Research Project 3288. New York: Columbia University.

Ladson-Billings, G. (1995). Toward a theory of culturally relevant pedagogy. *American Educational Research Journal, 32,* 465–491.

Lagan, J. (1982). *Reading and study skills* (2nd ed.). New York: McGraw-Hill.

Lakein, A. (1973). *How to get control of your time and life.* New York: P. H. Wyden.

Lambert, N., Nihira, K., & Leland, H. (1993). *AAMR Adaptive Behavior Scale—School: Examiner's manual* (2nd ed.). Austin, TX: Pro-Ed.

Lampert, M., & Clark, C. (1990). Expert knowledge and expert thinking in teachers: A response to Floden and Klinzing. *Educational Researcher, 19,* 18–25.

Lanauze, M., & Snow, C. (1989). The relation between first- and second-language writing skills. *Linguistics and education, 1,* 323–339.

Lancelotta, G. X., & Vaughn, S. (1989). Relation between types of aggression and sociometric status: Peer and teacher perceptions. *Journal of Educational Psychology, 81,* 86–90.

Larson, C. N., & Slaughter, H. (1984). The use of manipulatives and games in selected elementary school classrooms, from an ethnographic study. In A. E. Uprichard & J. V. Perez (Eds.), *Focus on learning problems in mathematics* (pp. 31–49). Framingham, MA: Center for Teaching/Learning of Mathematics.

Lazar, R. T., Warr-Leeper, G. A., Nicholson, C. B., & Johnson, S. (1989). Elementary school teachers' use of multiple meaning expressions. *Language, Speech, and Hearing Services in Schools, 20,* 420–430.

Leavell, A., & Ioannides, A. (1993). Using character development to improve story writing. *Teaching Exceptional Children, 25,* 41–45.

Leff, S., & Leff, R. (1978). *Talking pictures.* Milwaukee: Crestwood Company.

Lefkowitz, M. M., & Tesiny, E. P. (1985). Depression in children: Prevalence and correlates. *Journal of Consulting and Clinical Psychology, 53* (5), 647–656.

Lenz, B. K. (1983). Promoting active learning through effective instruction: Using advance organizers. *Pointer, 27* (2), 11–13.

Lenz, B. K., Alley, G. R., & Schumaker, J. B. (1987). Activating the inactive learner: Advance organizers in the secondary content classroom. *Learning Disability Quarterly, 10,* 53–67.

Lenz, B. K., Ehren, B. J., & Smiley, L. (1991). A goal attainment approach to improve completion of project-type assignments by adolescents with learning disabilities. *Learning Disabilities Research and Practice, 6,* 166–176.

Lenz, B. K., Ellis, E. S., & Scanlon, D. (1996). *Teaching learning strategies to adolescents and adults with learning disabilities.* Austin, TX: Pro-Ed.

Lenz, K., et al. (1993). *The course planning routine: A guide for inclusive planning* (Research Report). Lawrence: University of Kansas Center for Research on Learning.

Lenz, B. K., Schumaker, J. B., Deshler, D. D., & Beals, V. L. (1984). *The word identification strategy* (Learning Strategies Curriculum). Lawrence: University of Kansas.

Leon, J. A., & Pepe, H. J. (1983). Self-instructional training: Cognitive behavior modification for remediating arithmetic deficits. *Exceptional Children, 50,* 54–60.

Lerner, J. (1993). *Learning disabilities: Theories, diagnosis & teaching strategies* (6th edition). Boston: Houghton Mifflin.

Lerner, J. W., Lowenthal, B., & Lerner S. R. (1995). *Attention deficit disorders: Assessment and teaching.* Pacific Grove, CA: Brooks/Cole.

Leske, C. M. (1981). Prevalence estimates of communication disorders in the U.S.: Speech disorders. *ASHA, 23* (3), 217–225. Rockville, MD: ASHA.

Levin, J., & Nolan, J. F. (1991). *Principles of classroom management: A hierarchical approach.* Englewood Cliffs, NJ: Prentice Hall.

Lewis, R. B. (1993). *Special education technology: Classroom applications.* Pacific Grove, CA: Brookes.

Lewis, R. B., & Doorlag, D. H. (1995). *Teaching special students in the mainstream.* New York: Merrill.

Licht, B. G. (1983). Cognitive-motivational factors that contribute to the achievement of learning disabled children. *Journal of Learning Disabilities, 16,* 483–489.

Licht, B. G., & Kistner, J. A. (1986). Motivational problems of learning disabled children: Individual differences and their implications for treatment. In J. K. Torgesen & B. Y. L. Wong (Eds.), *Psychological and Educational Perspectives on Learning Disabilities* (pp. 225–255). Orlando, FL: Academic Press.

Link, D. B. (1980). *Essential learning skills and the low-achieving student at the secondary level: A rating of the importance of 24 academic abilities* (Unpublished master's thesis). Lawrence: University of Kansas.

Lloyd, J., Saltzman, N. J., & Kauffman, J. M. (1981). Predictable generalization in academic learning as a result of preskills and strategy training. *Learning Disability Quarterly, 4,* 203–216.

Loban, W. (1976). *Language development: Kindergarten through grade twelve* (p. 27), Res. Report #18. Urbana, IL: National Council of Teachers of English.

Lobovits, D. A., & Handal, P. J. (1985). Childhood depression: Prevalence using DSM-III criteria and validity of parent and child depression scales. *Journal of Pediatric Psychology, 10,* 45–54.

Loeber, R., Wung, P., Keenan, K., Giroux, B., Stouthamer-Loeber, M., Van Kammen, W., & Maughan, B. (1993). Developmental pathways in disruptive child behavior. *Development and Psychopathology, 51* (1/2), 103–134.

Lombroso, P. J., Pauls, D. L., & Leckman, J. F. (1994). Genetic mechanisms in childhood psychiatric disorders. *Journal of the American Academy of Child and Adolescent Psychiatry, 33* (7), 921–936.

Long, N. J., Morse, W. C., & Newman, R. G. (1980). *Conflict in the classroom.* Belmont, CA: Wadsworth.

Longstreet, E. (1978). *Aspects of ethnicity.* New York: Teachers College Press.

Lucas, T., Henze, R., & Donato, R. (1990). Promoting the success for Latino language minority students: An exploratory study of six high schools. *Harvard Educational Review, 60,* 315–334.

Luckasson, R., Coulter, D.L., Polloway, E. A., Reiss, S., Schalock, R. L. Snell, M. E., Spitalnik, D. M., & Stark, J. A. (1992). *Mental retardation: Definition, classification, and systems of supports.* Washington, DC: American Association on Mental Retardation.

Lundberg, I., Frost, J., & Peterson, O. (1988). Effects of an extensive program for stimulating phonological awareness in preschool children. *Reading Research Quarterly, 23* (3), 263–284.

Lusthaus, E., & Forest, M. (1987). The kaleidoscope: A challenge to the cascade. In M. Forest (Ed.), *More education integration* (pp. 1–17). Downsview, ONT: G. Allan Roeher Institute.

Lynch, E. W., & Hanson, M. J. (1992). *Developing cross-cultural competence: A guide for working with young children and their families.* Baltimore: Brookes.

Lyon, G. R. (1994). *Research in learning disabilities at the NICHD.* Bethesda, MD: National Institutes of Health.

Lyon, G. R., Newby, R. E., Recht, D. & Caldwell, J. (1991). Neuropsychology and learning disabilities. In B. Y. L. Wong (Ed.), *Learning about learning disabilities* (pp. 375–406). San Diego: Academic Press.

Lysynchuk, L. M., Pressley, M., & Vye, N. J. (1990). Reciprocal teaching improves standardized reading comprehension performance in poor comprehenders. *The Elementary School Journal, 90,* 469–484.

MacArthur, C. (1993). Beyond word processing: Computer support for writing processes. *LD Forum, 19,* 22–27.

Maclean, M., Bryant, P., & Bradley, L. (1987). Rhymes, nursery rhymes, and reading in early childhood. *Merrill-Palmer Quarterly, 33,* 255–281.

MacLeod, J. (1987). *Ain't no makin' it: Leveled aspirations in a low-income neighborhood.* Boulder, CO: Westview.

Madden, N. A., Slavin, R. E., Karweit, N. L., Dolan, L., & Wasik, B. A. (1991). Success for all. *Phi Delta Kappan, 72,* 593–599.

Maddux, C. D., Johnson, D. L., & Willis, J. W. (1992). *Educational computing: Learning with tomorrow's technologies.* Boston: Allyn & Bacon.

Maheady, L., Harper, G. F., & Sacca, M. K. (1988). Peer mediated instruction: A promising approach to meeting the needs of learning disabled adolescents. *Learning Disability Quarterly, 11,* 108–113.

Maher, F.A. (1987). Inquiry teaching and feminist pedagogy. *Social Education, 51,* 186.

Majsterek, D. J. (1990). Writing disabilities: Is word processing the answer? *Intervention in school and clinic, 26,* 93–97.

Mallory, B. L., & Kerns, G. M. (1988). Consequences of categorical labeling of preschool children. *Topics in Early Childhood Special Education, 8,* 39–50.

Mandler, J. M., & Johnson, N. S. (1977). Rememberance of things passed: Story structure and recall. *Cognitive Psychology, 9,* 111–151.

Mann, V. A. (1984). Longitudinal prediction and prevention of early reading difficulty. *Annals of Dyslexia, 34,* 117–135.

Mann, V. (1991). Language problems: A key to early reading problems. In B. Y. L. Wong (Ed.), *Learning about learning disabilities* (pp. 129–162). San Diego: Academic Press.

March of Dimes. (1992). *Public health education information sheet: Drinking during pregnancy.* White Plains: NY: March of Dimes Birth Defects Foundation.

Marland, S. (1972). *Education of the gifted and talented.* Report to the Congress of the United States by the U. S. Commissioner of Education. Washington, DC: U. S. Government Printing Office.

Marshall, H., & Weinstein, R. (1984). Classroom factors affecting students' self-evaluations: An interactional model. *Review of Educational Research, 54,* 301–326.

Martin, K. F., & Manno, C. (1995). Use of a check-off system to improve middle school students' story compositions. *Journal of Learning Disabilities, 28,* 139–149.

Masten, W. G. (1981). *Approaches to the identification of gifted minority students.* Paper for U.S. Department of Education, National Institute of Education). Education Resources Information Center (ED 234578).

Mastropieri, M. A., & Scruggs, T. E. (1989). Mnemonic social studies instruction: Classroom applications. *Remedial and Special Education, 10,* 40–46.

Mastropieri, M. A., Scruggs, T. E., & Shiah, S. (1991). Mathematics instruction for learning disabled students: A review of research. *Learning Disabilities Research and Practice, 6* (2), 89–98.

Mather, N. (1992). Whole language reading instruction for students with learning disabilities: Caught in the crossfire. *Learning Disabilities Research and Practice, 8* (4), 233–243.

Mather, N. & Lackowicz, B. L. (1992). Shared writing: An instructional approach for reluctant writers. *Teaching Exceptional Children, 25* (1), 26–30.

Mather, N., & Roberts, R. (1995). *Informal assessment and instruction in written language.* Brandon, VT: Clinical Psychology Publishing Company.

Mathes, P. G., & Fuchs, L. S. (1993). Peer-mediated reading instruction in special education resource rooms. *Learning Disabilities Research and Practice, 8* (4), 233–243.

Mathes, P. G., Fuchs, L. S., Fuchs, D., Hanley, A. M., & Sanders, A. (1994). Increasing strategic reading practice with Peabody Classwide Peer Tutoring. *Learning Disabilities Research and Practice, 9* (1), 44–48.

Mattingly, J. C., & Bott, D. A. (1990). Teaching multiplication facts to students with Learning Problems. *Exceptional Children, 56* (5), 438–449.

May. L. (1993). *Activities for assessing math performance.* Teaching K–8, 22.

Mayer, R. E. (1979). Twenty years of research on advance organizers: Assimilation theory is still the best predictor of results. *Instructional Science, 8,* 133–167.

McBurnett, K., Lahey, B., & Pfifner, L. (1993). Diagnosis of attention deficit disorders in DSM-IV: Scientific basis and implications for education. *Exceptional Children, 60* (2), 108–177.

McCaleb, J., & White, J. (1980). Critical dimensions in evaluating teacher clarity. *Journal of Classroom Interaction, 15,* 27–30.

McCormick, K. (1995). Translating theory into practice: Toward developing critically literate readings of literary texts. *ADE Bulletin* (110), 35–39.

McCormick, S., & Cooper, J. O. (1991). Can SQ3R facilitate secondary learning disabled students' literal comprehension of expository text: Three experiments. *Reading Psychology, 12,* 239–271.

McDaniel, T. R. (1993). Education of the gifted and the excellence-equity debate: Lessons from history. In C. J. Maker (Ed.), *Critical issues in gifted education: Program for the gifted in regular classrooms* (pp. 6–17). Austin, TX: Pro-Ed.

McDonald, D. (1989). A special report on the education of Native Americans: "Stuck in the horizon" [Special Report insert]. *Education Week, 7* (4), 1–16.

McDonnell, J., Wilcox, B., & Hardman, M. L. (1991). *Secondary programs for students with developmental disabilities.* Boston: Allyn & Bacon.

McGuffin, P., Asherson, P., Owen, M. J., & Farmer, A. (1994). The strength of the genetic effect: Is there room for an environmental influence in the etiology of schizophrenia? *British Journal of Psychiatry, 164* (5), 593–599.

McIntosh, R., Vaughn, S., & Bennerson, D. (in press). A social intervention to increase positive interpersonal interactions. *Teaching Exceptional Children.*

McIntosh, R., Vaughn, S., Schumm, J. S., Haager, D., & Lee, O. (1993). Observations of students with learning disabilities in general education classrooms. *Exceptional Children, 60* (3), 249–261.

McIntyre, T. (1992). *The behavior management handbook: Setting up effective management systems.* Boston: Allyn & Bacon.

McKenna, M. C., Stahl, S. A., & Reinking, D. (1994). Critical issues: A critical commentary on research, politics, and whole language. *Journal of Reading Behavior, 26* (2), 211–233.

McKinley, N., & Larson, V. Lord. (1991, November). *Seventh, eighth, and ninth graders' conversations in two experimental conditions.* Paper presented at the annual convention of the American Speech-Language-Hearing Association, Atlanta.

McKinney, J., Montague, M., & Hocutt, A. (1993). Educational assessment of students with attention deficit disorder. *Exceptional Children, 60,* 125–131.

McKnight, C. C., Crosswaite, F., Dossey, J., Kifer, E., Swafford, J., Travers, K., & Cooney, T. (1987). *The underachieving curriculum: Assessing U.S. school mathematics from an international perspective* (Report No. SE–047–822). New York: International Association for the Evaluation of Educational Achievement. (ERIC Document Reproduction Service No. ED 297 930)

McLaren, J., & Bryson, S. E. (1982). Review of recent epidemiological studies of mental retardation: Prevalence, associated disorders & etiology. *American Journal of Mental Retardation, 92,* 243–254.

McLaughlin, M. J., & Owings, M. F. (1992). Relationships among states' fiscal and demographic data and the implementation of P.L. 94–142. *Exceptional Children, 59* (3), 247–261.

McLeod, T. M., & Armstrong, S. W. (1982). Learning disabilities in mathematics-skill deficits and remedial approaches at the intermediate and secondary level. *Learning Disability Quarterly, 5* (3), 305–311.

McNeill, D. (1970). *The acquisition of language: The study of developmental psycholinguistics.* New York: Harper and Row.

McTighe, J. & Lyman, F. T., Jr. (1988). Cueing thinking in the classroom: The promise of theory-embedded tools. *Educational Leadership, 45* (7), 18–24.

Medical Research and Training Center in Rehabilitation and Childhood Trauma. (1993). *Facts from the National Pediatric Trauma Registry: Fact sheet 2.* Washington, DC: U.S. Department of Education.

Meinbach, A. M., Rothlein, L., & Fredericks, A. D. (1995). *The complete guide to thematic units: Creating the integrated curriculum.* Norwood, MA: Christopher-Gordon.

Menolascino, F. J., & Stark, J. A. (Eds.). (1988). *Preventive and curative intervention in mental retardation.* Baltimore: Brookes.

Menyuk, P. (1971). *The acquisition and development of language.* Englewood Cliffs, NJ: Prentice-Hall.

Mercer, C. D., Jordan, L., & Miller, S. P. (1994). Implications of constructivism for teaching math to students with moderate to mild disabilities. *Journal of Special Education, 28* (3), 290–306.

Mercer, C. D., & Mercer, A. R. (1993). *Teaching students with learning problems* (4th ed.). New York: Merrill/ Macmillan.

Mercer, C. D., & Miller, S. P. (1992). Teaching students with learning problems in math to acquire, understand, and apply basic math facts. *Remedial and Special Education, 13* (3), 19–35, 61.

Meyen, E. L., & Skrtic, T. M. (1995). *Special education and student disability: An introduction* (4th. ed.). Denver: Love.

Meyer, L. H., Peck, C. A., & Brown, L. (1991). *Critical issues in the lives of people with severe disabilities.* Baltimore: Brookes.

Michelson, L., & Mannarino, A. (1986). Social skills training with children: Research and clinical application. In P. S. Strain, M. J. Guralnick, & H. M. Walker (Eds.), *Children's social behavior* (pp. 373–406). Orlando, FL: Academic press.

Micklus, S. (1986). *OM program handbook.* Glassboro, NJ: OM Association.

Mihail, T. (1995). *Mental retardation: Beyond fear and low expectations.* Hammond, IN: Purdue University Calumet.

Miller, J. A. (1991, May 22). Chapter I: An educational revolution. *Education Week,* pp. 1–7, 9–10.

Miller, W. S., & Otto, J. (1930). Analysis of experimental studies in homogeneous grouping. *Journal of Educational Research, 21,* 95–102.

Moats, L. C., & Smith, C. (1992). Derivational morphology: Why it should be included in language assessment and instruction. *Language, Speech, and Hearing Services in Schools, 23,* 312–319.

Mobbs, F., Reed, V. A., & McAllister, I. (1993, May). *Rankings of the relative importance of selected communication skills in adolescent peer interactions.* Paper presented at the annual conference of the Australian Association of Speech and Hearing, Darwin, Australia.

Moffett, J., & Wagner, B. J. (1992). *Student-centered language arts, K–12* (4th ed.). Portsmouth, NH: Boynton/Cook.

Moll, L. C. (Ed.). (1990). *Vygotsky and education: Implications and applications of sociohistorical psychology.* Cambridge: Cambridge University Press.

Moll, L. C., & Greenberg, J. B. (1990). Creating zones of possibilities: Combining social contexts for instruction. In L.C. Moll (Ed.), *Vygotsky and education* (pp. 319–348). Cambridge: Cambridge University Press.

Molyneaux, D., & Lane, V. W. (1982). *Effective interviewing: Techniques and analysis.* Boston: Allyn & Bacon.

Montague, M. (1992). The effects of cognitive and metacognitive strategy instruction on the mathematical problem solving of middle school students with learning disabilities. *Journal of Learning Disabilities, 25,* 230– 248.

Montague, M., & Bos, C. S. (1986). Verbal mathematical problem solving and learning disabilities: A review. *Focus on Learning Problems in Mathematics, 8* (2), 7–21.

Montague, M., & Graves, A. (1993). Improving students' story writing. *Teaching Exceptional Children, 25*, 36–37.

Montgomery, M. S. (1994). Self-concept and children with learning disabilities: Observer-child concordance across six context-dependent domains. *Journal of Learning Disabilities, 27*, 254–262.

Moore, D. W., Readence, J. E., & Rickelman R. J. (1988). *Prereading activities for content area reading and learning* (2nd ed.). Newark, DE: International Reading Association.

Morales, D. (1992, June). Report examines gang activity. *Newsletter of Texas Commission of Alcohol and Drug Abuse, 1*, 8.

Moran, C., Stobbe, J., Baron, W., Miller, J., & Moir, E. (1992). *Keys to the classroom: A teacher's guide to the first month of school.* Newbury Park, CA: Corwin.

Morgan, H. (1980). How schools fail black children. *Social Policy, 10* (4), 49–54.

Morgan, T. D. (1993). Technology: An essential tool for gifted & talented education. *Journal for the Education of the Gifted, 16* (4), 358–371.

Morgan, S. R., & Reinhart, J. A. (1991). *Interventions for students with emotional disorders.* Austin, TX: Pro-Ed.

Morrice, C., & Simmons, M. (1991). Beyond reading buddies: A whole language cross-age program. *The Reading Teacher, 44* (8), 572–577.

Morrow, L. M. (1985). Retelling stories: A strategy for improving children's comprehension, concept of story structure and oral language complexity. *Elementary School Journal, 85*, 647–661.

Morrow, L. M. (1992). The impact of a literature-based program on literacy achievement, use of literature, and attitudes of children from minority backgrounds. *Reading Research Quarterly, 27*, 250–275.

Morrow, L. M. (1993). *Literacy development in the early years: Helping children read and write.* Boston: Allyn & Bacon.

Morrow, L. M., & Smith, J. K. (1990). The effects of group size on interactive storybook reading. *Reading Research Quarterly, 25* (3), 213–231.

Mtetwa, D., & Garofalo, J. (1989). Beliefs about mathematics: An overlooked aspect of student difficulties. *Academic Therapy, 24*, 611–618.

Muther, C. (1985c). What every textbook evaluator should know. *Educational Leadership*, 87–90.

Nagel, B. R., Schumaker, J. B., & Deshler, D. D. (1986). *The FIRST-letter mnemonic strategy* (Learning Strategies Curriculum). Lawrence, KS: Edge Enterprises.

Nahmias, M. (1995). *Project ADEPT.* Tucson: University of Arizona, Department of Special Education and Rehabilitation.

National Advisory Neurological Disorders and Stroke Council. (1990). *Implementation plan: Decade of the brain.* Bethesda, MD: National Institutes of Health.

National Center for Educational Research. (1990). *National education longitudinal study. A profile of the American eighth grader: NELS 88 student descriptive summary.* Washington, DC: U.S. Department of Education, Office of Educational Research and Improvement.

National Center on Educational Restructuring and Inclusion. (1994, Spring). National survey on inclusive education. *NCERI Bulletin*, (1), 3.

National Council of Teachers of Mathematics. (1989). *Curriculum and evaluation standards for school mathematics* (Report No. SE–050–418). Reston, VA: National Council of Teachers of Mathematics. (ERIC Document Reproduction Service No. ED 304 338)

National Education Goals Report. (1994). Washington, DC: National Education Goals Panel.

National Institute of Neurological Disorders and Stroke. (1988). *Developmental speech and language disorders: Hope through research* (NIH Publication No. Pamphlet 88–2757). Bethesda, MD: Author.

National Mental Health Association. (1986). *Severely emotionally disturbed children: Improving services under Education of the Handicapped Act (P.L. 94–142).* Washington, DC: Author.

Natrillo, G., McDill, E. L., & Pallas A. M. (1990). *Schooling disadvantaged children: Racing against catastrophe.* New York: Teachers College Press.

Nelson, J., Lott, L., & Glenn, H. S. (1993). *Positive discipline in the classroom.* Rocklin, CA: Prima.

Newland, E. (1932). An analytic study of the development of illegibilities in handwriting from the lower grades to adulthood. *Journal of Educational Research, 26*, 249–258.

Newman, F. M., & Wehlage, G. G. (1992–1993). Five standards of authentic instruction. *Educational Leadership, 50* (4), 8–12.

Nickel, D., Brand, M., & Middleton, G (1990). *Be a smooth talker.* Bellingham, WA: Voice Tapes, Inc.

Nieto, S. (1996). *Affirming diversity: The sociopolitical context of multicultural education* (2nd ed.). New York: Longman.

Noonan, M., & Siegel-Causey, E. (1990). Special needs of students with severe handicaps. In L. McCormick & R.L. Schiefelbusch (Eds.), *Early language intervention: An introduction* (2d ed., pp. 383–425). Columbus: Merrill.

Northcutt, L., & Watson, D. (1986). *Sheltered English teaching handbook.* San Marcos. CA: AM Graphics & Printing.

National Center for Educational Research. (1990). *National education longitudinal study. A profile of the American eighth grader: NELS 88 student descriptive summary.* Washington, DC: U.S. Department of Education, Office of Educational Research and Improvement.

Oakes, J. (1985). *Keeping track: How school structure inequality.* New Haven: Yale University Press.

Oakes, J. (1990). *Multiplying inequalities: The effects of race, social class, and tracking on opportunities to learn math and science.* Santa Monica, CA: RAND.

Oakes, J. (1992). Can tracking research inform practice? Technical, normative, and political considerations. *Educational Researcher, 21* (4), 12–21.

Oakes, J., Gamoran, A., & Page, R. (1991). Curriculum differentiation: Opportunities, consequences, and meanings. In P. Jackson (Ed.), *Handbook of research on curriculum.* New York: Macmillan.

Office of Scientific and Health Reports (1981). *Stuttering* (NIH Publication No. Pamphlet 81–2250). Bethesda, MD: National Institute of Neurological and Communicative Disorders and Stroke.

O'Flahaven, J. (1989). *An exploration of the effects of participant structure upon literacy development in reading group discussion.* Unpublished doctoral dissertation, University of Illinois-Champaign.

Ogbu, J.U. (1978). *Minority education and caste: The American system in cross-cultural perspective.* New York: Academic Press.

Ogbu, J. U. (1990). Minority education in comparative perspective. *Journal of Negro Education, 59*, 45–57.

Ogbu, J.U. (1992). Understanding cultural diversity and learning. *Educational Researcher, 21* (8), 5–14.

Ogle, D. (1986). KWL: A teaching model that develops active reading of expository text. *The Reading Teacher, 39*, 564–570.

Ogle, D. (1989). Implementing strategic teaching. *Educational Leadership, 46* (4), 47–48, 57–60.

Oishi, S., Slavin, R.E., & Madden, N.A. (1983, April). *Effects of student teams and individualized instruction on cross-race and cross-sex friendships.* Paper presented at the annual meeting of the American Educational Research Association, Montreal.

Okolo, C. M. (1992). The effect of computer-assisted instruction format and initial attitude on the arithmetic facts proficiency and continuing motivation of students with learning disabilities. *Exceptionality: A Research Journal, 3* (4), 195–211.

Okolo, C. M., Bahr, C. M., & Rieth, H. J. (1993). A retrospective view of computer-based instruction. *Journal of Special Education Technology, 12*, 1–27.

Olenckak, F. R., & Renzulli, J. S. (1989). The effectiveness of the schoolwide enrichment model on selected aspects of elementary school change. *Gifted Child Quarterly, 33,* 36–46.

Olsen, L. (1988). *Crossing the schoolhouse border: Immigrant students and the California public schools.* San Francisco: California Tomorrow.

Olson, R., Wise, B., Conners, F., & Rack, J. (1990). Organization, heritability, and remediation of component word recognition and language skills in disabled readers. In T. Carr & B. A. Levy (Eds.), *Reading and its development: Component skills approaches* (pp. 261– 322). New York: Academic Press.

Olympia, D., Jenson, W.R., Clark, E., & Sheridan, S.M. (1992). Training parents to facilitate homework completion: A model for home-school collaboration. In S.L. Christenson and J.C. Conoley (Eds.), *Home-school collaboration: Enhancing children's acadmic and social competence* (pp. 309–331). Silver Spring, MD: National Association of School Psychologists.

Ormrod, J.E. (1995) *Educational Psychology: Principles and applications.* Englewood Cliffs, NJ: Prentice Hall.

Osborne, A. G., & DiMattia, P. (1994). The IDEA's least restrictive environment mandate: Legal implications. *Exceptional Children, 61,* 6–14.

O'Shea, L. J., Sindelar, P. T., & O'Shea, D. J. (1987). The effects of repeated readings and attentioned cues on the reading fluency and comprehension of learning disabled readers. *Learning Disabilities Research, 2,* 103–109.

Otto, W. (1932), Wolf, A., & Eldrige, R. G. (1984). Managing instruction. In P. D. Pearson (Ed.), *Handbook of reading research* (pp. 799–828). New York: Longman.

Owens, Jr., R.E. (1988). *Language development: An introduction* (2nd ed.). Columbus, OH: Merrill.

Owens, Jr., R.E. (1995). *Language disorders: A functional approach to assessment and intervention* (2nd ed.). Boston: Allyn & Bacon.

Oyer, H.J., Crowe, B., & Haas, W.H. (1987). *Speech, language, and hearing disorders: A guide for teachers.* Austin, TX: Pro-Ed.

Palincsar, A. S. (1986). The role of dialogue in providing scaffolded instruction. *Educational Psychologist, 21* (1/2), 73–98.

Palmatier, R.A., & Ray, H.L. (1989). Sports talk: A dictionary of sports metaphors. New York: Greenwood.

Palmer, J.M. & Yantis, P.A. (1990). *Survey of communication disorders.* Baltimore: Williams & Wilkins.

Parker, B. N. (1989). *Gifted students in regular classrooms.* Boston: Allyn & Bacon.

Peal, E., & Lambert, W. (1962). The relation of bilingualism to intelligence. *Psychological Monographs, 7* (546), 1–12.

Pearl, R., Donahue, M., & Bryan, T. (1986). Social relationships of learning-disabled children. In J. K. Torgesen and B. Y. L. Wong (Eds.), *Psychological and Educational Perspectives on Learning Disabilities* (pp. 193–224). Orlando, FL: Academic Press.

Pearson, P. D., & Johnson, D. D. (1978). *Teaching reading comprehension.* New York: Holt, Reinhart, & Winston.

Pecyna-Rhyner, P., Lehr, D., & Pudlas, K. (1990). An analysis of teacher responsiveness to communicative initiations of children with handicaps. *Language, Speech, and Hearing Services in Schools, 21,* 91–97.

Pellegrini, A. & Galda, L. (1982). The effects of thematic fantasy plan training on the development of children's story comprehension. *American Educational Research Journal, 19,* 443–452.

Pennington, B. (1991). *Diagnosing learning disorders: A neuropsychological framework.* New York: Guilford Press.

Pepper, E.C. (1976). "Teaching the American Indian child in mainstream settings. In R.L. Jones (Ed.), *Mainstreaming and the minority child* (pp. 135–136). Reston, VA: Council for Exceptional Children.

Perfetti, C. A., Beck, I., Bell, L. C., & Hughes, C. (1987). Phonemic knowledge and learning to read are reciprocal: A longitudinal study of first grade children. *Merrill-Palmer Quarterly, 33,* 283–319.

Peterson, S. K., Mercer, C. D., & O'Shea, L. (1988). Teaching learning disabled students place value using the concrete to abstract sequence. *Learning Disabilities Research, 4,* 52–56.

Phillips, N. B., Fuchs, L. S., & Fuchs, D. (1995). Effects of classwide curriculum-based measurement and peer tutoring: A collaborative researcher–practitioner interview study. *Journal of Learning Disabiliites, 27,* 420–434.

Phillips, N. B., Hamlett, C. L., Fuchs, L. S., & Fuchs, D. (1993). Combining classwide curriculum-based measurement and peer tutoring to help general educators provide adaptive education. *Learning Disabilities Research & Practice, 8,* 148–156.

Piaget, J. (1955). *The language and thought of the child.* New York: Meridian.

Pinnell, G. S. (1990). Success for low achievers through reading recovery. Educational Leadership, 48 (1), 17–21.

Platt, J. J., & Spivack, G. (1972). Social competence and effective problem solving thinking in psychiatric patients. *Journal of Clinical Psychiatry, 28,* 3–5.

Ponchillia, S.V. (1993). The effects of cultural beliefs on the treatment of native peoples with diabetes and visual impairment. *Journal of Visual Impairments and Blindness, 87,* 333–335.

Powers, M. D. (1989). *Children with autism: A parents' guide.* Rockville, MD: Woodbine House.

Pressley, M. (1994). State-of-the-art-science primary grades reading instruction or whole language? *Educational Psychologist, 29* (4), 211–216.

Prewitt-Diaz, J. O., Trotter, R. T., & Rivera, V. A. (1990). Effects of migration on children. *The Education Digest* (55), 26–29.

Pugach, M. C., & Johnson, L. J. (1995). *Collaborative practitioners, collaborative schools.* Denver, Co: Love.

Putnam, M. L. (1992). Testing practices of mainstreamed secondary classroom teachers. *Remedial and Special Education, 13* (5), 11–21.

Putnam, M. L., Deshler, D. D., & Schumaker, J. S. (1993). The investigation of setting demands: A missing link in learning strategy instruction. In L. S. Meltzer (Ed.), *Strategy assessment and instruction for students with learning disabilities* (pp. 325–354). Austin, TX: Pro-Ed.

Quay, H. C., & Peterson, D. R. (1987). *Manual for the Revised Behavior Problem Checklist.* Coral Gables, FL: Author.

Quay, H. C., & Werry, J. S. (1986). *Psychopathological disorders of childhood.* New York: Wiley.

Radencich, M. C. (1992). Intergrated lesson plan formats: How do you fit it all in? *Florida Reading Quarterly, 29* (2) 15–17.

Radencich, M. C., Beers, P. C., & Schumm, J. S. (1993). *A handbook for the K-12 reading resource specialist,* pp. 119–120. Boston: Allyn & Bacon.

Radencich, M. C., & McKay, L. J. (Ed.). (1995). *Flexible grouping for literacy in the elementary grades.* Boston: Allyn & Bacon.

Rafferty, Y., & Rollins, N. (1989). *Learning in Limbo: Educational deprivation of homeless children.* New York: Advocates for Children of New York, Inc.

Ramirez, M. (1992, Winter/Spring). Executive summary, final report: Longitudinal study of structured English immersion strategy, early-exit and late-exit transitional bilingual education programs for language-minority children. *Bilingual Research Journal, 16* (1,2), 1–62.

Ramirez, M., & Castaneda, A. (1974). *Cultural democracy, bicognitive development and education.* New York: Academic Press.

Ramirez, J. D. & Merino, B. J. (1990). Classroom talk in English immersion, early-exit & late-exit transition bilingual education programs. In R. Jacobson & C. Faltis (Eds.), *Language distribution issues in bilingual schooling.* Clevedon: Multilingual Matters.

Ramirez-Smith, C. (1995). Stopping the cycle of failure: The Comer Model. *Educational Leadership, 52* (5), 14–19.

Raphael, T. E. (1982). Question-answering strategies for children. *The Reading Teacher, 36,* 188.

Raphael, T. E. (1984). Teaching learners about sources of information for answering comprehension questions. *Journal of Reading, 27,* 303–311.

Raphael, T. E. (1986). Teaching question-answer relationships revisited. *The Reading Teacher, 39* (6), 516–523.

Raphael, T. E., Englert, C. S., & Kirschner, B. W. (1986). *Students' metacognitive knowledge about writing* (Research Series No. 176). East Lansing: Michigan State University, Institute for Research on Teaching.

Rasinski, T. V. (1990). Investigating measures of reading fluency. *Educational Research Quarterly, 14* (3), 37–44.

Ratleff, J.E. (1989). *Instructional strategies for crosscultural students with special education needs.* Sacramento, CA: Resources in Special Education.

Raygor, A. L. (1977). The Raygor readability estimate: A quick and easy way to determine difficulty. In P. D. Pearson (Ed.), *Reading: Theory, research, and practice* (pp. 259–263). Twenty-sixth Yearbook of the National Reading Conference. Clemson, SC: National Reading Conference.

Read, C. (1971). Pre-school children's knowledge of English phonology. *Harvard Educational Review, 41,* 1–34.

Read, L.F. (1989). An examination of the social skills of blind kindergarten children. *Education of the Visually Handicapped, 20* (4), 142–155.

Readence, J. E., Bean, T. W., & Baldwin R. S. (1992). *Content area reading: An integrated approach* (4th ed.). Dubuque, IA: Kendall/Hunt.

Redl, F. (1959). The concept of the Life–Space Interview. *American Journal of Orthopsychiatry, 29,* 1–18.

Reed, V.A. (1994). *An introduction to children with language disorders* (2nd ed.). New York: Macmillan.

Reid, R., Maag, J. W., & Vasa, S. F. (1993). Attention deficit hyperactivity disorder as a disability category: A critique. *Exceptional Children, 60,* 198–214.

Reisner, H. (1988). *Children with seizure disorder: A parent's guide.* Kensington, UK: Woodbine House.

Renzulli, J. S., & Delcourt, M. A. B. (1986). The legacy and logic of research on the identification of gifted persons. *Gifted Child Quarterly, 30* (1), 20–23.

Renzulli, J. S., & Reis, S. M. (1991). The Schoolwide Enrichment Model: A comprehensive plan for the development of creative productivity. In N. C. Colangelo & G. A. Davis (Eds.), *Handbook of Gifted Education* (pp. 111–141). Boston: Allyn & Bacon.

Renzulli, J. S. & Smith, L. H. (1979). *A Guidebook for Developing Individualized Educational Programs for Gifted and Talented Students.* Mansfield Center, CN: Creative Learning Press.

Renzulli, J. S., Smith, L. H., & Reis, S. M. (1982). Curriculum compacting: An essential strategy for working with gifted students. *Elementary School Journal, 82,* 185–194.

Rex, E. J., Koenig, A. J., Wormsley, D. P., & Baker, A. J. (1994). *Foundations of braille literacy.* New York: American Foundation for the Blind.

Reyhner, J. (1992). American Indian bilingual education: The White House conference on Indian education and tribal college movement. *NABE News, 15* (7), 7–18.

Richard-Amato, P. (1988). *Making it happen: Interaction in the second language classroom.* White Plains, NY: Longman.

Richard-Amato, P.A., & Snow, M.A. (1992). Strategies for content-area teachers. In P.A. Richard-Amato & M.A. Snow (Eds.), *The multicultural classroom: Readings for content-area teachers* (pp. 145–163). White Plains, NY: Longman.

Ridley, C. A., & Vaughn, S. R. (1982). Interpersonal problem solving: An intervention program for preschool children. *Journal of Applied Developmental Psychology, 3,* 177–190.

Rikhye, C.H., Gotheif, C. R., & Appell, M.W. (1989). A classroom environment checklist for students with dual sensory impairments. *Teaching Exceptional Children, 22* (1), 44–46.

Riles, Lary P. (1972). C-71-2270 USC, 343 F. Supplement 130 (N.D. Cal. 1972).

Ringel, S.P. (1987). *Neuromuscular disorders: A guide for patient and family.* New York: Raven.

Riviera, D., & Deutsch-Smith, D. (1988). Using a demonstration strategy to teach middle school students with learning disabilities how to compute long division. *Journal of Learning Disabilities, 21,* 77–81.

Roberson, W., Gravel, J., Valcante, G., & Maurer, R. (1992). Using a Picture Task Analysis to Teach Student with Multiple Disabilities. *Teaching Exceptional Children, 24* (4), 12–16.

Roberts, J., & Crais, E. (1989). Assessing communication skills. In D. Bailey & M. Wolery (Eds.), *Assessing infants and preschoolers with handicaps* (pp. 337–389). New York: Macmillan.

Robertson, P., Kushner, M. I., Starks, J., & Drescher, C. (1994). An update of participation rates of culturally and linguistically diverse students in special education: The need for a research and policy agenda. *The Bilingual Special Education Perspective, 14,* 2–9.

Robinson, F.P. (1946). *Effective study.* New York: Harper & Brothers Publishing.

Robinson, R. (1993, February 25). P.C. Anderson students try hand at problem-solving. *Dallas Examiner,* pp. 1,8.

Rogoff, B., & Morelli, G. (1989). Culture and American children. *American Psychologist, 44,* 341–342.

Rohwer, W.D., & Harris, W. (1975). Media effects on prose learning in two populations of children. *Journal of Education al Psychology, 67,* 751–657.

Roland, B. H., & Robinson, B. E. (1991). Latchkey kids with special needs. *Teaching Exceptional Children, 23* (3), 34–35.

Romberg, T. A. (1993). NCTM's standards: A rallying flag for mathematics teachers. *Educational Leadership, 50* (5), 36–41.

Rooney, K., Hallahan, D., & Lloyd, J. (1984). Self-recording of attention by learning disabled students in the regular classroom. *Journal of Learning Disabilities, 17,* 360–364.

Rosenberg, M. S., Wilson, R., Maheady, L., & Sindelar, P. (1992). *Educating students with behavior disorders.* Boston: Allyn & Bacon.

Rosenshine, B., & Stevens, R. (1986). Teaching functions. In M. C. Wittrock (Ed.), *Handbook of research on teaching* (3rd ed., pp. 376–391). New York: Macmillan.

Rosman, N.P. (1994). Acute head trauma. In F.A. Oski, C. D. DeAngelis, R.D. Feigin, J. A. McMillan, & J. B. Warshaw (Eds.), *Principles and practices of pediatrics* (2nd ed., pp. 2030–2048). Philadelphia: J. B. Lippincott.

Ross, P. O. (1993). *National excellence: A case for developing America's talent.* Washington, DC: U.S. Department of Education.

Rourke, B. P. (1993). Arithmetic disabilities, specific and otherwise: A neuropsychological perspective. *Journal of Learning Disabilities, 26* (4), 214–226.

Routman, R. (1991). *Invitations: Changing as teachers and learners K–12.* Portsmouth, NH: Heinemann.

Rubalcava, M. (1991). *Locating transformative teaching in multicultural education.* Unpublished manuscript. University of California-Berkeley, Department of Anthropology, Special Project.

Rubin, H. (1988). Morphological knowledge and early writing ability. *Language and Speech, 31,* 337–355.

Rudolph, A. M., & Kamei, R. D. (1994). *Rudolph's fundmentals of pediatrics.* Norwalk, CT: Appleton & Lange.

Ruhl, K. L., Hughes, C. A., & Gajar, A. H. (1990). Efficacy of the pause procedure for enhancing learning disabled and nondisabled college students' long- and short-term recall of facts presented through lecture. *Learning Disability Quarterly, 13,* 55–64.

Ruhl, K. L., Hughes, C. A., & Schloss, P. J. (1987). Using the pause procedure to enhance lecture recall. *Teacher Education and Special Education, 10,* 14–18.

Rumberger, R. W. (1987). High school drop outs: A review of issues and evidence. *Review of Educational Research, 57* (2), 101–121.

Russo, D. C. (1991, November). *Behavioral treatment of pediatric head injury: Issues and outcomes.* Paper presented at conference on neurogenic developmental disorders, Niskayuna, NY.

Ryan, E. B., Weed, K. A., & Short, E. J. (1986). Cognitive behavior modification: Promoting active, self-regulatory learning styles. In J. K. Torgesan & B. Y. L. Wong (Eds.), P*sychological and Educational Perspectives on Learning Disabilities* (pp. 367–397). Orlando, FL: Academic Press.

Sacks, S. Z., & Gaylord-Ross, R. J. (1992). Peer-mediated and teacher directed social-skills training for blind and visually impaired students. In S. Z. Sacks, L. S. Kekelis, & R. J. Gaylord-Ross (Eds.), *The development of social skills by blind and visually impaired students.* New York: American Foundation for the Blind.

Salend, S. J. (1994). *Effective mainstreaming: Creative inclusive classrooms* (2nd ed.). New York: Macmillan Publishing Company.

Sander, E.K. (1972). When are speech sounds learned? *Journal of Speech and Hearing Disorders, 37,* 62.

Sanson, A., Smart, D., Prior, M., & Oberklaid, F. (1993). Precursors of hyperactivity and aggression. *Journal of the American Academy of Child and Adolescent Psychiatry, 32* (6), 1207–1216.

Santa, C. (1988). *Content reading including secondary systems.* Dubuque, IA: Kendall Hunt.

Santos, K. (1992). Fragile X syndrome: An educator's role in identification, prevention and intervention. *Remedial and Special Education, 13,* 32–39.

Sarcco, W. P., & Graves, D. J. (1985). Correspondence between teacher ratings of childhood depression and child self-ratings. *Journal of Clinical Child Psychology, 14,* 353–355.

Sattler, J. M. (1988). *Assessment of children* (3rd ed.). Boston: Allyn & Bacon.

Savage, R.C. (1993). Children with traumatic brain injury. *TBI Challenge! 1* (3), 4–5.

Scheuneman, R.S., & Lambourne, J. (1981). *Study skills for school success.* Tucson, AZ: Study Skills for School Success.

Schildroth, A., & Hotto, S. (1993). Annual survey of hearing-impaired children and youth: 1991–92 school year. *American Annals of the Deaf, 138* (2), 163–171.

Schildroth, A. N., & Hotto, S. A. (1995). Race and ethnic background in the annual survey of deaf and hard of hearing children and youth. *American Annals of the Deaf, 140* (2), 96–99.

Schiller, E., & Hauser, J. (1992). OSERS' initiative for meeting the needs of children with attention deficit disorders. *OSERS News in Print, 4* (3), 30–31.

Schloss, P. J., Alper, S., & Jayne, D. (1993). Self-determination for persons with disabilities: Choice, risk, and dignity. *Exceptional children, 60,* 215–225.

Schmitz, C. C., & Galbraith, J. (1985). *Managing the social and emotional needs of the gifted.* Minneapolis: Free Spirit.

Schnorr, R. (1990). "Peter? He comes and goes...": First graders' persepctives of a part-time mainstream student. *Journal of the Association for Persons with Severe Handicaps, 15,* 132–240.

Schroeder, H. (1993). Cerebral trauma: Accidental injury or shaken impact syndrome? *Headlines, 4* (5), 18–21.

Schultz, T. (1974). Development of the appreciation of riddles. *Child Development, 45,* 100–105.

Schumaker, J. B., Deshler, D. D., Alley, G. R., Warner, M. M., & Denton, P. H. (1982). Multipass: A learning strategy for improving reading comprehension. *Learning Disability Quarterly, 5,* 295–304.

Schumaker, J. B., Nolan, S. M., & Deshler, D. D. (1985). *The error monitoring strategy.* Lawrence, KS: Center for Research on Learning, University of Kansas.

Schumm, J. S. (1989). A-OK: A reading for revision strategy. *Reading: Exploration and Discovery, 10,* 26–34.

Schumm, J. S. & Lopate, K. (1989). An 8-step instructional plan for teaching notetaking skills to middle school students. *Florida Reading Quarterly,* 17–21.

Schumm, J. S., & Mangrum, C. T. (1991). FLIP: A framework for content area reading. *Journal of Reading, 35* (2), 120–124.

Schumm, J. S., & Radencich, M. (1992). *School power.* Minneapolis: Free Spirit Publishing.

Schumm, J. S. & Strickler, K. (1991). Guidelines for adapting content area textbooks: Keeping teachers and students content. *Intervention in School and Clinic, 27* (2), 79–84.

Schumm, J.S., & Vaughn, S. (1991). Making adaptations for mainstreamed students: General classroom teachers' perspectives. *Remedial and Special Education, 12* (4), 18–27.

Schumm, J.S., & Vaughn, S. (1992). Planning for mainstreamed special education students: Perceptions of general classroom teachers. *Exceptionality, 3,* 81–98.

Schumm, J. S., & Vaughn, S. (1992). Reflections on planning for mainstreamed special education students. *Exceptionality, 3,* 121–126.

Schumm, J. S. & Vaughn, S. (1995). *Using Making Words in heterogeneous classroom.* Unpublished manuscript.

Schumm, J. S., Vaughn, S., Haager, D., McDowell, D., Rothlein, L., & Saumell, L. (1995). General education teacher planning: What can students with learning disabilities expect? *Exceptional Children, 61* (4), 335–352.

Schumm, J. S., Vaughn, S., Haager, D., McDowell, D., Rothlein, L., & Saumell, L. (1995). Responsible inclusion for students with learning disabilities. *Journal of Learning Disabilities, 28* (5), 264–270, 290.

Schumm, J. S., Vaughn, S., & Leavell, A. G. (1994). Planning Pyramid: A framework for planning for diverse student needs during content area instruction. *The Reading Teacher, 47* (8), 608–615.

Schumm, J. S., Vaughn, S., & Saumell, L. (1992). What teachers do when the textbook is tough: Students speak out. *Journal of Reading Behavior, 24* (4), 481–503.

Schunk, D. H., & Rice, M. J. (1987). Enhancing comprehension skill and self-efficacy with strategy value information. *Journal of Reading Behavior, 19,* 285–302.

Schunk, D. H., & Rice, M. J. (1989). Self-efficacy and cognitive achievement: Implications for students with learning problems. *Journal of Learning Disabilities, 22,* 14–22.

Schunk, D. H., & Rice, M. J. (1991). Learning goals and progress feedback during reading comprehension instruction *Journal of Reading Behavior, 23,* 351–364.

Schunk, D. H., & Rice, M. J. (1992). Influence of reading comprehension strategy information on children's achievement outcomes. *Learning Disability Quarterly, 15,* 51–64.

Schuster, J. W., Stevens, K. B., & Doak, P. K. (1990). Using constant time delay to teach word definitions. *Journal of Special Education, 24,* 306–318.

Schwartz, S. E. (1977). *Real Life Math Program.* Austin: Pro-Ed.

Scott, C. M. (1988). Producing complex sentences. *Topics in Language Disorders, 8* (2), 44–62.

Scruggs, T. E., & Mastropieri, M. A. (1986). Improving the Test-taking skills of behaviorally disordered and learning disabled children. *Exceptional Children, 53,* 63–68.

Scruggs, T. E., & Mastropieri, M. A. (1988). Are learning disabled students "test-wise?": A review of recent research. *Learning Disabilities Focus, 3,* 87–97.

Scruggs, T. E., & Mastropieri, M. A. (1989). Reconstructive elaborations: A model for content area learning. *American Educational Research Journal, 26,* 311–327.

Scruggs, T. E., & Mastropieri, M. A. (1992). Classroom applications of mnemonic instruction: Acquisition, maintenance, and generalization. *Exceptional Children, 58,* 219–229.

Scruggs, T. E. & Mastropieri, M. A. (1993). Current approaches to science education: Implications for mainstream instruction of students with disabilities. *Remedial and Special Education, 14* (1), 15–24.

ss, L. W., & Readence, J. E. (1989). *Helping children learn to read* (2nd ed.). Englewood Cliffs, NJ: Prentice-Hall.

ears, P., & Barbee, A. (1977). Career and life satisfactions among Terman's gifted women. In J. Stanley, W. George, & C. Solano (Eds.), *The gifted and creative: A fifty-year perspective*. Baltimore, MD: Johns Hopkins University Press.

Seligman, M. (1991). Family systems and beyond: Conceptual issues. In M. Seligman (Ed.), *The family with a handicapped child*. (2nd ed., pp. 27–53). Boston: Allyn & Bacon.

Sexson, S. B., & Madan-Swain, A. (1993). School reentry for the child with chronic illness. *Journal of Learning Disabilities, 26,* 115–125.

Shanahan, T., Robinson, B., & Schneider, M. (1995). Integrating curriculum. *The Reading Teacher, 48* (8), 718–719.

Shaywitz, S., & Shaywitz, B. (1988). Attention deficit disorder: Current perspectives. In J. Kavanagh & J. Truss (Eds.), *Learning disabilities: Proceedings of the national conference* (pp. 369–567). Parkton, MD: York Press.

Shaywitz, S., Shaywitz, B., Fletcher, J. M. & Escobar, M. D. (1990). Prevalence of reading disability in boys and girls: Results of the Connecticut longitudinal study. *Journal of the American Medical Association, 264,* 998–1020.

Shea, T. M., & Bauer, A. M., (1991). *Parents and teachers of children with exceptionalities: A handbook for collaboration*. Boston: Allyn & Bacon.

Sheehan, J. G., & Martyn, M. M. (1970). Spontaneous recovery from stuttering. *Journal of Speech and Hearing Research, 13,* 279–289.

Sherman, A. (1994). *Wasting America's future: The Children's Defense Fund report on the costs of child poverty*. Boston: Beacon Press.

Shiah, R. L., Matsropieri, M. A., Scruggs, T. E., & Fulk, B. J. (1994). The effects of computer-assisted instruction on the mathematical problem solving of students with learning disabilities. *Exceptionality, 5* (3), 131–161.

Shipley, K., Maddox, M., & Driver, J. (1991). Children's development of irregular past tense verb forms. *Language, Speech, and Hearing Services in Schools, 22,* 115–122.

Shure, M. B., & Spivack, G. (1978). *Problem-solving techniques in childrearing*. San Francisco: Jossey-Bass.

Siccone, F. (1995). *Celebrating diversity: Building self-esteem in today's multicultural classrooms*. Boston: Allyn & Bacon.

Siegel-Causey, E., Guy, B., & Guess, D. (1995). Severe and multiple disabilities. In E. L. Meyen & T.M. Skrtic (Eds.), *Special education and student disability, an introduction* (4th ed.). Denver: Love.

Sigelman, C. K., Budd, E. C., Spanhel, C. L., & Schoenrock, C. J. (1981). When in doubt, say yes: Acquiescence in interviews with mentally retarded persons. *Mental Retardation, 19,* 53–58.

Simmonds, E. P. M. (1992). The effects of teacher training and implementation of two methods for improving the comprehension skills of students with learning disabilities. *Learning Disabilities Research and Practice, 7,* 194–198.

Simon & Schuster. (1983). *Misspeller's dictionary*. New York: Author.

Simpson, R. L. (1982). *Conferencing parents of exceptional children*. Rockville, MD: Aspen.

Simpson, R. L. (1988). Needs of parents and families whose children have learning and behavior problems. *Behavioral Disorders, 14,* 40–47.

Singer, H. (1986). Friendly texts: Description and criteria. In E. K. Dishner, T. W. Bean, J. E. Readence, & D. W. Moore (Eds.), *Reading in the content areas: Improving classroom instruction* (2nd ed.). (pp. 112–128). Dubuque, IA: Kendall Hunt.

Singer, H., & Donlan, D. (1989). *Reading and learning from text* (2nd ed.). Hillsdale, NJ: Erlbaum.

Sirvis, B. (1988). Physical disabilities. In E. L. Meyen & T. M. Skrtic (Eds.), *Exceptional children and youth: An introduction* (3rd ed., pp. 387–411). Denver: Love.

Sitlington, P. L., Frank, A. R., & Carson, R. (1992). Adult adjustment among high school graduates with mild disabilities. *Exceptional children, 59,* 221–233.

Skutnabb-Kangas, T. (1981, February). *Linguistic genocide and bilingual education*. Paper presented at the California Association for Bilingual Education, Anaheim, California.

Slavin, R. E. (1987). Ability grouping and student achievement in elementary schools: A best-evidence synthesis. *Review of Educational Research, 57* (3), 293–336.

Slavin, R. E. (1990). *Cooperative learning: Theory, research, and practice*. Englewood Cliffs, NJ: Prentice Hall.

Slavin, R. E. (1991). Synthesis of research on cooperative learning. *Educational Leadership, 48* (5), 71–82.

Slavin, R. E., Karweit, N. L., & Madden, N. A. (1989). *Effective Programs for Students at Risk*. Boston: Allyn and Bacon.

Slavin, R. E., Madden, N. A., Dolan, L. J., & Wasik, B. A. (1994). Roots and wings: Inspiring academic excellence. *Educational Leadership, 52* (3), 10–14.

Slavin, R. E., Madden, N. A., & Leavey, M. (1984). Effects of team assisted individualization on the mathematics achievement of academically handicapped and nonhandicapped students. *Journal of Educational Psychology, 76* (5), 813–819.

Sleeter, C. E., & Grant, C. A. (1993). *Making choices for multicultural education: Five approaches to race, class, and gender* (2nd ed.). New York: Merrill.

Smith, D., & Luckasson, R. (1995). *Introduction to Special Education: Teaching in an age of challenge* (2d ed.). Boston: Allyn & Bacon.

Smith, J. O., & Lovitt, T. C. (1982). *Computational Arithmetic Program*. Austin: Pro-Ed.

Smith, M. L., & Shepard, L. A. (1987). What doesn't work: Explaining policies of retention in the early grades. *Phi Delta Kappan, 69,* 129–134.

Smith, S. (1986). *No Easy Answers*. Cambridge, MA: Winthrop

Smith, T. M. (1994). Adolescent pregnancy. In R. J. Simeonsson (Ed.), *Risk, resilience, & prevention: Promoting the well-being of all children* (pp. 125–150). Baltimore: Paul H. Brookes.

Snyder, T.D. (1993). Trends in education. *Principal, 73* (1), 9–14.

Sobsey, D., & Wolf-Schein, E.G. (1991). Sensory impairments. In F.P. Orelove & D. Sobsey (Eds.), *Educating children with multiple disabilities: A transdisciplinary approach* (2nd ed., pp. 119–154). Baltimore: Brookes.

Speckman, N. J., Goldberg, R. J., & Herman, K. L. (1993). A exploration of risk and resilience in the lives of individuals with learning disabilities. *Learning Disabilities Research and Practice, 8,* 11–18.

Speece, D. L. (1994). The role of classification in learning disabilities. In S. Vaughn & C. S. Bos (Eds.), *Research issues in learning disabilities: Theory, methodology, assessment, and ethics* (pp. 69–82). New York: Springer-Verlag.

Spivack, G., Platt, J. J., & Shure, M. (1976). *The problem-solving approach to adjustment*. San Francisco: Jossey-Bass.

Spreen, O. (1988). *Learning disabled children growing up: A follow-up into adulthood*. New York: Oxford University Press.

Stahl, S. A. (1992). Saying the "p" word: Nine guidelines for exemplary phonics instruction. *The Reading Teacher, 45* (8), 618–625.

Stahl, S. A., McKenna, M. C., & Pagnucco, J. R. (1994). The effects of whole-language instruction: An update and a reappraisal. *Educational Psychologist, 29* (4), 175–186.

Stahl, S. A., Osborn, J., & Lehr, F. (1990). *Beginning to read: Thinking and learning about a print summary*. Urbana-Champaign, IL: Center for the Study of Reading.

Stainback, S., & Stainback, W. (1992). *Curriculum consideration in inclusive classrooms: Facilitating learning for all students*. Baltimore: Paul Brooks.

Stainback, W., & Stainback, S. (1990). *Support networks for inclusive schooling*. Baltimore: Paul H. Brookes.

Stallings, J. (1975). *Relationships between classroom instructional practices and child development* (Report No. PLEDE–C–75).

Menlo Park, CA: Stanford Research Institute. (ERIC Document Reproduction Service No. ED 110 200)

Stanovich, K. E. (1980). Toward an interactive compensatory model of individual fluency. *Reading Research Quarterly, 16,* 32–71.

Stanovich, K. E. (1986). Cognitive processes and the reading problems of learning-disabled children: Evaluating the assumption of specificity. In J. K. Torgesen & B. Y. L. Wong (Eds.), *Psychological and Educational Perspectives on Learning Disabilities* (pp. 87–131). Orlando, FL: Academic Press.

Stanovich, K. E. (1988). Explaining the differences between the dyslexic and garden-variety poor reader: The phonological-core variable-difference model. *Journal of Learning Disabilities, 21* (10), 590–604, 612.

Stanovich, K. E., & Siegal, L. S. (1994). Phenotypic performance profile of children with reading disabilities: A regression-based test of the phonological-core variable-difference model. *Journal of Educational Psychology, 86* (1), 24–53.

Stanovich, K. E., West, R. F., & Cunningham, A. E. (1991). Beyond phonological processes: Print exposure and orthographic processing. In S. A. Brady & D. P. Shankweiler (Eds.), *Phonological precesses in literacy—a tribute to Isabelle Liebermann* (pp. 219–235). Hillsdale, NJ: Erlbaum Associates.

Stein, N. L., & Glenn, C. G. (1979). An analysis of story comprehension in elementary school children. In R. O. Freedle (Eds.), *New directions in discourse processing (Vol. II)* (pp. 53–120). Norwood, NJ: Ablex.

Stephen, V. P., Varble, M. E., & Taitt, H. (1993). Instructional and organizational change to meet minority and at risk students' needs. *Journal of Staff Development, 14* (4), 40–43.

Stern, C. (1965). *Structural Arithmetic.* Boston: Houghton Mifflin.

Stevens, K. B., & Schuster, J. W. (1987). Effects of a constant time delay procedure on the written spelling performance of a learning disabled student. *Learning Disability Quarterly, 10,* 9–16.

Stevens, K. B., & Schuster, J. W. (1988). Time delay: Systematic instruction for academic tasks. *Remedial and Special Education, 9* (5), 16–21.

Stevens, L. J., & Price, M. (1992). Meeting the challenge of educating children at risk. *Phi Delta Kappan, 74* (1), 18–23.

Still, G. F. (1902). Some abnormal psychical conditions in children. *Lancet, i,* 1008–1012, 1077–1082, 1163–1168.

Stires, S. (1983). Real audiences and contexts for LD writers. *Academic Therapy, 18* (5), 561–568.

Strichart, S.S., & Mangrum, II, C.T. (1993). *Teaching study strategies to students with learning disabilities.* Boston: Allyn & Bacon.

Strickland, B. B., & Turnbull, A. P. (1990). *Developing and implementing individual education programs* (3rd ed.). Columbus, OH: Merrill.

Suddath, C., & Susnik, J. (1991). *Augmentative communication devices.* Reston, VA: The Council for Exceptional Children, Center for Special Education Technology.

Sugai, G. M., & Tindal, G. A. (1993). *Effective school consultation: An interactive approach.* Pacific Grove, CA: Brookes/Cole.

Sullivan, P., (1992). *ESL in context.* New York: Corwin Press.

Sumpton, M. R., & Leuking, E. M. (1960). *Education of the gifted.* New York: The Ronald Press Company.

Suritsky, S.K., & Hughes, C.A. (1996). Notetaking strategy instruction. In D. D. Deshler, E. S. Ellis, & B. K. Lenz (Authors), *Teaching adolescents with learning disabilities* (2nd ed.), p. 275. Denver: Love.

Svenson, O., & Broquist, S. (1975). Strategies for solving simple addition problems: A comparison of normal and subnormal children. *Scandinavian Journal of Psychology, 16,* 143–151.

Swain, M. (1986). Communicative competence: Some roles of comprehensible input & comprehensible output in its development. In J. Cummins & M. Swain (Eds.), *Bilingualism in education.* New York: Longman.

Swanson, H. L. (1993). Working memory in learning disabi[ ]subgroups. *Journal of Experimental Child Psychology, 5[ ],* 87–114.

Swanson, H. L., & Cooney, J. B. (1991). Learning disabilities and memory. In B. Y. L. Wong (Ed.), *Learning about learning disabilities* (pp. 103–127). Orlando: Academic Press.

Swanson, H. L., & Cooney, J. B. (1991). Learning disabilities and memory. In B. Wong (Ed.). *Learning about learning disabilities* (pp. 103–127). San Diego: Academic Press.

Swanson, M., McBurnett, K., Wigal, T., Pfiffner, L., Lerner, M., Williams, L., Christian, D., Tamm, L., Willcutt, E., Crowley, K., Clevenger, W., Khouzam, N., Woo, C., Crinella, F., & Fisher, T. (1993). Effect of stimulant medication on children with attention deficit disorder: A "review of reviews." *Exceptional Children, 60* (2), 154–162.

Swisher, K., & Deyhle, D. (1992). Adapting instruction to culture. In J. Reyhner (Ed.), *Teaching American Indian students* (pp. 81–95). Norman, OK: University of Oklahoma Press.

Tashie, C., Shapiro-Barnard, S., Dillon, A., Schuh, M., Jorgensen, C., & Nisbet, J. (1993). *Changes in latitudes, changes in attitudes: The role of the inclusion facilitator.* Durham, NH: Institute on Disability/UAP, University of New Hampshire.

Taylor, B., Harris, L. A., & Pearson, P. D. (1988). *Reading difficulties: Instruction and assessment.* New York: Random House.

Taylor, M. (1971). *Roll of thunder, hear my cry.* New York: Dial.

Terman, L. M., & Oden, M. H. (1951). The Stanford studies of the gifted. In P. Witty (Ed.), *The gifted child* (pp. 20–45). Boston: D.C. Heath and Company.

Tharp, R. G., & Gallimore, R. (1988). *Rousing minds to life: Teaching, learning, and schooling in social context.* Cambridge: Cambridge University Press.

Thomas, C. H. & Patton, J. R. (1990). Mild and moderate retardation. In J. R. Patton, M. Beirne-Smith, & J. S. Payne (Eds.), *Mental retardation* (2nd ed., pp. 197– 226). New York: Merrill/Macmillan.

Thornburg, K. R., Hoffman, S., & Remeika, C. (1991). Youth at risk: Society at risk. *The Elementary School Journal, 91* (3), 199–208.

Thornton, C. A., & Toohey, M. A. (1985). Basic math facts: Guidelines for teaching and learning. *Learning Disabilities Focus, 1,* 44–57.

Thornton, C. A., Tucker, B. F., Dossey, J. A., & Brazik, E. F. (1983). *Teaching mathematics to children with special needs.* Menlo Park, CA: Addison-Wesley.

Thurlow, M. L., Ysseldyke, J. E., & Silverstein, B. (1995). Testing accommodations for students with disabilities. *Remedial and Special Education, 16,* 260–270.

Tiedt, P. L., and Tiedt, I. M. (1995). *Multicultural teaching: A handbook of activities, information, and resources* (4th ed). Boston: Allyn & Bacon.

Tierney, R. J., Readence, J. E., & Dishner, E. K. (1990). *Reading strategies and practices: A compendium* (3rd ed.). Boston: Allyn & Bacon.

Tikunoff, W. J. (1983). *Compatibility of the SBIF features with other research instruction of LEP students.* San Francisco: Far West Laboratory.

Tollefson, N., Tracy, D. B., & Johnsen, E. P. (1982). *Self-control training of LD adolescents in a resource room setting* (Res. Report No. 69). Lawrence, KS: University of Kansas Institute for Research in Learning Disabilities.

Torgesen, J. K. (1982). The learning disabled child as an inactive learner: Educational implications. *Topics in Learning and Learning Disabilities, 2* (1), 45–52.

Torgesen, J. K. (1985). Memory processes in reading disabled children. *Journal of Learning Disabilities, 18* (6), 350–357.

Torgesen, J. K., & Goldman, T. (1977). Rehearsal and short-term memory in second grade reading disabled children. *Child Development, 48,* 56–61.

Towell, J., & Wink, J. (1993). *Strategies for monolingual teachers in multilingual classrooms.* Turlock, CA: California State

Stanislaus. (ERIC Document Reproduction Serve 9 797).

., Schloss, P. J., & Alper, S. (1994). Using self-aluation, and graphing to increase completion of ssignments. *Journal of Learning Disabilities, 27,*

ringer, D. J. (1982). Gifted students, regular students: Sixty ingredients for a better blend. *Elementary School Journal, 82,* 267–273.

Trimble, V. E. (1955). Provisions for gifted students in California public secondary schools. *California Guide Newsletter, 9,* 3–4.

Trotter, A. (1991). The sky's the limit when super students meet supercomputers. *Executive Educator, 13* (2), 17–18, 39.

Tucker, B. F., & Colson, S. E. (1992). Traumatic brain injury: A overview of school reentry. *Intervention in School and Clinic, 27* (4), 196–206.

Turnbull, H. R. (1990). *Free appropriate public education: The law and children with disabilities.* Denver, CO: Love.

Turnbull, A. P., & Turnbull, H. R. (1990). *Families, professionals, and exceptionality: A special partnership* (2nd ed.). Columbus, OH: Merrill.

Turnbull, H. R., Turnbull, A. P., & Wheat. (1992). Assumptions about parental participation: A legislative history. *Exceptional Education Quarterly, 3* (2), 1–8.

Turnbull, A. P., & Turnbull, H. R. (1993). Empowerment and decision-making through Group Action Planning. In *Life-long transitions: Proceedings of third annual parent/family conference* (pp. 39–45). Washington, DC: U.S. Department of Education.

Turnbull, A. P., Turnbull III, H. R., Shank, M., & Leal, D. (1995). *Exceptional lives: Special education in today's schools.* Englewood Cliffs, NJ: Merrill.

Tuttle, F. B., Becker, L. A., & Sousa, J. A. (1988). *Characteristics and Identification of Gifted and Talented Students.* Washington, D.C.: National Education Association.

Tyler, J. S. (1990). *Traumatic head injury in school-aged children: A training manual for educational personnel.* Kansas City: Children's Rehabilitation Unit, University of Kansas Medical Center.

Tyler, J. S., & Myles, B. S. (1990). Serving students with traumatic brain injury: A new challenge for teachers of students with learning disabilities. *LD Forum, 16* (1), 69–74.

Uhry, J. K. & Sheperd, M. J. (1990). Segmentational spelling instruction as part of a first-grade reading program: Effects on several measures of reading. *Reading Research Quarterly, 28,* 218–233.

United States Bureau of the Census. (1993). *Current population reports* (Series P–60, No. 181). Education Statistics on Disk. Washington, DC: U.S. Department of Education, Office of Educational Research and Improvement, National Center for Education Statistics.

United States Department of Education. (1990). *To assure the free, appropriate, public education of all handicapped children: Twelfth annual report to Congress on the implementation of the Education of the Handicapped Act.* Washington, DC: Office of Special Education Programs.

United States Department of Education. (1992). Rules and regulations. *Federal Register, 57* (189), 44800–44824.

United States Department of Education. (1993). *Fifteenth annual report to Congress on the implementation of the Individuals with Disabilities Education Act.* Washington, DC: U.S. Government Printing Office.

United States Department of Education (1994). *Annual report to Congress on the implementation of the Individuals with Disabilities Education Act.* Washington, DC: Author.

United States Department of Education (1994). *Sixteenth annual report to Congress on the implementation of the Education for All Handicapped Children ACT.* Washington, DC: U.S. Government Printing Office.

United States Department of Education (1995). *Annual report to Congress on the implementation of the Individuals with Disabilities Education Act.* Washington, DC: Author.

Unsworth, L. (1984). Meeting individual needs through flexible within-class grouping of pupils. *The Reading Teacher, 38* (3), 298–304.

Vacca, R. T., & Vacca, J. L. (1989). *Content area reading* (3rd ed.). Glenview, IL: Scott, Foresman and Company.

Valmont, W. J. (1995). *Creating videos for school use.* Boston: Allyn & Bacon.

Vandercook, T., York, J., & Forest, M. (1989). The McGill action planning system (MAPS): A strategy for building the vision. *Journal for the Association for Persons with Severe Handicaps, 14,* 205–215.

Vanderheiden, G. & Grilley K. (Eds). (1976). *Nonvocal communication techniques and aids for the severely physically handicapped.* Baltimore: University Park Press.

van Kleeck, A. (1990). Emergent literacy: Learning about print before learning to read. *Topics in Language Disorders, 10,* 25–45.

Van Reusen, A. K., & Bos, C. S. (1990). I PLAN: Helping students communicate in planning conference. *Teaching Exceptional Children, 22* (4), 30–32.

Van Reusen, A. K., & Bos, C. S. (1992). *Use of the goal-regulation strategy to improve the goal attainment of students with learning disabilities* (Final Report). Tucson, AZ: University of Arizona.

Van Reusen, A. K., & Bos, C. S. (1994). Facilitating student participation in individualized education programs through motivation strategy instruction. *Exceptional Children, 60* (5), 466–475.

Van Reusen, A. K., Bos, C. S., Schumaker, J. B., & Deshler, D. D. (1994). *The self-advocacy strategy for education and transition planning.* Lawrence, KS: Edge Enterprises.

Van Riper, C., & Emerick, L. (1984). *Speech correction: Principles and methods* (7th ed.), Englewood Cliffs, NJ: Prentice-Hall.

Van Strien, J. W., Stolk, B. D., & Zuiker, S. (1995). Hemisphere-specific treatment of dyslexia subtypes: Better reading with anxiety-laden words? *Journal of Learning Disabilities, 28,* 30–34.

Van Tassle-Baska, J. (1992). *Planning effective curriculum for gifted learners.* Denver, CO: Love Publishing Company.

VanTassel-Baska, J., Patton, J. M., & Prillaman, D. (1991). *Gifted youth at risk: A report of a national study.* Reston, VA: Council for Exceptional Children.

Vaughn, S. (1989). Gifted learning disabilities: Is it such a bright idea? *Learning Disabilities Focus, 4* (2), 123–126.

Vaughn, S., Bos, C., Harrell, J. E., & Lasky, B. A. (1988). Parent participation in the initial placement/IEP conference ten years after mandated involvement. *Journal of Learning Disabilities, 21* (2), 82–89.

Vaughn, S. R., Bos, C. S., & Lund, K. A. (1986).... But they can do it in my room: Strategies for promoting generalization. *Teaching Exceptional Children, 18,* 176–180.

Vaughn, S., Haager, D., Hogan, A., & Kouzekanani, K. (1992). Self-concept and peer acceptance in students with learning disabilities: A four- to five-year prospective study. *Journal of Educational Psychology, 84,* 43–50.

Vaughn, S., Hogan, A., Lancelotta, G., Shapiro, S., & Walker, J. (1992). Subgroups of children with severe and mild behavior problems: Social competence and reading achievement. *Journal of Clinical Child Psychology, 21* (2), 98–106.

Vaughn, S., & La Greca, A. (1993). Social skills training: Why, who, what, and how. In W. N. Bender (Ed.), *Learning disabilities: Best practices for professionals* (pp. 251–271). North Potomac, MD: Andover Medical.

Vaughn, S., & Lancelotta, G. X. (1990). Teaching interpersonal social skills to low accepted students: Peer-pairing versus no peer-pairing. *Journal of School Psychology, 28* (3), 181–188.

Vaughn, S. R., Lancelotta, G. X., & Minnis, S. (1988). Social strategy training and peer involvement: Increasing peer acceptance of a female, LD student. *Learning Disabilities Focus, 4,* 32–37.

Vaughn, S., McIntosh, R., & Spencer-Rowe, J. (1991). Peer rejection is a stubborn thing: Increasing peer acceptance of rejected students with learning disabilities. *Learning Disabilities Research and Practice, 6* (2), 83–88.

Vaughn, S. R., & Ridley, C. A. (1983). A preschool interpersonal problem solving program: Does it affect behavior in the classroom? *Child Study Journal, 13,* 1–12.

Vaughn, S. R., Ridley, C. A., & Bullock, D. D. (1984). Interpersonal problem-solving skills training with aggressive young children. *Journal of Applied Developmental Psychology, 5,* 213–223.

Vaughn, S. R., Ridley, C. A., & Cox, J. (1983). Evaluating the efficacy of an interpersonal skills training program with children who are mentally retarded. *Education and Training of the Mentally Retarded, 18,* 191–196.

Vaughn, S., & Schumm, J. S. (1994). Middle school teachers' planning for students with learning disabilities. *Remedial and Special Education, 15* (3), 152–161.

Vaughn, S., & Schumm, J. S. (1995). Responsible inclusion for students with learning disabilities. *Journal of Learning Disabilities, 28* (5), 264–270, 290.

Vaughn, S., Schumm, J.S., Klingner, J., & Saumell, L. (1995). Students' views of instructional practices: Implications for inclusion. *Learning Disability Quarterly, 18,* 239–248.

Vaughn, S., Schumm, J. S., Niarhos, F. J., & Daugherty, T. (1993). What do students think when teachers make adaptations? *Teaching & Teacher Education, 9,* 107– 118.

Vaughn, S., Schumm, J. S., Niarhos, F. J., & Gordon, J. (1993). Students' perceptions of two hypothetical teachers' instructional adaptations for low achievers. *The Elementary School Journal, 94,* 87–102.

Vaughn, S., et al. (1995). *Planning for academic diversity in America's classrooms: Windows on reality, research, change, and practice.* Lawrence, KS: University of Kansas Center for Research on Learning.

Vellutino, F. R. & Scanlon, D. M. (1987). Phonological coding, phonological awareness and reading ability: Evidence from a longitudinal and experimental study. *Merrill-Palmer Quarterly, 33,* 321–363.

Vellutino, F. R., Scanlon, D. M., & Tanzman, M. S. (1994). Components of reading ability: Issues and problems in operationalizing word identification, phonological coding, and orthographic coding. In G. R. Lyon (Ed.), *Frames of reference for the assessment of learning disabilities* (pp. 279–332). Baltimore: Brookes.

Vogel, S. A., Hruby, P. J., & Adelman, P. B. (1993). Educational and psychological factors in successful and unsuccessful college students with learning disabilities. *Learning Disabilities Research and Practice, 8,* 35–43.

Voltz, D. L., Elliott, R. N., & Cobb, H. B. (1994). Collaborative teacher roles: Special and general educators. *Journal of Learning Disabilities, 27* (8), 527–535.

Vygotsky, L. S. (1978). *Mind in society: The development of higher psychological processes.* Cambridge, MA: MIT Press.

Wacker, D. P., & Berg, W. K. (1984). Use of peer instruction to train a complex photocopying task to moderately and severely retarded adolescents. *Analysis and Intervention in Developmental Disabilities, 4,* 219–234.

Wagner, M. (1989, April). *The national transition study: Results of a national, longitudinal study of transition from school to work for students with disabilities.* Paper presented at the annual meeting of the Council for Exceptional Children, San Francisco, CA.

Wagner, R. K., & Torgesen, J. K. (1987). The nature of phonological processing and its causal role in the acquisition of reading skills. *Psychological Bulletin, 101,* 192–212.

Waldie, K., & Spreen, O. (1993). The relationship between learning disabilities and persisting delinquency. *Journal of Learning Disabilities, 26,* 417–423.

Walker, H. M., Colvin, G., & Ramsey, E. (1995). *Antisocial behavior in school: Strategies and best practices.* Pacific Grove, CA: Brooks/Cole.

Wallach, G. P., & Miller, L. (1988). *Language intervention and academic success.* San Diego: College Hill.

Wallerstein, J. S., & Blakeslee, S. (1989). *Second chances: Men, women and children a decade after divorce. Who wins, who loses—and why.* New York: Ticknor & Fields.

Walmsley, S. A. & Adams, E. L. (1993). Realities of "whole language." *Language Arts, 70,* 272–280.

Walp, T. P., & Walmsley, S. A. (1989). Instructional and philosophical congruence: Neglected aspects of coordination. *The Reading Teacher, 42,* 364–368.

Wang, M. C., & Birch, J. W. (1984). Comparison of a full-time mainstreaming program and a resource room approach. *Exceptional Children, 51,* 33–40.

Warren, D. W. (1994). *Blindness and children: An individual differences approach.* New York: Cambridge University Press.

Watkins, S. (Ed.). (1993). *Shy*HI resource manual.* Logan, UT: H.O.P.E.

Waxman, H. S. (1991). Reversing the cycle of educational failure for students in at-risk school environments. In H. C. Waxman, J. W. de Felix, J. E. Anderson, & H. P. Baptise (Eds.), *Students at risk in at-risk schools* (pp. 1–10). Newbury Park, CA: Sage.

Webb, N., & Cullian, L. (1983). Group interaction and achievement in small groups: Stability over time. *American Educational Research Journal, 20,* 411–423.

Webber, J., Anderson, T., & Otey, L. (1991). Teacher mindsets for surviving in BD classrooms. *Intervention in School and Clinic, 26* (5), 288–292.

Weinstein, G. & Cooke, N. L. (1992). The effects of two repeated reading interventions on generalizations of fluency. *Learning Disability Quarterly, 15,* 21–28.

Welch, M. (1992). The P.L.E.A.S.E strategy: A metacognitive learning strategy for improving the paragraph writing of students with mild learning disabilities. *Learning Disabilities Quarterly, 15,* 119–128.

Welch, M., & Link, D. P. (1989). Write, P.L.E.A.S.E.: A strategy for efficient learning and functioning in written expression (video cassette). Salt Lake City: University of Utah, Department of Special Education, Educational Tele-Communications.

Werner, O., & Begishe, K. (1968). *Styles of learning: The evidence for Navajo.* Paper presented at a conference on styles of learning in American Indian children, Stanford University, Stanford, CA.

West, J. F., & Idol, L. (1990). Collaborative consultation in the education of mildly handicapped and at-risk students. *Remedial and Special Education, 11,* 22–31.

West, J. F., Idol, L., & Cannon, G. (1988). *Collaboration in the schools: Communicating, interacting, and problem solving.* Austin, TX: Pro-Ed.

Westling, D. L. & Fox, L. (1995). *Teaching students with severe disabilities.* Englewood, NJ: Prentice-Hall.

Whipple, G. M. (1936). *The grouping of pupils. Thirty-fifth Yearbook of the National Society for the Study of Education (Part 1).* Chicago: University of Chicago Press.

White, B. (1975). Critical influences in the origins of competence. *Merrill-Palmer Quarterly, 2,* 243–266.

Wiggins, R. A. (1994). Large group lesson/small group follow-up: Flexible grouping in a basal reading program. *The Reading Teacher, 47,* 450–460.

Wigginton, E. (Ed.) *The Foxfire Series.* New York: Doubleday.

Wiig, E. H., & Semel, E., (1984). *Language assessment and intervention for the learning disabled* (2nd ed.). Columbus, OH: Merrill.

Wilcox, J., Sbardellati, E., & Nevin, A. (1987). Cooperative learning groups aid integration. *Teaching Exceptional Children, 20* (1), 61–63.

Williams, G. E., & Cuvo, A. J. (1986). Training apartment upkeep skills to rehabilitation clients: A comparison of task analytic strategies. *Journal of Applied Behavior Analysis, 19,* 39–51.

Williams, R., & Wolfram, W. (1977). *Social dialects: Differences vs. disorders.* Washington, DC: American Speech-Language-Hearing Association.

Willis, S. (1994). Teaching language-minority students: Role of native-language instruction is debated. *Update, 36* (5), 1,4–6.

Winebrenner, S. (1992). *Teaching gifted kids in the regular classroom.* Minneapolis: Free Spirit Publishing.

Wishom, P.M., Swaim, J.H., & Huang, A (1989). AIDS. *Middle School Journal, 20* (3), 3–7.

Wolery, M. (1989). Transitions in early childhood special education: Issues and procedures. *Focus on Exceptional Children, 22,* 1–16.

Wolery M., Cybriwsky, C. A., Gast, D. L., & Boyle-Gast, K. (1991). Use of constant time delay and attentional responses with adolescents. *Exceptional Children, 57,* 462–474.

Wolfram, W., Christian, D., & Adger, C.T. (in press). *Language variation in school and community.* Urbana, IL: National Council of Teachers of English.

Wong, B. Y. L. (1980). Activating the inactive learning: Use of questions/prompts to enhance comprehension and retention of implied information in learning disabled children. *Learning Disability Quarterly, 3,* 29–37.

Wong, B. Y. L. (1987). Directions in future research on metacognition in learning disabilities. In H. L. Swanson (Ed.), *Memory and learning disabilities: Advances in learning and behavioral disabilities* (Supplement 2) (pp. 335–356). Greenwich, CT: JAI Press.

Wong, B. Y. L. (1991). The relevance of metacognition to learning disabilities. In B. Y. L. Wong (Ed.), *Learning about learning disabilities* (pp. 231–258). Orlando: Academic Press.

Wong, B. Y. L. (1994). Instructional parameters promoting transfer of learned strategies in students with learning disabilities. *Learning Disability Quarterly, 17,* 110–120.

Wong, B. Y. L. & Jones, W. (1982). Increasing metacomprehension in learning disabled and normally achieving students through self-questioning training. *Learning Disability Quarterly, 5,* 228–240.

Wong, B. Y. L., & Wong. R. (1986). Study behavior as a function of metacognitive knowledge about critical task variables: An investigation of above average, average, and learning-disabled readers. *Learning Disabilities Research, 1,* 101–111.

Wong, B.Y.L., Wong,.R., Perry, N., & Sawatsky, D. (1986). The efficacy of a self-questioning summarization strategy for use by underachievers and learning disabled adolescents in social studies. *Learning Disabilities Focus, 2* (1), 20–35.

Wood, K. D., Lapp, D., & Flood, J. (1992). *Guiding readers through text: A review of study guides.* Newark, DE: International Reading Association.

Wood, M. M., & Long, N. J. (1994). *Life–space intervention: Talking with children and youth.* Austin, TX: Pro-Ed.

Wood, J. W., & Wooley, J. A. (1986). *Adapting textbooks. The Clearing House, 59,* 332–335.

Woodward, A., & Elliott, D. L. (1990). Textbook use and teacher professionalism. In D. L. Elliott and A. Woodward (Eds.), *Textbooks and schooling in the United States* (pp. 178–193). (Eighty-ninth yearbook of the National Society for the Study of Education, Part I). Chicago, IL: University of Chicago Press.

Woodward, J. & Carnine, D. (1993). Uses of technology for mathematics assessment and instruction: Reflection on a decade of innovations. *Journal of Special Education Technology, 12,* 38–48.

Work, R. S. (1994). Articulation disorders. In S. Adler & D. A. King, (Eds.), *Oral problems on children & adolescents* (1–17). Boston: Allyn & Bacon.

Workman, S. H. (1986). Teachers' verbalizations and the social interaction of blind preschoolers. *Journal of Visual Impairment and Blindness, 80* (1), 532–34.

Wright, C., & Bigge, J. L. (1991). Avenues to physical participation. In J. L. Bigge (Ed.), *Teaching individuals with multiple and physical disabilities* (3rd ed., pp. 132– 174). Englewood Cliffs, NJ: Merrill/Prentice Hall.

Wright, C. D., & Wright, J. P. (1980). Handwriting: The effectiveness of copying from moving versus still models. *Journal of Educational Research, 74,* 95–98.

Wyman, S. L. (1993). *How to respond to your culturally diverse student population.* Alexandria, VA: Association for Supervision and Curriculum Development.

Yang, H., & Wang, H. (1994). Special education in China. *Journal of Special Education, 28,* 93–105.

Yee, G. (1991). *The melting pot revisited: A literature review of current literature in multicultural education. Unpublished manuscript.* University of California-Berkeley Department of Anthropology, Special Projects.

Yopp, H. (1992). Developing phonemic awareness in young children. *The Reading Teacher, 45,* 696–703.

Yopp, H. & Troyer, S. (1992). *Training phonemic awareness in young children.* Unpublished manuscript.

York, J., & Vandercook, T. (1991). Designing an integrated program for learners with severe disabilities. *Teaching Exceptional Children, 23* (2), 22–28.

Young, M. J., & Riegeluth, C. (1988). *Improving the textbook selection process.* Bloomington, IN: Phi Delta Kappa Educational Foundation.

Ysseldyke, J. E., & Algozzine, B. (1990). *Introduction to special education* (2nd ed.). Boston: Houghton Mifflin.

Ysseldyke, J. E., Algozzine, B., & Thurlow, M. L. (1992). *Critical issues in special education* (2nd ed.). Boston: Houghton Mifflin.

Zabrucky, K. & Ratner, H. H. (1992). Effects of passage type on comprehension monitoring and recall in good and poor readers. *Journal of Reading Behavior, 24,* 373–391.

Zaragoza, N. (1987). Process writing for high-risk and learning disabled students. *Reading Research and Instruction, 26* (4), 290–301.

Zaragoza, N., & Vaughn, S. (1992). The effects of process instruction on three second-grade students with different achievement profiles. *Learning Disabilities Research and Practice, 7* (4), 184–193.

Zaragoza, N., & Vaughn, S. (1995). *Writing Workshop Manual.* Unpublished Manuscript.

Zentall, S. S., & Smith, Y. N. (1993). Mathematical performance and behavior of children with hyperactivity, with and without coexisiting aggression. *Behavior Research and Therapy.*

Zigler, E., & Burack, J. A. (1989). Personality development and the dually diagnosed person. *Research in Developmental Disabilities, 10,* 225–240.

Zigmond, N., & Baker, J. M. (1995). An exploration of the meaning and practice of special education in the context of full inclusion of students with learning disabilities. *Journal of Special Education, 29* (2), 1–25.

Zigmond, N., Levin, E., & Laurie, T. (1985). Managing the mainstream: An analysis of teacher attitudes and student performance in mainstream high school programs. *Journal of Learning Disabilities, 18,* 535–541.

Zimmerman, W. (1988). *Instant oral biographies: How to tape record, video or film your life stories.* New York: Guarionex Press.

Zipprich, M. (1995). Teaching web-making as a guided planning tool to improve student narrative writing. *Remedial and Special Education, 16* (1), 3–15, 52.

INDEX

AAMR Adaptive Behavior Scale—School, 230
Ability grouping, 53. *See also* Same-ability grouping
Absence seizures (petit mal), 264
Abstract concepts, 167–168, 253–254
Abstract knowledge, 276–277
Abstract skills, 223, 340, 440
Academic skills, low-level, 311
Acceleration, 336, 345, 346
Acceptance
    teacher, 110
    words of, 63
Accommodation
    for behavioral disorders, 201–210
    for communication disorders, 179–187
    content coverage versus, 109
    for cultural diversity, 298–302
    for dual sensory impairments, 221
    for emotional disorders, 201–210
    environmental, 237, 251, 267
    for gifted and talented students, 349–351
    for hearing impaired, 258–261
    in homework, 109–110, 146
    in instruction, 22–26
    for learning disabled students, 130, 137–148
    for linguistic diversity, 298–302
    for mentally retarded, 216, 221–241
    for personal learning styles, 237–238
    for physical disabilities, 266–269
    for severe disabilities, 216, 221–241
    for students at risk, 324–329
    for students with ADD, 130, 151–157
    in testing, 108
    for visually impaired, 251–255
    see also Adaptation
Acquired immunodeficiency syndrome (AIDS), 6, 265
Acronyms, for remembering, 143, 144, 501
Acrostics, for remembering, 501
Activity approach, 463–464
Adaptation
    models for instruction, 23–26
    see also Accommodation
Adaptive behavior and skills, 217
Adaptive behavior scale, 230
Adaptive physical education teachers, 247
Additive approach, 283, 284
Add-on programs, 319–320
Adler, Alfred, 76–77
Adolescent pregnancy, 315
Adolescents, 142
    with ADD, 150
    social skills program for, 89
Adopt-A-School programs, 324
Advance organizer, 140–141
Advocacy, 6, 84
Affixes, 171, 172
African Americans, 275

average achievement of, 275
behavior of, 78
culture of, 276
dialect of, 294, 296–297
expectations of, 77
intelligence testing of, 230
mentoring programs for, 323
perception of disabilities by, 240–241
AIDS. *See* Acquired immunodeficiency syndrome (AIDS)
Alliteration, 373, 376
Alphabetic principle, 367
American Association on Mental Retardation (AAMR), 217–218
American Printing House for the Blind, 249, 254–255
American Sign Language (ASL), 256, 260
Americans with Disabilities Act (ADA) (P.L. 101-336)
    history of, 6
Antonyms, 177
AOK strategy, 407, 409
Apprenticeship programs, 327
Articulation, 163, 228
    and English as a second language, 165
    regional dialects and, 165
Articulation disorders, 164–165
Asian Americans, 275, 293
    expectations of, 278
Assessment
    of behavioral and emotional disorders, 199–201
    of communication disorders, 178–179
    computer-managed, 147
    of essential skills, 224
    of functional skills, 224, 230, 233–234
    of gifted students, 355–357, 371–373
    of hearing impaired, 256, 258
    of learning disabled, 137
    of mentally retarded, 229–230
    of physically disabled, 266
    of prior knowledge, 350
    of reading, 371–373
    of severely disabled, 229–230
    students' perceptions of, 108
    of visually impaired, 249
    of writing, 372
Assessment portfolios, 481
ASSET, 89–90, 92
Assignment log, 155
Assignments. *See* Homework
Assignment sheet, 145
Assistive technology, 267
Association for Children with Learning Disabilities
    See Learning Disabilities Association
Association for Persons with Severe Handicaps (TASH), 218
Asthma, 261, 262, 263, 266
Asynchronous collaboration, 125

At-risk students. *See* Students at risk
Attention deficit disorders (ADD), 100, 130, 135, 148–157
    accommodations for students with, 130, 151–157
    adolescents with, 150
    characteristics of students with, 149–151
    definitions and types of, 148–149
    developmental features of, 149
    educational interventions with, 152–156
    effects of stimulant medications on students with, 156–157
    explaining to children, 150
    homework for students with, 152–154
    IDEA and, 148, 151
    instructional guidelines for students with, 151–157
    laws pertaining to, 151
    lesson plan for students with, 154
    prevalence of, 151
    sex differences in, 151
Attention span, 135, 153
Attitude goals, 370
Audiogram, 256
Audiologist, 256
Audiotaping, of textbooks, 478
Auditory readers, 249
Augmentative communication, 180, 181, 226–227
Authentic learning, 326–329
Authoring cycle, 397
"Author's chair," 410–411
Autism, 6, 21, 218–220, 225, 228, 240
    advice for teachers, 220
    Planning Pyramid for students with, 232
Automaticity, 378

Background knowledge, activating, 141
Balanced Reading instruction, 366
Barrier games, 182, 183
Basal programs, 387, 388
    critics of, 363–364
Basal readers, 363
    effective use of, 364
Basic interpersonal communication skills (BICS), 292
Basic skills
    on computers, 314
    in mathematics, 444–448
    substandard, 311
Beginning to Read: Thinking and Learning about Print (Adams), 367
Behavioral disorders, 61, 70
    accommodations for students with, 201–210
    anxiety-withdrawal, 198
    assessment of students with, 199–201
    causes of, 199
    changing behavior, 204–205, 206
    classification of, 195–196

541

Dual sensory impairments, 218, 221–222
  accommodations for students with, 221
Due process, 5–6
Dyscalculia, 132
Dysgraphia, 132, 419
Dyslexia, 132–133, 371
  genetic bases of, 137
  language-based, 133
  recordings for, 478
  visual-based, 133

Early intervention programs, 24, 320–322, 370
Echolalia, 228, 248
Eclectic programs, 363, 366
Ecological inventories, 230
Economic Opportunities Act, 310
Editing, 403, 407–410
  peer, 407–409, 410
Education
  bilingual, 274, 288, 294–297, 300
  cultural characteristics of, 278
  gifted, 335–337, 344
Educational Amendments Act (P.L. 93-380), 6
Educational assistants (EAs), 216 See also
  Paraprofessionals
Educationally disadvantaged, 309. See also
  Students at risk
Education and transition inventories, 496
Education for All Handicapped Children's
  Act (EAHCA)(P.L. 94-142), 6
  See also Individuals with Disabilities
  Education Act
Education Improvement and Consolidation
  Act (ECIA), 310
Education of All Handicapped Act Children's
  Amendments (P.L. 99-457), 6, 229
Effective schools, 102
Elaboration, 187
Elementary and Secondary Education Act
  (ESEA), 295, 310
Emotional disorders, 21, 70, 192
  accommodations for students with,
    201–210
  assessment of students with, 199–201
  causes of, 199
  classification of, 195
  definition of, 193
  identification of students with, 199–201
  prevalence of students with, 194–195
  teaching guidelines for students with,
    201–210
  types of, 195
  see also Behavioral disorders
Employment, 25
Empowering school culture, 281, 282
Enabling relationships, 169, 171
Encoding, 399
Encouragement, 63, 70
English
  official language of the U.S., 295, 297
  proficiency in, 289
  Sheltered, 298
  standard, 294
English as a second language (ESL), 165,
    169, 274
  goal of, 288
  historical perspective on, 294–297
  instruction in, 298–299
Enrichment programs, 336, 346–347, 349,
    357
Environmental accommodations, 237, 251,
    267
Environment-related factors, in planning, 38,
    39

Epilepsy, 220, 262, 264
Equity pedagogy, 281
Essay questions, 505
Essay writing, 414
Essential skills, assessment of, 224
Estimating, 445–446
European American culture, 77–78
  individuality in, 276
  learning styles in, 278
Expansion, 187
Expectations, 77–78, 84, 278
  for gifted and talented students, 334
  for students at risk, 324–325
Experientially-based instruction, 238–239
Explication, in text, 474
Expository text, 381
Expository writing, 414
Expressive language, 166
Extended practice, 144–146
Extinction, 74, 76
Eye contact, 81

Facilitator, 104
Failure. See Students at risk
Failure to shift operations, 449
Family adjustment, 113–114
Family collaboration, 28–29
Family instability, 313–315
Family mobility, 314
Family poverty, 313
FAST strategy, 86–88
FAST DRAW strategy, 451
Fetal Alcohol Syndrome (FAS), 218
Figurative language, 169
Final sounds, 165
Finger spelling, 257–258
First language, proficiency in, 289–290, 291,
    299
Flexible grouping, 56, 57–58
  planning for, 57–58
  principles of, 56
FLIP chart strategy, 474, 475
Fluency, 163
  in reading, 369
Fluency disorders, 165–166
Follow Through programs, 310
Fractions, 438, 447–448
Fractures, 262
Fragile health, 263
Friendly or considerate text, 474
Friendships, with mentally retarded, 225
Full-inclusion, 29–31
  advocates of, 29
  arguments for, 30
  see also Inclusion; Mainstreaming
Full-service schools, 322–323
Full-time placement, 9
Functional math activities, 239
Functional practice, providing opportunities
  for, 239–241
Functional skills, assessment of, 224, 230,
    233–234
Functional vision, 247
Funds of knowledge, 277, 290

Gender equity, 283
Gender roles, cultural characteristics of, 278
General education classroom
  adaptations for disabled students, 20
  adaptations for mentally retarded
    students, 231, 236–239
  adaptations for severely disabled
    students, 236–239
  inclusion in, 55–56

General education teachers
  advice for, 24
  responsibilities of, 17–26
  role of in IEP process, 16
Genetics
  and dyslexia, 137
  and reading disabilities, 133
Gifted and talented students, 6, 246, 334–357
  accommodations for, 349–357
  administrative arrangement for, 347–349
  assessment of, 355–357, 371–373
  characteristics of, 339–343
  classroom strategies and adaptations for,
    347
  creatively gifted or talented, 340–341
  definitions of, 337–339
  expectations for, 334
  federal definitions of, 338
  grading strategies for, 355–357
  high-tech alternatives for, 348
  identification of, 342–345
  inclusion programs for, 348–349
  instructional guidelines for, 349–357
  intellectually gifted, 340
  "invisible gifted," 341
  minority, 341, 342
  non-motivated, 309, 335, 341–342
  programs for, 337, 345–349
  referral of, 344–345, 346
  resource programs for, 347–348
  self-contained programs for, 348
  special programs for, 54
  stereotypes of, 339
Gifted education
  historical perspective on, 335–337
  nomination form for, 344
Giftedness, 222
  definitions of, 337–339
  see also Gifted and talented students
Gifted students. See Gifted and talented
  students
Glaucoma, 247
Goals
  cultural characteristics of, 278
  multicultural education, 282
  reading, 370
  setting, 494–496
"Graded" schools, 53
Graded system, 53
Grading, 106–108
  with cooperative learning, 61
  of gifted and talented students, 355–357
  reasons for, 108
Grammar, 171, 173
  Black Vernacular English, 165, 294,
    296–297
Graphing, 144
Graphophonic cues, 367
Group homes, 232
Grouping
  instructional, 52–58
  for math instruction, 446–447
  patterns, 58–63
  for reading instruction, 372
  strategies, 59
Group placement, criteria for, 59
Groups
  cooperative learning, 60–61
  random assignment, 60
  student-selected, 60
Guidelines, classroom, 73

Hands-on instruction, 238–239
Handwriting, 418–421
  fluency in, 421

Language development (*cont.*)
　　of hearing impaired, 256
　　of mentally retarded, 225–226
Language disorders
　　school-age, 166–167
　　severe, 180
　　see also Speech or language impairments
Language diversity
　　Black Vernacular English and Standard
　　　　English, 296
　　variation and dialect, 294
Language production, 166, 167
　　components of, 163
　　teaching, 182
Language skills
　　proficiency, 291–293
　　use, 174–175, 179
　　of visually impaired, 248
Large print books, 254
Latchkey children, 314
Latino Americans, 275
　　average achievement of, 275
　　culture of, 240, 279
　　family values in, 276
　　perception of disabilities, 240
Lau v. Nichols, 295, 297
Laws
　　on discrimination, 7
　　for equal educational opportunity, 310
　　mainstreaming and, 29
　　on special education, 5–17
Lead poisoning, 262
Learner characteristics, 289
Learning
　　bilingualism and, 291–292
　　connecting to reality, 327
　　demonstrating in multiple ways, 142, 143
　　and developmental process, 292–293
　　primary and secondary channels for, 249,
　　　　250
　　providing a framework for, 140–141
Learning community, creating, 80–81
Learning Disabilities Association (LDA), 131
Learning disabilities (LD), 130, 131–148
　　academic achievement of students with,
　　　　342
　　accommodations for students with,
　　　　137–148
　　assessment of students with, 137
　　characteristics of students with, 133–136
　　definitions and types of, 131–133
　　of gifted and talented students, 342
　　homework for, 479
　　identification of students with, 137
　　instructional guidelines for students with,
　　　　137–148
　　prevalence of, 136–137
　　reading instruction for, 362
　　spelling instruction for, 416, 417
　　writing instruction for, 399, 400–401
Learning disorders, 61
Learning Environment and Attitude Program
　　(LEAP) for Success, 464
Learning Media Assessment, 249, 250
Learning styles
　　of European Americans, 278
　　of Native Americans, 278
Learning to Read: The Great Debate (Chall),
　　367
Least restrictive environment
　　checklist for determining, 7, 9
　　concept of, 7–10
　　defined, 5
Lectures
　　instructional clarity in, 467–469

listener-friendly, 497–498
　　listening to, 497, 499
　　notetaking during, 497–500
　　pause procedure, 498
Legal blindness, 247
Legislation. *See* Laws
Leisure, cultural characteristics of, 278
Lesson co-planning and co-teaching, 105–106
Lesson planning, 47–52
　　software for, 49
　　for students with ADD, 154
Lesson Planning Form, 48, 50, 51
Lesson Planning Pyramid
　　example of, 50–51, 52
　　monitoring student learning during, 51
　　procedure for, 48–50
Lesson Reaction Sheets, 53
Leukemia, 262
Liberator, 181
Library visits, 328
Linguistic diversity, 287–297
　　accommodations for, 298–302
　　instructional guidelines for, 298–302
Linguistic input, 288–289
Listening, 153
　　effective, 110, 111
　　to lectures, 497, 499
　　to parents, 110, 111
　　to professionals, 110
Low vision, 247

McGill Action Planning System (MAPS), 232
Macroculture, 276
Magnet schools, 348
Main idea, finding, 141
Mainstream Assistance Team (MAT), 102
Mainstreaming, 29–31
　　advice for teachers, 4
　　consultation model for, 101
　　effectiveness of, 10
　　essential element of, 29
　　and inclusion, 29
　　law and, 29
　　successful, 31, 101
　　see also Full-inclusion; Inclusion
Mainstreaming Law. *See* Education for All
　　　　Handicapped Children Act (EAHCA)
　　　　(P.L. 94-142)
Maintenance bilingual education, 300
Maintenance checks, 146
Making Words, 375, 377
Management. *See* Classroom management;
　　Time management
Manuscript writing, 418, 419
MAPS. *See* McGill Action Planning System
　　(MAPS)
MARKER strategy, 494
"Marland Report," 337, 338
Mastery, in math, 442–443
Material/tangible reinforcement, 72
Math Blasters Plus, 146
Mathematical power, 429
Mathematics
　　behavior problems and, 432
　　computer-assisted instruction in, 147
　　demonstrating learning in, 143
　　and memory, 431–432
　　variables influencing ability in, 432
Mathematics instruction
　　activities for all learners, 434–443,
　　　　456–457
　　adapting basal materials for, 435–436
　　for comprehension, 440–441
　　computation skills, 429, 432–433, 437,
　　　　448–450

current trends in curriculum and,
　　　　429–431
　　establishing appropriate goals, 437–439
　　evaluating curricula, 434–435
　　feedback in, 439, 442
　　games, 442–443
　　guidelines for adequate, 434, 435
　　helping students acquire basic skills,
　　　　444–448
　　helping students develop problem-solving
　　　　skills, 451–453
　　monitoring and communicating progress,
　　　　443
　　national concerns about, 429
　　presenting mathematics concepts, 435
　　promoting positive attitudes, 443
　　providing appropriate, 439–442
　　providing practice, 442–443
　　standards for, 429, 430
　　for students with difficulties in, 431–434,
　　　　436–437
　　for students with learning problems, 429,
　　　　431
　　use of calculators in, 432–433
　　using manipulatives, 440
　　videos for fractions, 438
Mathematics skills
　　basic, 436, 442, 444–448
　　learning fractions, 447–448
　　prenumber skills, 444–445
　　understanding place value, 446–447
　　working with numeration, 445–446
"Matthew Effect," 373
Memory
　　idea retention for, 476
　　mathematics and, 431–432
　　problems, 449
　　strategies for remembering, 142–144,
　　　　500–502
　　using mnemonics, 143, 144, 501
Mental retardation, 10, 21, 113
　　accommodations for students with, 216,
　　　　221–241
　　assessment of, 229–230
　　causes of, 218, 222
　　characteristics of students with, 223–229
　　classification systems for, 218, 219
　　communication skills of students with,
　　　　225–229
　　cultural views of, 240
　　definition of, 217–218
　　degree of, 2218
　　developmental period of, 217
　　goals for students with, 239–240
　　identification of students with, 229–230
　　inclusion of students with, 216, 231, 237
　　instructional guidelines for students with,
　　　　231–241
　　intellectual functioning of students with,
　　　　223–225, 225
　　life functioning of persons with, 218
　　mild, 177
　　motor skills of students with, 225
　　prevalence of, 222–223
　　prevention of, 222
　　social skills of students with, 225
　　strategies for inclusion, 236
　　systems of support, 217
　　types of, 217–218, 220
Mentoring programs, 323
Metacognition, 369
Metadiscourse, in texts, 474
Metalinguistics, 175–176, 292
　　stages of development, 176
Metaphors, 169